Multidisciplinary Explorations of Corohysteria Caused by the COVID-2019 Pandemic

Multidisciplinary Explorations of Corohysteria Caused by the COVID-2019 Pandemic

Edited by
Abdul Karim Bangura

LEXINGTON BOOKS
Lanham • Boulder • New York • London

Published by Lexington Books
An imprint of The Rowman & Littlefield Publishing Group, Inc.
4501 Forbes Boulevard, Suite 200, Lanham, Maryland 20706
www.rowman.com

86-90 Paul Street, London EC2A 4NE

British Library Cataloguing in Publication Information Available

Library of Congress Cataloging-in-Publication Data

Names: Bangura, Abdul Karim, 1953- editor.
Title: Multidisciplinary explorations of corohysteria caused by the COVID-2019 pandemic / edited by Abdul Karim Bangura.
Description: Lanham : Lexington Books, [2022] | Includes bibliographical references and index. | Summary: "This book focuses on how mass hysteria has emerged among people across the globe due to reactions to news media reports and policies instituted by governments to address the challenges emanating from the COVID-19 pandemic"— Provided by publisher.
Identifiers: LCCN 2022005131 (print) | LCCN 2022005132 (ebook) | ISBN 9781666912197 (cloth) | ISBN 9781666912203 (ebook)
Subjects: LCSH: Hysteria (Social psychology) | COVID-19 Pandemic, 2020—Psychological aspects. | COVID-19 Pandemic, 2020—Influence. | Collective behavior.
Classification: LCC HM866 .M85 2022 (print) | LCC HM866 (ebook) | DDC 302/.17—dc23/eng/20220207
LC record available at https://lccn.loc.gov/2022005131
LC ebook record available at https://lccn.loc.gov/2022005132

To our coauthor Yakub Adams

Contents

Preface

As a recent and ongoing phenomenon, no comprehensive and multidisciplinary book exists on the Coronavirus Disease (COVID)-2019 pandemic as of this writing. This book, which is very likely to be the first of its kind on the topic, focuses on how massive hysteria (i.e., an exaggerated or uncontrollable emotion or excitement) has emerged among people across the globe due to reactions to news media reports and policies instituted by governments to address the challenges emanating from the virus. And, as stated by Isatu Ramatu Bangura in the introductory chapter of this book, COVID-2019 (or COVID-19 for short, the number 2019 or 19 representing the year it was identified) is an acronym for which "CO" stands for "Corona," "VI" for "virus," and "D" for "disease." She adds that the disease was first referred to as "2019 novel coronavirus" or "2019-nCoV."

Given its focus, the book is therefore suitable for the general public and as a main or supplementary text for undergraduate and graduate students taking courses in the Humanities and Sciences. It also will be useful to professors teaching related subjects and scholars doing research in these fields. In addition, policymakers in these areas will be interested in the valuable information that the book provides. Furthermore, relevant political activists and advocacy groups will be interested in the book to pursue their objectives.

The book is divided into 23 chapters. Chapter 1, "General Introduction," by Isatu Ramatu Bangura entails what the book is about, definition and detailed conceptualization of the term "Corohysteria," definitions of other major concepts related to COVID-2019, and justification and import of the book.

Chapter 2, "Coroeducation," by Ishmael I. Munene and Jafred Muyaka talks about how the global crisis posed by the COVID-2019 pandemic has engulfed Kenya's higher education in unprecedented dimensions that have led to hysteria. They argue that while previous crises have been predictable in terms of strategies, scope, impact, and span, the current one is unpredictable. They add that central to understanding aspects of its impact is to interrogate how Kenya's universities have reacted to the challenge COVID-2019 has presented. They further probe the policy decision-making, highlight the context of institutional responses and strategies, and finally speculate on lessons learned as well as the long-term impact.

Chapter 3, "Coroexpertise," by Joseph Lansana Kormoh is an interdisciplinary and exploratory approach to understand the various narratives used by experts to explain the nature of the COVID-2019 that have led to hysteria among people. While the interdisciplinary approach incorporates narratives of the COVID-2019 from medical science, from traditional medicine perspective, this chapter also investigates the problem which has not still been clearly understood even by the best medical experts across the globe. The chapter also offers some suggestions on how experts can disseminate information about the virus to their audiences.

Chapter 4, "Coroelitism," by Omosefe Oyekanmi examines how political leaders and government officials (members of the elite group) contracting COVID-2019 and the euphoria of the virus as a cleansing agent to purge the Nigerian space of corrupt and recalcitrant leaders are gathering momentum. She contends that this notion, however, is misleading, as only the political and privileged class has access to testing. Hence, the lower class, which constitutes the greater proportion of Nigeria's population, has thrown caution to the wind, barely adhering to all the basic hygiene and social distancing guidelines. This hysteria, sadly, she states, will create more poverty and deaths, except if the science of COVID-2019 changes to suit the wishes of a sizeable population in Nigeria.

Chapter 5, "Coropoverty," by Cecy Edijala Balogun looks at the global spread of the COVID-2019 and how it remains a source of fear for resource-poor populations whose livelihoods are already threatened by other socio-economic and political factors. She posits that fears of loss of employment, businesses, and other means of livelihood have been on the increase, raising concerns among the poor populations on how they would cope in the present circumstance, and especially in the lockdown policy that is adopted to curtail the spread of the pandemic. This chapter then interrogates the heightened hysteria among poor populations created by the COVID-2019 pandemic in Nigeria and the palliative measures taken by the state and national governments.

Chapter 6, "Corodemocracy," by Harrison Adewale Idowu studies how given the outbreak of the COVID-2019 and the World Health Organization's declaration of it as a global pandemic, governments across the globe have rolled out measures to curb the spread of the virus. Some measures, he points outs, include restrictions in movements and association and other impromptu decisions/actions without recourse to democratic tenets. These actions have led to hysteria among people. The chapter then seeks to interrogate, within the Nigerian context, the trends and patterns of democratic erosion in the face of COVID-2019, especially with respect to citizens' fundamental rights. It administered an online survey to citizens in order to unravel their perceptions of the extent of democratic erosion as a result of the COVID-2019.

Chapter 7, "Corofrontline," by Gregory Obinna Ugbo, Henry Chigozie Duru, and Chinwe Beatrice Ezeoke interrogates the scourge of the COVID-2019 pandemic being unprecedented in recent global disease outbreaks and has exposed the limit of international competencies in handling disease outbreaks. They note that at the forefront of containing the ravaging impact of the virus are healthcare providers that mediate between the members of public and the health challenges wrought by the pandemic, thereby suggesting the imperative of people-oriented communication (both verbal and non-verbal). This chapter therefore delineates how the frontline workers' communicative behaviors in terms of dressing, expressing personal concerns over their own safety, and general attitude to work have shaped public responses and perceptions of the pandemic. A qualitative research approach is adopted to analyze the experiences of COVID-2019 survivors in Nigeria.

Chapter 8, "Corophilanthropy," by Rosemary Oyinlola Popoola discusses the link between philanthropic gestures by selected Nigerians and the increasing hysteria over COVID-2019. The chapter poses and provides answers to the following questions: What is the relationship between public perception of philanthropic gesture and panic buying? What is the motivation for the donations? Is it altruism or attention seeking? Is the philanthropic gesture a form of spectacular performance in view of the mediatized nature of the giving? Is there a politics to the philanthropic gesture? By providing answers to these questions, this chapter contributes to existing knowledge on philanthropy in Africa while also providing new direction for researching philanthropy and humanitarianism in the continent.

Chapter 9, "Cororeligion," by Simon Gisege Omare broaches how the outbreak of the COVID-2019 led atheists to make the claim that the world does not need religion, the response of religious leaders to the claim, and how this has created hysteria among many people. He asserts that one must wonder about why religion has lost meaning in the contemporary world. This chapter therefore probes the question about how the church has involved itself in the fight against the COVID-2019 epidemic and challenges and prospects in Africa. Data for this chapter were collected through interviews and focus group discussions with purposively sampled respondents in Africa.

Chapter 10, "Coromathematics," by Abdul Karim Bangura delineates how mathematics is used for many purposes. He mentions that mathematics is utilized in everyday life for such simple purposes as telling time or counting the change that is returned by a cashier. In business, mathematics is prevalent in all exchange transactions. In industry, almost all companies depend on mathematics for their research and development. In science, mathematics pervades all aspects in the scientific fields. He also points out that now we see that since the outbreak of the COVID-2019 mathematics is being used to intensify hysteria among people. In this chapter, evidence is provided to demonstrate that most of the mathematical models that have been used to explain and predict the trends of the virus are faulty. In the end, more appropriate models and their attendant calculations are provided for a more rational understanding of the trends of the virus.

Chapter 11, "Coropsychology," by Pamela Anyango Oloo and Yakub Adams speaks about how the COVID-2019, a respiratory illness, is the first global pandemic of the era of independent social media. They maintain that incessant and mostly uncontrolled reporting of the illness' fatality dimensions is impacting the psychological wellness of the accessible populace. Additionally, they point out, the drastic measures to contain the spread of the virus are contrary to the norms of hitherto daily activities and this could cause anxiety over the illness. This chapter then examines the psychological ramifications and attendant coping mechanisms as manifest in the language use in reference to COVID-2019 fatalities and the interpretation of handwashing, social distancing, and quarantine.

Chapter 12, "Corolinguistics," by Abdul Karim Bangura investigates why language has always been a very important means of communication that is spoken or written through words, or expressed via the use of hand and figure gestures. Language plays an important role when we wish to express our thoughts and feelings. Thus, it is only inevitable that language has been used to express thoughts and feelings about the COVID-2019 that has led to a heightened hysteria among people. Thus, since linguistics is the scientific study of language, this chapter employs linguistic tools to examine the various ways language has been used to intensify the fears over the virus. The linguistic tools include oxymoron, euphemism, and metaphor.

Chapter 13, "Coroeconomics," by Alie Kunda explores the linkage between activities related to the production, consumption, and transfer of wealth apropos the advent of the COVID-2019, which has led to a great deal of hysteria among people. Thus, the chapter focuses on activities involving the making, distributing, selling, and purchasing of goods and services. This will allow readers to also understand how the COVID-2019 pandemic has impacted (a) how societies use scarce resources to produce valuable commodities and distribute them among different people to help them deal with the effects of the virus; (b) the variety of economic policies that have been implemented to deal with the impact of the virus; and (c) a focus on real life, since economics is focused on learning from case studies.

Chapter 14, "Coromedia," by Cecy Edijala Balogun analyzes how the use of the news media to disseminate information about the COVID-2019 pandemic is generating hysteria within different segments of societies. Such hysteria, she says, arises from frightening news media messages generated around the pandemic. She adds that the reportage of the predisposing poor health outcomes that reduce the survival rates of confirmed cases and the speculation of a global recession engender fear among those with poor health conditions and the large numbers of low-income earners who have lost their jobs. This chapter then assesses the extent to which the news media have contributed to the hysteria of the pandemic and the effects on select populations.

Chapter 15, "Corohistory," by Hadizat Audu Salihu comprises a review of how the histories of the deleterious effects of past pandemics have been used to characterize the emergence of the COVID-2019 which has fomented hysteria among people. She reveals that the outbreak and spread of pandemics have been part of human existence and narratives since the earliest times. She also notes that coronaviruses, which belong to a large family of viruses causing many illnesses in humans and animals, have been the cause of severe respiratory infections. They include the Middle East respiratory syndrome, the severe acute respiratory syndrome, and the COVID-2019. The chapter therefore traces the history of coronaviruses before the outbreak of the COVID-2019 in order to isolate the latter variant's actual impact on the minds of people.

Chapter 16, "Corolaw," by Osman Kabba talks about the legal battles that are brewing between governments and pharmaceutical companies about ownership and pricing of new inventions for the COVID-2019, even though the companies are taking grants from governments. This situation is causing hysteria among patients because of the possibility of very high costs of these vaccines and medicines should the companies not be regulated.

Chapter 17, "Coroexploitation," by Henrietta Eshalomi is about how the COVID-2019 pandemic has led to hysteria among people in terms of market exploitation in relation to demand and supply of goods and services in Nigeria. After a brief introduction, the chapter uses the theory of exploitation to deepen the analysis. It explores the underlying causes of price adjustments and exploitations in the face of the government-ordered restrictions and lockdown. The chapter also draws upon and analyzes empirical data from Lagos, Rivers, and Delta States using data collected via in-depth interviews with randomly selected traders and buyers of household essentials and services. Furthermore, the chapter highlights the different methods deployed in confronting these developments.

Chapter 18, "Coroweakstate," by Emmanuel Vincent Nelson Kallon explains how the characteristics of weak states are layered over time and how this connects with the heightened hysteria we are witnessing among people because of the COVID-2019. In particular, the chapter examines the pattern of institutionalized violence considered as a core feature of a weak state when the violence becomes reified and prominent within nation-states, particularly in states once conceived as institutionally and democratically reformed, when confronted with an internal difficulty. The chapter then builds on the emergence of the COVID-2019 scourge as a litmus test to argue that institutionally reformed nation-states can best be identified by their institutional behavioral patterns when confronted with an internal dilemma and not a prior taken-for-granted practice.

Chapter 19, "Cororacism," by JP Afamefuna Ifedi offers a critical appraisal of the intersection between the COVID-2019 pandemic and racism. He asserts that in the wake of the incidence of the pandemic, declared officially on March 11, 2020, some of the reactions and efforts to address it have degenerated to its racialization. He dissects the racist social, political, institutional dispositions, commentaries, and actions in relation to COVID-2019 in the United States and elsewhere, where the hysteria, angst, fear, unrest, and difficulties associated with the pandemic are exploited to foster political and social agenda. This situation, he argues, has led to the undermining of national and global responses to the virus.

Chapter 20, "Coroadaptation," by Feyisitan Ijimakinwa looks at how the COVID-2019 pandemic has unsettled the balanced life patterns of Nigerians in diverse contexts. The author proffers that the hysteria that trailed the outbreak resulted in impromptu adjustment and adaptation strategies. This chapter then entails an ethnographic analysis of societal responses and adaptations relating to the pandemic by individuals, homesteads, corporates, and religious organizations, among others. It also examines different coping strategies and actions by Nigerians against the backdrop of limited understanding of the virus and the implications. Secondary data drawn from the traditional and new media are shown to highlight the dangers inherent in the uninformed mitigation processes and ideas across different levels of Nigerian society.

Chapter 21, "Coropoliticaldiscourse," by Rachael M. Rudolph studies how since the outbreak of the COVID-2019 in China in December 2019, its subsequent spread across the globe, and the declaration of it as a pandemic on March 11, 2020, the world has witnessed a significant shift in how policymakers, news media, and the public frame the COVID-2019 discourse. This chapter traces a sampling of the coropoliticaldiscourse to highlight how some actors in Asia, Europe, and the Americas exploited the fear, panic, and hatred to push their own geopolitical agendas, exacerbate existing divisions, and limit a global response to address the greatest global health insecurity issue yet to emerge in the twenty-first century.

Chapter 22, "Coroinfodeluge," by Collence T. Chisita, Nyarai P. Chibanda, Cecilia T. Olugbara, and Moeketsi Letseka interrogates the nexus between the COVID-2019 pandemic that has resulted in the loss of lives, panic, and despair, on the one hand, and the overwhelming avalanche of information with which people fail to grapple, on the other hand. This scenario, the authors maintain, has been exacerbated by the proliferation of digital technologies and ubiquitous social media use. The authors then explore praxis-oriented strategies that are being used by librarians to overcome the COVID-2019 "infodemic." Using an interpretivist approach, the usefulness of multimodal literacies, including health, information, and digital literacies, will be investigated in this chapter.

Chapter 23, "Corolockdown," by John Idriss Lahai discusses how beyond the scientific justification for the COVID-2019 lockdowns lies the role of hysteria in the transformation of people's private spaces (homes) as prisons for the incarceration of disruptive attitudes toward the powers of governments and pharma industries. Writing from a Foucauldian methodical perspective, the author contends that corolockdown is a mechanism that unnaturally situates the "diseased bodies" of people as an existential threat to this power. It is not about "saving" people from self and others. It is about justifying, first, the necropolitical medical attitudes toward the anatomical bodies of people; and, second, securitizing hysterical politico-pharmaceutical attitudes toward their freedom. As such, argues the author, people's resistance to the corolockdown measures should be interpreted as a change in their sensibility toward what they perceive as a threat to their existence.

In order to ensure cohesion and coherence throughout the book, each chapter entails at least six sections. The first section introduces the topic covered; the second section discusses the theoretical framework upon which the chapter is systematically grounded; the third, fourth, and fifth sections entail pertinent case studies or issues pertaining to the COVID-2019 pandemic; and the sixth section draws a conclusion and offers recommendations based on the findings.

Abdul Karim Bangura
Washington DC, USA
Fall 2021

Acknowledgments

We, and hopefully many readers, owe gratitude to the following:

The Creator, for providing us the fortitude to do this work during this very challenging time.

The Ancestors, for providing us guidance, protection, and the willingness to seek verities.

Mwalimu Emmanuel D. Babatunde and Mwalimu Kelbogile T. Setiloane, for providing us intellectual and spiritual support for this and other projects.

My wonderful daughter, Isatu Ramatu Bangura, for designing the radiant image on the cover of the book.

The anonymous reviewers, for their suggestive evaluations. Asking difficult questions leads to better answers and clarifications.

Our immediate and global families, for their prayers and support.

Chapter 1

General Introduction

Isatu Ramatu Bangura

This book is about attempts to use the incidence of the Coronavirus Disease (COVID)-2019 to cause exaggerated or uncontrollable emotion or excitement among people. The now-oft-repeated narrative on COVID-2019 (or COVID-19 for short; the number 2019 or 19 representing the year it was identified) goes as follows. For the acronym COVID-2019, "CO" represents "Corona," "VI" for "virus," and "D" for "disease." The disease was first referred to as "2019 novel coronavirus" or "2019-nCoV." There are many types of human coronaviruses, including some that commonly cause mild upper respiratory tract illnesses (CDC, 2020a).

COVID-2019 is caused by a coronavirus: that is, any of a group of ribonucleic acid (RNA)—a nucleic acid present in all living cells—viruses that cause a variety of diseases in humans and other animals. Coronaviruses constitute a large family of viruses that are common in people and many different species of animals, including bats, camels, cats, and cattle. It is very rare that animal coronaviruses infect people and then spread between people such as with Middle East respiratory syndrome-related coronavirus (MERS-CoV), severe acute respiratory syndrome-related coronavirus (SARS-CoV), and now with this new virus named SARS-CoV-2. The SARS-CoV-2 virus is a betacoronavirus like MERS-CoV and SARS-CoV. All three of these viruses have their origins in bats. The sequences from U.S. patients are similar to the one that China initially reported, suggesting a likely single, recent emergence of this virus from an animal reservoir (CDC, 2020a).

At the early stage of the virus, many of the patients at the epicenter of the outbreak in Wuhan, Hubei Province, China, had some connection to a large seafood and live animal market, indicating an animal-to-person spread. Afterward, a larger number of patients reportedly did not have exposure to animal markets, thereby suggesting a person-to-person spread, which was later reported outside Hubei and in countries outside China, including the United States. As do some parts of the United States, some overseas destinations now have ongoing community spread with the virus that causes COVID-2019. Community spread denotes the fact that some people have been infected and it is not known how or where they became exposed (CDC, 2020a).

As of this writing, the clinical picture with regard to COVID-2019 is not completely known. Reported illnesses have ranged from very mild (including some with no reported symptoms) to severe, including illness resulting in death. What we do know for now is that most COVID-2019 illnesses are mild. A report from China suggests that serious illness occurs in 16 percent of cases. Older people and people of all ages with severe chronic medical conditions, such as heart disease, lungs disease, and diabetes, for instance, appear to be at higher risk of developing serious COVID-2019 illness. A Centers for Disease Control and Prevention (CDC) *Morbidity & Mortality Weekly Report* that looked at severity of disease among COVID-2019 cases in the United States by age group found that 80 percent of deaths were among adults 65 years and older, with the highest percentage of severe outcomes occurring in people 85 years and older (CDC, 2020a).

Since there was little to no pre-existing immunity against the new virus, it spread across the globe very quickly. The virus that causes COVID-2019 is blighting people and passing effortlessly from person to person. On March 11, 2020, the World Health Organization (WHO) declared the COVID-2019 outbreak a pandemic. This decision made COVID-2019 the first pandemic to be caused by a new coronavirus (CDC, 2020a).

Then we hear and read: "God is punishing us for having taking him out of our lives and living in sin," "the global order as we know it will be no more," "internationalism is dead and nationalism has emerged as its substitute," "about 70% of the people in the world will be infected by the time this virus is controlled," "many millions will die," "we must expect other new viruses that will be even deadlier," "millions will lose their jobs," "thousands of companies will go out of business," "unrest and disorder will take place in weak states," "democracy will be dead in many countries," "China invented the virus in order to cause economic havoc across the world that will allow it to dominate the global economy," "the United States invented the virus and launched it in China in order to put a brake to that country's challenge to the United States' dominance in the global economy," and so on. And the world knows the rest of the story; it replays every day and night on radio and television sets and social media across the globe. First, bodies are counted, tears are broadcast to boost ratings, and hearts and stomachs are assaulted. And all this time, where is the analysis? Where is the attempt to understand what keeps this wheel turning, or where to find the brake pedal? It is not there because most often with such emotionally charged issues analysis is condemned, as collusion and academics are pilloried as Benedict Arnolds for attempting to provide systematic explanations for what is plaguing our global society. But with no clear end in sight of the hysteria that has been whipped up over COVID-2019, perhaps it is time to abandon this policy of ignorance and really look at the struggle against the virus systematically.

This book brings together scholars from across the globe to examine the hysteria that has been conjured over COVID-2019 which is adversely affecting people culturally, psychologically, economically, politically, and socially. These scholars come from the Humanities and the Sciences. The topics covered are both disciplinary and thematic. In the rest of this chapter, an attempt is made to provide a broader understanding of the subject covered in the book by discussing the theoretical basis of hysteria and relevant epidemiological concepts of the COVID-2019.

HYSTERIA: A THEORETICAL DISCUSSION

To begin with, conceptually, *hysteria* informally refers to uncontrollable psychological overabundance. Contemporary medical professionals mostly ditch the concept *hysteria* when designating a diagnostic classification. Instead, they employ more exactly explicable terms to group disorders; these terms include *somatization* (the production of recurrent and multiple medical symptoms with no discernible organic cause), *conversion* (the manifestation of a mental disturbance as a physical disorder or disease), and *dissociation* (the separation of normally related mental processes, resulting in one group functioning independently from the rest, leading in extreme cases to disorders such as multiple personality) (Beattie and Lenihan, 2018; Adams and Sutker, 1984; the definitions in parentheses were self-generated by us using the *Google Online Dictionary*).

The term *hysteria* is traced to the Greek language and means "uterus." Nonetheless, the aforementioned contemporary denotation of the term is not equivalent to its Greek origin; instead, the ancient Greeks utilized the notion of "hysterical suffocation" to refer to a person feeling heat and lacking the capability to breathe. For the ancient Greeks, the uterus was believed to move through the body of a woman and subsequently chokes her and instigates diseases. Although this belief indicates a physical cause for all symptoms, connecting it to the uterus, however, means that hysteria can only occur among women (O'Brien, 2009; Gilman et al., 1993).

In earlier times, since hysteria was perceived to exist among women and, thus, the term *female hysteria*, its symptoms such as *anxiety* (a feeling of worry, nervousness, or unease, typically about an imminent event or something with an uncertain outcome), *dyspnea* (shortness of breath, which is an uncomfortable condition that makes it difficult to fully get air into the lungs), *fainting* (loss of consciousness for a short time because of a temporarily insufficient supply of oxygen to the brain), *insomnia* (habitual sleeplessness), *irritability* (the quality or state of having a tendency to be easily annoyed or made angry), *nervousness* (the quality or state of being easily agitated or alarmed, tending to be anxious or highly strung), and *sexually forward behavior* (using visual, verbal, written, or behavioral material or action with sexual undertones implying sexual intent in order to provoke sexual arousal) were all classified as female manifestations. Nonetheless, since these symptoms are similar to those of other more determinable diseases, later medical practitioners began to challenge the bona fides of the concept of hysteria and designated it as a cover term for a disease or period of sickness affecting the body or mind. Therefore, during the twentieth century, the term hysteria was employed to designate mental disorders as opposed to physical or uterine ones. In contemporary times the tag hysteria is utilized to characterize "mass hysteria"—that is, mass panic (Gilman et al., 1993; Maines, 1999; Tasca et al., 2012; the definitions in parentheses were self-generated by us using the *Google Online Dictionary*).

Next, the theory undergirding hysteria is traceable to the work of Austrian neurologist and founder of psychoanalysis Sigmund Freud (1856–1939). He began his analysis with the incidences of patients like Katherine who developed trouble breathing and apparitions of a dreadful face gazing at her after seeing her father sexually assaulting her cousin. The many tests done on these patients showed that the outcomes were not physically induced (Gray, 2016; Nicholson, 2017).

After a decade of his psychoanalytical practice, Freud concluded that underlying every hysterical symptom, such as *convulsion* (a sudden, violent, irregular movement of a limb or of the body, caused by involuntary contraction of muscles), *paralysis* (the loss of the ability to move, and sometimes to feel anything, in part or most of the body), *blindness* (the state or condition of being unable to see), *epilepsy* (a neurological disorder marked by sudden recurrent episodes of sensory disturbance, loss of consciousness, or convulsions, associated with abnormal electrical activity in the brain), *amnesia* (a partial or total loss of memory), and *pain* (physical suffering or discomfort), was a hidden trauma or series of traumas. In his many case examples, he conscientiously unearthed these initially concealed traumas (Nicholson, 2017; the definitions in parentheses were self-generated by us using the *Google Online Dictionary*).

At the end of his sojourn with French neurologist and professor of anatomical pathology Jean-Martin Charcot (1825–1893) during the winter of 1885–1886, Freud started having an interest in hysteria, even though his earlier work was mainly in the areas of neuropathology and general medicine. It was from the ideas of Charcot and his closest acolytes like French psychologist, philosopher, and psychotherapist Pierre Marie Félix Janet (1859–1947) and French anatomist, physiologist, sculptor, and anatomical artist Paul Marie Louis Pierre Richer (1849–1933) that Freud based his earlier analyses on hysteria in men, impact of subconscious notions, function of traumas, and psychological and sexual elements (Bogousslavsky and Dieguez, 2014).

Thereafter, Freud teamed up with Austrian physician Josef Breuer (1842–1925) to birth a theory of hysteria which comprised an amalgamation of Janet's "fixed subconscious ideas" and the concept of "pathological secret" proffered by Hungarian-Austrian neurologist Moriz/Moritz Benedikt (1835–1920). In 1895, the book titled *Studies on Hysteria* authored by Freud and Breuer was published. Entailed in the book are a joint introductory paper written in 1893 by the two authors; five individual essays on "hysterics"—four by Freud and one by Breuer; a theoretical paper by Breuer; and a therapy practice-oriented essay by Freud (Jones, 1964; Bogousslavsky and Dieguez, 2014).

Thereupon, Freud ended his collaboration with Breuer and ushered the concept of conversion of psychological problems into somatic manifestations, anchored on a solid foundation of "sexualization" of hysteria. Julien Bogousslavsky and Sebastian Dieguez describe this transformation of Freud's thought on hysteria as follows:

> Firstly, he believed that actual abuses had occurred in these patients (the "seduction" theory), but then blamed them for having deceived him on that issue, so that he subsequently launched a "fantasy" theory to explain the development of hysterical symptoms without the necessity of actual abuses. Like many of his contemporaries, and contrary to his claims, Freud did not follow a scientific process of verified experiments, but rather adapted his theories to the evolution of his own beliefs on psychological conditions, selectively emphasizing the aspects of his "therapies" with patients which supported his emerging ideas, with often abrupt changes in theoretical interpretations. While it remains difficult to get a clear, synthetic vision of what was Freud's definite theory of hysteria, it is obvious that hysteria really was the origin of what would become Freud's psychoanalytical theory. Indeed, psychoanalysis appears to have been initially developed by him largely in order to absorb and explain his many changes in the interpretation of hysterical manifestations. (Bogousslavsky and Dieguez, 2014, p. 109)

Nonetheless, according to Bogousslavsky and Dieguez, Freud's therapy, like Breuer's "talking cure," hinged upon bringing the original traumatic memory back into the patient's consciousness. The patient is "cured" once s/

he is freed from repression and the trauma ceases to cause hysterical symptoms (Bogousslavsky and Dieguez, 2014; Gray, 2016).

Also, a relatively recent study done by Timothy R. Nicholson and six of his colleagues discovered buttressing proof supporting the postulate that stressors at the time symptoms begin might be pertinent for some patients suffering from hysteria caused by psychological stress or trauma (Nicholson et al., 2016). Given the import of this study, it behooves us to restate its synopsis in the following paragraphs verbatim. In terms of the background and method, Nicholson et al. state the following:

> Background: Psychological models of conversion disorder (CD) traditionally assume that psychosocial stressors are identifiable around symptom onset. In the face of limited supportive evidence such models are being challenged. Method: Forty-three motor CD patients, 28 depression patients and 28 healthy controls were assessed using the Life Events and Difficulties Schedule in the year before symptom onset. A novel "escape" rating for events was developed to test the Freudian theory that physical symptoms of CD could provide escape from stressors, a form of "secondary gain." (Nicholson et al., 2016, p. 2617)

Regarding the results and conclusions:

> Results: CD patients had significantly more severe life events and "escape" events than controls. In the month before symptom onset at least one severe event was identified in 56% of CD patients—significantly more than 21% of depression patients [odds ratio (OR) 4.63, 95% confidence interval (CI) 1.56–13.70] and healthy controls (OR 5.81, 95% CI 1.86–18.2). In the same time period 53% of CD patients had at least one "high escape" event—again significantly higher than 14% in depression patients (OR 6.90, 95% CI 2.05–23.6) and 0% in healthy controls. Previous sexual abuse was more commonly reported in CD than controls, and in one third of female patients was contextually relevant to life events at symptom onset. The majority (88%) of life events of potential aetiological relevance were not identified by routine clinical assessments. Nine per cent of CD patients had no identifiable severe life events. Conclusions: Evidence was found supporting the psychological model of CD, the Freudian notion of escape and the potential aetiological relevance of childhood traumas in some patients. (Nicholson et al., 2016, pp. 2617–2618)

Finally, understanding hysteria, which is the pillar of the analyses in the present book, is requisite because, as Jonathan L. Freedman, for example, informs us, heightened hysteria can lead to *hysterical or conversion neurosis*: that is, "the development of an actual physical disability for no physical reason" (Freedman, 1978, p. 464). While this aspect has been discussed in passing, more needs to be said about it. Despite the lack of physical cause, a hysterical neurotic can become visually impaired, paraplegic, and so on. It is not the case whereby a person can pretend to be ill in order to avoid an unpleasant situation (Freedman, 1978), as when a nurse pretends to be ill in order to avoid dealing with COVID-2019 patients out of fear that s/he will be infected by the virus. Hence, as Freedman points out, whereas a healthy person knows that s/he is faking, does not actually get sick, and can stop acting anytime, the hysterical neurotic who has become visually impaired cannot see even if s/he wants to do so, and no degree of effort on his/her part will permit him/her to see (Freedman, 1978).

Indeed, several reports on the CDC website indicate that there have been many cases of hysteria related to reactions to the COVID-2019 pandemic. The sources for the hysteria include (a) depression and feelings of hopelessness when a person is infected by the virus, (b) isolation by family members and/or friends when one is infected, (c) negative information spread through the news media repeatedly, and (d) negative information coming from authoritative sources that have been politicized by the news media and social networks making the negative information ever present (CDC, 2020a).

RELEVANT EPIDEMIOLOGICAL CONCEPTS OF THE COVID-2019

In this section, relevant epidemiological concepts of the COVID-2019 are broached. What follows is based on information derived from the *CDC Self Study Text* (2020b), news accounts, and other sources. In order to make the discussion coherent, the rest of the narrative is divided into six separate but interrelated sections. It should be noted also that discussions of some of the related concepts are grouped together for cohesion.

Assessing a Community's Health

In order to assess a community's health, six questions are suggested and answers provided for them. The first question is this: What are the actual and potential health problems in the community? The actual and potential health problems are fever, cough, fatigue, lack of appetite, shortness of breath, mucus/phlegm, body aches, trouble breathing, constant pain or pressure in the chest, bluish lips or face, and sudden confusion (Cassoobhoy, 2020).

The second question is the following: Where are the health problems occurring? The cases are occurring all over the world, but specifically with respect to the United States, they are occurring mostly in Texas, Florida, California,

Washington State, Illinois, Indiana, Ohio, New York, Massachusetts, Rhode Island, and Connecticut (CDC, 2020b).

The following is the third question: Which population is at increased risk? The population that is at increased risk comprises those who are 65 years and older living in a nursing home or long-term care facility, with chronic lungs disease or moderate to severe asthma, serious heart conditions, immunodeficiency, severe obesity (body mass index of 40 or higher), diabetes, chronic kidney disease undergoing dialysis, or liver disease (CDC, 2020b).

The fourth question is as follows: Which health problems have declined over time? It seems that only fevers have declined over time (Bailey, 2020).

The following is the fifth question: Which health problems are increasing or have the potential to increase? The three that are increasing or have the potential to increase are pneumonia, myocarditis which is marked inflammation of the heart muscle, and high blood pressure (Lewis, 2020).

The sixth and final question reads as follows: How do these health patterns relate to the level and distribution of public health services available? These two aspects are related in that even though there have been many companies providing resources to state, local, ethnic/"tribal," and territorial public health officials, the cases are more prevalent where there aren't enough resources. This is why the United States Department of Health and Human Services (HHS), for instance, has made a 30-day commitment to help slow the spread of the COVID-2019 (HHS, 2020).

Making Individual Decisions

There are many individual decisions people can make to help to slow the spread of COVID-2019. These include (a) wearing cloth face coverings—homemade masks, scarves, bandanas—in public settings, such as the grocery store or a pharmacy, where other social distancing measures are difficult to maintain and when other masks are not available; (b) calling a primary care physician, the local public health department, or the local coronavirus hotline if one has been established; (c) staying home; (d) washing your hands; (e) maintaining aggressive social distancing; (f) changing clothes after going places; and (g) not touching your face (Pittalwala, 2020).

Completing the Clinical Picture

Data obtainable from reports and directives provided by health policy agencies allow for dividing the clinical manifestations of the disease according to the severity of the clinical pictures. The COVID-2019 may present mild, moderate, or severe illness. Among the severe clinical manifestations are severe pneumonia, acute respiratory distress syndrome, sepsis, and septic shock (Cascella et al., 2020).

The clinical picture of patients with COVID-2019 and with sepsis is particularly serious and characterized by a wide range of signs and symptoms of multi-organ involvement. They include respiratory manifestations such as severe dyspnea and hypoxemia, renal impairment with reduced urine output, tachycardia, altered mental status, and functional alterations of organs. When the disease results in complex clinical pictures of MOD (multiple organ dysfunction), then organ function support with respiratory support is mandatory (Cascella et al., 2020).

Searching for Causes and Public Health Surveillance

Coronaviruses are a family of viruses that can cause illnesses such as the common cold, SARS, and MERS. In 2019, a new coronavirus was identified as the cause of a disease outbreak that originated in China. The virus is now known as the SARS-CoV-2. The disease it causes is called COVID-2019. In March 2020, the WHO declared the COVID-2019 outbreak a pandemic (Mayo Clinic, 2020).

There are many types of public health surveillance. The first type is Virologic Surveillance, which is the percentage of specimens testing positive across laboratory types and the age of the person tested, if available. The second type is Outpatient and Emergency Department Illness Surveillances, each of which monitors a slightly different syndrome, and together provide a more comprehensive picture of mild to moderate COVID-2019 illness than either would individually. The third type is U.S. Outpatient Influenza-like Illness Surveillance Network, which provides data on visits for influenza-like illness (temperature of 100°F [37.8°C] or greater) and a cough and/or a sore throat (without a known cause other than influenza) to approximately 2,600 primary care providers, emergency departments, and urgent care centers in all 50 states, Puerto Rico, the District of Columbia, and the U.S. Virgin Islands. The last, but not the least, is Hospitalization Surveillance, whose rates are monitored through the COVID-2019-Associated Hospitalization Surveillance Network. It covers associated hospitalizations in more than 250 acute care hospitals in 99 counties in the 10 Emerging Infections Program states (CA, CO, CT, GA, MD, MN, NM, NY, OR, and TN) and four Influenza Hospitalization Surveillance Project states (IA, MI, OH, and UT). In total, approximately 10 percent of the U.S. population is covered by this surveillance system (CDC, 2020b).

Field Investigation, Analytic Studies, and Evaluation

The study of COVID-2019 clusters in Singapore found that the three clusters involved a Chinese tour group, company conference, and a church rather than simply household clusters. A total of 36 cases of individuals tested positive for COVID-2019, relating to Clusters A (11), B (20), and C (5), denoting the setting of transmission, respectively. Cluster A included individuals with interrelated interactions with the tour group. The only overlap in activities among Cluster C was that five of the patients visited the church at the same time (Lennon and Shah, 2020).

In terms of etiology, COVID-2019 is caused by a novel, enveloped single-stranded RNA virus (SARS-CoV-2). It is the seventh known coronavirus in humans and belongs to the same phylogenic family as the 2002 SARS and the 2012 MERS-Cov-2. It is presumed to have originated in bats, thereby giving a remarkable (89–96 percent) genetic homology; but for coronaviruses, SARS and MERS-CoV-2, the culprits of the two respiratory viral epidemics of the past two decades, similarly emerged from bats and infected civets (SARS) and camels (MERS-CoV-2) before spreading to humans (Oren et al., 2020).

As it concerns transmissibility and case fatality rates, the basic reproductive number ("R0"), a measure of the expected number of cases that is generated from one case, is estimated to be 1.5–3.0 for SARS-CoV-2 as opposed to 0.5–1.0 and 1.5–4.0 with MERS-CoV-2 and SARS, respectively. SARS had a 10 percent mortality rate while MERS-CoV-2 had a 34.4 percent mortality rate (Oren et al., 2020).

Most countries are utilizing some type of clinical and epidemiologic information to determine who should have testing performed. In patients with confirmed COVID-2019 diagnoses, the laboratory evaluation should be repeated to evaluate for viral clearance prior to being released from observation (Cascella et al., 2020).

Case Definitions

A suspect case is defined as (a) a patient with acute respiratory illness (fever and at least one sign/symptom of respiratory disease—e.g., cough, shortness of breath) and a history of travel to or residence in a location reporting community transmission of COVID-2019 disease during the 14 days prior to symptom onset; (b) a patient with any acute respiratory illness and having been in contact with a confirmed or probable COVID-2019 case in the last 14 days prior to symptom onset; or (c) a patient with severe acute respiratory illness (fever and at least one sign/symptom of respiratory disease—e.g., cough, shortness of breath, and requiring hospitalization) and in the absence of an alternative diagnosis that fully explains the clinical presentation. Probable case is defined as (a) a suspect case for whom testing for the COVID-2019 virus is inconclusive as reported by the laboratory or (b) a suspect case for whom testing could not be performed for any reason. A confirmed case is defined as a person with laboratory confirmation of COVID-2019 infection (WHO, 2020).

REFERENCES

Adams, H. E. and Sutker, P. B., eds. (1984). *Comprehensive Handbook of Psychopathology*. New York: Springer.

Bailey, R. (April 6, 2020). U.S. fever trends suggest COVID-19 rates could soon decline. Retrieved on April 19, 2020 from https://reason.com/2020/04/06/u-s-fever-trends-suggest-covid-19-rates-could-soon-decline/.

Beattie, M. and Lenihan, P. (2018). *Counseling Skills for Working with Gender Diversity and Identity*. London, UK: Jessica Kingsley Publishers.

Bogousslavsky, J. and Dieguez, S. (2014). Sigmund Freud and hysteria: The etiology of psychoanalysis? *Frontiers of Neurology and Neuroscience* 35:109–125. Retrieved on May 2, 2020 from https://www.ncbi.nlm.nih.gov/pubmed/25273494.

Cascella, M., Rajnik, M., Cuomo, A., Dulebohn, S. C. and Napoli, R. D. (April 6, 2020). Features, evaluation and treatment of coronavirus (COVID-19). Retrieved on April 19, 2020 from https://www.ncbi.nlm.nih.gov/books/NBK554776/.

Cassoobhoy, A. (April 17, 2020). Symptoms of coronavirus: Early signs, serious symptoms and more. Retrieved on April 18, 2020 from https://www.webmd.com/lung/covid-19-symptoms#1.

Centers for Disease Control and Prevention—CDC. (2020a). Situation summary. Retrieved on April 4, 2020 from https://www.cdc.gov/coronavirus/2019-ncov/cases-updates/summary.html#emergence.

Centers for Disease Control and Prevention—CDC. (2020b). *CDC Self Study Text*. Retrieved on April 19, 2020 from https://www.cdc.gov/.

Freedman, J. L. (1978). *Introductory Psychology*. Boston, MA: Addison-Wesley Publishing Company.

Gilman, S. L., King, H., Porter, R., Rousseau, G. S. and Showalter, E. (1993). *Hysteria Beyond Freud*. Berkeley, CA: University of California Press.

Gray, R. T. (2016). Freud and the literary imagination. University of Washington Faculty Web Server. Retrieved on May 2, 2020 from http://courses.washington.edu/freudlit/Hysteria.Notes.html.

Health and Human Services (HHS) Office & Public Affairs. (March 27, 2020). HHS Coronavirus (COVID-19) updates. Retrieved on April 19, 2020 from https://www.hhs.gov/about/news/coronavirus/index.html.

Jones, E. (1964). *The Life and Work of Sigmund Freud*. London, UK: Penguin Books.

Lennon, J. and Shah, R. (March 31, 2020). Investigation of COVID-19 clusters in Singapore. Retrieved on April 18, 2020 from https://www.2minutemedicine.com/investigation-of-covid-19-clusters-in-singapore/.

Lewis, D. K. L. (April 4, 2020). How does cardiovascular disease increase the risk of severe illness and death from COVID-19? Retrieved on April 18, 2020 from https://www.health.harvard.edu/blog/how-does-cardiovascular-disease-increase-the-risk-of-severe-illness-and-death-from-covid-19-2020040219401.

Maines, R. P. (1999). *The Technology of Orgasm: "Hysteria," the Vibrator, and Women's Sexual Satisfaction*. Baltimore, MD: The Johns Hopkins University Press.

Mayo Clinic. (April 15, 2020). Coronavirus disease 2019 (COVID-19). Retrieved on April 18, 2020 from https://www.mayoclinic.org/diseases-conditions/coronavirus/symptoms-causes/syc-20479963.

Nicholson, C. (November 16, 2017). Why Freud was right about hysteria. *The Conversation.* Retrieved on May 2, 2020 from https://theconversation.com/why-freud-was-right-about-hysteria-86497.

Nicholson, T. R., Aybek, S., Craig, T, Harris, T, Wojcik, W., David, A. S. and Kanaan, R. A. (2016). Life events and escape in conversion disorder. *Psychological Medicine* 46(12):2617–2626.

O'Brien, J., ed. (2009). *Encyclopedia of Gender and Society*. Thousand Oaks, CA: Sage Publications.

Oren, O. L., Kopecky, S. J., Gluckman, T. J., Gersh, B. S. and Blumenthal, R. (April 6, 2020). Coronavirus disease 2019 (COVID-19): Epidemiology, clinical spectrum and implications for the cardiovascular clinician. Retrieved on April 19, 2020 from https://www.acc.org/latest-in-cardiology/articles/2020/04/06/11/08/covid-19-epidemiology-clinical-spectrum-and-implications-for-the-cv-clinician.

Pittalwala, I. (April 6, 2020). Epidemiologist answers questions on COVID-19 ranging from grocery store visits to wearing masks and gloves. Retrieved on April 19, 2020 from https://news.ucr.edu/articles/2020/04/06/epidemiologist-answers-questions-covid-19-ranging-grocery-store-visits-wearing.

Tasca, C., Rapetti, M., Carta, M. G. and Fadda, B. (October 19, 2012). Women and hysteria in mental health. *Clinical Practice and Epidemiology in Mental Health* 8:110-119. Retrieved on April 30, 2020 from https://www.ncbi.nlm.nih.gov/pmc/articles/PMC3480686/

World Health Organization—WHO. (March 20, 2020). Coronavirus disease 2019 (COVID-19), *Situation Report–61*. Geneva, Switzerland. Retrieved on April 18, 2020 from https://www.who.int/docs/default-source/coronaviruse/situation-reports/20200321-sitrep-61-covid-19.pdf.

Chapter 2

Coroeducation

Ishmael I. Munene and Jafred Muyaka

If there is one event in the year 2020 that will forever be etched in our collective memories, it will be the outbreak of the Coronavirus Disease (COVID-2019) and its subsequent declaration as a global pandemic by the World Health Organization on January 30, 2020. First detected in Wuhan, China, on December 31, 2019, the pandemic has spread across the globe with devastating consequences on all spheres of human lives. From lockdowns to curfews to shelter-in-place restrictions in human movements, countries have sought to establish as much social distance between individuals as possible as they seek to contain the spread of this highly contagious and lethal pandemic. From Africa to Asia, from Americas to Europe, and from Australia to New Zealand, countries have sought to mitigate the effects of the pandemic through targeted legislation, law enforcement, and economic relief to the most vulnerable populations. But the effects of the pandemic are palpable all over: empty cities and towns, economic shutdowns and disruption of economic activities, large spikes in sudden unemployment, empty religious sanctuaries, and unoccupied educational establishments, among others. The global scale of the impact is unquestionable.

Of the many impacted institutions, educational establishments rank among the top. Schools, colleges, and universities enroll students in millions, making their closures or change of instructional mode extremely consequential for all stakeholders in the sector, including students, teachers, parents, and policymakers. The United Nations Education, Scientific and Cultural Organization (UNESCO) estimates that institutional closures had affected close to 1.37 billion students by March 24, 2020 (UNESCO, 2020). Higher education has taken a big hit with budget cuts, fall in enrollments, job losses, and unpaid furloughs that have affected both public and private universities on an unprecedented scale (Czerniewicz, 2020). This chapter explores the impact of COVID-2019 on higher education. Specifically, it looks at how universities in Kenya responded to the threat posed by the pandemic in the context of the government order that all educational institutions be closed and transition to other modes of instruction. By university, the authors refer to any Commission for University Education (CUE)-accredited degree-granting institution operating within Kenya. It excludes unaccredited universities as well as other tertiary educational institutions that award diplomas or associate degrees.

The chapter addresses two interrelated questions: (1) What does the order to shut down universities in Kenya during the COVID-2019 crisis imply for university autonomy? (2) In what ways and under what conditions have universities responded to this order to shut down? The shutdown order, though good in intent, is emblematic of the historical state incursion into university autonomy that has characterized state-university relations in the country. Furthermore, institutional responses to the shutdown have been contingent upon contextual variables, including ownership type and resource dependency with four levels of responses evident, namely strategic, incremental, partial paralysis, and complete paralysis. The authors employ a variety of data sources in this analysis, including Internet sources, personal communication with critical informants in the universities, important documents including memos, as well as our personal knowledge of the institutions as they responded to the threat posed by the COVID-2019 pandemic.

This chapter is important for several reasons. First, it is vital to appreciate how institutions are prepared to respond to emergency situations as the one posed by the COVID-2019 pandemic. Usually universities operate on an academic calendar without anticipating crisis that may render the calendar irrelevant if not unrealistic. The question becomes how well they are prepared to institute emergency measures to cope with the unfolding predicament and what short-term measures they can put in place to mitigate the disaster. This chapter allows us to gauge the various scenarios that Kenyan universities exhibited. Second, the analysis permits us to assess the effect of contextual variables in determining institutional responses to emergency crises. Ideally, it would be anticipated that all universities in a context would respond in a similar manner. However, this analysis enables us to link the varied institutional responses to institutional contexts. This is important for scholars with interest in institutional development, Resource Dependency Theory (RDT), as well as institutional isomorphism. Third, for policymakers, it is vital that they develop policies that would guide institutions in responding to emergency crises. Nations and institutions were caught off guard with the outbreak of the COVID-2019 pandemic. Many universities had never put in place emergency committees or procedures but have made decisions along the way. It is true no one can anticipate which crisis will arise, but simulating scenarios and developing reasonable response actions need to be encapsulated in institutional planning. The case analysis undertaken in this chapter should go a long way in shedding light on some of the pertinent issues to be considered in emergency planning.

The chapter begins with a brief overview of contemporary university education in Kenya which allows us to provide a brief historical context of university development in the country. This is followed by an examination of the government's decisions to shut down educational institutions in response to the pandemic. A critique of the decision enables us to locate the government's overreach in the context of the state's historical incursion into university governance and the attendant threat to institutional autonomy. Then there is a brief discussion of crisis management in higher education. An analysis of Kenya's situation points to a lack of preparedness by universities in handling crises such as COVID-2019 pandemic. The next sections provide illustrative cases of universities' responses to the government shutdown order. The various cases highlight the different approaches universities took and the context underlying those responses. The concluding section of the chapter offers lessons learned and the way forward in terms of universities responding to emergency crises.

THEORETICAL PERSPECTIVES

In this section, the authors elucidate the theories that inform our analysis of the different responses manifested by Kenyan universities in response to the closure order of the state. Why would universities in a similar context differ radically in their responses to an emerging crisis? How does context explain the varying responses? The authors situate the answers to these questions in two theoretical constructs that have been advanced to institutional behavior: that is, (1) RDT and (2) Institutional Isomorphism Theory (IIT). Although the authors choose to use these theories because they offer the best plausible explanations, we are cognizant that other plausible theories are available. Furthermore, it is our view that the two theories provide a very good complementary explanatory power in contextualizing institutional behavior during a crisis.

The RDT has its roots in the sociology of organizations premised around the view that organizations must transact with their environment in order to acquire resources. The theory, first expounded by Pfeffer and Salancik in their seminal work, *The External Control of Organizations: A Resource Dependence Perspective* (1978), asserts that an organization is defined by its contextual environment: that is, its ecology. Since the external environment has such power on organizations, Pfeffer and Salancik argue that managers can act to reduce dependency and environmental uncertainty. In this regard, power is critical to an organization's attempt to reduce others' power over it and to increase its power over others. Power allows for the control of vital resources. Put differently, according to RDT, relying on external resources, although useful, generates unequal power relations and dependency to the disadvantage of an organization. The resources an organization needs to survive may be scarce or in control by uncooperative actors, thereby threatening its very survival (Archibald, 2017). Not surprising, organizations develop adaptive strategies and internal structures to gain advantage in resource-related transactions. Among others, the strategies include taking political action, increasing the organization's scale of production, diversifying, and developing links to other organizations (Archibald, 2017).

Nonetheless, RDT is not without its skeptics who question whether it has overwhelming explanatory power even in situations where organizations engage in adaptive strategies to survive a hostile environment. Hillman, Withers, and Collins (2009), for example, document instances in which the theory does not provide sufficient explanation when organizations realign their internal and external strategies in order to survive. Of these instances, they cite mergers and acquisitions, joint ventures, board of directors' size and compositions, political action through campaign contributions, and executive succession. To fully explain these developments, RDT has to be juxtaposed with other theoretical lenses such as Institutional Theory, Stakeholder Theory, and Real Option Theory. In doing so, "the emergence of and advantages gained from these interdependency-reducing strategies may be better understood. The interaction of interdependent organizations and their environment is a dynamic, complex process requiring robust perspectives that can explain a broad range of outcomes" (Hillman, Withers and Collins, 2009, p. 1418). Additionally, since most RDT studies have been undertaken in the U.S. context, expanding rigorous research to test the theory in other national contexts will permit us to judge its efficacy in organizations in other cultural environments.

The other useful theory in this chapter, as stated earlier, is IIT. This theory seeks to explain the predictability or uniformity of organizational structures and behaviors in a cultural context. The theory was first articulated by DiMaggio and Walter in their seminal essay, "The Iron Cage Revisited: Institutional Isomorphism and Collective Rationality in Organizational Fields" (1983), in which they assert that previously organizational rationality emanated from the need for efficiency in the marketplace, but now it arises from institutional constraints imposed by the state and the professions. The need to achieve rationality during uncertainty and constraint leads to homogeneity of structure, otherwise known as institutional isomorphism. Rather than being an innovative process, isomorphism is a constraining process which, according to DiMaggio and Walter, "forces one unit in a population to resemble other units that face the same set of environmental conditions" (1983, p. 149). DiMaggio and Walter go on to argue that the bureaucratization of both the state and the corporation has been achieved and organizations are becoming more homogenous. The common denominator is that bureaucracy remains the common organizing form. Nonetheless, structural change in organizations is no longer driven by competition or need for market efficiency but rather by processes that do not make them more efficient but more similar.

DiMaggio and Walter (1983) identify three mechanisms through which isomorphic change occurs: (1) coercive isomorphism, (2) mimetic isomorphism, and (3) normative isomorphism. Coercive isomorphism denotes the pressures exerted on an organization by the one on which it is dependent. Coercive isomorphism could emanate from political pressure, legislative change, or even technological evolution. Mimetic isomorphism arises when an organization duplicates the practices of another it deems to be successful. This type of isomorphism is apparent where an organization lacks clear goals or how to accomplish them, and the successful organization appears to provide the appropriate model to emulate. Normative isomorphism is the pressure exerted on an organization by the professions, the concern being our values and broader social values. Norms are usually developed during education, training, and licensing of professionals. Other ways in which norms are transmitted are through inter-organizational networks that cut across different enterprises. Employees in an organization with similar qualifications or background view issues through the same lenses which enhance conformities. In all, isomorphism is both a state and a process.

One of the criticisms of institutional isomorphism is the absence of context in organizational analysis. There is an assumption that organizations in a particular region will be shaped equally by the same forces, thereby ignoring historical factors, traditions, and local political calculations. So, rather than speak of isomorphism, Hedgecoe (2012) speaks of "assumed isomorphism" to denote the possibility that organizations in a particular region may show similarities but underlying these are structural, functional, and organizational differences. Other scholars reject the idea that similar institutions in each sector will outright display isomorphic features, although the tendency to assume this is the case may be tempting. Levy (2004) contends that the private higher education sector displays wide differentiation than isomorphic tendencies and, therefore, institutional isomorphism lacks explanatory power. Also, Beckert (2010) argues that whereas there are powerful forces shaping organizational processes toward greater homogeneity, the same forces lead to organizational differentiation or heterogeneity. Organizational change, he reasons, does not necessarily occur in a uniform and linear fashion in favor of homogenization. He concludes that the idea of an "iron cage" could be a mirage.

Notwithstanding the misgivings expressed about both the RDT and the IIT, the authors feel that they are suitable for our analysis of Kenyan universities' responses to the COVID-2019 crisis. They may not fully capture all the nuances in similarities and distinctiveness, but they do help us to capture the broad contours of the universities' responses. Universities in Kenya display common organizational characteristics and behave in a similar manner with differentiation evidence based on ownership. Also, the authors can delineate responses to the crisis into categories which are due to contextual variables that are consistent with each of the strata. For these reasons, the authors are inclined to adopt these theories for their case analyses.

THE STATE OF UNIVERSITY EDUCATION IN KENYA

In this section, the authors provide a brief overview of the growth of university education in Kenya. The country's university sector has two structural categories: (1) the public and (2) the private universities. Furthermore, the authors examine the various typologies and key education indicators such as accredited universities in Kenya and student enrollment.

Growth of University Education in Kenya

With only one national public university (University of Nairobi) and one public constituent college (Kenyatta University College) in the 1970s, Kenya has invested heavily in university education and now boasts of the largest university education in East Africa. According to the CUE, there are 74 public and private universities authorized to operate in Kenya (CUE, 2020). These are 31 public chartered universities, 6 public constituent colleges, 18 private chartered universities, 5 private constituent colleges, and 14 institutions with letters of interim authority.

In terms of typology, universities in Kenya are categorized into two main strata: (1) the public and (2) private universities. The main source of funding for university operations has been used as a dichotomy to achieve this. Historically, funding sources for private universities have largely been from student fees. Although there are other sources such as tithes and endowments with varying levels of emphasis (UNESCO, 2005), the context has, however, changed with the entry of government sources. Since 2016/2017, the government partnered with private universities to admit government-sponsored (funded) students. During this time, the enrollment of public-funded students in private universities stood at 10,000.

Private universities in Kenya are not homogenous but present a complex heterogeneity in their composition. One easily identifiable category is religious-based private universities and non-religious-based private universities. From a broader sense, religious-based private universities refer to those private universities in Kenya that were established by or affiliated with religious institutions and were "not for profit" making. They constitute most of the private universities operating in the country. Of the 18 private chartered universities, 14 are affiliated with religious institutions. The sponsor religious institutions are known to have an influence on the teaching with infusion of their philosophical beliefs in the curricula. The non-religious-based private universities in Kenya are profit-making entities.

Over the years, Kenya's universities have experienced exponential growth in student enrollment. At independence, Kenya had only 571 students enrolled in University College Nairobi (Weidman, 1995). In 1983/1984, there were 7,418 students; in 1988/1989, the enrollment had risen to 21,846; and by 2000/2001, the enrollment had shot up to 59,193 (Sifuna, 1998; UNESCO, 2005). Currently, enrollment in Kenya's universities stands at 512,911; the majority of the students are enrolled in public universities (426,965 or 83.2 percent) while 85,946 (16.8 percent) in private universities (KNBS, 2019). Gender parity has not been achieved with the ratio of female students in public universities averaging 40.3 percent for the last three years compared to 47 percent for private universities.

Marginalization of women is also evident in the proportion of faculty. Data from CUE shows that women only make up 3,650 (30 percent) of the faculty staff (Too, Kandie and Oure, 2018). The figure is less for private universities (27 percent). Legally, public universities are operating within the provisions of the Constitution of Kenya (2010) which demands a representation of at least 30 percent of the either gender.

UNIVERSITIES CLOSURE AND THE AUTONOMY QUESTION

Our interest in this section is to problematize the COVID-2019-related universities shut down by the state action in the general context of university autonomy. As our analysis will illuminate, tensions between the state and the universities have brought to the forefront the tenuous nature of university autonomy in Kenya. On March 15, 2020, the president of the Republic of Kenya, Uhuru Kenyatta, ordered the closure of all learning institutions as a measure to contain the spread of COVID-2019, a surprise move that caught everyone off guard. He declared:

> We have suspended learning in all our education institutions with immediate effect. Consequently, and to facilitate a phased approach, primary and secondary day schools are to suspend operations from tomorrow. For those in boarding schools, the school administration should ensure students are home by Wednesday, while universities and tertiary institutions are to close by Friday. (Kabale, 2020, p. 1)

The public health interest in this measure is indisputable and, indeed, it was the right action to take. What is at stake, however, is the decision-making process and its implications for university autonomy. With the threat posed by this highly contagious pandemic, it was inevitable that instruction and student residential services could not proceed in the traditional mode due to the social distancing requirements in addition to high levels of hygiene observance. The state may have deemed it wise to move with haste and close all learning institutions, including universities, but this action robbed the institutions, which hitherto have made closure decisions under difficult conditions, the authority to determine the best course of action for their constituents, especially the students and the academic staff. They merely effected the government's order on closure.

The academic senate is the highest decision-making body on academic matters in Kenyan universities. Such matters include university closure, academic calendar, graduation, and award of degrees. The senate is chaired by the university vice chancellor (president) and is composed of the deputy vice chancellors; heads of faculties and directors of schools, institutes, and other academic units; heads of academic departments; and student representatives. Besides the senate, there are other university committees and sub-committees that are charged with important decision-making responsibilities for the smooth operations of the universities. The committee-style decision-making arrangement promotes wide consultation on critical issues and discourages the concentration of decision-making authority in a single individual. According to Sifuna, this arrangement "serves as a channel for the key players to exchange and communicate ideas and differences of opinion between the participating groups. It acts as an aid in the negotiation of outcomes" (2012, p. 123). With the unilateral closure, the government thwarted the age-old tradition of collegial decision-making within the universities on the best strategic direction to undertake in the context of the threat posed by COVID-2019 and the need to respect the academic calendar. Universities were denied the opportunity to deliberate and exercise discretion on class size for social distancing requirements, instructional delivery modes, research reorganization, residential requirements, and revision of the academic calendar, among others.

This abrogation of university internal decision-making prerogative has historical precedents. In 1988, the government ordered public universities to admit first-year students double their enrollment capacity to clear a backlog occasioned by a prolonged closure of the institutions. The universities were never warned to plan for the additional academic staff, classrooms, and residential facilities. The outcome was predictable: overcrowded facilities and deterioration in academic quality (Hughes and Mwiria, 1990). Another double admission occurred in the 1990/1991 academic year, barely three years after the first one. The need for this was necessitated by the country transitioning to a new education system that saw the elimination of the two-year advance level cycle of high school. Like the first double intake, universities were not given advance warning to plan for a first-year intake double their capacity (Sifuna, 1998). In both instances, the government took charge of making the critical decisions while letting the public universities manage the consequences of the state actions.

What do all these government interventions mean for university autonomy in Kenya? In broad terms, autonomy refers to self-government: that is, the ability accorded to universities to make decisions without outside interference. Berdahl (1990) makes a distinction between two forms of autonomy: (1) substantive autonomy and (2) procedural autonomy. Substantive autonomy is the ability of the university in its corporate form to determine its own goals and programs whereas procedural autonomy refers to how these goals will be attained. Substantive autonomy is the heart and soul of a university as it involves decisions that substantively focus on mission and goals of the universities, namely the academics. Procedural autonomy invites questions of funding, so the state has vested interests (Berdahl, 1990). What we see in the Kenyan case is the state's incursion into the realm of substantive autonomy by ordering university closure and determining the number of students to be admitted without input from the university community.

The government's order of university closure—public and private universities—embodies the unrestricted coercive power of the state to override institutional prerogatives and reshape the education landscape. Whereas governance is a complex broad term, the University Act No. 42 of 2012 looks at governance as formal and informal structures that allow universities to make decisions and to establish, implement, and continuously monitor the proper implementation of policies. These structures bestow authority to specific entities or persons to make decisions about university education. The state exercises external powers, either directly through decrees and pronouncements as was the case during COVID-2019 when universities were closed or indirectly through the state-appointed regulatory bodies such as CUE. In an ideal situation, universities have the freedom or autonomy to make decisions that represent the best interest of their institutions without any sort of interference from external or any non-university entities. The University Act No. 42 of 2012 further leaves the overall administrative management of universities in Kenya in the hands of the university councils. University councils are there to safeguard university autonomy particularly the influence from the state and at the same time, act as a platform for good governance (Mulinge et al., 2017). They ratify the decisions of the university senates to allow for implementation. As the supreme academic body of the university, senates plan for the yearly academic activities because they are responsible for all academic matters of the university. Therefore, the law when implemented in an ideal situation without the unrestricted coercive power of the state gives the university's internal structures to decide on university closure.

The government controls the state levers that extend the right to operate as a university. This includes the government-owned accreditation agency, CUE, and the Higher Education Loans Board (HELB) which are key drivers of university education in Kenya. CUE, on the one hand, ran by a five-member government-appointed commission board, has the sole mandate to grant provisional or full accreditations and to revoke them at its sole discretion among other responsibilities. It is also responsible for communicating government policy to university stakeholders. HELB, on the other hand, is a government agency responsible for providing education financing through loans and scholarships to all eligible students in accredited higher education institutions in Kenya. It is the first point of contact for students, whether in public or private universities, seeking financial aid to pursue higher education. For a university to lose CUE accreditation means the inability to attract HELB-funded students and the right to admit new students which is a significant blow. With these two instruments of university control, it is easy to see why universities had to kowtow to the government's order for immediate closure.

It is not just the coercive power of the state that CUE and HELB exemplify that is palpable; it is also the resource dependency on the economic might of the state that is demonstrated. Through CUE accreditation, universities have access to a huge student financial windfall which in the 2017–2018 academic year was Ksh. 11.3 billion (US$ 11.3 million) that financed 308,021 students (Higher Education Loans Board, 2018). With few other financing options available to students, HELB is a lifesaver for many university students and for a university's students to be locked out of access to this vital funding represents a significant financial hit for the institution.

Appointment to leadership positions in Kenya's public universities is a state prerogative. The president is responsible for naming chancellors of the universities who, although non-executive office holders, do exercise clout in university affairs owing to the political nature of their appointments. The government also appoints and recruits the executive leadership, the university councils, the vice chancellors, and their deputies. Out of the nine council members, who are responsible for overall administrative management of public universities in

Kenya, six are direct appointees of the cabinet secretary of education. The principal secretary in the ministry responsible for university education and the principal secretary in the ministry responsible for finance are the other two council members, again representing government interests. The vice chancellors and their deputies are appointed by the university councils, in consultation with the cabinet secretary of education, from a list of three candidates submitted by the Public Service Commission, another government entity. These appointive powers of the government in public universities translate into coercive influence over universities in specific policy directions. State-appointed university leadership is unlikely to second-guess let alone disobey government directive on university closure, irrespective of the threat it poses to university autonomy and the age-old tradition of internal consultations within the institutions.

CRISIS MANAGEMENT IN UNIVERSITY EDUCATION

The term "crisis" is a relative concept partly because of its interdisciplinary nature. However, scholars have built a general consensus that a crisis is highly unexpected and very uncertain in nature (Zamoun and Gorpe, 2018). We argue that crises unfold rapidly in such unpredictable patterns rendering decision-making process largely controlled by the top leadership. According to Coombs (2012), crises disrupt normal operations of an organization and if badly managed, their consequences can erode the hard-won reputation. In most literature on crisis management, crises are rare, significant, high impact, ambiguous, urgent, and involve high stakes (Zamoun and Gorpe, 2018; Coombs, 2012).

It is the conclusive conceptualization that a crisis is unexpected and uncertain which leaves most organizations unprepared for crisis management (Zamoum and Gorpe, 2018). These authors borrow the works of Coombs (2007) who looks at crisis communication as the perception of an unpredictable event, which if not well managed has the potential to negatively impact an organization's operations. Therefore, organizations such as universities have what it takes to plan early and strategize in order to reduce and manage the negative impacts of a crisis.

Crises in organizations have also been linked to failures in leadership. For instance, Gibson (2012) argued that an organization has to respond appropriately to an issue or an emergency that demands timely response and communication. Coombs (2012) further isolated three areas of operations in an organization that is always affected by a crisis. These are public safety, financial loss, and reputation loss. This means organizations, in times of a crisis, have to plan adequately to safeguard against financial losses, reputation, and guarantee public safety.

In the context of higher education, crises manifest when least expected and at times spontaneous affecting a few or most universities. Unfortunately, most leaders in the higher education sector, including universities, treat crises as rare occurrences or as anomalies and therefore lack response plans when they do occur (Zamoum and Gorpe, 2018). This is contrary to what Coombs (2007) observed when arguing for establishment of crisis management plans in learning institutions. According to Coombs (2007), crisis management ought to be mainstreamed as an integral part of university policy and admissions procedures because they help universities minimize the impact of catastrophic events such as mass murder, outbreak of pandemics, arson, among other crises. As a practice, various units within universities have to develop flexible crisis plans with various unit leaders having clarity on their roles and responsibilities.

Globally, universities experience either man-made or natural disasters. While man-made disasters are unfortunate occurrences linked to the activities of people, natural crises are events ranging from earthquakes, outbreak of pandemics, tornadoes, hurricanes, and floods (Lerbinger, 1997; Lindell, Prater and Perry, 2007). In African universities, the most common man-made disasters include violent strikes, murder associated with the ever-increasing threats caused by terrorists, suicides, arson, and attacks on university staff. Universities have a cardinal responsibility of protecting their employees when need arises. The conversations on what exists as plans to address a crisis that threaten the lives of the university community, such as the outbreak of COVID-2019 and terrorist attacks such as what happened in 2015 at Garissa University College in Kenya, have become common in university literature. Contrary to what a typical crisis management for a business entity will look like, universities' concept of 'duty of care' means crisis planning has to ensure reduced mortality and property damage in the event of an outbreak of a crisis. Kenya's university setup has little evidence of crisis planning because the plans emerge after the occurrence of an event and therefore are always unequipped to handle crises. For instance, it is after the Garissa University College attack that most universities in Kenya put up concrete walls around their campuses to protect the students and staff from external threats. In addition, there has been strengthening of security checks at most university gates and entry points, including the use of metal detectors. However, lack of preparedness when it comes to crisis management is not a challenge facing universities in Kenya alone. Coombs (2007) indicated that universities are underprepared and unprepared to create well-structured crisis management policies and procedures to address a man-made or natural crisis when they occur on campus.

Literature from the United States shows that a crisis management plan should be comprehensive, with clear assignments for leadership and including a review and evaluation component supported by training and coordination among all the units making up the university (Loner, 2014). This puts university leadership at the center of crisis management planning. Therefore, the success of a crisis management plan depends on the commitment of the top leadership. In the first stage, university leadership should be alert enough to detect early warning signs of a looming crisis. Attempts are made to detect the crisis and prevent it from happening. In the second stage, energy should be directed toward averting the crisis but equally prepare for a possible occurrence. The third stage involves what the institutions put in place just in case the crisis happens. The university reduces the risks by preparing strategically and tactfully. The efforts are to contain it and keep it from spreading to other parts of the institutions, including surrounding community. The fourth stage is the recovery stage where leaders and stakeholders are concerned with how to regain stable operations after the crisis. The fifth stage of crisis management is all about learning from the crisis where the leadership promotes learning by looking at the crisis from all angles (Wooten and James, 2008).

Crises have been part of the development of Kenya's higher education landscape, although with varying levels of magnitude. For instance, some universities in Kenya face a gaping budget deficit which is threatening their existence, student unrests that are sometimes violent and destructive, and dwindling student numbers leaving universities operating in perhaps the most trying moments, among others. However, recently Kenya's university education has been traumatized by catastrophic terrorist-related activities. The al-Shabaab attack on Garissa University College in north eastern Kenya killing 148 members of the university community has been referenced. The outbreak of COVID-2019 globally in late 2019 has reinforced the fragility of the university sector and heightened the need for crisis planning in Kenya's higher education system. The risk to individual safety that COVID-2019 posed to university staff meant they were among the risk areas for spreading the pandemic. Consequently, through a presidential decree, learning institutions in Kenya were closed on March 15, 2020.

UNIVERSITIES' RESPONSES TO THE COVID-2019 THREAT AND THE CONTEXT

In this section, the authors examine how universities responded to the short notice on closure. The authors have identified four typologies of immediate responses but make no claim that the contours of these are clear-cut. Indeed, there are many points of intersections where distinct differences cannot be discerned. Instead, what the authors have done is to identify broad patterns of similar immediate responses and use the main features to identify the four types of analysis along with the representative cases. The four broad patterns are labeled as (1) strategic intervention, (2) incremental intervention, (3) partial paralysis, and (4) complete paralysis.

Strategic Intervention: The Case of the United States International University-Africa

The United States International University-Africa (USIU), a part of the Alliant International University (formerly USIU) in San Diego, United States, is the premier private university in Kenya, founded in 1970. It was first accredited by the United States Western Association of Schools and Colleges (WASC) as part of USIU-San Diego and later chartered in Kenya by the Commission for Higher Education (CHE) in 1999. Therefore, it has dual accreditation, both in Kenya and in the United States. It has an enrollment of 6,508 students and representing 71 nationalities (United States International University-Africa, 2019). It has 14 undergraduate programs, 10 master's programs, and 3 doctoral programs primarily in business and psychology which are its central focus areas. Recently, it began offering health programs with the establishment of the School of Pharmacy and Heath Sciences and an undergraduate degree in Pharmacy. The university is largely a non-residential campus with accommodation facilities available in two residential buildings that can house only 256 students. A distinguishing characteristic of USIU is its cost which makes it the most expensive university to study in East Africa with its semester tuition fees (around US$1,526 for undergraduates) exceeding the total student fees of some private universities. It therefore attracts the sons and daughters of leaders in politics, business, and non-profit agencies who have the resources to meet the high cost of the tuition (Munene, 2009). Despite these features, Oketch (2004) contends that USIU's quality is not necessarily superior to that of other private universities in the country.

In human needs parlance, "strategic intervention" refers to the use of extraordinary skills to produce positive personal and cultural change. The course of human history provides examples whereby some individuals went beyond their own needs to secure positive change that transformed societies for the general good of a country. In Africa, a good example is Nelson Mandela, the first president of a democratic South Africa, who spent 27 years in prison for spearheading the struggle for the liberation of the Black people in that country. The authors use strategic intervention idiom for the USIU in the same context: that is, a systematic use of extraordinary skills and resources in a plan of action designed to transition university operations in an unprecedented direction following the COVID-2019 pandemic forced closure. The authors assert that the university leveraged its inbuilt advantages and has developed it over a considerable time to achieve this transition better than the rest of the universities in the country. The university's practices and procedures during this time reflect imitations of its American roots, especially its mother campus. It also reflects the high dependence on private resource financial resources of its affluent clientele.

In less than two weeks after the forced closure, the university moved swiftly and decisively to transition both instruction and business operations online. A complete shutdown of the university was out of question:

> Following the government directive to close schools, colleges and universities, USIU-Africa made the decision to continue its core business of teaching and learning according to the University's business continuity plan. To ensure that the process was as seamless as possible, the University partnered with Safaricom and Telkom to provide students with subsidized mobile data bundles to enhance E-learning and teaching. . . . The Vice Chancellor however, said despite the closure of the university, learning is still going on through the use of online learning platforms such as Blackboard as a mode of instruction, Zoom as a video conferencing tool and e-books, e-journals and other e-resources from the library to ensure academic continuity and maintain quality of education. "I am pleased that we were able to successfully complete the Spring semester online, including the end of term examinations for students. We are now in the final stages of preparing for the Summer Semester, and we look forward how best we can continue supporting our students," he added. (Muchiri and Odhiambo, 2020, p. 1)

Besides the instructional and operational contingency measures, the university also deployed resources to mitigate the psychosocial effects of the university closure and workplace transition along with the associated anxieties over the pandemic. The university's Counseling Department "has continued to offer counselling services to students, staff, faculty and even parents through calls, text messages, WhatsApp and even through platforms like Zoom" (Kung'u, 2020, p. 1). The counseling focuses on the following:

> Academic issues, financial challenges and fear of not being able to sit for end of semester exams, anxiety, loneliness, fear of discrimination, frustration with resuming with normal operations taking long, loss and grief through death of parents and family members, conflict with parents, relationship issues and continuity with education after academic dismissal are some of the issues that the Counseling Center has had to deal with during this period. (Kung'u, 2020, p. 1)

The university has kept constant communication with all stakeholders by updating them, through its website, social media outlets, and internal electronic communications, on latest developments on COVID-2019, safety measures to protect self and family, and the university's preparation for the summer and fall semesters.

The university also partnered with the Kenya Association of Manufacturers to develop a strategic guide to help the manufacturing sector cope with the new business environment. The document, *Readjusting Business Operations to Cope with COVID-2019 Crisis*, was prepared by a professor of marketing in the school of business. Among the issues covered in the guide are the current situation, business resilience, business response, business transition through crisis (resilience, return, re-imagination, and reform), and operations post-COVID-2019. In effect, USIU availed its academic resources through outreach to facilitate enterprises navigate the unknown consequences of the pandemic on both present and future operations.

Against the threat posed by COVID-2019, USIU has continued its operations with minimal interruptions. It is a feat unmatched by any other university in Kenya, public or private. What accounts for this level of success? Isomorphic tendencies and resource dependency factors underlie the reasons for the success in sustaining operations amid threats of a complete shutdown. The isomorphic forces at play in USIU lead to the university becoming similar in operations and practices to universities in the United States while dependence on elite private resources motivates it to exemplify distinctiveness from other private universities.

The first American isomorphic trend evident in USIU is institutional values that guide the university's operating philosophy. Organizational values have been defined variously, but, overall, denote the foundation upon which the organization is established and operates on. It is "what the people in the organization think is good for the organization, what needs to happen within the organization, and what might be needed with the organization in the future" (Cingula, 1992, pp. 499–500). Organizational values can be culturally bound as seen in the South African study of the social value of *ubuntu* philosophy on team effectiveness in an organization whereby survival, spirit solidarity, and compassion along with respect and dignity were considered (du Toit and Engelbrecht, 2006). USIU has five core values that define its operational ideals: (1) lifelong learning, (2) integrity, (3) innovativeness, (4) social responsibility, and (5) academic freedom (United States International University-Africa, 2019). These values, although useful, do not account for the success USIU has obtained during the COVID-2019-induced uncertainties. Other than innovativeness—introducing new methods and strategies that ensure quality, efficiency, effectiveness, and productivity—that emphasize procedures and operations, the rest focus on the essence of the university as an institution in Africa. In our view, it is the adoption of the values of the mother university, Alliant International University, which accounts for its resilience in uncertain time. These values, abbreviated as IMPACT, are the following:

- *Inclusion*: committed to inclusive excellence; include and engage the rich diversity of the Alliant community.
- *Mentorship*: foster learning, provide guidance, and create enabling environments that contribute to the success of students, colleagues, and university.
- *Passion*: bring enthusiasm, creativity, and authentic selves to work each day.
- *Accountability*: be responsible stewards of university time and resources; work with integrity and embrace the highest standards.
- *Communication*: be responsive, transparent, and respectful in our communication.
- *Teamwork*: collaborate across all university domains to develop innovative and multifaceted solutions to students, organizational, and community needs (Alliant International University, 2020, p. 1).

The swift transition to online instruction and operations, robust communications with key constituents, and the most advanced information technology of any university in Kenya are a clear manifestation of USIU emulating the values guiding the operations of its mother institution, Alliant International University. This mimetic process of values emulation allowed/allows USIU to replicate the Alliant International University model in its operational activities before and during the COVID-2019 pandemic.

Normative isomorphism at USIU is articulated through the American leadership at the executive level and the U.S. accreditation at the institutional level. Since its founding, the university has been headed by a professor recruited from an American university. One university head had a 21-year tenure that saw the massive transformation of the institution into a U.S.-style college, both in physical appearance and operations. As mentioned earlier, although the university is accredited in Kenya, it is also accredited in the United States by the WASC. The dual accreditation ensures that the American quality and practices in academic programing are not lost to clients who seek an American education. Of this dual accreditation, the university argues the following:

> It ensures that the best practices (required by the two agencies) which are more stringent and meticulous are applied to determine quality and standard. It is definite that an institution with a dual accreditation will meet higher standards of quality and effectiveness in its programs and, hence, the quality of its education is superior. The degree obtained is recognized in the regions covered by the accreditation bodies in question, giving it a global perspective. At some point in their education, some students may wish to transfer to a new university. Most often, these students wish to transfer the course credits they have already accumulated to the new university so that they will not have to repeat similar

> courses. Dual accreditation is an important factor when a university is deciding whether to accept transfer credit from a student's previous University. Most universities will not accept transferred course credits from an institution that has not earned appropriate accreditation status from accreditation agencies. Dual accreditation makes course credits more credible. (United States International University-Africa, 2019, p. 1)

The statement that "most universities will not accept transferred course credits from an institution that has not earned *appropriate accreditation* status from accreditation agencies" (emphasis ours) is a euphemism for a quality U.S. degree. In essence, both the leadership and the accreditation have ensured the professionalization of practices at USIU in tandem with operations at American universities. USIU's response to the threat posed by COVID-2019 mirrors the response in American universities.

The overarching context in which the isomorphic pressures influence operations at USIU to make it successful is resource dependency. Of the many private universities in Kenya, USIU and Strathmore Universities are the only ones that fit the "elite" mantra. Elite universities exist to provide a distinct university education at a high cost, akin to the high-cost universities in the United States and Latin America. They exist due to perceptions of decline in quality at public universities and seek to differentiate themselves from the low-cost demand-absorbing private university sector (Munene, 2009). To safeguard its elite status and continue to attract a high net worth client, USIU exemplifies "Americanism" both in its operations and curricular offering as expected by external stakeholders. In the absence of state financial support, the university is dependent on external resources generated through tuition fees, strong alumni, and some fundraising. Due to this level of external dependency, the university's operations cannot falter, let alone shutdown, which explains its unmatched success in transitioning from a physical to online campus during the COVID-2019 pandemic. In figure 2.1, the resource dependency context and isomorphic pressures influencing the success at USIU are graphically depicted, transitioning from a physical to online campus during the COVID-2019 pandemic.

Pressures at USIU-Africa

Incremental Intervention: The Case of Mount Kenya University (MKU)

The MKU is one of the 18 chartered private universities in Kenya. It started as a small computer training college and has grown over the years into a multi-campus private university. It also has footprints in Rwanda where it

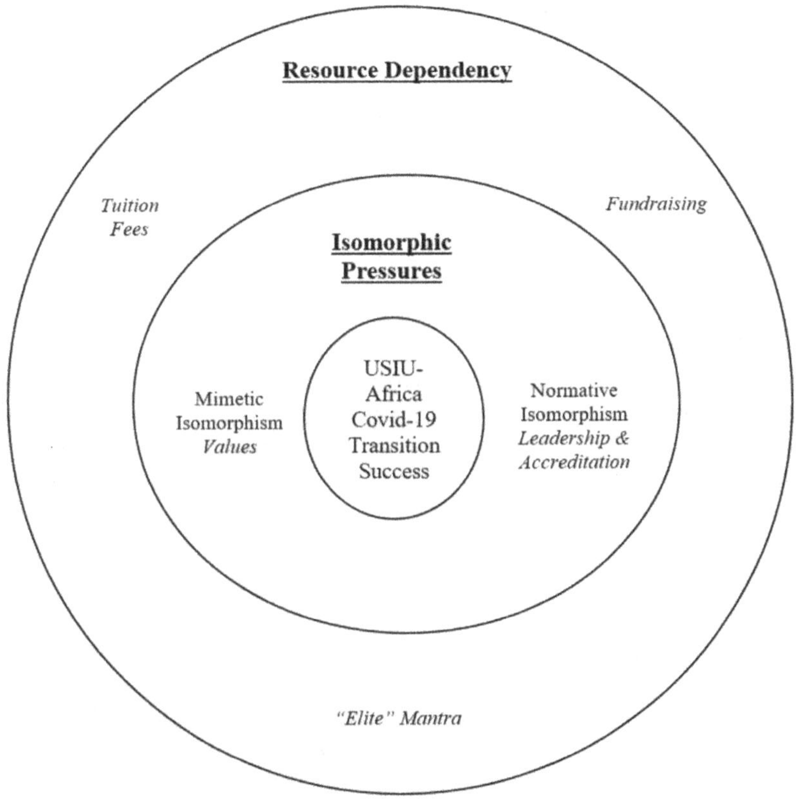

Figure 2.1 Resource Dependency and Isomorphic. *Source*: Self generated by the Authors.

runs the MKU Rwanda offshore campus. The university has over 30,000 students (MKU, 2020), making it one of the giant private universities in East Africa. MKU offers certificates, diplomas, undergraduate degrees, postgraduate diplomas, and postgraduate degrees. The university's significant contribution to the development of human resource capacity in the country is in the Bachelor's degree programs which have over 80 percent student enrollment (MKU, 2017).

Academic programs at MKU can be classified broadly into three categories based on modes of delivery. The first category is face-to-face that targets regular academic programs. This mode has three sets of regular students: those who attend (1) during the day, (2) during the evening, and (3) during the weekend (Mount Kenya University, 2020). The second category of programs utilizes the blended mode of study facilitated by the university's Digital Learning Management System platform. It targets students who are enrolled in the Distance Institutional-Based and Electronic Learning

(DIBEL) program. Under the blended learning format, online learning takes two-thirds of the course time (28 hours) and face-to-face the remaining 14 hours (MKU, 2020). The third category refers to the web-based mode of delivery whereby entire programs are fully on online platforms. The university has a directorate with the stated name, the Directorate of Open, Distance and Electronic Learning (ODeL) established to support distance learning and online instruction delivery.

The authors use incremental intervention to denote an intentional process whereby the university makes attempts to avoid a complete shutdown of its academic activities by enhancing the infrastructure available to reach all its students. Faced with a COVID-2019 shutdown threat, MKU enhanced its existing web-based instructional resources to transition the university operations to online platforms without changing the university's underlying values. In this way, the university avoided a complete shutdown that was evident in many other institutions. Online programs ran uninterrupted as emergency plans were made to transition the rest of the instruction from face-to-face to the online format.

MKU's incremental approach in shifting its programming to online offerings in order to avoid a complete shutdown of the university's activities can be accounted for by factors related to resource dependency (overdependence on their tuition fee paying students) and isomorphic forces (their practices and procedures that seem to imitate Kenya's public universities). Immediately after the closure of universities, the MKU senate met on March 16, 2020, and ratified the presidential edict, suspended face-to-face learning, and advised the students to leave the university latest by March 17, 2020. Part of the memorandum from the Vice Chancellor's Office reads as follows (Memorandum, Office of the Vice Chancellor, 2020, p. 1):

> Following the Presidential directive in response to the Coronavirus (COVID-2019) Pandemic, to suspend face-to-face learning in all institutions, the University Senate in a special meeting held on 16th March, 2020 has made the following resolutions:
>
> - That the University has extended the online learning platform to the regular students (day, evening, and weekend) to facilitate the learning process to complete the remaining part of the semester/trimester. When the University operations resume, students will be expected to sit for the January-April 2019/2020 semester/trimester examinations.
> - This is, therefore, to inform University stakeholders that the University has suspended the face-to-face learning with effect from Monday, 16th March, 2020. Students are requested to clear from the University premises by close of business on Tuesday 17th March, 2020 until further notice.

Nonetheless, the senate resolved to allow courses offered via online format to proceed uninterrupted. These are programs fully online and the online portions of the DIBEL programs. It was also resolved that examinations for the said programs be suspended until normal university operations resumed. This decision points to the challenges that the university faced in its ambition to transition programs to online platforms.

The Directorate of ODeL facilitated the seamless transition of MKU programs to online format. Unlike most public universities, MKU has a functional online platform and, therefore, programs under ODeL were not affected by the immediate closure. In addition, ODeL offered MKU a platform to commence the transition from face-to-face to an online environment course delivered in the traditional format. The university management was keen to leverage on this as evident in the communication to the stakeholders: "We are in the process of upgrading our systems to accommodate all regular students on the online platform where they will access the learning materials and also be able to have interactions with teaching staff. We expect that by Monday, March 23, 2020, all students will be able to access the e-learning resources" (Mount Kenya University, 2020, p. 1).

Access to appropriate and adequate online infrastructure remains a challenge as universities transition to online instruction platforms. This was anticipated by MKU and, as a mitigation measure, the university management collaborated with some of the Internet service providers to ensure that most students were reached. MKU signed a Memorandum of Understanding with a leading network provider in Kenya, Telkom Kenya, and equally sought the services of TV47 to supplement the online learning with televised lectures. The memorandum from the Vice Chancellor's Office noted "that online learning will be supplemented through televised lectures in collaboration with TV 47" and "that through the Memorandum of Understanding between MKU and Telkom Kenya, students will further be supported to access online learning resources" (Memorandum, Office of the Vice Chancellor, 2020, p. 1). Television coverage in Kenya is wider and has the capacity to reach most of households with relatively fewer challenges as compared to the other types of web-based learning. This equally circumvents the capacity hitch experienced by the faculty and students given that training on different forms of online instruction platforms was not prioritized. While all this demonstrated an eagerness to experiment with new instructional delivery modes, there was no evidence that the university had any robust strategy targeting faculty and students to ensure their readiness to engage with these instructional modes that included video conferencing and social presence in online teaching.

MKU's response is influenced by a mix of both normative values and resource dependency. The university derives its normative values from the founder, the vice chancellor, and recruitment of academic staff from public universities. The university's founder, its vision carrier, is a graduate of a Kenyan public university and his vision is to develop a university that mirrors the public ones in access and programming but is distinct through its innovativeness as in U.S. universities. The non-executive chancellor of the university is a long-serving U.S. professor, underscoring this orientation to the U.S. model. The public university values are conveyed by a long-service executive vice chancellor who was recruited from a public university where he had served as a dean and director of distance learning, and senior professors who were also sourced from public universities. This amalgam of values means that the university delicately straddles the line between a private innovative university and one that also mimics a public one.

Resource dependency both catalyzes innovativeness and constrains it. As a private university, it depends on private resources for most of its operations; hence, the development of a multi-campus university system with a huge online presence. The online campus targets private (self-sponsored) fee-paying students. The online campus allows the university to expand its tuition revenue resource beyond the vicinity of the university. It attracts working professionals and those unable to access the physical campus. The dependency on tuition revenue has allowed the university to develop a relatively robust online campus than found in public universities. Nevertheless, being a recipient of a sizable number of government-sponsored students, whose tuition fees is lower than that paid by privately sponsored students, the university is limited in the revenue it can generate from a segment of its student population. Lower tuition fees than would have been expected have constrained the university from developing a robust online campus in the manner of USIU. The authors capture the isomorphic and resource dependency influences on MKU in figure 2.2.

In summary, isomorphic forces, particularly the innovative leadership of MKU founder's appointment of foreign non-executive chancellors, brought the best university practices modeled along American-style universities into MKU. Even though dependency on fee-paying students has facilitated MKU to build an online infrastructure that helped it continue with instruction during COVID-2019 closure, normative values by top leadership and professors who were recruited from public universities coupled with the presence of government-sponsored students who paid lower tuition fees constrained MKU's efforts to build a robust ICT infrastructure comparable to USIU.

Partial Paralysis: The Case of Kenyatta University

Kenyatta University (KU) was established as the third public university in Kenya in 1985. Nonetheless, the authors trace its history to 1965 when the

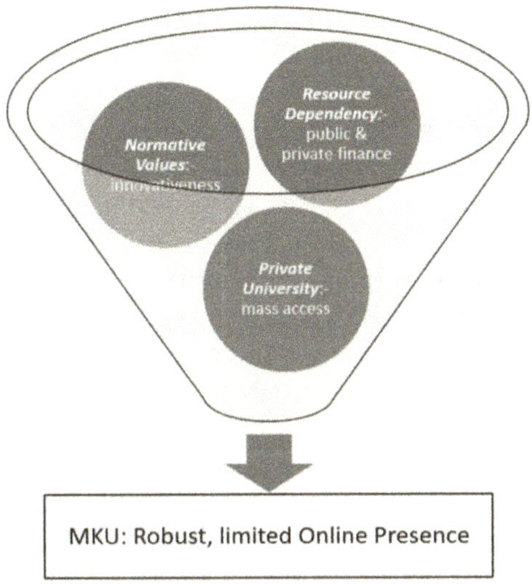

Figure 2.2 MKU Online Presence: Normative and Resource Dependency Influences.
Source: Self-generated by the Authors.

British government gave back the Templar Barracks in Kahawa to the then newly independent government (Mulinge et al., 2017). In 1970, it became a constituent college of the University of Nairobi (UoN) and renamed Kenyatta University College (KUC). As a college, KUC offered teacher training for certificate and diploma levels. The first set of Bachelor of Education students were admitted in 1972. In 1978, UoN moved its faculty of education to KUC, but it was not until 1985, through an Act of Parliament, that KUC was upgraded to fully fledged university status, thereby becoming the third public university after UoN (1970) and Moi University (1984).

Since its elevation, KU has grown massively in terms of student population and establishment of campuses. During the 2018/2019 academic year, KU was the second most populated university in Kenya with 64,599 students after UoN with 70,515 students (KNBS, 2019). KU has eight campuses spread across the country, namely (1) Nairobi City Campus, (2) Ruiru Campus, (3) Parkland Campus, (4) Kitui Campus, (5) Mombasa Campus, (6) Nakuru Campus, (7) Dadaab Campus, and (8) Embu Campus (KU, 2019).

Academic programs at KU have two modes of delivery. The first mode is face-to-face delivery which targets students enrolled in regular academic programs. Most of the academic programs at the university fall under this mode of delivery and comprises of students enrolled in regular and school-based programs. The second mode of delivery is for programs under the Digital School of Virtual and Open Learning (DSVOL). The digital school was established on June 30, 2014, and has been operational with an estimated student population of 9,853 (KU, 2020). This represented 15 percent of the total student enrollment in 2018/2019. The ratio of students under DSVOL is significant and the university set up regional learning centers across the country to provide critical support to enrolled students. The centers were established in Nairobi, Mombasa, Garissa, Embu, Nyeri, Nakuru, Kericho, Kisumu, and Kakamega (KU, 2020). These regional centers also work as examination sites for the DSVOL students.

We borrow the concept of paralysis as used in the medical field in describing the approach which universities took in dealing with their closure. From a medical perspective, a paralysis is a loss of muscle function in a part of the body. Therefore, partial paralysis signals loss of some control or function in a part of the body. In this case, when KU was faced with the COVID-2019 crisis, it lost its ability to operate normally, as there was a significant interruption to its university operations. As a consequence, it was forced to close face-to-face learning and only allowed online programs to proceed.

Among public universities' responses to the COVID-2019 pandemic, KU provided the most comprehensive directive to the university community prior to its decision to close the university. The first memorandum dated March 13, 2020, was advisory and enumerated the actions taken to support the government in containing the risks associated with the COVID-2019. Part of the compliance was to enforce the presidential directive that required a ban on international travel. The university equally resolved to prohibit gatherings including meetings within the university premises, designated its health facility as a key link with the university community members in case of an outbreak, earmarked entry points as screening areas, and provided hand washing in addition to the provision of hand sanitizer stations. The university's health unit established an isolation room to handle any suspected cases, trained health staff on screening and initial management of suspected cases, and also provided two dedicated phone numbers which were available to the university community for use in case of any emergency. Comprehensive as the communication was, this advisory focused on hygiene factors but made no provision for the contingency plans for academic services to be disrupted by university closure. KU's response to the presidential closure order was to put on hold face-to-face programs and only allow programs under DSVOL to proceed uninterrupted. A memorandum from the Vice Chancellor's Office dated March 16, 2020, read partly as follows (Memorandum Vice Chancellor's Office, March 16, 2020, p. 1):

> This is to notify all students that following the Presidential Directive on suspension of learning in Education Institutions due to the Coronavirus (COVID-2019) Pandemic, the University Senate met today and resolved to close the University until further notice with effect from tomorrow, Tuesday, 17th March, 2020. All

students are requested to clear and vacate from their respective Campus premises by 4:00 p.m. further to this:

- All resident students will be expected to remove their personal belongings from their rooms and hand over the keys to the Director of Accommodation Services.
- International students who either wish to travel back to their respective home countries or those who wish to stay on campus are expected to register with the Director of International Programmes and Collaborations.

KU's response in a full functioning online school alongside a closed face-to-face campus points to the normative values of its two past leaders and resource dependency forces interacting with the unique history of the university. Among the public universities in Kenya, KU was the first to develop online teaching and learning. It did so after it discarded the African Virtual University (AVU) of which it was the host in Kenya. Funded by the World Bank, AVU is a Pan-African project intended to provide an open and affordable distance learning institution to those seeking higher education and continuing learning. Through AVU, KU became the first university in the country to have a wireless Internet connection (although weak and poor as it relied on micro-wave link) which underlined the university's goal to become a digital campus. This is clearly articulated in the first strategic plan of the university (2005–2015). After the dissolution of AVU, KU established the Kenyatta University E-Learning (KUel) program under the Self-Sponsored Program in 2005 to provide online education (KU, 2020). No other public university at this time came to fathom online learning.

The key drivers of KU's entry into online/digital learning are the two long-serving vice chancellors—Professor George Eshiwani who initiated AVU and KUel and Professor Olive Mugenda who birthed DSVOL and headed the university for 22 years. Both are U.S. trained and maintained regular engagement with their U.S. alma maters along with other American universities. Their vision was to transform KU into an American-style university with an extensive online presence for those students who cannot enroll in full-time on-campus programs. It is this normative value of university access unrestrained by space and time that fueled the beginning and growth of an online campus by a Kenyan public university (KU, 2020).

Of all the public universities, KU was the most prepared to mitigate the COVID-2019-related closure by having at least 15 percent of the total student population enrolled in its digital school proceed online without interruption. Every online student at KU is provided with a dedicated tablet loaded with his/her courses. In addition, KU has a relatively good training program that has been in operation for lecturers since 2014. Equally, the staffing on the online program is robust to meet students' emerging concerns. KU's digital school was not experimenting with online offering but rather tapped into its already functional unit that had regional coordinators, content developers, teaching and quality assurance department, and ICT support staff, including tablet repair technicians to run an efficient program for its online courses (KU, 2020).

As a state-owned, state-funded university, KU largely depends on state apportionments. In addition, its first obligation is to admit government-sponsored students who are funded by the state-owned HELB. The tuition fee paid by these students is highly regulated by the state (the current tuition fee that students in KU pay was set about 31 years ago and is not in tandem with the current economic situation). Also, KU is cognizant about the fact that government-sponsored students are traditional students: they prefer the face-to-face on-campus residential student experience which contradicts the foundation of an online campus experience. Therefore, developing an online presence like USIU and MKU is constrained by this dependency on the state for capital development and operations.

KU illustrates how the normative values of the visionary leadership of its two leaders who sought to build a strong digital school have been central to KU establishing a good online presence. This circumvented the total shutdown of the university once the government declared all institutions closed. Nevertheless, we see how resource dependency on government funding has constrained the rapid expansion of the online presence at KU in contrast to USIU and MKU.

Complete Paralysis: The Case of Technical University of Kenya

The history of Technical University of Kenya (TUK) can be traced to May 29, 1961, when the Kenya Technical Institute was opened. It was later renamed the Kenya Polytechnic and registered in 1967 as a post-secondary educational institution with a capacity of 2,075 students. The niche of the institution comprised technical fields, mainly architecture, surveying, and planning (TUK, 2020). In 2007, it was made a constituent college of the UoN and then later elevated to a university status in line with the provisions of the 2012 University Act, with the mandate to offer higher education and research in technology. TUK received a government charter in January 2013. Student enrollment at TUK has been on the rise in the last three academic years to stand at 20,042 in the 2018/2019 academic year with male students at around 59 percent and female 41 percent. Although female enrollment over the three academic years is still lower than male students, TUK has contributed significantly to the enrollment of female students in the Science, Technology, Engineering, and Mathematics (STEM) programs in Kenya (KNBS, 2019).

TUK runs regular face-to-face academic programs in its three faculties, namely (1) Faculty of Engineering, Sciences and Technology; (2) Faculty of Social Sciences and Technology; and (3) Faculty of Applied Sciences and Technology. The niche of the university remains in STEM courses. At the time of the COVID-2019-induced closure, the university had not established online instruction; it lacked an appropriate ICT architecture that would have allowed the university to move its STEM programs to an online format. Programs in STEM have a practical component that necessitates access to laboratories and workshops for quality education.

The imagery of complete paralysis is used to denote an almost complete shutdown of the university's academic operations. The COVID-2019 crisis led to a shutdown of learning in the institution in complete contrast to the institutions analyzed previously. The university was closed until further notice, only allowing essential service providers who were non-academic staff to access the university. Students were advised to stay away from the university. The memorandum from the university management dated March 16, 2020, read in part as follows (TUK, 2020):

> Upon confirmation of the first case of the Coronavirus (COVID-2019) in Nairobi on Friday 13th March, 2020 and in compliance with the Presidential Directive of yesterday, Sunday 15th March, 2020, the University Management and Senate do advise as follows (TUK, 2020):
>
> - All lectures and examinations are suspended with immediate effect from today 16th March, 2020, until further notice.
> - All students are advised to stay away from the institution, until further notice.
> - The students in the university hostels are expected to vacate by Friday 20th March, 2020. However, students are encouraged to make plans to clear out from the premises as soon as possible.

Furthermore, besides non-essential staff, those not involved in security, finance, medical, mail, ICT, and telephone services were advised to take leave. The rest of the university community was advised to "work from home and stay at home as far as possible" and to "avoid unnecessary movements from home and observe all the preventive measures as provided by the Ministry of Health" (TUK, 2020). The advice to academic staff to take leave without contingency plans on how learning was to proceed going forward meant the university had put a halt to any form of learning.

We also situate the shutdown of TUK operations to normative factors centering on the disciplines and academic staff. As a technical training institution, TUK's educational model has been based on apprenticeship, a learning paradigm that elevates the integration of theoretical knowledge with practical application such as in the workshop or workplace. In this way, the apprentice gains performance skills like the practitioners in the field along with the tacit duties of the position for which s/he is training. The norms associated with this training orientation as espoused in STEM disciplines at TUK mean that online instruction has neither been promoted nor prioritized. For those developed universities, there has been adaption of freeware labs that allow students to complete their lab assignments through simulations, or sometimes use of pre-recorded videos in which instructors conduct experiments. Nonetheless, this approach goes against the general best practice of a student-centered approach that inculcates hands-on experiences espoused by TUK and underscored by the fact that globally only 3 percent of science and engineering programs were fully online (Mitchell, 2020).

The other source of normative forces that constrained TUK's capacity to move its courses to online offering has to do with its recent accreditation to full-fledged university status, an achievement obtained in 2013. Nonetheless, all the instructional staff members of the previous Kenya Polytechnic, a technical institution, were retained as members of the university academic staff. The university is still governed by norms and values of a technical institution in terms of teaching, assessment, and curriculum governance. The staff members inherited from the days of Kenya Polytechnic are easily amenable to online course development and teaching even where STEM theoretical courses can be offered online.

Conclusions and Recommendations: Contextualizing Responses and Lessons Learned

In this section, we draw conclusions and offer recommendations by synthesizing the analyses of the universities' responses to the COVID-2019-related closures through the contextual prisms as well as lessons learned for policy and practice. Of critical importance in this chapter was how the public and private universities in Kenya responded to the COVID-2019 crisis that threatened to shut down their entire operations. We interrogated the contexts by analyzing the ways and conditions under which the selected public and private universities mitigated the consequences of the pandemic to their academic programming. The purpose of this section then is to share best practices for handling crises and propose the way forward in terms of how universities ought to respond to emergency crises in future.

Context of Responses

That universities around the world were caught by COVID-2019 unprepared is hardly a surprise. Interestingly, although close to 60 percent of the universities across the globe reported some online presence, only 20 percent had full online courses of some form. The online offerings also had disciplinary and institutional differentiation with business studies, economics, education, and larger universities with a broad disciplinary scope being better prepared. In science and engineering, less than 3 percent of the programs were fully available online (Mitchell, 2020). These global statistics mirror the scenario that has visited the African higher education scene following the outbreak of the pandemic. The transition to online teaching laid bare the inequities between well-endowed regions and universities with robust ICT infrastructure within the same country, the state of poor instructional quality owing to lack of training in online pedagogy, and the financial troubles confronting tuition-dependent private universities (Mohamedbhai, 2020). No university was prepared for a crisis of this magnitude whose onset was so sudden and scope of impact so wide that administrators were left catching at the straws to ensure institutional survival.

The pedagogical challenges attendant to a sudden transition to online teaching without prior preparation and associated ecology have been laid bare in Kenya's universities. Whereas private universities have had a leg up due to their dependency on tuition fees, public universities have, overall, had a late start. Due to this late start, online teaching has turned out to be a "nightmare" for many public universities with most being unable to conduct their end of semester examinations online due to lack of expertise, appropriate learning management systems (LMSs), and constrained access to laptops by students (Oduor, 2020; Onyango, 2020). A lecturer in one of the public universities lamented the following: "Public universities are still struggling unlike private ones that established efficient online teaching years ago. We should explore ways of adding the cost of a laptop on fees and spread it across four years of the undergraduate course so that all students own this important gadget" (Onyango, 2020, p. 1). Our analysis in the foregoing sections has shown that private universities placed higher premium on online instructional delivery than their public counterparts due to isomorphic and resource dependency variables.

The universities' responses were dictated by the impacts of both isomorphic pressures and resource dependency needs. The two private universities analyzed, the USIU and MKU, had made good progress in online delivery due to consistent investment in information technology alongside LMSs, although USIU is way ahead in this investment. Without state funding, these universities depend on tuition fees paid by mostly self-sponsored students. USIU is a high-cost institution while MKU fees structure mimics that of public universities. Nonetheless, normative forces operating at the two institutions show some variation. At USIU, its American roots, its U.S. accreditation, along with a U.S. administrative leadership, ensure that it mirrors the instructional delivery practiced in the mother university in San Diego, the Alliant University. At MKU it is the founder and vision carrier's passion to develop a local innovative university coupled with the appointment of foreign non-executive chancellors that has propelled the university to reach its status in online offerings. Both USIU and MKU's investment decisions in online instructional delivery nurtured a market legitimacy focused on attracting private fee-paying students.

The responses of the two public universities analyzed, KU and the TUK, offer contrasting cases, both in terms of resource dependency and normative influences. KU pioneered the establishment of online teaching and wireless Internet connectivity among the public universities. It is also the only university in the country with a dedicated online school headed by an academic dean, a major feat for a public university which tends to focus on state-funded residential undergraduate students. This innovation is attributed to the normative values of its two long-serving, American-educated vice chancellors whose vision for the university is one that does not wholly depend on state funding but generates additional revenue while expanding university access to non-residential students unconstrained by time and space. Therefore, online instruction continued uninterrupted for programs in the online school while the rest of the university has been shut down. Normative values by leaders can, and do, circumvent limitations of state ownership. In contrast, TUK responded to the COVID-2019 closure in a state of almost complete paralysis with all instruction suspended: a consequence of the scientific and technical nature of the programs offered. As one of the technical colleges upgraded to university status, TUK's disciplinary values are based on the time-honored tradition of apprenticeship in which face-to-face instruction is the pedagogical norm. This historical position and disciplinary training norms have mitigated against transitioning instruction into an online format. The partial online offering at KU and the near-complete shutdown at TUK are characteristics of institutions with high state legitimacy that is largely state funded and mostly accessed by state-sponsored undergraduate students.

Whether the university responses typified market or state legitimacy, the universities operate in a context of limited autonomy. The closure of universities was an administrative edict from the state without reference to university leaders and their internal decision-making organs. Universities were not afforded any opportunity to make mission-critical decisions, such as transition to online instruction, examinations, and graduate research supervision, before the closure. This abrogation of internal decision-making authority runs counter to the need to safeguard university prerogatives in making decisions on academic affairs, a position espoused by the American Association of University Professors as follows:

> In certain situations, it is necessary to close a campus or move to online instruction to safeguard the health of the campus community. Faculty and academic staff—through their shared governance bodies or, when applicable, their unions—should be consulted on how best to implement this decision. In order to ensure full participation, administrations should share information with faculty and seek input from the appropriate faculty bodies. (Fichtenbaum, 2020, p. 1)

There is no doubt that COVID-2019 presented, and still presents, a serious threat to public health with schools and universities as high-density population zones providing opportunities for rapid spread. Nevertheless, unlike elementary and high schools where the government's direct involvement in administration is expected and accepted, universities are accorded latitude to make important decisions as self-governing entities. But this decision-making autonomy was thwarted by the government's closure declaration.

Lessons Learned and the Way Forward

The universities' responses to the impact of COVID-2019 provide valuable lessons on institutions' abilities to respond rapidly to unforeseen crises as well as strategies that need to be instituted to mitigate the adverse effects of such calamities. The immediate goal of a university in times of crisis is to protect the immediate stakeholders, staff, and students. Whereas the suggestions made are not necessarily specific to each institution explored in this chapter, they are broad-based enough to be customized to any Kenyan university based on its unique context. The COVID-2019 impact was felt across the entire spectrum of the universities in the country—old and new, rural and urban, as well as public and private. Importantly, the recommendations for managing crises in the universities echo, as will be evident, proposals made on handling emergencies in universities in countries with a longer tradition of higher education development. A graphic encapsulation of the key strategies is presented in figure 2.3.

Leadership is integral to any crisis response plan. In a national framework for decision-making during a crisis, the Australian government recommends that all organizations, including universities, establish a command structure that becomes the central authority as decision-making transitions from consultative to "command and control." A leader is designated to take authority over the crisis, provide directions to the crisis team, and provide rapid decision-making unencumbered by the need to consult (Australian Government, 2018). Writing in the U.S. context, Peatman recommends that in a crisis situation, "college presidents are the commanders of their universities, and all commanders have senior staff who are expected to competent during a crisis" (2017, p. 2) which reaffirms the central role a structured and

Figure 2.3 Proposed Way Forward for Universities in Crises Management. *Source*: Self-generated by the Authors.

dedicated leadership plays in its management. In a crisis context, the valued shared governance and consultative administrative model in the university may run counter to rapid decision-making that is necessary to arrest a fast-evolving crisis.

A prominent feature in Kenya's universities during crises is the absence of a crisis management committee with a designated leader. Crises are handled on an ad hoc basis by the universities' academic senates under the leadership of the vice chancellors. Throughout such crises, there is no point of focus where affected parties and stakeholders can gather reliable information, report evidence, and seek advice on the next course of action. In establishing a standing crisis management committee under the leadership of a deputy vice chancellor with representations from faculty and staff, Kenya's universities will be following the traditions established in many universities in Asia, Europe, and the United States. During a crisis, such a committee should, at the very minimum, be charged with developing a common operating picture, generating an initial press statement, identifying affiliated groups, codifying the essential tasks, aligning crisis events and normal university operations, and developing a plan to return to normalcy. This approach ensures that crisis management at the universities is proactive and enhances goodwill among all stakeholders.

The immediate paralysis that confronted universities as the COVID-2019 unfolded is the lack of information about its possible impact and longevity, besides the skills needed to handle its impact at the institutional level. It is this paralysis that confronted universities in the U.S. Gulf Coast in 2005 when hurricane Katrina plummeted the coastline and decimated institutions of higher education (Bakker et al., 2019). It is impossible to design appropriate response strategies in the absence of information about the possible impact a crisis will bring to bear on an institution. Decisions that university divisions and students will make will be based on access to requisite information provided by the institution. Since COVID-2019 was first identified in December 2019 up to when universities were ordered closed, there is no evidence that universities in Kenya provided any information on pandemic and possible response scenarios. One possible remedy is for universities in Kenya to be strategic in gathering information on potential threats, generating an assessment plan, and simulating the various possible response options. When the university stakeholders have such information, they can prepare appropriately. This risk assessment and management plan allows for a uniform and coordinated response both at the institution as well as nationally.

The swift transition to online (e-learning) instruction revealed another soft underbelly in Kenyan universities' instructional architectures. Online learning has inbuilt advantages in a pandemic context as it aligns with social distance, and it is not constrained by time and space. Prior to the pandemic, many universities in the country had ventured into online teaching but not in a systematic way. Nearly all of them used free web-based LMSs such as Moodle in which technical support is non-existent. Moreover, other than KU where online education is housed in a full-fledged school under an academic dean, other universities only have directorates overseen by a director. Due to this lower administrative position, e-learning is bereft of the clout needed to advocate for additional resources or to mainstream it in the entire university.

More problematic is the minimal attention paid to e-learning pedagogy due to the exclusive focus on technology and content production. A close examination of KU's DSVOL shows the preponderance of coordinators, administrative assistants, secretaries, and tablet repair technicians. Missing in the lineup are key personnel such as instructional designers and graphic designers who should be the core staff to facilitate pedagogically sound online classes. In a study of online teaching in both public and private universities in Kenya, Makokha and Mutisya establish that most lecturers used e-learning to mainly upload lecture notes and reference materials (Makokha and Mutisya, 2016). In other words, no instruction goes on, there is very little teacher-student interactions, social presence is absent, and synchronous engagement is hardly practiced. To ameliorate this challenge, universities need to reimagine e-learning through upscaling their administrative clout to a deanship or principal level, hiring and deploying instructional and graphic designers, and a robust program of training academic staff on the sound principles of online course design and delivery.

Finally, it is imperative that both the state and the universities envision crises as opportunities for strengthening institutional governance. By unilaterally ordering all universities closed, the government robbed the universities of an important moment to formulate their own plans and strategies for closing, rearranging the academic calendar, and establishing modalities for reopening. Not only were the universities left powerless, the government's unilateral decision to close the universities also negated the cardinal principle of university autonomy as it relates to internal decision-making on academic matters. In future, it is essential that the government provide space for universities to actualize responsible decision-making by allowing them to make decisions affecting internal academic matters during crises. Universities on their part need to nurture appropriate management of university affairs to demonstrate maturity in decision-making. Frequent disruptions of academic programs due to student, staff, and faculty strikes do not augur well for institutions seeking autonomy from the state.

REFERENCES

Alliant International University. (May 14, 2020). *Our Story*. Retrieved on April 5, 2020 from https://www.alliant.edu/why-alliant/our-story.

Archibald, M. (September 14, 2017). *Resource Dependency Thoery*. Retrieved on April 5, 2020 from https://www.britannica.com/topic/resource-dependency-theory.

Australian Government. (2018). *Decision Making During a Crisis: A Practical Guide*. Belconnen, Australia: Commonwealth of Australia.

Bakker, H. M., Kerstholt H. J., Van-Bommel, M. and Giebels, E. (2019). Decision-making during a crisis: the interplay of narratives and statistical information before and after crisis communication. *Journal of Risk Research* 22(11):1409–1424.

Beckert, J. (2010). Institutional isomorphism revisited: Convergence and divergence in institutional change. *Sociological Theory* 28(2):150–166.

Berdahl, R. (1990). Academic freedom and accountability in British universities. *Studies in Higher Education* 15:169–180.

Booker, L. (2014). Crisis management: Changing times for colleges. *Journal of College Admissions* 222:16–23.

Cingula, M. (1992). *Organizacijska Kultura v Implementaciji Poslovne Strategije. In Organizacija, Informatika, Kadri, 11. Posvetovanje Organizatorjev Dela.* Portorož, Slovenia: FOV.

Coombs, W.T. (2007). Crisis management and communications. Retrieved on 8 November 2021, from: http://www.instituteforpr.org/crisis-management-and-communications/.

Coombs, W.T. (2012). *Ongoing Crisis Management: Planning, Managing and Responding*, 3rd ed. Thousand Oaks, CA: Sage.

CUE. (May 1, 2020). *Commission for University Education*. Retrieved on April 5, 2020 from http://www.cue.or.ke/images/phocadownload/Accredited_Universities_in_Kenya_November_2017.pdf.

Czerniewicz, L. (April 30, 2020). The struggle to save and remake public higher education. *University World News*. Retrieved on May 2, 2020 from https://www.universityworldnews.com/post.php?story=20200428154746989.

DiMaggio, P. and Walter, P. (1983). The iron cage revisited: Institutional isomorphism and collective rationality in organizational fields. *American Sociological Review* 48:147–160.

du Toit, P. and Engelbrecht, A. (2006). The effects of social values of ubuntu on team effectiveness. *South Africa Journal of Business Managemen* 37(3):17–27.

Fichtenbaum, R. (March 10, 2020). *Statement on Covid-19 and the Faculty Role in Decision-Making*. Retrieved on June 25, 2020 from https://www.aaup.org/news/statement-COVID-2019-and-faculty-role-decision-making#.XvT7jOdlDIU.

Gibson P. (2012). Crisis Communication. Retrieved on June 25, 2020, from http://www.instituteforpr.org/crisis-management-and-communications/.

Hedgecoe, A. (2012). The problems of presumed isomorphism and the ethics review of social science: A response to Schrag. *Research Ethics* 8(2):79–86.

Higher Education Loans Board. (2018). *Publications*. Retrieved on May 8, 2020 from http://www.helb.co.ke/wp-content/uploads/2019/09/Annual-Report-2018.pdf.

Hillman, A., Withers, M. and Collins, B. (2009). Resource dependency theory: A review. *Journal of Management* 35(6):1404–1427.

Hughes, R. and Mwiria, K. (1990). An essay on the implications of university expansion in Kenya. *Higher Education* 19:215–237.

Kabale, N. (March 16, 2020). *All Schools Shut as State Moves to Curb Coronavirus Spread*. Retrieved on May 7, 2020 from https://www.nation.co.ke/news/All-schools-shut-State-moves-to-curb-coronavirus-spread/1056-5492446-cd94vk/index.html.

Kenya National Bureau of Statistics. (2019). *Economic Survey 2019*. Nairobi, Kenya: Government Printer.

Kenyatta University. (April 13, 2019). *Kenyatta University*. Retrieved on May 6, 2020 from http://www.ku.ac.ke/about-ku/ku-campuses.

Kenyatta University. (April 13, 2020). *Kenyatta University*. Retrieved on May 6, 2020 from http://www.ku.ac.ke/university-newsletters/101-schools/263-digital-school-of-virtual-and-open-learning.

KU. (February 26, 2020). *Kenyatta University's Digital School of Virtual & Open Learning*. Retrieved on May 11, 2020 from http://www.ku.ac.ke/dsvol/faculty-profile.

Kung'u, L. (April 27, 2020). Counselling department provides mental health support to students during COVID-2019 lockdown. Retrieved on May 13, 2020 from https://www.usiu.ac.ke/1800/counselling-department-provides-mental-health-support-students-during-COVID-2019-lockdown.

Lerbinger, O. (1997). *The Crisis Manager: Facing Risk and Responsibility*. Mahwah, NJ: Lawrence Erlbaum Associates.

Levy, D. (January 2004). *The New Institutionalism: Mismatches with Private Higher Education's Global Growth, Working Paper No. 3*. Retrieved on May 6, 2020 from https://www.albany.edu/dept/eaps/prophe/publication/paper/PROPHEWP18_files/PROPHE%20WP18.pdf.

Lindell, M., Carla, P., and Ronald, P. (2007). *Introduction to Emergency Management*. Hoboken, NJ: Wiley.

Makokha, G. and Mutisya, D. (2016). Status of E-learning in public universities in Kenya. *International Review of Research in Open and Distributed Learning* 17(3). Retrieved on May 29, 2020 from https://doi.org/10.19173/irrodl.v17i3.2235.

Mitchell, N. (June 9, 2020). Universities not ready for online learning—U-multirank. *University World News*. Retrieved on June 23, 2020 from https://www.universityworldnews.com/post.php?story=20200609183303614.

MKU. (April 6, 2018). MKU appoints a new chancellor. Retrieved on June 27, 2020 from https://mku.ac.ke/ebulletin/2018/04/06/mku-appoints-a-new-chancellor/.

Mohamedbhai, G. (2020). COVID-2019: What consequences for higher education in Africa? *International Higher Education* 102:30–32.

Mount Kenya University. (April 10, 2020). *Mount Kenya University*. Retrieved on June 27, 2020 from http://www.odel.mku.ac.ke/mku-open-distance-electronic-learning-odel/.

Muchiri, T. and Odhiambo, B. (March 28, 2020). USIU-Africa partners with Safaricom, Telkom to provide subsidized e-learning tariffs to students and faculty. Retrieved on May 12, 2020 from https://www.usiu.ac.ke/1772/usiu-africa-partners-safaricom-telkom-provide-subsidized-e-learning-tariffs-students-faculty.

Mulinge, M., Arasa, J. and Wawire, V. (2017). *The Status of Student Involvement in University Governance in Kenya: The Case of Public and Private Universities*. Dakar, Senegal: The Council for the Development of Social Science Research in Africa.

Munene, I. (2009). Anticipated developments: East Africa's private universities and privatisation of public universities in the global context. *Africa Education Review* 6(2):254–268.

Oduor, A. (May 26, 2020). Online teaching turns into nightmare for universities. Retrieved on June 23, 2020 from https://www.standardmedia.co.ke/article/2001372730/online-teaching-turns-into-nightmare-for-universities.

Oketch, M. (2004). The emergence of private university education in Kenya: Trends, prospects and challenges. *International Journal of Educational Development* 24:119–136.

Onyango, P. (May 16, 2020). Universities struggling with online teaching. Retrieved on June 23, 2020 from https://www.standardmedia.co.ke/article/2001371485/universities-grappling-with-online-teaching.

Peatman, S. S. (February 2, 2017). Responding to a crisis: Lessons for college leaders (Panel Interviewer). Retrieved on June 23, 2020 from https://www.academicimpressions.com/blog/responding-to-a-crisis-lessons-for-college-leaders/.

Pfeffer, J. and Salancik, R. (1978). *The External Control of Organizations: A Resource Dependence Perspective*. New York: Harper & Row.

Republic of Kenya. (2012). *The Universities Act No. 42 of 2012*. Nairobi, Kenya: Government Printer.

Sifuna, D. (1998). The governance of Kenyan public universities. *Research in Post-Compulsory Education* 3(2):175–212.

Sifuna, D. (2012). Leadership in Kenyan public universities and the challenges of autonomy and academic freedom: An overview of trends since independence. *Journal of Higher Education in Africa* 10(1):121–137.

Technical University of Kenya. (April 16, 2020). *Technical University of Kenya*. Retrieved on May 5, 2020 from http://tukenya.ac.ke/tu-k-profile.

Too, J., Kandie, A. and Oure, S. (2018). An analysis of gender dynamics and staffing in the university sector in Kenya. *1st Biennial Conference on the State of Higher Education in Kenya*. Nairobi, Kenya: Commission for University Education.

UNESCO. (2005). *Private Higher Education in Kenya*. Paris, France: UNESCO International Institute for Educational Planning.

UNESCO. (March 24, 2020). 1.37 billion students now at home as Covid-19 closures expand. Retrieved on May 1, 2020 from https://en.unesco.org/news/137-billion-students-now-home-Covid-19-school-closures-expand-ministers-scale-multimedia.

United States International University-Africa. (2019). *Summer 2019 Fact Sheet*. Retrieved on May 11, 2020 https://www.usiu.ac.ke/resource/summer-2019-fact-sheet#.

United States International University-Africa. (February 3, 2019). *Vision, Mission and Values*. Retrieved on May 14, 2020 from https://www.usiu.ac.ke/vision-mission-and-values/.

United States International University-Africa. (February 17, 2019). *USIU: Africa Overview*. Retrieved on May 15, 2020 from https://www.usiu.ac.ke/263/accreditations.

Weidman, J. (1995, April 4). Education policy analysis archives. Retrieved from *Diversifying Finance of Higher Education Systems in the Third World: The Cases of Kenya and Mongolia* on May 15, 2020 from https://epaa.asu.edu/ojs/article/view/648/770.

Wooten, L. and Erika J. (2008). Linking crisis management and leadership competencies: The role of human resource development. *Advances in Developing Human Resources* DOI: 10.1177/1523422308316450.

Zamoum K. and Gorpe T. S. (2018). Crisis management: A historical and conceptual approach for a better understanding of today's crises. Retrieved on October 26, 2021 from https://www.intechopen.com/chapters/60813.

Chapter 3

Coroexpertise

Joseph Lansana Kormoh

In this chapter, I use interdisciplinary and exploratory approach to explore the various narratives used by experts to explain the nature and character of the Coronavirus Disease (COVID)-2019 pandemic, which has led to hysteria among people. While the interdisciplinary approach incorporates narratives of the pandemic from medical science, traditional/herbal homemade remedies, and social media prescriptions, this chapter also investigates the problem which has still not been clearly understood even by the best medical experts across the globe on the nature and character of the pandemic. One of the problematics of the pandemic is information dissemination which has led to hysteria in the first place. This chapter draws from various disciplines such as communications, health, and sociology. The chapter also offers some suggestions/recommendations on how "experts" can disseminate information about the virus to their audiences to prevent hysteria.

The purpose of this research is primarily to examine the various explanations that have been given to the general public about COVID-2019. Thus, this chapter sets out to answer two questions about what this pandemic is all about and how people have suggested ways of handling it. The questions are the following: (1) How has the packaging of information about COVID-2019 created hysteria and panic in the public? (2) How has the information put out by so-called experts led to fatalities in the fight against the pandemic?

Clearly, the packaging and messaging on the virus have not only led to hysteria (as Isatu Ramatu Bangura discusses in the introductory chapter of this book), it has also created massive confusion in the minds of recipients of the messages put out by some of these so-called experts. In fact, some of the messaging on COVID-2019 has led to fatalities in certain countries. For example, the prescription of alcohol has led to overindulgence in certain parts of Africa which has affected people; but more striking was in

Iran where hundreds of Iranians have died and over 1,000 people fell ill after consuming industrial alcohol (methanol) amid false claims by some so-called experts that it can help cure COVID-2019 (BBC, 2020). Thus, in addition to fighting the virus that was killing many people in Iran, their government was now busy on another front fighting to cure the 1,000 and more people who had fallen ill after the consumption of methanol.

THEORETICAL FRAMEWORK: THEORIZING EXPERTISE

Definitions of "expertise" abound, but they usually revolve around the same kind of specialist knowledge or craft that a person or group of persons are said to possess. The opposite of an expert is either a layperson, an amateur, or perhaps even worse, a neophyte or a novice (Grundman, 2016). Close to the meaning of the word expert is the often-used synonym "a specialist." These characteristics of being a specialist apply to several roles in modern society, especially the professional and the scientist (Grundman, 2016).

Skovholt et al. (2016) and Grundman (2016) have postulated that the word "expertise" originated from a Latinate verb *experiri*, meaning "to try." An *expertus* is someone who is experienced, has risked and endured something, and is proven and tested. Closely related is the word *experimentum*. The semantic field opened up through this etymology which has led to an emphasis on tacit knowledge and experiments. All these expressions literally translate in English as "experienced in" or "having experience of" (Skovholt and Jennings, 2016). In this sense, therefore, an expert is perceived as someone who is skilled and well grounded in an accumulated set of experiences in that subject or domain. One of the first known written examples of the word "expert" appeared in 1374 in Geoffrey Chaucer's *Troilus II*. In that work, Chaucer described experts as those who acquired mastery through an accumulation of relevant experiences (Grundmann, 2016).

In theorizing "expertise," a critical question that comes to mind is the following: What/who are experts and what they do and what are their roles in the wider society? The main debate on experts revolves around the question of whether experts should have a privileged position in decision-making in society. In the light of this, one needs to understand expertise more deeply and contextualize it in modern society and the sociological literature (Grundmann, 2016). Grumman's framework "allows us to better understand how expertise emerges and how it works in society, what its main characteristics are, and how it relates to common notions of scientific and professional expertise" (2016, pp. 25–48).

Dear's definition of expert emphasizes the significance of personal experience and what he refers to as tacit knowledge. To him, it draws attention to the fact that an expert is defined by others as an expert (Dear, 2004). Thus, Dear argues that an expert is someone who is reckoned to be likely experienced in relevant matters. In effect, shared experience relies on the ability to recognize a kind of attribute or property that people ("experts") can be said to possess. Expertise, thus, resembles "tacit knowledge as understood by scholars in science studies" (Dear, 2004, pp. 206–207).

Judging from the preceding proposition, there is a fundamental difference between non-experts and experts, meaning that one is either an expert in a particular domain or not an expert at all. This also presupposes that experts are located in the sciences and they are equipped with technical skills and intellectual abilities which make their advice trustworthy. Additionally, experts are thought to have moral virtue, besides their technical competence and can also mediate between the production of knowledge and its application. They also define and interpret situations and set priorities for action (Collins, 2018; Laski, 2020; Nelkin, 1975; Shapin, 2008; Turner, 2001).

Skovholt et al. (2016) have established the point that a systematic definition of the term expert/expertise as it is in use today did not begin to emerge until well into the twentieth century when cognitive science revolution began. An earlier attempt to try to understand who or what an expert was came in 1966 when famous chess master Adriaan de Groot investigated mastery in his field. His main preoccupation was to try to understand whether chess masters used qualitatively different mental processes during their matches than their less expert counterparts (Skovholt et al., 2016). De Groot (1966) strikingly discovered that there are differences in the actual thought processes employed by novices and experts. He failed to see anything that would indicate why experts chose the "correct moves most of the time while novices chose the correct moves only some of the time" (De Groot, 1966, p. 3).

Owing to the fact that "expertise" is a complex construct, Skovholt et al. (2016) have observed that the clearest picture of expertise comes from the numerous research psychologists since the 1970s who devoted considerable time and energy describing the nuances of expertise. Chi, Glaser, and Farr (1988) are among those researchers who share a general consensus that experts can be identified by a limited set of well-studied and established characteristics that are generalizable across different domains.

Chi, Glaser, and Farr (1988) have identified a few characteristics of what they call expert performers. One of those characteristics is that "experts excel mainly in their own domain," although there is hardly any empirical evidence that an expert in one field cannot achieve expertise in other unrelated domains. Chi et al. also posit that "experts perceive large meaningful pattern in their domain," which infers that experts have the ability to see larger "global patterns where less experienced individuals might see fewer meaningful patterns or perhaps only chaos" (1988, p. 6).

Chi et al. (1988) also argue that experts are usually faster in performing the skills in their domain than novices. They further claim that experts have a superior memory than those who are not experts in that domain. Experts function in their domains with "automaticity," or as though "the skills required to excel come forth automatically, without a great deal of effort or thought. This occurs through thousands of hours of practice. Because experts' skills are so automatic, they have greater mental resources freed up for storage, retrieval, or other executive mental functions" (Chi et al., 1988, p. 6). Finally, they posit that experts see and represent a problem in their domain at a more principled level than novices and also that experts spend a great deal of time analyzing a problem qualitatively. Thus, experts have the ability to accurately predict a difficult problem and they are perceived as having greater knowledge base in their specific domain. They are deemed to "possess the ability to accurately assess a problem difficulty, have the advantage of knowing how much time they need to allocate to different aspects to complete the task" (Chi et al., 1988, p. 6).

Therefore, to become an expert, Collins (2018) has suggested that one should become embedded in the social life of the "domain," thereby acquiring what is to a large extent, tacit knowledge, so as to internalize the associated concepts and skillful actions to the point of fluency. However, current research has shown that there are many other fields where there is no scientific evidence that supposed expertise leads to superior performance (Collins, 2018). For example, one study has shown that psychotherapists who had advanced degrees and decades of experience were not reliably more successful in their treatment of randomly assigned patients than novice therapists with just three months of training (Ericsson et al., 2007). Also, there have been instances where expertise has shown decline with experience. For example, when a physician is out of training/practice for a period of time s/he may be less likely to unravel some strange characteristics of heart or lung diseases because they rarely encountered such diseases. Doctors quickly forget their characteristic features and have difficulty diagnosing them. Performance picks up only after the doctors undergo a refresher course (Ericsson et al., 2007).

The question now that begs for an answer in conceptualizing "expertise" is the following: How can one tell when one is dealing with a genuine expert? Ericsson et al. (2007) argue that real expertise must pass three tests. In the first place, it must lead to performance that is consistently superior to that of the expert's peers. Second, real expertise produces concrete results. Third, true expertise can be replicated and measured in the lab (Ericsson et al., 2007).

METHODOLOGY

The multidisciplinary approach is the overarching methodology in this piece to try to build up a balanced and nuanced presentation of the various explanations that are being put out about COVID-2019. Since the outbreak of the pandemic, many explanations have been put out and many messages have been sent out to explain the nature and character of the disease. This has not only been limited to scientific discussions, narratives, and counter-narratives, but to prescriptions of various methods by which COVID-2019 can either be prevented or perhaps even cured. This chapter uses interdisciplinary and exploratory approach to understand the various narratives used by 'experts' to explain the nature of the COVID-2019 that have led to hysteria among people.

Methodologically, attempts are made in this chapter to explore the various explanations about COVID-2019 from a variety of sources, including the use of scientific journals, individual videos and audios on social media, and also some personal interviews with some healthcare professionals and practitioners. In this work, an attempt is also made to explore some traditional/homemade and herbal/tropical medicine and the various interpretations and prescriptions to cure for COVID-2019. Some individuals who claim to have expert knowledge in traditional medicine are also quoted in this work to try to present a holistic picture of COVID-2019 messaging and how this has not only led to hysteria but also anxiety and sometimes even death. A key element in the research is to attempt to extend and deepen the understanding and study of the exercise of 'expertise' on the global pandemic and how some false messages about the disease have not helped in curbing the menace but how they have even exacerbated the current pandemic situation.

HISTORICAL BACKGROUND OF THE VIRUS

The history of the coronavirus has a fundamental feature in common with the disease itself. While the virus is conceived as mutating from one form to another thereby making the virus almost incomprehensible by the so-called experts, so is the history of the disease itself constantly being re-written. Many historical postulations have been made to try to explain the genesis of the disease. However, owing to the plethora of historical narratives, this work will only reference a few of such historical narratives. Thus, this work limits its historical narrative to where SARS-CoV-2 might have originated, 'how it compares with other viruses that cause major respiratory disease, and some of the treatments and vaccines currently being investigated to combat it' (Chaplin, 2020, pp. 23–28).

The coronavirus (CoV) has been identified as human pathogens as far back as the 1960s although some 'experts' have even identified a much earlier period in the 1930s (European Centre for Disease Prevention and Control (ECDPC), April 23, 2020). It is said to have first appeared in chickens. The virus is said to infect humans as well as a variety of animals, including birds and mammals. According to the World Health Organization (WHO), in the last 20 years, two zoonotic coronaviruses have emerged: SARS-CoV discovered in 2002, and belonging to *Betacoronavirus*, subgenus *Sarbecovirus*, and MERS-CoV discovered in 2012, belonging to *Betacoronavirus*, subgenus *Merbecovirus* (WHO, 2020). Both of them have led to disastrous human outbreaks. These were the severe acute respiratory syndrome (SARS) in 2003 and the Middle East respiratory syndrome (MERS) in 2012 (WHO, 2020).

In December 2019, a third novel coronavirus initially related to a cluster of pneumonia cases in Wuhan, China, was identified and named as SARS-CoV-2 (WHO, 2020). This new coronavirus is closely related to SARS-CoV and genetically clusters within *Betacoronavirus* subgenus *Sarbecovirus* (WHO). 'Based on a modelling study, SARS-CoV-2 could become the fifth endemic human coronavirus' (Kissler et al., 2020, pp. 860–868).

According to the WHO Coronavirus disease 2019 (COVID-2019) Situation Report 113 of May 12, 2020, the current COVID-2019 disease was formally made public on December 31, 2019, to the WHO. The health organization was officially notified about a cluster of cases of pneumonia in Wuhan city, which is home to 11 million people and which also doubles as the cultural and economic hub of central China. On January 5, 59 cases were known and none had been fatal (WHO, 2020). Ten days later, WHO was aware of 282 confirmed cases, of which four were in Japan, South Korea, and Thailand (WHO, 2020). The virus responsible was isolated on January 7 and its genome shared on January 12. According to the WHO Coronavirus disease 2019 (COVID-2019) Situation Report 113 of May 12, 2020, the cause of the SARS that became known as COVID-2019 was a novel coronavirus, SARS-CoV-2. By May 12, 2020, 82,591 new cases of COVID-2019 worldwide were confirmed daily and the death rate was over 4,200 per day (WHO, 2019).

Coronaviruses in Human Beings

Lu et al. (2019) suggest that 'SARS-CoV-2 originated in animals, probably bats, and was transmitted to other animals before crossing into humans at the Huanan wet market in Wuhan City.' Also, some scientific arguments suggest that there is some evidence that the intermediate vector may have been pangolin, a type of nocturnal anteater imported illegally for its flesh (Andersen et al., 2020). It has been suggested that this animal carries with it a type of coronavirus that is very similar to SARS-CoV-2 although it is said to differ in a crucial region that determines viral infectivity and host range. Thus, it has been argued that it is possible that the virus passed into humans and then, through adaptation as it infected more people, mutated to acquire the characteristics that made it spread so quickly (Andersen et al., 2020, pp. 450–452). SARS-CoV-2 is not the first coronavirus to cause "outbreaks of respiratory infection in humans. Six others have been identified so far, all believed to have originated in animals" (Corman et al., pp. 163–188).

According to the European Centre for Disease Prevention and Control (2019), there are four coronaviruses that are now endemic in humans and they cause 10–15 percent of common colds, mostly peaking between December and April in temperate climates. The European Centre for Disease Control suggests that the "NL63 and 229E probably came from bats; OC43 and HKU1 seem to have originated in rodents." Also, it is suggested that each of these conditions causes "mild symptoms, though OC43 has ancestry as a bovine coronavirus that may have caused a pandemic at the end of the 19th century" (European Centre for Disease Prevention and Control, 2019, p. 1).

SARS-CoV was the first to be recognized, occurring first in November 2002 in China (although not known at the time) and coming to the attention of WHO early in 2003 in Vietnam. The outbreak was largely over by July 2003 and the last cases were reported in China in April 2004. "This virus was responsible for SARS, a flu-like illness, although diarrhoea was common in it. It could progress to pneumonia and respiratory failure in two weeks and 25% of people infected required intensive care. A total of 8098 cases and 774 deaths were notified" (Hui and Zumla, 2019, pp. 869–889).

Also it has been argued that SARS-CoV appears to have originated in horseshoe bats and possibly transmitted to humans through palm civet cats, traded in China mostly for their meat to supplement their diet. However, the second serious infection due to a coronavirus was MERS. The MERS-CoV virus was first identified as the cause of a fatal infection in Saudi Arabia in 2012 which spread to 27 countries (Azhar et al., 2019). Thus, unlike the SARS, MERS is said to be still prevalent. By November 2019, 2,494 infections had been notified, of which 858 proved fatal (WHO, 2019). There is currently no evidence that any of the mutations identified since SARS-CoV-2 virus emerged in humans have altered the key characteristics of COVID-2019 (Wan et al., 2020).

CASE STUDY 1: MEDICAL SCIENCE AND COVID-2019: THE EPIDEMIOLOGY OF THE DISEASE

This first case study deals with the scientific explanations of the nature and character of the pandemic or the epidemiology of the disease. This portion is meant to discuss what medical science puts out as the important messages about COVID-2019 pandemic. However, owing to the fact that literature on the epidemiology of COVID-2019 is not in short supply, there will not be any detailed discussion on it in this chapter. Thus, an attempt is made here to just highlight a few scientific explanations that can fit into the overall discussions of "Coroexpertise" and by extension the wider context of "Corohysteria."

Several explanations have been given to describe the nature and character of the pandemic. Some have stated that like SARS, the MERS causes some flu-like illness with some symptoms, including acute respiratory distress, pneumonia, and even diarrhea in some people. According to the WHO, the "original source species is not known, but bats are the most likely. SARS-CoV-2 more closely resembles the bat wild virus than it does either SARS-CoV or MERS-CoV, strongly suggesting that it is a novel coronavirus in humans" (WHO, 2020). Some have argued that it is very likely that it was a mutation of this feature during human infection that led to the rapid spread of COVID-2019 in humans.

Channappanavar and Perlman (2017, pp. 529–539) have made the point that illness in humans regarding the virus is mostly 'respiratory or gastrointestinal infections, while symptoms can range from common cold to those of more severe lower respiratory infections.' Thus, according to the International Committee on Taxonomy of viruses, viral shedding occurs via "respiratory and digestive systems and transmission can occur through different routes: fomites, airborne or faecal-oral. Coronaviruses are enveloped positive stranded RNA viruses in the order of *Nidovirales*" (International Committee on Taxonomy of Viruses (ICTV), 2011). It further states that with their characteristic surface, the virions have a crown-like appearance under the electron microscope, which is why the viruses are named after the Latin word corona, meaning "crown" or "halo" (International Committee on Taxonomy of Viruses (ICTV), 2011). The "subfamily *Orthocoronavirinae* of the family *Coronaviridae* is further classified into four CoV genera: *Alpha-, Beta-, Delta-* and *Gammacoronavirus. Betacoronavirus* genus is further separated into five sub-general families of 'Embecovirus, Hibecovirus, Merbecovirus, Nobecovirus and Sarbecovirus'" (ICTV, 2020). Finally, according to the ICTV (2011), up to the present moment, seven coronaviruses have been identified which can infect humans. 'Common human coronaviruses *Betacoronavirus* HCoV-OC43 and HCoV-HKU1 as well as *Alphacoronavirus* HCoV-229E cause common colds but also severe lower respiratory tract infections in the youngest and oldest age groups, while *Alphacoronavirus* HCoV-NL63 is considered to be an important cause of (pseudo) croup and bronchiolitis in children.'

Coronavirus COVID-2019 Messaging and Its Effects on People

While messages put out so far by the CDC and WHO are important and helpful for the prevention and control of the pandemic, yet some of the messages have led to overwhelming fear and anxiety. Such fears have been spread among millions of people around the world which has led to serious circumstances such as mental health issues. Grohol (2020) argues that part of the fear and anxiety of so many people are perfectly reasonable and are a rational response to a terrifying pandemic. However, the point has been made that people should prepare themselves for months of physical not social distancing. This singular distinction between social and physical distancing has to a large extent also created some confusion in the minds of many people which is a major drawback on COVID-2019 messaging.

Furthermore, there has been a huge disparity in information dissemination at various levels or stages. There has not been a consistent and coordinated presentation of guidelines on the prevention and control of the pandemic which arguably has contributed not only to the confusion in the packaging of information and dissemination but also to the increase in the infection rate itself and anxiety in many people. A classic case is the use of the facemask. While the CDC and WHO are preaching the religious use of face masks, especially in public places, some 'Coro-experts' have argued that facemasks are not an effective means of controlling and preventing the pandemic. Also, some of these so-called experts have put out theories which have greatly undermined the fight against the pandemic. For example, there is the argument that if the masks work, why the lockdowns and social distancing? They argue that either the use of masks is not effective or lockdowns and social distancing are totally useless if masks do work. In the light of such confusing narratives about the nature and character of the pandemic and how to control it, this author argues that the best way out is to stick to the guidelines put together by the CDC and WHO.

The CDC and WHO guidelines state among others that it is always important to distance yourself from other people and to avoid touching one's face. Also, it is advised to stay at home if you are feeling sick. It is also advised that if you are coughing or sneezing, be sure to cover your mouth with your sleeve or a napkin or tissue. Throw the napkin or tissue into the trash afterward. Limit close contact with others as much as possible ("social distancing" as recommended by the CDC). The two organizations have recommended that the space between people must be 6 feet. It is also advised that people must continue to avoid non-essential travel, eating at bars and restaurants, gathering in larger groups, and so on. Finally, the CDC and WHO advise that if people experience symptoms such as fever, cough, and shortness of breath, especially if you have been in contact with a person who has been diagnosed with COVID-2019, or if you have recently traveled to an area that is highly infected with the disease, one should contact a doctor immediately. In order to avoid the possibility of spreading the disease, it is very important to call and consult with your doctor's office before going out to seek medical attention (WHO, CDC, 2020).

CASE STUDY 2: TRADITIONAL MEDICINE—HERBAL AND HOMEMADE

Remedies for COVID-2019

"Experts" in tropical/herbal and traditional medicine have also played a vital role in the search for the cure of COVID-2019. Some of their various prescriptions are detailed here for a clear understanding of how unscientific measures have been utilized in the fight against the pandemic. Clearly, some of these traditional or herbal remedies have ended up causing more harm than good although at the same time it has yielded some 'positive' outcomes in certain cases.

It is important to start from the premise that herbal and/or home remedies have been used for a very long time, probably from pre-literate times to contemporary period of the twenty-first century to cure diseases. In many societies, homemade remedies have been used to treat infections and viruses such as flu, fever, influenza, and many others including sexually transmitted infections. Thus, with the emergence of the deadly COVID-2019 pandemic, many so-called experts in traditional/herbal medicine have put out many 'curative' prescriptions that they purport can either prevent or even cure the disease. However, the point should be stressed here that some of the 'expert' advice of traditional 'doctors' about curing or preventing the coronavirus has had grave consequences on the lives of their patients, especially so when these remedies have no dosage prescriptions and have not been scientifically proven. Also, one of the biggest problems with using herbal medications is that many of these herbs and natural remedies are not only low-quality herbs, but some of these remedies are misused which could boost the immune system even more and lead to "a cytokine storm" (Ries, 2020). A few of such herbal/traditional medications are discussed below.

With the outbreak of the COVID-2019 pandemic, scientists and other individuals (herbal/traditional doctors) have been very busy finding an effective treatment and cure for the disease. In China, for example, health officials have been encouraging alternative types of medication, especially traditional herbal remedies to help combat this deadly pandemic. It is important to point out that herbs like ginger, licorice, and ephedra have been used for thousands of years to treat respiratory infections like pneumonia (Ries, 2020).

But although some of these herbal remedies may be beneficial for the cure and prevention of coronavirus, and although some people have claimed that these herbs have kept them healthy, the evidence is largely anecdotal and the science behind it remains scarce. It does not necessarily follow that because there have been some instances where herbal remedies have worked in the cure of other diseases; therefore it provides the same benefit for the coronavirus disease.

There is an array of herbal remedies that have been used for the cure and prevention of many viral and other diseases in the past. For example, ginger and honey wrap have been in wide use against nasty germs and infection spreading viruses. The unique combination of honey and ginger is believed to have the potential to effectively reduce symptoms of sore throat while at the same time serving as a soothing anti-inflammatory agent that strengthens one's immunity (TIMESOFINDIA.COM, 2020). Also, gargling with a solution of saltwater can be one of the best and trusted remedies to battle a sore throat and quash down germs and viruses. This remedy is however recommended for 3–4 days continuous use before it can yield the required results. It must however be remembered that although there are no convincing scientific proofs that saltwater can actually kill germs or the coronavirus, yet, saltwater can help reduce certain associated symptoms like swelling and irritation (TIMESOFINDIA.COM, 2020). It is also a good way to stay hydrated, which again is vital when you are going through a bout of cold, cough, or any viral infection.

Licorice root otherwise known as mulethi is a herb that is usually added to tea for the prevention and cure of viral infections. Tea is a sweet and spicy tea renowned for its fragrant aroma. Tea is made from a combination of black tea, cardamom, ginger, cinnamon, fennel, black pepper, and cloves, although star anise, coriander seeds, and peppercorns are also used. It's also a good reliever for the itchiness caused by a sore throat (TIMESOFINDIA.COM, 2020). Mulethi has also been found to contain helpful antiviral properties which target bad disease-spreading pathogens. It also produces healthy mucus, which softens the pain and roughness. The antioxidants in it take care of any free radicals which may harm your immunity (TIMESOFINDIA.COM, 2020).

Finally, there is the Triphala tea concoction which is recommended for immunity against viral infections. The widely held belief is that a strong immune system protects people from disease-causing bacteria and virus, which in turn keep them healthy and fit. Incidentally, this author has been tempted to use this concoction in the firm belief that it helps to prevent corona from invading one's system. Triphala tea is a traditional Ayurvedic mixture of herb, which is used for making medicines for centuries. It is mainly a mixture of three dried fruits—Indian gooseberry (*Emblica officinalis*), black myrobalan (*Terminalia chebula*), and Haritaki (*Terminalia chebula*) (TIMESOFINDIA.COM, 2020).

CASE STUDY 3: FREELANCE CORO-EXPERTS: SOCIAL MEDIA MESSAGING ON COVID-2019

Social media outlets have played a significant role in the spread of 'expert' knowledge on COVID-2019 although the bulk of the messages bother on falsehoods either deliberately or unconsciously. Thus, there is no gainsaying the fact that these falsehoods have exacerbated the situation which has made it difficult to prevent or curb this deadly pandemic. I argue that there are many deaths during this pandemic which have been a direct consequence of misinformation and falsehoods on social media. Thus, the core argument is that, if information had been properly managed, and if social media had not disrupted message packaging based on falsehoods on COVID-2019, many deaths could have been prevented.

As scientists and medical experts try to produce a cure or a vaccine to prevent COVID-2019, there has been a plethora of theories and non-evidence-based messages mostly bothering on misinformation circulating in the news and on social media about what might cure or prevent the deadly disease. At least 800 people may have died around the world because of coronavirus-related misinformation in the first three months of this year (BBC, August 12, 2020). Also, a study that was published in the *American Journal of Tropical Medicine and Hygiene* also estimates that about 5,800 people were admitted to hospital as a result of false information on social media (Islam et al., 2020).

Many have died from drinking methanol or alcohol-based cleaning products. In Iran, for example, where COVID-2019 had killed almost 2,400 people and had 32,332 people infected (BBC, 2020), social media had posed another serious threat to lives by publishing non-evidence-based information. In their desperate search for a cure, or a coping strategy for preventing or curbing the disease, families in Iran turned to fake remedies paraded on social media, including the use of alcohol, albeit banned in Iran. Many died from drinking methanol or alcohol-based cleaning products in the vain hope that the products can cure the virus.

The BBC reported in March 2020 that over 300 people were killed by drinking methanol (BBC, 2020). Also, citing a story published in the United Kingdom in February, the BBC stated that a British schoolteacher and others were able to cure themselves of COVID-2019 with whiskey and honey. Combined with the guidelines that alcohol-based sanitizers can be used as a hygienic measure against the virus, some have concluded, albeit erroneously, that drinking high-profile alcohol can kill the virus that causes the disease (BBC, 2020). Also, many of the victims who had suffered and continue to suffer had followed pieces of advice which most times resemble credible medical information. A classic case of such information is the suggestion that eating large amounts of garlic or ingesting large quantities of vitamins are great ways of preventing the infection. Some people following social media advice have even gone ahead drinking substances such as cow urine, eating goat feces, and many other dangerous substances. All these actions have potentially serious implications on the health of people (BBC, 2020).

SOME RECOMMENDATIONS ON THE DISSEMINATION OF INFORMATION ON COVID-2019

Information dissemination has been one of the thorniest issues, if not the major challenge to the fight against COVID-2019. This is partly as a result of the fact that there has emerged a preponderance of so-called Coro-experts who continue to package misinformation and disseminate them to the gullible and anxious public who are mostly fearful for their lives. Although most of the messages put out by these "experts" are not based on any solid scientific foundation, many people have tended to listen to these messages even where they turn out to be clear falsehoods with devastating consequences. This is a classic case of a drowning man will clutch at a straw.

Thus, I contend that the way and manner that governments communicate information about this pandemic can shape people's responses for the better. Since misinformation has tended to spread as fast as the disease itself, it is also plausible to argue that the quickest way out of the dangers of this pandemic is to put measures in place to tackle the issue of misinformation and replacing it with objective information.

Psychological and behavioral research has shown that the same objective information can elicit different responses when presented in different ways which reproduces an effect called "framing" (Kudrna and Schmidtke, 2020). Kudrna and Schmidtke argue that although we are unaware of any published research results that have tested framing effects in the context of COVID-2019, yet, framing messages differently have at least influenced the dissemination of information, from a psychological point of view. For example, in the United Kingdom, the government's initial messaging strategy emphasized personal decision-making, stating that people needed to stay at home in order to 'save lives.' But a later messaging strategy re-coined this same message which stressed that 'people will die' if they went out. This immediately had an effect on the behavior of so many people who were fearful of dying of

COVID-2019. Does flipping the vocabulary coin here matter? We, and others, suspect that it does (Kudrna and Schmidtke, 2020).

As important as information is in the fight against the corona pandemic, it is imperative that healthcare organizations, mass media, community-based organizations, and other important stakeholders build strategic partnerships and launch common platforms for disseminating authentic and correct public health messages. Also, advanced technologies like natural language processing or data mining approaches should be applied in the detection and removal of online content with no scientific basis from all social media platforms (Tasnim et al., 2020). Furthermore, these practices should be controlled with regulatory and law enforcement measures alongside ensuring telemedicine-based services providing accurate information on COVID-2019 (Tasnim et al., 2020).

Finally, although natural and homemade remedies have cured certain illnesses in the past, the point should be made that there has not been any scientific study or evidence that some, if not most of these remedies, can cure or even prevent COVID-2019. It is therefore prudent that each and every individual recipient of some of the messages, especially on social media, should only accept such messages with a pinch of salt. Anyone attempting to try any of the remedies prescribed in the mass media and indeed other media outlets must bear in mind that there is no cure or even a vaccine at the time of writing this piece for the disease and there has been no scientific investigation into the benefits or otherwise of some of these so-called remedies. In fact, the myth that consuming high-strength alcohol in the vain can cure COVID-2019 has not only led to so many deaths but also alcohol consumption is associated with a wide range of communicable and non-communicable diseases and mental health disorders. This can make a person more vulnerable to COVID-2019. In particular, alcohol compromises the body's immune system and increases the risk of adverse health outcomes. Therefore, people should minimize their alcohol consumption at any time, particularly during the COVID-2019 pandemic (WHO, 2020). Thus, if anyone is curious or inclined to use any herbal remedies, the best way to go is to consult a physician or naturopathic doctor who is well grounded in various herbs and their chemical properties.

CONCLUSION

This chapter has used interdisciplinary and exploratory approach to critically analyze the various narratives that have been put forward by so-called experts to explain the nature and character of COVID-2019. It has also explored some of the misinformation and falsehoods that have been directed at the public relating to perceived cure and preventive methods against the deadly pandemic. While the interdisciplinary approach has incorporated some narratives of COVID-2019 from medical science, traditional/herbal homemade remedies, and social media prescriptions, this chapter has brought to the fore questions which have still not been answered or clearly understood even by the best medical experts across the globe on the nature and character of the pandemic.

To critically analyze the concept of Coroexpertise, this chapter set out with a clear theoretical framework by theorizing what constitutes an expert, followed by a brief historical presentation/background of the disease. As observed earlier, the history of the coronavirus has a fundamental characteristic in common with the disease itself. The point has been made that while the virus is conceived as mutating from one form to another almost on a regular basis, thereby making the virus almost incomprehensible by the so-called experts, so is the history of the disease itself constantly being re-written.

In this chapter, I have approached the analysis from three main perspectives under the captions of three case studies with some suggestions and recommendations on the proper and reliable dissemination of information on COVID-2019. The chapter has also attempted to bring to the fore some of the deliberate attempts that have been made by certain individuals to deceive people into believing their 'expert' messages, especially on social media.

The first case study in this chapter has dealt with the scientific explanations of the nature and character of the pandemic or what is known as the epidemiology of the disease. The second case study dealt with 'experts' in tropical/herbal and traditional medicine who have also played a vital role in the search for the cure of COVID-2019. The third and final case study has dealt with freelance 'Coro-experts' on social media outlets and the role they have played in the spread of "expert" knowledge on COVID-2019. The chapter ends with some recommendations on the correct and appropriate dissemination of information on the pandemic.

It is important to conclude that while the disease continues to kill people in large numbers across the globe, some pieces of misinformation from so-called experts have not only exacerbated the situation by causing hysteria among people, it has also, in some cases, contributed to the death of many people as evidenced in Iran who were led into believing that the consumption of alcohol can cure and also prevent the infection of the virus.

REFERENCES

Andersen, K. G., Rambaut, A., Lipkin, W. I., Holmes, E. C. and Garry, R. F. (March 17, 2020). The proximal origin of SARS-CoV-2. *Nature Medicine* 26(4):450–452. Retrieved on August 3, 2020 from https://doi.org/10.1038/s41591-020-0820-9.

Azhar E., Hui, D. S. C., Memish, Z. A., Drosten, C. and Zumla, A. (December 2019). The Middle East Respiratory Syndrome (MERS). *Infectious Disease Clinics of North America* 33(4):891–905. Retrieved on August 28, 2020 from DOI 10.1016/j.idc.2019.08.001.

British Broadcasting Corporation (BBC). (August 12, 2020). Hundreds dead because of Covid-19 misinformation. Retrieved on August 30, 2020 from www.bbc.uk/world-53755067?fbclid=wAR2cK.

Channappanavar, R. and Perlman, S. (May 2, 2017). Pathogenic human coronavirus infections: Causes and consequences of cytokine storm and immunopathology. *Seminars in Immunopathology* 39(5):529–539. Retrieved on August 3, 2020 from http://doi: 10.1007/s00281-017-0629-x.

Chaplin, S. (May 2020) COVID-19: A brief history and treatments in development. *Journal of Prescribing and Medicines Management* 31:23–28. Retrieved on August 20, 2020 from https://doi.org/10.1002/psb.1843.

Chi, M. T. H., Glaser, R. and Farr, M. J., eds. (1988). *The Nature of Expertise*. Hillsdale, NJ: Lawrence Erlbaum Associates.

Collins, H. (1985). *Changing Order: Replication and Induction in Scientific Practice*. London, UK: Sage.

Collins, H. (2018). Studies of expertise and experience. *Topoi* 37, 67–77. Retrieved on July 10, 2020 from https://doi.org/10.1007/s11245-016-9412-1.

Corman V. M., Muth, D., Niemeyer, D. and Drosten, C. (2018). Hosts and sources of endemic human coronaviruses. *Advances in Virus Res*earch 100:163–88. Retrieved on July 10, 2020 from doi: 10.1016/bs.aivir.2018.01.001. Epub 2018 Feb 16.

De Groot, A. D. (1966). Perception and memory versus thought. In Kleinmuntz, B. (ed.), *Problem Solving Research, Methods and Theory*. New York: Wiley.

Dear, P. (2004). Mysteries of state, mysteries of nature: Authority, knowledge and expertise in the seventeenth century. In Jasanoff, S. (ed.), *States of Knowledge: The Co-Production of Science and the Social Order:* London, UK: Routledge.

Ericsson, A. K., Prietula, M. J. and Cokely, E. T. (2006). The making of an expert. *Harvard Business Review* 85:114–121, 193. Retrieved on August 23, 2020 from http://www.harvardbusinessonline.org.

European Centre for Disease Prevention and Control (ECDPC). (April 23, 2020). Coronavirus disease 2019 (COVID-19) in the EU/EEA and the UK, Retrieved on August 10, 2020 from https://www.ecdc.europa.eu/sites/default/Files/documents/covid-19-rapid-risk-assessment-coronavirus-disease-2019-ninth-update-23-april-2020.pdf.

Grohol, J. M. (March 2020). Coping with coronavirus (COVID-19): *Your Anxiety & Mental Health*. Retrieved on July 30, 2020 from https://psychcentral.com/news/coronavirus.

Grundmann, R. (September 27, 2016). The problem of expertise in knowledge societies. *Minerva* 55:25–48. Retrieved on August 10, 2020, from: DOI 10.1007/s11024-016-9308-7.

Hanson, M., Jennings, L. and Grier, T. (2016). A brief history of expertise. In Skovholt, T. M. and Jennings, L. (eds.), *Master Therapists: Exploring Expertise in Therapy and Counselling*. Oxford, UK: Oxford University Press.

Hui, D. S. C. and Zumla, A. (May 2020). Severe acute respiratory syndrome: Historical, epidemiologic, and clinical features. *Infectious Disease Clinics of North America* 33(4):869–889. Retrieved on August 10, 2020 from DOI: 10.1016/j.idc.2019.07.001.

International Committee on Taxonomy of Viruses (ICTV). (January 14, 2020). Virus taxonomy: The classification and nomenclature of viruses. Retrieved on July 10, 2020 from https://talk.ictvonline.org/ictv-reports/ictv_9th_report/.

Islam, S., Sarkar, T., Khan, S. H., Kamal, A.-H. M., Hasan, S. M. M., Kabir,Yeasmin, D., Islam, M. A., Chowdhury, K. I. A., Anwar, K. S., Chughtai, A. A. and Seale, H. (October 7, 2020). COVID-19–related infodemic and its impact on public health: A global social media analysis. *American Journal of Tropical Medicine and Hygiene* 103:1621–1629. Retrieved on October 30, 2020 from doi:10.4269/ajtmh.20-0812.

Kissler, S. M., Tedijanto, C., Goldstein, E., Grad, Y. H. and Lipsitch, M. (May 2020). Projecting the transmission dynamics of SARS-CoV-2 through the post-pandemic period. *Science* 368:860–868. Retrieved on August 22, 2020 from doi: 10.1126/science.abb5793.

Kudrna, L. and Schmidtke, K. A. (July 17, 2020). Changing the message to change the response: Psychological framing effects during COVID-19. *British Politics and Policy at LSE*. Retrieved on August 12, 2020 from https://blogs.lse.ac.uk/politicsandpolicy/changing-the-message-to-change-the-response-psychological-framing-effects-during-covid-19/.

Laski, H. J. (July 22, 2020). Limitations of the expert. *Society* 57:371–377. Retrieved on June 30, 2020 from https://doi.org/10.1007/s12115-020-00498-z.

Lu, R., et al. (February 22, 2020). Genomic characterisation and epidemiology of 2019 novel coronavirus: Implications for virus origins and receptor binding. *Lancet* 395:565–574. Retrieved on July 20, 2020 from https://www.who.int/emergencies/mers-cov/en.

Nelkin, D. (February 1, 1975). The political impact of technical expertise. *Social Studies of Science* 5:35–54. Retrieved on August 15, 2020 from https://doi.org/10.1177/030631277500500103.

Quincy, E., Imants, J., Dankbaar, B. and Segers, M. (2017). Designing education for professional expertise development. *Scandinavian Journal of Educational Research* 61:187–204. Retrieved on, July 12, 2020 from DOI: 10.1080/00313831.2015.1119729.

Ries, J. (April 15, 2020). Herbal remedies and COVID-19: What to know. *Health News*. Retrieved on August 12, 2020 from https://www.healthline.com/health-news/herbal-remedies-covid-19-what-to-know.

Shapin, S. (2008). *The Scientific Life: A Moral History of a Late Modern Vocation*. Chicago, IL: The University of Chicago Press.

Tasnim , S., Hossain, M. and Mazumder, H. (May 2020). Impact of rumours and misinformation on COVID-19 in social media. *Journal of Preventive Medicine and Public Health* 53(3):171–174. Retrieved June 30, 2020 from Doi: 10.3961/jpmph.20.094.

TIMESOFINDIA.COM. (June 16, 2020). COVID-19: Try these simple home remedies to treat a sore throat. Retrieved on August 14, 2020 from https://timesofindia

.indiatimes.com/life-style/health-fitness/home-remedies/covid-19-try-these-simple-home-remedies-to-treat-a-sore-throat/photostory/76402743.cms.

Turner, S. (February 2001). What is the problem with experts? *Social Studies of Science* 31:123–149. Retrieved August 21, 2020 from https://doi.org/10.1177/030631201031001007.

Wan Y., Shang, J., Graham, R., Baric, R. S. and Li, F. (March 2020). Receptor recognition by the novel coronavirus from Wuhan: An analysis based on decade-long structural studies of SARS coronavirus. *Journal of Virology* 94(7):9. Retrieved on July 21, 2020 from DOI:10.1128/JVI.00127-20.

World Health Organization (WHO). (May 18, 2004). Emergencies preparedness, response: Severe Acute Respiratory Syndrome (SARS). Retrieved on June 30, 2020 from https://www.who.int/csr/don/archive/disease/severe_acute_respiratory_syndrome/en.

World Health Organization (WHO). (March 11, 2019). Middle East Respiratory Syndrome Coronavirus (MERS-CoV). Retrieved on June 29, 2020 from https://www.who.int/emergencies/mers-cov/en.

World Health Organization (WHO). (January 9, 2020). WHO statement regarding cluster of pneumonia cases in Wuhan, China. Retrieved on June 30, 2020 from https://www.who.int/china/news/detail/09-01-2020-who-statement-regarding-cluster-of-pneumonia-cases-in-wuhan-china.

World Health Organization (WHO). (January 10, 2020). GCM teleconference—Note for the records. Subject: Pneumonia in Wuhan, China. Retrieved on June 29, 2020 from https://www.who.int/blueprint/10-01-2020-nfr-gcm.

World Health Organization (WHO). (January 12, 2020). Novel coronavirus: China, 2020. Retrieved on June 30, 2020 from: https://www.who.int/csr/don/12-january-2020-novel-coronavirus-china/en/.

World Health Organization (WHO). (January 20, 2020). Teleconference of the R&D blueprint GCM. pneumonia of unknown etiology in Wuhan, China. Geneva, Switzerland. Retrieved on June 21, 2020 from https://www.who.int/blueprint/prioritydiseases/Key-action/20-01-2020-nfr-gcm.pdf?ua=1.

World Health Organization (WHO). (January 21, 2020). Novel coronavirus (2019-nCoV). Situation Report, 1. Geneva, Switzerland. Retrieved on June 20, 2020 from: https://www.who.int/Docs/default-source/coronaviruse/situation-reports/20200121-Sitrep-1-2019-ncov.pdf? Sfvrsn=20a99c10_4.

World Health Organization (WHO). (May 12, 2020). Coronavirus Disease 2019 (COVID-19). Situation Report, 113. May 12, 2020. Retrieved on June 30, 2020 from https://www.who.int/emergencies/diseases/novel-coronavirus-2019/situationreports.

Chapter 4

Coroelitism

Omosefe Oyekanmi

The outbreak of Coronavirus Disease (COVID)-2019 at the end of 2019, and its spread across all continents and regions of the world by March 2020, did not only take the world by surprise but reawakened the discourse on elitist influence on countries' state capacity and national development. In Nigeria, the first case of coronavirus was recorded on February 28, 2020, in Lagos (NCDC, 2020). As of July 24, 2020, there are 39,539 confirmed cases, 845 fatalities, and 16,559 discharged cases of COVID-2019 in Nigeria (NCDC, 2020). The news of the disease in Nigeria attracted both confusion and controversy from her citizenry. This mixed reaction by citizens was informed by the enduring oppressive influence of the political class in exacerbating hardship and underdevelopment in the country in time past.

The complexities in Nigeria's social, economic, and political life are not just factored by primordial subjectivism like tribal and religious interventions, but by the influence of social formations at the base of Nigeria's polity. As such, since 1960 independence, the elite class has been very instrumental to the political power dynamics, finding expression in virtually all space in Nigeria's developmental discourse, which in the long run has brought untold hardship to a larger group of the Nigerian populace. According to Ojukwu and Shopeju (2010), the elite group has turned the Nigerian state into its main source of primitive wealth. This suggests that an elite advantage as a strategic instrument for driving the country forward may be difficult to achieve. Considering the clinical properties of COVID-2019 and its preventive measures, which require active state capacity and response to effect public health principles, the global pandemic presents a veritable tool for an elitist analysis in Nigeria's polity. As Nigeria joins the rest of the world to combat the COVID-2019 scourge, the hysteria of the virus as a disease targeting only political leaders and government officials in Nigeria has gathered momentum.

Although this notion compromises national and international efforts in managing the public health menace in Africa's most populous nation, it however reveals citizen's belief on the position of elitist/political class in influencing national development.

This chapter therefore seeks to interrogate the misleading narrative of the deadly coronavirus as a disease for the political elites only, thereby serving as a cleansing agent to purge the Nigerian space of corrupt and recalcitrant leaders. Although this object of enquiry is hinged on the narrative making the rounds in the country, a more analytical approach of coroelitism will be explored in the chapter.

Situating the discourse on the Elitist Theory, *coroelitism*, as used in this chapter, is derived from two words, "coro" and "elitism." Coro is culled from the novel virus coronavirus which originates from any of a group of ribonucleic acid—a nucleic acid present in all living cells—viruses that cause a variety of diseases in humans and other animals. Elitism according to Pareto is the reality of all societies, either developed or underdeveloped, simple or complex. Hence, elitism is a sociopolitical tool used by a privileged minority group (elites), armed with distinct features such as leadership abilities, knowledge and information, drive and ambition, to serve as societal agents for filtering broader notions of ethnicity, religion, and class to the larger society (Ojukwu and Shopeju, 2010). Accordingly, Nigeria's elites structure with the instrument of state apparatus and state's resources at their disposal accumulate wealth and seclude a greater fraction of the Nigerian society from development.

In the context of this chapter, elitism, as Aduloju (2017) affirms, refers to the political or governing class, that is, those who are at the top echelon of social, economic, and political power.

Coroelitism therefore refers to the state of affairs whereby Nigeria's political class, government officials who are usually the custodian and managers of national wealth and resources, becomes also the main persons contracting the coronavirus. This concept in the context of this chapter suggests that the notion of COVID-2019 pandemic as a disease exclusively for the political elites in Nigeria is a hysteria. This belief by some Nigerians is premised on an existing tradition of corrupt government officials navigating public good for a selected few. Furthermore, this chapter seeks to analyze government's response to the global pandemic, in view of the attendant consequences of elitist influence in governance. The chapter seeks to explore the following objectives: (a) to establish if the coronavirus is contracted by the political elites only in the Nigerian situation and the factors informing the hysteria of coroelitism and (b) to establish the relationship between coroelitism and the inequality gap in Nigeria, as well as the mechanism engaged by government officials/political class in the management of COVID-2019. The chapter therefore proposes that the management of COVID-2019 will influence positive elitist view toward national development. Thus, the importance of this chapter cannot be overemphasized, as an analysis of elitism in Nigeria is exigent for proffering solutions to the challenges of COVID-2019 and the complexities of the Nigerian situation that have exacerbated the management of COVID-2019. Considering the elitist tradition in Nigeria that circumvents Nigeria's resources for a selected few at the expense of infrastructural deficit, for an overwhelming impoverished population, the chapter is apt for various reasons. First, it is critical in understanding state's preparedness in responding to emergency situations. Second, it also helps to understand the effect of elitist decision on the general population in the long run. Third, the chapter affords the narrative that charts a course for re-positioning Nigeria's political class as instruments for driving development in Nigeria and lastly, it will equip policymakers and political elites with the necessary tools in developing policies that will situate institutions for national progress and development. The chapter adopts a descriptive case study research design. With Nigeria as its spatial scope, qualitative method forms the means of data gathering. Through textual and content analysis, newspaper reports and updates on government's policies on COVID-2019 were analyzed. Also, a close observation of events from February till the time of writing was reviewed and analyzed.

This chapter is divided into five sections. The first section begins with a brief historical development of elitism in Nigeria and its role in influencing national policies like COVID-2019. The second section assesses national responses to the management of COVID-2019 in Nigeria in the context of the principle of selective engagement, while the next section examines the maiden concept coroelitism as a hysteria in Nigeria. The fourth section examines the relationship between coroelitism and the inequality gap in Nigeria and the concluding section of the chapter makes recommendations for positive elitist engagement in emergency situations like COVID-2019 and beyond.

THEORETICAL DISCOURSE

As stated earlier in the introductory section, coroelitism is culled from two words, "coronavirus" and "elitism," with elitism as its theoretical underpinning. This section explicates the theory of elitism in analyzing the trajectory of COVID-2019 as an elitist disease in Nigeria. As a concept, the word elite became popular through the works of classical elitists like Vilfredo (1935), Gaetano (1939), and Robert (1911) by the end of the nineteenth and early twentieth century. Emerging from capitalism, its ideology on class distinctions in societies is based on the pursuit and promotion of mutually beneficial collective desires to improve the community in a subtle and unconscious emphasis on the self (Odubajo and Alabi, 2014). In other words, elitism is a political theory that rejects Marx's views of equality, suggesting that there will always be a minority elite ruling the majority. This minority elite, that is, the political class, breeds inequality (Albert, 2005). This according to Ake (1991), in the African scenario, is premised on the attitude inherited from colonial administration. He asserts that, rather than transforming the system to align with national progress, African independence political elites collided with their citizens in a bid to resist pressure for structural transformation and redistribution. Hence, the political class with the power acquired amasses public wealth for themselves and associates, which spirals into poverty, unemployment, inequality, and finally underdevelopment.

According to Parry (1976), Bottomore (1976), and Nwankwo (1997), elites are people who got their material empowerment through either talent, education, or influence and now exercise considerable influence over the political, cultural, economic, social, and intellectual life. Pareto's context of elitism gives more credence to the tone of this chapter. He affirmed that there are two groups of elites, the governing and non-governing elites. For him, both categories of elites are superior in any society. Similarly, most literature on elitism is based on classical and modern elitism. Classical elitism is based on the construct that, in determining the outcome *between state and society*, the notion of elite rule is inevitable as society is necessarily elite driven (Lopez, 2013). Hence, in the classical elitist literature, elites were often (but not only) defined through capacity, personality, and skill. On the other hand, modern concept of elites argues that elites control resources, key positions, and relating through power networks (Yamokoski and Dubrow, 2008). Furthermore, the Italian school of elitism, which influenced subsequent Western perspective of Elite Theory, is anchored on the following two major thoughts:

(1) Power lies in position of authority in key economic and political institutions.
(2) The psychological difference that sets elites apart is that they have personal resources, for instance, intelligence and skills, and a vested interest in the government; while the rest are incompetent and do not have the capabilities of governing themselves, the elite are resourceful and strive to make the government work. For in reality, the elite would have the most to lose in a failed state.

The preceding ideas by early thinkers on Elite Theory suggest that elites are aware of the influence of power and authority on key institutions, and since they possess the capability for driving leadership, their objective is then to make government work, especially with the elites losing out the more in the event of a failed state. Nevertheless, the dichotomy between government and governance, which the early thinkers did not put into account, makes it obvious that a working government may not translate to good governance for the majority. As Okeke (2017) posits, elitism in governance pays no heed to the real needs of the governed, as the superior class, which is usually found in government in any society, influences economic, political, and social factors created to suit the purpose of those in government. Accordingly, the basis of Elite Theory centers on the intricacies of elite behavior, its interaction, transformation, and the eventual contact between those instances and the reactions it produces (Lopez, 2013).

Bariledum and Vurasi (2013) aver that based on statutory, institutional, or ruling coalition status, political elites are custodians of decision-making power in the state and are able to influence policy decisions. This suggests that elites exercise influence on the people by controlling the ideological and philosophical direction of the society. Considering the two categories of classes in society, Genieys and Smyrl (2008) suggest that the basic elements shaping elitism must be emphasized. This suggestion infers that elements such as inequality, predominance, and organization represent a clear-cut demarcation between elites with influence and those without influence, as well as differentiating the "best" from the rest. Another dimension to elitism stems from the indispensability of elites in any society, and as a position of experts (Perreti, 2018), where every government or leadership has its brain trust that drives policies for the state. In this sense, elites engage their influence as positive energy for the state, such as restructuring of the world economy after the Second World War. Thus, in a modern nation, elite in all forms is a condition for success or failure, as in the case of Nigeria.

The complexity of Nigeria's situation in many ways is attributed to the conditions of failure of her elite system. It is further worrisome as Afuape (2012) submits that all classes of elites in the Nigerian society serve as a form of political decay. In the same vein, as Mosca, Pareto, and Michels, cofounders of the Italian school of elitism argued, the elite groups impose limit on what is possible. Limits imposed on genuine democratic systems are due to self-centered elites who circumvent resources and opportunities from the people (Higley and Burton, 1989). Assuaging to the above assertion, Akinbode succinctly affirms that

> Nigeria is structured as a series of concentric circles with political office holders and the civil service at the outer circle informing and influencing an inner elite core, which is not rule bound. This core is often termed the "cabal." That core is terrified of losing power, perks and influence all of which enable rent seeking. Meetings of the federal executive council have in previous regimes been described as a series of contract endorsing sessions. (2019, p. 9)

The cabal in Nigeria, which is the core of the concentric circle, imposes artificial limitation on the democratic system to continually gain monopoly of common good. The Elite Theory has been critiqued on several grounds, notably by the Marxist and pluralist schools of thoughts. The Marxist philosophical idea believes that class position is premised on the relationship to the means of production: that is, the bourgeoisie and the proletariat and not a factor of political, economic, social, and psychological resources. The pluralist also debunks the Elite Theory on the grounds that the state with several institutions, agencies, and departments cannot be controlled by a small group; hence, power is diffused among the different segments of the state. Another major critique of the Elite Theory hinges on the elites mismanaging the control of power, thereby personalizing state power without providing true democracy. Hence, the notion that only the smartest and strongest people are the best qualified to rule and control power is a major weakness of the theory of elitism. A synthesized notion of the different perspectives of elitism, referred to as new elitism, is the fact that, regardless of the regime type and structure of government, all political reality fits within the scope of Elite Theory, which has a causal effect on the relationship between state and society (Lopez, 2013).

DEVELOPMENT OF ELITISM IN NIGERIA

Before the influence of the West in shaping Nigeria's political development, there has been the "circulation of elites" as likened by Pareto till date, suggesting that the development of society and major changes that occur in them are a function of one elite replacing another in the order of time and event. Pre-colonial Nigeria was a blend of separate defined entities, governed by the existing structure of each society, usually based on the eldest in the family. The elite creation process was monarchical in nature in most part of the country, comprising of an elite system made up of kings, queens, chiefs, community leaders, and so on. The system in operation in the eastern part was however different from other regions, as there was a form of decentralized power bloc in that region. Notwithstanding, the category of elites in the monarchical system exercised both political and economic power and was able to converse with foreign merchants and colonial masters (Odubajo and Bamidele, 2014).

With Western interference into precolonial political system, the elitist system was altered, as the Europeans exclusively took over political and economic leadership of the country through slave trade and later colonialism. However, by 1922, the composition of elites in Nigeria changed slightly, with an introduction of indigenous representation in Nigeria's political leadership. Following the acceptance of Western civilization, a new trend of elites emerged, through the influence of Western education, which was instrumental to the struggle for independence.

Under Sir Hugh Clifford's constitution, where elective principle was first introduced, a small group of British educated Nigerians were co-opted into the political administration of Nigeria (Ogele, 2020), marking the beginning of indigenous elites in colonial administration. Although the elective principle introduced Nigerian elites into the political power play through the development of political parties, most Nigerians were still disenfranchised (Ogele, 2020). Between this period, major political parties like the Nigerian National Democratic Party, Northern People's Congress, and Action Group were crafted along ethnic formations on the basis of elite politics in those regions. This thereafter formed the cluster of power representation nationally, as the different colonial administrations had minimal indigenous representation in their cabinet. As Lloyd succinctly puts it, "throughout sub-Saharan Africa, political power has been rapidly passing from the colonial rulers to members of indigenous national elites—men who are predominantly young, highly educated and comparatively wealthy" (Lloyd, 1966, p. 1).

These privileged emerging local political elites further prompted nationalist movements both within and outside Nigeria for the struggle for independence. The struggle for 1960 independence was moved by a privileged few, who initially hoped on transforming the social, economic, and political sectors for national progress (Bariledum and Vurasi, 2013). Thus, according to Lloyd's assertion, there were two types of elites before the first civil war, "the traditional elite of the political office-holders of tribal societies, and the earlier westernized elite" (Lloyd, 1970, p. 14). Additionally, a third class of elites emerged from the military.

Similarly, with many disenfranchised, the political leadership of the entity called Nigeria was left in the hands of a selected few, who have had Western education from Europe and the United States. This culture groomed the elitist system in Nigeria throughout civilian and military administrations, whereby the circulation of few elites from one generation to another took root at the expense of an impoverished large population till date. In essence, the crop of modern-day elites in Nigeria's political system is a product of transferred control from previous generations. Accordingly, elites transform into the most important group in the society, occupying central positions of power and influence to set directional goals for the whole society and country (DFID, 2011). Invariably, the nature of the Nigerian state after independence guaranteed the petite-bourgeois class and its attendant client-patron relationship (Odubajo and Bamidele, 2014). Corroborating the above assertion, the united front against colonialist was not in isolation, it was based on a common enemy which had to be taken out. This explains the division and collapsed unity in the first republic among the elite formation, after the successful exit of the British in Nigeria. Hence, for over 60 years, each leading nationalist strives to achieve power using the people of his tribe as the base (Bariledum and Vurasi, 2013).

Basically, elites have considerably influenced national policies based on a favorable outcome for the political class. National policies like Operation Feed the Nation in 1976, Structural Adjustment Program in the 1980s, Roll Back Malaria formulated in 2001, National Economic Empowerment Development Strategy enunciated in 2004, and so on, were not in the best interest of the masses and, in essence, were either dead on arrival or short spanned. Again, these policies were created to fail, as they only served the political interest of public office holders who lacked continuation base for public policies and good governance capacity (Obamwonyi and Aibieyi, 2014). These programs expose the failure of the governing elites over the years in marshaling policies for productivity and development. It represents monumental waste of financial resources as well as clear demonstration of inadequacies in program planning and implementation (Egbue, 2009). In the same vein, the government has been criticized for adapting COVID-2019 lockdown policy in a country with majority of her citizenry depending on daily income jobs vis-à-vis an unstructured pattern of COVID-2019 palliative distribution. Similarly, economic assistance amid the pandemic reveals government's shortfalls, in Nigeria's social protection systems, with a possibility of excluding the country's poorest and most vulnerable people (Human Rights Watch, 2020).

As it stands, the elite group who has amassed wealth had nothing to lose in a lockdown policy compared to a vast majority of Nigerians working in the informal sector. For instance, in Lagos State, the economic center of Nigeria, 65 percent of the estimated 25 million workforce work in the informal sector, with lower income, lack of health insurance, pension, housing, and zero or insufficient saving (Human Rights Watch, 2020). In effect, the approach of the governing elites in managing the pandemic and many other social factors is imbued in selective engagement.

GOVERNMENT'S RESPONSE TO COVID-2019 IN THE PRINCIPLE OF SELECTIVE ENGAGEMENT

Since January 30, 2020, when COVID-2019 was declared as a Public Health Emergency of International Concern, the Nigerian government has closely monitored the ongoing outbreak which originated in Wuhan, China (OCHA Nigeria, 2020). On February 27, 2020, Nigeria recorded its index case of COVID-2019 in an Italian male national who works in Nigeria and was returning to Lagos on February 25, 2020. The government instituted a COVID-2019 Presidential Task Force response, which met regularly to review actions and inactions of government in mitigating the spread of the virus. Based on clinical properties of the virus, necessitating WHO basic health protocols of social distancing, personal hygiene, and community safety measures, the National Center for Disease Control moved to implement COVID-2019 guidelines in phases.

Considering Nigeria's population size, of about 200 million, highly populated densities, poor environmental sanitation, and continued operations of international flights, despite reporting an index case, Nigeria particularly became more vulnerable to the disease. Few weeks after the first recorded case was reported, Nigeria shut down her air space and land borders, like most other countries in the world. On March 18, 2020, international flights to Nigeria were banned from countries like China, United States, Italy, United Kingdom, and Iran—that is, countries with high rising cases of COVID-2019—and five days later, the total closure of air and land space was announced (Alagboso and Abubakar, 2020; IMF, 2020). Interstate travels were banned, with lockdowns enforced first in Lagos, Ogun, and Abuja and subsequently in some selective states in the North and across the country, where cases were on the rise. Social gatherings, religious gatherings, and schools were closed down. Economic activities watered down significantly, with the informal sector bearing the brunt (IMF, 2020). Oil prices fell by 45 percent to around US$ 30 per barrel in the first quarter of 2020 (Akanni and Gabriel, 2020). This downward slope in oil prices was a considerable threat to the intermediate economic growth achieved for many years by most African countries depending on oil as their mainstay (IMF, 2020). This in no small measure deepened the economic crises and created more vulnerabilities to poverty and crime. According to Elusoji (2020) amid COVID-2019, President Buhari affirms that Nigeria's revenues and foreign exchange earnings fell by 60 percent. By April 22, all states agreed to ban interstate travel for two weeks. Invariably, implicit social problems, such as insecurity, cybercrime, and gender-based violence, were aggravated as a result of the lockdown.

To mitigate these economic shocks, the federal government and Central Bank of Nigeria initiated programs and released funds and grants for critical healthcare support for states, especially Lagos which was the epicenter of the virus, with about 40 percent of COVID-2019 cases. Palliative measures in the form of grants and relief materials for the poorest household were also disbursed. Stimulus package for household, health sectors, SMEs, and so on, was discharged, and on March 24, an Economic Stimulus bill was passed. The federal government generated funds from private, bilateral and multilateral institutions like IMF, World Bank, and so on. Similarly, $3.4 billion was approved by the IMF as emergency funding (IMF, 2020), with the Nigerian government borrowing $4.34 billion from the domestic stock market to finance its budget, and projected borrowing in billion dollars from the African Development Bank and the World Bank. Following a 2.3 trillion economic sustainability plan by the Buhari government, the Central Bank of Nigeria created credit facilities up to 100 billion Naira for healthcare, 100 billion Naira for manufacturing, and 1 trillion Naira for the sectors (Eboh, 2020). These financial assistance and short-term mitigation though commendable are still below the threshold in fixing the squalor of an enduring elitist system. Basically, a good number of the extreme poor are not captured in the National Social Register (NSR). Forty percent of Nigeria's population (82.9 million) are poor, earning Nigeria the title of the poverty capital of the world (NBS, 2020). Hence, the measures taken by the government were not significant in cushioning the effect of COVID-2019 on a sizable extreme poor population, as the cash payment captured only a fraction of the poor. The lockdown strategy implored by government was in sharp contrast to the realities of the informal sector in Nigeria, which contributes about 65 percent of Nigeria's GDP and contributes more than 90 percent of the country's workforce (IMF, 2020). The lockdown policy, although adopted from Western nations like Canada, the United States, and Italy, was more successful given the depth of the social security system in operation, the robust national information management system, and the technological advancement in these countries. Again, the palliative measures and relief distribution were haphazard, as many citizens on the NSR did not receive the money promised by the government (Bosah, 2020).

Most of the relief materials were reserved for card-carrying members of political parties (Adelaja, 2020). More so, the distribution process for the palliatives was a mockery to the guidelines of social distancing protocols, as the sharing of materials often led to chaos, with the crowd scuffling over a portion of shared items (Okon, 2020). In essence, the distribution of relief materials and food items was not orderly, leading to more elites taking advantage of the system.

The inadequacy of cash transfers, food items, medical supplies, and trust in the government further increased crime rate and total negligence of COVID-2019 protocols. What this portends is that millions of Nigerians will be pushed into poverty adding to the overwhelming poor population. To a greater extent, the rate of temporary and permanent unemployment will increase exposing COVID-2019-induced vulnerable citizens to 'hunger virus' (Amzat et al., 2020).

Negating public health policies on COVID-2019, Nigerians conveniently tagged the virus as an elitist virus through social media handles (Nwaubani, 2020). Skits and short videos were made by citizens, referring to the virus as a 'big man disease' hunting for the corrupt politicians and political elites (Nwaubani, 2020), who have since independence engineered public policies for the good of themselves and associates. This hysteria gradually led to the negligence of COVID-2019 protocols and guidelines. As citizens claimed, the country has been hit by a worse virus "hunger virus" with greater implication worse than COVID-2019. It is important to state that advanced economies of the world also experienced the devastating impact of COVID-2019 on their economies and social systems, but the existing structures, institutions, and state capacity inherent in these countries before COVID-2019 cushioned the effect of the virus on the living conditions of their citizenry. By May 4, phase 1 of the three-phase economic reopening commenced. By June 2, phase 1 moved to phase 2, allowing most offices and schools to reopen, with partial restriction in place and the enforcement of the use of face masks or coverings in public. Subsequently, phase 3 opened on September 4 for a period of four weeks (IMF, 2020).

Likewise, the absence of accurate data across the country also limited Nigeria's ability to tackle the pandemic. Nigeria did poorly in the area of testing; the principle of selective engagement became evident as a criterion for testing and quality of healthcare given to COVID-2019 patients. As of September 14, 2020, with 442,075 samples tested, Nigeria has tested less than 1 percent of its population (NCDC, 2020), with political elites having more access to testing than any other citizen. According to Amzat et al. (2020), the first 30 days of COVID-2019 in Nigeria reflected an elitist representation of the disease distribution, as the majority of those who tested positive were returnees from abroad (NCDC, 2020). Consequently, the elite as the offshoot of the virus in Nigeria created the perception of the disease as an elitist disease among ordinary citizens.

THE HYSTERIA

Typically, various unscientific claims on the properties, probable causes, outcome, and cure of coronavirus circulated the country. Among such unfounded truth were the weather condition in Africa reduces the potency of the virus—claiming that the virus thrives in cold regions alone and cannot survive hot temperature; like any other flu disease, the virus cannot withstand the black skin; the virus can be cured with herbs and roots locally called "Agbo" in Nigerian parlance, and so on. Another unverified information is that the virus is an elitist disease and the general masses have nothing to worry about. These misconceptions filtering through social media spaces further complicate the entire process of public health management.

The hysteria of coronavirus as an elitist disease is a convenient anecdote fueling popular satisfaction that most of the cases and eventual deaths from the disease have so far been from the elite class who contracted the disease while abroad and spread it to ordinary citizens. The hysteria is couched on COVID-2019 as a "big man disease," claiming that the virus is not aiming for already oppressed and overwhelmed Nigerians, who lack access to testing and adequate healthcare. With the enduring influence of the elitist class on public good, the hysteria, patterned after Nigerians comic reaction of critical national issues, stems from aggrieved citizens over the high level of corruption and cost of governance at the detriment of poor citizens in a fragile state. Accordingly, as a means through which ordinary citizens seek to decipher and create meanings out of the reality that is definitely bizarre, humor and ridicule have paved its way into Nigeria's polity (Obadare, 2009). Afolayan (2013, p. 1) also adds that: "This perspective presumes not only that there is a comic dimension to the sociopolitical situation in Nigeria, but also that a pragmatic confrontation with this situation requires the hilarious—laughing it out—which preserves the health of the body while the political health of the state is being crafted."

Indeed, the hysteria is a mechanism of excitement for impelling the intensity of a population already enmeshed in several challenges of bad governance. The hysteria also emanates from the abrupt dependence of elites on the same inadequate medical services as the rest of the population (Campbell, 2020).

With less commitment from the government, Nigeria is already endemic with Lassa fever, malaria, cholera, and other environmental-induced diseases. The coming of COVID-2019 into Nigeria was therefore approached with much misgivings from citizens, given the inadequate availability of testing to non-political and influential citizens. More so, the role of the media in publicizing more elite cases of COVID-2019 made the assumption of COVID-2019 as an elitist disease a hysteria. The first recorded COVID-2019 death was Suleiman Achimugu, a former senior executive of the country's oil company; subsequently, the death of the alleged most powerful man in the country—chief of staff to President Buhari—Abba Kyari, a former governor—Abiola Ajimobi and a political chieftain of Nigeria's ruling party, state commissioners, federal senators, state parliamentarians, and political big-wits gave way to the hysteria of coroelitism. Similarly, with dozens of public officials testing positive, including state governors, federal lawmakers, and family members of the elites, the euphoria of a virus targeting only the political class became a convenient narrative for oppressed citizens. It is important to state why this may appear so, the slow pace of testing and the effect of the media made the euphoria probable (Mbachu, 2020).

As it appears, there are many more COVID-2019 cases in Nigeria than the reported number of cases. Some going undetected because of limited testing facilities, and other unreported cases of people not deemed newsworthy, like the alarming mysterious deaths rate in Kano State. However, from news coverage, Nigeria's elites would seem to be already disproportionately affected by the coronavirus (Campbell, 2020). In other words, factors that groomed the hysteria of coronavirus as an elitist disease in Nigeria were based on several factors. These include the recalcitrant position of the political elites to create positive indicators of development, a high level of mistrust for the system in time past, a labile policy frame on managing COVID-2019, passivity of the masses to critical national issues, and a pragmatic amusement as a solution to the general state of underdevelopment.

INEQUALITY IN NIGERIA AND THE HYSTERIA OF COVID-2019

The specific issues examined in this section bother around the enduring disparity between the political class and the larger population in informing the hysteria of coronavirus as an elitist disease in Nigeria. To this end, an exploratory analysis on corruption, poverty, a dismal health sector, unemployment, and a high illiteracy level in Nigeria, among others will be assessed in view of the inequality gap in Africa's most populous country.

The peculiarity of Nigeria's social formation, being bedeviled with inequality, reflects the wide gap between a few rich and an overwhelmingly poor population. As James succinctly puts it, "A small, emergent segment of the population—primarily politicians and former militants with access to government contacts and revenues—has grown spectacularly wealthy and powerful, while most Nigerians remain poor and beholden to the generosity of the elite" (2013, p. 208). Amid COVID-2019, the inequality gap became more apparent in the public management of the deadly virus, as well as the frenzy that originated from it. In essence, the inequality gap between the rich and the poor, in terms of educational levels, health, employment status, living condition, and quality of security, defines the protracted perception of the poor as marginalized, deprived, and insecure by an elitist few. The political elites in Nigeria have mismanaged and misappropriated public funds for a long time, whereas the poor have to scuttle for public good. Thus, the political leadership in Nigeria is motivated by self-interest and other primordial considerations, which takes precedence over the public (Yagboyaju and Akinola, 2019). Howbeit, the following numbers bring expression to the analysis in this section.

Indicating the disparity in healthcare between the masses and the political class, the health sector is in a state of comatose. In view of Nigeria's population figure of about 200 million, and a disproportionate 0.5 percent hospital beds per 1,000 persons, the health sector presents a wide margin between the political class and the masses (BudgIT, 2018). Similarly, a cursory look at these figures reflects a sharp contrast with the yet to be implemented National Health Act of 2015 that requires that 1 percent of government revenue is set aside for basic healthcare (BudgIT, 2018). The lack of political will to implement policies for the benefit of all informs the extended medical tourism approach by political elites from one administration to the other.

According to the 2019 Corruption Perceptions Index, Nigeria ranks 146th least corrupt nation out of 180 countries (Transparency International, 2020). In a purchase value information, Sandcastles data reveals that 800 Dubai properties linked to Nigerian politically exposed persons are estimated to be worth well over 146 billion naira (N) ($400 million) (as cited in Page, 2020). These estimates, according to BudgIT 2019 Approved Budget Analysis, amount to approximately two-thirds of the Nigerian army's annual budget and over three times the annual budget of the country's Independent National Electoral Commission (as cited in Page, 2020). Again, Nigeria with a huge human capital base and an avalanche of natural resources has an international ranking on illiteracy of 142 out of 165 countries (CIA World Factbook, 2020) and is the fourth most corrupt country in West Africa (Ayado,2020). The former governor of the Apex Bank, Sanusi Lamido Sanusi, stated that federal legislators gulp about 25 percent of federal government overheads (Ajani, Agande and Binniyat, 2020). This long trend of elitist domination, with its impact on the poorest population, reveals a traumatic relationship between politicians and the populace. This unequal relationship then produces a high level of passivity in the general populace, occasioned by a dismally low turnout in presidential elections, low contributions to national debates, and a humorous approach to national issues. For instance, the 2018 and 2019 pew research on Nigeria's satisfaction with their democracy reveals that 60 percent and 70 percent, respectively, for both years are not satisfied with the democracy in their countries, affirming that no matter who is elected, the trend remains the same. The survey went on to affirm that dissatisfaction with country's democracy is linked to the economic situation in that country. For Nigeria, 81 percent believe the economic situation is bad, so for those who think the national economy is bad are more dissatisfied with the democratic government (Wike and Schumacher, 2020).

The preceding discussion suggests that the government's effort in the Commitment to Reducing Inequality Index measures, such as social spending, taxation, and labor, exposes the action and inaction of the political class in failing the poorest people (Oxfam, 2018). The several parameters pointing to Nigeria as the largest economy in Africa are not been maximized by the elites to churn out her extreme level of inequality. More alarming is the annual cost for federal parliamentarians, in a country with the highest number of people living in extreme poverty and the majority of its population living on less than $2 a day. For annual cost of 109 Senators and 360 House of

Representatives comes to around ₦69 billion ($226 million) yearly, a sum sufficient to pay 191,954 civil servants the minimum wage (Stears Business, 2019). Similarly, the proposed capital expenditure for health or education in 2020 is ₦20 billion less than the annual salaries of the National Assembly (Stears Business, 2019).

Hence, subject to a relatively deprived population, the tagging of coronavirus as an elitist disease is a convenient claim, informed by aggrieved Nigerians who perceive the virus was brought into the country by recycled elites who have long benefited from the wealth of the nation. The budgetary allocation and social spending in critical sectors show the defect in infrastructural and developmental projects that can improve the living condition of a greater number of people and lift millions out of poverty, which is a critical objective of goal 10 of the UN Sustainable Developmental Goals.

Again, following the closure of local and international air space, Nigerians seemingly, experienced for the first time, an environment of equality. In most underdeveloped nations like Nigeria where the political class and public office holders underfund and circumvent public resources meant for capital projects like health institutions and education, politicians and family members travel abroad for healthcare and educational benefits at the detriment of an aching society.

Despite the availability of private jets, elitist influence on national resources, the political class for the first time was dissuaded from seeking medical care abroad due to the grim impact of the virus on advanced health systems like in China, the United States, and Italy. In other words, the ripple effect of poor government policy implementation in time past, evident in poor health facilities, ill-equipped educational system, infrastructural decay, high poverty rate, unemployment, and terrorism, was for the first time experienced by all, though for a short time. The stark reality of the impact of COVID-2019 on all influenced major actions taken by the political class. Assuaging to this, Cummings asserts that the political commitment to stop the spread of diseases like COVID-2019 is high. However, prior to COVID-2019 when the gap between the rich and the poor was very wide, the political commitment of public office holders was very low.

This is because most government officials were not in reality with the state of affairs in the country. Recently, Boss Mustapha, secretary to the Government of the Federation, who is also the head of the Presidential Task Fund on COVID-2019, confirmed the above assertion, when he stated that he did not know that the health sector was in such bad shape until he became the chairman of the Presidential Task Force on COVID-2019 (Iroanusi, 2020). This statement attests to the high level of disconnection between the political class and the masses. Although the inequality gap remains wide amid the pandemic, political elites have shown more commitment to the crisis than other prevalent national crisis, because COVID-2019 presents a greater threat to the elites than any other factor. In essence, until the air space is opened, wealthiest Nigerians and the political class are no longer able to seek health-care abroad. As such, since the elites are now dependent on internal health-care and cannot escape poor sanitation, densely populated cities, a large and vulnerable informal economy, and weak public health (Cummings, 2020), the attention of political office holders has been drawn inward, with elitist interest as the driver.

CONCLUSION AND RECOMMENDATIONS

This chapter has been an exposition on the critical analysis of the influence of Nigeria's political elites in driving policies amid the realities of COVID-2019. Like most countries of the world, the Nigerian government has risen to the occasion. Several policies, both external and locally generated, were enforced to mitigate the impact of COVID-2019 on lives and livelihood. Factored by insincerity of the government to deliver on public good in time past, it was stated that citizens' trust level on public office holders waned. With several myths, misinformation, cynicism, and hysteria on coronavirus, COVID-2019 guidelines were in conflict with several unorthodox doctrines. Among such, as the chapter accounts, is the claim that the virus is a disease contracted by political elites only in Nigeria, name calling the virus 'big man disease.' Evidently, the virus is being contracted by both political elites and ordinary citizens in Nigeria and elsewhere, as the virus can be contracted by anyone who is exposed or has had contact with an infected person, regardless of race, tribe status, age, or religion.

The chapter identified that the hysteria of coroelitism in Nigeria is premised on the perception of aggrieved citizens on the existing traditional domination of wealth by a circulation of few elites against an impoverished greater population. In essence, the notion hinges on the popular satisfaction of a misleading narrative by the masses. Within the first few weeks of the first recorded case in Nigeria, the chapter submits that the testing rate for ordinary citizens in comparison to the elite class was low. Stating that, the media blaring of infected elites compared to many unannounced COVID-2019-related cases and deaths was overwhelming. These scenarios alongside the long-standing marginalization of the masses by the political elites across regions and administrations presented unscientific claims of the virus as elitist.

The implication, therefore, is that these factors invariably affected government's effort in curbing the spread and managing the socioeconomic effects of the virus on the masses. First, most citizens became more susceptible to poverty, due to the lockdown policies that crippled daily income businesses. Once more, as citizens threw caution to the wind due to the fear of 'hunger virus,' the possibility of ordinary citizens contracting the virus increased. Factored by several undocumented cases and death in Nigeria, due to an ailing health system in the face of numerous life-threatening diseases like malaria, typhoid, cholera, and Lassa fever more people are likely to get infected with COVID-2019 without proper medical attention and documentation.

While countries with high development index and high allocation to social spending cushioned the effect of the pandemic on its citizenry, Nigerian citizens were more vulnerable to adversity, poverty, and insecurity. The reality of the hysteria brought to the fore for the first time the dependence of the powerful, rich, and poor on the same inadequate medical and health facilities.

Conclusively, as against the postulations of reputable agencies on public health, thankfully, Africa, and particularly Nigeria, has not witnessed a surge in COVID-2019 cases. As in the case of Nigeria the cases have been decreasing, even though the testing capacity is still less than 1 percent of total population. Although much is still unknown, given that COVID-2019 is still undergoing clinical trials. The chapter concludes that, at the time of writing, the decrease in COVID-2019 cases in Nigeria so far has no scientific base with the actions or inactions of Nigeria's political class or her citizenry.

It is recommended therefore that the elite formation in Nigeria should be re-distributed to capture all groups and constituent units in the country, by ensuring free, fair, and credible elections, as well as restructuring the present skewed/expensive federal and presidential systems. Similarly, the opportunities presented by the pandemic should not be misused; government should pursue policies with even development and progress across the country. The Nigerian government should embark on development projects and programs that are of priority to the welfare and security of citizens, by strengthening the independence of regulatory institutions on effective transparency and proper accountability on public goods.

With much of the outcome of COVID-2019 in Nigeria being packaged under divine providence and luck, this should however not invalidate the elitist repressive approach to governance in Nigeria and its attendant consequences on the masses. The present status of COVID-2019 in Nigeria, however, presents a window for further research on unraveling the downward slope in COVID-2019 cases in Nigeria. While COVID-2019 in Nigeria may appear containable, despite the challenges, the disease is real and can be contracted by anyone. Thus, the political class must seize the opportunity presented by the pandemic to establish and sustain resilient measures for future natural disasters in order to mitigate the effects of the artificial social structures in the society.

REFERENCES

Adelaja, B. (April 12, 2020). COVID-19 relief items chaos: 300 persons get one loaf of bread, two sachets of tomato Paste. *Vanguard Newspaper*. Retrieved on June 25, 2020 from https://www.vanguardngr.com/2020/04/covid-19-relief-items-chaos-300-persons-get-one-loaf-of-bread-two-sachets-of-tomato-paste-2/

Afolayan, A. (2013). Hilarity and the Nigerian condition. *The Journal of Pan African Studies*, 6(5):156–174.

Afuape, S. (2012). Effects of elitism and external debt crises on Nigerian citizenry. *Journal of Politics & Law* 5(4):136–146.

Ajani, J., Agande, B. and Binniyat. L. (December 4, 2010). National Assembly overhead: when figures don't lie. *Vanguard Newspaper*. Retrieved on May 22, 2020 from https://www.vanguardngr.com/2010/12/national-assembly-overhead-when-figures-don%E2%80%99t-lie/

Akanni, L. O. and Gabriel, S. C. (2020). *The Implication of Covid19 on the Nigerian Economy*. Centre for the Study of the Economies of Africa (CSEA). Retrieved on July 6, 2020 from http://cseaafrica.org/theimplication-of-covid19-on-the-nigerian-economy/

Ake, C. (1991). Rethinking African democracy. *Journal of Democracy*, 2(1):32–44.

Akinbode, A. (October 31, 2017). Building elite consensus in Nigeria. *Centre for Public Policy Alternative*. Retrieved on September 9, 2020 from http://cppar-esearch.org/nu-en-pl/building-elite-consensus-nigeria/

Alagboso, C. and Abubakar, B. (June 2, 2020). The first 90 days: How has Nigeria responded to the COVID-19 outbreak? #COVID19NaijaResponse. *Nigeria Health Watch*. Retrieved on August 16, 2020 from https://medium.com/@nigeriahealth-watch/the-first-90-days-how-has-nigeria-responded-to-the-covid-19-outbreak-covid19naijaresponse-a0974493efa6

Amzat, J., Aminu, K., Kolo, V. I., Akinyele, A. A, Ogundairo, J. A. and Danjibo, M. C. (2020). Coronavirus outbreak in Nigeria: Burden and socio-medical response during the first 100 days. *International Journal of Infectious Diseases* 98:218–224.

Ayado, S. (January 23, 2020). Knocks as Nigeria ranks 4th most corrupt country in West Africa. *Business Day*. Retrieved on May 15, 2020 from https://businessday.ng/africa/article/knocks-as-nigeria-ranks-4th-most-corrupt-country-in-west-africa/

Bariledum, K. and Vurasi, S. S. (2013). Political elites and the challenges of national development: The Nigeria experience. *European Scientific Journal* 9(31).

Bosah, C. (April 20, 2020). Palliatives without relief. *ThisDay Newspaper*. Retrieved on August 16, 2020 from https://www.pressreader.com/nigeria/thisday/20200422/281668257118609

BudgIT. (First Quarter of 2018). *Nigeria: Health Budget Analysis: Policy Brief*. Retrieved on August 12, 2020 from https://yourbudgit.com/wp-content/uploads/2018/04/Nigeria-Health-Budget-Analysis.pdf

Campbell, J. and McCaslin, J. (April 28, 2020). How Nigeria has responded to Covid-19 so far. Retrieved on August 12, 2020 from https://www.cfr.org/blog/how-nigeria-has-responded-covid-19-so-far

Cummings, C. (May 5, 2020). Nigeria's Response to Covid-19. Effective states and inclusive development. Retrieved on August 17, 2020 from http://www.effective-states.org/will-nigerias-success-in-stamping-out-ebola-help-it-to-stop-the-spread-of-covid-19-too/

DFID. (2011). *The Politics of Poverty: Elites, Citizens and States*. Addis Ababa, Ethiopia: The Department for International Development.

Dixit, S., Ogundeji. Y. K. and Onwujekwe, O. (July 2, 2020). How well has Nigeria responded to Covid-19. Retrieved on August 20, 2020 from https://www.brookings.edu/blog/future-development/2020/07/02/how-well-has-nigeria-responded-to-covid-19/

Eboh, C. (March 18, 2020). Update 1-Nigeria cenbank to inject 1 trln naira into coronavirus-hit economy. Retrieved from https://in.reuters.com/article/nigeria-economy/update-1-nigeria-cenbank-to-inject-1-trln-naira-into-coronavirus-hit-economy-idUSL8N2BB8IZ

Egbue, N. C. (2009). Elite perceptions of poverty and Nigeria's poverty reduction research: a theoretical orientation. *International Journal of Development and Management Review* 4(1):50–62.

Genieys, W. and Smyrl, M. (2008). Inside the autonomous state: Programmatic elites in the reform of French health policy. *Governance* 21(1):75–93.

Higley, J., and Burton, M. G. (1989). The elite variable in democratic transitions and breakdowns. *American Sociological Review* 54(1):17–32.

Human Rights Watch. (April 14, 2020). Nigeria: Protect most vulnerable in COVID-19 response. Retrieved on August 4, 2020 from https://www.hrw.org/news/2020/04/14/nigeria-protect-most-vulnerable-covid-19-response

Idike. A. N. (2014). Rising inequality and the challenge of change in Nigeria. *International Journal of Humanities and Social Science* 4(9):207–213.

International Monetary Fund (IMF). (2020). Policy responses to COVID-19: Policy tracker. Retrieved on July 12, 2020 from https://www.imf.org/en/Topics/imf-and-covid19/PolicyResponses-to-COVID-19

Iroanusi., Q. E. (April 10, 2020). I never knew Nigeria's healthcare infrastructure was in such bad state—SGF. *Premiumtimes*. Retrieved December 12, 2020 from https://www.premiumtimesng.com/health/health-news/387036-i-never-knew-nigerias-healthcare-infrastructure-was-in-such-bad-state-sgf.html

James, S. (February 18, 2013). In Nigeria, oil divides the rich and poor. Retrieved on August 5, 2020 from https://www.pri.org/stories/2013-02-18/nigeria-oil-divides-rich-and-poor

Lawson, M. and Martin, M. (October 8, 2018). The Commitment to Reducing Inequality Index *Oxfam Report*. Retrieved on July 12, 2020 from https://oxfamilibrary.openrepository.com/bitstream/handle/10546/620553/rr-commitment-reducing-inequality-index-2018-091018-en.pdf

Lloyd, P. (1970). The Study of the Elite. In P. Lloyd (ed.), *The New Elites of Tropical Africa*. Oxford, UK: Oxford University Press.

Lopez, M. (2013). Elite theory. *Sociopedia. ISA* 1–12.

Michels, R. (1911). *Political Parties*. New York: Free Press.

Mosca, G. (1939). *The Ruling Class*. New York: McGraw-Hill Publishing Company.

National Bureau of Statistics (NBS). (2020). 2019 Poverty and inequality in Nigeria. *Executive Summary*. Abuja, Nigeria. Retrieved on August 12, 2020 from file: ///C:/Users/USER/Downloads/2019%20POVERY%20AND%20INEQUALITY%20IN%20NIGERIA%20(1).pdf

Nigeria Centre for Disease Control (NCDC). (September 14, 2020). *Covid-19 Nigeria*. Abuja, Nigeria. Retrieved on September 16, 2020 from https://covid19.ncdc.gov.ng/

Nwaubani, A. T. (April 22, 2020). Coronavirus: Why some Nigerians are gloating about Covid-*BBC News*. Retrieved on August 8, 2020 from https://www.bbc.com/news/world-africa-52372737

Obadare, E. (2009). The uses of ridicule: Humour, 'infrapolitics' and civil society in Nigeria. *African Affairs* 108(431):241–261.

Obamwonyi, S. E. and Aibieyi, S. (2014). Public policy failures in Nigeria: Pathway to underdevelopment. *Journal of Policy and Development Studies* 289(1849):1–10.

Odubajo, T. and Bamidele, A. (2014). The elite factor in Nigeria's political-power dynamics. *Journal of Studies in Social Sciences* 8(1):121–139.

Ogele, E. P. (2020). Elitism, election, and governance in Nigeria's fourth republic: A study of Rivers state from 2003–2019. *Journal of Law and Global Policy* 5(1):1–13.

Okeke, R. C. (2017). Elitism, local governance and development in Nigeria. *Speciality Journal of Politics and Law* 2(3):62–72.

Okon, D. (April 19, 2020). Lamentation still trails Lagos, FG's palliative package as middlemen hijack programme. *Business Day*. Retrieved on May 16, 2020 from https://businessday.ng/features/article/lamentation-still-trails-lagos-fgs-palliative-package-as-middlemen-hijack-programme/

Olisah, C. (June 11, 2020). Senate passes the revised N10.8 trillion 2020 budget. *Nairametrics*. Retrieved on July 8, 2020 from https://nairametrics.com/2020/06/11/senate-passes-the-revised-n10-8-trillion-2020-budget/

Page, M. (March 19, 2019). Dubai property: An oasis for corrupt Nigeria's political elites. *Carnegie Endowment for International Peace*. Retrieved on May 8, 2020 from https://carnegieendowment.org/2020/03/19/dubai-property-oasis-for-nigeria-s-corrupt-political-elites-pub-81306

Pareto, V. (1935). *The Mind and Society* (A. Bongiorno and A. Livingston, Trans.). London, UK: Jonathan Cape.

Parry, G. (1976). *Political Elite*. London, UK: George Allen and Unwin.

Proshare. (June 19, 2020). Coronanomics (13)—Nigeria: The budget, the people and poverty. *Proshare Intelligent Investment*. Retrieved on September 1, 2020 from https://www.proshareng.com/news/Nigeria%20Economy/Coronanomics-13-Nigeria-The-Budget--The-People-and-Poverty/51687#

Stears Business. (October 15, 2019). How much does lawmaking cost Nigerians? Retrieved on June 27, 2020 from https://www.stearsng.com/article/how-much-does-lawmaking-cost-nigerians?fbclid=IwAR0-04DOf-YdVHXTW-xUWaiyyTfMUNxJqeM04oElxTR6f7GE6pzNZH4i4zQ

The Assembly. (October 17, 2019). How much does lawmaking cost Nigerians? Retrieved on July 13, 2020 from http://theassemblyng.com/index.php/2019/10/17/how-much-does-lawmaking-cost-nigerians/

Transparency International. (2020). Corruption Perception Index. Retrieved on July 10, 2020 from https://www.transparency.org/en/countries/nigeria

Transparency International. (July 16, 2020). Nigeria, IMF and Covid-19: How Nigeria could avoid waste and corruption when spending billions in IMF emergency assistance during Covid-19. Retrieved on August 2, 2020 from https://www.transparency.org/en/blog/nigeria-imf-covid-19

United Nations Office for the Coordination of Humanitarian Affairs (OCHA). (March 14, 2020). National interim guidelines for clinical management of COVID-19. Retrieved on September 16, 2020 from https://reliefweb.int/report/nigeria/national-interim-guidelines-clinical-management-covid-19

Wike, R. and Schumacher. S. (February 27, 2020). Satisfaction with democracy. Pew Research Centre. Retrieved on May 10, 2020 from https://www.pewresearch.org/global/2020/02/27/satisfaction-with-democracy/pg_2020-02-27_global-democracy_03-3

Yagboyaju, D. A. and Akinola, A. O. (2019). Nigerian state and the crisis of governance: A critical exposition. *SAGE Open* 9(3):2158244019865810.

Yamokoski, A. and Dubrow, J. K. (2008). How do elites define influence? Personality and respect as sources of social power. *Sociological Focus* 41(4):319–336.

Chapter 5

Coropoverty

Cecy Edijala Balogun

This chapter describes how the Coronavirus Disease (COVID)-2019 outbreak in Nigeria generated anxieties about the expected impact of the disease on the livelihood of the Nigerian population. The anxieties stem from the high rate of poverty in the country, coupled with other social challenges that put the livelihoods of the poor and vulnerable at risk. Poverty is not peculiar to Nigeria as it is a global challenge, and the seriousness that the global community places on poverty was amplified in the United Nations Sustainable Development Goals that prioritized poverty eradication as the first of the 17 goals of the Agenda 2030.

Since 2000, giant strides have been made toward the reduction of extreme poverty worldwide (UN, n.d.). Such global strides notwithstanding, the poverty rate in Nigeria is persistently on the increase. Nigeria has the second highest level of poverty globally after India (World Bank, 2019) and, alongside the Democratic Republic of Congo, accounts for 23 percent of the world's poor (UNDESA, 2019a). The high level of poverty in Nigeria has been a long-standing subject for debate and a social concern even before the outbreak of COVID-2019. The National Bureau of Statistics (NBS, 2020a) report revealed that 40.1 percent of the Nigerian population are living below the international poverty line, representing 82.9 million people, that is, more than one-third of the country's population of over 200 million people, further confirming the state of poverty in Nigeria.

However, the outbreak of COVID-2019 heightened the anxieties of the state of poverty in Nigeria, with concerns about the expected impact of the disease on the well-being of the poor and those who, as a result of exposure to the challenges that will arise from the outbreak in the country, will also become vulnerable to poverty. These anxieties raised serious questions among the Nigerian public, such as how will poor and vulnerable households survive the pandemic considering the poor health systems and services in the country? How will people access and be able to afford proper healthcare in the event of contagion given the poor state of the healthcare sector and the high costs of healthcare in the country? How many people have the economic and social capacities to cushion the likely impact of COVID-2019 on their well-being? How will the poor comply and survive the national lockdown and movement restrictions in the midst of increasing national poverty? How prepared is the government to mitigate the likely impact of COVID-2019 on the citizens? Given the neglect that the masses are subjected to by the corrupt political class and public office holders, does the government have the political will and sympathy to address the social issues that may arise as a result of the disease outbreak and to provide adequate palliatives to mitigate the impact on the well-being of the citizens?

Although the basis for these questions is as a result of the poverty situation that is evident in the country, a grounded approach is necessary to support or refute the fears that are associated with the outbreak of the pandemic and its attendant effect on the Nigerian populace. Hence, the chapter will interrogate the poverty situation in Nigeria from the multidimensional perspective of living standards, health and education, the impact of COVID-2019 on the already poor state of things in the country, the response of the government in mitigating the impact of COVID-2019 on the Nigerian population, and the implications for policymakers on issues that concern public health and livelihood security.

Coropoverty describes the fear, agitation, panic, and anxiety of loss of well-being due to the coronavirus pandemic. It is a concept that defines the fears that stem from the outbreak of COVID-2019 and the likely impact on the livelihoods of people, and concerns that COVID-2019 will increase vulnerability to poverty.

The chapter will understudy the poverty situation in Nigeria by attempting to address three critical questions concerning the COVID-2019 outbreak in the country: (1) What is the poverty situation in pre-COVID-2019 Nigeria? (2) How is COVID-2019 contributing to the poverty situation in Nigeria? (3) What are the responses to mitigate the impact of COVID-2019 on the populace?

Based on the narratives of poverty in Nigeria, the chapter argues that COVID-2019 will further worsen the incidence of poverty in the country, given the containment measures that further threaten the livelihood of the citizens, especially those who are employed in the informal sector and depend on daily means of livelihood for their survival. Additionally, the chapter contends that poverty thrives in Nigeria because of the structural failures that limit the potentials of the citizens to achieve their socioeconomic aspirations.

This chapter uses secondary data from various information sources, such as the Internet, reports, and publications of the NBS, World Health Organization (WHO), United Nations, World Bank, articles, and personal observations of the dynamics of the issues surrounding the pandemic outbreak, to situate how the disease contributes to poverty in Nigeria.

To fully understand whether the hysteria that has emerged from the outbreak of the disease and its likely impact on the wellbeing of the Nigerian populace is justifiable, a situational analysis of the socioeconomic environment in which the average Nigerian interacts and generates his/her means of livelihood and the capacity of the healthcare system to respond to the health needs of the populace is imperative. Furthermore, narratives that arise from the investigation will help to inform policymakers on critical areas of concern that have implications for the well-being of the Nigerian populace.

The rest of the chapter will address the theoretical discussions on poverty from a multidimensional viewpoint; the poverty situation in Nigeria will cover living standards including food security, access to sanitation and other infrastructures, unemployment situation, health, and educational systems; the impact of COVID-2019 along the identified dimensions of poverty; the government's response to cushion the effect of COVID-2019 in Nigeria; and the recommendations for policymakers and areas for future research.

THEORETICAL DISCUSSION OF POVERTY

This section focuses on the theoretical discussion of the concept of poverty from a multidimensional perspective. Although poverty in the chapter will be viewed from a multidimensional perspective, the discourse will be grounded within the Structural Theory of Poverty. This is because poverty in the Nigerian context anchors on the structural systems in the society as a major driver.

The concept of poverty implies deprivation of the necessities of life needed for the well-being of an individual, family, or society. Poverty describes a lack of capability to obtain and utilize resources that are necessary for a fulfilling life in terms of food, shelter, health, and empowerment to adequately compete and survive in society.

Poverty was traditionally defined as the absence of economic resources (income) that are available for consumption or expenditure and this was premised on the belief that income level could capture a variety of household needs whether as nutrition, clothing, or housing (Alkire and Santos, 2013). However, using income alone as a measure for poverty was critiqued as income does not capture the non-monetary aspects of needs or deprivations that individuals experience and so lacks sufficient evidence as a determinant of the well-being of people (Sen, 1985, cited in Sameti, Esfahani and Haghighi, 2012). Social issues such as poor health, lack or limited access to education, limited access to empowerment opportunities, concerns on safety, and participation in society which gives a sense of fulfillment, cannot be measured using monetary indicators, and such deprivations present a sense of social exclusion and insecurity for individuals. Furthermore, the economic improvement of a family does not necessarily reduce other deprivations like malnutrition and child mortality (Oxford Poverty and Human Development Initiative (OPHI), n.d.).

The problems that the poor encounter are multifaceted; encompassing poor health, lack or limited access to education, poor living standards, lack of empowerment opportunities, limited or lack of access to decent work, exposures to violence, lack of access to credit needed to improve living standards, and lack of capacities and opportunities to participate in the development of the societies in which they live (Bradshaw, 2006; Walker, 2015; OPHI, n.d.). The multidimensionality of poverty was explained by the United Nations Development Program in collaboration with the OPHI at the University of Oxford using the Multidimensional Poverty Index (MPI) that measures poverty along three key indicators of living standard, health, and education (Alkire and Santos, 2010). The multidimensional view of poverty proffers that access to basic human needs such as sanitation, clean water supply, adequate housing, balanced diet, healthcare, education, and security is necessary for a decent living. The perspective also portrays poverty as a problem that affects different aspects of the lives of people (Darlington, 2002, cited in Sameti, Esfahani and Haghighi, 2012; World Bank, 2020a).

The structural failures of the Nigerian system remain a key factor that exposes the populace to poverty. The failure of the government to provide public facilities that are necessary to enhance the potentials of individuals and households to invest and maximize their capacities for development and prosperity remains a key driver of poverty in Nigeria. The persistent rising rates of poverty are not necessarily because of the unwillingness of the people to work, but the absence or limited opportunities for improvement due to poor commitment of the government to provide the enabling environment for self-development and private investors' interventions in the employment sector. The social, economic, and political environment in Nigeria limits the socio-economic performance of citizens, and any attempt to resolve the problem of poverty in Nigeria must consider an overhauling of the structures that are in place, which can either enhance or limit people's access to, ability to pay for and utility of public facilities that can bring about a change in their well-being. Hence, the aptness of the Structural Theory of Poverty as the basis for describing poverty in Nigeria.

Structural theories originated from scholars like Clark (1965) who attempted to explain racial inequalities as a structural problem. The theory attributes poverty to the economic, political, and social discriminations of the society (Bradshaw, 2006; Sameti, Esfahani and Haghighi, 2012). The proponents of poverty as a structural problem believe that poverty is due to the workings of the political, social, and economic systems that limit the opportunities and resources of people, thereby truncating their chances of achieving the desired level of living for self-fulfillment.

The economic system contributes to poverty by making it difficult for people to achieve their economic aspirations irrespective of their competence and the efforts they put in (Bradshaw, 2006). Economic structures such as economic growth and development, industrialization, and spatial and skills mismatch, and social structures like geographic disadvantages such as rural or slum environment, residential discrimination, urbanization, and demographic transitions, predispose populations to poverty (Brady, 2018). Davies and Moore (1945) cited in Sameti, Esfahani, and Haghighi (2012) also argued that the conversion of one's talent to skills and knowledge depends on the training acquired and that people should be motivated with higher wages and privileges to undergo training as the wage for labor is proportional to the amount of training acquired and the individual's sacrifice.

Bradshaw (2006) identified three strategies that can be used to change the systems that constitute barriers to poverty reduction: through the actions of the social movements in communities, who can mobilize the community to action for the desired change; developing alternative institutions that have access and the necessary innovations to create the needed livelihood and employment opportunities, health and educational facilities, and other necessities that will enhance the well-being of the poor; development of pro-poor policies that are aimed at employment creation, provision of social protection, effective access to education and healthcare facilities, and so on. Failure of the government to pay attention to the relatedness and interactions of the structures that exist in the society leads to inequality and increased poverty for disadvantaged marginalized populations.

The contributory roles of the structural failures of systems to the socioeconomic challenges that predispose populations to poverty have been cited in the literature. Poor public structures contribute to poor employment opportunities (Mouw, 2000, cited in Brady, 2018) and facilitate poverty at family levels (Harknett and McLanahan, 2004, cited in Brady, 2018). Ananat (2011) and Massey (2016) cited in Brady (2018) also argued that the interactions of economic variables and geographic locations contribute to poverty. In a contrary vein, Brady, Kaya, and Beckfield (2007) faulted the Structural Theory of Poverty by arguing that the effects of structures on poverty depend on time and location. They noted that while economic development could lead to poverty reduction in developing countries, its performance for developed countries as a tool for poverty reduction has diminished in recent decades. Brady

(2018) also contended that the effect of structures on poverty is determined by the political and institutional systems that exist in the society.

Based on the complexities of poverty that encompass various aspects of the life of an individual, family, or society, a multidimensional approach to poverty is considered prime for the Nigerian society, taking into cognizance the varied dimensions of deprivations that threaten the survival of the citizens. Poverty in the Nigerian context can be explained quite well by using the Structural Theory of Poverty because of the systemic failures that are evident in the country, especially in the areas of infrastructure, healthcare, education, food security, living conditions, and employment, all of which have placed the country lower in the global poverty rankings.

THE POVERTY SITUATION IN PRE-COVID-2019 NIGERIA

The hysteria that trailed the outbreak of COVID-2019 in Nigeria anchors on evidential situations of poverty in Nigeria. Although Nigeria has the largest economy in Africa, with an estimated GDP of $522 billion (USAID, 2019), the level of poverty is the highest in the continent and the second highest globally after India (World Bank, 2020a). A recent report of the NBS (2020a) showed that 40.1 percent of households in Nigeria are living below the national poverty line representing 4 in 10 people which is almost half of the country's population. Additionally, inequality in Nigeria, which is put at 35.1 percent (NBS, 2020a), indicates serious inequality gaps along socioeconomic lines and geographical locations. The glaring levels of poverty and inequality, which is expressed by the uneven distribution of wealth, access to social services coupled with the myriad of social problems in the country, engendered the hysteria of worsening well-being due to the COVID-2019 outbreak in the country.

Hence, this section focuses on a situational analysis of poverty in Nigeria before the outbreak of COVID-2019 using the multidimensional components of living standards, health, and education. The wholesomeness of Nigerian society is anchored on the collective performance of these components in serving societal well-being.

The Poverty of Living Standards in Nigeria

The UNDESA (2019b) World Populations Prospect estimated the population of Nigeria to be over 200 million and this is projected to increase to over 400 million by 2050. While the population growth in Nigeria is seen as a demographic dividend that can be harnessed for the development of the country, the living condition of a larger category of the populace speaks contrary. The sorry state of the living condition of the average Nigerian makes the exploding population in the country a social emergency. The attainment of food security and access to basic amenities like electricity, clean water, clean cooking fuel, and adequate sanitation have continued to elude a large number of households. The poor economic policies of the government that hardly address the socioeconomic concerns of the poor, embezzlement of public funds by public office holders, insecurity that has continued to reduce the economic resources and means of livelihoods of individuals and communities and which has led to the displacements of millions of families, and so on, are major issues that undermine the development of critical infrastructures that are required to improve the living standards of the poor in Nigeria.

Food insecurity in Nigeria has been a persistent problem due to the joint effects of climate change evident in the high incidences of flooding, desert encroachment, irregular rainfall patterns, crop failures; low use of improved farming practices; insecurity; and the poor commitment of the government to research and development as a way of addressing the challenges to food insufficiency (International Food Policy Research Institute [IFPRI], 2020; PricewaterhouseCoopers [PwC], 2020). Food insecurity is particularly critical in the northern region which is ridden by insurgency, armed bandit attacks, farmers and herders' clashes and communal clashes, and so on, resulting in the destruction of farmlands, rustling of animals, and kidnapping of rural farm families who are the primary producers of food in the country. An estimated 5 million people in 16 northern states were affected by food shortages in 2018 (PwC, 2020).

The large number of people living in slums, with poor sanitation, also indicates the poor living condition in Nigeria. An estimated 42 million people in Nigeria live in slum environments (Assessment Capacities Project (ACAPS), 2020), which is almost a quarter of the country's population. Slum dwellers in Nigeria constitute the poorest of the poor, lack adequate sanitation facilities, clean water, nutrition, and are partakers of most of the social vices in the Nigerian society. The NBS (2020b) report also indicated that 25 percent of the population lack standard sanitation facilities and are involved in open defecation, which is prevalent in slum areas and constitutes health risks to the slum dwellers. Additionally, amenities such as power supply, clean water, and clean cooking fuel are in short supply in Nigeria. For example, electricity supply constitutes a major barrier to the survival of businesses in the country. Even though NBS (2020b) report indicated that about 63 percent of households in Nigeria have access to electricity, the frequency and adequacy of power have been a major constraint to the survival of businesses in the country for decades, especially for small businesses that provide livelihoods to majority of the citizens.

The absence of structures to create employment opportunities for the teeming workforce in the country is the enabler of the poor working conditions that mark the Nigerian work environment. Even though the informal sector employs about 93 percent of the country's workforce (International Labor Organization (ILO), 2020), most of them are daily income earners with low income, as they lack the financial resources to improve their means of livelihood. Structural failures also account for the high rates of unemployment in the country, which was put at 23.1 percent and as high as 55 percent among the youth (NBS, 2018). The high rate of unemployment, coupled with the containment measures imposed by the government that resulted in the closure of businesses, posed additional issues of concern following the outbreak of the disease in Nigeria. The possible increase in crime rate as a result of the lockdown and related measures, given the various socioeconomic concerns in the country, presented causes for tensions following the outbreak of COVID-2019 in Nigeria.

Health Poverty in Nigeria

The poor state of the health sector also posed concerns that trailed the COVID-2019 outbreak in Nigeria. The sector has been largely neglected by the government, and over the years, the Nigerian political class, wealthy public officials, and private individuals have taken to medical tourism for their health needs, leaving the health systems in the country in a sorry state. From understaffing, poor infrastructural development, high cost of healthcare, to poor funding; the health sector in Nigeria is far from having the potential to accommodate large outbreaks of COVID-2019 in the country. The WHO (2018), in the rating of Health Systems Performance, ranked Nigeria poorly due to observations in critical health indicators such as the overall life expectancy, morbidity and mortality rates which are lower than the regional averages. Nigeria has the second-largest number of people living with HIV/AIDS after South Africa accounting for 9 percent of the global HIV burden and also the highest incidences of malaria globally, which account for the primary cause of child morbidity and mortality, representing more than half (51.7 percent) of health concerns in the country (USAID, 2014; 2019; NBS, 2020b).

The commitment of the government to the health sector has been poor. For example, the budgetary allocation for health for 2020 was a meager 4.16 percent of the total budget, which is a far cry from the 15 percent recommendation of the WHO (BudgIT, 2020), for a country with a population of over 200 million people, with high incidences of maternal and child-related deaths, malaria, and HIV/AIDs. The poor commitment of the government to funding the health sector is the driver of the high cost of healthcare, such that medicine stores and chemist shops are the preferred points of call in times of ill health than hospitals, especially for poor households (NBS, 2014). Additionally, health insurance is basically beyond the reach of a vast majority of the populace, particularly the informal sector employees (ILO, 2020), and since out-of-pocket payments put pressure on their limited resources, self-medication and use of informal health facilities are prevalent among the Nigerian public. This reduced utilization of healthcare facilities in the country further reduced the rating of the country by the WHO, as Nigeria's health utilization is rated 44 percent, which is lower than the regional average of 48 percent (WHO, 2018).

The absence of infrastructures affects service delivery. The limited number of health workers, especially doctors, constitutes another challenge that the health sector in the country has been grappling with over the years. The doctor-to-patient ratio in Nigeria is 1:2,500 compared to the 1:1,000 recommendation of WHO (BioSpectrum, 2018), which is outrageously low in comparison to the over 200 million population of the country. Most of the medical doctors that are trained in Nigeria migrate to higher-paying countries due to poor remuneration and poor working conditions. The limited available doctors are mostly concentrated in the tertiary health institutions in urban areas (WHO Global Health Workforce Alliance, GHWA, 2008). Hence, it is obvious that the state of the health system in Nigeria justifies the fears of the populace; with the political class and wealthy public office holders patronizing healthcare in other countries on the one hand, and the generality of the populace lacking in access to adequate healthcare further brings to light the inequality divide that exists along socioeconomic lines, as an enabler of poverty in the country.

The Poverty of Education in Nigeria

The educational sector in Nigeria has severally been described as an emergency due to the persistent neglect by the government, both at the national and state levels. The government-run public schools are poorly staffed, poorly financed and managed, and lack adequate educational and instructional facilities (USAID, 2014). The poor commitment of the government to the development of the country's human capital placed Nigeria as the country with the highest number of out-of-school children globally, accounting for 20 percent of out-of-school children in the world (World Economic Forum, 2020). An estimated 10.5 million children are out of school in Nigeria, even though primary and post-primary education in the country are free (United Nations Children Education Fund [UNICEF], 2020a).

In most public schools in Nigeria, there are limited classrooms to cater for a large number of students, factored by population growth and the failure of the government to provide adequate resources to accommodate the population dynamics facing the educational sector in the country. The situation is even worse in the rural areas, where students are forced to learn in very poor environments that are lacking in essential infrastructural and learning facilities. The effect of the population dynamics in the educational sector is also observed in the teacher-student ratio in the government-owned schools, where class populations are over 100 and a teacher has to assess over 500 students, limiting the teachers' performance as their effectiveness is challenged by their capacity to teach and assess large numbers of students with limited available resources.

The budgetary allocation to the sector has been on the decline, decreasing from 12.28 percent in 2015 to 6.48 percent in 2020 (BudgIT, 2020), whereas the United Nations Educational, Scientific and Cultural Organization recommendation for adequate funding of education is between 15 percent and 20 percent (Hussain, 2020). The poor funding of the sector contributes to the poor performance of education in Nigeria, evident in the limited number of teachers, as cases abound where unqualified teachers are engaged to teach subjects for which they have not been trained. The result has been poor academic performance of the students that characterizes the educational system, as poor funding limits the compliance of schools to international best practices, which has continually resulted in the low ratings of Nigerian educational institutions at the global scale.

In addition, the educational curricula hardly incorporate aspects of learning that drive the contemporary world of work, such that the high turnout of graduates from the higher institutions constitutes a greater portion of the unemployed, due to lack of competence that is required for employability or self-employment. To survive, such graduates have resorted to working in underemployed conditions with reduced remunerations, which further reduce their socioeconomic development, making them vulnerable to poverty.

The correlates of poor living standards, health, and education as indicators of poverty are well grounded in literature. Bloom and Lucas (1999) contended that the health status of individuals and populations depends on such factors as a high living standard (nutritious food, clean water, adequate clothing, and shelter). The prevalence of hunger predisposes the health of families to diseases and affects the educational prospects and socioeconomic well-being of the family (WHO, 2014). Also, Roberts (2018) argued that poverty is both a cause and consequence of poor health, and the WHO (2014) also alluded to the contributory role of poverty to poor health which prevents people from accessing healthcare services as a result of poor financial capacities since the poor usually lack the resources to access health services and the quality and quantity of food required to maintain good health. The World Bank (2018a) correlated education and other poverty indicators, attributing the poor performance of students to poor health and nutrition of children, among other factors.

However, the multidimensional approach to poverty reduction has been critiqued for its inability to allow a substitution between dimensions and the lack of a direct income measure for the indicators (Walker, 2015). Gweshengwe (2019) argued that the limited criteria in the measurement of the indicators of the MPI are not exclusive, stating that malnutrition and mortality which are captured in the indicators do not exclusively describe poor health conditions since other health issues are left out which are equally critical for development. Ravallion (2011) contended that the components of standard of living that are captured in the MPI are not exclusively covered while in the argument of Santos, Lugo, Lopez-Calva, Cruces, and Battiston (2010), limiting the educational indicator to access to schooling is not sufficient to determine educational performance which is more explicitly explained by the cognitive ability of individuals.

Taken as a whole, in the Nigerian context, the multidimensionality of poverty fits perfectly well as poverty affects all aspects of the individual life, factored by the structural problems in the country, such as poor leadership, neglect of the social welfare of the populace by the political class, and systemic corruption that has continued to cripple developmental efforts through the diversion of public funds for self-aggrandizement. The narratives of the structural failures in Nigeria that expose people to incidences of poverty justify the anxieties and outcry that welcomed the COVID-2019 outbreak in the country. The fears of the masses cannot be said to be unfounded when the system prevents their self-fulfillment and, in the event of COVID-2019, obviously spells a new level of hardship for the common Nigerian, who hardly has enough sustenance that guarantees a good lifestyle for self-development.

IMPACT OF COVID-2019 IN NIGERIA

In Nigeria, the impact of COVID-2019 on the health status of the society has been minimal, given the relatively low number of cases recorded in terms of contagion and fatalities, when compared to global statistics from other countries, particularly the Western countries. Nevertheless, the pandemic has highly impacted the poverty situation in the country. The social or physical distancing, lockdown of public places, interstate movement restrictions, and the border closures that were imposed by the government to reduce the spread of the disease brought about a series of agitations as there was a near-total shutdown of socioeconomic activities, posing threats to the livelihoods of citizens. This section will further situate the impact of COVID-2019 in Nigeria around the components of living standards, health, and education.

Impact of COVID-2019 on Living Standards in Nigeria

For the average Nigerian, the impact of the containment measures imposed to check the spread of COVID-2019 was well felt. Living is first of all possible when there is food security. The containment measures affected the distribution of food items, resulting in inflation. Food inflation rose from 14.7 percent in December 2019 to 15 percent as of April 2020 (PwC, 2020) and by August 2020, it has risen to 16 percent (Trading Economics, 2020). There was also a hike in food prices, which was as high as 80–120 percent in major cities like Lagos and Abuja (PwC, 2020). Additionally, the World Bank (2020a) report indicated that the closure of schools affected the nutrition of about 7 million children who partake in the school feeding program of the government. The threat to food security of households as a result of the containment measures confirmed the fears that trailed the outbreak of the disease. The fear of dying of hunger coupled with the problem of dwindling resources due to the containment measures led to situations where the existence of the disease in the country was doubted. The frustration and increased impoverishment, with the poor response of the government in providing palliatives to mitigate the disease impact on the food security of the people, led to situations where caution was thrown to the wind, as social distancing and other containment measures were violated in search of means of survival.

Projected estimates on Nigeria indicated that about 5 million people are expected to be pushed into poverty due to COVID-2019 and the containment measures adopted by the government through disruption of economic activities of households, with increased vulnerability to food insecurity (IFPRI, 2020; International Monetary Fund, IMF, 2020; World Bank, 2020a). The impact of COVID-2019 was worse in the northern part of the country, especially the North-east where the number of people in need of humanitarian support increased from 7.9 million at the beginning of 2020 to 10.6 million, and an estimated 7 million people likely to become food insecure compared to the 3.7 million before the pandemic outbreak in the country (The United Nations Office for the Coordination of Humanitarian Affairs (UNOCHA), 2020).

Additionally, loss of jobs and means of livelihood, especially for the informal sector employees, portrayed the high sensitivity of livelihoods to COVID-2019 in Nigeria. NBS (2020c) report for Q3 2020 indicated a 15.8 percent reduction in the number of people in employment compared to the previous quarter and that the unemployment rate, which was 23.1 percent in Q3 2018, increased to 27.1 percent in Q2 2020 while the underemployment rate increased from 20.1 percent in Q3 2018 to 28.6 percent in Q2 2020. The combined impact of COVID-2019 on food security, employment, and other means of livelihood will further increase people's vulnerability to poverty.

Impact of COVID-2019 on Health in Nigeria

Incidences of COVID-2019 outbreak in Nigeria have been low, compared to global narratives. As of September 18, 2020, there are 56,735 confirmed cases, 48,092 discharged cases, and 1,093 fatalities in Nigeria (NCDC, 2020). The impact of COVID-2019 on the health security in Nigeria was not necessarily in contracting the disease, but the exposure of the populace to other health challenges due to the poor state of the health system and the handling of non-COVID-2019-related ailments in the country.

The poor state of the health sector in Nigeria was exposed by the outbreak of COVID-2019 in the country. Shortages of personal protective equipment (PPE) for health personnel raised concerns on the safety of health workers, both at the isolation centers where COVID-2019 cases were being treated and in other health facilities. As a way of protecting themselves from contracting the disease, due to the shortages of PPEs, the effectiveness of the Nigerian health systems was put to test. Patients with other ailments were denied healthcare by medical personnel due to fear of contracting the disease; in some cases, patients were prevented from entering health facilities and told to state their reason for visits and drugs prescribed without proper diagnosis. There were also reported cases of individuals who died due to their inability to access medical attention as and when needed. In other instances, health workers bore the cost of PPEs to ensure safety, as the poor response of the government to their protective needs led to the death of several health workers in Nigeria. As of July 2020, over 800 health workers had contracted the virus and 14 fatalities of doctors have been recorded (Punch, 2020). The limited availability of PPEs that limits the capacity of medical personnel to carry out their duties led to a series of threats, actual instances of industrial actions, and instances of medical personnel who attempted resignation due to the fear of contracting the disease, a sorry case for a country that is suffering from understaffed health system.

Among the Nigerian populace, apart from the challenge that shortages of face masks and hand sanitizers created, the fear of contagion led to situations where people resorted to self-medication rather than visiting healthcare facilities. Past experiences of the poor state of health infrastructures and healthcare delivery, the negative narratives that surrounded the dreariness of contracting the disease, coupled with the belief that medical attention for COVID-2019 cases was focused on the political elite and other wealthy citizens who could no longer embark on medical tourism due to the lockdown measures, several cries of patients in isolation centers, who complained of neglect and poor treatment also contributed to such fears in the country.

Situations where people take to self-medication and the buying of unrecommended drugs further exposed the health security of the Nigerian populace to vulnerability. Also, when a diagnosis is not conducted on patients to ascertain their health situation before remotely recommending medication to them, or rejection of patients by health facilities under the guise of fear of contracting the virus, put the lives of countless Nigerians at risk of dying from health situations that would have been preventable.

Impact of COVID-2019 on Education

COVID-2019 outbreak in Nigeria resulted in the complete halting of school activities at all levels, affecting the education of over 50 million children (UNICEF, 2020b). While remote learning facilities were employed in several countries to combat the impact of COVID-2019 on the education of millions of students due to the lockdown, the possibility of remote learning in Nigeria was crippled by the inability of the government to quickly address the situation due to the absence of structures that can cushion the effect of unexpected emergencies like COVID-2019. Although there were attempts at remote learning in a few states with the support of private agencies and organizations using radios, televisions, and Internet-aided facilities, the effectiveness of such attempts is questionable. Such attempts also threw up another dimension of inequality, as school-age children from disadvantaged backgrounds were denied opportunities to learn during the period of school closures in the country.

The adequacy, accessibility, and affordability of communication mechanisms that can enhance remote learning, given the containment measures that prevented teacher-student closeness, also posed a challenge to remote learning as an alternative for engaging students during the lockdown. The barrier of poor Internet connectivity in the urban areas and the near to non-existent communication infrastructures in very remote rural communities as well as epileptic power supply narrowed the benefits that remote learning offers as an educational alternative during the COVID-2019 lockdown in Nigeria. Even for private tertiary institutions that attempted online classes, it was not without challenges, since parents were made to bear the extra burden of providing Internet connectivity tools for their children, further putting pressure on their dwindling economic resources occasioned by the COVID-2019 outbreak.

The impact of COVID-2019 on poverty in Nigeria was amplified by the Food and Agriculture Organization (FAO) (2020), stating that persistent food insecurity will increase the vulnerability of households and in worse scenarios will result in situations where negative coping mechanisms may be adopted to mitigate the impact on livelihoods such as reduction in the number of meals, selling off family assets to raise funds to meet more pressing obligations or to reduce the burdens of indebtedness, and increase in school drop-outs. The UN (n.d.) also stated that the overburden on the health systems due to COVID-2019 and the inability to access medical attention for non-COVID-2019-related ailments could result in increased deaths from preventable or treatable health conditions.

RESPONSES TO COVID-2019 IN NIGERIA

The United Nations Development Systems (UN, 2020) identified five pillars of responses that are essential in mitigating the impact of COVID-2019: health first (which prioritizes the protection of health services and systems during the crisis); protecting people (including social protection and basic services); economic response and recoveries (entail protecting jobs, small- and medium-sized enterprises, and the informal sector workers); macroeconomic responses and multilateral collaboration; and social cohesion and community resilience.

The responses of the government in mitigating the impact of COVID-2019 in Nigeria were met with mixed feelings. While some measures are praiseworthy, in some other areas, doubts abounded about the commitment of the government toward addressing the myriad of problems that have continued to undermine the socioeconomic well-being of the poor in the country, which is worsened by the COVID-2019 outbreak.

Health Responses

On February 28, 2020, when the disease first broke out in Nigeria, the Nigerian Centre for Disease Control (NCDC) activated a multi-sectoral Emergency Operations Center (EOC) at level 3, which is the highest emergency level in Nigeria in coordination with the state public health EOCs (NCDC, 2020a). A contingency fund of N984 million ($2.7 million) was released to the NCDC; an additional N6.5 billion ($18 million) was distributed for purchasing more testing kits, opening isolation centers, and training medical personnel; and a grant of N10 billion ($28 million) was further released to Lagos State government to increase its capacity for containment of the outbreak (IMF, 2020), as the state was the epicenter of the disease in the country. In addition to the efforts of the government, private individuals, and companies, bilateral and multilateral organizations also contributed to mitigating the disease impact in Nigeria.

Shortages of health workers, limited testing kits, laboratories, PPE, and so on marred the government's responses to mitigating the impact of COVID-2019 in Nigeria. For example, while 955 oxygen cylinders were required, 446 were available; 15,762 oxygen tubes are required in isolation centers, only 6,383 were available; 300 ventilators were needed with only 72 on the ground; about 263,463 examination gloves were needed but only 38,549 were available; 36,519 face shield were required with only 2,945 available; 243,960 surgical masks were needed with only 37,047 available for use as of September 17, 2020 (NCDC, 2020b). Additionally, while about 959 doctors were required in the management of COVID-2019 cases, only 630 doctors were available as of September 17, 2020 (NCDC, 2020b).

The low response of the government is also revealed by the number of people tested for COVID-2019 in Nigeria. As of September 17, 2020, only 482,321 people have been tested (NCDC, 2020b) in a country with over 200 million people, whereas in South Africa, with a population of about 58 million people, more than 2 million people have been tested for the virus. The fear of exposure to the virus, especially as a result of reports in media sources about accusations of negligence by people whose family members were isolated for the virus and died due to lack of proper care and treatment in isolation centers, discouraged many people from taking the test.

Social Protection Responses

In a bid to mitigate the impact of COVID-2019 on the populace, several efforts were made to provide social protection to poor and vulnerable households in Nigeria. The government provided 77 million metric tons of grains from the national grain reserve and other food items which were distributed to poor and vulnerable households as well as cash transfers of N20,000 using the National Social Register (Human Rights Watch, 2020; PwC, 2020). State governments, private individuals, religious bodies, and nongovernmental organizations also supported the efforts of the government by providing food items and other necessities to households as safety nets. Palliatives were also made available in the forms of improved seedlings, reduction in the price of inputs such as fertilizers, subsidized farm implements, and free or affordable extension services at the national and state levels (PwC, 2020).

However, the social protection efforts of the government were flawed due to the small number of households that benefited in comparison to the number of poor people in the country. The National Social Register in Nigeria only contains 2.6 million registered households. Even though the government planned to increase the number of registered households to 3.6 million

(IMF, 2020), the effort remains ineffective, for a country with a population of over 200 million with more than 82 million people living below the national poverty line (NBS, 2020a). The distribution of palliatives was also marred by lack of transparency, accountability, and corruption (Dixit, Ogundeji and Onwujekwe, 2020; Human Rights Watch, 2020) as government officials were accused of appropriating palliatives for personal use or distribution among their cronies, calling to question the transparency of the government in implementing the social protection measures for the benefit of the populace. The accusations of corruption in the distribution of palliatives were confirmed following the discovery of several warehouses where palliatives were stored across different parts of the country, which were looted by starving individuals, following the End SARS protest in Nigeria. This further confirms the poor commitment of the government to addressing the hunger and food insecurity that followed the outbreak of COVID-2019 in Nigeria.

Economic Responses

The Federal Executive Council approved the sum of N2.3 trillion stimulus package (1.6 percent of GDP) to cushion the impact of COVID-2019 on the businesses of the citizens. The stimulus package included an initial approved N500 billion (0.34 percent of GDP) intervention fund which was meant to support healthcare facilities, provide relief for taxpayers, and incentivize employers to retain and recruit staff during the lockdown. The 2020 budget was reduced by cutting non-essential capital spending by N1.5 trillion (about 1 percent of GDP) while import duty waivers were introduced for pharmaceutical firms (IMF, 2020). The CBN also approved the disbursement of N75 billion loan guarantee scheme that was implemented under the Nigerian Incentive-based Risk Sharing System for Agricultural Lending to boost the agricultural sector (PwC, 2020), and a targeted credit facility was provided to support households, micro, small and medium enterprises (SMEs) that are affected by the COVID-2019 outbreak in Nigeria (Human Rights Watch, 2020; PwC, 2020).

An Emergency Economic Stimulus Bill 2020 was passed which provided for 50 percent tax rebates to businesses that are registered under the Companies and Allied Matters Act (CAMA) as a way of preventing employers of labor from retrenching workers in the formal sector. Programs such as the provision of increased housing, roads, facility maintenance, and labor interventions were taken into consideration by the Nigeria Economic Sustainability Plan (PwC, 2020). State governments also put several measures in place to mitigate the impact of the disease on households. For instance, tax reliefs were implemented in some states to help private individuals and businesses recover from the lockdown effects.

Unfortunately, the poor may not benefit much from the government's economic responses for several reasons. Firstly, accessing the loans that were provided by the CBN may not be feasible for poor and vulnerable households who lack the necessary collateral required for the loan. Secondly, the informal sector workers may not be able to access the provisions captured by the stimulus bill since most of them are not officially registered with CAMA, putting them at disadvantaged positions with respect to the social, economic, and legal protections that accrue to registered companies.

Macroeconomic Responses and Multilateral Collaboration

As a way of revamping the economy from the near-collapse state due to the COVID-2019 lockdown, macroeconomic policies were equally implemented in Nigeria. The CBN reduced interest rates on all applicable CBN interventions from 9 percent to 5 percent, created a N50 billion ($139 million) targeted credit facility, N100 billion support to the health sector, and efforts are also in motion to raise $50 million to support physical infrastructures of healthcare centers in Local Government Areas and the existing Social Investment Programs (IMF, 2020).

Funds were also raised through collaboration with private companies, bilateral and multinational donors to augment the efforts of the government. The IMF provided an emergency support fund of $3.4 billion, the European Union contributed €50 million, while the United States supported the country by providing ventilators to the isolation centers (Dixit, Ogundeji, and Onwujekwe, 2020). The African Development Bank also approved a loan of $288.5 million for the COVID-2019 response support program in Nigeria (African Development Bank, 2020). The private sector in Nigeria was also mobilized to establish the Coalition Against COVID-2019 which has so far contributed over $72 million used for purchasing food items and medical facilities that are distributed to different parts of the country (Dixit, Ogundeji and Onwujekwe, 2020).

Social Cohesion and Community Resilience

The practice of social cohesion in the COVID-2019 era was changed by the social distancing measures that became necessary to reduce human contact as a way of containing the spread of the disease. The government's efforts at building social cohesion cannot be said to be successful during the COVID-2019 lockdown in Nigeria. This is because several cases of social unrest and criminal activities that threaten the peaceful cohesion of communities abounded. Terror attacks on communities by Boko Haram, Bandits, and herdsmen as well as incidences of kidnapping and killings continued unabated. The law enforcement agents also contributed to the threats to social harmony during the lockdown, as several harassments and extrajudicial killings were announced; stranded citizens who, in a bid to survive the harsh economic situations enabled by the lockdown, were constantly harassed, and in some cases killed by law enforcement agents in different parts of the country. As of March 30, 2020, BBC (2020) reported that 12 people were killed by security forces in a bid to enforce the lockdown measures. The National Human Rights Commission also reported that during the same period, over 100 complaints were made against harassment by security agents (BBC, 2020).

Surviving COVID-2019 in Nigeria, amid scarce resources and the low response of the government to the number of people needing social protection and alternative means of income due to the hardship that spans the lockdown period, was a mission that the poor set out to achieve. Several coping measures were employed to reduce the impact of COVID-2019 by individuals and households such as cutting down of family's budget, reduction in family meals, and reduced spending on essential needs. With the shortages of hand sanitizers and face masks following the outbreak of the pandemic, it was easy for individuals to key into opportunities that the shortages in the PPEs offered. Local production of hand sanitizers and face masks helped to assist families to adjust to the effect of COVID-2019 on their livelihoods. For those who were employed in the informal sectors and who could no longer work due to the movement restrictions, alternative means of livelihood such as farming and engagement in new businesses to raise income for family sustenance were embarked upon.

CONCLUSION AND RECOMMENDATIONS

No doubt, COVID-2019 significantly impacted the Nigerian populace, lending its contributions to the high rates of poverty that the society was already grappling with before the outbreak of the disease in the country. COVID-2019 in Nigeria exposed the poor state of the available structures to combat not only the health issues generated by the disease but also the socioeconomic challenges of the populace, the majority of whom cannot weather the effect on their livelihood due to their poor resource base. As a way of confirming or refuting the hysteria that COVID-2019 will dwindle the resource base of families and further increase the poverty situation in the country, the chapter considers the poverty situation in Nigeria pre-COVID-2019, the impact of COVID-2019 on the socioeconomic well-being of the populace, and how the government has responded to mitigating the impact of the disease on the populace.

The study revealed that poverty has been embedded in Nigeria before the outbreak of COVID-2019, with over 80 million people, representing 40.1 percent of the population living below the national poverty line and that poverty affected every aspect of the life of the populace: from poor living condition evident in the high level of food insecurity, poor sanitation especially among slum dwellers, and the IDPs' limited access to electricity, water, and clean cooking fuels. The limited employment opportunities, limited access to financial resources, and the inadequate and poor working public infrastructures that could boost the livelihood opportunities of households are also in short supply in Nigeria.

The poor state of healthcare systems and services also contributes to the poverty outcome in Nigeria. The limited health infrastructures and poor funding drive the understaffing of the health sector, contributing to the poor performance of the sector. The poor state of health accounted for the low ranking of the country in the global community, as the country accounts for a high proportion of people living with HIV/AIDS, as well as having high rates of maternal and child mortality and morbidity in the world. The study also established that poverty in Nigeria contributed to the poor performance of the educational sector, which lacks adequate funding, staffing, and instructional materials and accounts for the country's ranking as having the highest number of out-of-school children in the world.

Furthermore, the containment measures that were imposed by the government, especially the lockdown and movement restrictions, impacted the livelihood of the populace, confirming the agitations that the COVID-2019 outbreak will increase the poverty narratives in the country. The food security in the country was seriously affected by the containment measures; there was a hike in food prices leading to food inflation that threatened the food security of an estimated 7 million people. The rise in the unemployment rate from 23.1 percent in 2018 to 27.1 percent by the second quarter of 2020 further confirmed the agitations that the disease outbreak will make more people to become vulnerable to poverty.

Shreds of evidence on the outbreak of COVID-2019 in Nigeria showed that the impact of the disease on the health security of Nigerians was low compared to global narratives. This is not to say that the impact of the disease was not felt. Its impact on the health of the citizens was rather observed in the management of patients with non-COVID-2019 ailments and the limited supply of PPEs to health workers that threw up anxieties about their safety. The focus of the government on COVID-2019 patients at the expense of other health issues of the public, especially in the inefficient provision of PPEs for medical personnel across health systems that led to situations where patients were denied medical care, was a risk that was not anticipated nor sufficiently addressed by the government.

On the educational front, the outbreak of the disease truncated the education of over 50 million school children. The inadequate Internet facilities in the educational sector crippled the benefits that Internet-enabled remote learning offered during the COVID-2019 lockdown in the country. The absence of remote learning facilities led to a near-collapse of the education sector throughout the lockdown period, with only a limited number of students benefiting from remote learning alternatives.

The study also found that the government responded to the mitigation of COVID-2019 in several ways. The health sector was mobilized through the NCDC which coordinated the public health sectors of the respective states. Funds were made available to the sector by the government and supported by private companies, bilateral and multilateral organizations. However, the efforts of the government in the health response to the disease were marred by the shortage of health workers, limited testing kits, and PPEs. The testing capacity of the government to ascertain the exposure rate of the populace was low when compared to the population in the country.

Palliatives in the forms of food items, cash transfers, and agricultural inputs were provided by the government and private bodies as a way of mitigating the impact of the disease on the livelihood of the populace. The quantity of social safety net provided was insignificant in comparison to the over 80 million people living below the national poverty line and the number of people, who, as a result of the lockdown and other measures, became vulnerable to poverty. Interest rates on lending were reduced, credit facilities were provided, and promise to improve the physical infrastructures in the country were made by the government.

The series of social unrests, with which Nigeria has come to be described also furnished the stress emanating from COVID-2019 and these threatened the social cohesion of the society. The kidnappings, Boko Haram and bandits' attacks, armed robbery, and extrajudicial killings were commonplace throughout the lockdown. On the part of individuals and families, to survive the effect of food insecurity and low income occasioned by the containment measures, family budgets were cut, with spending reduced to only essential needs like food. Livelihood options such as the production of face masks and hand sanitizers and involvement in farming activities were used to mitigate the impact on livelihoods.

The evidential impacts of COVID-2019 on the Nigerian populace as outlined above established that poverty in Nigeria is multidimensional and is a factor of the structural failures in the country as the absence of developmental structures hinders the self-development of any people. Food insecurity will not only affect the health status of the people but also increase incidences of crime and insecurity, and social security efforts that are not inclusive and effective will end up exposing the entire country to increased social problems.

The failure of the government to adequately equip the health systems with the necessary PPEs will not only expose health workers but also deny the poor, who already lack access to adequate healthcare due to the poor staffing of the health sector. Self-medication that stems from the inability to access healthcare during the COVID-2019 outbreak can further expose citizens to other diseases which may compromise their health status. The lopsided access to educational facilities, especially remote learning tools during the lockdown period, will further increase the inequality in the country.

Recommendations for Policymakers

From the foregoing, grounding the poverty and associated problems in Nigeria as emanating from the poor public structures is imperative as the absence of structures that provide platforms for development leaves a population continually undeveloped. Any effort that is aimed at addressing poverty in Nigeria must, first of all, focus on providing adequate structures. This is necessary, as the well-being of the populace is key to the nation's survival in the post-COVID-2019 era. Hence, to address the structural problems that predispose the Nigerian public to poverty outcomes, the following recommendations are put forth:

(a) The structural problems that drive poverty in Nigeria should be addressed by developing pro-poor policies and programs that provide the enabling environment for people to live, engage in livelihood activities, and develop themselves for a better life.
(b) The government should improve the living conditions of the poor by providing public infrastructures that will enhance access to clean water and sanitation facilities for poor communities and slum environments.
(c) To revamp the public infrastructures such as healthcare facilities and educational facilities, there is a need for the government to allocate more resources taking into cognizance, the growing population in the country which is presently putting pressure on public facilities.
(d) Finally, the health security of the country is key to the wealth of the country. The long-standing crisis of inadequate medical doctors has to be addressed if the endemic challenges of poor healthcare will be addressed through adequate remuneration of medical staff and provision of healthcare facilities that guarantee the safety of health personnel in the

discharge of their duties. The reduction in the cost of healthcare will help to increase health utilization in Nigeria.

Areas of Future Research

Based on the findings in the preceding sections, the following areas are recommended for future research:

(a) There is a need to investigate the effectiveness of the government's palliatives in changing the poverty narratives in post-COVID-2019 Nigeria.
(b) The long-standing mistrust of the government in providing public good was a key factor that generated hysteria about the outbreak of COVID-2019 in Nigeria. Several promises were made by the government toward addressing critical infrastructures in the country. Research is needed to investigate the commitment of the government toward the provision of such infrastructures.

REFERENCES

Alkire, S. and Santos, M. E. (2010). *Multidimensional Poverty Index. Oxford. The Oxford Poverty and Human Development Initiative*. University of Oxford. Retrieved on June 7, 2020 from www.ophi.org.uk.

Alkire, S. and Santos, M. E. (2013). A multidimensional approach: Poverty measurement and beyond. *Soc. Indic Res* 112:239–257. Retrieved on June 7, 2020 from https://doi.org/10.1007/s11205-013-0257-3.

Ananat, E. O. (2011). The Wrong side(s) of the track: The causal effects of racial segregation on urban poverty and inequality. *American Journal of Applied Economics* 3(2):34–66. Retrieved on July 10, 2020 from https://doi.10.1257/app.3.2.34.

Assessment Capacities Projects (ACAPS). (2020). *COVID-19 in Nigeria. Vulnerabilities to COVID-19 and Containment Measures. Thematic Report.* Retrieved on September 17, 2020 from http://www.acaps.org/.

BioSpectrum. (September 17, 2018). Aster DM healthcare partners with Nigerian university hospitals. Retrieved on September 21, 2020 from https://www.biospectrumasia.com/news/49/11703/aster-dm-healthcare-partners-with-nigerian-university-hospital-.html.

Bradshaw T. K. (2006). *Theories of Poverty and Anti-Poverty Programs in Community Development. RPEC working paper no. 06-05 February 2006 Rural Poverty Research Centre.* Retrieved on June 10, 2020 from http://www.rprconline.org/.

Brady, D. (2018). Theories of the causes of poverty. *Annual Review of Sociology* 45:155–175. Retrieved on July 10, 2020, from https://doi.org/10.1146/annurev-soc073018-022550

Brady, D., Kaya, Y. and Beckfield, J. (2007). Reassessing the effect of economic growth on well-being in less developed countries, 1980–2003. *Studies in Comparative International Development* 42:1–35. Retrieved on July 12, 2020, from https://doi.10.1007/s12116-007-9003-7.

Bloom, G. and Lucas, H. (1999). *Health and Poverty in Sub-Saharan Africa. IDS Working Paper 103*. Retrieved on June 14, 2020 from www.ids.ac.uk.

British Broadcasting Corporation (BBC). (April 16, 2020). Coronavirus: Security forces kill more Nigerians than COVID-19. Retrieved on 23, September 2020 from https://www.bbc.com/news/world-africa-52317196.

BudgIT. (2020). *2020 Budget. Analysis and Opportunities*. Retrieved on August 16, 2020, from https://yourbudgit.com/wpcontent/uploads/2020/03/2020-Budget-Analysis.pdf.

Dixit S., Ogundeji, K. Y. and Onwujekwe. O. (July 2, 2020). How well has Nigeria responded to Covid-19? Retrieved on September 8, 2020 from www.brookings.edu.

FAO (2020). *FAO in Emergencies. Nigeria*. Retrieved on September 15, 2020 from http://www.fao.org/emergencies/countries/detail/en/c/213439.

Gweshengwe, B. (2019). A critique of the income poverty line and global multidimensional poverty index. *Southeast Asia: A Multidisciplinary Journal* 19:37–46. Retrieved on July 27, 2020 from www.researchgate.net/publication.

Human Rights Watch. (April 14, 2020). Nigeria: protect most vulnerable in COVID-19 response. Extended lockdown threatens the livelihoods of millions. Retrieved on September 17, 2020 from www.hrw.org.

Hussain, A. T. (2020). *Education and Covid-19 in Nigeria. Tackling the Digital Divide. World Literacy Foundation*. Retrieved on September 29 2020 from https://worldliteracyfoundation.org/education-and-covid-19-in-nigeria/.

International Food Policy Research Institute (IFPRI). (2020). *Impacts of Covid-19 on Food Security. Panel Data Evidence from Nigeria. IFPRI Discussion Paper 01956*. Retrieved on September 29, 2020 from https://www.ifpri.org/publication/impacts-covid-19-food-security-panel-data-evidence-nigeria.

International Labor Organization (ILO). 2020. *ILO Terms of Reference. A Rapid Diagnostics Assessing the Impact of COVID-19 on Enterprises and Workers in the Informal Economy in Nigeria*. Retrieved on September 29, 2020 from http://www.ilo.org/wcmsp5/groups/public/---Africa/---ro-abidjan/---iloabuja/documents/genericdocument/wcms_749091.pdf.

International Monetary Fund (IMF). (2020). Retrieved on May 22, 2020, from www.imf.org.

National Bureau of Statistics (NBS). (2014). *LSMS—Integrated Surveys on Agriculture General Household Survey Panel 2012/2013*. Retrieved on September 29, 2020 from www.nigerianstat.gov.ng.

National Bureau of Statistics (NBS). (2018). *Labour Force Statistics—Volume I: Unemployment and Underemployment Report. (Q4 2017–Q3 2018)*. Retrieved on September 29, 2020 from www.nigerianstat.gov.ng.

National Bureau of Statistics (NBS). (2020a). *2019 Poverty and Inequality in Nigeria: Executive Summary*. Retrieved on June 7, 2020 from www.nigerianstat.gov.ng.

National Bureau of Statistics (NBS). (2020b). *Nigerian Living Standards Survey. A Survey Report by the Nigerian National Bureau of Statistics in collaboration with the World Bank*. Retrieved on July 23, 2020 from www.nigerianstat.gov.ng.

National Bureau of Statistics (NBS). (2020c). *Labor Force Statistics: Unemployment and Underemployment Report. Abridged Labor Force Survey under COVID-19. Q2 2020*. Retrieved on July 23, 2020 from https://nigerianstat.gov.ng/elibrary.

Nigerian Centre for Disease Control (NCDC). (2020a). *Weekly epidemiological report*. Retrieved on June 15, 2020 from https://ncdc.gov.ng/reports/246/2020-february-week-7.

Nigerian Centre for Disease Control (NCDC). (2020b). *COVID-19 Nigeria*. Retrieved on June 15, 2020 from https://covid19.ncdc.gov.ng/.

Oxford Poverty and Human Development Initiative (OPHI). (n.d.). *Policy – A Multidimensional Approach*. Retrieved on June 23, 2020 from www.ophi.org.uk.

PricewaterhouseCoopers (PwC). (2020). *Responding to the impact of COVID-19 on food security and agriculture in Nigeria*. Retrieved on September 29 2020 from https://www.pwc.com/ng/en/assets/pdf/impact-covid19-food-security-nigeria.pdf

Punch (October 7, 2020). COVID-19: 319 doctors infected, 14 dead as 33 states owe N5,000 monthly hazard allowances. July 29, 2020. Retrieved on October 7, 2020 from https://healthwise.punchng.com/covid-19-319-doctors-infected-14-dead-as-33-states-owe-n5000-monthly-hazard-allowances/.

Ravallion, M. (2011). On multidimensional indices of poverty. *Journal of Economic Inequality* 9: 235–248. Retrieved on July 5, 2020 from https://link.springer.com/article/10.1007/s10888-011-9173-4.

Roberts, S. (2018). *Key Facts: Poverty and Poor Health*. Retrieved on May 7, 2020 from www.healthpovertyaction.org.

Sameti, M., Esfahani, R. D. and Haghighi, H. K. (2012). Theories of poverty: A comparative analysis. *Kuwait Chapter of Arabian Journal of Business and Management Review* 1(6). Retrieved on June 18, 2020 from https://www.arabianjbmr.com/pdfs/KD_VOL_1_6/4.pdf.

Santos, M. E., Lugo, M. A., Lopez-Calva, L. F., Cruces, G. and Battiston, D. (2010). Refining the basic needs approach: A multidimensional analysis of poverty in Latin America. In Bishop, J. A. (ed.), *Studies in Applied Welfare Analysis: Papers from the Third ECINEQ Meeting*. London, UK: Emerald Group Publishing Limited. Retrieved on May 24, 2020 from www.researchgate.net.

Trading Economics. (2020). *Nigeria Food Inflation 1996–2020 Data*. Retrieved on September 16, 2020 from https://tradingeconomics.com/nigeria/food-inflation.

United Nations (UN). (n.d.). *Ending Poverty*. Retrieved on May 20, 2020 from www.un.org.

United Nations (UN). (2020). *A UN Framework for the Immediate Socio-Economic Response to COVID-19*. Retrieved on August 8, 2020 from www.un.org.

United Nations Children Education Fund (UNICEF). (2020a). *UNICEF Nigeria*. Retrieved on September 22, 2020 from https://www.unicef.org/nigeria/education.

United Nations Children Education Fund (UNICEF). (2020b). *The state of the world's children. 2017 children in a digital world*. Retrieved on October 4, 2020 from https://www.unicef.org/publications/index_101992.html.

United Nations Department of Social and Economic Affairs (UNDESA). (2019a). *World Economic Situation and Prospects: October 2019 Briefing No. 131.* Retrieved on May 29, 2020 from www.un.org.

United Nations Department of Economic and Social Affairs (UNDESA). (2019b). *World Population Prospects 2019: Data Booklet.* Retrieved on August 23, 2020 from www.population.un.org>files.

United Nations Office for the Coordination of Humanitarian Affairs (UNOCHA). (2020). *Situation Report—Highlights. 14 September 2020. Nigeria Humanitarian Situation.* Retrieved on September 29, 2020 from https://reliefweb.int/country/nga.

United States Agency for International Development (USAID) Nigeria. (2014). *The Ripple Effect of COVID-19 on Economic Activities, Livelihoods and Food Security in East Africa and the Great Lakes.* Retrieved on July 18, 2020 from www.reliefweb.int>files>resources.

United States Agency for International Development (USAID) Nigeria. (2019). *Global Health.* Retrieved on July 20, 2020 from www.usaid.gov.

Walker, R. (2015). *Multidimensional Poverty. GSDRC Professional Development Reading Pack No. 22. Birmingham, UK: University of Birmingham.* Retrieved on June 25, 2020 from www.gsdrc.org.

World Bank. (January 9, 2019). Half of the world's poor live in just 5 countries. Retrieved on May 15, 2020 from www.Blogs.worldbank.org.

World Bank. (2020a). *Understanding Poverty.* Retrieved on May 20, 2020 from www.worldbank.org.

World Bank. (June 26, 2020b). Nigeria's economy faces the worst recession in four decades, says new World Bank report. Retrieved on July 7, 2020 from www.worldbank.org.

World Economic Forum. (2020). Covid-19 has exposed the education divide in Nigeria. This is how we can close it. Retrieved on September 29, 2020 from https://www.weforum.org/agenda/2020/06/education-nigeria-covid19-digital-divide/.

WHO Global Health Workforce Alliance (GHWA). (2008). *HRH Country Profile: Nigeria, WHO GHWA, 2008).* Retrieved on September 29, 2020 from https://www.who.int/workforcealliance/countries/nga/en/.

World Health Organization (WHO) Africa. (2014). *The Health of the People. What Works. The African Regional Health Report.* 2014. Retrieved June 3, 2020 from www.who.int.

World Health Organization (WHO) Africa. (2018). *The State of Health in the WHO Africa Region: An Analysis of the Status of Health, Health Services and Health Systems in the Context of the Sustainable Development Goals.* Retrieved on June 6, 2020 from www.afro.who.int.

Chapter 6

Corodemocracy

Harrison Adewale Idowu

The outbreak of the Coronavirus Disease (COVID)-2019 pandemic had not only ensured that the world was brought to its knees following several measures put in place to contain the spread of the virus but had also triggered a lot of political and socioeconomic issues. While social and physical distancing, lockdown, and travel restrictions have been touted as the most effective means to curb the spread of COVID-2019 and flatten the curve, some governments had taken undue advantage of these measures (Diamond, 2020; Nyei, 2020). This has been demonstrated in the abuse of citizens' rights in several contexts like unlawful detentions, shooting rubber bullets at lockdown defaulters, and meting out other inhumane treatments on them. Generally, while these abuses are condemnable, they are even more so for democratic governments, where human rights to life, association, fair hearing, and human dignity, among others, are guaranteed (Nyei, 2020). Nevertheless, democratic governments have been found culpable in either restriction or outright violation of these rights in the guise of containing the spread of COVID-2019. These acts of democratic erosion, especially with respect to human rights abuses and restrictions which occurred in the process of implementing safety and quarantine policies occasioned by the COVID-2019 pandemic, are what is meant by "Corodemocracy."

In Africa, evidence abound on how governments took undue advantage of the emergency situation occasioned by the pandemic, to expand their partisanship nature and curtail free speech of the opposition and those individuals and groups criticizing their policies. In South Africa and Liberia, for instance, the governments had criminalized the activities of individuals and/or groups who publish deceptive statements about the COVID-2019 situation in the countries or those who criticized the governments' policies aimed at containing the virus, and those who spread "fake news" about the COVID-2019 situation in the countries (Nyei, 2020). Explicitly, the Liberian government had warned its citizens that "you cannot have 100 percent rights that you may exercise during normal times. . . . Liberia is technically at war [with COVID-2019]." This statement paints a general picture of the situation across countries, as several governments have openly likened the COVID-2019 pandemic to a war situation. In the United States, Algeria, Tunisia, Nigeria, and Hungary, the situation was the same.

Whereas the COVID-2019 pandemic potentially poses a threat to the "health of the state," as such, the rules and guidelines put in place to contain the virus spread and protect human lives from the pandemic are not out of place, albeit efforts to enforce them had seen to the appalling rate of disrespect for human rights. As such, global COVID-2019 responses had resulted in restrictions of human rights like freedom of movement, assembly, and expression (Human Rights Watch, 2020a); arbitrary detention, ill-treatment of citizens, torture, and in some cases, the violation of the right to life or death (Diamond, 2020).

The United Nations Declaration of Human Rights of 1948 guarantees that the human rights of citizens be protected at all times, with the exception of circumstance which is injurious to the life of the state (United Nations, 1949). Even in such a circumstance, the rule provides that enough scientific evidence to warrant such temporary restrictions must be provided. Such exceptional restrictions are possible where there is the need to protect public health and where the state is under an emergency situation which threatens the life of the state (Human Rights Watch, 2020a). For these to occur, however, such restrictions must be "necessary, proportionate, non-discriminatory, limited in duration and measures must be in place to guide against excesses" (Human Rights Watch, 2020a, p. 1; Perelman, 2020, p. 1; UN, 1984, p. 1). Albeit no matter the circumstance, human rights laws stipulate that certain rights like those to life, prohibition against torture and ill-treatment, and the right not to be arbitrarily detained must be in place at all times (Delvac, 2020; Perelman, 2020). Quite contrastingly, efforts to implement COVID-2019 policies by state governments had resulted in the violation of these "untouchable" rights in many countries across the globe. Despite these provisions, across democratic governments the world over, from the United States to Turkey, Algeria, and Nigeria, among others, there had been incidents of human rights abuses by the very government which has the onus of protecting these rights. The exception to human rights restrictions does not cover most of the rights violated in the cause of enforcing COVID-2019 lockdown policies (Delvac, 2020). Safe to say therefore that the pandemic has seen to the erosion of democratic tenets across democratic states.

It is undisputed that democratic tenets are not confined to human rights alone, as COVID-2019 pandemic has also seen the arbitrary postponement of democratic elections, without any rescheduled date in sight. It has seen elections conducted under "new" and unpopular conditions, and the promulgation and rule by decrees and anti-democratic laws by democracies (Diamond, 2020). The COVID-2019 situation had also ensured that citizens suspended ongoing peaceful movements and were unable to begin fresh ones for their personal safety (Nyei, 2020). While some of the actions by democratic governments are justifiable, given the emergency situation that the pandemic created, the fact remains also that most "autocratic governments" disguised as democracies had taken undue advantage of the pandemic situation to unleash the autocratic nature in them. Particularly of interest in this chapter are the disrespect, undermining, abuse, and restrictions on the rights of citizens by democratic governments in the course of implementing quarantine and safety rules to contain the spread of COVID-2019. This is particularly important as the protection of human rights is both globally recognized and binding by the UN Declaration of Rights, and it is guaranteed by democracies.

While human rights abuses across the world were not new before the outbreak of COVID-2019, the pandemic had ensured that it took a new dimension and became more pronounced and rampant. Given the preponderance of misuse of emergency power that the COVID-2019 situation occasioned, the UN high commissioner for human rights, Bachelet, had warned state governments on the danger of this. According to her, "emergency powers should not be a weapon governments can wield to quash dissent, control the population, and even perpetuate their time in power. . . . They should be used effectively to cope with the pandemic—nothing more, nothing less" (Perelman, 2020, p. 1).

In Nigeria, the most populous Black nation in the world, and the most populous country in Africa, cases of democratic erosion had continued unabatedly in the form of human rights abuses and restrictions in the course of implementing lockdown and social distancing rules occasioned by the pandemic. This had even seen to the molestation of frontline workers like health workers and journalists. While the COVID-2019 has generated a lot of scholarly and public debates on its socioeconomic effect on people's lives and countries' economies, scanty empirical attention has been given to the "Corodemocratic" issues, especially as it relates to human rights abuses and restrictions within the Nigerian context. This chapter is therefore significant as it empirically appraises within the Nigerian context the rate of democratic erosion measured through human rights violations and restrictions in the course of implementing COVID-2019 safety and quarantine policies. The chapter therefore interrogates the following issues: What are the various civil and social human rights abuse/restrictions occasioned by COVID-2019 pandemic in Nigeria? What is the level of human rights abuses amid COVID-2019 in Nigeria? What gender is more affected by the human rights abuses/

restrictions occasioned by COVID-2019 in Nigeria? These are the questions to which the chapter provides answers.

The remaining part of the chapter is structured as follows. The next section presents a theoretical discourse on democracy and human rights, while the third section presents the methodological approach adopted. The subsequent section tracks some global incidents of human rights abuses in the course of implementing COVID-2019 safety and quarantine policies across democracies, while the fifth section presents and analyzes data collected from Nigerians. The last two sections are on findings, and conclusion and recommendations, respectively.

DEMOCRACY AND HUMAN RIGHTS: THEORETICAL DISCOURSE

Democracy is a system of government of, by, and for the people. It is a governance system which prioritizes the people and rules by their consent. Democracy guarantees and protects the rights of the people. According to the United Nations' Guidance Note on Democracy (2009), democracy refers to governance, respect for human rights and fundamental freedom, accountability in decision-making process, and end endorsement of institutions and practices. It is a system of government where the interest of the people is prioritized by the state. For this chapter, democracy implies a system of government which guarantees and safeguards respect for human rights and fundamental freedom. Human rights are those essential rights which humans are entitled to. Kirchschlaeger (2014, p. 113) defines human rights as "those rights that belong to everyone as a member of the human race, regardless of skin color, nationality, political convictions or religious persuasion, social standing, gender or age." This presupposes that human rights are non-discriminatory, they apply to all humans. In a democracy, human rights are incorporated in the national constitution as fundamental human rights.

While respect for human rights entails states' refrainment from violating the rights, protecting human rights entails states' prevention of human rights violation by third parties (Landman, 2018; Payne, 2000). To fulfill human rights implies states' commitment to the investment in and implementation of policies to ensure the realization of human rights (Koch, 2005; Landman and Kersten, 2016). Human rights could be civil, political, economic, social, or cultural (Landman, 2018, p. 50). Human rights are as follows:

> Universal (every human being is a right holder), categorical (every human being has these rights, they cannot be denied to anyone), egalitarian (every human being has the same rights), individual (human rights apply to every human being

> as individual and protect the latter from violations by a collectivity, recognizing at the same time the important role of a collectivity for the individual), fundamental (human rights protect basic and essential elements of human existence), indivisible (the whole catalogue of human rights must be respected, they are complementary), and they make legitimate demands with corresponding position positive and negative duties. (Kirchschlaeger, 2014, p. 116)

This chapter focuses on civil and social rights which have to do with rights to life, prohibition against torture and ill-treatment, right not to be arbitrarily detained, liberty (UN, 1949, Art. 3); freedom of religion in community with others (UN, 1949, Art. 18); freedom of movement (UN, 1949, Art. 13.1); education (UN, 1949, Art. 26.1); freedom of peaceful assembly and association (UN, 1949, Art. 20.1); freely participate in community (UN, 1949, Art. 27.1); and work and protection against unemployment (UN, 1949, Art. 23.1).

It is undisputed that human rights are not exclusive to democracies, albeit, human rights-democracy proponents like Matthews (2019), Gallagher (2008), Kirchschlaeger (2014), Hills (2016), Gould (2004), and Landman (2018) have consistently linked human rights' protection with democracies, and deemed such rights as more pronounced and secured in democracies. This is correct to the extent that, although democracy is not mentioned in the United Nations Charter on the Declaration of Human Rights, it nonetheless recognizes the will of the people in its opening words as "we the people of the United Nations" (Gallagher, 2008). This suggests that even though the word "democracy" was not referenced, it directly places the onus of human rights protection on the government which respects the will of the people (democracy). In its World Conference on Human Rights (1993), the United Nations explicitly stated the relationship between human rights and democracy. It avers that "democracy . . . and respect for human rights and fundamental freedoms at the national and international levels should be universal and conducted without conditions attached" (UN, 1993, paragraph 8).

From the late 1980 onward, democracy has been increasingly referred to as a system of government and a value related to human rights (Gallagher, 2008, p. 2), as such, human rights and democracy have become intrinsically linked. This reaffirms the argument that human rights protect democratic process (Kirchschlaeger, 2014, p. 114). A state which is truly democratic is therefore the one in which all human rights are respected and protected. The tenets of democracy such as universal suffrage, non-discrimination, the rule of law, and institutions of democracy engender the promotion and protection of human rights. Confining democracy strictly to the electoral process, as one which allows the people to choose their leaders in periodic, free and fair elections, without recourse to the status of human rights, falls short of a truly democratic state. For as Gallagher (2008, p. 2) argued, and rightly so, "true democracy goes much deeper than the electoral process. . . . It would be a serious mistake to imagine that freely elected governments are a guarantee of individual rights."

The fact that governments are freely elected does not therefore guarantee that such governments will respect and protect human rights. Given this, democracy must be conceived beyond free electoral process to the protection of rights. As we shall soon highlight, evidences across democracies where freely elected governments have abused human rights in various dimensions clearly put this position into limelight. Human rights protection has been consistently used as an indicator to gauge democratic performance and the strengths and weaknesses of such a democratic state (Matthews, 2019, p. 7). Such human rights indicators have sought to evaluate state activities or policies against human rights norms, standards, and values, in order to assess the state of promotion and implementation of human rights in a democratic state (UNOHCHR, 2012, p. 16). Therefore, while assessing democracies, consideration is given to among other factors like the protection, promotion, and enforcement of human rights, and individual freedoms (Freedom House, 2019; World Justice Project, 2018). Nevertheless, the universality and generalization of these human rights indicators across the board has been queried (cf. Davis et al., 2012, p. 4; Merry, 2011). To buttress this position, Hill (2016) opined that the respect for human or personal integrity is a prerequisite for claims to democratic practice; hence, his argument that democracy and human rights are mutually constitutive.

Whereas such strong links have been normatively made on democracy and human rights, the debate over the complementarity of the duo remains largely contested (Matthews, 2019). According to Matthews (2019), this contestation has persisted, owing to the confusion and lack of conclusiveness over the underpinnings of political, economic, social, civil, and cultural rights; and arguments over which of these rights are critical to the promotion of democracy and those eligible to benefit from them. Some proponents of this school of thought have submitted that too much emphasis is placed on the need for the state to desist from indulging in acts which abuse or restrict human rights and individual freedoms. The obvious from this emphasis is that they portray rights as though essential, but as mere tools in the state (Kurki, 2011). Rather than such an individualistic approach which seems to set the state against citizens, Kurki (2011) avers that the advancement of human rights and the recognition and respect for human rights by the state could be pursued in such a way as to promote, more holistically, a democracy which protects the interest of all (the state and the citizens). The much emphasis on the need for the state to respect and protect rights appears to set the state against the people, encouraging a frosty relationship between the people and the state.

The universality/cultural relativism of human rights in democracy has also resulted in a divided debate among human rights-democracy proponents. According to Matthews (2019, p. 7), this has resulted in "conceptual and substantive" universality of human rights. While conceptual universality posits that every human is entitled to human rights equally on the basis of being human beings, substantive universality concerns whether the recognition of human rights in institutional framework of the UN Declaration of Human Rights is really equally applicable to everyone (Donnelly, 2007; Gould, 2004). This dimension of the debate puts strain on the straightforward relationship between democracy and human rights. Culturally, human rights application is argued to be relative to culture, as such, their application cannot be the same across cultures. Despite these contestations, Gould (2004) posits that the most important thing is that human rights promotion within a democracy ought to take cognizance of the equality of all humans as carriers of an inherent human dignity. This is the point that this chapter clings unto, that human rights must be equally applied to all humans by the virtue of being human beings, irrespective of the numerous positions and the universal/cultural relativist debate. This holds even in the face of a pandemic and while trying to protect the people from the virus.

Globalization has contributed in no small measure to upset the relationship between democracy and human rights (Matthews, 2019). To a large extent, the interference of powerful states and international institutions has the ability to impede state's capacity to pursue the advancement of human rights vigorously (Evans, 2001). For instance, given the outbreak of COVID-2019, the World Health Organization had come up with safety and quarantine policies to contain the spread of the virus. These policies which restrict certain citizen rights are binding on all member states, as such, they are persuaded to implement these policies. In this circumstance, state's capacity to protect human rights to the fullest is impeded. This is the situation most countries, including Nigeria, found themselves. While the policies were not designed to strategically violate and abuse certain human rights, albeit their implementation across countries has seen the wanton abuse of human rights. This is the globalization effect. For as Matthews (2019, p. 8) puts it, "while the human rights framework is predominantly state-centric, the human rights challenges it seeks to address are not exclusively national." This paints the COVID-2019 pandemic situation, which is not exclusively a national issue, but a global one requiring global response.

The contestations over human rights and democracy notwithstanding, this chapter anchors democracy as the surest means for the protection of and respect for human rights. As such, pandemic or no pandemic, democracies are expected to promote and protect the fundamental human rights of citizens. In the face of the COVID-2019 pandemic therefore, and in state efforts to implement safety and quarantine policies, democracy like Nigeria is expected to protect and respect human rights and avoid abuses like arbitrary detention, torture, killings, and restriction in freedom of religion and association, and freedom of movement, among others. This is correct to the extent that "democracy remains the most suitable vehicle to advance the full range of civil, political, economic, social and cultural rights towards ensuring that everyone is able to enjoy the material, social, economic and political benefits that democracy seeks to deliver" (Matthews, 2019, p. 8). This is also the position of Landman (2018) who avers that democracy is superior to other forms of government in terms of protecting and respecting human rights.

METHODOLOGY

The chapter adopts the descriptive survey research design and the quantitative method, using primary and secondary data to ascertain the level of human rights abuses and restrictions in the process of enforcing COVID-2019 safety and quarantine rules in Nigeria. The methodological approach is designed to interrogate how much citizens felt that their fundamental human rights (civil and social) guaranteed in democracy were violated by the state in its efforts to enforce COVID-2019 safety and quarantine rules in order to contain the spread of the virus in Nigeria. To adhere to safety and quarantine rules occasioned by the COVID-2019 pandemic, the opinions of Nigerians were randomly sampled using an online survey. A structured survey titled "Corodemocracy" was administered via e-mail addresses, WhatsApp, Twitter, Facebook, and other social media platforms. The survey consisted of two sections (A and B). Section A collected data on the sociodemographic information of respondents, while section B collected data on human rights abuses/restrictions occasioned by the COVID-2019 pandemic in Nigeria.

Using the Research Advisor's Sample Size Table (2006), at confidence level of 95 percent and margin of error of 5 percent, a corresponding sample size for the over 200 million population of Nigeria was adopted. Therefore, the sample size for the study was 384 (see Research Advisor Sample Size Table, 2006). Responses to the survey were collated and retrieved within a period of two month from August 3 to October 3, 2020. At the close of the survey exercise, a total of 310 responses representing 80.7 percent of the original sample size were retrieved for analysis.

Data were analyzed using the descriptive (tables, frequencies, percentages, mean, and charts) and inferential (Chi-square and ANOVA) statistical technique of the Statistical Package for Social Science (SPSS). The level of human rights abuses recorded in the course of enforcing COVID-2019 lockdown rules in Nigeria was ascertained using a Likert scale of 13 items and the mean score of responses. Each item had a range of possible responses from "Neutral" to "Strongly agree," with corresponding scores ranging from 0 to 4. Mean scores which fell below the criterion mean of 2 or equal to 2 were deemed to be low level of human rights abuses/restrictions, while mean scores above the criterion mean of 2 were deemed to be high level of human rights abuses/restrictions.

GLOBAL TRACKING OF CORODEMOCRACY

The outbreak of COVID-2019 in December 2019 in Wuhan city of China and its subsequent spread to other parts of the globe had ensured the global approval of certain safety and quarantine rules to contain the spread of the virus. Nevertheless, such rules have seen to the flagrant abuse and restrictions of human rights even in democratic states where human rights are supposedly better protected and respected. Whereas social and physical distancing and other quarantine policies put in place to contain the COVID-2019 pandemic have been lauded as the best means to flatten the pandemic curve, the fact remains that, as much as they restrict people's movement, they constitute a violation of the UN Declaration of Human Rights (Delvac, 2020; UN, 1949). According to Delvac (2020), COVID-2019 safety and quarantine rules continue to violate rights to freedom of movement, freedom of peaceful assembly and association, liberty, education, work and protection against unemployment, freely participate in community, freedom of peaceful assembly and association, and freedom of religion in community with others. While the United Nations leaves room for such restrictions in circumstances which pose threat to the health of the state, it however advocates for an unhindered, uncompromised, and continuous respect for human dignity (UN, 1984). Furthermore, while the COVID-2019 crisis qualifies as a "special situation" recommended by the UN, and therefore warrants the safety and quarantine measures put in place to contain the virus, the implementation of these rules had seen to the wanton abuse of human dignity (Delvac, 2020) across democracies. This section attempts a tracking of some of these human rights abuses which took place across the globe amid the pandemic.

To contain the spread of COVID-2019 in the Philippines, the country's president had announced that lockdown violators could be shot and in fact, police had placed violators in animal cages and subjected them to physical punishments and posted the recordings online to shame violators (Heijmans et al., 2020). These are clearly disrespect for human dignity. The situation is similar in Brazil where lockdown violators were been held feet bound in public square (Martinez, 2020). In South Africa, reports show how the police deployed physical punishments, including the use of rubber bullets and water cannons, on quarantine violators in the country (Heijmans et al., 2020). Indian and Britain have had police beating those flaunting quarantine rules, while others had been subjected to inhumane treatments like squats push-ups, crawl, or roll on the floor. The countries also proposed, threatened, and imposed imprisonment on violators (Assuncao, 2020). People diagnosed with COVID-2019 or showing symptoms of it, but had refused to quarantine, could face a three-year jail term in Mexico (Heijmans et al., 2020). In violation of freedom of worship with community, pastors and imams were arrested and detained in Nigeria and Senegal for violating COVID-2019 restrictions in places of worship.

Overzealous security abuses leading to the death of at least 12 citizens violating safety and quarantine rules were recorded in Kenya, Guinea, Nigeria, Rwanda, South Africa, and Zimbabwe (France 24, March 28, 2020; Punch, May 14, 2020). The use of drones to monitor those infected with the virus whether they are self-isolating, to take the temperature of citizens, and enforce stay-at-home orders in Italy, India, France, and the United States were criticized by civil rights advocates and groups as "invasive and pose constitutional dangers" (Phillips, 2020). Laws and decrees were promulgated in Bolivia, Poland, and South Africa to criminalize fake news on COVID-2019 or punish anyone criticizing government policies toward addressing the pandemic (Freedom House, 2020; Open Democracy, 2020). Such laws and decrees threaten freedom of expression which constitutes a part of human rights. In Nigeria, Izuora (2020) reports cases of arbitrary arrests of lockdown violators and seizure and demolition of commercial properties by a state governor amid the COVID-2019 pandemic.

Press freedom, a germane ingredient in any democracy, has also been threatened by the COVID-2019 pandemic. Across the world, including the United States and India, journalists were "harassed, detained, fined and imprisoned for their reporting" about the COVID-2019 situation in their countries (Truong, 2020). Some suffered such ill-treatments for being on duty during the lockdown periods. The attack on free press amid the pandemic is particularly a cause for concern because free press is an instrument to preserve human rights. For as rightly argued by Truong (2020), "Without free and independent media serving as watchdogs, citizens in some countries will be left with diminished freedoms when COVID-2019 crisis ends, damaging democracy in ways that will be difficult to undo."

Relying on data from the V-Dem's (2020) Pandemic Backsliding Risk Index, Shenga (2020) found among Eastern and Southern African states that only Malawi introduced emergency measures during the pandemic, which did not pose any threat to democracy. Whereas Burundi and Tanzania imposed measures which had medium threat to democratic norms, the likes of Botswana, Kenya, Mozambique, Namibia, Rwanda, South Africa,

Uganda, Zambia, and Zimbabwe had pandemic emergency measures which posed high risk to democracy. These risks to democratic norms occasioned by the pandemic emergency measures were demonstrated through restrictions in media freedom, punishments for violation of restrictions on media freedom, limitations of electoral freedom, limitation of the role of the legislature, restrictions on judicial oversight, and arbitrary and abusive enforcement (Shenga, 2020).

El Salvador arbitrarily detained lockdown violators in "containment centers," Honduras temporarily restricted freedom of speech rights guaranteed in the country's constitution in order to address the spread of misinformation about the pandemic, and the Venezuelan government harassed and detained journalists to silence criticism of its pandemic policies (Washington Office on Latin America (WOLA), 2020). When low-income citizens took to the streets to protest continuous stay-at-home policy and demanded food from the Honduras government, the government deployed the military police to confront and assault the protesters (WOLA, 2020). In Uganda, police forced women to undress in public as punishment for breaking COVID-2019 lockdown rules; police injured children and shot a man while enforcing the lockdown in South Africa (Human Rights Watch, 2020). According to the United Nations (2020, p. 8), the COVID-2019 crisis has seen the rise in unemployment and food insecurity, and widespread closure of schools—a situation which has interrupted the education of over 1 billion people worldwide. These are both deprivation of right to work and employment and the right to education.

DATA PRESENTATION AND ANALYSIS

This section deals with analysis and interpretation of data obtained from the respondents on the level of human rights abuses during the enforcement of COVID-2019 lockdown in Nigeria. A total of 310 responses were retrieved at the end of the online survey, representing 80.7 percent of the sample size adopted for the study. The results are represented and analyzed using descriptive (tables, frequencies, percentages, graphs, mean, and standard deviation) and inferential (Chi-square) statistical techniques of SPSS.

Descriptive Analysis

Table 6.1 and figure 6.1 show that male respondents have the highest population of the sampled respondents with 172 males, representing 55.5 percent of the respondents. Also, 12 respondents, representing 3.9 percent of the sampled respondents, preferred not to disclose their gender. With respect to

Table 6.1 Sociodemographic Characteristics of Respondents

Gender	*Frequency*	*Percentage (%)*
Female	126	40.6
Male	172	55.5
Prefer not to say	12	3.9
Total	310	100.0
Age Group		
18–25	77	24.8
26–35	141	45.5
36–50	72	23.2
Above 50	20	6.5
Total	310	100
Region		
South West	203	65.5
North West	4	1.3
North East	8	2.6
North Central	43	13.9
South-South	37	11.9
South East	15	4.8
Total	310	100
Employment Status		
Employed	128	41.3
Self-employed (Business)	57	18.4
Student	87	28.1
Unemployed	38	12.3
Total	310	100

Source: Online Survey Conducted by the Author (2020).

age, respondents who fell between ages 26 and 35 years made the highest population of the respondents, with 141 of them constituting 45.5 percent of the total respondents' population. Respondents above the age of 50 made the lowest population of the respondents, with 20 of them representing 6.5 percent of the sampled respondents.

The table also shows that most respondents are resident in the Southwestern region of Nigeria, with 203 respondents constituting 65.5 percent of the sampled respondents coming from that region. Northwest had the lowest representative of respondents, with only four respondents representing 1.3 percent of the total sampled population. The table and graphical presentation show that 128 respondents, making 41.3 percent of the sampled respondents, are employed. The employed constitute the highest number of the sampled respondents. Also, 38 respondents, representing 12.3 percent of the total respondents, are unemployed, and they make the lowest population of the sampled respondents. Other data on the sociodemographic characteristics of the respondents are presented in table 6.1 and figure 6.1.

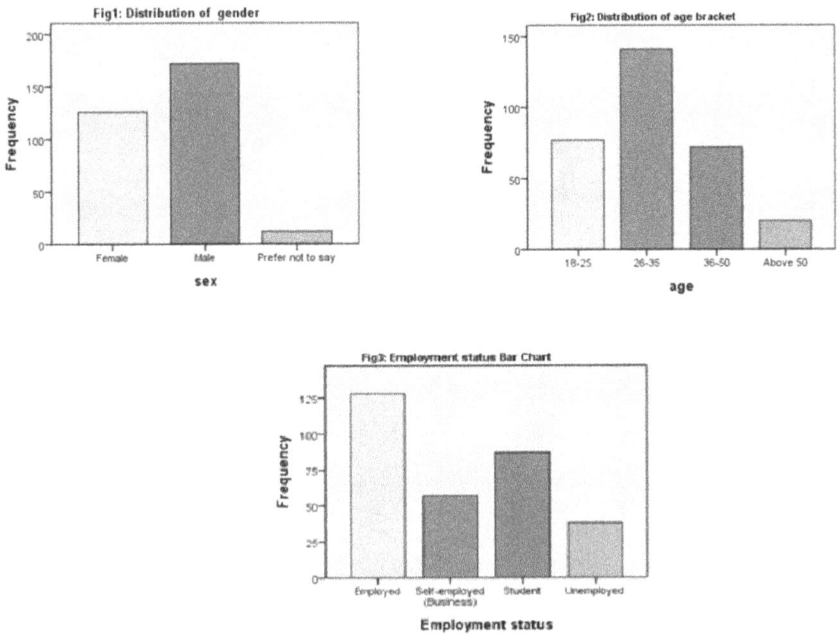

Figure 6.1 Graphical Presentation of Sociodemographic Characteristics of Respondents. *Source*: Self-generated by the Authors.

Various Forms of Human Rights Abuses/Restrictions Occasioned by COVID-2019 Pandemic in Nigeria

Based on table 6.2, table 6.3 shows the status of all the civil and social rights tested. The table reveals that all of the rights tested were abused during the COVID-2019 lockdown in Nigeria.

Level of Human Rights Abuses/Restrictions Occasioned by COVID-2019 Pandemic in Nigeria

Derived from additive index of all constructs measuring human rights abuses during COVID-2019 lockdown in Nigeria, table 6.4 shows the level of such abuses resulting from restrictions during this period. The total obtainable score is 52, therefore respondents with score below average, that is, below 26 were categorized as having low level of human rights abuse during COVID-2019 lockdown in Nigeria, otherwise, they experienced high level of human rights abuse. Consequently, while about 37 percent of respondents in this survey experienced low level of human rights, 63 percent experienced high level of human rights violations.

Table 6.2 Frequency Distribution Tables of Respondents for Human Rights Abuses/Restrictions during COVID-2019 Lockdown in Nigeria

Response	*Neutral (0)*	*Strongly Disagree (1)*	*Disagree (2)*	*Agree (4)*	*Strongly Agree (5)*	*Total N (%)*	*Mean (SD)*
1. I feel my right to worship in the community of others was violated during COVID-2019 lockdown	55(17.7)	57(18.4)	72(23.2)	97(31.3)	29(9.4)	310(100)	1.9(1.2)
2. I was maltreated or detained by law enforcement agents for violating COVID-2019 lockdown rules	52(16.8)	115(37.1)	28(9)	98(31.6)	17(5.5)	310(100)	1.5(1.0)
3. I know/heard of someone maltreated or detained by law enforcement agents for violating COVID-2019 lockdown rules	32(10.3)	43(13.9)	122(39.4)	33(10.6)	80(25.8)	310(100)	2.6(1.3)
4. I was tortured for violating COVID-2019 lockdown rules	46(14.8)	137(44.2)	17(5.5%)	102(32.9)	8(2.6)	310(100)	1.4(0.9)
5. I know/heard of someone tortured for violating COVID-2019 lockdown rules	31(10)	47(15.2)	124(40)	43(13.9)	65(21)	310(100)	2.5(1.3)
6. I know/heard of someone killed for violating COVID-2019 lockdown rules	52(16.8)	90(29)	57(18.4)	68(21.9)	43(13.9)	310(100)	1.8(1.3)
7. I feel my freedom of movement was abused during COVID-2019 lockdown	30(9.7)	44(14.2)	116(37.4)	64(20.6)	56(18.1)	310(100)	2.4(1.2)
8. I feel my freedom of association was violated during COVID-2019 lockdown	34(11)	49(15.8)	101(32.6)	66(21.3)	60(19.4)	310(100)	2.3(1.3)

9. I feel my right to education is being restricted by COVID-2019 lockdown	41(13.2)	43(13.9)	75(24.2)	55(17.7)	96(31)	310(100)	2.5(1.4)
10. I feel COVID-2019 lockdown rules restricted my liberty	36(11.6)	33(10.6)	114(36.8)	43(13.9)	84(27.1)	310(100)	2.6(1.3)
11. I lost my job because of COVID-2019 lockdown	70(22.6)	100(32.3)	30(9.7)	84(27.1)	26(8.4)	310(100)	1.5(1.2)
12. I know/heard of someone who lost their jobs during COVID-2019 lockdown	21(6.8)	32(10.3)	110(35.5)	16(5.2)	131(42.3)	310(100)	3.0(1.2)
13. I feel all the restrictions during COVID-2019 lockdown were not necessary to contain the spread of the virus	26(8.4)	93(30)	57(18.4)	89(28.7)	45(14.5)	310(100)	2.0(1.2)

SD: Standard Deviation.
Source: Online Survey Conducted by the Author (2020).

Table 6.3 Checklist of Various Human Rights (Civil and Social) Abuses during COVID-2019 Lockdown in Nigeria

Human Rights	*Remarks*
Right to worship in the community of others	Abused
Right not to be arbitrarily detained	Abused
Prohibition against torture and ill-treatment	Abused
Right to life	Abused
Right to liberty	Abused
Freedom of movement	Abused
Right to education	Abused
Freedom of peaceful assembly and association	Abused
Right to freely participate in community	Abused
Right to work and protection against unemployment	Abused

Source: Online Survey Conducted by the Author (2020).

Table 6.4 Level of Human Rights Abuses/Restrictions Occasioned by COVID-2019 Pandemic in Nigeria

Level of Human Rights Abuses/Restrictions	*Frequency (N)*	*Percentage (%)*
Low	114	36.8
High	196	63.2
Total	310	100.0

Source: Online Survey Conducted by the Author (2020).

Also, from table 6.5, it can be seen that the mean rating of the levels of abuse/restriction for all the human rights tested, except for the rights to worship, and to life, is above the criterion mean of 2, indicating that those rights were highly violated/abused during the implementation of COVID-2019 safety and quarantine rules in Nigeria. Nevertheless, while the personal experiences of respondents as touching arbitrary detention, torture, and protection against unemployment are below the criterion mean of 2, indicating low level of abuses from personal experiences, the reports on incidents heard or known by respondents as touching these rights were above the criterion mean of 2, showing that those rights were highly abused, even though they were not experienced by the respondents themselves. On the perception of the respondents on whether the restrictions were not necessary during the lockdown to contain the spread of the pandemic, the score fell below the criterion mean of 2; hence, preponderance of opinion suggests that the restrictions were necessary.

The Gender Most Affected by Human Rights Abuses/ Restrictions Occasioned by COVID-2019 Pandemic in Nigeria

In an attempt to assess the relationship between human rights violations during COVID-2019 lockdown and gender of respondents, table 6.6 reveals that

Table 6.5 The Level of Human Rights Abuses/Restrictions Occasioned by COVID-2019 Pandemic in Nigeria

Response	*Mean*	*Std. Deviation*	*Remarks*
I feel my right to worship in the community of others was violated during COVID-2019	1.9	1.2	Low
I was maltreated or detained by law enforcement agents for violating COVID-2019 lockdown rules	1.5	1.0	Low
I know/heard of someone maltreated or detained by law enforcement agents for violating COVID-2019 lockdown rules	2.6	1.3	High
I was tortured for violating COVID-2019 lockdown rules	1.4	0.9	Low
I know/heard of someone tortured for violating COVID-2019 lockdown rules	2.5	1.3	High
I know/heard of someone killed for violating COVID-2019 lockdown rules	1.8	1.3	Low
I feel my freedom of movement was abused during COVID-2019 lockdown	2.4	1.2	High
I feel my freedom of association was violated during COVID-2019 lockdown	2.3	1.3	High
I feel my right to education is being restricted by COVID-2019 lockdown	2.5	1.4	High
I feel COVID-2019 lockdown rules restricted my liberty	2.6	1.3	High
I lost my job because of COVID-2019 lockdown	1.5	1.2	Low
I know/heard of someone who lost their jobs during COVID-2019 lockdown	3.0	1.2	High
I feel all the restrictions during COVID-2019 lockdown were not necessary to contain the spread of the virus	2.0	1.2	Low

Std. Deviation = Standard Deviation.
Source: Online Survey Conducted by the Author (2020).

Table 6.6 Results from Chi-square Test Showing the Association between Human Rights Abuse and Gender during COVID-2019 Lockdown

	Abuse Level			
Gender	*Low*	*High*	*Total*	*Chi-square*
Female	43(34.1)	83(65.9)	83(100.0)	$\chi^2 = 0.692$
Male	66(38.4)	106(61.6)	172(100.0)	$df = 2$
Prefer not to say	5(41.7)	7(58.3)	129(100.0)	$p = 0.707$
Total	114(36.8)	196(63.2)	310(100.0)	

Source: Online Survey Conducted by the Author (2020).

Table 6.7 Result from ANOVA Showing the Difference in Average Human Rights Abuse by Gender of Respondents during COVID-2019 Lockdown

Gender	*Mean*	F	*Prob* > F
Female	28.1	0.52	0.589
Male	27.8		
Prefer not to say	25.7		
Total	27.8		

Source: Online Survey Conducted by the Author (2020).

with a Chi-square value of 0.692 and a *p*-value (0.707) greater than level of significance (0.05), there is no statistically significant association between gender and human rights abuse during COVID-2019 lockdowns. However, as against the 66 percent of females who experienced high human rights abuse, 62 percent of male respondents had high human rights violations during COVID-2019 lockdown in Nigeria.

Hypothesis Testing

The null and testing hypotheses for this study are the following:

H_0: Females are more affected by human rights abuses/restrictions occasioned by COVID-2019 pandemic in Nigeria
H_1: Females are not more affected by human rights abuses/restrictions occasioned by COVID-2019 pandemic in Nigeria

The results from the ANOVA test shown in table 6.7 reveal the average human rights abuse during COVID-2019 lockdown score for female respondents as 28 while those of males and respondents who preferred not to say as 28 and 26, respectively. Additionally, with *F*-value of 0.52 and a *p*-value of 0.589 which is greater than the level of significance (0.05), there is no statistically significant difference in the average human rights abuse score during the lockdown in Nigeria. In essence, there is not enough evidence to accept the null hypothesis (H_0) and conclude that females are more affected by human rights abuses/restrictions occasioned by COVID-2019 pandemic in Nigeria. I therefore conclude that females were not more affected by human rights abuses/restrictions occasioned by COVID-2019 pandemic in Nigeria.

DISCUSSION OF FINDINGS

The chapter set out to appraise within the Nigerian context, the rate of democratic erosion measured through human rights violations and restrictions in the course of implementing COVID-2019 safety and quarantine rules. This was with the aim to identify the various civil and social human rights abuse/restrictions occasioned by COVID-2019 pandemic in Nigeria, examine the level of such abuses, and determine the gender which was more affected by the abuses/restrictions.

With respect to the civil and social rights abused/restricted during the COVID-2019 safety and quarantine implementation in Nigeria, the chapter finds that the entire 10 of such rights identified by this study were abused during the period. These rights included the right to worship in the community of others, the right not to be arbitrarily detained, prohibition against torture and ill-treatment, the right to life, and right to liberty. Others include freedom of movement, right to education, freedom of peaceful assembly and association, right to freely participate in community, and right to work and protection against unemployment. At least one Nigerian suffered or heard/knew others who suffered at least one of these rights abuses. To the extent that human rights protection has been consistently used to gauge democratic performance, and to know the strength and weakness of democracies (Freedom House, 2019; Gallagher, 2008; Matthews, 2019, p. 7; World Justice Project, 2018), this chapter finds that the Nigerian democracy is weak, as it cannot absorb the type of shock occasioned by COVID-2019 pandemic, resulting in the flagrant abuses and restrictions in human rights. This finding corroborates the ones by Nyei (2020), Diamond (2020), Human Rights Watch (2020a), and Delvac (2020), who observed that the COVID-2019 crisis has resulted in abuses and restriction of civil and social rights across many democracies around the world.

The chapter further reveals that the level of human rights abuses and restrictions occasioned by the implementation of COVID-2019 safety and quarantine rules in Nigeria was high. The high level of abuses was found with all the civil and social rights studied, except the rights to worship, and to life. This high level of abuses was either directly experienced by respondents or they heard or knew someone who suffered such high-level abuses. This finding also aligns with other studies across democracies during the pandemic. For instance, Freedom House (2020), Open Democracy (2020), and Heijmans et al. (2020) found gross abuses in human rights in the Philippines, South Africa, and Mexico. Martinez (2020) also observed high level of human rights abuses in the implementation of COVID-2019 safety and quarantine rules in Brazil. Similar findings were also made about human rights abuses occasioned by the pandemic in India and Britain (Assuncao, 2020; Phillips, 2020; Truong, 2020); the United States and France (Phillips, 2020; Truong, 2020); Bolivia and Poland (Freedom House, 2020; Open Democracy, 2020); and El Salvador, Honduras, and Venezuela (WOLA, 2020).

Specifically, the revelation on the high level of civil and social rights abuses and restrictions occasioned by the COVID-2019 crisis in Nigeria corroborates that of Izuora (2020) and the Punch (May 14, 2020), who observed the arbitrary arrests and/or death of lockdown violators, including the seizure and demolition of commercial private properties in Nigeria. Nyei (2020), Human Rights Watch (2020a), and Delvac (2020) also recorded cases of high-level human rights abuses and restriction in the wake of COVID-2019 pandemic. Shenga (2020) made a similar finding across Eastern and Southern Africa, where emergency measures put in place during COVID-2019 lockdown posed a threat to democracy, with Malawi being the only exemption. The United Nations (2020, p. 8) specifically notes that the COVID-2019 pandemic has resulted in loss of jobs and widespread school closure. This corroborates the high rate of restrictions in the right to work and employment, and the right to education, occasioned by COVID-2019 pandemic in Nigeria.

Also, findings show that there is no significant relationship between human right abuses during the COVID-2019 restrictions in Nigeria and gender. Male and female citizens had roughly equal shares of the high level of abuses in Nigeria. This finding is congruent with the conceptual universalists' idea of human rights which posit that every human (irrespective of gender, age, or race) is entitled to equal human rights on the basis of being a human. Conversely, the finding also allays the doubt of the substantive universalists about whether human rights as contained in the UN Declaration are really equally applicable and guaranteed to everyone, irrespective of age, gender, or race (cf. Donnelly, 2007; Gould, 2004). This study finds that there was no gender-based discrimination with respect to the human right abuses experienced during the COVID-2019 lockdown in Nigeria.

CONCLUSION AND RECOMMENDATIONS

The chapter has been able to appraise the level of civil and social rights abuses and restrictions experienced by citizens in the course of enforcing COVID-2019 safety and quarantine rules in Nigeria. Like in other democracies across the world, the Nigerian democracy could not guarantee the protection of human rights as a result of the COVID-2019 pandemic. Human rights (all of the civil and social rights) were arbitrarily abused and restricted, including the right to life. These revelations suggest that the COVID-2019 pandemic has resulted in democratic erosion in the form of human rights abuses, violations, and restrictions. It also reveals that democracy is still very much fragile in Nigeria, and this is also the case for many democracies around the world, as any little shock as the COVID-2019 crisis presents is capable to disrupt critical democratic tenets like the respect for and protection of human rights. The preponderance of civil and social rights abuses during the COVID-2019 lockdown periods has also exposed the lip service many democratic leaders pay to democratic tenets and revealed their true status as "authoritarian" leaders disguised in democratic systems, as the case of Nigeria and other democracies clearly show in this chapter.

The chapter recommends a recommitment by leaders in democracies across the world and the African continent, including those in Nigeria, to the very germane and critical democratic tenet of the respect for and protection of human rights at all times and in all circumstances. While the United Nations Declaration of Human Rights provides that certain rights could be restricted when a situation threatens the health of the state like the COVID-2019 did, certain rights are, however, "untouchable," regardless. Democratic leaders must thus learn to adhere to this rule and ensure the protection of rights to life, prohibition against torture and ill-treatment, and the right not to be arbitrarily detained in the face of COVID-2019 and any other future pandemics and emergency crisis for that matter. Sadly, all of these "untouchable" rights were abused in the course of implementing the COVID-2019 safety and quarantine rules in Nigeria and many other democracies. Truly, while COVID-2019 poses threat to the health of nations, it does not warrant the killing, torture, ill-treatment, and arbitrary detention of lockdown violators as experienced in the Nigerian democracy and elsewhere.

Like the United Nations advised, restrictions to human rights in periods of emergencies like the COVID-2019 presents must be "necessary, proportionate, non-discriminatory, limited in duration and measures must be in place to guide against excesses." For future occurrences, Nigerian leaders, and indeed, other democratic leaders must learn to put measures in place to guide against such excesses experienced in the course of implementing COVID-2019 safety and quarantine rules. Citizens must also learn to obey, as much as possible, safety and quarantine rules laid down by democratic governments in times of national and/or global emergencies to safeguard their health and lives. By so doing, the cases of excesses and human rights abuses in the implementation process will be reduced to a minimum.

While this chapter has appraised democratic erosion in the wake of COVID-2019 crisis, the focus is largely on the Nigerian democracy. Future research intervention could expand this scope to cut across several democracies, most likely in comparative perspective. Also, whereas this chapter has focused on the violation and abuses in civil and social rights, the author is not oblivion of the fact that democracy goes beyond the protection of human rights to include other issues like periodic, free, fair, and credible elections, among other issues. Future research endeavors should attempt to expand the scope further to cover these other issues. Furthermore, although human rights cut across civil, political, economic, social, and cultural rights, this chapter has beamed the light on civil and social rights abuses. This could be extended to political, economic, and cultural rights in future research attempts.

REFERENCES

Assuncao, M. (March 21, 2020). Hefty fines, jail time, expulsion: How governments around the world are dealing with people who ignore quarantine orders. *New York Daily News*. Retrieved on August 20, 2020 from https://www.nydailynews.com/coronavirus/ny-coronavirus-hefty-fines-jail-time-expulsion-quarantine-orders-20200321-03ucbid5vvhsxkcbzahpikcqci-story.html.

Davis, K. E., Kingsbury, B. and Merry, S. (2012). Introduction: global governance by indicators. In K. Davis, A. Fisher, B. Kingsbury and S. E. Merry (eds.), *Governance by Indicators: Global Power through Quantification and Rankings*. Oxford, UK: Oxford University Press.

Delvac, K. S. (2020). Human rights abuses in the enforcement of Coronavirus security measures. *The National Law Review x* (213). Retrieved on August 10, 2020 from https://www.natlawreview.com/article/human-rights-abuses-enforcement-coronavirus-security-measures.

Diamond, L. (June 13, 2020). Democracy versus the pandemic: The Coronavirus is emboldening autocrats the world over. *Foreign Affairs*. Retrieved on September 10, 2020 from https://www.foreignaffairs.com/articles/world/2020-06-13/democracy-versus-pandemic.

Donnelly, J. (2007). The relative universality of human rights. *Human Rights Quarterly* 29:281–306.

Evans, T. (2001). If democracy, then human rights? *Third World Quarterly* 22(4):623–642.

France 24. (March 28, 2020). Virus prevention measures turn violent in parts of Africa. *France 24*. Retrieved on September 20, 2020 from https://www.france24.com/en/20200328virus-prevention-measures-turn-violent-in-parts-of-africa.

Freedom House. (2019). Freedom in the world: 2019. Retrieved on August 30, 2020 from https://freedomhouse.org/report/freedom-world/freedom-world-2019.

Freedom House. (May 14, 2020). Bolivia: Supreme decree threatens freedom of expression. Retrieved on August 28, 2020 from https://freedomhouse.org/article/bolivia-supreme-decree-threatens-freedom-expression.

Gallagher, A. (2008). *The United Nations, Democracy and Human Rights*. Oslo, Norway: The Norwegian Center for Human Rights.

Gould, C. (2004). *Globalizing Democracy and Human Rights*. New York: Cambridge University Press.

Heijmans, P. J., Pradhan, B. and Bax, P. (April 2, 2020). Locked in cages, beaten and shamed: Virus laws lead to abuses. *Bloomberg*. Retrieved on August 30, 2020 from https://www.msn.com/en-us/news/world/locked-in-cages-beaten-and-shamed-virus-laws-lead-to-abuses/ar-BB122Uas?ocid=spartandhp.

Hill, D. (2016). Democracy and the concept of personal integrity rights. *The Journal of Politics*. 78(3):822–835.

Human Rights Watch. (April 14, 2020). *Covid-19 offers chance to address human rights concerns. Human Rights Watch*. Retrieved on September 20, 2020 from https://www.hrw.org/news/2020/04/14/covid-19-offers-chance-address-human-rights-concerns.

Izuora, Y. (May 14, 2020). Civil society coalition fights Rivers governor for subverting rule of law. *Oriental News*. Retrieved on September 30, 2020 from https://orientalnewsng.com/civil-society-coalition-fights-rivers-governor-for-subverting-rule-of-law/.

Kirchschlaeger, P. G. (2014). The relation between democracy and human rights. *Globalistics and Globalization Studies* 2014:112–125.

Koch, I. E. (2005). Dichotomies, trichotomies, or waves of duties? *Human Right Law Review* 5(1):81–103.

Kurki, M. (2011). Human rights and democracy promotion: Reflections on the contestation in, and the political-economic dynamics of rights promotion. *Third World Quarterly* 32(9):1573–1587.

Landman, T. (2018). Democracy and human rights: Concepts, measures and relationships. *Politics and Governance* 6(1):48–59.

Landman, T. and Kersten, L. (2016). Measuring human rights. In Goodhart, M. (ed.), *Human Rights Politics and Practice* (3rd ed.). Oxford, UK: Oxford University Press.

Martinez, J. (April 9, 2020). In Columbia, citizens are bound by their feet for quarantine violation. *The Rio Times*. Retrieved on September 30, 2020 from https://www.ritimesonline.com/brazil-news/Mercosur/in-columbia-citizens-are-bound-by-their-feet-for-quarantine-violation/.

Matthews, T. (2019). *To Be Equal and Free: The Nexus between Human Rights and Democracy*. Berlin, Germany: Heinrich-Boll-Stiftung Foundation.

Merry, S. (2011). Measuring the world: Indicators, human rights, and global governance. *Current Anthropology* 52(3):83–95.

Nyei, I. A. (May 27, 2020). The use of emergency powers during COVID-19 and its implications for stability in Africa. *ACCORD*. Retrieved on September 11, 2020 from https://www.accord.org.za/analysis/the-use-of-emergency-powers-during-covid-19-and-its-implications-for-stability-in-africa/.

Open Democracy. (2020). The Coronavirus crisis affects us all. Retrieved on September 28, 2020 from https://www.opendemocracy.net/en/corona-virus-crackdown-democracy

Payne, L. (2000). *Uncivil Movements: The Armed Right Wing and Democracy in Latin America*. Baltimore, MD: John Hopkins University Press.

Perelman, M. (May 15, 2020). Some governments 'using' Covid-19 to stifle dissent, UN human rights chief warns. *France 24*. Retrieved on September 20, 2020 from https://www.france24.com/en/20200515-some-governments-using-covid-19-to-stiffle-dissent-un-human-rights-chief-warns.

Phillips, K. (May 3, 2020). Police agencies are using drones to enforce stay-at-home orders, raising concerns among civil rights groups. *USA Today*. Retrieved on August 30, 2020 from https://www.usatoday.com/story/news/politics/2020/05/03/coronavirus-police-use-drones-enforcement-privacy-concerns/305907300/.

Punch. (May 14, 2020). Lockdown: Protesters reopen Mosques in Guinea. Retrieved on September 30, 2020 from https://punchng.com/lockdown-protesters-reopen-mosques-in-huinea/.

Research Advisors. (2006) Sample size table. Retrieved on August 25, 2020 from http://research-advisors.com/tools/SampleSize.htm.

Shenga, C. (2020). *The Risk of Covid-19 Pandemic Emergency Measures to Democratic Standards in Eastern and Southern Africa*. Maputo, Mozambique: Center for Research on Governance and Development.

Truong, M. (2020). Media restrictions today will harm democracy tomorrow. *Freedom House*. Retrieved on September 30, 2020 from https://freedomhouse.org/article/media-restrictions-today-will-harm-democracy-tomorrow.

United Nations. (1949). *Universal Declaration of Human Rights*. Geneva, Switzerland: United Nations.

United Nations. (September 28, 1984). UN Commission on Human Rights, the Siracusa Principles on the limitation and derogation provisions in the international covenant on civil and political rights. E/CN.4/1985/4. Retrieved on September 30, 2020 from https://www.refworld.org/docid/4672bc122.html.

United Nations. (1993). *World Conference on Human Rights: Vienna Declaration and Program of Action*. 32 I.L.M.1667. Geneva, Switzerland: United Nations.

United Nations. (September 15, 2009). Guidance note of the Secretary General on democracy. Retrieved on September 21, 2020 from https://www.un.org/democracyfund/sites/www.un.org.democracyfund/files_attach/UNSG%20Guidance%20Note%20on%20Democracy-EN.pdf.

United Nations OCHR. (2012). *Human Rights Indicators: A Guide to Measurement and Implementation*. Geneva, Switzerland: United Nations.

United Nations. (2020). *Covid-19 and Human Rights: We Are All in This Together*. Geneva, Switzerland: United Nations.

V-Dem. (2020). *Democracy Report 2020: Autocratisation Surges, Resistance Grows*. Gothenburg, Sweden: Democracy Institute.

World Justice Project. (2018). *World Justice Project Rule of Law Index: 2017–2018*. Washington, DC: World Justice Project.

Chapter 7

Corofrontline

Gregory Obinna Ugbo, Henry Chigozie Duru, and Chinwe Beatrice Ezeoke

The scourge of the Coronavirus Disease (COVID)-2019 pandemic is unprecedented in recent global disease outbreaks and has exposed the limit of the human competencies in handling disease outbreaks (Verhoeven, Tsakitzidis, Philips and Royen, 2020). At the forefront of containing the ravaging impact of the virus are healthcare providers that mediate between the members of public and the health challenges wrought by the pandemic, thereby suggesting the imperative of people-oriented communication (both verbal and nonverbal). This chapter therefore seeks to interrogate how the frontline workers' communicative behaviors in terms of dressing, expressing personal concerns over their own safety, and general attitude to work may have shaped patients' responses to their condition.

The content of this chapter is purely theoretical and relied on testimonies of COVID-2019 survivors in Nigeria, as reported in the mainstream and social media, to theorize patients' experiences within the context of their interactions and/or communication with healthcare providers in an uncertain health emergency. Again, in the context of this chapter, the term "frontline workers" is used interchangeably with "healthcare providers/workers/givers" which include the doctors, nurses, midwives, pharmacists, and other medical personnel who render direct health services to patients in hospitals. Before delving into the main discourse, however, it makes sense to first discuss the concept of communication that undergirds the analysis.

THE CONCEPT OF COMMUNICATION

Communication is an ever-present and inevitable component of social life. As a concept, it has been differently defined by various scholars (Okunna and Omenugha, 2012; Daramola, 2003). This multiplicity and variety of definitions stem from the multidimensional and dynamic nature of communication. Basically, communication is an interaction that results in exchange of information, ideas, feelings, emotions, knowledge, and understanding between individuals (Okunna and Omenugha, 2012; Baran, 2010). Berry (2007) describes communication as a bridge to a relationship that requires the parties to have a shared understanding of meanings ascribed to words, sounds, and gestures. In a nutshell, communication is a means to a common understanding.

Humans communicate in a number of complex ways, which broadly speaking can be verbal or non-verbal. While verbal messages involve the use of words (spoken or written), non-verbal messages can be transmitted through body postures, facial expressions, gestures, symbols, colors, and even clothing, all of which communicate loads of meaning (Okunna and Omenugha, 2012; Rogers, 1996, as cited in Berry, 2007). Similarly, communication can be symmetrical (two-way) or asymmetrical (one-way or top-down). In a symmetrical communication, there is a shared sense of equal engagement such that the individuals involved in the communicative act have control over the flow of the conversation. In 1954, American psychologist Charles Osgood espoused what became a classical model of two-way symmetrical communication. There he conceived ideal communication as happening in a dialogic context where each of the two parties is at the same time the sender and the receiver. Stated differently, the model eliminates the rigid boundary between the sender and the receiver as the two parties alternate between the two roles: one originates while the other receives at this moment, and the next moment, the initial receiver becomes the originator and vice versa (Daramola, 2003).

On the other hand, asymmetrical communication is top-down or unidirectional where power dynamics are more emphatically expressed (Fairclough, 1989). A typical example is where a boss is giving instruction to a subordinate or the sort of chain of commands in regimented organizations like the military or police force. The kind of communication in a conference, seminar, or workshop where an individual talks to others and where there may not be opportunities for interaction can also be classified as an asymmetrical communication.

THE ROLE OF COMMUNICATION IN HEALTHCARE

No aspect of human social life can exist outside the possibilities and limitations created by communication given that communication is the ultimate enabler of social interaction. Therefore, healthcare, as a social endeavor, integrally involves communication in various ways and forms (Ha and

Longnecker, 2010). When we discuss communication within the health sector as an exchange of message between healthcare givers and patients or their relatives, we are concerned with how the actors, through such exchange, create the messages that inform and shape their lives (Stay and Ruben, 2015). Broadly speaking, such communication may be verbal, non-verbal, or simultaneously both (Berry, 2007).

Effective communication plays a vital role in healthcare delivery. Hence, among the six competency areas in medical practice as introduced by the Accreditation Council for Graduate Medical Education, three center on communication skills. Discussing this prime place of communication in clinical context, Jahan and Siddiqui (2019) observe that communication between a doctor and a patient critically influences health outcomes. Consequently, such communication ought to be very robust and comprehensive. The authors argue that when there is a good communication between a patient and a healthcare provider, patient's satisfaction is enhanced. This submission is quite persuasive. Thus, the "art of medicine is intricately tied to the art of communication" and "communication is central in patient-doctor interactions" (Teutsch, 2003). Previous studies indicate that a properly managed doctor-patient relationship has the potency to contribute to patient's management of deadly diseases, for example, diabetes, especially when it includes involving the patient in decision-making (DiMatteo, 1997; Suchman, Branch and Matthews, 1995; Suchman and Matthews, 1988; Greenfield et al., 1988). Agreeing with this submission, Stay and Ruben (2015) note that effective communication generally results in patient's willingness to disclose personal information, improved accuracy in diagnosis and treatment, improved connection and interaction between patients and healthcare givers, increased effectiveness in utilizing available medical facilities and healthcare options, better adherence or commitment in treatment regimens or prescriptions, improved clinical outcomes, and fostering of general well-being and improved health. Teutsch (2003) lists the components of effective communication to include the following: (a) setting the right tone, (b) interpreting communication cues accurately, and (c) listening actively.

Notably, communication in healthcare contexts is unique in its strategy and goal; it is professionally and systematically guided and aimed at engendering the best medical outcome for the patient. Importantly, it is intimate and involving a great deal of trust (Chandra, Mohammadnezhad and Ward, 2018). One of the common experiences of any individual in need of medical care is that they get to meet a doctor and/or any other healthcare service provider. Their meeting inevitably results in communication—a solicitation of information (from the doctor or healthcare provider), the giving out of the same (by the patient), and an expert opinion reply to the information received. At this point, one of the core areas of the medical profession has been established.

Beyond verbal and (non-verbal) communication, a relationship between two persons (who might be strangers to each other) has been formed: one where there is need for some level of intimacy up to that of physical examination of the patient's body (Adelman, Greene and Ory, 2000).

What physician-patient communication entails is far from just a lab-coated person and a sick person chattering away, rather, it is a well-calculated effort geared toward patient's satisfaction and in the long run, the delivery of quality healthcare. The ability of a doctor or any other healthcare provider to gather useful information on how a patient feels will help in correct diagnosis, treatment, and further counseling. Hence, patient-healthcare giver communication is fundamentally a problem-solving transaction. Thus, such communication may also be termed *therapeutic communication* being that it "is intended to help patients/clients cope with problems, relate with another, adapt to what cannot be changed, and face obstacles to one's self-realization" (Igbinlade et al., 2020, p. 1). It is also for this reason that the role of communication in healthcare has been described by scholars as both a problem and potential solution (Stay and Ruben, 2015). When efficiently managed, it provides solution, but when the reverse is the case, problem results. Hence, professional and academic literature has variously viewed communication as a symptom, partial cause, and potential cure to patients' medical conditions (Chandra et al., 2018; Berry, 2007). From the potential solution perspective, healthcare providers who communicate well with patients achieve more positive medical outcomes and create an overall satisfaction in patients, themselves, and patients' relatives (Berry, 2007). Through efficient communication, such elements of healthy interpersonal relationship, including empathy, tolerance, and non-judgmental listening, are enhanced and these are consistent with healthcare giver's experiences in practice. Where the professional bond that ordinarily should exist between patients and their healthcare givers is lacking, relationship and opportunities for a satisfactory health service delivery will be strained (Steinmetz and Tabenin, 2001).

Importantly, communication in healthcare contexts is ideally not a one-off thing, but aimed at building a relationship between a patient and the healthcare giver. This relationship is imperative given the often continuous, intimate, and trust-based nature of clinical services. Through such relationship, healthcare workers are able to elicit a greater level of cooperation from the patients who are now actively involved as equal partners in their own treatment. Good communication builds confidence and greater level of rapport between patients and healthcare givers which is required for relaxed medical procedures (Ha and Longnecker, 2010; Berry, 2007). Extant research evidence suggests that healthcare givers and patients' relationship have a psychological impact on patients' recovery (Ruchinskas and Alonzo, 2005). Effective communication goes a long way in lubricating the relationship, and by implication, brings about general satisfaction in health services delivered and obtained. Thus, literature in medical sciences has identified the therapeutic effect of cordial and mutual communication between patients and healthcare givers (Ruchinskas and Alonzo, 2005). Healthy doctor-patient relationship is fostered and established through appropriate communication skills (Steinmetz and Tabenin, 2001).

But how may healthcare providers bring about this effective communication, cordial relationship, and consequently patients' satisfaction? Beck et al. (2002) did an extensive review on the role of communication in medical care. They highlighted the relevance of previous works on the verbal and non-verbal behaviors of physicians in primary healthcare settings and went on to list the following behaviors that had been linked to patient satisfaction: the ability to understand a patient's situation, courtesy, friendliness, reassurance, support, encouragement, giving more explanations, laughing and joking to release tension (Beck et al., 2002). From these studies, it is safe to state that patients need to be comfortable with discussing their issues with their healthcare providers. To give them the assurance that they are in safe hands, healthcare providers can only get better at communicating with them.

Worthy of note is the fact that certain patients may prove particularly difficult to handle. This may be as a result of the patient's medical condition, unusual expectations, demands, temperament, or emotions, which may make the client more difficult to handle than an average patient. Fortunately, good communication is an effective panacea here. Compatibility analysis conducted by Steinmetz and Tabenin (2001) concluded that strong communication skills are vital in building trust and coping with difficult patients. Patients under different conditions react and respond differently to treatments. The reactions could range from violent agitation, aggression, verbally abusive, unsolved repeated complaints, high level of anxiety, and outright indifference or withdrawal in responding to diagnostic investigations. When healthcare givers are confronted with some of the difficult reactions from patients, communication becomes a bridge of understanding between them.

CONSEQUENCES OF INEFFECTIVE COMMUNICATION IN HEALTHCARE DELIVERY

As earlier admitted, while communication will significantly advance healthcare when appropriately and competently managed, it could achieve the opposite when the reverse is the case (Jahan and Siddiqui, 2019; Chandra et al., 2018). For one, badly managed communication between a patient and a healthcare giver could upset calmness and cooperative disposition of a patient. It takes a relaxed patient to interact with their healthcare providers meaningfully. Patients who are already stressed out and anxious about their health conditions will naturally relapse in confusion or hysteria with a healthcare giver that lacks adequate communication skills to address their conditions.

Other consequences of poor communication include patients' withdrawal from an ongoing medical procedure or not seeking further medical services in case of new developments in health conditions; patients not disclosing vital health information that would have aided treatment and services; patients showing unwillingness to comply with prescriptions or recommended health behavior and treatment; and in extreme cases poor communication can result in more complications leading to trauma, depression, and death (Berry, 2007). According to Berry (2007), effective communication entails "imparting the right information, to the right people, in the right way, at the right time" (p. 4). Therefore, the goal of the communicative relationship between the physician and the patient is to provide better healthcare. Correct drug prescriptions from physicians are helpful for recovery from ailments, but patient dissatisfaction arising from poor communication of the way they actually feel to these physicians or healthcare providers has been known from previous studies to hamper this smooth recovery process (Jahan and Siddiqui, 2019; Chandra et al., 2018).

Unfortunately, the manner of communication between doctors and patients is still a major cause of patient dissatisfaction. Interestingly, most complaints about doctors concern poor communication and failure to listen, rather than competence or more technical aspects of consultations (Chandra et al., 2018).

FACTORS AFFECTING COMMUNICATION IN HEALTHCARE

Communication does not occur in a vacuum. Like every other social process, it is entrapped in a complex web of social variables that condition and are conditioned by it (Okunna and Omenugha, 2012; Baran, 2010; McQuail, 2010; Daramola, 2003). Here we will be concerned with those variables that need to be understood and controlled by healthcare givers toward optimizing communication as a component of health service delivery. These include (a) sensitivity of health condition; (b) language, culture, and demographics; (c) balance of power; and (d) mediation.

Sensitivity of Health Condition

Certain health situations pose greater sensitivity than others. A typical case is communicable diseases where the need to balance the safety of healthcare workers with the need to avoid stigmatization of patients inevitably creates tensions of values. In the case of COVID-2019, for instance, the patient may feel the burden of isolation and social distance, if not stigmatization, especially as they are confronted with healthcare givers veiled in personal protective equipment (PPE), while the healthcare provider may also have to deal with the two competing instincts of self-preservation and optimal care delivery (Verhoeven, Tsakitzidis, Philips and Royen, 2020). Besides the communicable factor, severity of a disease is also an important variable heightening sensitivity in patient-caregiver communication. Diseases that involve much suffering or with a clear risk of death are more likely to heighten anxiety in patients, so demand greater communication skills on the part of the caregiver. Arguably, COVID-2019 poses such challenge (Verhoeven et al., 2020). Similarly, certain health services pose particular challenge to patient-healthcare giver communication due to the privacy of the focus of the engagement. An example is pregnancy and sexuality-related services where the healthcare provider will ideally be systematic and cautious in handling communication to as much as possible minimize intrusion (Fairclough, 1989).

Language, Culture, and Demographics

The three related variables of language, culture, and demographics also influence communication between a patient and a healthcare giver (Steinmetz and Tabenin, 2001). Language plays a part in effective communication and so does culture (Cioffi, 2003). Patients are not a monolith; they are a heterogeneous set of human beings, with different backgrounds, cultures, educational qualifications, and belief systems. The need for the healthcare provider to prepare for encounters with such varied people cannot be overemphasized. The healthcare giver needs to communicate with them and at their level too.

A study done in Australia primarily concerning the communication of nurses with patients that were of different cultures and spoke other languages, other than English, showed how frustrating it could be for both the nurses who would love to explain medical procedures in English to non-English-speaking patients and the culturally and linguistically diverse patients who would love to better explain to the nurses how bad they feel or how painful a procedure is for them (Cioffi, 2003). Findings of the study underscore the need for better communication, hence its recommendations of heavier involvement of bilingual nurses in Australian hospitals and maternity houses. Another study in Spain by Pino-Postigo (2017) shows how language differences between doctors and foreign patients affect treatment and eventual recovery. The study confirmed that a Spanish doctor's diagnosis of a foreign patient's ailment can be hindered in a situation where the interview begins in Spanish and slowly transitions to English, because the patient is not well versed in Spanish. Then at some point, there's a complete breakdown in communication due to the confusion that has arisen from the language switching. It ends up affecting the diagnosis because some vital details were missed in the process. Similarly, a study that compared the level of satisfaction gained from race-concordant and race-discordant medical visits of African Americans to physicians in the United States showed a huge level of disparity between the time spent during such medical visits to White physicians and those of the African American race. Results showed race-concordant visits (i.e., between members of the same race) were longer and yielded better health results. However, this was not really a matter of differences in ethnic affiliations, but more of the physician's personal decision and ability to communicate better. Medical visits that had physicians discussing on a common cultural plane, for example, what is happening in the economy or the neighborhood, surely had better care results, as did patient participation in decision-making (Cooper et al., 2003).

Age has also been established as an influential demographic variable in patient-healthcare giver communication. A study explored the realities of physician communication with older patients. There happened to be an existing anomaly with handling older people. The study referred to this as *Ageism*—that is, a system of belittling old people's situation and which (the study claims) is prevalent in the medical profession (Adelman et al., 2000). It can be seen in the way their sicknesses are not dealt with as vigorously as those of younger patients, as well as the tendency to carelessly attribute their illnesses to old age, instead of getting results from a proper diagnosis. The study found that there were a couple of inhibitors to a smooth, mutually beneficial physician-older patient interaction. One of the inhibitors is that there is the prevalence of the "third-person in the medical encounter" who always accompanies the older patient to the medical visits. According to Adelman et al. (1987), it is either the "third person" is an advocate, a passive participant, or an antagonist. The latter not being beneficial to the physician-older patient interaction at all. The study concluded that there is an obvious need to re-strategize when communicating with older patients. Elsewhere, there is also empirical evidence of under-disclosure of fact on the part of old people during clinical consultation. A survey of 200 older diabetic patients on a medical visit shows that 50 percent of them did not disclose medical topics they were really pressed to discuss, while 60 percent did not get to discuss important psychosocial matters (Rost and Frankel, 1993). All these indicate the need for enhanced strategies in communicating with older patients.

In a nutshell, demographics are of significant impact on patient-healthcare giver communication. It influences behavior of both the parties as well as impacts understanding and trust (Chandra, Mohammadnezhad and Ward, 2018).

Balance of Power

As earlier noted, relationships are established in the course of a patient's interaction with a healthcare giver, mainly through communication. This relationship, to a large extent, shapes the dispositions and expectations of the parties in the communicative engagement. However, the type of relationship that emerges is typically asymmetrical, meaning that power and expertise are usually not evenly distributed in such interactions and engagements (Molina-Mula and Gallo-Estrada, 2020; Kędzior, 2015; Stay and Ruben, 2015). In clinical settings, doctors and other health personnel occupy a special position of power and respect given their exclusive claim to expertise in health service matters (Stay and Ruben, 2015; Ha and Longnecker, 2010). This unequal relationship tends to largely exclude the patient in the process of appraising and taking decisions on the patient's condition (Molina-Mula and Gallo-Estrada, 2020; Kędzior, 2015; Stay and Ruben, 2010; Fairclough, 1989). Molina-Mula and Gallo-Estrada (2020) observe that nurses have been found to treat their patients as "passive subjects" who should only be seen but not heard. This philosophy of clinical communication and engagement has been termed the biomedical approach as against the humanistic approach. The biomedical approach views patient-healthcare giver communication from the narrow perspective that considers the healthcare giver as possessing unimpeachable expertise and unquestionable moral authority to diagnose and prescribe treatment to a "helpless" patient. The humanistic approach, on the other hand, views the healthcare giver as empathetically working with the patient to get a complete understanding of their condition. In the former case, the healthcare giver talks *to* the patient, while in the latter, the healthcare giver talks *with* the patient (Pino-Postigo, 2017).

Hence, the intricacies of this imbalance and power play need to be fully understood to improve the overall quality of healthcare available to patients for a better clinical outcome. Molina-Mula and Gallo-Estrada (2020) in this vein argue that balance of power in the patient-healthcare giver communication enables the patient have a say in the decisions taken, while the health professional acts more like a witness who observes the patient's experience while offering useful professional guidance. This approach aligns with the contemporary perspective to communication which recognizes the empowered audience who has the agency and autonomy in the communicative contract. In other words, patients are not merely passive recipients of medical information, rather, they actively engage in creating messages and meanings that best suit their health needs and aspirations (Dunu and Ugbo, 2018; Okunna and Omenugha, 2012; McQuail, 2010; Berry, 2007).

The imperative of paying attention to the problem of power dynamics in clinical communication is heightened by the fact that patients have, more than ever, become empowered to seek out health information on their own. This is made possible by the availability of the Internet with its limitless pool of health resources, many of which are presented in a manner that will suit the comprehension of non-experts. As such, doctors no longer enjoy that monopoly as the sole purveyors of health communication that the patient must consult. As rightly stated by Stay and Ruben (2015), "the consumer community has already become quite multidisciplinary in its use of health sources, services, and settings." Consequently, the top-down asymmetric orientation to communication will not always suit the present-day clinical setting where the patient is getting increasingly sophisticated.

Unfortunately, most communications in the health setting are hierarchical with the senior doctors dominating in the interactions (Berry, 2007). The prevailing top-down (doctor for instance talking 'to' and not 'with' patients) communication pattern in hospitals negates the stark reality of today's active audience in the communication setting. In such instances, communication outcomes are essentially shaped by the "predispositions and susceptibilities" of the receiver (who is the patient or the patient's family) rather than the message sender (the healthcare givers) (Stay and Ruben, 2015).

Mediation

In communication context, mediation refers to a situation whereby a message does not get to its target directly but reaches them through a medium. In this case, what occurs is known as *mediated communication*. The medium can be radio, television, phone, and the Internet, among others (Okunna and Omenugha, 2012; McQuail, 2010). The advancement in the information and communication technologies, especially the Internet, has led to the availability of mediated alternatives to the physical face-to-face contacts between patients and their healthcare providers in a conventional hospital setting. Thus, telemedicine is becoming an influential new culture in the health service sector (Zayapragassazan and Kumar, 2016). While this innovation is definitely solving problems of cost and distance, there is a concern as to its effect in the patient-healthcare giver communication being that where physical presence is dispensed with, intimacy, trust, and correct diagnosis can be adversely affected (Gillman-Wells, Sankar and Vadodaria, 2020). In a nutshell, presence or absence of mediation is a critical factor in the outcome of any communication between health personnel and patients.

PATIENTS-HEALTHCARE PROVIDERS' COMMUNICATION: COVID-2019 AS A SPECIAL CASE

The COVID-2019 which started as a mere outbreak in Wuhan, China, eventually took the world by storm and off guard as it quickly metamorphosed to the scale of a global pandemic. On January 30, 2020, the World Health Organization (WHO) declared it as a Public Health Emergency of International Concern (WHO, 2020b). Today, virtually all nations of the world are engaged in the fight against the disease.

But why does COVID-2019 merit a special consideration in the discourse of patient-healthcare giver communication? The first reason, of course, is the monumental challenge posed by the disease. It has a high infection rate with one not needing a direct physical contact with a carrier to become infected. This further results in rapid growth in the number of cases with the attendant stress on health facilities, bringing to question human capacity to contend with some of the existential challenges confronting it. In fact, as earlier observed, the challenge posed by COVID-2019 to health infrastructure globally is unprecedented in history (Verhoeven et al., 2020). This situation will most likely shake patients' faith in the ability of the health system to provide the direly needed succor. These, combined with the absence of any proven cure as well as continuous deaths recorded from the pandemic, create and sustain a pervading atmosphere of anxiety with potentially serious effect on the efficacy of patient-healthcare giver communication. As has been noted, seriousness and likely outcome of a health condition are a strong variable shaping the atmosphere and hence the result of clinical communication.

Also, a strong factor here is the novelty of COVID-2019. Epidemiological information was still emerging and with uncertainties here and there, especially in the early days of the pandemic, thus heightening the "fear of the unknown." This situation immerses in the trending tales of woes and deaths to intensify tensions and create a communication challenge in the face of people's anxiousness to understand what is happening (Rubinelli, Myers, Rosenbaum and Davis, 2020). Evidently, an individual who contracts the disease is most likely to have even a worse personal experience of these pervading social tensions, and which will definitely impact the orientation of their communication with healthcare providers.

The foregoing brings to scrutiny the communicative competencies of health professionals. There is now a large body of empirical evidence to show that healthcare providers who communicate well with patients make more accurate and complete diagnoses, are more likely to detect distress in patients, and keep patients more satisfied and less anxious (Reuben, 2016; Berry, 2007). Their patients are also more likely to follow recommended advice and treatments, and have improved health indices and recovery rates (Molina-Mula and Gallo-Estrada, 2020). On the contrary, patients who are already stressed as a result of their illness or anxiety associated with it can easily get agitated and irritated at the same time if the healthcare provider does not create the best impression in the first place (Teutsch, 2003). Similarly, when healthcare givers experience prolonged engagement in their duty post, stress may set in and could negatively affect their relationship and communication with patients (Adams and Walls, 2020). No doubt, COVID-2019 care got many healthcare workers engaged beyond their normal duty routines.

Incidentally, research efforts and discourses have focused on the experiences of healthcare givers who risk their lives amid a lack of adequate protection in the face of deadly disease outbreaks, including COVID-2019 (Gillman-Wells et al., 2020; Liu et al., 2020; Verhoeven et al., 2020). However, what appears to be lacking is a focus on patients' experiences in their transactions with these health experts. This is very necessary because clinical services are inevitably bilateral; the continuous mutual interaction between patients and experts implies that the experiences of each party invariably impact those of the other. This chapter, therefore, intends to fill this gap by focusing on the communicative experience of COVID-2019 patients. How do patients react to the communication by caregivers? How do they perceive the conduct of caregivers toward them? What is their impression of the caregivers' appearance in the PPE? Do all these increase hysteria and panic in the patients? Or boost the patients' confidence and sense of safety?

THEORETICAL PERSPECTIVES

A number of theoretical perspectives are germane for understanding COVID-2019 patients' role and behavior in the context of the communication occurring between them and healthcare personnel. First is the Symbolic Interactionism Theory which views symbols and their interpretation as the basis of social interaction. By symbols are meant anything to which we attach meaning (Redmond, 2015; Doda, 2005). In the context of COVID-2019 care, symbols will include words, gestures, and any other form of expression from healthcare workers and patients, health workers' kits (by way of PPE), the isolation center, the ward, the drugs, and other procedures administered, as well as any other thing or action which is of communicative value to the actors.

Symbolic Interactionism Theory holds that our actions are determined by the way we "read" (interpret) symbols around us. These symbols constitute our reality, dictating how we react to things and other persons. They are the ultimate stimuli provoking our actions and conducts. In other words, there is no reality outside these symbols; they constitute the mirror through which we view our world. George Herbert Mead, a pioneering figure in the evolution of Symbolic Interactionism Theory, argued that in the course of our daily living, we purposively and creatively respond to our social environment. These responses constitute our "self" and this "self" is a social product—a creation of social stimuli. In other words, the "self" is not entirely self-made but socially created (Griffin, Ledbetter and Sparks, 2015). The implication is that we act based on our perception of the outside world, a perception that may not necessarily correspond with the objective reality (Hewitt, 2002; Dong, 2008; Doda, 2005).

In the course of interactions, social actors do continuously 'reach consensus' on the meanings of symbols. This agreement is what makes mutual understanding possible. Thus, there are no fixed meanings antedating social interactions, rather meanings are products of the social interactions themselves. It is these mutually agreed symbols that are invoked from time to time to bring about communication (Dong, 2008).

Symbolic Interactionism Theory has been applied in the study of patient-healthcare giver relationship to analyze how the parties' interpretation of the other's speech and conduct advances or undermines fruitful engagement (Kędzior, 2015). Hence, in the context of this chapter, this theory becomes useful for understanding how interpretation of symbols by COVID-2019 patients may have affected their reactions in the course of receiving care from health personnel.

Also relevant to COVID-2019 patients' response to cues of healthcare givers in the course of clinical transactions is the Health Belief Model (HBM). The model describes how individuals may or may not be moved to take positive health actions based on the presence of certain factors. It identifies these factors to include, among others, how much a person sees self as vulnerable to a health problem (perceived susceptibility), how much serious they consider such health problem (perceived severity), and how much effective they consider a recommended remedy (perceived benefit of taking action) (Glanz, Rimer and Lewis, 2002; Rosenstock, 1974). In the context of COVID-2019 care, a patient's view as to their susceptibility to whatever damage attendant on being a carrier as well as the severity of such damage (which may include death) will likely influence their reaction to the communicative acts of healthcare provider. The same applies to the patient's perception regarding the benefit of recommended actions. These will be determining factors, first, in the extent of anxiety a patient may suffer, and second, in the patient's willingness to completely rely on and cooperate with healthcare experts who now become the direly needed helpers. More pointedly, the patient's perceived susceptibility and perceived severity regarding their condition are likely to heighten or reduce anxiety, while their perceived benefit of taking recommended actions is as well likely to heighten or reduce trust, receptiveness, and calmness toward the treatment offered.

Therefore, from the perspective of Symbolic Interactionism Theory, these perceptions constitute the patients' interpretations of the relevant symbols as communicative agents, and which will in turn influence their responses to clinical procedures. This way, a meeting point is established between the Symbolic Interactionism Theory and the HBM for the purpose

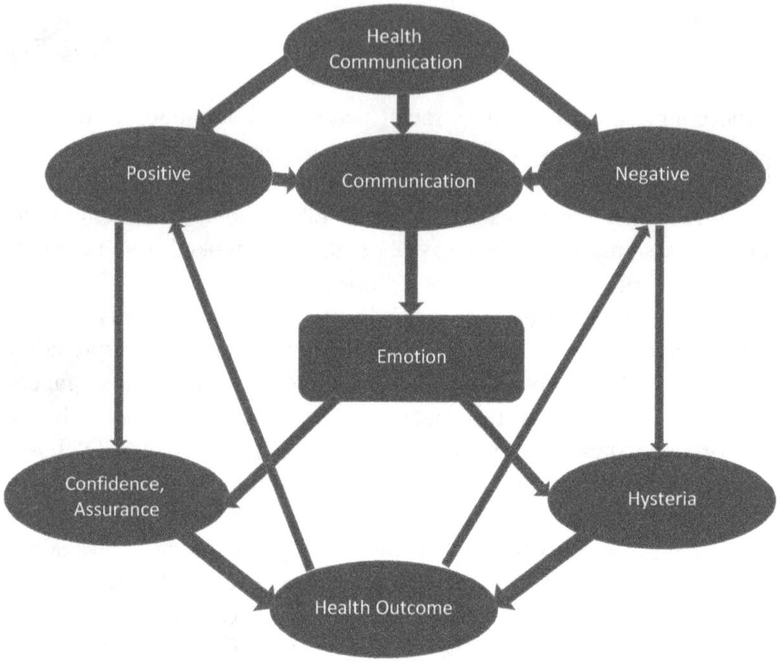

Figure 7.1 Hypothetical Model of Communication Impact in Health Communication. *Source*: Self-generated by the Authors.

of understanding patients' conducts in the context of COVID-2019 clinical communication.

Consequently, the hypothetical model shown in figure 7.1 illustrates the probable outcomes of patient-healthcare providers interactions/communication under certain conditions. It shows that health communication (in the context of patient-healthcare giver interactions) if appropriately managed is likely to lead to positive emotions of confidence and assurance in the patient. On the contrary, if this communication is not properly managed, negative emotions of anxiety, fear, and hysteria become probable.

COVID-2019 CARE, CLINICAL COMMUNICATION, AND PATIENTS' REACTIONS: THE NIGERIAN EXPERIENCE

Nigeria has had her own fair share of the COVID-2019 scourge. As of Monday, November 2, 2020, there were 62,964 confirmed cases of infection in the country. Recorded deaths from the disease stood at 1,146, while 58,790 patients had been treated and discharged; active cases stood at 3,028 (Nigeria

Centre for Disease Control, NCDC, 2020). However, with just 627,600 persons tested in a country of close to 200 million populations, there have been concerns that the infection rate is being grossly underreported. But the bottom line remains that Nigeria, like many other countries, is experiencing the burden of this novel pandemic. In this section, we focus on the communicative experience of patients in their transactions with healthcare givers with a view to understanding how this may have advanced or undermined positive clinical engagement and/or outcome. This will be done under four themes emerging from the reported experiences of patients as follows: (a) the diluted presence, (b) the "hostile" presence, (c) intimacy versus professional distance, and (d) imperative of an expanded communication space.

The Diluted Presence

One significant aspect of the experience of COVID-2019 patients is related to the 'unusual' look/appearance of healthcare givers who, as a matter of safety protocol, must appear in PPE comprising coverall suit, head cover, face cover, goggles, hand gloves, and rubber boots. The kits tended to 'dilute' their presence from the perspective of the patient being that the closeness and intimacy that are natural with face-to-face contact were undermined or diminished. This was evident in the accounts of some of the survivors of COVID-2019.

Emmanuel "Manny" Asika recalled the initial difficulty of coming to terms with healthcare givers "whose faces you cannot see" (Nigerian Health Watch, 2020, p. 1). He described this as "strange" and "difficult to stay with initially." Oluwaseun Ayodeji Osowobi similarly referred to "a very shaky start" before things started going fine with the communication between her and the healthcare providers. Even though she did not exactly attribute this to the PPE worn by these personnel, the presence of this factor became clear in her later admission that relationship was ultimately built with the healthcare providers "irrespective of the fact that one does not exactly have a clear view of the countenance of these doctors and other experts" (Mbah, 2020, p. 1).

In the same vein, an anonymous survivor who spoke to the press recalled that in his initial anxiety over his condition, he felt the need to be reassured that all would be fine. The first doctor that he encountered tried to encourage him, but the fact that he could not have a real facial contact with these personnel became disadvantageous. According to him, "I knew he was reassuring me, his tone sounded quite confident. However, deep inside me, I was a little unsettled by this thought that I was not able to see his face, "how sure am I he is not being pretentious, trying to give me a hope that doesn't exist? That was how I sincerely felt" (Muhammad and Bunu, 2020, p. 1). In other words, this patient was implying that being able to have a face-to-face contact with the medical personnel would have enabled him better assess the genuineness of his reassurance.

The limiting effect of PPE on patient-healthcare giver communication has been documented in literature. Verhoeven et al., in their study of impact of the COVID-2019 pandemic on the core functions of Flemish general practitioners engaged in primary care, found that protective measures which include PPE adversely affected communication in physical consultations. One of their respondents admitted that "it is more difficult to show empathy [to patients] with these masks" (2020, p. 4). Similarly, Liu et al. (2020) found that wearing of protective gear intensified work stress on the health personnel by causing difficulty in walking and sweating which undermined communication with patients.

What all these sum up to is "dilution" of presence of a healthcare giver. In other words, the contact between the healthcare provider and the patient is caught up in a liminal space of presence-absence. Thus, the patient (like the anonymous COVID-2019 survivor quoted above) may find self in a dilemma of belief versus unbelief, trust versus distrust, and confidence versus doubt. All this will likely sustain or intensify anxiety.

Worthy of note, however, is the fact that the patients eventually felt satisfied with their communication and relationship with healthcare givers in spite of this initial challenge of 'diluted' presence. All of the patients whose accounts were found by these writers testified to this. For example, Salihu Umar eventually found the doctors to be "most empathic and humane" (WHO, 2020a). An anonymous survivor described the health personnel as "so cooperative and so wonderful" (Muhammad and Bunu, 2020). From the perspective of the Symbolic Interactionism Theory, this later favorable perception by the patients may be explained as a function of their eventual positive interpretation of the symbols offered by the healthcare givers—their words, gestures, and even protective kits. In this context, the PPE is seen no longer as a communication barrier, but a necessary component of the due care needed by the patients from the health personnel, which they (the patients) must cope with. This also aligns with the position of the HBM that a person is likely to cooperate with a required health process to the extent they are convinced that it is an effective way to solving a given health problem (perceived benefit of taking action).

The "Hostile" Presence

"Hostile" presence denotes the tendency of the appearance and distancing conduct of healthcare givers, especially within the context of their full-body covering, to induce anxiety in patients. Such appearance and conduct may have the effect of driving it home unequivocally to the patients that they are carriers of a deadly infectious disease who must be avoided by others. An incident in Abia State, South-East Nigeria, illustrates this point vividly. On May 28, 2020, the state government declared a man, by the name Emmanuel Ononiwu, wanted for refusing to present himself to be taken to an isolation center for treatment. The man, whose samples had been taken, tested and confirmed negative, was said to have been informed of the result and told to wait for the health team that would convey him to the isolation center. However, this patient, who had been cooperative all along, upon sighting the health team, took to his heels and went into hiding. The state government noted that findings showed that he ran away due to the anxiety that seized him upon encounter with the health personnel in PPE (Eze, 2020). In other instances, patients were reported to have escaped from isolation centers—a development that might also not be unconnected with the feeling of being in a hostile environment (Mosadomi et al., 2020).

Also, an important instance is the experience of a patient who happened to be the index case in the South-East state of Anambra. This man, while at the isolation center, spoke to the press through his phone insisting he was not infected and had been forcefully brought to the isolation center. The state government, in its own account, stated that the index case had gone into hiding as soon as he was informed of his result but was eventually found in a hotel room and taken to the treatment center. It described the man's reaction as stemming from his anxiety over his condition. A more detailed account given by the patient later tended to confirm that his anxiety stemmed, partially or wholly, from the appearance of the health personnel. He reported how some persons "covered from head to toe like masquerades" came into his private ward and inserted a long instrument into his nose (Odogwu, 2020).

Some other survivors who spoke to the media or via the Internet noted how the appearance and distancing conduct of the health staff tended toward a 'hostile' presence. Osowobi, for instance, recalled how she got to an isolation center, but there was no one there to receive her. After she waited in the ambulance for 2 hours, a nurse finally came out and treated her "like a plague." She said she had "sat at the ambulance as though rejected" (Ifijeh, 2020). Interestingly, the patient noted, however, that things eventually went well in spite of "a very shaky start," as she started working smoothly with the health personnel (Mbah, 2020). Ojo Damilare, another survivor, noted that the knowledge that one is being avoided, cannot be approached or touched by others without full-body covering was "indeed nauseating and despairing." However, he admitted that this feeling defused with time as he began to appreciate all that the professionals were doing to make him better, which helped him "keep positive all through" (Healthwise, 2020).

Nonetheless, the fact that these survivors eventually settled to calmly cooperate with their healthcare givers may again be a function of change in their interpretation of the symbols (represented by the healthcare givers' protective kits and general distancing conduct). Seeing these as a necessary component of the care they require would have, from the point of view of Symbolic Interactionism Theory, calmed them and made them cooperative. As the patient Osowobi put it, "I was . . . able to see how much they were trying their best to provide top-notch service to everyone at the center, including myself." Osowobi initially felt distant from the healthcare givers. Similarly, the fact that some of the patients were willing to 'endure' the ordeal of the 'hostile' presence of health workers may be attributable to their perception of susceptibility and perception of severity, which the HBM describes as key determinants of health behavior. This is evident in the testimony of Salihu Umar and Ojo Damilare who noted that despite initially feeling unease with the things around them at the treatment center, they knew they had no choice than to cooperate with the protocols in the face of the threat of survival they saw in COVID-2019 (Healthwise, 2020; WHO, 2020a).

Intimacy versus Professional Distance

Fairclough (1989) notes the culture of maintaining a "professional distance" as typically found among physicians in engaging with their patients. This culture, for instance, requires a doctor to frankly disclose fully to a patient their real health conditions no matter how unpalatable this will sound to them. In other words, the doctor should not be emotionally involved. Such "professional distance" also manifests when a doctor, as is typically the case, tries not to sound too intrusive while discussing something that may be sexually sensitive. Citing an example with communication between a gynecologist and a patient, Fairclough observes that such a doctor will likely say "the vagina" instead of "your vagina" as a way of maintaining professional distance and avoiding much intrusion.

Professional distance may be in conflict with the need for a healthcare giver to fully connect with a patient who is in need of emotional support. It may also undermine the development of the required clinical intimacy between the patient and the healthcare giver which will enable the patient to freely disclose fully whatever the health expert may need to know. An extensive review by Beck et al. (2002) on the verbal and non-verbal behaviors of physicians in primary healthcare settings found verbal behaviors that had been linked to patient satisfaction to include the ability to understand a patient's situation, courtesy, friendliness, reassurance, support, and encouragement; giving more explanations, laughing and joking, just to release tension. Similarly, Igbinlade et al. (2020) report that studies have shown that patients are mostly satisfied when healthcare givers show empathy, politeness, and active listening. All this underscores the vital place of patient-healthcare giver intimacy in realizing effective clinical engagement.

Testimonies of COVID-2019 survivors show that health personnel appeared to have favored intimacy over professional distance in relating with their patients, and which helped nurture favorable patient-healthcare giver relationships as well as calmed anxiety. Salihu Umar recalled: "The doctors gave me some counselling and assured me of their commitment to making sure we make it out of the isolation centre healthy" (WHO, 2020a). Counseling and assurance of commitment might not have featured in that patient-doctor transaction if the physicians had stuck rigidly to their formal professional routines. Osowobi revealed that

> we [the healthcare givers and I] were able to build a relationship as things went by . . . I had one doctor's number, so I would text him to tell him of my symptoms or call him if I was feeling a certain way. When I was still vomiting, I would text him to say, "Help me, I don't want to die." Some of the nurses would come in and encourage me, say a word of prayer with me. (Mbah, 2020, p. 1)

The preceding excerpt clearly paints a picture of closeness and intimacy prevailing over professional distance. The communication the patient had with her healthcare givers was far from being restricted to strictly clinical matters. And the patient really found this helpful in her condition. Another survivor, Emmanuel Asika's account made a similar impression:

> We were so impressed that we created the video appreciating the doctors, nurses, cleaners and all the support staff. It went viral. Despite the far from perfect conditions they never had sour dispositions, they were very friendly, supportive and professional. I would rate them 9.5 out of 10. We had their numbers on speed dial and they were available 24/7 to respond to us. Treatment was personalised, so it was not one-size-fits-all. For instance, people who had underlying conditions had a separate treatment regime. When I was nauseous and was constantly vomiting, I was placed on a special diet plan that included oats and custard. When I was recovering, I asked for noodles (Indomie) and they were quick to prepare it even as I dictated how I wanted it cooked. They went out of their way to make us comfortable. It was amazing. (Nigerian Health Watch, 2020, p. 1)

Also, an anonymous patient who spoke to the media upon his discharge from an isolation camp recalled that the "doctors have been so cooperative and so wonderful. We have exchanged phone numbers with them, anytime we need something, we call them and they are at our service. Above all, the doctors have been so caring" (Muhammad and Bunu, 2020).

Nonetheless, it is pertinent to point out that this impression of the patients about the healthcare givers would not have been so if the parties had not shared common symbols and common interpretations regarding what it means to be caring, empathic, and loving. For instance, the fact that Osowobi felt loved and comforted when the nurses came to "say a word of prayer" with her whenever she became anxious of dying meant that praying with one was interpreted by both parties as a demonstration of love and empathy. This is to be expected in a country like Nigeria where religiosity and prayer are a dominant feature of people's life. The Symbolic Interactionism Theory holds that in interacting between themselves, individuals borrow their symbols and interpretations thereof from their society and its culture (Dong, 2008; Doda, 2005).

The Imperative of Expanded Communication Space

An important idea emerging from the testimonies of COVID-2019 survivors is the imperative of expanding their communication space beyond the bilateral clinical encounters with experts. The necessity of ensuring a favorable mental state for the patients meant that communicating with other persons such as fellow patients, family, and friends was as much important as the communication with caregivers themselves. This expanded communication space was vital for checking anxiety in the patients.

Describing how she settled in the isolation center, Osowobi revealed how such expanded communication space worked for her and other patients: "After two hours, I was taken to my space. I felt lonely, bored, and disconnected from the outside world. Few days after, another patient came in. We bonded. Days later, patients trooped in" (Ifijeh, 2020). Even after she tested positive, other patients wanted her to remain in the same ward with her. "For them, I was a beacon of hope," she said (Salaudeen, 2020). An unnamed patient among the 11 discharged from the Infectious Disease Centre, Yaba Mainland Hospital, Lagos, on May 28, 2020, recalls: "Initially, I found it hard to settle into the facility. In fact, the first two days I spent here was so lonely for me, but I gradually settled and found a companion in my fellow ward mates" (Adeniyi, 2020). The therapeutic effect of the interaction among patients is also evident in the account of Asika:

> Some of us who were up to it tried to keep fit during the period. We would walk round the large tent in the mornings. This routine was repeated in the afternoons and evenings. In between, we had vibrant conversations on politics, economics, and religion, to name a few topics. There were a range of emotions at the centre; anxiety, solidarity, optimism. There was also a lot of spirituality—we had people who functioned as resident imams and pastors. (Nigerian Health Watch, 2020, p. 1)

A study conducted by Kędzior (2015) among cardiovascular patients in a Polish hospital found that fraternization among patients and eventual formation of a "community" (of patients) were a factor in their ability to settle and defeat anxiety. Communicating with relative and friends outside the isolation centers is also vital for handling anxiety in the patients as can be seen in the following submission by Salihu Umar:

> It was quite depressing, being confined in a facility away from family and friends. It was the first time I was in that kind of situation. I was always (up and about) and suddenly I couldn't move. From face timing (online chatting) with my family to tweeting and linking up with friends to sending emails. There was no time my kids missed me for one day. We were always connected. (WHO, 2020a, p. 1)

According to Ojo Damilare, his first reaction the moment his test result was communicated to him was to speak with his mother. Speaking to a relative was the first instinctual response to a situation of intense anxiety. "I was totally confused and did not know what to make of the situation," he said (Healthwise, 2020). Inside the isolation center, Damilare's expanded communication space included not just friends and family, but also his church:

> Whilst at the Centre, I remained very positive and did not see myself as one with any ailment. I was listening to my music, working as I had my laptop and my internet with me whilst remaining active on social media and engaging with friends and family who continued to encourage me. I also participated in the Hallelujah Challenge by Nathaniel Bassey and joined various Instagram Live Sessions of my church (RCCG Throne Room, Abuja). This was my routine every day whilst at the Centre. (Healthwise, 2020, p. 1)

From the perspective of Symbolic Interactionism Theory, these relatives and friends are people with whom the patients have over the years developed common symbols and common interpretations, which in turn engender intimacy. The same applies to the co-patients with whom they bonded in the treatment centers. Evidently, words of encouragement and similar gestures of empathy tend to be more strongly felt when they come from someone with whom one shares a common understanding and have built closeness and intimacy. This underscores the need to complement clinical communication (patient-healthcare giver exchange) with extra-clinical communication (involving relatives, friends, and others) as a way of managing anxiety in patients, especially when such patients have to be isolated from the outside world.

CONCLUSION AND RECOMMENDATIONS

From the foregoing discourse, it is clear that communication between patients and healthcare givers is a very key variable in the management of anxiety in patients in times of medical crises such as the COVID-2019 pandemic. The COVID-2019, given its novelty and effect, is generating so much mass hysteria. When communication is appropriately managed in medical context like the COVID-2019 pandemic, the mental health of patients is more likely to be in a favorable state, and this will play an important role in the treatment and healing process. However, it is important to note that patient-healthcare giver communication is dynamic, and its management requires a good understanding of each specific clinical situation and what it demands, the peculiar condition of an individual patient, as well as the potential challenges posed by factors like physical appearance (clothing) and distancing conduct of healthcare givers, the culture of professional distance, and the limited impact of clinical communication (which creates the need for an expanded communication space that will integrate non-clinical actors like family and friends).

Even though this chapter relied on secondary sources—media and Internet report of accounts of COVID-2019 survivors—the discourses have the added advantage of offering some insight into one of the factors that can influence the extent of public hysteria arising from the pandemic. This is the factor of public knowledge—what members of the public are able to learn (via the media and the Internet) about the experiences of patients inside the isolated centers. Such information and the interpretation thereof are critical to their reactions to the situation. Incidentally, the findings here suggest that the information coming from the media and the Internet about patients' experiences has tended to paint a largely positive picture regarding treatment and recovery, thus are more likely to de-escalate than heighten public hysteria—other things being equal. Therefore, beyond the immediate communicative functions of healthcare givers in managing health conditions, a huge responsibility toward managing public anxiety in moments like the COVID-2019 pandemic rests on the shoulders of the media and other persons involved with information dissemination. They should endeavor to report patients' experiences and other issues around the pandemic in ways that will likely de-escalate rather than heighten public anxieties.

Based on the discourses so far in this chapter, the following recommendations are put forward:

(a) Health professionals should always prioritize individualism as against paternalism in communicating with patients. Individualism is the practice of recognizing and treating the patient as an individual with a unique personal disposition, preferences, and views, and which must be put into consideration in providing care to them. On the contrary, paternalism sees the health personnel act like an all-knowing "father" who has the exclusive capacity to tell what is good for the patient. Modern healthcare service is shifting from paternalism to individualism given the realization that it is much more productive engaging patients via two-way symmetrical communication than the one-way top-down approach (Ha and Longnecker, 2010). Such an approach to patient-healthcare giver communication helps deepen understanding, douses tension, and generally improves clinical experience. This is evident in the testimonies of former COVID-2019 patients presented earlier.

(b) Training of healthcare professionals should emphasize the above-stated approach to clinical communication. Would-be healthcare givers should be equipped with requisite skills and the proper orientation for optimal application of the two-way symmetrical model of clinical communication, especially in very sensitive and potentially tensed clinical situations such as provided by COVID-2019 care.

(c) There is a need for prior orientation of patients on what to expect in certain sensitive clinical situations such as represented by COVID-2019 treatment. Preferably before such patients are admitted at isolation/treatment centers, they should be well instructed on the need to remain calm and cooperative in the face of the mental stress of isolation and distancing practices of healthcare givers such as wearing of PPE. Such prior orientation will contribute in preparing them psychologically for their treatment experience, thus helping to control tension and eliciting cooperation toward a more effectual care. This will be similar to the counseling received by individuals before HIV testing and possibly treatment to prepare them psychologically for what they might meet ahead.

(d) There is a need for empirical studies focusing on the communicative experiences of patients on the one hand and those of healthcare givers on the other hand in the context of COVID-2019 care. Empirical data on these experiences will serve as a more reliable basis for improving training, policy, and practice in healthcare delivery as it regards patient-healthcare giver's relationship.

REFERENCES

Adams, J. G. and Walls, R. M. (2020). Supporting the health care workforce during the COVID 2019 global epidemic. *JAMA* 323(15):1439–1440.

Adelman, R., Greene, M. G. and Charon, R., (1987). The physician-elderly patient-companion triad in the medical encounter: The development of a conceptual framework and research agenda. *Gerontologist* 27:729–734.

Adelman, R. D., Greene, M. G. and Ory, M. G. (2000). Communication between older patients and their physicians. *Clinics in Geriatric Medicine* 16(1):1–24.

Adeniyi, O. (April 4, 2020). Discharged coronavirus patient narrates experience. *NaijaNews*. Retrieved on July 3, 2020 from https://www.naijanews.com/2020/04/02/discharged-coronavirus-patient-narrates-experience/.

Baran, S. J. (2010). *Introduction to Mass Communication, Media Literacy and Culture* (6th ed.). New York: McGraw-Hill.

Beck, R., Daughtridge, R. and Sloane P. D. (2002). Physician-patient communication in the primary care office: A systematic review. *JABFP* 15(1):25–38.

Berry, D. (2007). Health communication theory and practice. In Payne, S. and Horn, S. (eds.). *Health Psychology*. Berkshire, UK: Open University Press.

Chandra, S., Mohammadnezhad, M. and Ward, P. (2018) Trust and communication in a doctor-patient relationship: A literature review. *Journal of Healthcare Communications* 3(36):1– 6.

Cioffi, R. N. J. (2003). Communicating with culturally and linguistically diverse patients in an acute care setting: Nurses' experiences. *International Journal of Nursing Studies* 40(3):299–306.

Cooper, L. A., Router, D. L., Johnson, R. L., Ford, D. E., Steinwachs, D. M. and Power, N. R. (2003). Patient-centered communication, ratings of care and concordance of patient and physician race. *Annals of Internal Medicine* 139(11):907–916.

Daramola, I. (2003). *Introduction to Mass Communication* (2nd ed.). Lagos, Nigeria: Rotham.

DiMatteo, R. (1997). Health behavior and care decisions: An overview of professional-patient communication. In *Handbook of Health Behaviour Research II: Provider Determinants*. New York: Plenum Press.

Doda, Z. (2005). Introduction to sociology. Retrieved on August 20, 2020 from https://www.cartercenter.org/resources/pdfs/health/ephti/library/lecture_notes/health_science_students/ln_sociology_final.pdf.

Dong, X. (2008). Symbolic Interactionism in sociology of education textbooks in mainland China: Coverage, perspective and implications. *International Education Sociology* 1(3):14–20.

Dunu, I. V. and Ugbo, G. O. (2018). South-East Nigerian women's perceptions and responses: Alternative views to gender-based advertising messages? *International Journal of Journalism and Mass Communication* 4(1):50–60.

Eze, J. (May 28, 2020). Abia declares COVID-2019 patient wanted. *Premium Times*. Retrieved on July 3, 2020 from https://www.premiumtimesng.com/regional/ssouth-east/395056-abia-declares-COVID-2019-patient-wanted.html.

Fairclough, N. (1989). *Language and Power*. New York: Longman.

Gillman-Wells, C.C., Sankar, T. K. and Vadodaria, S. (2020). COVID-2019 Reducing the risks: telemedicine is the new norm for surgical consultations and communications. *Aesthetic Plastic Surgery*. Retrieved on August 20, 2020 from https://doi.org/10.1007/s00266-020-01907-8.

Glanz, K., Rimer, B. K. and Lewis, F. M. (2002). *Health behavior and health education. Theory, Research and Practice*. San Francisco, CA: Wiley & Sons.

Greenfield, S., Kaplan, S.H., Ware, J.E. and Yano E.M. (1988). Patients' participation in medical care: Effects on blood sugar control and quality of life in diabetes. *Journal of General International Medicine* 3(5):448–457.

Griffin, A., Ledbetter, A. and Sparks, G. (2015). *A First Look at Communication Theory* (9th ed.). New York: McGraw-Hill Education.

Ha, J. F. and Longnecker, N. (2010). Doctor-patient communication: A review. *Ochsner Journal* 10(1):38–43.

Healthwise (2020). What COVID-2019 infection taught me: Abuja lawyer. Retrieved on August 20, 2020 from https://healthwise.punchng.com/what-COVID-2019-infection-taught-me-abuja-lawyer/.

Hewitt, J. (2002). *Self & Society* (9th ed.). New York: Allyn & Bacon.

Ifijeh, M. (March 30, 2020) 'Call Me Survivayo', Discharged COVID-2019 patient narrates experience. *This Day*. Retrieved on August 20, 2020 from https://www.thisdaylive.com/index.php/2020/03/30/call-me-survivayo-discharged-COVID-2019-patient-narrates-experience/.

Igbinlade, A. S., Anyebe, E. E., Olorukooba, H., Yusuf, A. G. and Jobin, J. (2020). Level of nurse-patient therapeutic communication: Perspectives of nurses and patients in a tertiary hospital in North West Nigeria. *Journal of Nursing and Midwifery* 1(1):1–7.

Jahan, F. and Siddiqui, H. (2019). Good communication between doctor-patient improves health outcome. *European Journal of Medical and Health Sciences* 1(4):332–341.

Kędzior, B. (2015). Becoming an inpatient: A symbolic-interactionist study in a polish hospital. *Zoon Politikon* 6:237—255. Retrieved on April 30, 2020 from https://www.civitas.edu.pl/wp-content/uploads/2015/03/Bozena-Kedzior_-ok.pdf.

Lewis, D. (2012). Humanism and the art of medicine. *Momentum* 1(2):12–17.

Liu, Q., Luo, D. Haase, J. H., Guo, Q., Wang, X. Q., Liu, S., Xia, L., Liu, Z., Yang, J. and Yang, B. X. (2020). The experiences of health-care providers during the COVID-2019 crisis in China: A qualitative study. *Lancet Glob Health* 8(e7):90–98.

Mbah, F. (April 7, 2020). Nigeria COVID-2019 survivor: 'An experience I don't wish it on anyone.' *Aljazeera*. Retrieved on July 15, 2020 from https://www.aljazeera.com/news/2020/4/7/nigeria-COVID-2019-survivor-an-experience-i-dont-wish-on-anyone.

McQuail, D. (2010). *McQuail's Mass Communication Theory* (6th ed.). London, UK: Sage.

Molina-Mula, J. and Gallo-Estrada, J. (2020). Impact of nurse-patient relationship on quality of care and patient autonomy in decision-making. *International Journal of Environmental Research and Public Health* 17(3):1–24.

Mosadomi, W. Agbakwuru, J., Ajayi, O., Ojomoyela, R. and Abubakar, S. (March 2, 2020). Commercial driver escapes isolation centre in Bida, declared wanted. Retrieved on July 15, 2020 from https://www.vanguardngr.com/2020/04/coronavirus-positive-man-escapes-from-isolation-centre/.

Muhammad, H. M. and Bunu, Y. (2020). Updated: Discharged COVID-2019 patients narrate experience, say it is real. Retrieved on August 20, 2020 from https://yenlive.com/news/index.php/news/2914-updated-discharged-COVID-2019-patients-narrate-experience,-say-it-is-real.

Nigeria Centre for Disease Control, NCDC (2020). COVID-2019 Nigeria. Retrieved on September 30, from https://covid19.ncdc.gov.ng/.

Nigerian Health Watch. (2020). Courage, community, care: How I defeated COVID-2019– Manny Asika. Retrieved on September 25 from https://nigeriahealthwatch.com/courage-community-care-how-i-defeated-COVID-2019 percentE2 percent80 percent8A- percentE2 percent80 percent8Amanny-asika/.

Odogwu, O. (April 12, 2020). Index case, Anambra govt disagree over status. *Daily Sun*. Retrieved on July 15, 2020 from https://www.sunnewsonline.com/index-case-anambra-govt-disagree-over-status/.

Okunna, C. S. and Omenugha, K. A. (2012). *Introduction to Mass Communication* (3rd ed.). Enugu, Nigeria: New Generation Books.

Pino-Postigo, A., (2017). Challenges in doctor-patient communication in the province of Malaga: A multi-lingual crossroads. *Procedia – Social and Behavioral Sciences* 237:992–997.

Redmond, M. V. (2015). Symbolic interactionism. *English Technical Reports and White Papers, 4*. Retrieved on Juky 15, 2020 from http://lib.dr.iastate.edu/engl_reports.

Reuben, B. D. (2016). Communication theory and health communication practice: The more things change, the more they stay the same. *Health Communication* 31(1):1–11.

Rosenstock, I. (1974). Historical origins of the health belief model. *Health Education Monographs* 2(4):311–334.

Rost, K. and Frankel, R. (1993). The introduction of the older patients' problems in the medical visit. *Journal of Aging and Health* 5(3):387–401.

Rubinelli, S. Myers, K., Rosenbaum, M. and Davis, D. (2020). Implications of the current COVID-2019 pandemic for communication in healthcare. *Patient and Counseling Education* 103(6):1067–1069.

Ruchinskas, R. and Alonzo, G. E. D. (2005). Patient-physician communication : Why and how. *Journal of the American Osteopathic Association* 105(1):13–18.

Salaudeen, A. (March 31, 2020). 'I thought I was going to die': Nigerian coronavirus survivor shares her experience. *CNN*. Retrieved on July 15, 2020 from https://edition.cnn.com/2020/03/31/africa/nigeria-COVID-2019-survivor/index.html.

Stay, T. and Ruben, B. D. (2015). Communication theory and health communication practice : the more things communication theory and health communication practice: The more things change, the more they stay the same. Retrieved on August 20, 2020 from https://doi.org/10.1080/10410236.2014.923086.

Steinmetz, D. and Tabenin, H. (2001). The 'difficult patient' as perceived by family physicians. *Family Practice* 18(5):495–500.

Suchman, A. and Matthews, D. A. (1988). What makes the patient-doctor relationship therapeutic? Exploring the connexional dimension. *International Medicine Journal* 108(1):125–130.

Suchman, A. L., Branch, W. T. and Matthews, D. A. (1995). The role of the medical interview in the physician's search for meaning. In Lipkin, M., Putnam, S. M. and Lazare, A. (eds.), *The Medical Interview: Clinical Care, Education and Research*. New York: Springer-Verlag.

Teutsch, C. (2003). Patient-Doctor communication: Prepublication draft from author that meets upload guidelines, ResearchGate. *Medical Clinics of North*

America. Retrieved on July 15, 2020 from https://www.researchgate.net/publication/9006103_Patient-Doctor_Communication.

Verhoeven, V., Tsakitzidis, G., Philips, H. and Royen, P. V. (2020). Impact of the COVID-2019 pandemic on the core functions of primary care: Will the cure be worse than the disease? A qualitative interview study in Flemish GPs. *BMJ Open*, 10doi:10.1136/bmjopen-2020-039674.

World Health Organization, WHO. (2020a). 'Let's fight this together,' urges Nigerian COVID-2019 survivor. Retrieved on August 20, 2020 from https://www.afro.who.int/news/lets-fight-together-urges-nigerian-COVID-2019-survivor.

World Health Organization, WHO. (2020b). COVID-2019 Public Health Emergency of International Concern (PHEIC) Global research and innovation forum. Retrieved on August 20, 2020 from https://www.who.int/publications/m/item/COVID-2019-public-health-emergency-of-international-concern-(pheic)-global-research-and-innovation-forum#:~:text=On percent2030 percent20January percent202020 percent20following,of percent20International percent20Concern percent20(PHEIC.

Zayapragassazan, Z. and Kumar, S. (2016). Awareness, knowledge, attitude and skills of telemedicine among health professional faculty working in teaching hospitals. *Journal of Clinical and Diagnostic Research* 10(3):1–4.

Chapter 8

Corophilanthropy

Rosemary Oyinlola Popoola

This chapter examines the link between the public hysteria about the Coronavirus Disease (COVID)-2019 and the politics of philanthropic gestures by selected Nigerians. "Corophilanthropy" is a combination of two words, "Coro" and "Philanthropy." Coro is an abbreviation for coronavirus and philanthropy is a word that is generally used to describe a charitable endeavor, while hysteria describes the obsessive and compulsive fear, fright, and anxieties that characterized COVID-2019 in Nigeria. Corophilanthropy therefore refers to the charities or giving "hysteria" that characterized Nigeria's digital, social, economic, political, and religious spaces between the period that the index case of COVID-2019 was reported and when the nationwide lockdown was imposed in Nigeria. There are signs to show that the COVID-2019 pandemic has stirred up a "new" wave of charitable giving across Nigeria as elsewhere.

The philanthropic donations among others were to cushion the effects of the palpable economic downturn on the less privileged, underserved groups and communities, given the stay-at-home COVID-2019 advisory from the state and federal governments (FGs), geared toward "flattening the curve" as well as supporting governments' effort at combating the health emergency caused by the pandemic. These donations came from politicians, celebrities, renowned clergy men and women, corporations, and businessmen and women. It included cash, medical supplies such as ventilators, hand sanitizers, "giveaways" (crediting individual bank accounts), food banks (sharing food items and basic necessities), and other social welfare programs.

Though the COVID-2019 philanthropy in Nigeria was widely covered by the media, several questions remain unanswered about these waves of unprecedented charitable gestures that cut across various classes, religions, and socioeconomic statuses. Therefore, this chapter poses the following questions: what is the relationship between public perception of philanthropic gestures, panic buying, and hysteria in the minds of the public? How did the COVID-2019 spark off these philanthropic acts of giving that cut across different political, sociocultural, and religious divides, especially the kind that has not been seen in recent Nigerian history? What was the motivation for these donations? Were the philanthropic gestures a form of spectacular performance in view of the mediatized nature of the giving? Were the donations based on altruism or attention seeking? In what ways did the pandemic spark off or awaken a "new wave" of corporate social responsibility (CSR) among corporations and individuals including celebrities. Did these donations come out of fear of an impending danger or a routine expression of CSR? Was it reactionary or proactive? Did the philanthropic gestures have some political undertones?

One must bear in mind that leadership ineptitude in Nigeria has made structured social security or welfare system a Herculean task. Coupled with this are institutional decay, allegations and counter-allegations of corruption against state humanitarian agencies, lack of accountability and transparency about how donations to governments were spent, reluctance of some donors to redeem their pledges, as well as the events that followed the philanthropic gestures such as retrenchment of staff and salary cuts by institutions, corporations, and individuals who gave. In this chapter, based on participant observation, content analysis, and ethnography, I show in this chapter that philanthropy during the coronavirus pandemic (especially in the stated period) in Nigeria was performative.

Note that the idea of performance was introduced to gender studies through the works of Judith Butler and it has been applied to philanthropic studies by Zhulina (2018). Zhulina defines "philanthropy as a host of processes, practices and conflicting ideologies that performatively give rise to the economic effect known as philanthropy" (Zhulina, 2018, p. 51). Arguably, Littler's argument suffices here that philanthropy is the "public displays of support for the afflicted and a way for 'philanthropists' to raise their profiles above the zone of the crudely commercial into the sanctified, quasi-religious realm of altruism and charity, whilst revealing or constructing an added dimension of compassion and care that defines a personality" (Littler, 2008, p. 327).

Over the years, scholars (Bishop and Green, 2008; Repo and Yrjölä, 2011; Bell, 2013; Daley, 2013; Budabin and Richey, 2018) have examined the varying intersections of philanthropy and humanitarianism. Specific focus has been on impact assessment and motivation for philanthropy and humanitarianism. In the area of motivation, scholars (Yrjölä, 2009; Wirgau, Farley, and Jensen, 2010; Richey and Ponte, 2012) have questioned the extent to which the Global North philanthropy and humanitarianism in Africa are motivated by altruism, and the extent to which they are attention seeking or an extension of the notable capitalist influence. However, limited attention has been paid to philanthropy and humanitarianism of Africans in Africa.

For instance, significant empirical works have been done on the philanthropic exploits of the Bill and Melinda Gates Foundation, the Rockefeller Foundation (Eisenberg, 2006; Saltman, 2010; Youde, 2013), as well as Western celebrities in Africa (Repo and Yrjölä, 2011; Budabin and Richey, 2018), with less consideration given to the responses of African philanthropists to Africa's humanitarian problems. Arguably, this is because philanthropy is seen as the exclusive preserve of Western agents or actors in Africa.

As a departure from the focus on Western philanthropy and humanitarianism in Africa, this chapter focuses on philanthropy and humanitarian of Africans in Africa, particularly the contributions of Nigerian philanthropists during the COVID-2019 pandemic. This study contributes to existing knowledge on philanthropy in Africa and provides new directions for researching philanthropy and humanitarianism in the continent. This chapter sits at the crossroads of multiple fields in the humanities and the social sciences—from political science, media, development, and psychology to sociology of everyday life and history. What's more, it provides an African- and indeed a Nigerian-centered perspective to global narratives and studies on philanthropy and humanitarianism while extending the scope of research in the area.

The chapter is organized into six sections. After this introductory section, the next section examines the theoretical discourse on philanthropy, drawing extensively from secondary literature. The section that follows examines the link between philanthropic gestures and hysteria in Nigeria's public domains. The section after that reviews selected case studies of philanthropic gestures during the COVID-2019 pandemic, grouped under pre-selected themes: from the secular (i.e., government palliatives and politicians' acts of philanthropy) to the sacred (i.e., coming from religious leaders) and to those of celebrities and corporations.

PHILANTHROPY: A THEORETICAL DISCUSSION

The precise meaning of *philanthropy* is a matter of some contentions within contemporary academic circles, since its definition is largely dependent on the particular subject of focus (Sulek, 2010). Jon Van Til defines philanthropy "as the voluntary giving and receiving of time and money aimed (however imperfectly) toward the needs of charity and the interests of all in a better quality of life" (1990, p. 34). Also, Schervish defines "philanthropy as a social relation governed by a moral obligation that matches a supply of private resources to a demand for unfulfilled needs and desires that are communicated by entreaty" (1998, p. 600). A broader definition sees it as "voluntary contributions (money, goods, time/expertise) to the public good, given by individuals and organizations and dominantly benefitting the public good" (Schuyt, 2009, p. 18). One of the most widely accepted of the numerous definitions of philanthropy is the one employed by Lester Salamon who defines it as "the private giving of time or valuables (money, security, property) for public purposes" (1992, p. 10). This study holds that philanthropy is the love for mankind and various acts of improving the situations of others through charitable donations. However, the concept has undergone significant changes through history and in ways that illuminate both contemporary and academic understandings of the term. Yet, the modern view of philanthropy "took shape in the years between 1885 and 1915 as multimillionaires such as Andrew Carnegie, John D. Rockefeller, and other rich men and women sought practical, socially useful ways of disposing of [their] surplus wealth" (Bremner, 1994, p. 159).

Corophilanthropy as used in this context means the donation or charities that dominated the COVID-2019 lockdown in Nigeria. Importantly, "giving back to the society has been contentious ever since philanthropy first became an organized enterprise of managing surplus wealth" (Zhulina, 2018, p. 52). Proponents argue that it enables one institution, even with modest resources, to simultaneously, and over time, test and support disparate organizations and interventions (Grady, 2014). Philanthropic foundations have made important contributions to development, particularly in agriculture, family planning, and infectious diseases control (Scott, Adelman, Sebag, and Ruiz, 2003).

Philanthropy is frequently seen as a part of companies' CSR or corporate citizenship initiatives (Carroll, 2018). Carroll further argues that it fulfills businesses' discretionary responsibility of becoming good corporate citizens, since philanthropic activities are voluntary, guided only by businesses' desire to engage in social activities that are not mandated, not required by law, and not generally expected in an ethical sense (Carroll, 2018). It is even viewed principally as "gap fillers" for official development assistance. In the explanations of Schultz (2015), the scholar opines that the merits of philanthropy include the diversification of the sources of funding, the virtues of citizen engagement, the benefits of private entrepreneurship in identifying needs and responding to them effectively, and advantages related to the tax system. As noted by Grady (2014), it is directed at supporting individual and collective human initiatives and ingenuity.

Conversely, critics claim that it is a cultural weapon in promoting the values of unbridled capitalism. For example, Zhulina (2018) argues that it is vulnerable to being used performatively to sway the public to embrace capitalist values. The scholar continues this line of thought saying that it is yet another process by which the values and assumptions of the so-called free market are performatively reproduced (Zhulina, 2018). Supporting the argument of Zhulina (2018), Massing notes that philanthropy is "one of the principal ways in which the super-rich not only 'give back' but also exert influence, thus becoming political activism in its own right" (2016, p. 1). It can thus perform the role of "conscience money" by smoothening over the detrimental economic effects triggered by the financial elites (Shaw, 1901, p. 14). Philanthropy is the vehicle used by industrial capitalism to justify its economic injustices, while presenting itself as the only viable economic and political system. In the estimation of Zhulina (2018), although it masquerades as a benevolent gift for the common good, its goal is often nothing less than the aggressive control of public policy and the prevention of an equitable redistribution of wealth. That is why it can be used to influence politics, scientific research, and artistic creation. For example, in *Dark Money: The Hidden History of the Billionaires Behind the Rise of the Radical Right*, Jane Mayer shows how the Koch family has "weaponiz[ed] philanthropy" in "the war of ideas" (2016, p. 31). The Koch brothers have bankrolled the Tea Party, lobbied against restrictions on carbon emissions, and funded think tanks that deny climate change, all the while presenting their libertarian activism "as philanthropy, leaving almost no money trail that the public could trace" (Mayer, 2016, p. 6). Critics further argue that the disadvantages of philanthropy include "the lack of formal public accountability on behalf of donors, aspects related to aggrandizement of wealthy large-scale donors, frequent fluctuations in size and direction of donations which may lead to poor reliability from the grantees' point of view, and the risk that the philanthropic system can perpetuate inequalities" (Schultz, 2015, p. 6). The next section interrogates the intersections of COVID-2019 with humor, hysteria, and panic buying.

PHILANTHROPIC GESTURES AND COVID-2019 IN NIGERIA: FROM HUMOR TO HYSTERIA

At the beginning of 2020 when news filtered into Nigeria about coronavirus in China and Italy, COVID-2019 seemed a distant phenomenon for Nigeria. However, the first confirmed case of coronavirus in Nigeria was announced on February 27, 2020, when an Italian citizen in Lagos tested positive for the virus (Alagboso and Abubakar, 2020b). On March 9, 2020, a second case of the virus was reported in Ewekoro, Ogun State, and was a Nigerian citizen who had contact with the Italian citizen (PM News, 2020). The index case and the subsequent ones that followed led to three distinctive stages of emotional responses in Nigeria vis-à-vis skepticism, humor, and hysteria. When the index case was reported in Lagos State, Nigerians thought it was a foreign disease that would not have a foothold in the country. This belief was further affirmed with mixed roots of the identity of the driver that drove the first victim from Murtala Muhammed International Airport, Lagos, to a company in Abeokuta. While blogsite used the picture of a man who lived in Delta State as the picture of the driver, the alleged driver soon came out to say he was not the individual who drove the victim to Lagos as he had not been to Lagos in two years (Tijani, 2020). This news of mixed identity affirmed Nigerians' belief that the illness/pandemic was not real and if it were real like Ebola, it would be instantly out of Nigeria and defeated like Lassa fever. This, combined with the public distrust for government, led to the proliferation of memes and comedy skits that sought to play down the reality of the pandemic.

Studies on humor in Nigeria are numerous and scholars (Obadare, 2009; Nneji, 2013; Filani, 2017; Okunola, 2018) have examined varying intersections of humor with politics and the civil societies in Nigeria. Markedly, one of the memes and comedy skits that was proliferated on the Nigerian digital space was the one done by a popular comedian called 'Fatboiz comedy.' In the comedy skit, the coronavirus flew into the country and on its way, from what seemed like an airport, met the Ebola virus and Lassa fever who were calling its attention to the danger in entering Nigeria and advising it not to do so. The virus ignored them and proceeded into the country. Its first encounter was with children who avoided it; subsequently, it found its way into the body of a fat guy who refused to succumb to the virus through hard work, advantage of the hot climate, traditional herbal medicine (Agbo), and the resilience of a big man. The virus therefore ran back to Lassa fever and the Ebola virus to tell them that what they said about Nigeria was true. The video which portrayed the resilience and invincibility of Nigeria to pandemics and epidemics was widely shared across various social media space and digital apps. In another skit, the virus flew into the country and called the Ebola virus to announce its arrival. The Ebola virus exclaimed, asking why the virus went into Nigeria. The Ebola virus told COVID-2019 that Nigerians were resilient people who would not succumb to the virus but make everything miserable by making jokes, memes, and skits about it. Consequently, COVID-2019 was seen fleeing the country. Memes and skits like these were not unusual or uncommon during the early stage of COVID-2019 infection in Nigeria.

However, what began as humor turned to hysteria in the weeks after the first index case was diagnosed, as the news of the number of deaths increased in Nigeria and around the world, and as local and international news media reported COVID-2019 deaths in countries that Nigeria considered advanced. From skepticism and humor, Nigerians moved to hysteria as they saw in the news and read about the severity of the pandemic around the globe. This reality led to panic, anxiety, fear, and hysteria among the public. More so, as the news of the impending lockdown filtered into the public sphere, public hysteria was heightened by several factors.

First was the closedown of schools, religious centers, and public gatherings, and subsequently, the closure of international airports. It is important to note that in over a century and since the Spanish flu pandemic, a time that most Nigerians alive now did not witness (about 60 percent of the Nigerian population are youth between 25 and 40 years of age), the magnitude of the present COVID-2019 lockdown could be described as unprecedented and strange.

Secondly, the closedown of schools brought the pandemic closer home for many Nigerians. Children staying at home during a normal school session was new, particularly as this has raised the costs of feeding and living for many families. Several memes and WhatsApp messages of parents lamenting and overwhelmed with children at home filled the digital media space. Third, the closure of public gatherings, including religious centers, further heightened the hysteria as the feeling of uncertainty, panic, and fear pervaded everywhere. The religious outlook of the nation fueled the growing fear about the pandemic as religious conscientiousness and spiritual interpretations of the pandemics dominated the public sphere. This spiritual dimension gained momentum with the closure of the Vatican and Saudi Arabia, raising public hysteria and palpable tension among adherents of the faiths. The shutdown of churches was new and uncommon; weekend parties and gathering which Nigerians are well known for were also suspended. More so, the shutdown of all airports means that for many people, their families were locked out and stranded in many countries of the world.

Even more, what many Nigerians thought was going to be a lockdown of few days and weeks extended into months. The apogee of public hysteria over coronavirus was the deaths of prominent Nigerians and the mysterious or unexplained deaths in Northern Nigeria. The line of prominent death started with Abba Kyari, the chief of staff to the president but considered to be the de facto president, and Senator Isiaka Abiola Ajimobi—former governor of Oyo State. It included prominent leaders and elites in Northern Nigeria notable among whom were six professors of Bayero University, Kano. Among them were a former Grand Khadi, a former State chairman of State Universal Basic Education Board, former commissioner of education, and a renowned professor of Economics, Prof. Ibrahim Ayagi (Ibrahim, 2020).

Significantly, the rude shock that followed the death of Abba Kyari awakened many Nigerians to the reality of coronavirus and heightened fear. There was public outcry especially because of the lack of social distancing at his burial and also the viral video of one of the pall-bearers who was seen removing his personal protective equipment (PPE) and discarding it openly in violation of NCDC burial protocols (Adeoye et al., 2020). This event led to online and offline outrage and the video raised public anxiety and fear over possible transmission and community spread of the virus. The incident and the public hysteria that followed made the NCDC team to visit the burial site and decontaminate it (Punch New, 2020).

Fundamentally, if the death of Abba Kyari heightened public anxiety, the inability of stakeholders and sympathizers to follow the due process during his burial increased hysteria. As a matter of fact, the news about "mysterious" deaths in Kano was the apogee of COVID-2019 hysteria in Nigeria. Kano is one of Nigeria's oldest commercial cities and one of the biggest in West Africa, with a huge population that usually shapes electoral results in Northern Nigeria. Kano has a population of over 9 million according to 2006 census. When the spate of these "mysterious" deaths began, the Kano State Government attributed it not to the coronavirus, but hypertension, diabetes, meningitis, or acute malaria. Yet, the gravediggers of the city said they were working overtime (Adebayo, 2020). For instance, Ali, a gravedigger at the Abattoir Graveyard, told the BBC: "We have never seen this, since the major cholera outbreak that our parents tell us about. That was about 60 years ago" (Izundu, 2020, p. 1). More so, the only death register available allegedly contained lower numbers than the real picture across the state.

Pointedly, the public hysteria was heightened by the statement of the Kano State's commissioner for information, Muhammad Garba, who said that the government was conducting "verbal autopsies" to ascertain the cause of the deaths (Human Right Watch, 2020, p. 1). Given how incredible verbal autopsies can be, Nigerians online and offline used the period to denigrate and lampoon such unreliable line of evidence as a political statement. The statement alongside the viral video of mass burial in Kano increased the level of hysteria in other states of the federation which forced many of them to tighten interstate movement restrictions to ensure that people coming from the Northern Nigeria did not infiltrate their states, thereby increasing the rate of infection (Njoku, Olaniyi, Msugh, Ityokura, Akhaine and Wantu, 2020). Additionally, if the statement of verbal autopsies increased public hysteria, the alleged deception, denial, defiance, denunciation, and disagreement of Kano State Government with the NCDC and the Presidential Task Force on COVID-2019 further exacerbated it. The State Governor, Abdullahi Umar Ganduje, continued to deny the link to coronavirus despite the surge in deaths (Izundu, 2020). It is pertinent to note that he labeled the deaths "mysterious deaths."

Primarily, public hysteria over Kano's "mysterious deaths" was validated by the location of the state, its population, and connectivity to the rest of the Northern region. If Kano became another epicenter of the pandemic, its contagion effect on the rest of the region might be devastating. "If Kano falls, the whole of the Northern Nigeria falls. The whole of Nigeria falls,"

Dr. Yusuf said. "It spreads into the whole of West Africa and the whole of Africa" (Maclean, 2020, p. 1). These mysterious deaths included prominent northerners including three Emirs, or traditional Muslim rulers, and a former health minister (Maclean, 2020). More so, reports of hundreds of more people dying "mysteriously" in Nigeria's northern states of Jigawa, Yobe, Sokoto, and Katsina extremely raised the level of public hysteria and forced President Muhammadu Buhari to declare a total lockdown of Kano State and sent the Presidential Task Force on COVID-2019 to ascertain the situation.

Furthermore, the palpable hysteria was further fueled by the decadence in the health sector and a confirmed fear that Nigeria lacked critical health infrastructures needed to contain or accommodate patients, should the invasion transform into a health crisis beyond the infrastructural capacity of the country's health sector. Importantly, decades of under-investment in healthcare and gross under-supply of modern equipment, medicines, and chemicals have rendered the nation's healthcare system one of the most vulnerable to the pandemic. According to reports, the ratio of doctors to patients is 4:10,000 (Adegoke, 2019). Additionally, WhatsApp messages that spread conspiracy theories and distrust for government also intensify the hysteria. "WhatsApp is the medium of choice for older Nigerians spreading fake news" according to the Business and Human Rights Center (2020, p. 1) and "WhatsApp messages started to spread misleading information about the coronavirus" (Romm, 2020, p. 1). The implications of the hysteria are numerous but fundamentally it led to panic buying. Newspapers and the digital media were replete with reports of panic buying that characterized the period of COVID-2019 pandemic in Nigeria. This led to hike in prices of necessities and household commodities (Salau and Akinfenwa, 2020; Okeafor, 2020).

If the coronavirus stirred public hysteria, the philanthropic gestures that were to support government and citizen in combating COVID-2019 raised more contentions and concern just as the coronavirus. The next section is a case study and interrogation of COVID-2019 philanthropy in Nigeria. The section examines the politics of philanthropic gestures by Nigerians along four thematic areas vis-à-vis philanthropic gesture by governments and politicians, religious groups, the private sectors such as banks and big corporations, as well as Nigerian celebrities in the entertainment sector.

Case Study 1: Government Palliatives, Public Distrust, and Politics of Political Philanthropy

The rider to the title of this subsection was the response of a Lagos resident interviewed by a foremost Nigerian newspaper *The Guardian*, when asked about the impact of government's COVID-2019 palliatives on vulnerable groups and indigent citizens. The skepticism and pessimism expressed by this respondent are not unusual for the average Nigerian across the 36 states of the federation. Following the index case of COVID-2019 in Nigeria on February 27, 2020, and the partial lockdown and subsequent total lockdown announced by government at all levels, the FG rolled out several palliative measures to cushion the effects of hardship on the citizens. Palliative measures announced by the FG included the continuation of the school feeding program even though the schools remained closed, the immediate payment of the conditional cash transfers for the next two months to the beneficiaries, the deployment of relief materials to residents of satellite and commuter towns/communities around Lagos and Abuja, and a three-month moratorium on loans to all: TraderMoni, MarketMoni, and FarmerMoni beneficiaries (Agbedo, Anazia, Awodipe, Odia, Diamond, Adeowo and Ezeilo, 2020). The FG further directed that a parallel moratorium be given to all FG funded loans issued by the Bank of Industry, Bank of Agriculture, and the Nigeria Export Import Bank. This was followed by cash transfer and sharing of food to component states in the federation. Lagos State, for instance, received 6,000 bags of rice and two truckloads of vegetable oil from the FG for distribution to the poor and the vulnerable in the state on April 10, 2020. Abia State received 1,825 bags of rice and 32 kegs of 25-liter vegetable oil. Lagos State also announced an economic stimulus package for residents, targeting 200,000 households in the first phase (Agbedo, Anazia, Awodipe, Odia, Diamond, Adeowo and Ezeilo, 2020). These food packs are produced for six-person households and are meant to last for at least 14 days.

While media reports of the palliatives stirred up hope among the citizens, the realities of the distribution of these palliatives are worth exploring. Many of the government's palliatives did not get to most Nigerians. What is more puzzling is the fact that the distribution process—which often led to chaos—violated the guidelines of social distancing as it often attracted huge crowds scuffling for a share. The zenith of the performativity of government's palliatives and philanthropic gestures was that most of the food items sent to several states were declared not fit for human consumption; they had decayed. Hence, some states rejected the food items: Ondo, Oyo, and Rivers states rejected bags of rice on account of poor quality and weevil infestation (Alagboso and Abubakar, 2020). Though critics initially claimed that the rejection had political undercurrent, subsequent rejections by other states dislodged the political interpretation and vindicated the submission of states which rejected the palliatives. More so, Abia State received 551 bales of fairly used clothes out of which 49 bales were bad (Agbedo, Anazia, Awodipe, Odia, Diamond, Adeowo and Ezeilo, 2020). More disheartening is the politicized and partisan process taken to distribute the palliatives. Respondents in the interview done by *The Guardian* newspaper said the following:

> The food was shared to party members, and we didn't get because we are not members of the party. (Guardian, 2020, p. 1)

> They said they are sharing food, but if you don't have a party card, you won't get. They brought rice to Agboyi, the woman that was in charge divided it and said it was for party people and started sharing a DeRica (a unit of measurement) to people. (Guardian, 2020, p. 1)

> The palliatives that got to us was very meager and they just shared it amongst staff that belonged to the All Progressives Congress (APC) party. I can tell you very confidently that we didn't share anything to the general public except maybe an individual or politician did that privately. But if we are talking about official palliatives, there was nothing like that. In fact, for most of the staff here, they didn't get any palliatives of any kind. The only thing I can say the staff got from the chairman of Isolo LCDA, Shamsudeen Olaleye, was N2,500 each, which was paid into their accounts. (Guardian, 2020, p. 1)

The same story resounded in Ekiti, Plateau, Imo, Abia, and Cross River states (Ukwu, 2020). The palliatives were politicized, and states which were not on lockdown received government palliatives ahead of those that were the epicenter of the COVID-2019 lockdown. A social media user commented thus: "I've never seen a government more fraudulent and shameless as the FG of Nigeria. How can you lockdown three states and be sharing money in states that aren't on lockdown? Why embezzle at every chance y'all [*sic*] get?" (Okon, 2020, p. 1). This biased approach to the distribution of the relief packages was affirmed by the report of the International Center for Investigative Reporting (ICIR). According to the ICIR Publication which revealed data of the beneficiaries of the relief, of the 35 states and the Federal Capital Territory, North West region had the highest number of households benefiting from the cash transfer with a number of 561,758 households. "Others were North Central—321,434, North East—109,442, South-South—67,696, South West—37,904, and South East—27,977 households. Top five states with the highest number of beneficiaries are Katsina—133,227, Zamfara—130,764, Jigawa—99,044, Kano—84,148, and Plateau—78,430" (Okon, 2020, p. 1).

Beyond the insincere nature and process of distributing the stimulus, the accusation and counter-accusation of corruption, lack of transparency, and accountability on the total cost of the palliatives raise more questions. While the Minister of Humanitarian Affairs, Sadiya Farouq, said the government spent over 100 million naira, human rights groups and citizens asked a plethora of questions on who received the palliatives? How were the palliatives distributed? How were the recipients determined and identified? What database did the Ministry of Humanitarian Affairs rely on to draw the list of the recipients? Ms. Farouq once suggested that the Ministry would adopt three methods to distribute the palliatives across the country. First, the use of the National Social Register. Second, the use of verified Bank Verification Numbers. Third, phone recharge ratio, that is, those who recharged above N100 will be unworthy to receive cash from the FG (Sanni, 2020). It remains debatable whether these criteria were used or not. It remains contentious how recipients received the transfer given that almost half of the active population of Nigeria do not have bank accounts. The Nigeria Inter-Bank Settlement System shows that despite the 11.33 percent surge in active bank accounts in 2019, the country still has 40 million unbanked population (Okafor, 2020). The insistence of the Humanitarian Minister to continue to school feeding program for pupils at home even when schools were closed raised further suspicion and continued to affirm public suspicion about the insincerity of the government in power.

This is exacerbated by the corruption charges that bedeviled many government ministries and parastatals, as many of them allegedly used the COVID-2019 situation to siphon money. For instance, the acting managing director of the Niger Delta Development Commission, Kemebradikumo Pondei, admitted that the commission spent N1.5 billion on staff as 'COVID-2019 relief funds' despite the fact that staff received salaries during the months quoted (Akinpelu, 2020). The increasing level of hunger was confirmed by several outcries in many viral videos online. One respondent to *The Guardian* interview said: "The lockdown really affected me so much that I was very broke. I went to bed without eating most of the days. But I did not receive any foodstuffs from government" (Agbedo, Anazia, Awodipe, Odia, Diamond, Adeowo and Ezeilo, 2020, p. 1).

In general, the distribution of most of the government palliatives received bad reviews and reprimand nationwide. More so, the social menace and insecurity stirred by delinquent youths during the lockdown affirmed that governments (both states and federal) have not been sincere in the way they handled the welfare of the citizens. One Million Boys, a gang of armed youths terrorized Lagos, Ogun, and Ibadan by raiding and robbing homes, maiming people, raping women, and dropping threatening notes in many communities (Thomas-Odia, Diamond, Adeowo and Ezeilo, 2020). Specifically, in Lagos, another group of deadly and notorious youth-gang called the Awawa boys created insecurity, tension, fear, and panic for residents of Agege, Agidingbi, Ogba, Ifako Ijaiye, Iyana-Ipaja, and Abule Egba.

If governments' strategy for distributing COVID-2019 palliatives raised numerous unanswered questions, that of politicians was filled with political theatrics as politicians engaged to outdo and prove that their opposition was not doing enough for the electorate or their communities. Politicians who gave during the COVID-2019 lockdown in Nigeria included former vice president and presidential aspirant, Alhaji Atiku Abubakar, who was one of the first politicians to give after his son contracted the virus.

Specifically, the centers of the political theatrics were Kogi, Rivers, and Calabar, although that of Kogi stood out. Kogi attracted intense rivalry between its governor, Bello Yahaya, and Senator Dino Melaye. Dino Melaye through several philanthropic gestures went to great lengths to demonstrate that the pandemic was real and that Nigerians in the state were suffering under the Kogi State Government. Paradoxically and in another turn of event, Senator Dino Melaye, who gave philanthropic gestures aimed at encouraging people to stay at home during the pandemic, soon joined the bandwagon of conspiracy theorists claiming that the pandemic was engineered against Africans and that it was linked to 5G technology (Ikeke, 2020). While his counterparts in Calabar and Rivers did not deny the existence of the virus, they however differed on government's solutions and appropriate responses to the pandemic. While the Rivers State Government was suspicious of the FG and institutions such as the NCDC, Kogi insisted that there was no index case in its state (Odogun, 2020). Yahaya Bello once remarked that "it is a disease that has been imported, propagated and forced on the people for no just cause . . . as COVID-2019 is only out to create fear, panic; orchestrated to reduce and shorten the lifespan of the people" (Odogun, 2020, p. 1).

Significantly, the distribution of palliatives was partisan and politicians replaced empathy and responsible leadership with political theatrics. Again, the post-lockdown actions of government further affirmed that government philanthropy was performative and lacked altruism. It appears what the government gave to the citizen with one hand it took with another hand. For instance, the Federal Government of Nigeria, through the Government Enterprise and Empowerment Program, has provided COVID-2019 relief loans for about 87,614 traders across 20 states. The FG also announced that the second phase of the loans would be the disbursement to 412,368 traders across the country in a bid to restart economic productivity as the government eased the economic lockdowns which heavily affected the informal and formal sectors. Yet, the same government increased fuel price and electricity tariffs. Given the importance of fuel and electricity as basic infrastructures for business and economic growth, the increase in the cost of fuel and the hike in electricity tariff could cripple business, increase the cost of doing business, and impoverish the already poor citizens who derive their sustainability from daily businesses.

Case Study 2: Religious Leaders—Piety or Performance?

The philanthropic gestures of religious leaders raised more questions and contentions than raised by the performative philanthropic actions of governments and politicians. Is it premised on altruism or attention seeking; is it based on piety which is expected of religion or performance? Following the total lockdown and ban on religious gatherings in churches and mosques, leaders of megachurches began to show solidarity toward government, church members, and the communities at large. Churches such as the Living Faith Church popularly called Winners Chapel (of Bishop David Oyedepo), the Redeemed Christian Church of God (of Pastor Enoch Adeboye), the Common Wealth Zion known as COZA (of Reverend Biodun Fatoyinbo), and the Daystar Christian Centre (of Pastor Sam Adeyemi) gave ventilators, ambulances, and medical supplies, including masks to government at various levels (Ngozi and Abiaziem, 2020). The Province of Lagos, Church of Nigeria (Anglican Communion) donated the sum of N5 million to Ogun State Government to tackle the coronavirus pandemic.

The Redeemed Christian Church of God donated 11 intensive care units with ventilators to Lagos, Ogun, and Plateau states to improve the medical response to the disease (Ngozi and Abiaziem, 2020). The Dunamis International Gospel Centre donated medical equipment and relief materials worth millions of naira to the Federal Capital Territory, Abuja, to help fight the outbreak of the novel coronavirus (Kwen, 2020). Also, the Living Faith Church Worldwide also known as the Winners Chapel International donated state-of-the-art ambulances and test kits and other medical supplies to Lagos and Ogun state governments in the midst of the pandemic (Sahara Reporter, 2020). Medical equipment were also donated which included 10 cartons of disposable face masks, 40 pieces of infrared thermometers, 2 cartons of blood pressure monitors, 20 cartons of latex hand gloves, and 500 pieces of PPE, among other medical items (Taiyese, 2020). Beyond giving to government, many of these churches gave to members and their immediate communities.

The place of religion and religious institutions is a field that has been widely covered by academic studies. Specifically, Ebenezer Obadare in his seminal work *Pentecostal Republic* (2018) examines the hegemonic roles of megachurches in every facet of the Nigerian public and private existence. While the appraisal and critique of religious institutions in Nigeria remain largely inconclusive, the paradox of religious piety demonstrated by them through giving during the pandemic was soon contrasted by conspiracy theories and skepticism that church leaders and Muslim clerics began to raise about the validity of the pandemic. They called it a 'plandemic' and not a pandemic. This conspiracy theory was fueled by unconfirmed allegations that the pandemic was an antichrist virus. This position was amplified by ideas of eschatology that suggest that the pandemic was an antichrist agenda to give people the sign about the second coming of Christ. While the pandemic is yet to be over, several questions remain unanswered. Why did religious centers give if they believe the pandemic was not real? What motivated their philanthropic gesture? Was the philanthropic gesture an outcome of pressure from the public who expected piety of religion or a drive by religion institutions to use philanthropy to drive positive public relations at a time of increasing resentment against religious institutions or another CSR of religious institutions? The answers to these questions are outside the scope of this chapter.

Case Study 3: Corporations and CSR—Good Samaritan or Robbing Peter to Pay Paul?

Philanthropy and humanitarianism gestures as expression of social corporate responsibility (SCR) and solidarity from individuals, big corporation, organization, and global foundations have been major features of corporate governance for many centuries. Through several centuries, it has become an expected response in situation of conflict, post-conflict, natural disasters, and in times of global health pandemic like COVID-2019, among others.

In Nigeria, as COVID-2019 cases rise, the Central Bank of Nigeria (CBN) and the private sector, led by Nigerian richest man Aliko Dangote Foundation, and Access Bank, set up a coalition aimed at raising N120bn toward the fight against COVID-2019 in Nigeria. The goal of the coalition was to provide support for healthcare facilities, increase capacity for testing, treatment, and training centers across the country during the crisis (Iwouah, 2020). Contributors who donated some amount of money included but not limited to Aliko Dangote (N2 billion), Mike Adenuga (N3 billion), Femi Otedola, chairman of Forte Oil (now Ardowa Plc), Folorunsho Alakija, chairman of United Bank of Africa ('UBA') Tony Elumelu, Jim Ovia (Zenith Bank), and Oba Otudeko (N1 billion). The CEOs of Access Bank and Guaranty Trust Bank gave N1 billion each; Abdul Rabiu the founder of BUA group and the third richest man in Nigeria according to Forbes gave 1 billion naira (Sule, 2020).

Existing research into the motivations for corporate philanthropy provides a mixed evidence concerning the degree to which philanthropy is motivated by strategic concerns (Brammer, Millington, and Pavelin, 2006). The philanthropic gesture of each corporation raises fundamental questions, even though each will require unique interrogation. Why did Access Bank give to the COVID-2019 and subsequently made the staff bear the burden through salary cuts and proposed retrenchment? More so, the post-philanthropic actions of some of the corporations affirmed an earlier argument that the philanthropic gesture was performative. It can be likened to robbing Peter to pay Paul. For instance, after Access Bank donated to the COVID-2019 funds, the bank without the consent of her customers deducted outrageous stamp duties from its customers' accounts which led to widespread outbursts from the general public (Benson, 2020).

Subsequently, the bank implemented a 30 percent salary cut for its staff and was on the verge of retrenching over 75 percent of its staff until the intervention by the CBN stopped the bank from doing so. Additionally, many of the organizations that gave were unsustainable and on the verge of collapse even before the COVID-2019 invasion. Many gave to follow the philanthropic rituals that follow a crisis and for some, it was a public relations attempt to curry public support. Herbert Wigwe, the group managing director of Access Bank, in a video message to his staff said the company no longer needed security guards, cleaners, and tea girls. The paradox of the situation was that while on the one hand Access Bank was involved in philanthropic gestures, on the other hand, the bank was reliving the security guards, cleaners, and tea girls of their jobs. This is evidently contrary to justice for the poor employees who relied on meager salaries for their well-being.

Importantly, the philanthropic gestures were done to engender goodwill, promote positive corporate image, and enhance acceptability by the public. More so, there is a capitalist dimension to philanthropy since most big corporations give to their community not out of altruism, but to exploit the tax advantage that SCR confers. Since most of the companies donating would be exempted from taxes, what the companies are 'giving back to the society' in one hand would be collected back with the other hand. In 2018, the CBN claimed that it had recovered N65 billion from commercial banks for wrongful deductions and illegal charges on deposits of customers and other transactions during the period 2012–2018 (Ojekunle, 2018). Again, in February 2020, CBN reported it had also recovered N60 billion in excessive charges imposed on customers by some Nigerian banks (Oliseh, 2020). This "robbing Peter to pay Paul" approach makes a mockery of the philanthropic and CSR initiatives of Nigerian banks.

It should be noted that the COVID-2019 philanthropic gestures significantly focused on urban center. Likewise, momentary humanitarian reliefs did not necessarily aim at tackling the structural inequalities that COVID-2019 magnified. Sule (2020) argues that the complicity of corporate elites in the existing structural inequality makes their philanthropic gesture performative. For instance, in the build-up to the 2019 general elections, President Muhammadu Buhari named Chief Aliko Dangote and Femi Otedola as advisers on his re-election campaign (Ibukun, 2018). Sule argues against corporate philanthropic gesture which he termed 'Nigeria's Big Philanthropy Industrial Complex (NBPIC).' In his view,

> big philanthropy covers a multitude of sins and is insufficient to resolve Nigeria's structural challenges. Though the NBPIC might be united in its desire to give back to the society, yet it has little or nothing to say about its members giving up their privileges and restructuring the economic and political system,

> which currently works for the fortunate few, and not the unfortunate many. At face value, big philanthropy appears to benefit the masses; however, a closer examination would reveal that the donation has some anaesthetizing qualities, which ease the short-term pain, but does not address the root cause of the problem. (Sule, 2020, p. 1)

Case Study 4: Celebrities: Between Altruism and Attention Seeking

Scholars in Europe and America (Bell, 2013; Bulck, Claessens, and Panis, 2015; Jeffreys and Allatson, 2015; Littler, 2015; Budabin and Richey, 2018) have studied the intersection between celebrities' philanthropy and humanitarian gestures while their African and indeed Nigerian scholars have paid limited attention to this branch of scholarship, though Nigerian celebrities' philanthropic gestures are widely reported in the newspapers and on social media. As a matter of fact, the social media is filled with news of celebrities' interventions in social economic realities of vulnerable Nigerians whose stories made it to social media or headline news. The news items include those about Taju, a five-year-old boy who was unable to read; Nollywood actress and director, Funke Akindele, who helped Taju to read; Success Adegor, a young girl who was sent home from school due to her parents' inability to pay the school fees; and the celebrities who mobilized to help Success.

The period of COVID-2019 has not been different as celebrities turned out both online and offline to give various forms of palliatives to vulnerable groups. For instance, Michael Colins Ajereh, a music artist and director (also known as Don Jazzy), gave out cash, including N100,000 to an old woman who wanted to have sex with any man in order to survive and raise her grandchildren (Tolu, 2020). Also, the Tonto Dikeh Foundation, in collaboration with Prosperity for Africa, set up a 'raw food bank drive for 5,000 Nigerians' (Punch, 2020). Other celebrities who helped with cash as relief funds in this period included DJ Jimmy Jatt, Runtown, Peruzzi, and Tunde Ednut, among others (Tolu, 2020). Importantly, as the philanthropic gestures of governments and churches were said to be performative too, that of celebrities seemed to be lacking in altruism, thus raising the question of motivation and impact. It is difficult to situate giving by celebrities as altruism because the mediatized nature of their philanthropic gesture in some ways mirrors public performance.

Celebrity philanthropy is a contested topic among scholars who study the phenomenon in Europe and North America. Scholars who support philanthropy like Bishop and Green (2008) argue that celebrity philanthropy leverages on "fame" to promote humanitarian values and global citizenship. Furthermore, celebrity engagement raises the public profile of a given social issue, intensifies campaign for social cause and its host organization, attracts extra media coverage, magnets old audience and entices new audiences, simplifies campaign issues, encourages sponsorship from private and public organization, and raises public awareness (Bishop and Green, 2008). It is a known fact that celebrity philanthropy can draw the attention of the global community to an important global cause; act as interface between publics, elite, political movement, and international organizations; and may be able to translate and communicate complex issues in politics, economics, or related areas into understandable terms (Jerslev, 2014). Celebrity philanthropy in the absence of government support, or sometimes in support with it, can offer help to troubled areas and regions such as war-torn zones, victims of natural disaster, and people in rural slums, among others. According to Mediatrust (2007), a United Kingdom organization that works on communication skills, celebrity involvement in philanthropy "can help in harnessing public opinion and participation, repositioning an organisation in the public's perception, [and] strengthening a long running campaign" (Littler, 2008, p. 242).

Conversely, critics of celebrity philanthropy opine that it reinforces inequality, consumerism, and corporate capitalism because it is motivated by media stations' desire for a story and the attention-driven culture of the celebrity industry. It is also condemned for hiding the unequal nature of trade and business relationships (Žižek, 2006; Nickel, 2012; Kapoor, 2013; Rojek, 2014). Thorup argues that it is one of the ways through which "the global attention-economy needs an explicated moral dimension in order to appear legitimate" (2013, p. 570). It is therefore tainted by self-promotion, branding, and the spread of Western ideals (especially capitalism).

CONCLUSION AND RECOMMENDATIONS

This chapter has examined the linkages among the COVID-2019 pandemic, public hysteria, and philanthropic gesture. It has revealed that although news about COVID-2019 was initially approached with the usual humorous or comic reactions to major events in Nigeria, this was soon turned to hysteria. The fear of an impending danger led to panic buying and subsequent philanthropic gestures from multiple sectors. The central argument of this chapter is that the philanthropy recorded during the crisis was performative, lacking in any form of altruism. It was mediatized philanthropic ritual that was not aimed at structurally addressing fundamental issues of inequality, vicious poverty, and infrastructural decay. This is because it did not address inherent systemic issues that have turned the Nigerian health sector to a graveyard due to neglect by successive administrations, corruption, and a lack of a long-term vision for healthcare in the country. While philanthropic gesture should be applauded, its politicized nature makes it almost ineffective. For instance, most of the isolation centers that were constructed from funds from philanthropic gestures are now shutdown due to the dwindling cases of coronavirus in Nigeria. More so, post-COVID-2019 realities, events, and activities by government show that government is not interested in the health, well-being, security, and welfare of her citizens.

Nigeria's first lady Aisha Buhari was flown abroad for treatment despite annual budgeting and special votes for the Aso Rock Clinic. Since the relaxation of COVID-2019 lockdown, the government is yet to present a strategic vision for the health sector. Health professionals remain underpaid even as government and its health minister continue threatening to replace serving health professionals with youth corps members (because of industrial actions) and yet hinder the immigration of health officers to other parts of the world.

The inherent problems of the Nigerian health sector are beyond the scope of this chapter. Nonetheless, the study offers the following recommendations for coordinated and strategic philanthropy, seeking to offer lasting solutions to systemic and structural inequities, poverty, and decay that COVID-2019 palliatives seek to alleviate:

- The isolation centers should be converted into hospitals to increase the number of available healthcare facilities and improve the doctor–patient ratio.
- The nation should develop a rewarding remuneration scheme to encourage health workers and reduce brain drain within the sector.
- It is high time Nigeria had a holistic and strategic vision and plan for the health sector that guarantee universal health coverage for all Nigerians.
- The nation needs a philanthropic gesture that is geared toward addressing structural and systemic inequalities rather than palliatives that are cosmetic.
- Social justice must become a pillar of governance in Nigeria.

REFERENCES

Adebayo, B. (June 9, 2020). Over half of April's unexplained deaths in Nigeria's Kano state due to coronavirus, health minister says. CNN. Retrieved on June 15, 2020 from https://edition.cnn.com/2020/06/09/africa/nigeria-spike-in-deaths-covid/index.html.

Adegoke, Y. (April 24, 2019). Does Nigeria have too many doctors to worry about a 'brain drain'? Retrieved on June 30, 2020 from https://www.bbc.com/news/world-africa45473036#:~:text=The percent20NMA percent20says percent20there percent20are,wait percent20hours percent20to percent20be percent20seen.

Adeoye, G., Atoyebi, O., Olokor, F., Adepegba, A., Nwogu, S., Adesomoju, S., Aworinde,T., Ajaja, T. and Ojerinde, D. (April 19, 2020). Coronavirus: Quarantine attendees of Kyari's burial, experts tell FG. Retrieved on June 30, 2020 from https://healthwise.punchng.com/coronavirus-quarantine-attendees-of-kyaris-burial-experts-tell-fg/.

Agbedo, O., Anazia, D., Awodipe, T., Thomas-Odia. I., Diamond, M., Adeowo. A. and Ezeilo, O (August 8, 2020). FG's COVID-2019 palliatives: Why Nigerians are not feeling the impact. Retrieved on September 15, 2020 from on https://guardian.ng/saturday-magazine/fgs-COVID-2019-palliatives-why-nigerians-are-not-feeling-the-impact/.

Akinpelu, Y. (July 20, 2020). We used N1.32 billion, not N1.5bn to take care of ourselves as COVID-2019 palliative—NDDC Chief. Retrieved on August 15, 2020 from https://www.premiumtimesng.com/news/top-news/402101-we-used-n1-5bn-to-take-care-of-ourselves-as-COVID-2019-palliative-nddc-md.html.

Alagboso, C. and Abubakar, B. (June 2, 2020a). Coronavirus: Why Nigeria's rice handouts aren't going down well. Retrieved on June 15, 2020 from https://www.bbc.com/news/world-52488923.

Alagboso, C. and Abubakar, B. (June 2, 2020b). The first 90 days: How has Nigeria responded to the COVID-2019 outbreak?#COVID19Naija.Response. Retrieved on June 15, 2020 from *Nigeria Health Watch.* https://medium.com/@nigeriahealthwatch/the-first-90-days-how-has-nigeria-responded-to-the-COVID-2019-outbreak-covid19naijaresponse-a0974493efa6.

Bell, K. M. (2013). Raising Africa? Celebrity and the rhetoric of the white savior. *PORTAL Journal of Multidisciplinary International Studies* 10(1):1–23.

Benson, E. A. (June 22, 2020). Access Bank tells customers it's time to accrued stamp duty charges. Retrieved on June 30, 2020 from https://nairametrics.com/2020/06/28/access-bank-rescinds-decision-on-collection-of-accrued-stamp-duty-from-customers/.

Bishop, M. and Green, M. (2008). *Philanthrocapitalism: How the Rich Can Save the World and Why We Should Let Them.* Edinburg, UK: A & C Black Publishers.

Brammer, S., Millington, A. and Pavelin, S. (2006). Is philanthropy strategic? An analysis of the management of charitable giving in large UK companies. *Business Ethics: A European Review* 15(3):234–245.

Bremner, R. H. (1994). *Giving: Charity and Philanthropy in History*, New Brunswick, NJ: Transaction Publishers.

Budabin, A. C. and Richey, L. A. (2018). Advocacy narratives and celebrity engagement: The case of Ben Affleck in Congo. *Human Rights Quarterly* 40(2):260–286.

Bulck, V. H., Claessens, N. and Panis, K. (2015). World relations and development issues: Framing celebrity philanthropy documentaries. In Jeffreys, E. and Allatson, P. (eds.). *Celebrity Philanthropy.* Bristol, UK: Intellect Books.

Business and Human Rights Center, 2020 Nigeria. (October 22, 2019). Use of WhatsApp among older generations contributing to spread of fake news, includes company comments. Retrieved on September 15, 2020 from https://www.business-humanrights.org/en/latest-news/nigeria-use-of-whatsapp-among-older-generations-contributing-to-spread-of-fake-news-includes.

Carroll, A. B. (2018). Strategic philanthropy. In Kolb, R. W. (ed.), *Sage Encyclopedia of Business Ethics and Society*. Thousand Oaks, CA: Sage Publications.

Daley, P. (2013). Rescuing African bodies: celebrities, consumerism and neoliberal humanitarianism. *Review of African Political Economy* 40(137):375–393.

Eisenberg, P. (2006). The Gates-Buffett merger isn't good for philanthropy. *Chronicle of Philanthropy* 20:262–279.

Filani, I. (2017). Politics of humour and political humour in Nigerian stand-up comedy. *Israeli Journal for Humour Research* 6(1):93–109.

Grady, H. (2014). Philanthropy as an emerging contributor to development cooperation. United Nations Development Programme (UNDP). Commissioned by the United Nations Development Program as a Background Paper for the conference International Development Cooperation: Trends and Emerging Opportunities – Perspectives of the New Actors in Istanbul, June 2014.

Guardian. (August 8, 2020). FG's COVID-2019 palliatives: Why Nigerians are not feeling the impact. Retrieved on September 30, 2020 from https://guardian.ng/saturday-magazine/fgs-COVID-2019-palliatives-why-nigerians-are-not-feeling-the-impact/.

Human Rights Watch. (May 1, 2020). Fears of COVID-2019 outbreak in Nigeria's Kano State. Retrieved on June 15, 2020 from https://www.hrw.org/news/2020/05/04/fears-COVID-2019-outbreak-nigerias-kano-state.

Ibrahim, N. (May 7, 2020). Kano records death of seventh professor. Retrieved on 15 June 2020 from https://www.premiumtimesng.com/news/top-news/391751-kano-records-death-of-seventh-professor.html.

Ibukum, Y. (December 28, 2018). Nigeria's Dangote named as Buhari election campaign adviser. Retrieved on June 15, 2020 from https://www.bloomberg.com/news/articles/2018-12-28/nigeria-s-dangote-named-as-buhari-election-campaign-adviser.

Ikeke, N. (April 4, 2020). Dino Melaye under attack for saying coronavirus deaths caused by 5G mobile networks. Retrieved on June 15, 2020 from https://www.legit.ng/1318203-dino-melaye-attack-coronavirus-deaths-caused-by-5g-mobile-networks.html.

Iwuoha, B. B. (May 11, 2020). Dangote: Mobilising private sector support in effort to fight against COVID-2019. Retrieved on June 2020 from https://www.africanleadershipmagazine.co.uk/dangote-mobilising-private-sector-support-in-fight-against-COVID-2019/.

Izundu, C. (April 28, 2020). What is behind Nigeria's unexplained deaths in Kano? Retrieved on May 15, 2020 from https://www.bbc.com/news/world-africa-52454259 BBC_News

Jeffreys, E. and Allatson, P. (2015). *Celebrity Philanthropy*. Bristol, UK: Intellect Books.

Jerslev, A. (2014). Celebrification, authenticity, gossip. *Nordicom Review* 35:171–186.

Kapoor, I. (2013). *Celebrity Humanitarianism: The Ideology of Global Charity*. London, UK: Routledge.

Kwen, J. (March 24, 2020). Dunamis Church donates Coronavirus precautionary kits to FCTA, equipment to Abuja Hospital. Retrieved on April 15, 2020 from https://

businessday.ng/coronavirus/article/dunamis-church-donates-coronavirus-precautionary-kits-to-fcta-equipment-to-abuja-hospital/.

Littler, J. (2008). "I feel your pain": Cosmopolitan charity and the public fashioning of the celebrity soul. *Social Semiotics* 18(2):237–251.

Littler, J. (2015). The new Victorians? Celebrity charity and the demise of the welfare state. *Celebrity Studies* 6(4):471–485.

Maclean, R. (May 17, 2020). COVID-2019 outbreak in Nigeria is just one of Africa's alarming hot spots. Retrieved on June 15, 2020 from https://www.nytimes.com/2020/05/17/world/africa/coronavirus-kano-nigeria-hotspot.html.

Massing, M. (January 14, 2016). How to cover the one percent. *The New York Review of Books*. Retrieved on February 15, 2020 from http://www.nybooks.com/articles/2016/01/14/how-to-cover-the-one-percent/.

Mayer, J. (2016). *Dark Money: The Hidden History of the Billionaires Behind the Rise of the Radical Right*. New York: Doubleday.

Nickel P. M. (2012). Philanthromentality: Celebrity parables as technologies of transfer. *Celebrity Studies* 3(2):164–182.

Njoku, L., Olaniyi, S., Ityokura, M., Umeh, K., Akhaine, S. and Wantu, J. (May 8, 2020). South East, South South clamp down on Almajrai relocating from North. Retrieved on June 15, 2020 from https://guardian.ng/news/south-east-south-south-clamp-down-on-almajirai-relocating-from-north/.

Nneji, O. M. (2013). Nigerian jokes as humour construction: A semantico-pragmatic study. *International Journal of Research in Arts and Social Sciences* 5:117–129.

Obadare, E. (2009). The uses of ridicule: Humour, 'infrapolitics' and civil society in Nigeria. *African Affairs* 108(431):241–261.

Obadare, E. (2018). *Pentecostal Republic: Religion and the Struggle for State Power in Nigeria*. London, UK: Zed Books.

Odogun, G. (June 30, 2020). COVID-2019 only out to create fear, panic—Yahaya Bello. Retrieved on July 15, 2020 from https://punchng.com/COVID-2019-only-out-to-create-fear-panic-yahaya-bello/.

Ojekunle, A. (19 July 2018). Nigerian banks illegally charged customers over N65 billion in 6 years. Retrieved on 15 from August 2020 from https://www.pulse.ng/news/finance-nigerian-banks-illegally-charged-customers-over-n65-billion-in-6-years/k97lj1x.

Okafor, E. (February 12, 2020). Nigeria records 11 percent increase in active bank accounts but 45m remain dormant. Retrieved on June 15, 2020 from https://businessday.ng/financial-inclusion/article/nigeria-records-11-increase-in-active-bank-accounts-but-45m-remain-dormant/.

Okeafor, P. J. (March 30, 2020). COVID-2019: Panic-buying in Nigeria and nearest shops for stock buying. Retrieved on June 15, 2020 from https://naijauto.com/market-news/COVID-2019-panic-buying-in-nigeria-and-nearest-shops-for-buying-6419.

Okon, D. (April 19, 2020). Lamentation still trails Lagos, FG's palliative package as middlemen hijack programme. Retrieved on June 15, 2020 from https://businessday.ng/features/article/lamentation-still-trails-lagos-fgs-palliative-package-as-middlemen-hijack-programme/.

Okunlola, O. L. (2018). (Un)funny laughter: Sexist humour and the discursive production of femininity in Nigerian stand-up comedy. The 61st Annual Meeting of the African Studies Association, Atlanta, GA.

Oliseh C. (February 21, 2020). Excess charges: CBN return over N60 billion to customers. Retrieved on June 15, 2020 from https://nairametrics.com/2020/02/21/excess-charges-cbn-return-over-n60-billion-to-customers/.

PM News. (March 9, 2020). Nigeria records second case of Coronavirus. Retrieved on March 10, 2020. Coronavirus: Nigeria's Access Bank announces salary cuts to curb job loss. Retrieved on June 15, 2020 from https://www.pmnewsnigeria.com/2020/03/09/breaking-nigeria-records-second-case-of coronavirus/.

Punch. (May 10, 2020). COVID-2019 celebrity givers. Retrieved on June 10, 2020 from https://punchng.com/COVID-2019-celebrity-givers/

Repo, J. and Yrjölä, R. (2011). The gender politics of celebrity humanitarianism in Africa. *International Feminist Journal of Politics* 13(1):44–62.

Richey, L. A. and Ponte, S. (2012). Brand Africa: Multiple transitions in global capitalism, *Review of African Political Economy* 39:135–150.

Rojek, C. (2014). "Big citizen" celanthropy and its discontents. *International Journal of Cultural Studies* 17(2):127–41.

Romm, T. (March 2, 2020). Fake cures and other coronavirus conspiracy theories are flooding WhatsApp, leaving governments and users with a 'sense of panic'. Retrieved on June 15, 2020 from https://www.washingtonpost.com/technology/2020/03/02/whatsapp-coronavirus-misinformation/.

Saharareporters, New York. (March 31, 2020). Coronavirus: Lagos, Ogun to receive ambulances, test kits from Oyedepo. Retrieved on June 15, 2020 from http://saharareporters.com/2020/03/31/coronavirus-lagos-ogun-receive-ambulances-test-kits-oyedepo.

Salamon, L. M. (1992). *America's Nonprofit Sector: A Primer.* New York: Foundation Center.

Salau, G. and Akinfenwa, G. (March 26, 2020). Lagosians embark on panic-buying, cash withdrawal. Retrieved on June 15, 2020 from https://guardian.ng/news/lagosians-embark-on-panic-buying-cash-withdrawals/.

Saltman, E. K. J. (2010). From Carnegie to Gates: The Bill and Melinda Gates Foundation and the venture philanthropy agenda for public education. In E. K. Philips (ed.), *The Gates Foundation and the Future of US Public Schools.* New York: Routledge.

Sanni, K. (April 15, 2020). Nigeria: COVID-2019—Only 25 percent of Nigerians will get relief items—Minister. Retrieved on June 15, 2020 from https://allafrica.com/stories/202004160046.html.

Scott, S., Adelman, C., Sebag, R. and Ruiz, C. A. (2003). Philanthropic foundations and development co-operation. *DAC Journal* 4(3):73–148.

Schervish, P. (1998). Philanthropy. In Wuthnow, R. (ed.), *Encyclopedia of Politics and Religions.* Washington, DC: Congressional Quarterly Press.

Schultz, G. (2015). What legitimizes philanthropy? M.A. Thesis, Department of Philosophy Submitted to Prof. Daniel Attas, Department of Philosophy Hebrew University of Jerusalem, Israel.

Schuyt, B. M. (2009) *Giving in the Netherlands*. Gouwenberg en R.H.F.P. Bekkers (eds.). Den Haag: Reed Business.

Shaw, G. B. (1901). *Socialism for Millionaires*. London, UK: The Fabian Society. Retrieved on June 15 2020 from https://digital.library.lse.ac.uk/objects/lse:duf537zem.

Sule, A. O. (May 27, 2020). The case against Nigeria's big philanthropy industrial complex (NBPIC). Retrieved on June 15, 2020 from https://www.proshareng.com /news/Products percent20& percent20Services/The-Case-Against-Nigeria-s Big-P hilanthropy-Industrial-Complex--NBPIC-/51268.

Sulek, M. (2010). On the modern meaning of philanthropy. *Nonprofit and Voluntary Sector Quarterly* 39(2):193–212.

Taiyese, N. (April 04, 2020). How faith based organizations support the containment of COVID-2019 in Nigeria. Retrieved on June 15, 2020 from https://www.proshareng.com/news/Faith percent20& percent20Religion/How-Faith-Based-Organi zations Support-The-Containment-of-COVID-2019-in-Nigeria/50295.

Thomas-Odia, I., Diamond, M., Adeowo, A. and Ezeilo, O. (April 18, 2020) Insecurity worries Lagos, Ogun residents than COVID-2019. Retrieved on June 15, 2020 from https://guardian.ng/news/insecurity-worries-lagos-ogun-residents-than-COVID-2019/.

Thorup, M. (2013). Pro bono? On philanthrocapitalism as ideological answer to inequality. *Ephemera* 13(3):555.

Tijani, M. (March 3, 2020). Nigerian taxi driver threatens to spread coronavirus? Retrieved on June 15, 2020 from https://factcheck.afp.com/story-originated-parody -account-no-driver-threatening-spread-COVID-2019-across-nigeria.

Tolu, O. (April 14, 2020). Coronavirus: What has Nigerian celebrities done? Retrieved on June 15, 2020 from https://everyevery.ng/coronavirus-what-has-nigerian-celebrities-done/

Ukwu, J. (June 12, 2020). COVID-2019: Benue state govt. rejects FG's rice donation. Retrieved on June 15, 2020 from https://www.legit.ng/1353549-COVID-2019 -benue-state-govt-rejects-fgs-rice-donation.html.

Uma, N. and Abiaziem, C. (May 3, 2020). COVID 19: Are churches' donations to government misplaced priorities? Retrieved on June 15, 2020 from https://www .independent.ng/COVID-2019-are-churches-donations-to-government-misplaced -priorities/.

Wirgau, J. S., Farley, K. W. and Jensen, C. (2010). Is business discourse colonizing philanthropy? A critical discourse analysis of (PRODUCT) RED. *Voluntas: International Journal of Voluntary and Nonprofit Organizations* 21(4):611–630.

Youde, J. (2013). The Rockefeller and Gates Foundations in global health governance. *Global Society* 27(2):139–158.

Yrjölä, R. (2009). The invisible violence of celebrity humanitarianism: Soft images and hard words in the making and unmaking of Africa. *World Political Science* 5(1):279–292.

Zhulina. A. (2018) Performing philanthropy from Andrew Carnegie to Bill Gates. *Performance Research* 23(6):50–57.

Žižek, S. (2006). The liberal communists of Porto Davos. *In These Times*, 11 April. Retrieved on June 15, 2020 from http://www.inthesetimes.com/site/main/article /2574/.

Chapter 9

Cororeligion

Simon Gisege Omare

This chapter explains how religion involved itself in the fight against the Coronavirus Disease (COVID)-2019 pandemic in Africa. It explains the effects of the disease on religion, discusses the interpretation of Christian religions on the cause of COVID-2019, and explains the response of various churches to the outbreak of the pandemic. By corroreligion, I intend to determine the interaction between religion and COVID-2019 from the perspective of Christians in Africa. The chapter is intended at answering the question, how did the outbreak of COVID-2019 affect religion, how did Christian religions interpret the cause of COVID-2019, and how did churches respond to the outbreak of the COVID-2019 pandemic? The assumption is that religion is the key to determining the interpretation and response of people toward new phenomena. If the interpretation is wrong, many people in different religions will respond negatively. Health is one of the key elements of society, and religion influences the response of people toward health matters.

The chapter recognizes the role of religion during pandemics. It analyzes how religion involved itself in the fight against the COVID-2019 pandemic in Africa. It takes a case of Christianity in Africa since Christians are the majority. It recognizes the idea that Africans are notoriously religious as John Mbiti (1969) puts it. John explains that whatever Africans do is influenced by religious beliefs; the way they act, eat, walk, and speak is influenced by their religious beliefs. The chapter is guided by the functional theory of sciences where it holds that religion has a function in society. One of the functions is to influence people's behavior and response toward health concerns. We hold that, for the world to manage this COVID-2019 pandemic and any pandemic in future, there is need to understand people's religious beliefs and teach religious leaders more about the cause and control of pandemics. This is important as the faithful will get the correct information, and they will be involved to offer solution and control of any pandemics in future.

This chapter begins by discussing the methodological and theoretical approaches. Later, it discusses the effects of religion, how Christian religions interpreted the cause of COVID-2019, and how churches responded to the outbreak of the COVID-2019 pandemic.

METHODOLOGICAL AND THEORETICAL APPROACHES

To begin with, this study employs qualitative methodology: that is, the emphasis is on words instead of numerical values. The data informing the chapter was collected through interviews and focus group discussions from purposively sampled respondents in Africa and analyzing literature reviews on Christianity and COVID-2019.

Next, the study is guided by the Structural Functionalist Theory that was developed by Emile Durkheim (1858–1917) and expounded by Brownsław Malinowski (1884–1942), Talcott Parsons (1902–1979), and Alfred Reginald Radcliffe-Brown (1881–1955) (Bajpai, 1996). This theory emphasizes the organic unity of society. The structural functionalists opine that a society is made up of various elements. Each of the different elements of a society has a function that contributes to the preservation of the structural survival and the coherence of the society as a whole. If one of the organs fails, the whole system will either collapse or be forced to readjust. Society's survival depends on the harmonious interaction of its various elements. All elements in a social system have functional unity as they work together without conflicts. These elements include the structure (social organizations and institutions) and their functions (patterns of social behavior) (Durkheim, 1915). These parts of the society are interrelated; a change in any part affects all others. The theory is equated to the human body that is made up of different organs which are necessary for the body's survival. If one of the organs is removed, the human being will either die or will not function normally.

For Durkheim, religion is a social phenomenon and the social function of religion is to act as a lubricant and glue to the social process. It is likened to glue in the sense that it binds an individual to the society, and a lubricant as it provides legitimation and authority for the social structure and moral order, which facilitates the smooth functioning of society. Therefore, religion acts as the mechanism for the imposition of the society's authority. Later, Malinowski added that a social phenomenon such as religion fulfills a function in relation to human psychological needs (Malinowski, 1948). He claims that religion has a function of providing psychological safeguards against fear of death and give humans a feeling of mastery of their fate. Taking a different approach Radcliffe-Brown analyzed the social structural pattern of societies with regard to overall cohesiveness and functioning with regard to religion in maintaining social order (Brown, 1952). Lastly, Parsons describes the main function of religion as being the creation of cultural values, beliefs, and symbols (Parsons, 1944). According to him, ritual action and religious belief are forms of symbolic statement about social order.

In society, social systems work to maintain equilibrium after external shocks disturb the balance among social institutions (Merton, 1968). Such social equilibrium is achieved through socialization of members of the society into the basic values and norms of that society so that consensus is reached. Where socialization is insufficient, social control mechanisms exist to restore conformity or to segregate the nonconforming individuals from the rest of society (Merton, 2004, pp. 894–900).

This study examined religious beliefs through the principles of Structural Functionalist Theory so as to investigate the role it plays toward health. The research made a conclusion that religion has a function toward health through its teachings. Specifically, it indicated that religion has a role toward management and control of COVID-2019. It reinforces and defines acceptable behavior and response toward pandemics positively and negatively, just like a double-edged sword. It is a social control mechanism that tries to restore conformity to basic values and norms of a society with regard to health patterns.

COVID-2019'S EFFECTS ON RELIGION

Religion is a way of life for African people; Africans are notoriously religious (Mbiti, 1969). Majority of Africans identify themselves as Christians (6 in every 10 people), while 3 in 10 are Muslims (Pew Research Center, 2018). Further, about 3 percent do not identify with any religion while a similar percentage follows African religion. Hindus, Buddhists, and Jews make up less than 1 percent of the sub-Saharan African population. How did the outbreak of COVID-2019 affect Christianity in Africa? This study uses cases of the African Christian population to make arguments.

When news spread about the eruption of COVID-2019 in China in February 2020, the world population was shocked, including Christians in Africa (Parsitau, 2020). Parsitau further notes that, as a response to the foregoing, many pastors from Pentecostal Churches in Africa such as Emmanuel Makandiwa of Zimbabwe prophesied to their members that the disease would not come to Africa (Asamoah-Gyadu, 2020). Most of the pastors assured their Christians that God will deliver them in times of crisis and resorted to fasting and prayers which remained unsuccessful (Asamoah-Gyadu, 2020). One wonders why such a prophecy and its possible effects on the preparedness to the prevention of the spread of the disease. Most African governments relaxed and Africans made claims that the disease would not kill Africans but only the Whites as many claimed that African people's blood had immunity against the virus. Therefore, as the rest of the world was taking precaution, Africans relaxed with allegations that the climate in Africa is too hot for the virus to thrive (Bukhari et al., 2020). A famous Kenyan Pentecostal clergyman went public claiming that coronavirus is a hoax and refused to cancel his church services (Parsitau, 2020). The outbreak of COVID-2019 brought confusion among Africans, hence a setback to the African governments in their efforts to control the spread of the virus. Most African governments forced religions to close their churches and worship services; this affected socialization through religion since it is a social phenomenon that deals with a group of people.

Due to the rapid spread of the disease, the World Health Organization (WHO) declared COVID-2019 a pandemic in March 11, 2019 (WHO, 2020). As a result, some people started blaming religions for the spread of the virus (Parsitau, 2020). In order to control the spread, worship places were closed. For instance, the Church of the Nativity in Bethlehem was shut down temporarily after a congregant contracted the virus (Aljazeera, 2020). In the United States, 38 percent of believers at a rural church at Arkansas were confirmed COVID-2019 positive and three persons died (James et al., 2020). On the other hand, in South Korea, the secretive Shincheonji Church of Jesus service became a breeding ground for the infection (Eunha et al., 2020). The services held by a Christian group in South Korea formed the epicenter of the massive outbreak in early February (Sang-Hun, 2020). The COVID-2019 did not affect only Christians; infections also occurred during a four-day pilgrimage to Malaysia in late February where some infected Muslims spread the virus to citizens of six other countries in Asia, through contact (Ananthalakshmi, 2020). In this case, the Muslims contracted the virus in a mosque in Kuala Lumpur. In the United States, there was transmission among mourners attending a Christian funeral in Dougherty County, in the state of Georgia, with an infection rate that was two times higher than that of New York City (as of April 1, 2020) (Barry, 2020). In Bnei Brak, the country's largest ultra-orthodox city (in the North-West suburbs of Tel Aviv) 35–40 percent of the population tested positive (BBC, 2020).

The foregoing selected incidents led to cancelation of worship services in many countries with an opinion that religious gatherings were an avenue to spread the virus; African countries such as Kenya followed suit (The Guardian, 2020). Closure of worship places was not taken lightly as many Christians expressed dissatisfaction—not forgetting that some of their trusted leaders had prophesied that the disease would not affect them. For instance, many Christians expressed displeasure when the Milan Cathedral was open to tourists but not to worshippers. At the same time, religious services were also canceled at Venice, hence banning Easter festivities and masses among the many cases worldwide (The Guardian, 2020). Several worshippers were deprived of the opportunity to attend their crucial religious rituals such as Easter Monday, Good Friday, and pilgrimage to Mecca, among others. The foregoing affected the ritual dimension of religion as many religious rituals were dropped, for instance, as a control for the spread; Rabbis in many parts of the world discouraged their followers from hugging and shaking hands (Schechter, 2020). In Houston in the United States, Pastor Joel Osteen of Lakewood Church, who appeals to several worshippers (up to 50,000), closed the church (Parke, 2020). Similarly, the celebrated mega-church preacher T. D. Jakes of Potter's House suspended his church services (Akpan, 2020). Scientists warned that holy water is not a hand sanitizer and prayer is not a vaccine; all people were encouraged to take safety measures (Parsitau, 2020). The closure of churches affected the source of income for pastors negatively and closure of businesses owned by churches such as hotels, schools, and colleges. This pandemic affected the church negatively economically.

Consequently, what happened after the closure of the worship places? An assumption is made that the functions of religion were interfered with. The outbreak of coronavirus and the response of religion seem to have affirmed with the claim made by atheists and scientists that religion has become outdated and it has to pave way for science to take over the world. They resonated with James George Frazer's claim that religion is in a process of evolution (from Magic-Religion-Science) (Frazer, 1936). Frazer's theory was a general development of approaches of thought from the magical to the religious and, finally, to the scientific. This seems to have affected religion negatively as some people lost their faith in religion. Many ask, does it mean religion deals with worship only? We can argue that religion is multidimensional and worship is a singular element of religion, and failure to attend religious services is not a valid claim to dismiss religion; one can worship from anywhere including their own houses or offices or cars as God is omnipresent.

Most presidents of African countries such as Uhuru Kenyatta, the president of the Republic of Kenya, assembled religious leaders to pray against the attack of COVID-2019 and its negative economic impacts (Parsitau, 2020). When the first case was reported in March 2020 in Kenya, all citizens panicked leading to intensified prayers and fasting. Most Christians associated and blamed the devil for the spread of the disease (Parsitau, 2020). Subsequently, the religious leaders and their worshippers were surprised when the same governments which were seeking God's intervention declared an order against public worship in mosques and churches. As such, the Kenyan government banned all social gatherings, including the regular Sunday religious worship service on March 15, 2020 (Parsitau, 2020). Banning of religious services was a surprise as to many it was a sign of 'side-lining' and 'rejecting' God more, especially the idea of not choosing religion as an essential service just like other services such as the services of health workers was not welcome to many Kenyans. The foregoing claim was made despite news spreading that several priests dying after contracting the virus worldwide (Bramstedt, 2020). A question arises, if the virus didn't spare God's servants, how about the followers? The virus infected people without discrimination, hence need to seek for universal protection of humans. It was indicated that no amount of prayers could help cure the virus (COVID-2019) just like other earlier infectious diseases such as Ebola and HIV AIDS in Africa (Parsitau, 2020).

Pastors who had claimed to have the power of healing the virus retreated into their cocoons just like other worshippers. The atheists responded by criticizing the relevance of religion in seeking for the solution to COVID-2019; instead they gave credit to efforts of science in the search for the cure (Parsitau, 2020). During interviews, most pastors defended the previous by saying, 'being religious does not mean that one is not bound to challenges of the world.' In defense, they gave an example of Job who was a man of God but went through temptations from the devil (Osei, 2020). The Bible gives a story of a man known as Job. Job was righteous and godly, he was "blameless and upright," a man who "feared God and shunned evil" (Job 1:2). He was greatly tested by God who allowed the devil to bring suffering to Job through diseases, loss of property, death of family members, and even more greatly blessed by God after persevering. Pastors claimed that, just like Job, COVID-2019 came to test the faith of Christians. They encouraged Christians to keep praying to strengthen their faith.

Despite many Africans seeking the intervention of God, it seems their God couldn't hear them; the virus kept spreading. Tanzania's president John Pombe Magufuli who was a committed Christian refused to close worship places. He said, 'God will save Tanzania from this disease, I will not close worship places just like our neighboring countries' (Kombe, 2020). Despite Magufuli informing the public that one of his sons had contracted the disease, his faith was unshaken. Unfortunately, Magufuli later succumbed to the disease. He claimed holy places are places of God and told his fellow Tanzanians not to be afraid of worshipping Him. He further alleged that corona cannot survive in the body of Christ; it will burn. As an example, he took the Holy Communion (Otieno, 2020). In response, Tanzanians composed songs praising their president for the bold step. In support of President Magufuli, Josephat Gwajima, a Tanzanian pastor who had mocked Kenya and Rwanda over the measures they had taken to curb the spread of COVID-2019, retracted his words after his country recorded 53 new cases on the Friday of April 17, 2020 (Otieno, 2020). The pastor claimed that the spike in the two countries was due to the nations enforcing strict rules to battle COVID-2019 which included banning church gatherings. "They are being tested but there are no healings there because they are not going to church, what stupidity is that?", the pastor claimed (Otieno, 2020). The reality was that corona was in Tanzania just like other countries. The main reason why the numbers were not realized was that the country stopped testing.

COVID-2019 heightened the politics of supremacy among religionists and atheists. Under normal circumstances, basing on the pain and struggle which worshippers go through, the crucial role of religion in the control and search for the solution to coronavirus is questionable yet the holy books indicate that the Supernatural Being hears prayers. The moment disasters arise and Christians suffer like other people, questions arise on whether God hears their prayers. The challenging point is when one sees non-believers enjoying healthy life while Christians are suffering. In cases of diseases, all people turn to science for solution, therefore, during such times, science appears to be the more reliable solution than religion. Science has repeatedly sought cures for pandemics. Taking the case of central Africa, the truth is that antiretroviral drugs and the Ebola vaccine have given a new lease of life to millions of people around the world, not religion. It can be predicted that it is science that will come up with a cure and not religion. As a response to these, Christians claimed that scientists are men and women of God. We have scientists who are Christians at the same time, not forgetting that religion deals with the spiritual realm which scientists cannot address. They were given authority by God to act as co-creators (Hicks, 2019). Religion deals with the psychological concerns of humans toward health which is crucial to healing. Both religionists and scientists need to work hand in hand in solving this COVID-2019 pandemic. In all, COVID-2019 affected religion economically, socially, and politically.

Interpretation on the Cause of COVID-2019 and Clergy in Drama over Prophecies and Healing

Jesus Christ promised his disciples gifts of the holy spirits such as the gift of prophecy, wisdom, miracles, healing, discerning, speaking in tongues, interpretation, and healing (1 Corinthians 12:8–10). Christians believe that their pastors are blessed with the same gifts. Through the gifts, they can perform miracles. On May 16, 2020, a megachurch pastor, Franklin Ndifor of Cameroon, who claimed he could cure COVID-2019 by laying hands on hundreds of followers, died from the virus (Stone, 2020). Ndifor is the founder of Kingship ministry church based in Bonaberi in the fourth district of Douala. Franklin's followers were surprised how their chosen healer, a man of God, could die from a disease he had claimed to have power over. The followers blocked entrances to his residence praying for his resurrection. This raised criticism from atheists who asked how God would allow a man chosen by Him to die out of a disease that is meant for 'sinners.'

Some Christians interpreted that COVID-2019 as God's punishment for those who oppose Jesus (Kettley, 2020). Sebastian analyzes a book authored by Billy Prewitt, author of *The Coronavirus in Biblical Prophecy*, who believes that God unleashes his vengeance upon mankind through different signs. The author claims there is a relationship between coronavirus and the biblical plagues of Egypt. He concludes that God has sent the coronavirus to punish and persecute Christians. Ralph Drollinger, the Christian clergy of the former president of the United States, Donald Trump's Cabinet, echoes this claim that it was a punishment (Naughtie, 2020). Drollinger in a post entitled "Is God Judging America Today?" explains that "America is experiencing the consequential wrath of God"—that is, a punishment for violating the Bible's teachings on godly behavior. Ralph implied that homosexuality could be one of the causes of the coronavirus epidemic in the United States. Robert Jeffress, a Christian minister close to Trump, traced the origin of the disease to sin and quotes Romans 8:19–21 to justify his claim (Jeffress, 2020). He further argues that pandemics, earthquakes, cancer, birth defects, and every other malady all traces back to the original sin. He explains that sickness and calamity were never a part of God's original plan for this world. Later, a poll report done in the United States indicated that 63 percent of Americans claimed the pandemic is a "wake-up call" from God and "signs of coming judgment" (Fox6, 2020).

T. B. Joshua, a Nigerian pastor who is widely known as a holy prophet of God in Nigeria and claimed to be divinely inspired, predicted that the coronavirus pandemic would be over by March 27, 2020, several days before a lockdown was imposed on the states of Lagos, Ogun, and the capital Abuja (Orjinmo, 2020). Joshua said, "By the end of this month, whether we like it or not, no matter the medicine they might have produced to cure whatever, it will go the way it came," to applause from his congregation. When March 27 passed the televangelist was mocked for his "false prophesy."

As earlier said, the famous pastor T. B. Joshua of Nigeria was branded a liar for the false prophecy on when COVID-2019 would end. After realizing that his prophecy did not come to pass, Joshua changed tune by saying, "What I meant was that the virus would be halted where it began, and in Wuhan it has stopped." Joshua even prophesied the date on which the virus was to end on March 27, 2020 (Adekaye, 2020). We are not sure, but it is rumored that Joshua succumbed to the disease. Some pastors such as Chris Oyakhilome of the Christ Embassy linked the virus to 5G networks and alleged that it was part of a plot to create a "new world order" (Orjinmo, 2020). Such views were rejected by scientists, who said the idea of a connection between COVID-2019 and 5G was "complete rubbish" and biologically impossible.

COVID-2019 led to the development of prophecies that created fear in many people leaving them more confused (Hackernoon, 2020). Hackernoon explains that some churches started teaching that the 666 prophecy in the Bible and the mark of the beast had been fulfilled through COVID-2019. The Bible in the book of Revelation 13:16–18 explains that Satan will create a mark in his name and that all people will receive the mark on their right hands or on their foreheads, so that they could not buy or sell unless they had the mark. The mark is prophesied to be a number which is the name of the beast or the number of its name. The Bible warns that, let the person who has insight calculate the number of the beast, for it is the number of a man. Hackernoon further noted that there was fear and panic among Christians when Bill Gates suggested that all people should be given a vaccination; those who would have had the vaccination should be implanted with microchips. Preachers referred to the Microsoft's U.S. Patent WO 2020 060606 entitled Cryptocurrency System Using Body Activity Data as the framework of a global financial scheme aimed to influence buying and selling that integrates technology with the human body (Hackernoon, 2020). In order to force all people to get the vaccine, he suggested that anybody without the microchips should not be allowed to access essential services. By coincidence, his words were reflected when Israel's prime minister Benjamin Netanyahu wanted all children to be micro-chipped, in the name of protecting public health (Armstrong, 2020). Some Christians in Africa doubted the existence of the disease due to such prophecies—this made it a challenge for governments in Africa to control the pandemic. COVID-2019 is a new viral disease that generated anxiety and rumor mongering among the people (Ogila, 2020). Such interpretations through rumors and theories made religion a laughing stock in Africa. Many warned if religion cannot be contained, it can lead to the further spread of the disease just like in eighteenth-century central Russia where the plague epidemic of 1770–1772 claimed over 100,000 lives in Moscow. The plague spread when the faithful queued to kiss icons contaminated by the bacteria (Kahan, 1979).

RESPONSE OF RELIGION TO COVID-2019

While public worship sessions were temporarily discouraged, religious institutions sought new ways of providing their services. Most churches utilized the Internet; they utilized platforms such as Zoom, WhatsApp, Facebook, and YouTube to live-stream prayer services. For the first time, most Catholics worshipped their masses online (Parsitau, 2020). This affirms the crucial role of science in religion. Many people sat home and enjoyed online worship services. Churches utilized money transfer services to collect offerings. For instance, most televangelists in Kenya such as Bishop Mark Kariuki introduced MPESA money transfer service to collect offerings. Christian-owned radio stations such as Sayare in Kenya were the most efficient media for reaching out to communities and sharing vital information to widen community audience in all languages in East Africa (Okoth, 2020). During their broadcasts, they relayed information to their worshippers on how to protect themselves from the virus. We identify one of the oldest churches in Nairobi, Christ Is the Answer Ministries, that runs television, radio, and online broadcasts reaching around 200,000 people on Sundays (Okoth, 2020). The church encouraged people to wash their hands, sanitize, to keep distance, and stay at home. Through this, they were able to help the government to achieve its objective of slowing down and eventually stopping the transmission of the virus.

Some religions helped to donate food and money to those affected by the virus. Churches made donations to the government and financially stricken worshippers in a move that is likely to see them retain popularity. To avert the spread of COVID-2019, Catholic Relief Services (CRS) and their partners worked in more than 30 countries to support populations that were identified to be in high risk, such as elderly people, vulnerable children, and caregivers (USAID, 2020). In Kenya, CRS provided COVID-2019 training in Nairobi and Kisumu for 3,000 healthcare workers. CRS launched programs to conduct community awareness, equip their health workers and facilities. World vision, a faith-based organization, assisted in supplying food and other essential items to those affected by COVID-2019 in different countries such as the Democratic Republic of the Congo, Kenya, Senegal, and South Africa. The organization identified the most vulnerable children and families in their communities through local churches to serve the neediest families.

Religious and other community leaders played a role in promoting messages of unity among their community members and emphasized the importance of preventing the social stigma of affected people and groups. They encouraged community members to show empathy with others and understand the virus itself (UNICEF, 2020). Religious leaders tried to promote positive behavior and beliefs in times of crisis. After the outbreak of COVID-2019 there were tensions arising due to claims that COVID-2019 was sent by evil forces or as a punishment sent by God for sin and disobedience (Global Voices, 2020). Such rumors led to panic and suspicion, leading to strategies to eliminate those portended to have done serious crimes such as witchcraft and prostitution. Most religious leaders and communities of faith led the way in finding new ways to serve, unite, and stem the spread of the virus. Religious leaders and communities were instrumental in advocating and taking action to avoid scapegoating and build harmony in society during this time of heightened stress and tension.

Many surveys in the world indicate that religious leaders are the most trusted leaders in the world. Throughout history, most people started mistrusting their governments during pandemics. During pandemics, trust is important for public health interventions, economic and social dislocations that accompany them. Such a case was seen when Litzman, the ultra-orthodox Israeli minister of health, was asked whether confinement in Israel will last until Passover. He replied that "the Messiah will come and take us out of this the way [God] He took us out of Egypt. Soon we will be freed and the Messiah will come and redeem us for all the evils of the world." By a cruel twist of fate, the minister later tested positive for COVID-2019, obliging Prime Minister Benjamin Netanyahu and other politicians and security officials who had been in contact with him to go into quarantine (Estrin, 2020). It can be observed that religious leaders can encourage positive behavioral changes by example and by preaching, for instance, about the value of physical distancing and wearing a mask, since they are trusted by their communities. At the same time, religious communities, in turn, need to earn the trust of public health authorities.

Religious leaders and actors re-examined religious rituals and practices in order to minimize risks of transmission of the virus (Jaja, 2020). Most rituals which went against social distancing were relooked at. For example, the Catholic Church changed the mode of administering sacraments. The religious leaders emphasized hygiene and created awareness on the importance of frequently washing hands with warm water and soap, to help prevent the spread of the virus. Adequate running water and soap as well as hand sanitizers were availed at several stations within the worship premises. This is a sign that they heeded the call of scientists and assisted to seek control of the spread of the disease. Rituals that involved interring the dead were either abolished or modified to prevent the spread of the virus.

Churches, mosques, synagogues, temples, and other sacred spaces continued to serve the community. They provided prayer services and rituals that helped people to connect with their faith. Most religions recognized that faith is an important support and coping mechanism, especially in a time of crisis and uncertainty. Pope Francis exemplified the pastoral leadership as he invited Christians to a kind of "solidarity in place," encouraging them to check on friends and family by phone or Internet, or to deliver groceries to those in need. His lovely *Urbi et Orbi* blessing on March 27 offered the consolation and encouragement to many people (Pope Francis, 2020).

In Kenya, Christianity was an avenue for politicians to break the COVID-2019 protocols. Kenya's deputy president was seen moving from one church to another in the name of fundraising for churches. While in the fundraising, people never wore masks, never kept social distance, and shook hands in the open. Such careless behaviors made many Kenyans to be worried when they realized that some of those who the deputy president shared podium contracted the coronavirus, leading to death of some individuals such as the African Independent Pentecostal Churches of Africa Bishop, Rev. Stephen Ng'ang'a, who succumbed to coronavirus a few days after hosting Kenya's deputy president William Ruto on Sunday, October 4 in Kenol, Murang'a County (Gitau, 2020). Later, the Matungu MP Justus Murunga who had hosted the deputy president in a church fundraising died also due to coronavirus a few weeks afterward.

Spirituality helps people to find meaning and maintain hope in the face of threats and disrupted lives (Parsitau, 2020). Normally, when people are afraid and lonely, they seek comfort and explanations for their suffering, as well as glimpses of hope. Greg Epstein (Radar, 2020), the Humanist chaplain at Harvard University, has observed that people find comfort in knowing that they are enduring the current crisis together and in their common vulnerability. Even as the pandemic highlights injustices and wrongs in society, people look to faith teachings for inspiration for the path forward. Christian religious traditions remind people that their forebears were tested and emerged stronger from past trials, providing some reassurance that they will in this crisis, too.

The danger of mutual distrust was evident during the 2014 Ebola outbreak in West Africa when measures by officials in Guinea and Sierra Leone to cremate or swiftly bury the dead, in order to contain the spread of Ebola, generated fear and suspicion in many West African communities (Dockins, 2014). Those who led burial procedures—outsiders dressed in protective gear that resembled spacesuits—were blocked from entering many Ebola-affected communities and some faced violent, even deadly, physical attacks (Jallow, 2014). In late 2014, public health officials and religious leaders with the WHO worked together to produce a protocol for culturally sensitive burials for Ebola victims that may have saved thousands of lives (Mazumdar, 2017). Similar trust challenges surrounded COVID-2019 health directives like contact tracing, which has raised legitimate concerns about privacy, and they seemed to deny families and religion time to accord their final respect to the dead.

CONCLUSION AND RECOMMENDATIONS

This chapter on corroreligion reveals that religion has involved itself in the fight against the COVID-2019 pandemic in Africa. The outbreak of COVID-2019 affected religion negatively in Africa economically and socially. Christian religions interpreted the cause of COVID-2019 differently and the various interpretations have the potential of interfering with the control of COVID-2019. Different churches responded in different ways to cope and fight the spread of the COVID-2019 pandemic.

The study was guided by the functional theory of social sciences that led us to conclude that religion is the key to determining the interpretation and response of people toward COVID-2019. Through the principles of Structural Functionalist Theory the research made a conclusion that religion has a function toward health through its teachings. Specifically, it indicated that religion has a role toward management and control of COVID-2019. Further, it reinforces and defines acceptable behavior and response toward pandemics positively and negatively, just like a double-edged sword. It is a social control mechanism that tries to restore conformity to basic values and norms of a society with regard to health patterns.

The study recommends that the fight against COVID-2019 cannot be achieved if we cannot involve religionists as stakeholders. This is because they involve the attitudes of people toward the cause, control, and prevention of diseases. Scientists cannot succeed in solving health matters such as the search for a cure and control of the spread of dangerous diseases minus involving the spirituality of the people whom they are serving. Failure to accommodate the spirituality of the targeted audience may prevent effective implementation of whatever measures scientists may need for effective control, management, and prevention of the spread of coronavirus and other pandemics. We recommend that for the world to manage this COVID-2019 pandemic and any pandemic in future, there is need to understand people's religious beliefs and doctrines in matters of health. After understanding, scientists should teach religious leaders more about the cause and control of the specific pandemics. This is important as the faithful will get the correct information, and they will be involved to offer solution and control of any pandemics in future without conflicts.

There is need for a universal model on how to include religion in the fight against pandemics. As much as science is searching for a vaccine for coronavirus, religion also gives hope to the patients; offers therapy to affected families; provides scientists with operational ethics; and becomes an avenue to train and educate people on the prevention, control, and spread of diseases. Both science and religion are crucial in the fight against coronavirus.

During this research, it was revealed that much of the Christian traditions in Africa are influenced by indigenous African beliefs. Therefore, some African cases of corroreligion may not be universal. There is need for more studies about the involvement of indigenous African religionists in the control and prevention of COVID-2019.

REFERENCES

Adekaye, M. (March 26, 2020). Nigerians remind T. B. Joshua of his prophecy on coronavirus. Retrieved on October 15, 2020 from https://www.guardian.ng/life/nigerians-reminds-t-b-joshua-of-his-prophesy-on-coronavirus.

Akpan, N. (March 14, 2020). Popular pastor suspends church activities over coronavirus. Retrieved on September 29, 2020 from https://www.firstreportsonline.com/popular-pastor-suspends-church-activities-over-coronavirus.

Allison, J., Eagle, L., Phillips, C., Hedges, D. S., Bodenhamer, C., Brown, R., Wheeler, J. G. and Kirking, H. (May 22, 2020). COVID-19 attack rate among attendees at events at a church—Arkansas. Retrieved on May 29, 2020 from https://www.cdc.gov/mmwr/volumes/69/wr/mm6920e2.htm.

Armstrong M. (March 11, 2020). Netanyahu of Israel suggests micro chipping kids and mandatory vaccines begin. Retrieved on May 5, 2020 from https://www.armstrongeconomics.com/world-news/conspiracy/netanyahu-of-israel-suggests-microchipping-kids.

Ananthalakshmi, J. A. A. (March 17, 2020). How mass pilgrimage at Malaysian mosque became coronavirus hotspot. Retrieved on May 5, 2020 from https://www.reuters.com/article/us-health-coronavirus-malaysia-mosque-idUSKBN2142S4.

Asamoah-Gyadu, J. K. (2020). *Dealing with a Spiritual Virus: Whither the Prophetic?* Accra, Ghana: Trinity Theological Seminary, Legon.

Bajpai, S. R. (1996). *Methods of Social Survey and Research*. Kanpur, India: Kitab Ghar Publishers.

Barry, E. (March 30, 2020). Days after a funeral in a Georgia town, coronavirus 'hit like a bomb.' Retrieved on April 2, 2020 from https://www.nytimes.com/2020/03/30/us/coronavirus-funeral-albany-georgia.html.

Bramstedt, K. A. (September 14, 2020). COVID-19 as cause of death for Catholic priests in Italy: An ethical and occupational health crisis. *Health and Social Care Chaplaincy* 8(2). Retrieved on October 15, 2020 from https://www.journals.equinoxpub.com/HSCC/article/view.

British Broadcasting Corporation (BBC). (April 3, 2020). Coronavirus: Ultra-orthodox Israeli town of Bnei Brak under lockdown. Retrieved on July 7, 2020 from https://https://www.bbc.com/news/world-middle-east-52149316.

Brown, A. R. R. (1952). *Structure and Function in Primitive Society*. New York: Free Press.

Bukhara, Q., Massaro, J. M., D'Agostino Sr. R. B. and Khan, S. (2020). Effects of weather on coronavirus pandemic. *MIT Libraries*. Retrieved on July 7, 2020 from https://dspace.mit.edu/handle/1721.1/126462.

Dockins, P. (August 2, 2014). Traditional burials hamper Ebola fight. Retrieved on July 12, 2020 from https://www.voanews.com/africa/who-traditional-burials-hamper-ebola-fight.

Durkheim, E. (1915). *The Elementary Forms of the Religious Life: A Study in Religious Sociology*. New York: Macmillan.

Estrin, D. (April 1, 2020). Israel faces challenges in fighting coronavirus in ultra-orthodox communities. Retrieved on April 4, 2020 from https://www.kpbs.org/news/2020/apr/01/israel-faces-challenges-in-fighting-coronavirus.

Fox6. (May 17, 2020). Poll: 63 percent of religious Americans believe COVID-19 pandemic is message from God for humanity to change. Retrieved on April 4, 2020 from https://www.fox6now.com/news/poll-63-of-religious-americans-believe-covid-19-pandemic-is-message-from-god-for-humanity-to-change.

Frazer, J. G. (1936). *The Golden Bough: A Study in Comparative Religion*. London, UK: Macmillan Publishers.

Gitau, M. (November 14, 2020). Bishop, who hosted DP Ruto in chaos-hit Murang'a fundraiser dies, gets buried in low-key ceremony. Retrieved on October 12, 2020 from https://www.k24tv.co.ke/news/bishop-who-hosted-dp-ruto-in-chaos-hit-muranga-fundraiser-dies-gets-buried-in-low-key-ceremony-28365.

Global Voices. (March 25, 2020). Across Africa, COVID-19 heightens tensions between faith and science. Retrieved on 25 March 2020 from https://www.globalvoices.org/2020/03/25/across-africa-covid-19-heightens-tension-between-faith-and-science/.

Hackernoon. (May 3, 2020). The Bible's 666 Mark of The Beast prophecy: COVID-19 coronavirus vaccinations & crypto currency. Retrieved on May 15, 2020 from https://www.hackernoon.com/covid-19-and-the-bibles-666-prophecy-zb2432po.

Hicks, R. (January 2, 2019). *Co-Creators With God: Learn How To Create The Abundant Life Jesus Came To Give You!* Jericho, NY: Ryan Hick's Publishers. Retrieved on October 2, 2020 from https://www.kobo.com/ww/en/ebook/co-creators-with-god-learn-how-to-create-the-abundant-life-jesus-came-to-give-you.

Jaja, I. F., Anyanwu, M. U. and Jaja, C-J. I. (May 27, 2020). Social distancing: How religion, culture and burial ceremony undermine the effort to curb COVID-19 in South Africa. Retrieved on October 30, 2020 from https://www.tandfonline.com/doi/full/10.1080/22221751.2020.1769501.

Jallow, M. (July 29, 2014). Health workers pay the ultimate price in the fight against Ebola. Retrieved on September 20, 2020 from https://www.intrahealth.org/vital/health-workers-pay-ultimate-price-fight-against-ebola.

Jeffreys, R. (March 9, 2020). Is the coronavirus a judgment from God. Retrieved on June 15, 2020 from https://www.firstdallas.org/blog/is-the-coronavirus-a-judgment-from-god/.

Kahan, A. (1979). Social aspects of the plague epidemics in eighteenth-century Russia. *Economic Development and Cultural Change* 27(2):255–266. Retrieved on November 7, 2020 from https://www.jstor.org/stable/1153439.

Kgatle, M. S. (2017). The unusual practices within some neo-Pentecostal churches in South Africa: Reflections and recommendations. *HTS Teologiese Studies/Theological Studies* 73:3–8.

Kenya Open Data Survey. (October 21, 2009). *Census, Volume 2, Table 12: Population by Religious Aliation, Kenya Open Data*, last modified 2014. Retrieved on August 15, 2020 from https://www.opendata.go.ke/-Environment-AndNatural-Resources/2009-Census-Volume-2-Table-12-Population-byReligi/jrmn-krnf.

Kettley, S. (March 22, 2020). Coronavirus in the Bible: Bizarre claim virus is punishment for Christian persecution. Retrieved on May 5, 2020 from https://www.express.co.uk/news/weird/1258745/Coronavirus-Bible-virus-punishment-God-Christian-persecution-COVID-19.

Kombe, C. (March 27, 2020). Tanzanian president criticized for refusing to close places of worship. Retrieved on June 20, 2020 from https://www.voanews.com/

science-health/coronavirus-outbreak/tanzanian-president-criticized-refusing-close-places-worship.

Marshall, K. (May 26, 2020). What religion can offer in the response to COVID-19. Retrieved on May 26, 2020 from https://www.worldpoliticsreview.com/articles/28789/what-religion-can-offer-in-the-response-to-covid-19.

Mazumdar, T. (June 22, 2017).Ebola virus burial teams may have 'saved thousands of lives.' Retrieved on May 10, 2020 from https://www.bbc.com/news/health-40375693.

Mbiti, J. S. (1969). *African Religions and Philosophy*. London, UK: Heinemann.

Merton, R. K. (1968). *Social Theory and Social Structure*. New York: Free Press.

Naughtie, A. (March 26, 2020). Coronavirus; Trump cabinet's pastor blames gay people for 'wrath of God.' Retrieved on July 20, 2020 from https://www.independent.co.uk/news/world/americas/coronavirus-trump-pastor-homophobic-ralph-drollinger.

Ogila, J. (May 13, 2020). Covid-19 is not 666 where are Christian theologians to educate the world? Retrieved on July 7, 2020 from https://www.standardmedia.co.ke/article/2001371223/covid-19-is-not-666-where-are-christian-theologians-to-educate-the-world.

Okoth, D. O. (September 4, 2020). Radio and pandemics. COVID 19 in East Africa. How vernacular radio are influencing social and behavior change. Retrieved on July 10, 2020 from https://www.comminit.com/media-development/content/radio-and-pandemics-covid-19-east-africa-how-community-and-vernacular-radio-are-influenc.

Orjinmo, N. (April 8, 2020). Coronavirus: Nigeria's mega churches adjust to empty auditoriums. Retrieved on August 10, 2020 from https://www.bbc.com/news/world-africa-52189785.

Osei, S. (March 27, 2020). How one pastor is comforting his members during the COVID-19 pandemic? Retrieved on September 7, 2020 from https://www.theundefeated.com/features/how-one-pastor-is-comforting-his-members-during-the-covid-19-pandemic.

Otieno, I. (April 18, 2020). Pastor who mocked Kenya's Covid-19 cases embarrassed. Retrieved on August 20, 2020 from https://www.kenyans.co.ke/news/52204-tanzanian-pastors-mockery-kenyas-covid-19-cases-leaves-egg-face.

Parke, C. (March 12, 2020). Joel Osteen's Houston Mega church cancels public Sunday service over coronavirus. Retrieved on June 15, 2020 from https://www.foxnews.com/us/coronavirus-update-houston-texas-joel-osteen-lakewood-church-cancel-sunday-service.

Parsitau, D. (March 23, 2020). Religion in the age of coronavirus. Retrieved on April 20, 2020 from https://www.theelephant.info/features/2020/03/23/religion-in-the-age-of-coronavirus.

Parsons, T. (1951). *The Social System*. Glencoe, NY: Free Press.

Patterson, D. K. (1983). The influenza epidemic of 1918–19. *The Journal of African History* 24(4):489.

Pew Research Center. (August 22, 2018). The world's most committed Christians live in Africa, Latin America and the U.S. Accessed on August 20, 2020. https://www

.pewresearch.org/fact-tank/2018/08/22/the-worlds-most-committed-christians-live-in-africa-latin-america-and-the-u-s.

Pope Francis. (March 27, 2020). Urbi et Orbi address on coronavirus and Jesus calming the storm. Retrieved on April 4, 2020 from https://www.americamagazine.org/faith/2020/03/27/read-pope-francis-urbi-et-orbi-address-coronavirus-and-jesus-calming-storm.

Radar. (April 24, 2020). Faith and purpose during the coronavirus pandemic. Retrieved on April 20, 2020 from https://www.wgbh.org/news/lifestyle/2020/04/24/faith-and-purpose-during-the-coronavirus-pandemic.

Sang-Hun, C. (May 22, 2020). Church is at center of coronavirus outbreak in South Korea. Retrieved on October 15, 2020 from https://www.nytimes.com/2020/02/21/world/asia/south-korea-coronavirus-shincheonji.html.

Sanneh, L. (1983). *West African Christianity: The Religious Impact.* Mary Knoll, NY: Orbis Books.

Schechter, D. (November 11, 2020). Synagogues and Jewish institutions discuss how to take community precautions as COVID-19 spreads globally. Retrieved on November 18, 2020 from https://www.Ihpemory.org/being-Jewish-in-the-time-of-coronavirus.

Shim, E., Tariq, A., Choi, W., Lee, Y. and Chowell, G. (2020). Transmission potential and severity of COVID-19 in South Korea. *International Journal of Infectious Diseases* 93:339–344.

Stone, M. (May 18, 2020). Mega church pastor who claimed he could cure COVID-19 dies from Virus. Retrieved on May 23, 2020 from https://www.patheos.com/blogs/progressivesecularhumanist/2020/05-Megachurch-Pastor-who-claimed-he-could-cure-COVID-19-Dies-from-Virus.

The Guardian. (March 14, 2020). Religious festivals cancelled or scaled back due to coronavirus. Retrieved on April 20, 2020 from https://www.theguardian.com/world/2020/mar/14religious-festivals-cancelledor-scaled-back-due-to-coronavirus.

UNICEF, 2020. Coronavirus (COVID-19) global response situation reports humanitarian action for children. Retrieved on November 11, 2020 from https://www.unicef.org/appeals/covid-19/situation-reports.

USAID. (July 14, 2020). Faith based organizations in the front lines of COVID-19. Retrieved on August 24, 2020 from https://www.crs.org/media-center/news-release/faith-based-organizations-front-lines-covid-19.

World Health Organization (WHO). (March 12, 2020). WHO announces COVID-19 outbreak a pandemic. Retrieved on May 20, 2020 from https://www.euro.who.int/en/health-topics/health-emergencies/coronavirus-covid-19/news/news/2020/3/who-announces-covid-19-outbreak-a-pandemic.

Yakubu, N. (March 16, 2020). Duncan-Williams declare thirty-days fasting, prayers against coronavirus. Retrieved on March 16, 2020 from https://www.youtube.com/watch.

Chapter 10

Coromathematics

Abdul Karim Bangura

As I relay in my books titled *African Mathematics: From Bones to Computers* (Bangura, 2011) and *The African Mother Tongue and Mathematical Ideas* (Bangura, 2020), mathematics is used for many purposes. It is utilized in everyday life for such simple purposes as telling time or counting the change that is returned by a cashier. In business, mathematics is prevalent in all exchange transactions. In industry, almost all companies depend on mathematics for their research and development. In science, mathematics pervades all aspects in the scientific fields. Now we see that since the outbreak of the Coronavirus Disease (COVID)-2019, mathematics is being used to intensify hysteria—that is, an exaggerated or uncontrollable emotion or excitement—among people. The two aspects that have witnessed a proliferation of hysteria are (1) the reporting of COVID-2019 data by the news media and (2) attempts at mathematical projections.

In this chapter, evidence is provided to demonstrate that most of the mathematical approaches and models that have been used to explain and predict the trends of the virus are faulty. Thereafter, a more appropriate model and its attendant calculations are provided for a more rational understanding of the trends of the virus. In the end, conclusion is drawn and recommendations are made. Before doing all this, however, I will first discuss the General Mathematical Theory upon which the discussion that follows is grounded.

GENERAL MATHEMATICAL THEORY

The analysis in this chapter is grounded on General Mathematical Theory, which can be commonly defined as a supposition or a system of ideas intended to explain the abstract science of number, quantity, and space, especially one based on general principles independent of these aspects. Thus, a mathematical theory is customarily an archetype and conjecture which frequently ignores real physical attributes. As August Stern cogently illustrates this point, "a ball is not a perfect sphere and there is no point like mass and no absolutely smooth surface without friction" (2000, p. 1). For a discipline that dates back to 3000 BC in Ancient Kemet/Egypt, there are to be expected many mathematical theories (for more on this, see Bangura, 2011), as we will see later. The focus here, however, is mainly on General Mathematical Theory due to space limitation and to prevent a perfunctory exercise in trying to discuss all of the existing theories, albeit brief definitions will be provided for them.

Thus, to begin with, General Mathematical Theory hinges upon axioms: that is, statements or propositions which are regarded as being established, accepted, or self-evidently true. It can also be a corpus of knowledge such as known denotations and axioms. Concomitantly, a specific mathematical theory can be employed to broach a part of mathematical inquiry within that theory (Nelson, 2014).

Next, 72 different mathematical theories have been identified. The following is a listing of these theories with brief statements of their foci:

1. Algebraic K-theory focuses on assigned objects referred to as K-groups in the sense of abstract algebra.
2. Almgren–Pitts Min–Max Theory focuses on generalizing George David Birkhoff's method for constructing simple closed geodesics on the sphere in order to construct embedded minimal surfaces in arbitrary 3-manifolds. A manifold is a collection of points forming a certain kind of set, such as those of a topologically closed surface or an analogue of this in three or more dimensions.
3. Approximation Theory focuses on how functions can best be approximated with simpler functions and to quantitatively characterize the errors introduced.
4. Asymptotic Theory focuses on describing limiting behavior.
5. Automata Theory focuses on abstract machines and automata, in addition to the computational problems that can be solved employing them.
6. Bifurcation Theory focuses on changes in the qualitative or topological structure of a given family (e.g., the integral curves of a family of vector fields) and the solutions of a family of differential equations.
7. Braid Theory focuses on the basic groups of a configuration space or braid relations that are kept as pictures in the mind only to guide intuition.
8. Brill–Noether Theory focuses on special divisors on a curve *C* that reveal more well-matched functions than would be found.

9. Catastrophe Theory focuses on dynamical systems—that is, phenomena characterized by sudden shifts in behavior arising from little changes in situations.
10. Category Theory focuses on mathematical structure and its concepts vis-à-vis a labeled directed graph referred to as a category, whose nodes are referred to as objects and whose labeled directed edges are referred to as arrows or morphisms.
11. Chaos Theory focuses on states of dynamical systems whose seemingly random states of disorder and irregularities are frequently controlled by deterministic laws that are quite responsive to inceptive states.
12. Character Theory focuses on a function on the group that links to each group element the indication of the correlate matrix.
13. Choquet Theory focuses on measures which have assistance on the furthermost points of a convex set C.
14. Class Field Theory focuses on the abelian extensions of local fields, global fields of positive characteristic, and number fields.
15. Coding Theory focuses on the attributes of codes and their attendant fitness for specific applications.
16. Cohomology Theory focuses on the succession of abelian groups connected to a topological space.
17. Computation Theory focuses on problems to be solved on a computational model by utilizing an algorithm, how they can be efficiently solved, or to what degree.
18. Deformation Theory focuses on infinitesimal conditions connected with varying a solution P of a problem to moderately different solutions $P\varepsilon$, where ε is a small number or vector of small quantities.
19. Dimension Theory focuses on the least number of coordinates needed to identify any point within it.
20. Distribution Theory focuses on items that generalize the classical idea of functions in mathematical analysis.
21. Elimination Theory focuses on algorithmic techniques used to get rid of some variables between polynomials of several variables, so that systems of polynomial equations can be solved.
22. Extremal Graph Theory focuses on how global properties of a graph affect local substructure.
23. Field Theory focuses on a set through which addition, subtraction, multiplication, and division are defined and behave as do the corresponding operations on rational and real numbers.
24. Galois Theory focuses on the nexus between Field Theory and Group Theory.
25. Game Theory focuses on mathematical models of strategic interchanges among rational decision-makers.

26. Graph Theory focuses on mathematical structures used to devise pairwise relations between things.
27. Grothendieck's Galois Theory focuses on the basic group of algebraic topology in the context of algebraic geometry.
28. Group Theory focuses on algebraic constructions called groups accordingly.
29. Hodge Theory focuses on the cohomology groups of a smooth manifold *M* employing partial differential equations.
30. Homology Theory focuses on connecting a series of algebraic objects like abelian groups or modules to other mathematical objects like topological spaces.
31. Homotopy Theory focuses on conditions in which maps emerge with homotopies (relations that exist between two mappings in topological spaces if one mapping can be deformed in a continuous way to make it coincide with the other) between them.
32. Information Theory focuses on quantifying, storing, and communicating information.
33. Invariant Theory focuses on actions of groups in terms of algebraic differences.
34. K-theory focuses on a ring brought about by collections of a vector over a topological space or scheme.
35. Knot Theory focuses on mathematical knots: that is, closed, non-self-intersecting curves that are embedded in three dimensions and cannot be untangled to produce simple loops.
36. L-theory focuses on the K-theory (i.e., a ring brought about by collections of a vector over a topological space or scheme) of quadratic forms.
37. Local Class Field Theory focuses on abelian extensions of local fields: that is, fields which are complete in terms of absolute values or discrete valuations with finite residue fields.
38. M-theory focuses on consistent versions of Superstring Theory: that is, an endeavor to explicate every particle and basic force of nature in one theory by modeling them as vibrations of tiny supersymmetric strings.
39. Matrix Theory focuses on tables comprising expressions, numbers, or symbols organized in rows and columns.
40. Measure Theory focuses on assigning a number to a suitable subset of a set.
41. Model Theory focuses on the link between formal theories and their delineated models.
42. Morse Theory focuses on the topology of a manifold and the analysis of the differentiable functions on that manifold.
43. Module Theory focuses on the generalization of the idea of vector space over a field.

44. Network Theory focuses on graphs as portrayals of either symmetric or asymmetric relations between discrete objects.
45. Nevanlinna Theory focuses on the asymptotic placement of solutions of the equation $f(z) = a$, as a varies.
46. Number Theory focuses on integers and integer-valued functions.
47. Obstruction Theory focuses on an invariant that is cohomological: that is, a series of abelian groups related to a topological space.
48. Operator Theory focuses on linear operators on function spaces.
49. Order Theory focuses on the instinctive idea of order (i.e., the degree of complexity of an equation, expression, etc., as denoted by an ordinal number) utilizing binary relations.
50. Percolation Theory focuses on the response of a network when nodes or links are extracted.
51. Perturbation Theory focuses on approximate solutions to problems, beginning from the exact solutions of related, simpler problems.
52. Probability Theory focuses on the determination of a mathematical likelihood by expressing it through a set of axioms.
53. Proof Theory focuses on proofs (i.e., series of stages in the resolution of mathematical or philosophical problems) as formal mathematical objects whose analyses are facilitated by mathematical techniques.
54. Quantum Theory focuses on the physical attributes of nature at the scale (i.e., a system of numerical notation in which the value of a digit depends upon its position in the number, successive positions representing successive powers of a fixed base) of atoms and subatomic particles.
55. Queue Theory focuses on the mathematical prediction of waiting lines.
56. Recursion Theory focuses on computable functions (i.e., the formalized analogues of the intuitive idea of algorithm) and Turing degrees (i.e., a set of natural numbers that measures the level of algorithmic unsolvability of the set).
57. Representation Theory focuses on abstract algebraic structures whose elements are characterized as linear transformations of vector spaces.
58. Ring Theory focuses on algebraic structures in which addition and multiplication are explained and possess characteristics that are like those operations delineated for the integers.
59. Scheme Theory focuses on the enlarged idea of algebraic variety.
60. Seiberg–Witten Theory focuses on the calculation of an exact low-energy effective action.
61. Semigroup Theory focuses on algebraic structures embodying sets with connected binary operations.
62. Set Theory focuses on sets: that is, collections of distinct entities regarded as units, being either individually specified or, more usually, satisfying specified conditions.

63. Sheaf Theory focuses on locally defined data linked to the open sets of a topological space.
64. Singularity Theory focuses on spaces that are almost, albeit not completely, manifolds.
65. Spectral Theory focuses on eigenvalues of linear operators. An eigenvalue is a set of values of a parameter for which a differential equation has a nonzero solution (an eigenfunction) under given conditions.
66. String Theory focuses on how strings (i.e., physical entities) grow through space and interact with one another.
67. Surgery Theory focuses on the construction of one finite-dimensional manifold from another in a controlled manner.
68. Theory of Equations focuses on algebraic equations also referred to as polynomial equations.
69. Topos Theory focuses on the objects of topos (i.e., sheaves of sets), or a mathematical universe, which provide a general framework in which one can do mathematics.
70. Transcendental Number Theory focuses on the qualitative and quantitative analyses of numbers that are not solutions of any polynomial equation with integer coefficients.
71. Twistor Theory focuses on the arena from which space-time should arise.
72. Type Theory focuses on a formal system in which every term has a "type" that elucidates its denotation and the operations that may be done on it.

In sum, the foregoing mathematical theories, which together constitute the General Mathematical Theory, are quite useful for explaining the dynamics, structures, five basic notions, that is, (1) identity, (2) intersection, (3) negation, (4) conversion of a relation, and (5) relation in general, generalization of a problem, communication, mechanics, representation of groups, and providing general solutions to phenomena.

REPORTING COVID-2019 DATA BY THE NEWS MEDIA

A detailed analysis of how the news media have reported COVID-2019 data would require an encyclopedia. For the sake of brevity, I briefly discuss in this section the following aspects in a deductive (moving from the general to the specifics) and sequential order: (a) global coverage, (b) coverage in a developed nation—the United States, and (c) coverage in a developing nation—Nigeria. In the end, I briefly allude to the factors that underlie the manner the news media have reported the data.

Global Coverage

From Sintia Radu, we learn that the global coverage of the COVID-2019 pandemic has included deceptive data with racist connotations in certain instances. As the global media struggle to comprehend the virus and its attendant data, media experts have both praised and condemned the media for their reporting. Analysts say that the media have paid little attention to the real stories patients tell and instead focus more on spheres that have not even been exposed to the virus (Radu, 2020).

Radu adds that since the outbreak of the virus, the global media have constantly reported on the causes of the virus, the number of people that have been infected, and the number that have died. Informing the public that the virus originated in China, the media have also inundated audiences with very frequent live updates on the number of infected and dead patients (Radu, 2020), while relatively little is said about the overwhelming majority of the patients who recover from the virus.

Also, according to Radu, the media coverage has been asymmetrical across the globe and has included overdramatized features. She cites sources that say "Attention to how media messages address the virus, its transmission and risk varied significantly across types of coverage and by the nation that produces it" and "coverage has been inflammatory, particularly across social media and other unsubstantiated sources, which are unfortunately often taken as fact" (Radu, 2020, p. 1).

Coverage in a Developed Nation: The United States

To begin with, employing "multiple, computer-assisted content analytic" techniques on newspaper and television news coverage of COVID-2019 data between March and May 2020, P. Sol Hart, Sedona Chinn, and Stuart Soroka (2020) demonstrate how the news media have politicized and polarized the United States through their reporting. Their discovery is that while politicians appear in newspaper coverage more regularly than scientists, both politicians and scientists are more equally featured in network news. The high degree of politicization and polarization in the initial news coverage of COVID-2019, they argue, might have led to the polarization in attitudes among U.S. citizens toward the virus (Hart et al., 2020).

Next, Hart and his coauthors mention that by the end of May 2020, the news media reported that 6 million people had been infected and 369,000 had died from the virus worldwide. These authors also note that the news media reported that the United States had the largest infection rate of 1.8 million people and 100,000 deaths (Hart et al., 2020). Graphs were even presented comparing the infection and death rates in the United States, which has almost 331 million people, with countries that have very small populations.

Also, Hart and his colleagues point out that due to the way the news media have reported COVID-2019 data in terms of political responses, public perceptions in the United States have been divided across political ideological lines. For instance, the authors note that "83% of Republicans rate President Donald Trump's response to COVID-2019 as good or excellent, whereas only 18% of Democrats do so" (Hart et al., 2020, pp. 680–681).

In addition, Hart and his fellow authors indicate that American citizens' perceptions in terms of actions and scientists in dealing with the pandemic have been polarized. They state that, for example, "while in 2019 Democrats had greater confidence than Republicans that both medical scientists and scientists in general would act in the best interests of the public, this difference dramatically widened in April 2020, especially with respect to medical scientists, as Democratic confidence increased while Republican confidence remained flat" (Hart et al., 2020, p. 681). Hart and his coauthors further state that with "regard to protective actions, a minority of Republicans, compared to a majority of Democrats, felt that social distancing was helping a lot to slow the spread of coronavirus, that there was insufficient testing for coronavirus, and that more people needed to follow social distancing guidelines" (Hart et al., 2020, p. 681).

I must also mention here that a polarization has emerged in terms of how African Americans are being blamed by many people from other racial groups for the pandemic in the United States due to how the news media report COVID-2019 data pertaining to the group. For instance, the news media have been saying that African Americans are six times more likely to die from the virus than Whites. Then as one reads or listens as the story is told, one sees or hears that the estimate is based on "incomplete data" from "Chicago" (see, for example, a *Chicago Tribune* article republished in *The Gazette*, 2020). Yet, one notices that Washington, DC, where African Americans make up the largest racial group of 45.4 percent (42.5 percent White [37.3 percent non-Hispanic White and 5.2 percent Hispanic White], 4.1 percent Asian, 4.4 percent some other race, 0.3 percent Native American and Alaskan Native, 0.1 percent Pacific Islander, and 3.3 percent from two or more races) have a low death rate from COVID-2019.

Coverage in a Developing Nation: Nigeria

Oberiri Destiny Apuke and Bahiyah Omar (2020) start off by providing a brief chronology of how the COVID-2019 pandemic was reported in Nigeria's newspapers. The arrangement of the dates and detections of the infections in the order of their occurrence is as follows: (a) on February 27,

2020, the first case of the disease was reported when an Italian in Lagos tested positive for the virus; (b) on March 9, 2020, a second case of the virus was reported in Ewekoro, Ogun State, when a Nigerian who had visited an Italian tested positive; and (c) on May 21, 2020, it was reported that 4,971 individuals were infected, 164 had died, and 1,070 had recovered from the virus (Apuke and Omar, 2020).

Next, Apuke and Omar tell us that unlike the Nigerian newspapers' coverage of other infections such as the Flu, the newspapers highlighted that COVID-2019 is an unparalleled peril. This characterization of the virus, the authors say, further exaggerated the panic, stress, and hysteria that followed the coverage, since the news media are perceived to be a reliable source of health information (Apuke and Omar, 2020).

Overall, according to Apuke and Omar, the Nigerian newspapers did well apropos to their coverage of the pandemic which, in turn, led to awareness. Nonetheless, the authors note, the coverage lacked depth as most of the reported stories were short and mostly straight news. They add that the most cited entities by the newspapers were the Nigeria Centre for Disease Control and government officials. They also mention that most of the stories were frightening and caused anxiety. They further point out that the most frequently covered topics were about the death rates in the country and concerns about Nigeria's preparedness, while very little attention was paid to topics on sensitizing and educating the public (Apuke and Omar, 2020).

Factors that Underlie the Manner the News Media Have Reported the Data

There are a number of reasons for the shortcomings of the news media's reporting of COVID-2019 data noted in the preceding subsections. First, many journalists have a knack for Yellow Journalism—that is, reporting that is based upon sensationalism and unrefined magnification. This proclivity makes many journalists use exciting or shocking stories or language at the expense of accuracy in order to provoke public interest or excitement. It also makes them be offensively coarse when reporting the news.

Second, the news media are highly competitive. Thus, they have a strong desire to be more successful than others in the industry. This disposition leads journalists to rush and be the first to tell a story, even before getting complete data.

Third, the news media have agendas that they promote. They have plans of things to be done or problems to be addressed. They also have underlying intentions or motives. Consequently, journalists are vigorous in furthering, supporting, or actively encouraging the progress of their plans, intentions, or motives.

Fourth, many journalists are inclined to see the world through the standpoints of their employers. This natural survival tendency of journalists to keep their jobs makes them to neglect the fact that while their employers hire them, they do not own them.

Fifth, many journalists are not the most knowledgeable individuals when it comes to numbers because most of the students who major in journalism and other communication areas in the United States, for example, and most probably the other countries across the globe, are those with the lowest grade point averages (GPAs) and scholastic aptitude test (SAT) scores as compared to those who major in the sciences with higher GPAs and SAT scores. Also, communication programs have very weak mathematics requirements in their curricula.

ATTEMPTS AT MATHEMATICAL PROJECTIONS

Many mathematical projection models for COVID-2019 in the United States have been developed. Nonetheless, only two of these have been the most referenced by government officials and the news media. One of these projections is the Institute for Health Metrics and Evaluation (IHME) Model also called "The Chris Murray Model" based at the University of Washington. This model employs the following technique:

> COVID-2019 case and mortality data covering from February 1, 2020 to September 21, 2020 and a deterministic susceptible, exposed, infectious and recovered (SEIR) compartmental framework to model possible trajectories of severe acute respiratory syndrome coronavirus 2 (SARS-CoV-2) infections and the effects of non-pharmaceutical interventions in the United States at the state level covering from September 22, 2020 through February 28, 2021. (IHME, 2020, p. 1)

In March 2020, IHME published its first iteration of its COVID-2019 projections model. It projected that more than 400,000 people would die from the virus in the United States by November 1, 2020 (IHME, 2020). This projection was cited by the White House and many news media outlets. But by October 2, 2020, the IHME revised its projection down to 234,981 deaths by the same date. Its recent projection is that there would be 360,000 deaths by January 1, 2021 (IHME, 2020).

The deterministic SEIR compartmental model being utilized by IHME requires the use of differential equations to simulate an epidemic. Its computation is based on the following logic:

> Individuals experience a long incubation duration (the "exposed" category), such that the individual is infected but not yet infectious. For example chicken pox and even vector-borne diseases such as dengue hemorrhagic fever have long incubation duration where the individual cannot yet transmit the pathogen to others. [Also] recovered people may become susceptible again (recovery does not confer lifelong immunity). For example, rotovirus and malaria are diseases with long incubation durations, and where recovery only confers temporary immunity. (IDM, 2020, p. 1)

A major question that emerges here then is the following: What is a differential equation and what are its limitations? To begin with, a differential equation can be generally defined as that calculation which involves derivatives of a function or functions. The derivative of the function is derived by d*y*/d*x*, where d = derivative, *y* = the dependent variable, and *x* = the independent variable. Put differently, it is defined as the calculation that contains derivatives of one or more dependent variables with respect to one or more independent variables. There are two types of differential equations. One is the partial differential equation that involves partial derivatives. The other is the ordinary differential equation that does not involve partial derivatives.

Next, in terms of the limitations of differential equations, two are well known. One limitation is that "some differential equations are not as well-behaved, and show singularities due to a failure to model the problem correctly, or a limitation of the model that was not apparent" (Harten, 2018, p. 1). The other limitation is that "some differential equations can be solved analytically in closed-form, but most have to be approximated by numerical procedures, which can be unstable" (Harten, 2018, p. 1).

The other projection model is the one by the Johns Hopkins University Coronavirus Resource Center (CRC). It is based on the COVID-19 Testing Insights Initiative that reflects the significant changes that have taken place in both the testing landscape and the data environment in the United States. The following are the changes that have led to the differences between the initiative's calculations and some state estimates (CRC, 2020):

(a) The test of positivity is a measure of testing capacity that reveals important contexts about case totals and trends, but it does not show how widespread the virus is in communities.
(b) The technique being employed to calculate positivity hinges upon the lack of federal standards which leads to significant differences in how states report testing data; the CRC's data scientists and epidemiologists believe that a "people-centered calculation" allows users to determine whether states are testing widely in order to identify infections that may be taking place; and by looking at the percentage of people who

test positive, the CRC's personnel can also determine whether there are testing participation, access, or capacity problems that must be resolved.

(c) The focus of the technique is on the number of people that are actually tested, not the number of tests administered.

(d) The technique will not catch repeat tests done on the same individual if states report data on the number of people tested.

The preceding shortcomings notwithstanding, the CRC believes that it is imperative to continue calculating and tracking each state's test positivity while making every effort to use the best data available and monitoring the data environment and making needed changes (CRC, 2020).

Also, utilizing available data from multiple sources, the CRC has what it calls "COVID-19 Data in Motion," which is a "60-second, daily summary of the most important data on COVID-19 in the United States, updated every morning" (CRC, 2020, p. 1). It then uses 7-day averages to make its projections as follows:

> The CRC calculates the rolling 7-day average separately for daily cases and daily tests, and then for each day calculate the percentage over the rolling averages. Some states may be calculating the positivity percentage for each day, and then doing the rolling 7-day average. The reason why we use our approach is because testing capacity issues and uneven reporting cadences create a lot of misleading peaks and valleys in the data. Since we want to give a 7-day average, it is more fair to average the raw data and then calculate the ratios. Otherwise, days when a large number of negative tests are released all at once—and positivity is going to be very low—will have the same weight as days when data was steadily released, and the overall result is going to be lower. Our approach is applied to all our testing data to correct for these uneven data release patterns. (CRC, 2020, p. 1)

A profitable question to be raised is as follows: What is a rolling average and what are its limitations? For starters, according to Paul J. Lavrakas,

> A rolling average, also referred to as a moving average, is a type of chart analysis technique used to examine survey data collected over extended periods of time. . . . It is typically utilized to smooth out data series. The ultimate purpose of a rolling average is to identify long-term trends. It is calculated by averaging a group of observations of a variable of interest over a specific period of time. Such averaged number becomes representative of that period in a trend line. It is said that these period-based averages "roll," or "move," because when a new observation is gathered over time, the oldest observation of the pool being

averaged is dropped out and the most recent observation is included into the average. (Lavrakas, 2008, p. 768)

Next, a rolling average possesses a number of limitations. First, it always stays within a past level. Second, it calls for extensive record keeping of past data, which can be quite expensive and time consuming. Third, it gives equal weight to each of the values utilized in the calculation, while most reasonable data are more significant to current situations. Fourth, it excludes data outside the average period.

A major problem with the preceding projection models is that they rely heavily on spurious data from the discredited World Health Organization (WHO), many research organizations, the Red Cross, the Census American Community Survey, and the Bureau of Labor Statistics. The data are highly prone to double-counting: that is, a case is counted in more than one of these sources. Even more troubling is that the data are based on confirmed and also presumptive positive cases.

Another serious problem is that modeling a COVID-2019 projection is empirical: that is, knowledge is derived from sense experience. As such, a researcher wants to know what needs to be included in an epidemic model to match real-world data. Unfortunately, one cannot know everything about an epidemic, especially this new COVID-2019, or the data may not be available.

In addition, it behooves me to mention here other factors John P. A. Ioannidis, Sally Cripps, and Martin A. Tanner (2020) posit for why making projections for the COVID-2019 has been problematic. They are as follows: (a) "poor data input," (b) "wrong modeling assumptions," (c) "high sensitivity of estimates," (d) "lack of incorporation of epidemiological features," (e) "poor past evidence on effects of available interventions," (f) "lack of transparency," (g) "errors," (h) "lack of determinacy," (i) "consideration of only one or a few dimensions of the problem at hand," (j) "lack of expertise in crucial disciplines," (k) "groupthink and bandwagon effects," and (l) "selective reporting" (Ioannidis et al., 2020, p. 1).

A BOX-JENKINS MONTE CARLO TYPE MATHEMATICAL PROJECTION

For starters, on March 27, 2020, I made the point on my Facebook page that as a scientist, I was more afraid of the flu that had killed more than 48,000 people from January 21 to March 27, 2020, compared to a bit over 1,000 who had died from COVID-2019 during the same period in the United States (for the data, see CDC, 2020). I argued that the data being bandied around by the news media were spurious because they really do not understand what the data actually mean, and relying on the specious data from the WHO was an anathema. The only accurate data are those from the Centers for Disease Control and Prevention (CDC). But because the data are finessed backward, which takes a couple of days, and do not support the news media's knack for sensationalism, they are not well consulted.

Next, I demonstrated in my MATLAB Box-Jenkins Monte Carlo (a time series simulation method used to forecast with limited information) type mathematical projection models (soon to be presented) that the probability of an individual dying from COVID-2019 in the United States is very low. While waiting for robust longitudinal data to engage in more sophisticated mathematical computations, the following are what were available from the CDC for March 26, 2020:

Reported Cases: 68,440
Reported Deaths: 994 or 1.5 percent
Infected People Who Had Not Died: 67,446 or 98.5 percent

Thus, the mathematical calculations of the probability of dying from the COVID-2019 versus dying from the flu in the United States as of March 25, 2020, are the following:

P(COVID-2019 Deaths): 819 / 331,002,651 = 0.000002
P(Flu Deaths): 23,000 / 331,002,651 = 0.000069

The mathematical calculations of the probability of dying from COVID-2019 in Washington, DC, are as follows:

Number of Confirmed Infections = 401
Number of Deaths = 9
DC Population = 633,427
Probability of a DC Resident Dying from COVID-2019:
P(Death COVID-2019): 9 / 633,427 = 0.000014 = 0.0014 percent
Percentage of Infected Residents Dead: 9(401) = 2 percent
Percentage of Infected Residents Not Dead: 392(401) = 98 percent

On April 13, 2020, I stated that we now had robust longitudinal data for more sophisticated mathematical analyses. There were two potential data sets that were applicable for a Box-Jenkins projection and Monte Carlo type analysis. They both covered from January 12 to March 31, 2020, which means 81 daily data points. But because the first data set was cumulative, it had only 71 daily data points. The second data set, which was based on the date of illness onset, covered the entire 81 data points and, thus, more tenable for mathematical analyses.

The first data set is the cumulative total number of COVID-2019 cases by report date, covering from January 12 to March 31, 2020, at 4 pm ET (n = 186,101). Given their nature, some of these data had been vulnerable to double-counting. These are the ones bandied around by journalists because they are not trained mathematicians and thrive on emotional sensationalism. No wonder the uninitiated reader/hearer gets hysterical.

The second data set is the COVID-2019 cases by date of illness onset, covering from January 12 to March 31, 2020, at 4 pm ET (n = 47,923). These data are free of double-counting and, therefore, more tenable for serious mathematical analyses.

The data on deaths are cumulative for the obvious reason that they cannot, like the other data, be collected at the point of testing. Besides, a significant amount of the earlier data that were collected on deaths has been found to have been based on misdiagnoses. Thus, not even a mathematical correlation test can be done on these data because there are no matching vector points with any of the other data sets.

From my preliminary observation, I had stated that the spike we saw earlier was based more on the fact that we now have better instruments to determine the existence of the virus in minutes. The highest spikes took place between March 9 and 21, 2020. They started receding on March 22 and have been doing so significantly from March 26 to the present (see figure 10.1). I have been running the data via my MATLAB program every day for more accurate analyses.

The following Box-Jenkins results were yielded using both simple and linear lagged time series models:

No seasonality or trend is present
Initial Value Series = 591.95062
Dynamic Flux Estimation: 80
Sum of Squared Error: 57,079,017.126
Alpha: 0.1

Given the preceding results, I therefore proffered that ceteris paribus, for the next 18 days of the month, from April 3 to 20, the rates should seesaw with 11 days of increases and 7 days of decreases. For the last 10 days of the month, from April 21 to 30, we should see significant and uninterrupted decreases. Since I posted the preceding results, my model projections for the month of April were 100 percent accurate and supported by the data later posted at the CDC website which I monitor daily and post the results on Facebook.

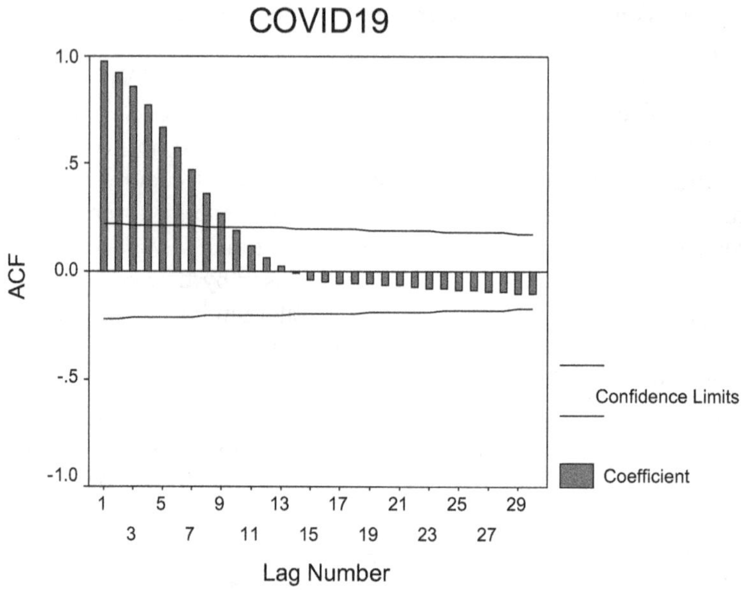

Figure 10.1 COVID-2019 Lagged Time Series for the United States.

My most recent analysis of the CDC data on COVID-2019 in the United States for November 16, 2020, still supports my assertion that the probability of an individual in the country dying from the virus is still very low. The following are the statistical results that support my postulation:

Number of Confirmed Infections = 10,984,398
Number of Deaths = 245,470
U.S. Population = 331,746,299

Probability of an Individual in the United States Dying from COVID-2019:

P(Death COVID-2019): 245,470 / 331,746,299 = 0.00074 = 0.074 percent
Percentage of Infected Individuals in the United States Dead: 245,470(10,984,398) = 2.2 percent
Percentage of Infected Individuals in the United States Not Dead: 10,738,928(10,984,398) = 97.8 percent

CONCLUSION AND RECOMMENDATIONS

Seeing and hearing the decontextualized COVID-2019 data for the United States and many Asian and European countries being bandied around by the news media, the governments across Africa, a continent with countries (with the exception of South Africa due to its weather conditions) that have the smallest numbers of travel-related cases, joined the bandwagon of locking down and forcing their citizens to practice "social distancing." The notion of "social distancing" itself is an oxymoron, as "social" means the need for companionship and "distance" denotes staying away from people. It is also contrary to the community-centered culture of Africans.

Besides, most of the African countries neither have the new instruments to test for the virus nor the new vaccines to prevent and medicines to treat it if detected. In most of Africa, a house built for 10 people is occupied by 40 or more people with one toilet. So, if even one person in a household has COVID-2019 during a lockdown, the government might as well just go and shoot everyone in that house to save them from the ensuing agony.

Also, we now see many African governments using the COVID-2019 pandemic to upend democracy and suppress the freedom of people, leading to economic depression and heightened hysteria. These governments are not even giving people food and other basic necessities to survive. In fact, it has been very well demonstrated that the virus does not thrive in hot weather. So, as stated earlier, most of the comparatively very small numbers of cases in Africa, with the exception of South Africa as mentioned earlier, are travel related. Thus, a recommendation for African governments is to address the problem at the ports of entry into their countries.

Given the findings in the preceding sections, I proffer in the rest of this section two additional recommendations. First, there is a need for the use of more sophisticated mathematical techniques to model COVID-2019 projections. Among these techniques are the following: (1) Autoregression, (2) Autoregressive Moving Average, (3) Autoregressive Integrated Moving Average, (4) Seasonal Autoregressive Integrated Moving-Average, (5) Seasonal Autoregressive Integrated Moving-Average with Exogenous Regressors, (6) Vector Autoregression, (7) Vector Autoregression Moving-Average, (8) Vector Autoregression Moving-Average with Exogenous Regressors, (9) Simple Exponential Smoothing, and (10) Holt Winter's Exponential Smoothing (for details on these techniques, consult Brownlee, 2018 and updated 2020).

Second, in order for journalists to be able to report COVID-2019 and other numerical data adequately, they need to be trained in an Introduction to Mathematical Proof course, which will allow them to make inferential arguments for mathematical statements and show that the stated assumptions logically guarantee the conclusion. The course will also force them to take the mathematical prerequisites, which are Calculus II, Introduction to Linear Algebra, and Multivariable Calculus. The topics covered in an Introduction to Mathematical Proof course normally include (a) Introduction to Sets—Set Operations, De Morgan's Law; (b) Some Logic—Direct Proofs, Contrapositive Proofs, Proofs by Contradiction, Quantifiers, Impact of Change of Quantifiers, Order of Quantifiers and Negations on Meaning of Statements, Disproving Statements; (c) Applied Proof Techniques—Divisibility, Real Number Properties, Set Equalities, and Equivalence Relations; (d) Cardinality—Size of Sets, Countability, and Bernstein's Theorem; (e) Induction—First Principle of Finite Mathematical Induction, Second Principle of Finite Mathematical Induction, and Applications; (f) Sequences—Definition of Limit, Convergence, Monotone Convergence Theorem, and Bolzano-Weierstrass Theorem; (g) Completeness—Greatest Lower Bounds, Least Upper Bounds, and Cauchy Sequence; and (h) Functions—Injective, Surjective and Bijective Functions, Continuous Functions with Sequence Definition, and Continuous Functions with Epsilon/Delta Definition (for more details on this course's requirements, see, for example, UMCP Mathematics Department, 2020). In sum, what these techniques will do for a journalist is to help him/her know how to prove something in many different ways by mastering direct proof, proof by contradiction, and proof by induction.

REFERENCES

Apuke, O. D. and Omar, B. (October 21, 2020). How do Nigerian newspapers report COVID-19 pandemic? The implication for awareness and prevention. *Health Education Research* 35(5):471–480

Bangura, A. K. (2011). *African Mathematics: From Bones to Computers*. Lanham, MD: University Press of America/Rowman and Littlefield Publishing Group.

Bangura, A. K. (2020). *The African Mother Tongue and Mathematical Ideas*. Wilmington, DE and Malaga, Spain: Vernon Press.

Brownlee, J. (August 6, 2028, updated August 20, 2020). 11 classical time series forecasting methods in Python. *Machine Learning Mastery*. Retrieved on November 20, 2020 from https://machinelearningmastery.com/time-series-forecasting-methods-in-python-cheat-sheet/.

Centers for Disease Control and Prevention (CDC). (2020). *Coronavirus Disease 2019 (COVID-19)*. Retrieved on January 27, 2020 onward from https://www.cdc.gov/coronavirus/2019-ncov/cases-updates/index.html.

Chicago Tribune. (April 7, 2020). African Americans 6 times more likely than whites to die from coronavirus, Chicago statistics show. Republished in *The Gazette*. Retrieved on November 19, 2020 from https://www.thegazette.com/subject/news/health/african-americans-6-times-more-likely-than-whites-to-die-from-coronavirus-chicago-statistics-show-20200407.

Coronavirus Resource Center (CRC). (2020). *COVID-19 Data in Motion*. Retrieved on November 18, 2020 from https://coronavirus.jhu.edu/.

Hart, P. Sol, Chinn, S. and Soroka, S. (August 25, 2020). Politicization and polarization in COVID-19 news coverage. *Science Communication* 42(5):679–697.

Harten, L. (December 27, 2018). What are the advantages and disadvantages of differential equations? *Quora.* Retrieved on November 17, 2020 from https://www.quora.com/What-are-the-advantages-and-disadvantages-of-differential-equations.

Institute for Disease Modeling (IDM). (2020). SEIR and SEIRS models. *Malaria Model.* Retrieved on November 17, 2020 from https://docs.idmod.org/projects/emod-malaria/en/latest/model-seir.html.

Institute for Health Metrics and Evaluation (IHME). (2020). COVID-19 projections. *Measuring What Matters.* Retrieved on November 17, 2020 from http://www.healthdata.org/.

Ioannidis, J. P. A., Cripps, S. and Tanner, M. A. (August 25, 2020). Forecasting for COVID-19 has failed. *International Journal of Forecasting.* doi:10.1016/j.ijforecast.2020.08.004. Retrieved on November 18, 2020 from https://www.sciencedirect.com/science/article/pii/S0169207020301199?via%3Dihub.

Lavrakas, P. J., ed. (2008). *Encyclopedia of Survey Research Methods.* Thousand Oaks, CA: Sage Publications.

Nelson, S. (2014). Theorems and theories. *Internet Archive Way Back Machine.* Retrieved on November 14, 2020 from https://web.archive.org/web/20140819090102/http://www.esotericka.org/cmc/tth.html.

Radu, Sintia. (February 7, 2020). How global media covers the coronavirus. *U. S. News.* Retrieved on November 19, 2020 from https://www.usnews.com/news/best-countries/articles/2020-02-07/how-the-global-media-covered-stories-about-the-coronavirus-outbreak.

Stern, A. (2000). *Quantum Theoretic Machines.* North Holland, The Netherlands: Elsevier BV.

University of Maryland College Park (UMCP) Department of Mathematics. (2020). Math 310: Introduction to mathematical proof. Retrieved on November 20, 2020 from https://www-math.umd.edu/offered-courses/378-math-310-introduction-to-analysis.html.

Chapter 11

Coropsychology

Pamela Anyango Oloo and Yakub Adams

In his eighth national address to the people of Kenya on the state of the Coronavirus Disease (COVID)-2019 pandemic, President Uhuru Muigai Kenyatta of the Republic of Kenya said the following: "The whole world is walking through the valley of the shadow of death" (Kenyatta, 2020, p. 1). This biblical analogy succinctly summarizes the perception by most world governments toward COVID-2019 as well as the potential generation of anxiety and inherent hysteria among people. Kenya's chief administrative secretary of health echoed similar sentiments when, in the daily briefing on June 20, 2020, she observed that the COVID-2019 pandemic had had a great impact on the health, socioeconomic, and psychological aspects of the population, "not only because of the morbidity or mortality it causes . . . but also because of the insidious psychological suffering that results from the response against the pandemic" (Ministry of Health, 2020a, p. 1).

This chapter is hinged on the premise that time and again human beings are faced with adverse effects of novel diseases that highly threaten their existence and create instability and apprehension globally. The essence of fear, especially of the incomprehensible, normally portends issues of panic and anxiety which lead to possible psychological and physical hysterical reactions. Pandemics, all over the world and for eons, have emerged as serious health hazards to humanity. These pandemics enhance, to greater levels, human morbidity and mortality rates and impact severely the psychological, socioeconomic, and political activities of individuals and the world nations at large. The continued emergence of pandemics is in total disregard to the perceived medical technological advancements humans have managed to put in place. This belies the expectations that with such technological growth seen in the medical field, for instance, pandemics should be things of the past or if they appear, be crushed swiftly from the onset. However, severe disease outbreaks have always dogged human survival and perseverance. The noteworthy ones include deadly disease outbreaks such as smallpox, bubonic plague, the Spanish flu, typhus, the plague of Justinian, malaria, Ebola, AIDS, and most recently, COVID-2019. Currently, the world is facing the infectious wrath of the novel COVID-2019.

According to the World Health Organization (WHO) (2020), the COVID-2019 is an infectious disease caused by a newly discovered coronavirus. The WHO adds that the COVID-2019 virus spreads primarily through droplets of saliva or discharge from the nose when an infected person coughs or sneezes. Most people infected with the COVID-2019 virus will experience mild to moderate respiratory illness and recover without requiring special treatment. According to the Centers for Disease Control and Prevention (CDC) (2020), the youth and young adults are noted to have the lowest mortality rates from COVID-2019 but they are not immune to its consequences, including mental health and psychological well-being. However, older people and those with underlying medical problems like cardiovascular disease, diabetes, chronic respiratory disease, and cancer are more likely to develop serious illness.

The outbreak of COVID-2019 is traced to Wuhan city of China, probably in December 2019 when a group of people were detected to have pneumonia of unknown cause. The outbreak was mainly linked to the owners of businesses in Wuhan fish market. By March 20, 2020, the WHO declared COVID-2019 a pandemic. Since its emergence, the disease has spread to many countries and nations outside of China. According to the Consumer News and Business Channel (CNBC, 2020), the virus presents evidence of person-to-person transmission, and the infection rate notably spiked by mid-January 2020. Currently, the disease is all over the world in Europe, Asia, America, and Africa among other continents (Okal et al., 2020). COVID-2019 is a contagious new strain of coronavirus that has not been previously identified in humans and has no known cure. Anybody is notably susceptible to catching the virus.

COROPSYCHOLOGY: A HYSTERICAL PERSPECTIVE

The response by most world governments toward the disease has reached hysterical levels and the people are practically faced with monstrous feelings about COVID-2019. Kenya, like other governments, has implemented certain preventive protocols suggested to enhance prevention and the slowing down of person-to-person virus transmission. Such preventive measures include washing of hands with soap and running water or using a sanitizer, wearing of face masks while in the public places or among people, social distancing, self-quarantine, staying at or working from home, contact tracing, and isolation, among others. Health departments have implemented these preventive measures so as to ensure the containment of COVID-2019. As can be noted, these protocols are new and extremely strange to the people. Subsequently, families and individuals are bound to go through a lot of adjustments because their normal schedules are severely disrupted. Thus, there was a birth of "the new normal" which may impact the psychological wellness of the populace in many stressful ways. Literature indicates that psychologists often emphasize processes that occur inside the individual, including perception, cognition, motivation, and emotion, and the antecedents and consequences of these processes. In analyzing interaction, their focus is often on how aspects of self, attitudes, and interpersonal perception influence behavior.

The psychological implications of the novel coronavirus on the people are here referred to as Coropsychology. This coined terminology alludes to corona and psychology which construes a meaning of imaginary hyper responses to the COVID-2019 pandemic. The drastic measures to contain the spread of the virus are contrary to the norms of hitherto known daily activities and this could cause disturbing mental health issues such as deadly anxiety, panic disorder, and depression among the people over the strange illness. This chapter seeks to examine the psychological implications as manifest in people's reactions in reference to COVID-2019 eventualities. The focus would also be on the practical interventions and administrative policies to deter the coropsychological challenges experienced by the people.

Emanating from the ongoing narrative, this chapter explores the resultant psychological effects of COVID-2019 and the attendant coping mechanisms. This is determined as manifest in the language used in reference to COVID-2019 fatalities and the interpretation of containment measures such as hand washing, social distancing, quarantine, and home-based care of those who test positive for COVID-2019 but present mild or no symptoms at all. Additionally, there is an investigation of how the population responds to the various levels of the adverse measures implemented by governments to curb the spread of this disease. It also strives to find out the psychological implications of these measures. The big question is: How do the implications of and the measures in place to contain the pandemic demonstrate hysteria with possible debilitating psychological results?

In order to avail answers to these concerns, the study focused chiefly on the Kenyan scenario to provide the experiences based on the concept of Coropsychology, which will be used to refer to the psychological consequences of COVID-2019 on the accessible populace. In addition, the case of Tanzania is explored and used as an illustration of an alternative response to the pandemic that sharply contrasts the Kenyan experience and response. While COVID-2019 is a respiratory illness that presents with fairly ordinary symptoms such as fever, cough, difficulties in breathing, and shortness of breath, it may sometimes prove fatal. Nonetheless, majority of those who contract the virus recover from the illness. It is the global containment measures outlined by the WHO and cascaded to all countries irrespective of geographical, social, and economic contexts that cause untold suffering and mental anguish to the citizenry. The pandemic is characterized by reported large numbers of infection cases and deaths, broadcast daily by the media, and social disruptions, economic losses, and anxiety and uncertainty about the future, resulting in emotional strain and fear about contagion, loss of lives and livelihoods. COVID-2019 and the containment measures instituted impose irreversible psychological impacts on human societies.

The following key question is explored: What is the response to COVID-2019 by both the government and the general population and how has this response impacted the life of the general population? The novelty around COVID-2019 creates a mix of feelings, notably anxiety, fear, doubt, worry, sadness, anger, loss of control, helplessness, hopelessness in both response and mitigation efforts. This is evident at both the governmental and general population levels. There is anxiety on the return to normalcy, given that the "normal" has disrupted lives, economies, and social relationships. Consequently, coping with all the changes occasioned by COVID-2019 has taken a toll on the psychological makeup of people, leading to mental issues such as depression. While the COVID-2019 pandemic has spread to almost all nations and territories in the world, its effects across these regions are evidently disproportionate.

Africa has recorded considerably lower numbers in terms of infections and fatalities compared to other regions. While this has largely been attributed to low testing capacity, questions abound as to why people are not falling ill in large numbers or flocking to hospitals seeking treatment or even just collapsing dead on the streets since they would be sick anyway even in the absence of testing for COVID-2019. This then begs the question: Does Africa have much reason to fear COVID-2019 as much as regions that have recorded higher infection and fatality rates? Is it a mark of hysteria to copy and paste containment measures in total disregard of the geographic, social, and economic contexts in which lives are lived? In Africa, given that daily life and livelihoods happen in the streets, the calls for preventive isolation, working from home, staying at home, and instituting lockdowns have put people's livelihoods and survival at risk. Additionally, they constrain access to affordable food.

Coropsychology is here examined in relation to the COVID-2019 illness fatalities and the interpretation of the non-pharmaceutical containment interventions of hand washing, social distancing, and quarantine with reference to the four key actions in the management of COVID-2019 infections, namely test, isolate, find (contact tracing), and quarantine. A presentation of a different approach from Tanzania, a neighboring country to Kenya, is also highlighted to demonstrate the disproportionality in the response to COVID-2019.

METHODOLOGICAL AND THEORETICAL APPROACHES

For starters, data are analyzed within the framework of the Health Belief Model (HBM) and Cognitive Dissonance Theory. The chapter examines how the use of expectations (also frames) is employed to make sense of daily life situations and the changes therein in the context of COVID-2019. This is cognizant of the fact that frames or expectations are not innate and that they are constructed based on previous experience—from media or personal encounters.

Next, the theoretical framework for this chapter is based on psychology, specifically health psychology. Subsequently, theories dealing with perceptions of health and well-being are used to unravel and explain the psychological impact of COVID-2019 on the general population. The chapter draws from the cognitive theories and employs the HBM and Cognitive Dissonance Theory with a view to understanding and explaining the psychological impact on the general population due to the containment measures outlined to stem the spread of COVID-2019. While the former will expose the perceptions on severity and susceptibility to COVID-2019, the latter will explain the attendant anxiety and mental anguish that the information, communication, and containment measures of COVID-2019 have on the populace and the mental stress that individuals go through when they encounter information on COVID-2019 that is inconsistent with their values and beliefs.

THE HEALTH BELIEF MODEL

The Health Belief Model (HBM) is a health behavior change model that is used to predict individuals' responses and change in behavior to prevent diseases (Chin and Mansori, 2019). It was developed by Becker (1974) from the work of Rosenstock (1966) and postulates that personal beliefs influence health behavior. Additionally, a person's behavior can be predicted and explained on the basis of how vulnerable the individual considers themselves to be. Vulnerability is expressed in the HBM through risk (perceived susceptibility) and the seriousness of consequences (severity). These two vulnerability variables need to be considered before a decision and action can take place. The major assumption of this model is that in order to engage in healthy behaviors, key groups need to be aware of their risk for severe or life-threatening diseases and perceive that the benefits of behavior change outweigh potential barriers or other negative aspects of recommended actions (Schiavo, 2019).

The overall premise of the HBM is that knowledge and information facilitated through messages, channels, and spokespeople will bring change (Andreasen, 1995). The framework is often used to explain why individuals change or maintain specific health behaviors. The underlying concept of the HBM is that health behavior is determined by personal beliefs or perceptions about a disease and the strategies available to decrease its occurrence (Hochbaum, 1958). It addresses the individual's perceptions of the threat posed by a health problem (susceptibility, severity), the benefits of avoiding the threat, and factors influencing the decision to act (barriers, cues to action, and self-efficacy). The model has six main constructs or tenets, namely perceived susceptibility, perceived severity, perceived benefits, perceived barriers, cues to action, and self-efficacy (Morowatisharifabad et al., 2018; Schiavo, 2019).

Perceived susceptibility or personal risk refers to an individual's perception or assessment of whether (s)he is at risk of contracting an illness or health problem. For this assessment, the individual must feel that they are at risk if they continue engaging in certain behavior. For example, by not taking preventive measures, such as hand washing or wearing a face mask, a person would feel that they would be putting themselves at risk of contracting COVID-2019. When an intervention increases the perception of risk, that is, the chances of contacting or developing a disease are believed to be greater, health behavior changes (Sheeran, Harris and Epton, 2014). The greater the perceived risk, the greater the likelihood of engaging in behaviors to decrease the risk. When individuals believe they are not at risk or have a low risk of susceptibility, unhealthy behaviors tend to result (Marmarà, Marmarà and Hubbard, 2017).

Perceived severity refers to the subjective feeling on whether the specific illness or health problem can be severe or serious or is life threatening, and therefore worthy of one's attention. Hence, it is an individual's belief about the seriousness or severity of a disease. Severity perception is usually not only pegged on medical information or knowledge but may also proceed from the beliefs held by an individual on the consequences an illness is likely to have on him or her. For example, a common cold is perceived as a relatively minor ailment which is not life threatening at all. It is believed to run its course and clear on its own with rest and no medication and does not prevent one from going about their daily activities (Cal and Bahar, 2018; Chin and Mansori, 2019; Didarloo, Nabilou and Khalkhali, 2017).

Perceived benefits are an individual's perception of the advantages of adopting recommended actions to reduce the risk for disease severity, morbidity, and mortality or one's opinion of the value or usefulness of a recommended action in reducing the risk of contracting an illness. It constitutes an individual's conclusion as to whether the new behavior is better than what he or she is already doing. An individual must be convinced that change in behavior will have "benefits," which need to outweigh the "barriers." For example, an individual needs to have reason to believe that going into self-isolation or quarantine if they experience symptoms of COVID-2019 outweighs the need to go out and earn a living if they are self-employed or run a business. With reference to wearing face masks, people will identify barriers to wearing them, such as feeling suffocated, being cumbersome, and that they are too costly to procure. Barriers to frequent hand washing with soap and running water include lack of water and soap. New recommended behavior is adapted when the perceived benefits outweigh the consequences of continuing the old behavior (Centers for Disease Control and Prevention, 2004). Similarly, the new behavior will decrease the chance of developing a disease when easily taken up (Akhondali, Dianat and Radan, 2015; Soriano et al., 2018).

Therefore, perceived barriers are the individual's perceptions of the costs of and obstacles to adopting recommended actions and include economic costs as well as other kinds of lifestyle sacrifices. They refer to an individual's opinion as to what will stop him or her from adopting the new behavior. Change and adoption of new ways of living are difficult to embrace and perceived barriers are the most significant construct in behavior change (Janz and Becker, 1984). Barriers constitute elements such an inconvenience, price, limited information on a particular event, fear of unknown, and many more (Chin and Mansori, 2019).

Individuals weigh up the costs and benefits (Naidoo and Wills, 2000) or pros and cons of performing a behavior before embracing a particular approach. These could include how "susceptible" they feel about contracting an illness such as COVID-2019, how "severe" the consequences of having COVID-2019 are, how 'susceptible' they are to contracting COVID- 2019 without wearing a mask or maintaining social distancing, and how "severe" the consequence will be on their health status. All the parameters are brought to bear in explaining the perceptions of the population toward COVID-2019 in terms of the severity of the illness, their susceptibility to infection, perceived barriers to observing the non-pharmaceutical interventions, as well as voluntary testing.

Cues to action are public or social events that can signal the importance of taking action, for example, when one knows an individual who tests positive for COVID-2019 then that would be a cue for them to take necessary precautions. These cues need to be relevant to the context in which individuals operate as factors that start a person on the way to changing behavior.

Self-efficacy is an individual's confidence in their ability to independently and successfully adopt and sustain the recommended behavior. In the context of COVID-2019, an individual must be confident in their ability to wear a face mask consistently and correctly while in public places, to consistently wash their hands with soap and running water, and to maintain social distancing (Rosenstock, Strecher and Becker, 1988; Bandura, 1977).

From another perspective, there are modifying variables which are the personal factors that affect whether the new behavior is adopted by an individual and the factors include demographic variables such as age, gender, marital status, and ethnicity; sociopsychological variables such as peer group and social class; and structural variables such as knowledge and past experience that influence how a person perceives the disease severity, threats, and susceptibility (Rosenstock, 1974). Modifying variables, cues to action, and self-efficacy are then said to affect perception of disease in terms of susceptibility, seriousness, benefits, and barriers and, therefore, influence behavior. In the context of COVID-2019, persons who are advanced in age and with underlying medical conditions are said to be more susceptible to death arising from COVID-2019-related complications. Consequently, younger people with no underlying conditions may have a low perception of their risk to the illness and ignore the precautionary containment measures aimed at curbing the spread of COVID-2019.

The HBM focuses on individual behavior to the exclusion of other factors such as friends, family, and social norms which have an impact on individual behavior. When internal and external expectations are at variance, there will be dissonance in an individual, which the HBM fails to address. Additionally, the role of cultural contexts is missing and in non-Western populations such as Kenya, this theory is less culturally sensitive (Lin et al., 2005). In the context of COVID-2019, containment measures promote individualism and remove emphasis on family or group behaviors, for example, in the case of isolation, quarantine, and social distancing (Airhihenbuwa and Obregon, 2000). The theory seems to ignore the environmental context in which health behaviors occur. To mitigate this limitation, this chapter incorporates the Cognitive Dissonance Theory.

The Cognitive Dissonance Theory was developed by Festinger (1957) arising from his interest in people's susceptibility to field forces and states that the state of cognitive dissonance occurs when people perceive that a pair of cognitions is inconsistent. The theory holds that when an individual holds two or more elements of knowledge that are relevant to each other but inconsistent with one another, a state of discomfort is created, known as dissonance (Harmon-Jones and Harmon-Jones, 2007). Dissonance is experienced when cognitions about oneself either conflict or contradict. As such, cognitions regarding inconsistencies in the behavior or attitudes of others are likely to result in the experience of dissonance. Dissonance occurs when a person holds two or more contradictory beliefs, ideas, or values; or participates in an action that goes against one of these three and experiences psychological stress because of that. According to this theory, when two actions or ideas are not psychologically consistent with each other, people do all in their power to change them until they become consistent. The discomfort is triggered by the person's belief clashing with new information perceived, and they consequently strive to find ways to resolve the contradiction to reduce their discomfort (Festinger, 1957).

Festinger (1957) contends that human beings strive for internal psychological consistency in order to function mentally in the real world and that a person who experiences internal inconsistency tends to become psychologically uncomfortable and is motivated to reduce the cognitive dissonance. Festinger (1957) identifies different relation types between internal cognition and external reality: consonant, irrelevant, and dissonant. A relationship of consonance exists where two cognitions or actions are consistent with each other, irrelevant relationship where two cognitions or actions are unrelated to each other, and dissonant relationship where two cognitions or actions are inconsistent with each other.

PERCEPTIONS OF COVID-2019

This section examines the perceptions and reactions to COVID-2019 and the containment measures. The point of departure entails the key actions advanced to curb the spread of COVID-2019, that is, test, find, isolate, and quarantine, as well as the containment measures of frequent hand washing with running water and soap or use of hand sanitizers, social distancing, and consistent and correct wearing of face masks while in public places. Cases will be used to illustrate the various standpoints. This section seeks to explain how people generally understand disease and illness and specifically how they perceive COVID-2019, how disease is mediated and understood, and how this in turn impacts health-related behavior. The thesis here according to Quinn (2018) is that human beings intuitively categorize diseases and illnesses according to certain predispositions and when they encounter a phenomenon that goes against their lived experiences, a gap opens up between the expectations of what a disease is and the condition that they are faced with, in this case COVID-2019. Quinn (2018) further states that it is within this gap that harm may occur at different levels: institutionally in the form of dismissals from employment, breakdown of marriages and relationships, as well as adoption of measures that are contrary to peoples' known and comfortable ways of living; and psychologically in the form of self-doubt and depression which contradicts these conceptualizations.

A gap realized between these two creates tension (Quinn, 2018) which if not addressed may culminate in hysterical reactions. Notably, health problems often bring ambiguity, loss of control, feelings of threat, as well as making life chaotic and unpredictable. Perceptions then come in to interpret these experiences. Perceptions are self-regulation processes that take place in face of health threats with patients striving to feel like survivors rather than victims (Benyamini, 2011). This is the case being witnessed in the COVID-2019 scenario where peoples' understanding of the disease and illness largely contradicts the information they encounter on the same, leading to a gap which in this context is identified as hysteria. In this section we distinguish between disease and illness and how each of these is perceived. Additionally, we examine the two in the context of COVID-2019 and how the perceptions constitute hysteria. The key questions here will be: How does a sick person understand their disease? How does this (mis)understanding influence their (health) behavior? We begin by exploring definitions and conceptualizations of disease and illness.

Disease is perceived as constituting the central facts that inform the medical view which can be measured, quantified, and somehow touched by apparatus and observation (Marinka, 1975). Diseases are observable, universal, comparable, and consistent malfunctions that manifest as deviations from biological and physical norms and are professionally diagnosed conditions (Wikman et al., 2005). One key distinction of disease is its disabling nature: that a person with a disease must be disabled or impaired in some way and be prevented from going about their normal, daily activities. The fact that an individual has a disease or not is for doctors and laboratory technicians to establish, and this can barely be disputed (Boyd, 2000).

Illness, on the other hand, refers to a feeling internal to the person concerned—the patient—and is inconsistent, personal, and subjective. It is an underworld of experience which is a subjective, personal process and entry to it for outsiders is entirely reliant on the ways in which the individual chooses to or is able to communicate their experience (Marinka, 1975) because illnesses are self-reported bad health (Wikman et al., 2005). Illnesses are manifest differently in each individual even where several individuals have the same disease. The implication of this definition is that it is entirely up to the individual as to whether or not they are ill and the notion "illness" cannot be externally imposed on or decided for a patient. While disease is objective, illness is subjective. This distinction is key in unraveling perceptions of COVID-2019 and the containment measures advocated to curb its spread, notably quarantine.

Quarantine has been used as a containment measure to curb the spread of COVID-2019 and entails the separation and restriction of movement of persons who may have been exposed to the coronavirus in order to prevent the spread of COVID-2019. The general expectation of quarantine was that a medical approach would be adopted in its implementation, with strict observance of all measures to prevent chances of contracting COVID-2019. In most instances this was not the case. In Kenya, people were put in mandatory quarantine at their own cost, with unexplained extensions of the quarantine period, leading to a lot of psychological anguish. Many of Kenyans placed in mandatory quarantine had been arrested for flouting curfew regulations and were placed in mandatory quarantine, instead of being taken to court to answer for their transgressions, as would be expected. Given that perceptions of illness are largely sociocultural, a lot of people were at pains to reconcile their being in quarantine while not ill, at least not exhibiting any symptoms of illness and the need to be out there fending for their families, earning a living, and going about their normal daily routines. This caused many of them to escape from quarantine centers. For instance, in the month of April 2020 alone, 50 people escaped from the Kenya Medical Training Centre, Nairobi, 36 from Mandera, and 12 from Migori Township (Rahman and Shaban, 2020). The conflict between peoples' expectations and experiences creates a psychological tension leading to hysteria, in line with Showalter (1997) who identifies the existence of disaffected and isolated patients as a key ingredient for modern hysteria in health. Conflicting notions of illness may also create very unpleasant emotions, raise moral issues, disturb patient's self-image, and estrange him from his community (Frank, 1995). The reactions of the Kenyan people placed in quarantine for varied reasons conform to the HBM vulnerability tenet which states that a person's behavior can be predicted and explained on the basis of how vulnerable the individual considers themselves to be. These people were in panic and scared of the incomprehensible coronavirus.

Even with a proclamation from the WHO indicating that dead bodies were "generally not infectious" (WHO, 2020a, p. 1), Kenya's Ministry of Health issued guidelines on handling human remains infected with COVID-2019 which emotionally impacted negatively on the bereaved persons. Among these was the requirement that the body "must be disposed of or buried by the family as soon as possible under supervision of the health care professional, the local health care committee and a religious leader . . . within two days to avoid community practices that would result in more infections through contact" (Ministry of Health, 2020b, p. 11). However, the practice on the ground departed sharply from these guidelines, driven by fear and hysteria rather than fact. Four cases illustrate this. Scenario One: There was the burial of a man who hailed from Siaya County. Having traveled with his family from Mombasa County (then a hot spot for COVID-2019), he was involved in an accident in Kisumu County but proceeded to his home county, Siaya. While there, he was taken ill, having complained of chest pains and difficulties in breathing. He died while undergoing treatment in a health facility in Siaya County. He was buried in a body bag, hurriedly on the same day, at dawn, in a shallow grave without a coffin, by health officials clad in hazmat suits.

This burial was devoid of religious rites and in total contravention of the guidelines issued by the Ministry of Health, taking place in the absence of close family members, leaving them severely traumatized. Soon after, members of his family were taken into quarantine since they "had been in contact" with a COVID-2019 patient. However, all of them tested negative for COVID-2019. Upon their release from quarantine, they sought legal orders to exhume the body of their loved one to accord him "a decent sendoff" with the befitting cultural and religious rites. These orders were not granted. Additionally, they demanded an autopsy to establish the actual cause of death of their kin. Clearly, they were in doubt of the COVID-2019 narrative given that having been in very close contact with the deceased, none of them tested positive for COVID-2019 as was expected.

Scenario Two: This case involved a young man from Meru County, Kenya, who was forced to spend a night with the casket bearing remains of his wife under a lorry in a police station. Having lost his wife to cancer in Malindi County, he left in a bus bearing the body of his late wife accompanied by mourners for burial in Meru County. The funeral entourage was denied entry into Meru County and ordered back to Malindi. The casket was offloaded from the bus and put in a police vehicle with only the widower accompanying it and driven to the police station. Unable to get transport home from the police station, the young man spent a rainy night alone with the casket, taking shelter under a lorry in the police station, and later ordered to go into self-quarantine after the burial. Having been left with a six-month-old infant and having nursed his wife for two years, this experience left the young man severely traumatized.

Both cases present scenarios where there is dissonance between known and lived experiences and the current reality. In the Kenyan and indeed the African context, funerals are largely communal activities where the departed are given an elaborate and dignified sendoff. Indeed, the WHO (2020a) takes this into account when it recommends that "the dignity of the dead, their cultural and religious traditions and their families should be respected and protected throughout" (WHO, 2020a, p. 1).

Scenario Three: In Kenya, there have been cases where individuals or their kin dispute the alleged COVID-2019 test positive results. A case in point is that of a mother to a member of parliament who was buried hurriedly at night in early June 2020, having been declared a COVID-2019 case. However, results of a test conducted at a different facility released after her burial indicated that she had tested negative for COVID-2019. The member of parliament appearing before the parliamentary health committee lamented that he was unable to accord his late mother the dignity of a proper funeral when she was buried hurriedly and wondered how many voiceless Kenyans had had to contend with inaccurate diagnoses for COVID-2019 and possibly quarantined.

Scenario Four: A popular television actor and comedian in Kenya died in mid-July 2020 due to COVID-2019-related complications. Accounts by the family indicated that the actor, who had earlier tested positive for COVID-2019 and was self-isolating, was rushed to hospital after developing breathing difficulties. It is said that he died in the car while awaiting admission to a city hospital.

The cases above clearly illustrate hysteria, both on the part of the general population and the government through various agencies. The handling of the COVID-2019 cases has had the net result of stigmatizing the condition, causing people to behave irrationally when faced with COVID-2019 patients and situations. As of September 22, 2020, the Kenyan Ministry of Health issued revised guidelines on burial protocols. In this revision, family members would take up active roles in the burials of their loved ones who had died of COVID-2019-related complications and the "men in white" referring to the health officials donning white personal protective equipment would no longer take charge of the burials. While this is a welcome move, a lot of damage has been done to those whose loved ones had died earlier and proves that the initial reaction was hysterical and based on fear rather than on fact.

COMMUNICATION OF THE PANDEMIC AND CONTAINMENT MEASURES

According to Crokett, Kappes, and Nuberger (2018), many of the most serious global threats today involve a high degree of uncertainty, and COVID-2019, which is currently ravaging the world, is no exception. This uncertainty has an impactful effect on the psychological demeanor of the affected people. Crokett et al. (2018) add that the uncertainty inherent in infectious diseases provides the ideal conditions for their spread, hence risk-seeking decisions in social situations. The uncertainty can lead to anxiety which is a major public health repercussion. Subsequently, the feelings of uncertainty during pandemics can increase people's vulnerability to feelings of stress and even mental health problems. As a consequence, rapidly expanding mass hysteria and panic regarding COVID-2019 may beget enduring psychological problems in the public from all the socioeconomic domains, which could potentially be even more detrimental in the long run than the virus itself (Depoux et al., 2020). Mass fear of COVID-2019, termed as "Coronaphobia," has possibly generated a plethora of psychiatric manifestations across the different strata of the society also coined as "Coropsychology."

To this end, the WHO (2020b) advocates for communication of verified information concerning the origin, spread, and containment measures related to the COVID-2019 pandemic with the sole intention, among others, of assuaging the psychological well-being of the people. Indeed, on the day COVID-2019 was officially declared a global pandemic, the director general of the WHO called upon all nations to "strike a fine balance between protecting health, preventing economic and social disruption and respecting human rights" (WHO, 2020b, p. 1). Thus, all communication aimed at informing the population on the pandemic and the adoption of mitigation strategies must take care not to injure their psychological well-being. To communicate about the pandemic is one thing and to achieve its objectives is another thing. Zarocostas (2020) cites WHO (2020) which referred to some forms of COVID-2019 communication as "Coronavirus infodemic" akin to breeding fright and panic by laying out unchecked mind-boggling rumors, flamboyant news propaganda, and sensationalism. Hence, "Coronavirus infodemic" demonstrates the growing ecosystem of misinformation and public distrust which in turn is bound to create hysteria among an already scared people.

Notably, the way information is delivered to the people is of significance during such pandemics. This direction follows the overall premise of the HBM in that knowledge and information facilitated through messages, channels, and spokespeople will bring change (Andreasen, 1995). Like previously known pandemics, it is definite that the speed and scale of the advent and spread of COVID-2019 breed uncertainty and emotional disruption. How organizations communicate about it can create clarity, build resilience, catalyze positive change, or end up disastrous. Moreover, with COVID-2019 being a novel disease, people are bound to experience a lot of anxiety leading to hysteria due to panic on all spheres of life. Sensational relaying of both verified and unverified information is bound to negatively impact the people and the fight against the pandemic. Governments and their machineries are mandated to inform the public about the continued fight against the pandemic as well as the fatalities and recoveries realized from the disease.

Mendy et al. (2020) assert that when information is unavailable or inconsistent and people feel unsure about what they know, behavioral science points to an increased human desire for transparency, guidance, and making sense of what has happened. They add that at such times, the words and actions of those with technical knowledge can help keep people safe, help them adjust and cope emotionally, and finally, help them put their experience into context—and draw meaning from it. The health and government officials who have the mandate to ensure information is delivered to the people have to do it rightly taking into consideration the oft resultant hysterical reactions.

For guidance, WHO (2020c) produced a document for those countries preparing for the outbreak and those with confirmed cases. The document contained checklists for risk communication and community engagement (RCCE) readiness and initial responses to the COVID-2019 outbreak on how to implement effective RCCE strategies that will help protect the public's health. This interim WHO document recommends that one of the most important and effective interventions in public health response to any event is to proactively communicate the risks involved, what is known, what is unknown, and what is being done to get more information, with the objectives of saving lives and minimizing adverse consequences.

As a focus of this narrative, the Kenyan government has implemented several prevention measures to curb ongoing COVID-2019 infections in the country and to reduce importation of the virus from the neighboring countries. Some of these risk management protocols include the temporary closure of schools and workplaces, encouraging people to work from home, travel restrictions, cancellation of mass gatherings, social distancing, avoidance of handshakes, kissing and hugs, frequent washing of hands with soap and running water, use of sanitizers, wearing of face masks, border closures, and closing the airspace. The government has also provided guidance for the provision of essential services, minimizing crowds within social facilities, intense laboratory surveillance to pick up COVID-2019 cases in the community, selected cessation of movements in some counties, and imposing night curfew for a period of time in a bid to flatten the epidemic curve and stop the spread. These measures were put in place to protect the people against infection with the novel virus. Majority of Kenyans adhered to these measures albeit hysterically to protect themselves so as to reap the perceived benefits of the behavior. According to the HBM, perceived benefits are an individual's perceptions of the advantages of adopting recommended actions to reduce the risk of disease severity, morbidity, and mortality, or one's opinion of the value or usefulness of a recommended action in reducing the risk of contracting an illness. The Ministry of Health has also initiated various aspects of communication channels and methods to communicate information to local residents through reliable messages. The channels include the use of websites, local newsletters, community notice boards, community group contacts, leaflets and posters, roadshow announcements, billboards, mobile phone SMSs, and the use of the mass media.

The containment measures by the Kenyan government were implemented on a population that was clearly not used to the new normal lifestyle. With the announcement of the first confirmed case of COVID-2019 infection, Kenyans went into panic mode of buying and stocking up on food items. This was behavior copied from people in other countries who had an earlier experience of COVID-2019. The net result of this behavior was the hiking of the cost of essential commodities. Additionally, people kept off the streets and took shelter in their homes. This initial reaction was also because the people perceived the disease as a death sentence, a perception gathered from mainstream and social media about massive deaths happening in Europe (especially Italy then) and the United States. With such streaming of information on coronavirus, the people were thrown into hysteria and hence became psychologically unsteady and extremely fearful. There was also immense emotional disturbance due to the fears and anxieties of infection with COVID-2019 and the challenges brought about by the novel lifestyle. Social distancing and ban on gatherings, even at funerals, resulted in various traumas including complicated grief and separation. The concept of adjusting to social distancing and self-quarantining as a society would easily create anxieties in families who had hitherto led a different lifestyle they were comfortable with. These measures were rushed by the government and health officials in a knee jerk reaction to the COVID-2019 leading to hysteria among much of the Kenyan population. The Kenyan population responded to these measures with a feeling of panic. This was enhanced by the general feeling of susceptibility in the face of a hitherto unknown disease. Their response could be grounded within the HBM which asserts that the greater the perceived risk, the greater the likelihood of engaging in behaviors to decrease the risk. This was especially noted among Kenyans in March 2020, that being the time of announcement of the first confirmed COVID-2019 case in Kenya.

In Kenya, like other parts of the world, the way that experts, officials, and leaders talk with and to the public about this medical and social crisis matters. The country's population depends on information from those experts and government officials to easily comprehend matters to do with COVID-2019 and to make decisions about what they should do to avoid trauma and hysteria. However, the communication from these groups, at times, posed more of a threat than a solution to the same target consumers of the information. For instance, the daily updates of COVID-2019 infection numbers, fatalities, and recoveries communicate a frightening dimension to the general understanding of the virus's spread, creating an air of anxiety and even traumatic experiences. In the updates, the government officials made expressions such as the following:

> "We must rise up to the occasion and be responsible people, failure of which, this disease will decimate our society." "If you treat this disease normally, it will treat you abnormally." "The whole world is walking through the valley of the shadow of death." (MOH, 2020c, p. 1)

The preceding utterances coming from those mandated with ensuring Kenyans are informed about the disease actually instilled fear in the people. Using expressions such as "decimate," "abnormally," and "shadow of death" could easily send the people into panic mode. Such articulations did create a sense of fear and anxiety, especially to a population which did not have enough verifiable information about the novel virus. In Kenya, the Cabinet Secretary (CS) for health was referred to, in Swahili, as *Yule mtu wa corona* loosely translated as "That Corona person" which indicated that if you see the CS then you see COVID-2019. He portended a foreboding effect on the Kenyan people that seemingly preferred the other health officials to address them instead of him. To be nicknamed as such showed that the people equated him with the disease and had mentally associated him with negativity.

An opinion poll carried out in Kenya between March 13, 2020, and April 2, 2020, found that majority of Kenyans find the Ministry of Health's updates on COVID-2019 alarming, unnecessary, and stressful. The Infotrak poll shows 75 percent of Kenyans are worried while 63 percent say the virus has affected personal finances. The poll also shows that 82 percent of Kenyans feel anxious and stressed and that show that financial and psychological burden has taken a toll on the majority of Kenyans. It is also noted that in an opinion poll by Trends and Insights for Africa conducted between June 2 and June 15, 2020, 78 percent of respondents said they find news on the pandemic stressful while 48 percent find it confusing. In this poll, up to 81 percent of the respondents feel anxious and stressed about the virus while 63 percent feel confined and trapped as 61 percent and 52 percent of the sampled respondents feel lonely and helpless, respectively.

Apart from the traditional mode of communication used to inform the people, there is also the digital form which encompasses the social media. It has transformed the way people get information and it is highly accessible, usually at the click of the button. There is, therefore, the increase in news consumption which has given rise to debate about the quality of information users come across. A study published by the *British Medical Journal* found more than one in four of YouTube's most viewed COVID-2019 English videos contain misleading or inaccurate information. The journal adds that as social media continues to grow as a source of health information, misinformation on COVID-2019 is reaching far more people than previous public health crises like swine flu, Zika, and Ebola. Hence, for every expert trying to pass accurate and verifiable COVID-2019 information, there are many social media users spreading rumors, sensationalism, and other forms of disinformation. Such misinformation bombardment from social media actually changes the way society is perceiving and responding to the disease. This sensational reportage creates a worrying trend where people exhibit fear and anxiety. One such widely circulating message stated:

> Corona virus [*sic*] before it reaches the lungs it remains in the throat for four days and at this time the person begins to cough and have throat pains. If he

> drinks water a lot and gargling with warm water and salt or vinegar eliminates the virus. Spread this information because you can save someone with this information. (Dorn, 2020, p. 1)

This post, alongside numerous others, could have reached hundreds, if not thousands, of people, given the possibility that it was shared and liked severally. The net result of this is the hysterical rush to acquire the ingredients for the concoction, in total disregard to the side effects they may have on those on other medical conditions and medication. Also, "expert" suggestions on what constitutes a perfect diet to avert COVID-2019 (notably a concoction of ginger, garlic, and lemon) are triggers of panic buying!

From the foregoing, it is undoubtedly clear that psychological complications of COVID-2019 communication are evident. It is, therefore, in good stead that crisis communication must adopt a strategy that does not spur hysterical reactions. It is important for communicators to give the people what they really need to hear at the right time and ensure that there are different channels of discourse to enhance people's coping mechanisms. When people are under hysterical conditions and their psychological stability is disturbed, their ability to think rightly and comprehend information is greatly reduced. This calls for communication being made in a simple, straightforward, and clear way for easy understanding.

The COVID-2019 containment measures advocated for by the WHO (2020) may not necessarily be universal as cultures and people differ from region to region. The African continent in general and Kenya in particular have a different reaction to, for instance, the concept of social distancing. The government of Kenya should adapt these containment measures in such a way that they do not jeopardize the people's normal lives. It is noted that most of these measures if implemented as structured by the WHO lead to mental health issues of anxiety, stress, and trauma.

TANZANIA: CALM AMID A RAGING STORM

As the COVID-2019 pandemic struck Asia, Europe, and North America early in the year 2020, the Africanews (2020) reports the WHO as forecasting that Africa would be next in reporting infections from the virus. When sub-Saharan Africa recorded its first COVID-2019 death, the head of the WHO urged the continent to "prepare for the worst" (Africanews, 2020, p. 1). This observation from the WHO set the stage for panic and hysterical reactions from both governments and individuals in Africa. However, in contrast to other world continents, Africa in September 2020 was still lagging behind the global curve for coronavirus infections and deaths. Experts had repeatedly warned about the perils for Africa given its weak health infrastructure, poverty, conflicts, poor sanitation, and urban congestion. As of December 19, 2020, the COVID-2019 confirmed cases in Africa stood at 1.2 million with recoveries at 231, 126, and only 30,071 fatalities (WHO COVID-19 Dashboard, 2020). These are statistics way below numbers of COVID-2019 infections and fatalities in countries such as the United States and Brazil. The rate of infections and deaths in Africa has fallen below the scientific predictions of health experts within and without Africa.

Different countries have responded differently and have on their own adapted WHO guidelines to the pandemic. These variations are informed by the various styles of leadership and governance among leaders around the world. From the varied approaches, we posit that some of the world governments have created a series of hysteria triggers while other nations border on an almost skeptical approach to virus containment. In Tanzania, President John Pombe Magufuli has continuously looked at COVID-2019 as a war and not a health calamity requiring structured scientific consultation. This has led the approach to handling the pandemic a governmental rather than a focused health responsibility. Tanzania, an East African country neighboring Kenya, had their first confirmed case of COVID-2019 infected person on March 16, 2020, as announced by the Tanzanian Minister for Health. The Tanzania government spokesperson also tweeted that the government was prepared with isolation centers and isolation hospitals which was a strategic approach to reduce the levels of panic and any possible hysterical reactions.

From the onset, the Tanzanian Ministry of Health informed the public that there was no need to panic. However, like most citizens worldwide, normal life seemed to have changed overnight and there was clear frenzy and panic among the Tanzanians. Majority of Tanzanians rushed to shops to stock up on food items, drinks, and other basic necessities as they feared the worst out of the novel virus. This was also noted in the high demand for face masks and hand sanitizers from most of the country's pharmacies. This flurry of activities and scramble for these items caused prices of the hitherto remotely used products to skyrocket! The emergence of the virus in Tanzania equally caused a lot of reactions on social media by the netizens where expressions of fear and panic were demonstrated.

As a cautionary measure, the prime minister of Tanzania quickly directed that all primary and secondary schools, colleges, and other institutions of higher learning be closed for one month to help curb the spread of the deadly virus. The prime minister also banned football leagues, sports, music events, political meetings, and community events. The responses to the announcement of the first infection in Tanzania portrayed a typical hysterical reaction from both government and the citizens as seen in other COVID-2019 hit countries. The publicized use of a raft of WHO-recommended COVID-2019 containment measures was subsequently adopted by Tanzania as was happening in other African and world countries. The measures meant to slow down the spread of the virus included social distancing, contact tracing, travel restrictions, and hand washing, among others. The Tanzanian president implored the media houses and religious leaders to assist in popularizing messages of COVID-2019 prevention.

All of these initial reactions from the government and the common Tanzanians were a replication of the hysterical response experienced elsewhere in the rest of the infected nations of the world. However, things seemed to drastically change in the Tanzanian COVID-2019 response scenario. The government, led by the president himself, began sending mixed signals which practically dismissed the information about the pandemic. Even though learning institutions were closed and public gatherings banned, the other sections of public life remained open, including places of worship. There was open skepticism by the government which pointed to doubting the existence of the deadly pandemic! These half-hearted containment measure strategies supposedly lowered the panic level of Tanzanians and the initial hysteria dissipated. These actions conform to the Cognition Dissonance Theory principle which asserts that discomfort is triggered by the person's belief clashing with new information perceived, and they consequently strive to find ways to resolve the contradiction to reduce their discomfort (Festinger, 1957).

What became very obvious in Tanzania was a non-official position by the government on conspiracy theories, tight control over information, and aversion to science. There was enhancement of religious devotion and natural remedies as direct cures for the virus. The country's president encouraged citizens to continue attending churches and mosques because COVID-2019 is "satanic" and "cannot live in the body of Christ . . . it will burn instantly" (Magufuli, 2020, p. 1). In a further show of religious devotion, the government announced three days of national prayer against COVID-2019. The government also portrayed the virus as easily curable with the president recommending steam inhalation as a "scientific treatment." The president also added: "Let's stop scaring each other, it's too much . . . this is the right time for all of us, regardless of one's religion to extend our prayers to God and work hard so that we build our own economy. We can't surrender to Coronavirus, because this too shall pass" (Magufuli, 2020, p. 1).

This approach was meant to downplay the ravages of COVID-2019 and ensure Tanzanians were devoid of any panic, depression, and hysterical repercussions. To the Tanzania government, therefore, the way to fight COVID-2019 is to dispel fear and panic among the people and reinforce their faith. The approach concurs with the argument made by the Cognitive Dissonance Theory stating that a relationship of consonance exists where two cognitions or actions are consistent with each other, irrelevant relationship where two cognitions or actions are unrelated to each other, and dissonant relationship where two cognitions or actions are inconsistent with each other. The Tanzanian approach seemed to be contradicting the scientific inclination as encouraged by the WHO.

As a report by Freedom House (2020) states, the Tanzanian government has increasingly sought to obstruct access to public information in recent years. This could be confirmed during the pandemic. Unlike other nations, for instance, Kenya, the Tanzania government does not update the public on the status of COVID-2019 pandemic issues. The last COVID-2019 public updates had confirmed positive cases to be slightly over 500 with 16 deaths in the month of May 2020. Since then, there has been no more reportage of the COVID-2019 status in Tanzania. This goes contrary to the fact that almost all African countries and the world at large release daily updates, including the current number of infections, fatalities, and recoveries. The dearth of information concerning the pandemic in Tanzania was a reverse to what was happening in Kenya which maintained the updates. This could have positive results as the citizens will not focus on the daily corona test results, hence not experience hysteria and panic attacks.

The conspiracy theories were initiated by the country's president himself by claiming that the testing tools were returning fake results. This was after the claim that non-human samples from a pawpaw and a goat had been assigned human pseudonyms and tested for COVID-2019 had posted COVID-2019 positive results. This revelation led to the opening up the economy, even for tourists, under normal and regular pre-COVID-2019 border rules. Such moves indicated that the government was not considering COVID-2019 as an existing pandemic and that the positive cases could be negative after all. The Tanzanian government could have been ensuring that they do away with any form of coropsychological panic or hysteria by alluding to possible non-existence of the COVID-2019 pandemic. This perspective is highlighted by Festinger (1957) who contends that human beings strive for internal psychological consistency in order to function mentally in the real world and that a person who experiences internal inconsistency tends to become psychologically uncomfortable and is motivated to reduce the cognitive dissonance. The only dissenting voices in Tanzania were the opposition party, civil society, and some celebrities who took it upon themselves to sensitize the public about the pandemic. These concerns followed fears that the effect of the pandemic in Tanzania could be more widespread than the government is telling the people. Unconfirmed reports of bodies of coronavirus victims being buried at night were spreading. Such assertions did not deter most Tanzanians from moving on, normally, with their lives.

On June 9, 2020, the government declared that COVID-2019 had been eliminated from Tanzania by the powers of God (BBC, 2020). This meant that life returned to normalcy almost three months after the first positive case of the virus was announced. The hitherto closed schools, colleges, and universities were ordered reopened from June 1, 2020, as well as the resumption of sporting activities. On August 22, 2020, Simba Sports Club, a football club in Tanzania, celebrated Simba Day which is an annual day for honoring the club's success after concluding the season and is also used to unveil their new signings to the fans before the new season kicks off. On that day, the Benjamin Mkapa Stadium was full to capacity with the fans hardly observing any of the WHO-recommended COVID-2019 containment measures. Apart from sporting activities and resumption of the education sector, bars and eateries were allowed to fully open their businesses. The year 2020 being an election year for Tanzania, the country had been in campaign mode with political rallies being attended without any observation of the containment measures. Tanzania is completely back to the normal ways! These normal life measures also followed the opening of the country to tourists and the lifting of a restriction that required tourists to undergo the mandatory 14-day quarantine when they visit the country. The government intimated that these measures were to return the country back to normalcy and they assured the public that the number of positive cases has reduced a great deal with more people recovering from the infection.

The manner in which the Tanzania government has handled the COVID-2019 pandemic managed to calm the population even as the UN anticipated that COVID-2019 would have a devastating impact on Tanzania's economy, the incomes of businesses and individuals, and the government's ability to provide social and economic services (Godo, 2020). The declaration by Tanzania that the country was COVID-2019 free created a diplomatic rift with Kenya which continued testing cargo truck drivers entering Kenya from Tanzania. Kenya actually closed the borders with Tanzania due to the fear of coronavirus transmission. Kenya had considered Tanzania as not serious with handling the pandemic. Kenya's continued testing of drivers from Tanzania angered the Tanzania regime who retaliated against Kenyan truck drivers by banning even cargo trucks from entering Tanzania.

It is a fact that Tanzania's unorthodox approach to COVID-2019 appeared awkward in response to the pandemic and exhibited a lack of medical direction, but its uniqueness demonstrated the need for governments to form context-specific protocols for the containment of the virus.

CONCLUSION AND RECOMMENDATIONS

In this section, we draw conclusions based on our analysis and make recommendations that would inform policy in the management of pandemics in a manner that shields the general population from psychological harm. These aspects are presented in sequential order.

This chapter has explored the psychological ramifications of COVID-2019 on the populace within the Kenyan and Tanzanian context. Our analysis has revealed that the response by the authorities to COVID-2019 caused great human, social, and economic disruption. The population was generally thrust into the throes of uncertainty with no psychological preparation at all of what lay ahead the COVID-2019 journey. The announcement of the first COVID-2019 case in Kenya was followed by a series of closures, bans, restrictions, as well as verbal threats in the event of non-compliance with the outlined measures. The closures of learning institutions and businesses led to loss of lives and livelihoods, while the reference to and framing of COVID-2019 led to stigmatization of those who were infected and affected by the disease. People were subjected to disruption in normalcy, forced to spend a lot of time out of their normal areas of operation, causing feelings of anxiety, fear, worry, and lack of self-control.

The basic question on everyone's mind is when will all this end? There have been cases of COVID-2019-driven suicide cases, the notable one being a woman of South African origin who committed suicide in an isolation facility in Nakuru town. The rejection and denials of positive test results for COVID-2019 are a clear pointer to the effects of stigmatization on those who test positive for COVID-2019. The resort to violence to enforce compliance with the restrictions such as dawn to dusk curfew caused untold trauma to the offenders who were quickly whisked into quarantine at their own cost, having been assumed to have been exposed to the virus.

In conclusion, we pose this question: Given the mildness of the infection in majority of those who contracted the virus and the fairly low fatality rates (0.16 percent in Kenya at the time of this writing), were all the energies put in the name of containment necessary? We propose that the answer is clearly no. The rates of infection and fatalities, compared with other diseases such as malaria and other immediate threats to life such as floods, famine, and starvation, make the measures instituted to prevent the spread of COVID-2019 more of fear mongering and unnecessary hyping of a disease that, though highly infectious, is not necessarily deadly. From forced quarantine and isolation at peoples' expense, causing people untold physical, mental, and financial suffering, we are back to home-based care, pointing to the fact that all the drastic containment measures of quarantine and isolation in the Kenyan context were drastic and unnecessary, and that the response to the pandemic was driven more by fear rather than by fact, in turn instilling fear in the population. People feared not the virus itself but the consequences arising from infection with the virus, notably being placed in quarantine and being traced as a contact of one who had tested positive for COVID-2019.

Arising from the foregoing, several recommendations are proposed with a view to lessening the psychological effects of a pandemic on the population. To begin with is the need for the contextualization of a pandemic in order to customize the responses. This entails the adoption of local solutions to localized contexts and situations. The response needs to take into account the specific community needs in context. For example, lockdowns as instituted in other parts of the world are not workable in the Kenyan context as well as other countries such as Tanzania, given the predominantly outdoor nature of lives and eking out livelihoods. Second, there is need to communicate explicitly and unambiguously about C0VID-2019 so as to address the fears and anxieties arising from the novel COVID-2019 disease. This would go a long way in forestalling the attendant stigma around the disease. Additionally, the use of stigmatizing language needs to be avoided. There is need to embrace language that communicates the disease as something that we can live with, given that it is now endemic. The communication needs to build trust and confidence in individual and collective ability to live with the disease as well as to garner and provide the much-needed social support.

REFERENCES

Africanews. (March 9, 2020). On Covid-19, Africa must 'prepare for the worst now' WHO says. Retrieved on June 12, 2020 from www.africanews.com.

Airhihenbuwa, C. O. and Obregon R. (2000). A critical assessment of theories/models used in health communication for HIV/AIDS. *Journal of Health Communication 5 Supplementary* 5:1–15.

Ajzen, I. and Fishbein, M. (1980). *Understanding Attitudes and Predicting Social Behavior*. Hoboken, NJ: Prentice-Hall.

Akhondali, Z., Dianat, M. and Radan, M. (2015). Effect of health belief model based training on performance of women in breast self-examination. *Electronic Physician* 7(1):971–976.

Andreasen, A. R. (1995). *Marketing Social Change: Changing Behavior to Promote Health, Social Development and the Environment*. San Francisco, CA: Jossey-Bass.

Bandura, A. (1977). Self-efficacy: Toward a unifying theory of behavior change. *Psychological Review* 84:191–215.

BBC. (June 8, 2020). Coronavirus: John Magufuli declares Tanzania free of Covid-19. Retrieved on August 5, 2020 from https://www.bbc.com/news/world-africa-52966016

Becker, M. H. (1974). The health belief model and sick role behavior. *Health Education and Behavior* 2(4):326–327.

Benyamini, Y. (2011). Health and illness perceptions. In Friedman, H. S. (ed.), *The Oxford Handbook of Health Psychology*. Oxford, UK: Oxford University Press.

Boyd, K. M. (2000). Disease, illness, sickness, health, healing and wholeness: Exploring some elusive concepts. *Medical Humanities* 26:9–17.

Cal, A. and Bahar, Z. (2018). Use of the Health Belief Model in the prevention of lymphedema after breast surgery. *Progress in Health Science* 8(1):176–181.

Centers for Disease Control and Prevention—CDC (September 18, 2020). *Morbidity and Weekly Report*. Retrieved on July17, 2020 fromhttps://www.cdc.gov/mmwr/volumes/69/wr/mm6937e4.htm.

Chin, J. H. and Mansori, S. (2019). Theory of planned behavior and Health Belief Model: females' intention on breast cancer screening. *Cogent Psychology* 6(1):1647927.

CNBC (January 30, 2020). CDC confirms first human to human transmission. Retrieved on August 15th 2020 from https://www.cnbc.com/2020/01/30/cdc-confirms-first-human-to-human-transmission-of-coronavirus-in-us.html.

Cooper, J. (2007). *Cognitive Dissonance: Fifty Years of a Classic Theory*. London, UK: Sage Publications.

Crokett, M., Kappes, A. and Nuberger, A. (August 27, 2018). Pandemics and the psychology of uncertainty. Retrieved on September 17, 2020 from https://www.weforum.org/agenda/2018/08/the-psychology-of-pandemics/pdf.

Dadipoor, S., Mehraban, A., Aghamolaei, T. and Ramezankhani, A. (2017). Prediction of birth type based on the health belief model. *Journal of Family and Reproductive Health* 11(3):159–164.

Depoux, A., Martin, S., Karafillakis, E., Preet, R., Wilder-Smith, A. and Larson, H. (2020). The pandemic of social media panic travels faster than the COVID-2019 outbreak. *Journal of Travel Medicine* 27(3):taaa031. Retrieved on July 15, 2020 from https://doi.org/10.1093/jtm/taaa031.

Didarloo, A., Nabilou, B. and Khalkhali, H. R. (2017). Psychosocial predictors of breast self-examination behavior among female students: An application of the health belief model using logistic regression. *BMC Public Health* 17(1):1–8.

Dorn, S. (March 21, 2020). Don't believe these fake coronavirus stories on social media. Retrieved on July 3, 2021 from https://nypost.com/2020/03/21/dont-believe-these-fake-coronavirus-stories-on-social-media/.

Festinger, L. (1957). *A Theory of Cognitive Dissonance*. Stanford, CA: Stanford University Press.

Frank, W. (1995). *The Wounded Storyteller: Body, Illness and Ethics*. Chicago, IL: The University of Chicago Press.

Freedom House. (2020). *Country Status Report: Tanzania*. Retrieved on August 5, 2020 from https://www.freedomhouse.org.

Godo, E. (May 20, 2020). COVID-19 Innovation challenge in Tanzania. Retrieved on August 23, 2020 from https://thepalladiumgroup.com/news/COVID-2019-Innovation-Challenge-in-Tanzania.

Harmon-Jones, E. and Harmon-Jones, C. (2007). Cognitive dissonance theory after 50 years of development. *Zeitschrift für Sozialpsychologie* 38:7–16.

Hochbaum, G. M. (1958). *Public Participation in Medical Screening Programs: A Sociopsychological Study*. Washington, DC: US Government Printing Office.

Janz, N. K. and Becker, M. H. (1984). The health belief model: A decade later. *Health Education Quarterly* 1(1):1–47.

Kamagi, D. (March 23, 2020). No need to panic, JPM calms nation. Retrieved on May 20, 2020 from https://dailynews.co.tz/news/2020-03-235e7848c9780c6.aspx.

Kenyatta, U. (May 16, 2020). The Sixth Presidential Address on the Coronavirus Pandemic at State House. Retrieved on August 17, 2020 from https://www.president.go.ke/2020/05/16/the-sixth-presidential-address-on-the-coronavirus-pandemic-at-state-house-nairobi-16th-may-2020/.

Lin, P., Simoni, J. and Zemon, V. (2005). The health belief model, sexual behaviors and HIV risk among Taiwanese immigrants. *AIDS Education and Prevention* 17(5):191–215.

Marinka, M. (1975). Why make people patients. *The Journal of Medical Ethics* 1:81–84.

Marmarà, D., Marmarà, V. and Hubbard, G. (2017). Health beliefs, illness perceptions and determinants of breast screening uptake in Malta: A cross-sectional survey. *BMC Public Health* 17:416.

Mendy, A. Lass, S. M. and van Akin, K. (April 17, 2020). *A Leader's Guide: Communicating with Teams, Stakeholders and Communities during COVID-2019.* Retrieved on August 5, 20202 from https://www.mckinsey.com/business-functions/organization/our-insights/a-leaders-guide-communicating-with-teams-stakeholders-and-communities-during-COVID-2019.

Ministry of Health (June 20, 2020a). Status update on Covid-19 in the Country and response measures. Retrieved on July 20, 2020 from https://www.health.go.ke/wp-content/uploads/2020/06/COVID-19-Press-Statement-June-20-2020.pdf.

Ministry of Health (2020b). Interim Guidelines on Handling of Human Remains Infected with COVID-9 in Kenya. Retrieved on July 20, 2020 from www.health.go.ke.

Ministry of Health (March 22, 2020c). Kenya reports eight more cases of coronavirus. Retrieved on April 20, 2020 from www.health.go.ke.

Morowatisharifabad, M. A., Amani, F., Kaseb, F. and Namayandeh, S. M. (2018). Predictors of healthy nutrition behaviors among elderlies of Kalat County based on Health Belief Model. *Elderly Health Journal* 4(1):11–17.

Okal, B. O., Kodak, B. O., Yakub, A. and Okello, J. (2020). Implications of coronavirus (COVID-2019) on the stability of the Luo cultural funeral ceremonies in Kenya. *EAS Journal of Humanities and Cultural Studies* 2(2):98–104.

Quinn, S. H. (2018).*What do we talk about when we talk about disease?* Doctoral Thesis (PhD), UCL (University College London).

Rahman, A. and Shaban, A. (May 10, 2020). Kenya Coronavirus updates from March to April 2020. Retrieved on October 20, 2020 from https://www.africanews.com/2020/05/1-/enforcement-of-coronavirus-lockdown-turns-violent-in-parts-of-africa.

Rosenstock, I. M. (1966). Why people use health services. *Milbank Memorial Fund Quarterly* 44:94–127.

Rosenstock, I. M. (1974). Historical origins of the health belief model. *Health Education Monographs* 2:328–335.

Rosenstock, I. M., Strecher, V. J. and Becker, M. H. (1988). Social learning theory and the health belief model. *Heath Education and Behavior* 15(2):175–183.

Schiavo, R. (2013). *Health Communication: From Theory to Practice*. San Francisco, CA: Jossey-Bass.

Sheeran P., Harris, P. R. and Epton, T. (2014). Does heightening risk appraisals change people's intentions and behavior? A meta-analysis of experimental studies. *Psychology Bulletin* 40(2):511–543.

Showalter, E. (1997). *Hystories: Hysteria, Gender and Culture*. London, UK: Pan Books Limited.

Soriano, E. C., Pasipanodya, E. C., LoSavio, S. T., Otto, A. K., Perndorfer, C., Siegel, S. D. and Laurenceau, J. P. (2018). Social constraints and fear of recurrence in couples coping with early stage breast cancer. *Health Psychology* 37(9):874–884.

Tafti, A., Rahaei, Z., Shahi, M. A. and Hakimi, T. (2018, May). The effect of educational program on the prevention of pediculosis in primary school fifth grade students: An application of the health belief model *Journal of Social Behaviors and Community Health* 2(1):134–143.

The Independent (June 26, 2020). Medics urge government to emulate Tanzania, Burundi on COVID-2019 management. Retrieved on July **2nd** 2020 fromhttps://www.independent.co.ug/medics-advise-govt-to-emulate-tanzania-burundi-on-COVID-2019-management/.

Wang, W. L., Hsu, S. D., Wang, J. H., Huang, L. C. and Hsu, W. L. (2014). Survey of breast cancer mammography screening behaviors in eastern Taiwan based on a health belief model. *Kaohsiung Journal of Medical Sciences* 30(8):422–427.

WHO Coronavirus Disease. (2020). *COVID-19 Dashboard*. Retrieved on December 21, 2020 from www.who.int.

Wikman, A., Marklund, S. and Alexanderson, K. (2005). Illness, disease and sickness absence: An empirical test of differences between concepts of ill health. *The Journal of Epidemiological Community Health* 59:450–454.

World Health Organization. (March, 24 2020a). *Infection Prevention and Control for the Safe Management of a Dead Body in the Context of COVID-19. Interim Guidance*. Retrieved on May 2, 2020 from www.who.int.

World Health Organization. (March 11, 2020b). WHO Director-General's opening remarks at the media briefing on COVID-2019-11.Retrieved on May 5, 2020 fromhttps://www.who.int/dg/speeches/detail/who-director-general-s-opening-remarks-at-the-media-briefing-on-COVID-2019-11.march.2020.

World Health Organization. (2020c). *RCCE Action Plan Guidance. COVID-19 Preparedness and Response*. Retrieved on June 3, 2020 from www.who.int

World Vision—Tanzania. (May 27, 2020). World Vision is complimenting the Tanzanian government's efforts in fighting COVID-2019. Retrieved on June 29, 2020 from https://www.wvi.org/stories/tanzania/world-vision-complimenting-tanzanian-governments-efforts-fighting-COVID-2019.

Zarocostas, J. (2020). How to fight an infodemic. *The Lancet* 395(10225):676.

Chapter 12

Corolinguistics

Abdul Karim Bangura

It is well known that language has always been a very important means of communication, and it is spoken or written through words, or the use of hand or figure gestures. Language plays an important role when we wish to express our thoughts and feelings. Thus, it is only inevitable that language has been used to express thoughts and feelings about the Coronavirus Disease (COVID)-2019 that has led to a heightened hysteria among many people; thus, Corolinguistics. Since linguistics is the scientific study of language, this chapter employs linguistic tools to constitute the analytical method to examine the various ways language has been used to intensify the fears over the virus. These linguistic tools include communication misfires, neologisms, and interpersonal communication.

Before proceeding any further, it makes sense to provide general definitions of the aforementioned concepts right away for the sake of coherence. First, *communication misfires* refer to stating things the sender of a message (i.e., speaker/writer/hand signer) did not intend. Second, *neologisms* are newly coined words, expressions, and usages. Third, *interpersonal communication* denotes the process, through verbal and non-verbal messages, by which two people interchange facts provided or learned about something or someone; emotional states or reactions; and what are meant by words, texts, concepts, or actions.

But, prior to exploring the preceding aspects, I will first explain the General Linguistic Theory upon which their analyses in this chapter are situated. This is imperative for the theoretical grounding of the ensuing examination.

GENERAL LINGUISTIC THEORY

To commence with, while there is a consensus that General Linguistic Theory is about a system of ideas intended to explain the scientific study of language and its structure, especially one based on general principles independent of the things to be explained, there is, however, great variation in the ways it is characterized, with some overlaps. Francis P. Dinneen, S.J. (1967 and 2007), for instance, portrays General Linguistic Theory as involving the systematic investigation of (a) the study of linguistics; (b) language as a system of sounds; (c) language as a system of forms; (d) ancient linguistics; (e) some medieval routs of traditional grammar; (f) etymology and historical linguistics; (g) works of great linguists such as Ferdinand de Saussure, Edward Sapir, Leonard Bloomfield, Bronislaw Malinowski, John Rupert Firth, and Louis Hjelmslev; (h) transformational grammar; (i) after aspects; and (j) different constants.

Also, John Lyons (1971) delineates General Linguistic Theory as including the scientific inquiry of (a) the study of language, (b) the structure of language, (c) the sounds of language, (d) general principles of grammar, (e) grammatical units, (f) grammatical structure, (g) grammatical categories, (h) grammatical functions, (i) general principles of semantics, and (j) semantic structure. In addition, D. Terence Langendoen (1998) represents General Linguistic Theory as entailing the systematic study of (a) goals of the theory, (b) expression and meaning, (c) morphs and morphemes, (d) the lexicon, (e) morphology and syntax, (f) recursion, (g) movement and deletion, (h) universal grammar, (i) generative grammar, and (j) Optimal Theory. Furthermore, Hans-Jörg Schmid (2012) outlines General Linguistic Theory as covering the scientific analysis of theories in the following subdisciplines of linguistics: (a) grammar and lexicology, (b) semantics, (c) cognitive linguistics, (d) psycholinguistics, (e) pragmatics, (f) variational linguistics and sociolinguistics, and (g) historical linguistics.

Next, 48 specific theories can be considered as components of the General Linguistic Theory. A full discussion of these theories would necessitate a book in its own right. Only brief descriptions of their foci are presented here for succinctness. They are the following:

1. Accelerated Language Deaths Theory of Abdul Karim Bangura focuses on how globalization and the new world order have impacted certain sociological factors (migration, industrialization, school language, urbanization, prestige, and smaller population) and, they, in turn, have led to and will continue to lead to the rapid demise of many languages across the world.
2. Basic Linguistic Theory focuses on the fundamental concepts that are generally employed in the grammatical description of languages and in linguistic typology.

3. Bow-wow Theory focuses on the idea that the first human languages developed as onomatopoeia: that is, the imitations of natural sounds.
4. Cartesian Linguistics Theory focuses on the universal characteristics of grammatical structure that are common to all languages and reflect some basic features of the mind.
5. Causal Theory of Reference focuses on how words or phrases used to describe things or to express concepts obtain particular referents based on evidence.
6. Contrastivism Theory focuses on how knowledge attributions have a ternary structure of the form "S knows that p rather than q."
7. Cratylism Theory focuses on how the unstable nature of ideas, words, and communications leaves them basically baseless and, feasibly, incapable of supporting logic and reason.
8. Decreolization Theory focuses on how over time a Creole language reconverges with the lexifier from which it first sprung.
9. Descriptivist Theory of Names focuses on how the denotation or semantic content of a proper name is identical to the representations linked with it by speakers, while their referents are deduced to be the objects that fulfill these representations.
10. Direct Reference Theory focuses on how the denotation of a term or statement hinges upon what it designates in the universe.
11. Distributionalism Theory focuses on how language could be analyzed as an inevitable procedure, explained by the external circumstances of its manifestation.
12. Double Articulation Theory focuses on the utilization of combinations of a small number of meaningless elements (phonemes, i.e., sounds) to produce a large number of meaningful elements (morphemes, i.e., words).
13. Dramatism Theory focuses on the examination of human relationships through the utilization of language.
14. Epistemicism Theory focuses on facts about the perimeters of an indeterminate predicate which we cannot possibly locate.
15. Expressivism Theory focuses on the denotation of moral language.
16. Functional Linguistics Theory focuses on how the practicality of a language and its constituents are the means to comprehending linguistic procedures and arrangements.
17. Government and Binding Theory focuses on (a) the abstract syntactic relation applicable to the assignment of case—that is, government; and (b) the connections among pronouns and the expressions with which they are co-referential—that is, binding.
18. Inferential Role Semantics Theory focuses on the denotation of a statement with its relationship to other statements.

19. Integrational Linguistics Theory focuses on the systematic features of language systems and the phenomenon of language variability in an integrated manner.
20. Integrational Theory of Language focuses on the difference between theories of language and theories of language descriptions.
21. Integrationism Theory focuses on the novel involvement by communicators within contexts and the declination of rule-based models of language.
22. Jakobson's Functions of Language Theory focuses on how a successful act of verbal communication can be delineated.
23. Langue and Parole Theory focuses on the abstract, systematic rules and norms of a signifying system.
24. Levels of Adequacy Theory focuses on the hierarchy of degrees of sufficiency for assessing grammars.
25. Linguistic Determinism Theory focuses on the notion that language and its structures restrict and dictate human knowledge or thought, in addition to thought processes such as designation, recognition, and recollection.
26. Literary Nominalism Theory focuses on the linkages among some features of nominalist philosophy, literary works, and theology.
27. Logical Atomism Theory focuses on the notion that logical analysis is in a way a falsification.
28. Logical Positivism Theory focuses on the proposition that only statements that can be verified via direct observation or logical proof are meaningful.
29. Mediated Reference Theory focuses on the thought that words or phrases refer to something in the external world, albeit there is more to the denotation of a name than simply the object to which it calls attention.
30. Mimetic Theory of Speech Origins focuses on the elements that led to the changes of language in human ancestors.
31. Nominalism Theory focuses on the existence of general or abstract words or phrases and predicates while rejecting the existence of universals and abstract objects.
32. Non-cognitivism Theory focuses on the meta-ethical perspective that ethical sentences do not communicate propositions and, therefore, they can neither be true nor false.
33. Origin of Language Theory focuses on evidence from the fossil record, archaeological digs, contemporary language diversity, language acquisition, and comparisons between human language and systems of communication existing among animals.
34. Phallogocentrism Theory focuses on the privileging of the masculine in the making of meaning.

35. Picture Theory of Language focuses on Ludwig Wittgenstein's characterization of linguistic reference and meaning.
36. Quietism Theory focuses on the notion that the value of philosophy is mostly therapeutic in alleviating incertitude in the linguistic and conceptual frameworks of other subjects.
37. Reism Theory focuses on the postulate that only concrete material things exist.
38. Schneider's Dynamic Model Theory focuses on how a language develops as a process of "competition-and-selection" and how particular linguistic aspects develop.
39. Semantic Externalism Theory focuses on how the denotation of a word or phrase is influenced, entirely or to some extent, by aspects that are external to the speaker.
40. Semantic Holism Theory focuses on how a particular component of language, whether it is a word, phrase, or a complete sentence, can only be comprehended via its connections to a previously understood larger component of language.
41. Semiotic Theory of Charles Sanders Peirce focuses on semeiotics: that is, the study of signs and symbols and their use or interpretation.
42. Structuralism Theory focuses on the proposition that features of human culture such as language ought to be understood by way of their relationship to a larger system.
43. Supposition Theory focuses on providing explanations of ideas similar to modern interpretations of modality, plurality, reference, and tense within an Aristotelian milieu.
44. Symbiotic Theory focuses on memes as isofunctional neuroanatomical units that correlate with linguistic signs and symbols and their use or interpretation.
45. Symbiosism Theory focuses on the belief that language is an organism housed in the human brain and that language is a memetic life form.
46. Symbol Theory of Semiotics focuses on three clear-cut classes of signs: (1) icons, (2) indexes, and (3) symbols.
47. Theory of Descriptions focuses on the proposition that the syntactic configuration of descriptions is deceptive, since it does not match up with their logical and/or semantic structure.
48. Two-dimensionalism Theory focuses on how to determine the sense and reference of a word and the truth-value of a sentence.

Together, the aforementioned theories, which comprise the General Linguistic Theory, are beneficial for recognizing, mapping out, and explicating the underlying precepts and procedures of how things operate in languages. They are also quite profitable for answering the primary twin questions of General Linguistic Theory: (1) What is language? (2) What features must a learner possess in order to learn and use a language?

COMMUNICATION MISFIRES

According to John Hampton, the five communication misfires are the following: (1) what a sender is thinking makes no sense to the receiver of the message but the sender, (2) a sender says/writes/hand gestures too much and makes things more complicated, (3) a sender does not control the tone of the message, (4) a sender replaces words with symbols or other sounds, and (5) a receiver makes too many assumptions even before the sender says/writes/hand gestures a message (Hampton, 2016).

The ensuing dialogue reveals how the term *mask* vis-à-vis the facial masks that have become mandatory in most countries when a person is in public spaces makes no sense to some people. The discourse took place on Facebook as follows:

Gbanabom Hallowell: Mask? I don't know who first called it MASK; the better word should have been BANDANA (save your knowledge of what bandana means). Mask? I'm not comfortable with such a public register. To call it MASK was a grayish attempt at being terroristic with the innocent world. There is a whole political linguistic subterfuge surrounding COVID-2019. Language experts failed us woefully in that respect.

Alpheus Rogers: I too am not comfortable with such a register, MASK. I'm not comfortable either with the register BANDANA. It is semantically misplaced to use the word "bandana" with regard to COVID-2019 when a bandana is worn on the head, which I think has nothing to do with keeping the spread of the virus at bay. Mask when used as a noun could mean an object to hide one's real identity. What I think Gbanabom is attempting to do is to provoke an intellectual discussion for language and communication experts as to their analyses in relation to masks, bandanas, COVID-2019, and the like from semantic, pragmatic, and syntactic viewpoints. Interesting indeed!

Momoh Juana: Gbanabom not having the background like you linguists, I would adopt a social science research approach. For the purpose of fighting COVID-2019, a mask is a piece of material used to cover your nose and mouth to protect you from being infected.

Peter Andersen: Perhaps because mask is also a verb, as in to mask one's face. It is also some 200 years older than the word bandana, and being less specific it has picked up wider variations or connotations. In my understanding, anything which has elastic or cloth ties is not a bandana, which is a single strip of cloth.

Gbanabom Hallowell: Thanks for that Peter. And for that reason that I fear the word mask I had found a way to prefer bandana. In linguistic elasticity, bandana is not only feminine and gentle at the same time, it carries the day. Bandana could begin from the neck right down to one's mouth. But thanks Peter you are always engaging.

Peter Andersen: Gbanabom Hallowell, I never thought of bandana as feminine. That's what cowboys wore (or wear) when riding the range, which could be dusty work.

Gbanabom Hallowell: Peter, therefore as I stated from a less cosmopolitan American culture, I've also negotiated that it could be gentle if you will as well from the Taekwondo culture made it masculine or Indian and Indonesian.

Peter Anderson: Gbanabom Hallowell, the only bandanas in our house—somewhere—belong to my son, who was a Scout first in Sierra Leone and then here. He put away his Scout uniform for (American) football gear.

Gbanabom Hallowell: Peter Andersen, in that case bandana could be unisexual.

Abdul Karim Bangura (the author of this chapter): Kohthoh Agba Gbanabom Hallowell, from a linguistic perspective, the word "mask" is fraught with too many syntactic, semantic, and pragmatic "Wahalas" (i.e., big problems). Let me give you just a couple of examples: (1) some adjectives for "mask" include bland, official, tanned and forgettable, hairy orange, pleasant, optimistic, loose and pliable, savage, hairy, suave facial, devilish waxen, gory and devilish, hideous comic, still soft and likable, identical blank, true schizoid, tasteful, pleasant, carefully haughty, skillful, etc.; (2) a "mask" also usually represents a supernatural being, an ancestor, and a fanciful or imagined figure, and it can further represent a portrait. Thus, the localization of a particular spirit in a specific mask must be considered a highly significant reason for its existence. Our leaders and news media personalities lacking the aptitude to use a more appropriate term or coin a more fitting neologism, we are stuck with the ambiguous term.

Karamoh Kabba: Abdul Karim Bangura, isn't why it's often called facial mask?

Abdul Karim Bangura: Karamoh Kabba, long time. Nice try, but the adjectival creates another labyrinth of problems as "facial" has numerous denotations and connotations of or affecting the face from Numismatics, Geometry, Mountaineering, Astronomy, Architecture, Clock-making, Cards, and Military.

Sheikh Kamarah: Gbanabom, I know your goal here is to trigger some intellectual discussion. But tell me, what have language experts got to do with the use of "mask" in this case? It is not the job of language experts to create words; they study the nature of human language, and its functions and uses in human society. Mask began its life in Medieval Latin (*masca*?), in the sixteenth century, traveled through Italian (*maschera*), then middle French (*masque*), and found itself in English. It simply meant "a guard or cover for the face." Like any word in any language, the connotative meanings of "mask" are many because a linguistic unit derived its meaning from the context and situation in which it finds itself. If you were to carefully study the various and varied connotations of "bandana," you will quickly drop the idea of replacing "mask" with it. Troublesome poet, leave "mask" alone.

Gbanabom Hallowell: You win this debate.

Abdul Karim Bangura: You concede too soon, Kohthoh Agba Gbanabom Hallowell. Sheikh Kamarah should have stuck to restating what is well known about the etymology of the term "mask." But he had to overreach and say that "It is not the job of language experts to create words." On this, he is quite wrong. Linguists have been on the forefront in making neologisms and developing languages for a very long time. For example, the Danish linguist Otto Jespersen developed Novial, a constructed international auxiliary language for universal communication among speakers of different languages.

Adding to my point about Gbanabom Hallowell conceding too soon on the preceding debate, I will share here a great lesson the revered linguist and my former professor at Georgetown University, the late Deborah Schiffrin, taught me: that is, although speakers/writers exhibit a preference for disagreement, they do not use that disagreement to reach common ground of winning or losing a debate. Rather, the topic of disagreement is merely the indispensable medium through which the lively exchange of speech/writing unfolds. And although speakers/writers display commitment to their own assertions and lack of alignment with each other, such participation frameworks are fluid and vulnerable: argumentative frames, stances, and alignments end as quickly and unpredictably as they begin. In addition, the use of openly competitive forms of talk/writing actually rests on underlying assumptions of cooperation and protection of speaker/writer selves—hardly the sort of contest that would be created by serious challenges and threats. And finally, the disagreements in the data seem to be valued as processes and activities in their own right whereas serious fights might be valued for their outcome, but not for their process.

Also, reflecting on the misfires taking place in discourses surrounding the COVID-2019 pandemic, Toyin Oluwagbemi-Jacob makes a salient point about the phenomenon on Facebook. As he puts it, "I thought it was only in Africa where the proverbs that people that are eating do not talk. Seems the alloys for power always blind until one is out or in the opposition to align with popular views but so long as leaders remain in power it serves just the few rich and opportune. May God help His own."

One more case of communication misfire is how some leaders in Africa conflated the notions of National Emergency and State of Emergency in mimicking what was done by President Donald Trump to address the pandemic in the United States. On the one hand, the National Emergencies Act (Pub. L. 94–412, 90 Stat. 1255, enacted September 14, 1976, codified at 50 U.S.C. § 1601–1651) is a U.S. federal law passed to end all previous national emergencies and to formalize the emergency powers of the president. The act empowers the president to activate special powers during a crisis but imposes certain procedural formalities when invoking such powers. The perceived need for the law arose from the scope and number of laws granting special powers to the executive in times of national emergency. Congress can terminate an emergency declaration with a joint resolution signed into law. Powers available under this act are limited to the 136 emergency powers Congress has defined by law (Simonova and Sobel, 2020).

On the other hand, State of Emergency refers to "a situation of national danger or disaster in which a government suspends normal constitutional procedures in order to regain control" (Lexico, 2020, p. 1). A state of emergency is a situation in which a government is empowered to perform actions or impose policies that it would normally not be permitted to undertake. A government can declare such a state during a natural disaster, civil unrest, armed conflict, medical pandemic or epidemic, or other biosecurity risk.

NEOLOGISMS

As David Crystal informs us, neologisms are birthed when people acknowledge altered situations in the external environment which attain some prevalence within a speech community. He adds that only some neologisms will survive in a speech community, but it is impossible to predetermine which ones will survive and which ones will die (Crystal, 1992).

Even the title of this book, *Corohysteria*, and the titles of the attendant chapters—Coroeducation, Coromathematics, Corolinguistics, Cororeligion, Coropsychology, Corophilanthropy, Coroexpertise, Coropoverty, Corodemocracy, Coroelitism, Corofrontline, etc.—are neologisms reflecting the various aspects that have been affected by COVID-2019 and led to hysteria among many people. The following is a presentation of neologisms that I coined and shared on Facebook, and they are being used by many participants on the medium:

Corocliche: If one person out of 1,000,001 dies, it is "one too many." But you never hear 1,000,000 "too many recovered." Like any cliché, this one is overused and betrays a lack of original thought.

Coronaphobia: An extreme or irrational fear of or aversion to anything with the name Corona, including the Corona Beer that has nothing to do with the virus.

Coronaphobist: A person who recklessly flacks the fear of the virus.

These are two terms being used mostly by decision-makers relating to policies designed to limit the spread of the COVID-2019 virus that have acquired new meanings:

Social distancing: As mentioned earlier, this is a COVID-2019 oxymoron in the sense that a person cannot be "social" (i.e., needing companionship) while "distancing" (i.e., being far off or remote in position or nature) himself/herself from other people. Akin to any other oxymoron, this one is a figure of speech in which apparently contradictory terms appear in conjunction.

Lockdown: This term generally refers to the confining of prisoners to their cells, typically after an escape or to regain control during a riot. But as a policy to limit the spread of the COVID-2019 virus, the term now also refers to citizens isolating themselves in their homes and immediate environments as a precaution against the virus.

What follows is a neologism that reflects a novel meaning to the usage of the expression dealing with living in the capital city of Nairobi versus living in a village. In the advent of the COVID-2019 pandemic, living in Nairobi is no longer seen as an advantage over living in a village because of the higher number of infections from the disease in the former compared to the latter. It was submitted on Facebook by Naomi Lanoi, a doctoral candidate at Egerton University:

Before corona, homies would scare the village in us by saying, "I live in Nairobi." Not anymore. The villagers now have the say.

INTERPERSONAL COMMUNICATION

Ronald B. Adler and Neil Towne apprise us that social scientists (especially linguists) call interpersonal communication a "dyad" and frequently employ the adjective "dyadic" to modify it. After discussing the ambiguity involved in determining what is interpersonal communication in terms of the number of people involved and the setting in which a communication takes place (private or public), the coauthors make the following distinction: "*interpersonal communication* . . . occurs when people regard one another as unique persons, whereas in *impersonal communication* they treat each other more like objects" (Adler and Towne, 1993, p. 17). They then go on to provide the following instructive anecdote to underpin their point:

> Philosopher Martin Buber captured the difference between interpersonal and impersonal relationships in the title of his book *I and Thou*. Buber wrote in

> German, where the word "Thou" translates into the intimate form of address "du." In French and Spanish, the word is "tu." The familiar and formal ways of saying "you" capture the difference between interpersonal and impersonal relationships. In these languages the more intimate pronoun expresses a different kind of relationship—one that ideally possesses some qualities that [are] the essence of interpersonal communication. (Adler and Towne, 1993, pp. 17–18)

I must add to the preceding excerpt that the formal form for "you" in German is *sie*; in Italian, it is *lei*; and in Spanish, it is *usted.*

In the succeeding interchange, we can discern the occurrence of successful interpersonal communication between Chan, a small retail store owner in my neighborhood, and me. The conversation took place at his store on May 17, 2020, and I posted it on Facebook the same day as follows:

Abdul Karim Bangura: Good afternoon Chan. How are you doing?

Chan: Good afternoon Liu Zhi (or Liu Chih, who was a great *Chinese* Sunni *Muslim scholar* and philosopher of the Qing Dynasty belonging to the Huiru (*Muslim*) school of Neoconfucian thought). It has been a while.

Abdul Karim Bangura: I stopped by several times to buy my usual items, but your store was closed.

Chan: Oh well, you know we had to obey the mayor's lockdown rule since she said that our business is not essential.

Abdul Karim Bangura: That is the problem with dumb rules. The makers never go around and ask people to determine what is essential and not essential to them. They sit in their offices or homes and rely on lazy advisers to tell them. Most of the news media are not essential, but they have not been shut down and continue to give bad and fake news and spread fear among the people. Why did you decide to open your store today?

Chan: I had to take the risk and open my store because the bill collectors never took a coronavirus break.

Abdul Karim Bangura: Yes, yes, yes, I understand. These lawmakers never think about our having to pay bills and do not think that the check President Trump sent a person would not last for even a week.

Chan: My wife and I were talking about you the day after the travel ban to China was imposed that your travel there and fieldwork on Hongwu Emperor Zhu Yuanzhang (the founding Muslim Emperor of the Ming Dynasty) has been messed up. I was so upset to see some of my people beating and mistreating Blacks in my country. No Chinese Muslim would do something like that as it is against the Islamic teachings and practices.

Abdul Karim Bangura: Yes, it was quite unfortunate that some Chinese would do things that will make all Chinese look bad. And, it is happening at a time when some Buddhist scholars have been speaking out against the institutional racism people of color face in economics, employment, and housing in China.

Chan: Knowing how you are not timid about raising sensitive issues for debate and making good suggestions, your public lectures in China which were to be televised would have made a difference.

Abdul Karim Bangura: I hope so. But I see that you are not wearing a mask. Are you not afraid of being arrested?

Chan: I will take a chance of being arrested for not wearing a mask than being arrested on charges that I am a Chinese agent wearing a mask to spread the virus, as the Chinese government is being accused of doing, or being shot on the excuse that I am a bank robber. But I see that you are not wearing a mask either.

Abdul Karim Bangura: Just like you, I am also afraid that as a darker-skin Black male, the police may shoot me 41 times like they did Mamadou Diallo in New York some years ago if I wore a mask walking around this city.

Chan: Yes, I remember that madness to this day. It is pure evil to shoot anyone 41 times. How many times must you kill a person? It is as if to say that if you were born again 40 times, we will kill you again 40 times.

Abdul Karim Bangura: Bye Chan. See you again soon.

Chan: Yes, bye. Have a great day.

The subsequent stretch of discourse reveals that impersonal communication prevailed between the mayor of Washington, DC, Muriel Bowser, and me. She was my neighbor and our Ward Four representative at the DC City Council. In fact, she used to visit my house when she was running for both offices. I even suggested that she run for the Mayor's Office when the mayor that preceded her, Adrian Fenty, got into political trouble.

Mayor Bowser was the initiator of the communication when on April 24, 2020, she sent out the following e-mail to Washington, DC, residents via her official listserv:

> Dear Washingtonians,
>
> Please help spread the word: free COVID-19 testing is available for DC residents. Health care providers across the District have free testing for COVID-19 and the District is operating free testing sites at the United Medical Center in Ward 8 and at the UDC Bertie Backus campus in Ward 5. (A list of testing locations can be found on coronavirus.dc.gov/testing.)
>
> Additionally, we need residents to know that it is not just people with fever, cough, or shortness of breath who are being tested. Over the past several weeks, more symptoms related to COVID-2019 have been identified. So, if you feel sick, call a doctor or call the testing hotline and let a medical professional advise

you on next steps. We are sending out information by mail and making phone calls, but we also ask that when you call seniors in your life, you share this information with them and give them the phone number for our COVID-2019 testing hotline: 1-855-363-0333.

Testing and contact tracing will be critical at every stage of our response and recovery. In order to flatten the curve and contain the virus, we need to know who has COVID-2019 and who has been exposed to it. That is why we continue to look for ways to expand testing in DC and why, this week, we established a Contact Trace Force at DC Health.

We are all eager to get to the other side of this. To enter the next stage of our response, we need to see a consistent downward trend in new cases for at least 14 days. You can track DC's curve HERE. Remember: your continued sacrifices are saving lives. Continue to stay at home except for essential activities, continue to practice proper social distancing, and when you go out, wear a face covering.

We are all in this together, and we will get through it together.

Sincerely,
Muriel Bowser

That same day (i.e., April 24, 2020), I received another e-mail with a one-sentence directive from the mayor. It is as follows:

Free COVID-19 Testing Is Available

Muriel Bowser
Ward 4

On April 30, 2020, I replied to the mayor as follows:

Good Greetings Mayor Muriel Bowser:

I pray that you and your loved ones are doing very well. Out of respect for your office and personhood, I have stayed out of your affairs in running this city which has been my home for almost 45 years. But when you seem to be oblivious to our personal freedoms vis-à-vis the Coronavirus Disease (COVID)-2019, it behooves me to suggest that you reopen our city as soon as possible.

For starters, there was no reason for you to threaten people with arrests because of your dubious "lockdown" and oxymoronic "social distance" policies for which there is no incontrovertible empirical evidence that they have been effective. Most Washingtonians are civil and law-abiding citizens who respect the policies of their mayors. The few who will flout such policies will do so regardless of your threats.

Next, you have overstated the ramifications of the COVID-2019 in our city. Given the available data, which must be taken with a grain of salt as there is the possibility of misdiagnoses, false-positive and false-negative cases during the earlier stages of the data collection process, the following is what can be discerned for Washington, DC:

Given
Total Estimated Population: 702,455
Number of Confirmed Cases of COVID-2019: 4,323
Number of Deaths from COVID-2019: 224
Number Recovered from COVID-2019: 660

Thus,
Probability (P) of a DC resident dying from COVID-2019: 224 / 702,455 = 0.00032
Probability (P) of a DC resident catching COVID-2019: 4,323 / 702,455 = 0.006
Percentage of infected people who have died from COVID-2019: 5.18%
Percentage of infected people who have NOT died from COVID-2019: 94.82%

In essence, the other very serious ramifications, which are too many to list here, which have resulted from the "lockdown" and oxymoronic "social distance" policies far outweigh those of COVID-2019. And I do not want to hear the tired old parlance that "If even one person dies, it is one person too many," for it accentuates the negative as people would not say the 4,099 that have NOT died out of the 4,323 infected are 4.099 too many, which is accentuating the positive. So, please, reopen our city as soon as possible.

In Peace Always,
Karim/. Ward-4 Resident

After not receiving a reply to my foregoing e-mail for over two weeks, I sent a follow-up e-mail on May 2, 2020. It was precipitated by her statement in her first e-mail about relying on healthcare professionals for her decision-making on the pandemic. It reads as follows:

Good Greetings Mayor Muriel Bowser:

I pray that this follow-up E-mail finds you and your loved ones well. Your most recent E-mail on the COVID-2019 entails your conundrum on this issue: i.e. relying on your healthcare professionals to make decisions. Shouldn't health-care professionals stick to their mundane duties and systematic policy-making remain the domain of policy scientists? Also, what services have you provided residents to meet their basic human needs? Do you really believe that the $1,200 stimulus check from President Trump is enough to sustain most of the people in this city given how long you have shut it down?

Simple logic and the empirical evidence behoove you to open up our city as soon as possible. The costs of its prolonged closure have surpassed that of the Coronavirus COVID-2019 itself.

In Peace Always,
Karim/.

I must mention here that I sent my two e-mails to Mayor Bowser to both his direct and office addresses. It is also evident from my e-mail that I used a mixture of formal and informal tones to encourage interpersonal communication. Both tactics, obviously, did not work.

CONCLUSION AND RECOMMENDATIONS

From January to April 2020, the sales of Corona Beer and the stocks of its distributor, Constellation Brands, plummeted due to the negative news being bandied around about the COVID-2019 on a daily basis, and many people came to associate the beer with the name of the virus. For example, in the United States, the ensuing hysteria led 38 percent of beer drinkers surveyed to say that they want nothing to do with Corona Beer. The distributor had to engage in a massive advertisement campaign to inform the public that *Corona*, which has a Latin origin that means "crown," has no connection whatsoever to the virus (Bajic, 2020).

So a pertinent question that can be raised here is the following: Why did terms such as "corona beer virus," "beer virus," and "beer coronavirus" become prevalent on the Internet, for instance? The answer to this question lies in what I stated at the beginning of this chapter: that is, language has always been a quite salient tool of communication and, thus, plays a major part in our expression of thoughts and feelings. Consequently, it is only inescapable that language has been used to express thoughts and feelings about the COVID-2019, some of which have led to a heightened hysteria among people. And, since linguistics involves the scientific study of language, this chapter is titled Corolinguistics accordingly.

Also, as demonstrated in the preceding sections, Corolinguistics has been quite applicable in analyzing the three linguistic aspects that are evident in the discourse on COVID-2019 and have been the foci of this chapter: that is, (1) communication misfires, (2) neologisms, and (3) interpersonal communication. The ultimate question then is as follows: What can be done to assuage the hysteria that these aspects cause? The rest of this section entails three recommendations related to the three aspects.

First, communication misfires can be alleviated by providing COVID-2019 information in such a lucid manner that even the least educated person can understand what is communicated. Messages should be developed in a simple way, albeit not losing the primary idea. While a message sender cannot determine how receivers will interpret what is transmitted, significant efforts should be made to frame the tone of the message in a pleasant manner. And, receivers must never make a priori assumptions of the senders' knowledge: allow them to tell you what they know and do not know.

Second, negative effects of neologisms can be attenuated by coining or using new words that clearly communicate not only the bad aspects of COVID-2019 but also the good things that are being done to combat the virus. The following suggestion and questions recommended by Richard Nordquist comprise a good guide for developing neologisms:

> Before grabbing the latest usage, ask yourself a few questions. Is it likely to pass the test of time? If not, are you using it to show just how cool you are? Has it already become a cliché? Does it do a job no other word or expression does just as well? Does it rob the language of a useful or well-liked meaning? Is it being adapted to make the writer's prose sharper, crisper, more euphonious, and easier to understand—in other words, better? Or to make it seem more with it (yes, that was cool once, just as cool is cool now), more pompous, more bureaucratic or more politically correct—in other words, worse? (Nordquist, 2019, p. 1)

Third and finally, interpersonal communication can be enhanced and impersonal communication palliated by communicating about aspects of COVID-2019 in various constructive ways. To begin with, more focus should be placed on the disease itself and less so on the conflicting numbers on the infected and dead. Next, the discourse should be sincere instead of being wily. Also, communicators should be empathetic as opposed to being dispassionate. In addition, communicators should be accommodating toward others. Furthermore, communicators should value themselves and their own knowledge and skills. Moreover, communicators should employ affirming answers.

I end this chapter on a positive note by providing one example indicating that despite the numerous negative news about COVID-2019 with which we are being bombarded each day, many people have found ways to cope with it. The following are some from among the many jokes relating to the disease posted on Facebook by Margaret Bulimu, a doctoral candidate at the University of Witwatersrand in South Africa, as her coping mechanism. They are presented here after she gave me written permission:

(a) I heard that Corona Virus will kill people alphabetically. I feel sorry for Abigail.
(b) Please don't react to my posts without washing your hands.

(c) Government giving 100M to musicians. Are those Kenyans stuck in China going to eat and sleep lyrics?
(d) Coronavirus is just a virus on steroids.
(e) Been here in my manger just thinking about the closure of airports because of COVID-2019. What if, God forbid, a relative died now? How would I travel?
(f) So we all now know how it feels to be locked up for something you didn't do.
(g) Who names these viruses? We get attacked by something we don't know and it already has a name.
(h) A Nigerian pastor has challenged fellow pastors to donate church halls as isolation centers. What say Kenyan counterparts?
(i) I already ate 15 times, took 10 naps, watched 6 movies, and it's still today. #Lockdownlife

Indeed, the aphorism that humor lightens your burden and laughter is the best medicine is not farfetched. It is sorely needed during these days of COVID-2019 to help one escape from hysteria.

REFERENCES

Adler, R. B. and Neil T. (1993). *Looking Out/Looking In: Interpersonal Communication*. Fort Worth, TX: Harcourt Brace Jovanovich College Publishers.

Bajic, J. (April 6. 2020). Corona Beer vs coronavirus: Effects on the company's brand and its response. *Lexocology*. Retrieved on November 26, 2020 from https://www.lexology.com/library/detail.aspx?g=77d1fb22-64e2-4f7b-b886-ef40db6d0772.

Buber, M. (1970). *I and Thou* (translated from German by W. Kaufmann). New York: Scribner.

Crystal, D. (1992). *An Encyclopedic Dictionary of Language and Languages*. Cambridge, MA: Blackwell Publishers.

Dinneen, S. J., F. P. (1967). *An Introduction to General Linguistics*. New York: Holt, Reinhart and Winston, Inc.

Dineen, S. J., F. P. (2007). *General Linguistics*. Washington, DC: Georgetown University Press.

Hampton, J. (November 7, 2016). 5 common communication misfires. *Fast Company*. Retrieved on November 21, 2020 from https://www.fastcompany.com/3065149/5-common-communication-misfires-and-how-to-avoid-them.

Langendoen, D. T. (1998). Linguistic theory. In Bechtel, W. and Graham, G. (eds.). *A Companion to Cognitive Science*. Oxford, UK: Blackwell.

Lexico. (2020). State of emergency. *Oxford English and Spanish Dictionary, Thesaurus, and Spanish to English Translator*. Retrieved on November 25, 2020 from https://www.lexico.com/en/definition/state_of_emergency.

Lyons, J. (1971). *Introduction to Theoretical Linguistics*. Cambridge, UK: Cambridge University Press.

Nordquist, R. (February 28, 2019). How neologisms keep English alive. ThoughtCo. Retrieved on November 26, 2020 from https://www.thoughtco.com/neologism-words-term-1691426.

Schmid, H. -J. (2012). Linguistic theories, approaches and methods. In Middeke, M., Müller, T., Wald. C. and Zapf, H. (eds.), *English and American Studies: Theory and Practice*. Stuttgart-Weimar, Germany: J. B. Metzler.

Simonova, M. and Sobel, M. (April 2, 2020). Federal executive emergency authorities to address COVID-19. *Lawfare*. Retrieved on November 25, 2020 from https://www.lawfareblog.com/federal-executive-emergency-authorities-address-covid-19.

Chapter 13

Coroeconomics

Alie Kunda

This chapter investigates the linkage between activities related to the production, consumption, and transfer of wealth apropos the advent of the Coronavirus Disease (COVID)-2019 that has led to a great deal of hysteria among many people. Thus, the analytical approach of the chapter focuses on activities involving the making, distributing, selling, and purchasing of goods and services. This will allow readers to also understand how the COVID-2019 pandemic has impacted (a) how societies use scarce resources to produce valuable commodities and distribute them among different people to help them deal with the effects of the virus; (b) the variety of economic policies that have been implemented to deal with the impact of the virus; and (c) a focus on real life, since economics is focused on learning from case studies.

Thus, the major concepts in this chapter are (a) hoarding, (b) price gouging, (c) market volatility, (d) job loss, and (e) unemployment. In order to facilitate clarity from the start, I will define these concepts here. First, *hoarding* refers to amassing a commodity that is perceived to be valuable and hiding or storing it away. *Price gouging* is sellers trying to take unfair advantage of consumers during an emergency or disaster by greatly inflating prices for crucial consumer goods and services. *Market volatility* denotes a demand for a particular commodity or service changing rapidly and unpredictably, especially for the worse. *Job loss* means disappearance of paid positions of regular employment because of basic structural economic changes as different from impermanent swings in demand. *Unemployment* signifies the state of being without a paid job but available to work.

Before broaching the aforementioned themes, the General Economic Theory will be propounded first. This is necessary to give the reader an idea about how the exploration thereafter is established.

GENERAL ECONOMIC THEORY

For starters, General Economic Theory can be basically defined as an idea or a structure of ideas envisaged for elucidating the production, consumption, and transfer of wealth based on general postulates independent of these aspects. Next, the theory is segmented into two constituents. One constituent is *Microeconomic Theory* which is concerned with single factors and the effects of individual decisions. The other constituent is *Macroeconomic Theory* which is concerned with large-scale or general economic factors such as interest rates and national productivity.

Also, at least 47 main specific economic theories have been noted to compose the General Economic Theory. They are the following with the aspects they investigate:

(1) Asset-Based Welfare Theory investigates poverty eradication in an economy via the redistribution of productive assets instead of income.
(2) Bayesian Regret Theory investigates the expected difference (i.e., the "regret") between the utility of a Bayesian strategy (whereby an individual must specify type spaces, strategy spaces, payoff functions, and prior beliefs, and then employ a complete plan of action that covers every contingency that might arise for every type that player might be) and that of the optimal strategy (i.e., the one with the highest expected payoff).
(3) Cartel Theory investigates associations of manufacturers or suppliers that seek to maintain prices at a high level and restrict competition.
(4) Circular Cumulative Causation Theory investigates how the central variables of a phenomenon and their linkages are delineated with the premise that a change in one form of an institution will lead to successive changes in other institutions.
(5) Cluster Theory investigates how concentrating industries in particular regions leads to several advantages.
(6) Credibility Theory investigates the emergence and evolution of societal institutions or social rules.
(7) Dahrendorf Theory investigates the desirability of diversity in economic policies across time and space based on local needs.
(8) Demand-Pull Theory investigates why when the demand for goods and services exceeds existing supplies leads to inflation.

(9) Developmentalism Theory investigates the idea that fostering a strong and varied internal market and imposing high tariffs on imported goods constitute the best way for less developed economies to develop.
(10) Dispersed Knowledge Theory investigates the idea that no one agent possesses all of the necessary information on the factors that influence prices and production in every part of a system.
(11) Economic Transformation Theory investigates the process of transferring labor and other resources from lower- to higher-productivity sectors and raising productivity growth within a sector.
(12) Engineering Economics Theory investigates the economic choice among technically feasible alternatives so that scarce resources can be allocated rationally.
(13) Guild Socialism Theory investigates how through an implicit contractual relationship with the public, workers can control an industry via trade-related guilds.
(14) Harmonies of Political Economic Theory investigates the ability and inventiveness of the complex social mechanism.
(15) Hiding Hand Theory investigates the intersection between ignorance vis-à-vis perceiving future obstacles when one decides to launch a project and the rational choice to take on that project.
(16) Hubbert Peak Theory investigates how the rate of petroleum production is liable to follow a bell-shaped curve for any given geographical area, ranging from a particular oil-producing region to the world as a whole.
(17) Identity Economics Theory investigates how given monetary incentives and their identities, people make economic choices.
(18) Incomplete Contracts Theory investigates why it is impractical for contracts to specify what should be done in every possible contingency.
(19) Indigo Era Theory investigates how the new epoch of economies and economics based on creativity, ideas, and innovation is replacing that which is based on the possession of natural resources.
(20) Kenneth Boulding's Evolutionary Theory employs evolutionary methodology to investigate the know-how processes used to metamorphose an economy for employment, firms, growth, industries, institutions, production, and trade within via the actions of diverse agents from experience and interactions.
(21) Khazzoom–Brookes Theory investigates how increased energy efficiency is inclined to usher increased energy consumption.
(22) Least-Cost Theory investigates why firms tend to look for locations with the lowest transport and labor costs.
(23) Legal Origins Theory investigates the idea that civil law and common law, which comprise the two key legal traditions or origins,

fundamentally shape lawmaking and dispute adjudication and have not been amended after the inceptive external relocation by Europeans.

(24) Liquidity Premium Theory investigates the difference between two types of financial securities, such as stocks, that have all of the same standards with the exception of liquidity.

(25) Local Multiplier Effect Theory investigates the additional economic boon an area receives from money spent in the local economy.

(26) Lucas Wedge Theory investigates how much higher gross domestic product (GDP) would be if it grows as fast as it should.

(27) Market Design Theory investigates the establishment of markets of specific properties.

(28) Mutualism Theory investigates the notion of a socialist society based on free markets and usufructs: that is, the rights to enjoy the use and advantages of another's property short of the destruction or waste of its substance.

(29) O-ring Theory of Economic Development investigates how tasks of production must be carried out dexterously together so that any of them can be of high value.

(30) Pain of Paying Theory investigates the negative, natural instinctive states of mind a person undergoes when paying for a good or service.

(31) Product Life-cycle Theory investigates how early in a product's life-cycle all of the components and labor connected to that product came from the location where it was designed.

(32) Rational Inattention Theory investigates the consequences of the cost of information collection on decision-making.

(33) Regenerative Economic Theory investigates the goods and services the earth makes available.

(34) Relative Income Theory investigates how a person's settled way of feeling about consumption and saving is shaped more by his/her income in relation to others than by abstract living standard.

(35) Rent-gap Theory investigates the process of gentrification: that is, the activity whereby the character of a poor urban area is changed by wealthier people moving in, improving housing, and attracting new businesses, while displacing current inhabitants.

(36) Shale Band Theory investigates the span of world oil prices that can hold up present levels of U.S. shale oil extraction using hydraulic fracturing techniques.

(37) Social Gravity Theory investigates the nexus between social structure and socioeconomics by utilizing the now well-known theory of Newtonian gravity: that is, every mass attracts every other mass in the universe, and the gravitational force between two bodies is proportional to

the product of their masses and inversely proportional to the square of the distance between them.

(38) Social Metabolism Theory investigates the collection of steady, continuous stream of materials and energy that happen between (a) nature and society, (b) between different societies, and (c) within societies.

(39) Split Labor Market Theory investigates racial/ethnic strains and labor market division by race/ethnicity in regard to social structure and political power instead of individual-level prejudice.

(40) Theories of Poverty investigate (a) for the developing countries, cultural features that delay development; and (b) for the developed countries, social and political features that maintain poverty and perceptions that the poor have a notable effect on the formation and implementation of programs geared toward alleviating poverty.

(41) Theory of Conjoint Measurement investigates continuous quantity: that is, a property that can exist as a multitude (i.e., a large number of elements) or magnitude (i.e., the great size or extent of an element).

(42) Theory of Interstellar Trade investigates how goods in transit can be calculated when the goods travel at close to the speed of light.

(43) Theory of Storage investigates (a) when supplies of a commodity at hand are high and the working inventories of commercial consumers of the commodity are kept to a minimum accordingly; and (b) when supplies are fixed and purchasing managers set up production inventory levels to guarantee accessibility.

(44) Three-sector Theory investigates how an economy's undertaking moves from the primary to the secondary and then to the tertiary sector.

(45) Toothpaste Tube Theory investigates how growing pressure eventually propels some sort of release, as in the case of exports when home demand is squeezed and exports are forced out.

(46) Tournament Theory investigates conditions whereby wage differences are based on the relative differences among individuals as opposed to marginal productivity.

(47) Vanishing Hand Theory investigates how at first the Visible Hand is existent when industries need managerial collaboration and vertical amalgamation for long-term growth. But, in due course, this hand gradually becomes weak and metamorphoses to a more Invisible Hand whereby specialization makes it possible for economic factors affecting the price of, demand for, and availability of a commodity to synchronize more strongly.

I must also mention here that there are numerous other specific theories classified under the following subcategories: (a) 51 Finance Theories, (b) 29 Macroeconomic Theories, (c) 14 Microeconomic Theories, (d) 25 Social

Choice Theories, (e) 17 Taxation Theories, and (f) 79 Economic Value Theories. All of these theories and the ones discussed combine to form the General Economic Theory. In addition, these theories, following Lloyd G. Reynolds (1985a,b), among many other economists, permit an analyst to employ logical reasoning in order to make factual predictions.

HOARDING AND PRICE GOUGING

As Daniel J. Smith points out, when buyers encounter a catastrophe or dilemma, they develop a high propensity to hoard essential goods. Unable to produce and supply these goods in a timely manner in the face of the growth in desire, one way sellers try to limit the hoarding is to charge high prices for the goods, leading to price gouging. This situation tends to get buyers angry and call for stern laws to stop price gouging (Smith, 2020).

Nonetheless, Smith delineates a number of positive aspects of price gouging. First, high prices force some buyers to buy goods they really need and leave those they do not need for other buyers. This situation deters buyers from unnecessarily hoarding goods. It also dissuades buyers from placing the goods into lower-value uses (Smith, 2020). For example, charging $20.00 for a small jar of vapor rub that used to sell for $3.00 would force the typical buyer to ponder about buying an extra jar, thereby leaving more vapor rubs for those buyers who actually need them to relieve their coughs caused by minor throat and bronchial irritation associated with the common cold and those who need them to temporarily relieve minor aches and pains of muscles and joints.

Second, according to Smith, even buyers outside an affected area also economize on their buying because of higher prices. He cites the example of "the increased demand for building materials for rebuilding New Orleans after Hurricane Katrina [which] drove building material prices up across the nation, leading unaffected consumers to delay less essential building or remodeling projects" (Smith, 2020, p. 1). He adds that putting limits on purchases, even though the intention is good, does not work well as buyers can easily get around the restriction by getting different family members to buy the goods or by splitting up their shopping into different trips or to different stores (Smith, 2020).

Third, Smith posits that the production and supply of needed goods to an affected area can be stimulated by higher prices. This is because it could take many weeks for producers to get more raw materials, increase production, and supply needed goods to those affected areas. Also, having to pay workers for overtime work; suppliers having to be motivated in order to make more raw materials; and having to operate machinery more rigorously, which results in high operating costs in addition to wear and tear, make driving up short-term production very costly (Smith, 2020).

Fourth, Smith states that sellers will divert goods to affected areas where they are needed the most when the prices for those goods are higher. For instance, the higher prices will propel sellers that are not in the affected areas to buy the needed goods and rent trucks to transport them to those areas (Smith, 2020).

Fifth, paradoxically, contends Smith, prices will eventually be pushed back down as the higher prices lead to an increase in the supply of the needed goods as more sellers are attracted to producing and supplying the goods. Price-gouging laws which seek to keep prices lower in spite of the increase in demand of the goods, he also argues, would lead to shortages because they would not deter hoarding. This shortcoming would in turn discourage manufacturers from making the goods, thereby leading to shortages (Smith, 2020).

Finally, however, Smith makes the salient point that concern of providing relief for low-income residents emerges whenever there is a disaster. Nonetheless, these residents get very little relief when the shelves in stores are empty in the face of anti-price-gouging laws. It is only by allowing the price system to work and providing charity assistance to low-income residents would they become better off (Smith, 2020).

In the rest of this section, we will see how COVID-2019-related hoarding precipitated price gouging and its effects and responses in the United States and the People's Republic of China (PRC), two countries among the hardest hit by the virus. The two cases are presented separately for lucidity. The examination of each case will proceed in three steps. First, the nature of the hoarding and price gouging will be delineated. Second, the government's policy against the practice will be outlined. Third, an example of the practice and how it was addressed by a government agency will be outlined.

The Case of the United States

To begin with, in terms of the nature of the hoarding and price gouging of COVID-2019-related products in the United States, the law firm of SmithAmundsen LLC informs us that price gouging in the country is an "anti-competitive conduct" and is right now a serious issue due to the pandemic. The virus' impact on various supply and demand factors and the hoarding and price gouging of medical supplies and other crucial products have emerged as major concerns for state and federal authorities. Indispensable supplies of goods needed to fight the virus do not reach people and professionals that desperately need them due to the practice of hoarding and price gouging. Right now, there is an increased demand for and a shortage of certain necessary items like hand sanitizers, ventilators, and personal protective equipment (PPE)—that is, face masks, gloves, and other medical supplies. Healthcare professionals on the frontline need these supplies to fight the virus and protect themselves. A number of healthcare professionals are getting sick because of the lack of sufficient PPE and other vital medical supplies. For example, in New York, two nurses and a world-acclaimed pediatric neurosurgeon have died as a result of the virus (SmithAmundsen, 2020).

The law firm goes on to apprise us that on April 1, 2020, the U.S. federal government reported that it had nearly exhausted its supply of PPE. Consequently, federal and state authorities turned to anti-price-gouging laws to protect their supplies of crucial materials. On March 23, 2020, President Donald Trump signed an executive order mandating the United States Department of Justice (USDOJ) to deal with the hoarding and price gouging of necessary health and medical supplies. The executive order, which was authorized under the Defense Production Act, forbids anyone from amassing identified materials that are more than the reasonable demands of business, personal, or home use; or for the purpose of resale at prices that are more than the current market prices (SmithAmundsen, 2020).

The president's executive order and similar state laws across the United States protect the following medical supplies from hoarding and price gouging: (a) N-95 face masks, (b) portable ventilators, (c) disinfecting devices, (d) medical gowns, (e) medical gloves, (f) surgical face masks, (g) sterilizers, and (h) drug products with active ingredient chloroquine phosphate or hydroxychloroquine. A total of 34 states have price-gouging laws covering these supplies. These laws as a general rule ban an increase in price that is more than a particular threshold or "cap," commonly a maximum percentage increase from the price immediately preceding the state of emergency. Price-gouging laws typically extend for a period of time after a declared state of emergency (commonly 30 days unless extended). In addition, 48 states have declared a "state of emergency" in response to the outbreak of the virus (SmithAmundsen, 2020).

Next, as it concerns the U.S. government's policy against hoarding and price gouging of COVID-2019-related products, Attorney General William Pelham Barr, as secretary of the USDOJ, stated the following in a memorandum sent to U.S. attorneys across the country: "We will aggressively pursue bad actors who amass critical supplies either far beyond what they could use or for the purpose of profiteering. Scarce medical supplies need to be going to hospitals for immediate use in care, not to warehouses for later overcharging" (USDOJ, 2020, p. 1). The agency also encourages citizens to report practices of hoarding or price gouging of critical supplies to the National Center for Disaster Fraud by calling its National Hotline at 1.866.720.5721 or by submitting the Center's Web Complaint Form (USDOJ, 2020).

Also, vis-à-vis an example of a matter dealing with hoarding and price gouging of COVID-2019-related products, the United States Immigration and Customs Enforcement (USICE) tells us about an investigation of 66-year-old Richard Schirripa, also referred to as "the Mask Man," a licensed pharmacist in New York City who was charged with violating the Defense Production Act by hoarding and price gouging scarce N95 masks. The joint operation by USICE, Homeland Security Investigations New York's Dark Web and Cryptocurrency Task Force, the United States Postal Inspection Service, and the Drug Enforcement Administration charged Schirripa as follows (USICE, 2020):

> (1) hoarding and price gouging of thousands of N95 masks in late March and April 2020, in violation of the Defense Production Act (DPA); (2) lying to officers of the Drug Enforcement Administration (DEA) on two occasions in early 2020; and (3) causing Medicare and Medicaid to be billed for prescriptions based on false representations, from 2014 to 2019, as well as the unauthorized use of his pharmacy patients' identifying information in connection with his health care fraud scheme. (USICE, 2020, p. 1)

The one count of violating the Defense Production Act carries a maximum sentence of one year in prison. Each of the two counts of making false statements carries a maximum sentence of 5 years in prison, making a total of 10 years for the two counts. The one count of healthcare fraud carries a maximum sentence of 20 years in prison. And, the one count of aggravated identity theft carries a mandatory minimum sentence of two years in prison, which must run consecutively to any other sentence of imprisonment. As of this writing, the case against Schirripa is still under litigation. As with every criminal complaint in the United States, the charges are not evidence of guilt. Schirripa is presumed innocent and entitled to a fair trial at which the government has the burden of proving his guilt beyond a reasonable doubt (USICE, 2020).

The Case of the PRC

To commence with, apropos to the nature of the hoarding and price gouging of COVID-2019-related products in the PRC, Tung and his coauthors explain that since the outbreak of the virus, the hoarding and price gouging of daily necessities and personal or medical protective goods has become a common issue in the country due to supply shortages combined with high demand. While some provinces such as those in Hong Kong have allowed free market prices, others have either put in place new emergency laws and countermeasures or enhanced their existing laws to discourage the hoarding and price gouging of such products (Tung et al., 2020).

Tung and his colleagues proceed to point out that penalties can be severe when an entity is found guilty of engaging in hoarding and price gouging in the PRC. The punishments include huge fines, impoundment of illegal gains, nullification of business licenses, and imprisonment of the perpetrators. In order to facilitate the production of the needed goods in an orderly manner, regulators and enforcement agencies in the country have shown their resolve to fight hoarding and price gouging. Concomitantly, manufacturers and distributors have also become quite watchful of the enforcement trend and pay attention to the latest updates to ensure their compliance in order to avoid the severe penalties (Tung et al., 2020).

In addition, Tung and his partners note that even though "anti-price-gouging laws" have been in place in the PRC, emergency courses of action were also instituted by the government in January 2020 in order to deal with the COVID-2019 outbreak. The main goal of these actions is to firm up supplies and guarantee market order (Tung et al., 2020).

Next, in reference to the PRC government's policy against hoarding and price gouging of COVID-2019-related products, the law firm Proskauer Rose LLC tells us that the policy is centered on the country's Price Law that was enacted on December 29, 1997. Also, other price-gouging practices are treated as anti-monopoly, unfair competition, or consumer protection concerns within the ambit of the country's Anti-Monopoly Law, Anti-Unfair Competition Law, or Consumer Rights and Interests Protection Law (Proskauer Rose LLC, 2020).

Also, according to the law firm, the Price Law mandates that, with certain exceptions, businesses operating in the PRC are required to set prices for their goods and services based on the costs of manufacturing, operation, and market supply and demand. Thus, reasonable price increases due to rising costs or changes in market supply or demand are permitted. This does not, however, account for the limited number of goods and services that are subject to government-set prices or government-guidance prices (Proskauer Rose LLC, 2020).

In addition, the law firm enlightens us about some types of "unfair price behaviors" that are forbidden by the government of the PRC. They include (a) fabricating and/or disseminating price increase information to drive up prices; (b) hoarding commodities with tight supply or abnormal price fluctuations; (c) using other price-gouging practices to push up commodity prices excessively; (d) using misleading or false pricing practices; (e) covertly manipulating prices by raising or reducing grade levels of goods or services; and (f) illegally seeking exorbitant profits, even absent any market power (Proskauer Rose LLC, 2020).

Furthermore, the law firm illuminates that in order to "deter hoarding and price gouging" of sorely needed COVID-2019-related products, in February 2020, the Chinese government put in place additional measures to intensify the application of the Price Law and other related rules and mandates. For instance, the China State Administration for Market Regulation (SAMR), which is responsible for enforcing the Price Law, issued the Guidance on Investigation and Handling of Illegal Acts of Price Gouging during the Novel Coronavirus Pneumonia Epidemic Prevention and Control Period, simply referred to as the "SAMR Guidance." This guidance entails detailed rules on the application of the Price Law and determination of illegal price gouging for products related to the prevention of the virus (Proskauer Rose LLC, 2020). The following are the practices deemed as "excessive pricing as illegal price gouging" in the SAMR Guidance:

> Selling the same product in such a manner that results in the margin between the seller's cost and the selling price being significantly higher than that of the last actual transaction on or before January 19, 2020 (being the day immediately prior to the Chinese government's official declaration of the Novel Coronavirus as a Class B level communicable disease); or otherwise selling products at a margin above levels determined as acceptable by the local counterparts of SAMR. Although SAMR has not issued national guidance on acceptable margins, local governments have set thresholds ranging between 15% and 35%. (Proskauer Rose LLC, 2020, p. 1)

Moreover, the administrative penalties for violating these laws are the following: (a) restitution; (b) confiscation of any illegal gains and a fine up to five times of the illegal gains, capped at RMB 3 million, or approximately US$450,000, if there is no illegal gain; (c) halting business operation pending rectification; and/or (d) revocation of business licenses. Those individuals who engage in more serious violations such as a large amount of illegal gains or causing significant market disruption may be imprisoned for up to five years or longer for "extremely serious" violations. Also, consumers affected by a price-gouging practice have the right to file civil lawsuits against violators to recover losses caused by the violation (Proskauer LLC, 2020).

Also, regarding an example of an occurrence of hoarding and price gouging of COVID-2019-related products, Tung and his coauthors relay that on January 29, 2020, Nanchang Municipal Market Supervision Bureau served a Notification on Hearing of Administrative Punishment to a drugstore in Jinxian County and fined it RMB 3 million, which is the highest amount for such an offense. The drugstore was illegally hoarding masks and other epidemic protective products and price gouging. A total of 224 pieces of absorbent gauze masks and 320 bottles of disinfectant were confiscated. It was determined that in its effort to make excessive profit, the drugstore publicly sold epidemic prevention-related commodities at a margin ranging from 50 percent to 130 percent beginning on January 22, 2020, even though there was no substantial change in purchasing cost, which activities fall within the purview of Article 2(2) of the Measures for the Implementation of Administrative Punishments on Price-related Illegal Acts. The highest fine of RMB 3 million was imposed because the hoarding and gouging were regarded as very serious (Tung et al., 2020).

MARKET VOLATILITY

The wealth management company Genève Invest inculcates us about five major factors that cause market volatility. The first factor discussed is investor concern. This element has to do with investors worrying about their investments and the prices of bonds and equities are impacted. For instance, investors who are concerned about losing money may sell their bonds and securities out of fear that their values will fall. The inclination can indeed cause prices to plummet (Genève Invest, 2020).

The second factor broached concerns the occurrence of political events in countries across the globe. By way of illustration, when a major politician assumes office or gives a speech about the economy, investors tend to respond in expectation of new policies or changes to those in place that they perceive will affect the market (Genève Invest, 2020).

The third factor propounded is in regard to natural disasters. Markets may become more volatile in reaction to natural disasters that affect natural resources, the flow of goods and services, or money supply (Genève Invest, 2020).

The fourth factor discussed relates to major events in foreign markets (Genève Invest, 2020). Since American businesses, for instance, depend on relationships with businesses in the Middle East, major events in Middle Eastern markets can affect American markets as well. For example, a significant drop in the value of Saudi Arabian stocks may trigger an increased volatility in American stocks.

The fifth factor proffered is about public relations issues. This type of volatility usually occurs when a particular sector of the market is affected which will not impact the whole bond and stock market. Hence, prices of a large company's stocks often drop when it experiences a public relations disaster (Genève Invest, 2020).

Also, from Stacy Rapacon, we learn about (a) whether market volatility is a negative or positive thing, (b) how market volatility is measured, (c) what a normal amount of market volatility is, (d) why market volatility is rising and whether investors should be worried, and (e) what all this talk about market volatility means for investors. To begin with whether market volatility is a negative or positive thing, Rapacon says that the phenomenon can be both negative and positive. On the negative side, the steep and inverse gallops of the stock market can be quite frightening for timorous and many neophyte investors. In addition, by the time one learns about how volatile a market is in the news, it is usually when volatility is high, which may be a sign "for a bear market, or a period when major indexes drop by 20 percent or more. That's what happened recently, when the longest bull market in history transitioned to a bear market after concerns about the economic impact of the coronavirus brought major market indexes down 20 percent from recent highs" (Rapacon, 2020, p. 1). A *bear market* is a market in which prices are falling, thereby encouraging selling; and a *bull market* a market in which share prices are rising, thereby encouraging buying.

On the positive side, certain acute spikes ascend toward the bull market territory, not descend toward bear market territory. Thus, an individual who has investments in a market and stocks ascend on a sprint will be joyful for the price spikes. But even when the prices of stocks drop, an investor who believes that there will be a turnaround, as it has happened on many occasions, will still see the drop as an opportunity to buy stocks for future profits. Thus, as Rapacon puts it, "The truth is that a normal level of market volatility can be both good and bad. It's the very heart of investing, keeping everyone's money moving and giving investors a chance to make good on the classic investing directive to buy low and sell high" (Rapacon, 2020, p. 1).

Next, about how market volatility is measured, Rapacon identifies several computational techniques. One technique involves analyzing daily, weekly, or monthly price swings. For this, analysts compute the "standard deviation" (i.e., a quantity calculated to indicate the extent of deviation for a group as a whole), which is the most frequently utilized gauge of market volatility. It is derived by using the S&P (Standard and Poor) 500 Stock Index, a representative for the entire U.S. stock market, and computing how each monthly return varies from the year's average monthly return (Rapacon, 2020).

Another technique entails calculating daily price movements. For instance, a significant movement "in the value of the S&P 500—notably higher or lower than the average 0.66 percent daily move, according to data from Adviser Investments—on any given day is likely to make headlines" (Rapacon, 2020, p. 1). Some analysts usually count the number of days major indexes go through significant swings in a particular span as another way to calculate market volatility. On average, the S&P's value, for example, changes by 1 percent or more 52 days of the year. Hence, a much greater frequency than that reflects "extra volatility" (Rapacon, 2020).

The other technique requires calculating future volatility, which is also referred to as “implied volatility.” This statistic is calculated by the Chicago Board Options Exchange’s Volatility Index, also referred to simply as the “VIX” or “the investor fear gauge.” It is an estimate of the anticipated performance of the S&P 500 over the next 30 days, based on “put and call options.” These options are “investors’ agreements to, respectively, sell and buy investments at specified prices on or before a particular date. (But they’re not binding: that is, ordering a put option gives you the chance to sell, but does not require you to do it.) When the VIX is rising, volatility is rising” (Rapacon, 2020, p. 1).

Also, in regard to what a normal amount of market volatility is, Rapacon explicates that over time, the American credit rating agency S&P Global Ratings’ 500 long-term average standard deviation has been 15.6 percent. In recent years, it has been noticeably below average. In 2017, for instance, the S&P’s standard deviation nosedived as low as 6.7 percent, marking the second-lowest level since 1957. The S&P moved by 1 percent or more on only nine trading days that same year (i.e., 2017). Thus, when volatility returned to the historic average in 2018, those “normal” levels were jarring to many investors (Rapacon, 2020).

In addition, as it pertains to why market volatility is rising and whether investors should be worried, Rapacon illuminates that “uncertainty” (i.e., the state of not being completely confident or sure of something) is a key source of market volatility, especially in the current milieu of COVID-2019. In the United States, for example, the precariousness of market volatility is compounded by the federal government’s decisions on interest rates amid the travails of the 2020 presidential election that have investors fretting about the future of the stock market which keeps heaving (Rapacon, 2020). Consequently, Rapacon makes the following observation:

> If volatility is high for a stock that means it could be a risky bet because of wild price swings. And if volatility is high for the overall market, get ready to swoon (and not in a celebrity-sighting kind of way): Experts often point to high market volatility as an indicator that a big drop and potential bear market is on the way. . . . This lines up with what history shows: When the VIX is on the rise, the S&P 500 index typically falls. And higher levels of volatility tend to indicate greater short-term losses. What’s important to remember, though, is what else history reveals. After each of these periods of increased volatility and losses, the stock market has rebounded to unprecedented heights. (Rapacon, 2020, p. 1)

Furthermore, vis-à-vis what all this talk about market volatility means for investors, Rapacon says that it denotes that when investors are making long-term investing plans, it behooves them to seriously consider market volatility as part and parcel of participating in bonds and stock markets. This does not, however, imply that they should be frenetically examining the daily price swings of the markets on a daily basis and acting correspondingly. Instead, they must expect the turbulences and plan on addressing them in a rational manner. In essence, market volatility should be considered as a normal phenomenon (Rapacon, 2020).

The rest of this section entails brief examinations of the effects of COVID-2019-related market volatility on (a) the oil and gas market and (b) the precious metals market. They are presented separately for the sake of clarity.

Oil and Gas Market

To begin with, the Organization for Economic Cooperation and Development (OECD) points out that the fossil market is encountering structural decline because of the negative effects the COVID-2019 pandemic is having on oil-exporting developing countries. While some of these countries may be able to withstand the present predicament if they have sovereign wealth funds or reasonably low public debt levels, most of the weak ones that are resource dependent and were already facing high levels of public debt and underlying economic and social weaknesses will have a very difficult time withstanding the turmoil. This is mainly because, in recent years, oil-exporting developing countries have used their oil collateral to heavily borrow short-term and expensive private loans on non-concessional terms (OECD, 2020).

Next, we glean from James Thompson that the COVID-2019 pandemic has contributed significantly to the volatility of the world oil and gas market. Upstream operators in the oil and gas extraction and petroleum exploration industries have been affected greatly by the turbulent oscillations in demand conditions and prices. Since travel activity constitutes more than half of the global oil demand, travel restrictions instituted in early 2020 in attempts to contain the spread of the virus led to a huge decline in the demand for fuel. The enormous decline in turn has led to significant drops in oil and gas prices. Thus, the International Energy Agency, for example, estimates that "global oil demand to fall by 8.4%, from 100.1 million barrels per day in 2019, to an average 91.7 million barrels per day in 2020" (Thompson, 2020, p. 1).

Also, Thompson apprises us that in order to address the impact of the COVID-2019 pandemic on the oil and gas market, apropos the declines in demand conditions and price, the Organization of the Petroleum Exporting Countries (OPEC) and other major oil-producing countries such as Malaysia, Mexico, and Russia (together referred to as OPEC+) slashed their oil production. The objective was to bring supply and demand conditions into equilibrium and stability to the price. Accordingly, the group "cut oil production by 9.7 million barrels per day in May of 2020 before scaling back cuts to 7.7 million barrels per day in August as demand conditions stabilized" (Thompson, 2020, p. 1).

In addition, according to Thompson, considering that the United States and some countries in Europe are again adumbrating large numbers of COVID-2019 cases, there is significant uncertainty for the oil and gas market in the short run. As countries reenact various states of lockdown, there is bound to be renewed pressure on the demand conditions and fuel price. Nonetheless, since OPEC+ countries have demonstrated the discipline to cut oil production and stabilize price, they will again do the same in the short term (Thompson, 2020).

Precious Metals Market

To start with, coauthors Jason Sappor, Thomas Rutland, Gregory Rodwell, Alice Yu, Luke Nickels, and Ronnie Cecil tell us that reactions toward the COVID-2019 pandemic have given rise to a significantly volatile precious metals market. They predict that the situation will lead exploration budgets to decline by 29 percent in 2020, which will consequently have a quite negative impact on many precious mineral operations. They also point out that national and provincial closures such as the ones that were instituted in Canada, Mexico, Peru, and South Africa have contributed a great deal to the volatility (Sappor et al., 2020).

Next, the coauthors indicate that since January 2020, the decline in purchases of precious metals caused by the COVID-2019 pandemic's economic impact in turn led to a notable decline in the prices for these goods. The attendant uncertainty has caused declines in the prices of base metals in line with copper, "as is traditionally the case in times of uncertainty, whose price has decreased by 22% since January 2, 2020, while iron ore, zinc, lead and nickel have all fallen by 10%–20% over the period. Cobalt and lithium carbonate prices have fallen by just 5% and 8%, respectively, over the same period" (Sappor et al., 2020).

Furthermore, the coauthors reveal that even though the price for gold declined in the first quarter of 2020, it rebounded significantly because of the demand for bigger financial investment. The price of silver, however, sank to an 11-year low because of lesser industrial demand, even though it had enjoyed record retail investments. The price for the platinum group metals has taken quite a wallop due to the lockdowns enacted in South Africa and the huge decline in auto sales across the world. The turmoil has bred a nervous equilibrium, albeit it has not upended either the upward price directions for rhodium and palladium or the downward price direction for platinum (Sappor, 2020).

Nonetheless, as the Exchange Traded Funds (ETF) Trends opines, opportunities tend to emerge for precious metals when uncertainty is present in capital markets. The resulting volatility from the uncertainty is inclined to direct investors to precious metals. For example, gold provides investors with a proxy to variegate their holdings and it "marches to the beat of its own drum compared to the broader market" (ETF Trends, 2020).

JOB LOSS AND UNEMPLOYMENT

To get going, Jennie E. Brand talks about job loss and unemployment being reflexive and obstreperous phenomena that can greatly affect the career paths of an employee. The two phenomena are being noticed more nowadays because of their occurrences among an increasing number of constituents of the labor force. They can lead to "long-term earnings losses, and lower job quality; declines in psychological and physical well-being; loss of psychosocial assets; social withdrawal; family disruption; and lower levels of children's attainment and well-being" (Brand, 2015, p. 359). Even when reemployment alleviates "some of the negative effects of job loss, it does not eliminate them"; nonetheless, "contexts of widespread unemployment, although associated with larger economic losses, lessen the social-psychological impact of job loss" (Brand, 2015, p. 359).

Next, according to Melinda Smith, Jeanne Segal, and Lawrence Robinson, it is a very stressful experience for anyone to be "laid off, downsized, forced to take early retirement, or see contract work dry up" (Smith et al., 2020, p. 1). A person who loses a job also suffers financial angst and deteriorating mood, mental and emotional health, and relationships (Smith et al., 2020).

In addition, Smith and company point out that a person's job is frequently more than just a way s/he sees himself/herself; it also shapes the way other people perceive him/her. Even in a situation where a person may not love his/her job, it most probably gave him/her a means of social expression and an organization, inspiration, and significance to his/her life. For the person to lose a job suddenly could leave him/her feeling irate, melancholic, or tormented. S/he might even doubt his/her identity, lamenting about all that s/he lost, or feeling apprehensive about what the future may hold (Smith et al., 2020).

Furthermore, Smith et al. allude to the fact that based on the circumstances that lead a person to lose a job, s/he may believe that s/he has a personal failure or error, betrayed by his/her employer, or lack power over his/her life's course. The person can feel quite overwhelmed if s/he does not employ the right coping techniques to ease his/her anxiety and stress (Smith et al., 2020).

Moreover, in addition to the personal costs, there are also a number of societal costs associated with job loss and unemployment. First, Stephen D.

Simpson mentions that the ubiquity of unemployment can propel people to demand that their governments put in place protectionist measures and strict immigration restrictions. A major consequence of protectionism is tit-for-tat retaliations, which can reduce trade that can in turn be harmful to the economic well-being of the trading partners (Simpson, 2020).

Second, as Simpson points out, the way people interact with one another is another societal cost that can result from job loss and unemployment. High unemployment, for instance, yields higher crime rates and less volunteerism. Some people engage in criminal activities in order to meet their economic needs when they lack wage-paying employment. Others may not engage in volunteer work because of the psychological effect of being unemployed (Simpson, 2020).

Third, Tejvan Pettinger asserts that when there are high job loss and unemployment, governments must borrow more because fewer people would be paying taxes and the unemployed would spend less, thereby resulting in a decline in tax revenues. As a consequence, governments must spend more on unemployment and related benefits (Pettinger, 2019).

Fourth, Pettinger states that high job loss and unemployment usher a lower GDP for the economy. High job loss and unemployment are signs of an economy being inefficient and performing below full capacity. The results are lower output and incomes, as the unemployed would lack the capacity to buy many goods. A negative multiplier effect (i.e., "when an initial withdrawal of spending from the economy leads to knock-on effects and a bigger final fall in real GDP") would result as the unemployment rate rises (Pettinger, 2019, p. 1).

Fifth, as stated by Pettinger, high job loss and unemployment can lead to a multiplication of social problems. Places where job loss and unemployment are high, particularly among the youth, are likely to experience more crime and vandalism. The situation can lead to isolation and strains in incorporating the unemployed youth into society (Pettinger, 2019).

Sixth and finally, Pettinger notes that high job loss and unemployment do serve as catalysts for political instability. He cites two examples of this episode: (1) the mass unemployment in the 1930s that led to social unrest in the United States and (2) the unemployment rate of 6 million that gave rise to Adolf Hitler and the Nazi Party in Germany (Pettinger, 2019).

Discussed in the rest of this section is the nexus between the COVID-2019 pandemic and job loss and unemployment in Africa and Europe. The two continents are broached separately for cohesion.

Africa

To get underway, the Anadolu Agency estimates that 4.5 million jobs will be lost in 2020 across Africa as a result of travel-related restrictions enacted in the continent in response to the COVID-2019 pandemic. The agency notes a statement made by the Air Transport Action Group (ATSG) that of Africa's 7.7 million aviation-related jobs, approximately 4.5 million jobs are expected to be lost in 2020 in the aviation industry, in addition to other aviation-related industries (Anadolu Agency, 2020).

Next, the agency points out that about 172,000 jobs in the aviation industry in Africa are expected to be lost by the end of 2020. The figure represents about 40 percent of the continent's 440,000 aviation jobs. With respect to the aviation industry's share in the African economy, it is estimated that the continent's GDP will fall by up to $37 billion: that is, 58 percent lower compared to pre-COVID-2019 levels (Anadolu Agency, 2020).

Also, the agency notes that the ATSG report came at a time when 31 African countries were reopening their borders to regional and international air flights many months after closing their skies in response to the COVID-2019 pandemic. Yet still, 22 African countries are imposing mandatory 14-day quarantines on travelers, a policy regarded by the International Air Transport Association (IATA) as preventing people from traveling. The IATA therefore recommends that systematic testing of travelers before departure be done to ensure safety without imposing quarantines (Anadolu Agency, 2020).

In addition, regarding the consequences and a plausible policy response to the very large number of job loss and unemployment in the aviation industry in Africa due to the COVID-2019 pandemic, the agency quotes Muhammad Albakri, IATA's regional vice president for Africa and the Middle East, of stating the following:

> The breakdown in air connectivity in Africa has severe social and economic consequences for millions. No income means the lack of a social safety net for many. Governments need to do all they can to reconnect the continent safely. Keeping borders closed, or imposing measures such as quarantines, that deter air travel, will result in many more livelihoods being lost and further economic shrinkage along with hardship and poverty. (Anadolu Agency, 2020, p. 1)

Furthermore, in South Africa, for which more reliable statistical data are available compared to other countries in Africa, the British Broadcasting Corporation (BBC) reports that the country was among the first states in the world to implement lockdowns in order to attenuate the spread of the COVID-2019 virus. South Africa's policy banned everything from alcohol and cigarette sales to dog walking. The constraints have been moderated slowly; and, on September 20, 2020, the overnight curfew was lessened, gatherings were permitted at 50 percent of a venue's capacity, and limitations on the sale of alcohol were mollified (BBC, 2020).

As a result of the drastic lockdown policy, in the second quarter of 2020 alone, the South African economy lost approximately 2.2 million jobs. The number represents the country's largest job loss since it started conducting its employment survey in 2008. In essence, the restrictions that were put in place to stop the spread of the COVID-2019 virus instead led to the contraction of the country's economy at an atypical level. The reasons for these outcomes, according to the BBC, are as follows: (a) "most businesses were shut for five weeks from March 27, 2020"; (b) South Africa's implemented "one of the strictest lockdowns in the world"; (c) "the number of people who have not been economically active indicated an even more dramatic economic decline"; and (d) "between March and June [of 2020] that figure increased by 5.3 million people to 20.5 million" (BBC, 2020, p. 1).

Europe

For starters, according to David McHugh and Helena Alves, by August 2020, the unemployment rate for the entire European continent had grown five months in a row due to policies instituted to combat the spread of the COVID-2019 virus. In the 19 countries that utilize the Euro currency, the unemployment rate jumped from 8 percent in July to 8.1 percent in September 2020 and the number of people who lost their jobs increased by about 251,000 to 13.2 million during that same period. The job loss was expected to continue to grow across the continent as the European governments would not be able to continuously provide financial resources indefinitely to support businesses that are being hampered by the implemented restrictions (McHugh and Alves, 2020).

In their efforts to addresses the challenges, the European governments have earmarked trillions of Euros to assist businesses and launch or enhance programs to keep workers on payrolls. For instance, in Germany, which has the continent's largest economy, about 3.7 million people remain on a furlough support program that pays more than 70 percent of a worker's salary for short hours or no hours of work. As the number of people infected by the COVID-2019 virus continues to grow in Germany, the government has extended the furlough support program to the end of 2021. Also, the European Central Bank has imbued the economy with 1.35 trillion Euros (McHugh and Alves, 2020).

Also, as Michael Kahn points out, the COVID-2019 pandemic has eliminated the initial horizontal support of the jobs ladder for many young Europeans, a situation perceived by some economists as having the likelihood of disrupting the long-term employment and earnings prospects for these young Europeans. While youth unemployment has long beset Europe, lasting for many years following the 2008–2009 global financial crisis that affected southern countries such as Spain and Greece the hardest, the early signs of the current pandemic-related job loss and unemployment among young workers suggest that the situation will get worse (Khan, 2020).

In addition, we learn from Khan that even though the total unemployment rate for the European Union in May 2020 increased modestly by 0.1–6.7 percent because of the furlough and short-time work programs that were implemented, still the unemployment rate of workers under the age of 25 skyrocketed three times as fast by 0.3 percent points to 15.7 percent. The conundrum of this situation is that there is a significant correlation between youth unemployment and economic growth. Hence, the greater the decline of the overall economic growth, the greater the ramification will be on young workers. For example, "before the COVID-2019 outbreak, the Czech Republic had the lowest youth jobless rate in Europe of barely 5 percent following a protracted economic boom. Yet by May of 2020, unemployment among those aged 15–24 jumped by over a half to 34,000" due to the economic decline impelled by the pandemic (Khan, 2020, p. 1).

CONCLUSION AND RECOMMENDATIONS

It is quite evident from the analyses in the foregoing sections that policies implemented to combat the spread of the COVID-2019 virus and its attendant predicaments have engendered the following three aspects: (1) hoarding and price gouging, (2) market volatility, and (3) job loss and unemployment across the globe. Also evident is that by employing the General Economic Theory, instead of a specific economic theory, both the microeconomic and macroeconomic features of the three aspects are delineated. So a question that arises here is the following: What can be done to mitigate these coroeconomic problems? The rest of this section encompasses recommendations for the three aspects in sequential order.

First, as it pertains to hoarding and price gouging, a two-pronged approach is needed. One prong would entail a massive public education campaign via television, radio, print media, and billboards highlighting the ills of the practice. The other prong would involve enacting and enforcing stringent laws that would punish perpetrators expeditiously.

Second, in terms of market volatility, since it can never be eliminated, the goal would be to lessen it. Thus, the following three strategies suggested by Ken Faulkenberry would be quite prudent:

(1) "Employ Fundamental Value Analysis: The kind of stock market volatility you really want to avoid is downside volatility. All major market tops coincide with high valuations. This makes fundamental value strategies an important part of investing. These tools can guide you away from

over-priced investments that are prevalent at market tops" (Faulkenberry, 2020, p. 1).

(2) "Have a Maximum Drawdown Plan: Have [this] policy as a part of your risk management plan. A large part of your asset allocation strategy should be based on how you will manage and minimize a portfolio drawdown. It is large portfolio drawdowns that destroy your long-term returns" (Faulkenberry, 2020, p. 1).

(3) "Use a Tactical Asset Allocation Strategy: A fixed or strategic asset allocation makes little sense because we know valuation is the biggest determinant of your long-term investment returns. Once you are empowered with the knowledge from fundamental value analysis and have mapped out your risk management plan you can choose an appropriate asset allocation" (Faulkenberry, 2020, p. 1).

Third and finally, as it relates to job loss and unemployment, the strategy being employed by the European Union countries mentioned earlier is a profitable one. The governments of these countries assist businesses and have launched or enhanced programs to keep workers on payrolls. Furlough support programs that pay more than 70 percent of a worker's salary for short hours or no hours of work are needed across the globe. Also, the following strategies suggested by Michelle Evermore would be quite helpful: (a) "increase funding to meet higher unemployment insurance demand," (b) "adopt work-sharing [as an] alternative to layoffs," (c) "waive work-search and waiting week requirements," (d) "clarify good cause to quit," (e) "reform disaster unemployment insurance," and (f) "boost unemployment insurance recipiency" (Evermore, 2020, p. 1).

REFERENCES

Anadolu Agency. (October 1, 2020). COVID-19: Some 4.5M African jobs to be lost in 2020. Retrieved on November 30, 2020 from https://www.aa.com.tr/en/africa/covid-19-some-45m-african-jobs-to-be-lost-in-2020/1992666#.

Brand, J. E. (2015). The far-reaching impact of job loss and unemployment. *Annual Review of Sociology* 41:359–375.

British Broadcasting Corporation (BBC). (September 29, 2020). Coronavirus lockdown costs South Africa millions of jobs. Retrieved on November 15, 2020 from https://www.bbc.com/news/world-africa-54343598.

Exchange Traded Funds (ETF) Trends. (October 12, 2020). Volatility could open opportunities for precious metals in 2021. *Nasdaq Latest News*. Retrieved on November 30, 2020 from https://www.nasdaq.com/articles/volatility-could-open-opportunities-for-precious-metals-in-2021-2020-10-12.

Faulkenberry, K. (2020). 3 ways to reduce the effects of stock market volatility. *Arbor Investment Planner*. Retrieved on November 30, 2020 from https://www.arborinvestmentplanner.com/stock-market-volatility/.

Genève Invest (2020). How to identify and avoid risky stocks and bonds. *Genève Invest Wealth Management*. Retrieved on November 15, 2020 from https://www.geneveinvest.com/market-volatility/.

Khan, M. (July 9, 2020). Coronavirus 'Class of 2020': Europe's lost generation? *Reuters*. Retrieved on November 30, 2020 from https://www.reuters.com/article/us-health-coronavirus-unemployment-youth/coronavirus-class-of-2020-europes-lost-generation-idUSKBN24A0LN.

McHugh, D. and Alves, H. (October 1, 2020). Unemployment marches higher in Europe as pandemic grinds on. *Associated Press*. Retrieved on November 30, 2020 from https://apnews.com/article/virus-outbreak-pandemics-europe-archive-unemployment-33474f925f42bc63df440b2d49c6936c.

Organization for Economic Cooperation and Development (OECD). (September 30, 2020). The impact of coronavirus (COVID-19) and the global oil price shock on the fiscal position of oil-exporting developing countries. *OECD Policy Responses to Coronavirus (COVID-19)*. Retrieved on November 15, 2020 from https://www.oecd.org/coronavirus/policy-responses/the-impact-of-coronavirus-covid-19-and-the-global-oil-price-shock-on-the-fiscal-position-of-oil-exporting-developing-countries-8bafbd95/.

Pettinger, T. (June 28, 2019). Economic costs of unemployment. Economics Help. Retrieved on November 30, 2020 from https://www.economicshelp.org/macroeconomics/unemployment/costs/.

Proskauer Rose LLC. (November 19, 2020). International spotlight: Price gouging restrictions in China. *Minding Your Business Blog*. Retrieved on November 30, 2020 from https://www.proskauer.com/blog/international-spotlight-price-gouging-restrictions-in-china.

Rapacon, S. (March 16, 2020). What is market volatility? *Money Basics*. Retrieved on November 30, 2020 from https://www.acorns.com/money-basics/what-is-market-volatility-/

Reynolds, L. G. (1985). *Macroeconomics: Analysis and Policy*. Homewood, IL: Richard D. Irwin, Inc.

Reynolds, L. G. (1985). *Microeconomics. A & I*. Homewood, IL: Richard D. Irwin, Inc.

Sappor, J., Rutland, T., Rodwell, G., Yu, A., Nickels, L. and Cecil, R. (April 15, 2020). COVID-19 impacts to metals prices: Volatility is here to stay. *S&P Global Market Intelligence*. Retrieved on November 15, 2020 from https://www.spglobal.com/marketintelligence/en/news-insights/research/covid-19-impacts-to-metals-prices-volatility-is-here-to-stay-part-1.

Simpson, S. D. (September 24, 2020). The cost of unemployment to the economy. *Investopedia*. Retrieved on November 15, 2020 from https://www.investopedia.com/financial-edge/0811/the-cost-of-unemployment-to-the-economy.aspx.

Smith, D. J. (April 17, 2020). Crisis economics: Price gouging laws perpetuate the hoarding of goods and create shortages. *Nashville Business Journal*. Retrieved on

November 15, 2020 from https://www.bizjournals.com/nashville/news/2020/04/17/crisis-economics-price-gouging-laws-perpetuate-the.html.

Smith, M., Segal, J. and Robinson, L. (2020). Job loss and unemployment stress. *Help Guide*. Retrieved on November 15, 2020 from https://www.helpguide.org/articles/stress/job-loss-and-unemployment-stress.htm.

SmithAmundsen LLC. (2020). Hoarding and price gouging: Antitrust concerns amid COVID-19. JD Supra. Retrieved on November 15, 2020 from https://www.jdsupra.com/legalnews/hoarding-and-price-gouging-antitrust-85028/.

Thompson, J. (November 18, 2020). Spillover: Oil and gas market volatility due to COVID-19 pandemic. *Interactive Biodiversity Information System World*. Retrieved on November 25, 2020 from https://www.ibisworld.com/industry-insider/analyst-insights/spillover-oil-and-gas-market-volatility-due-to-covid-19-pandemic/.

Tung, T., Hickin, Lewis, J. M. and Pu, L. (April 20, 2020). Ensuring the price is right—PRC measures to combat price gouging during the COVID-19 crisis. *Mayer Brown*. Retrieved on November 15, 2020 from https://www.mayerbrown.com/en/perspectives-events/publications/2020/04/ensuring-the-price-is-right-prc-measures-to-combat-price-gouging-during-the-covid-19-crisis.

United States Department of Justice. (June 16, 2020). Combating price gouging and hoarding. Retrieved on November 15, 2020 from https://www.justice.gov/coronavirus/combattingpricegouginghoarding.

United States Immigration and Customs Enforcement (May 26, 2020). NYC pharmacist charged with hoarding and price gouging of N95 masks. *Cyber Crimes*. Retrieved on November 15, 2020 from https://www.ice.gov/news/releases/nyc-pharmacist-charged-hoarding-and-price-gouging-n95-masks.

Chapter 14

Coromedia

Cecy Edijala Balogun

Social media platforms played an unprecedented role in disseminating information about the likely causes of the Coronavirus Disease (COVID)-2019, its modes of contagion, its preventive and protective measures, and its trends in terms of how it spread across the globe. This is because of the ease of information transfer and the popularity of social media platforms among populations, generational groups, and social strata, aided by the advancements in digital technology which has made it easy to send text messages, video clips, and voice notes.

News about the dynamics of the outbreak, transmission, and effect of the coronavirus pandemic as it spreads across continents raised diverse dimensions of hysteria in Nigeria. Stories and videos in social media platforms on the causes, effect, and treatment methods; the insufficiency or unavailability of medical test kits; and the predisposing poor health outcomes that reduce the survival rates of confirmed cases, and so on, caused fears among those with health situations, and even the healthy felt threatened or panicky as a result of such media news about the disease outbreak. The exponential increase in death rates as a result of the disease generated emotional and psychological trauma. Audio and video clips of the loneliness suffered by isolated infected patients as a result of the contagious nature of the disease were freely circulated; viral messages of the impossibility of family contact with infected persons created scary images in the minds of recipients of such news.

The authenticity or otherwise of circulated social media messages can impact public perception of social events and can affect how people respond to issues of public health. With the outbreak of the COVID-2019 pandemic, this becomes a serious problem given that COVID-2019 is a public health issue, and in the event of poorly managed information transfer, the health security of the public could be compromised. The independence in sending and receiving information that social media networks allow makes them viable sources of misinformation and misconceptions about COVID-2019, particularly in Nigeria. Given the social challenges that the country has been grappling with, negative COVID-2019 narratives in the country produced fears, then doubts and mistrust about the authenticity, prevalence, and severity of the disease in Nigeria. Doubts and mistrust were engendered by the poor responses of the government to addressing the myriads of social challenges that are facing the country in the past and the poor handling of measures that could mitigate the impact of the disease on the livelihoods of the populace.

Hence, this chapter focuses on the role of social media in the management of the COVID-2019 outbreak in Nigeria; how social media were used to misinform the Nigerian public; and the misconceptions about COVID-2019 due to such misinformation that created anxieties in the society, the effect of such misinformation on public trust in government's efforts aimed at containment of the disease, and what was done by the government to curtail the spread of misinformation about COVID-2019 in Nigeria.

Coromedia explains the exaggerated and uncontrolled panic that ensued after the outbreak of COVID-2019 due to the manner social media reported the pandemic. It describes the agitations that stem from social media framing of COVID-2019 that portrays the disease as a death sentence for those who are unfortunate enough to be victims of the disease, unverified preventive measures and treatments, and how the public reacted to such social media reports in responding to COVID-2019 in Nigeria.

The chapter attempts to situate COVID-2019 around social media perspective about the spread and containment of the disease in Nigeria by providing answers to three questions: (1) How did social media contribute to information dissemination about the spread and containment of COVID-2019 in Nigeria? (2) How did social media contribute to the misinformation and misconception of COVID-2019 in Nigeria and how did such misinformation affect public opinion about the reality of COVID-2019 in Nigeria? (3) How did the government manage COVID-2019 misinformation in Nigeria?

The agitations that trailed the outbreak of COVID-2019 in Nigeria provide the basis for this chapter which argues that social media reportage of COVID-2019 contributed to the anxieties about the disease outbreak and that misinformation has a negative effect on public perception of issues that affect the social well-being of the society.

The chapter explores secondary sources of information from the website of the Nigerian Communications Commission (NCC), articles, publications, and personal observations about the dynamism of COVID-2019 scenarios in Nigeria.

Studies about COVID-2019 will not be complete without an understanding of the role social media played in the reportage of the disease outbreak in Nigeria. This is because an individual or societal perception, attitude, or behavior toward public health is paramount to achieving results for efforts aimed at combating a global pandemic like COVID-2019. This chapter will provide evidence on how social media narratives about COVID-2019 affected public opinion about the disease outbreak in Nigeria, the effect of such reportage on public attitude toward the disease, and how the government attempted to contain public misinformation. The chapter will inform policymakers on the need to leverage the dynamics in information consumption and how social media platforms can be managed to curtail misinformation about issues that pose threat to national social security, while at the same time, maximizing the benefits that they provide in building social networks.

The theoretical basis for the chapter is the Media Effect Theory and this will focus on how media frames determine the public response to social events in society. The rest of the chapter will focus on the roles social media played in informing the Nigerian public about the spread and containment of COVID-2019, how social media were used to misinform the Nigerian public about the disease, misconceptions that were spread as a result of such misinformation, and the attendant effect of social media reportage of COVID-2019 on the perception of the Nigerian society, the management of misinformation in Nigeria, the recommendations for policymakers, and areas for future research.

THEORETICAL DISCUSSION OF MEDIA EFFECT

Media remain the primary source of providing information to the public and how such information is constructed or framed determines how the public will react to the disseminated information, thereby underscoring the relevance of media in shaping public opinion. The theoretical basis for this chapter is therefore anchored on the Media Effect Theory. While delving into the theory, the concepts of media, social media, and media frames are clarified.

Media Effect Theory

Media play an important role in depicting how society works by informing the public of happenings within and around society. Media influence and stimulate the ideas and thoughts of individuals and societies and determine how people react to events that occur around them. Media also depict different means of communication that were first used in the 1920s to reach a large audience through mass media sources like newspapers, radio, television, and films (McQuail, 2010, cited in Valkenburg, Peter, and Walter, 2016). Advancements in technology have widened media sources to include the

Internet and social media networks, which have increasingly contributed to media connectivity and have reduced the world to a global community due to the speed and coverage of social media networks in information sharing globally.

Social media have been conceptualized by various authors. Social media are social user-driven networks and websites that facilitate the communication of media content to a broad audience (Kappor et al., 2017 in Saheed and Dumebi, 2020). Social media are digital communication forums that allow individuals and groups to interact and share ideas and knowledge using texts, voice, or visual messaging applications. They are computer-mediated tools or web-based applications and platforms which are developed to provide profiles that allow shared and participatory communication that involve others in the creation, organization, sharing, finding, and using of information (Boyd and Ellison, 2008; Saheed and Dumebi, 2020). They are powerful communication tools that make use of pictures, videos, live streaming of events, and voice notes to disseminate information and have greatly influenced societal narratives in unprecedented ways. The positive uses of social media notwithstanding, the freedom of communication they permit has been exploited by individuals, who take advantage of the attribute to circulate information that has not been scientifically or empirically verified by authorities, such that social media are increasingly being used for circulating misinformation or fake news.

The way media content is framed is an important tool in the construction of messages. Media frames influence the choices people make about the information they receive and the interpretation ascribed to such information. Media frames express the thoughts of people, including their mental interpretations and simplification of realities (Druckman, 2001a), and determine public actions and reactions to constructed messages (Druckman, 2001b). Media frames affect the perception and response of the public to circulated messages and the effect of such frames is observed when the emphasis on a public issue that is of relevant consideration makes recipients of information pay attention to these considerations when forming their own opinion (Druckman, 2001a).

There are two schools of thought on how media frames affect the recipients of the intended information. Proponents of one of the schools of thought contend that different frames make individuals subject their opinions to different considerations without considering the overall opinion, while the other school of thought contends that individuals base their opinions on the overall opinion with less attention to the underlying considerations.

Media effect theories have undergone several phases depending on the emerging media technologies, the cultural environment and the methods, the perspectives or ideologies of the researcher, although the boundaries of these phases are not clearly demarcated (Borah, 2016). Harold Lasswell is recognized as the main proponent of the Media Effect Theory (Borah, 2016). In his theory, Lasswell's arguments were based on Freudian psychology, pragmatism, and political science, and he argued that society and individuals could be controlled by a minority through propaganda (Borah, 2016).

One of the features of media effect theories that consider the media and non-media factors that define the conditions under which media affect the response of the audience to receive information is the selectivity of media use (Valkenburg et al., 2016). The selectivity of media use proposes that people only consider a limited number of messages from an array of messages that are of interest to them and that the messages they select are those that can influence them. The selectivity paradigm gave rise to the Uses and Gratification Theory (Katz et al., 1973, cited in Valkenburg et al., 2016) and the Selective Exposure Theory (Knobloch-Westerwick, 2015, cited in Valkenburg et al., 2016).

The uses and gratification and the selective exposure theories propose that individuals select media based on their needs which are determined by psychological and social factors and that media use determines the consequences of the decision reached in using a media source (Valkenburg et al., 2016). However, the theories are different in that the Uses and Gratification Theory views media users as rational and aware of their selection motives whereas Selective Exposure Theory argues that media users are not often aware or not fully aware of their selection motives.

The selectivity approach to media use emerged in the 1940s as a new paradigm that proposes that media investigation should focus on 'what people do with the media' rather than 'what media do to people' (Katz, 1959, cited in Valkenburg et al., 2016). The selectivity theories contend that individuals shape their media effects through the choices they make in selecting media use. Valkenburg and Peter (2013a) cited in Valkenburg et al. (2016) identified the following three factors that influence selective media use:

(1) *Dispositional factors*: Valkenburg and Peter (2013a) cited in Valkenburg et al. (2016) argued that dispositions of the audience, which range from more distal and stable factors such as temperament, personality, and gender to more proximal and transient factors such as beliefs, motivations, and moods, lead to selectivity in media use. Anchoring on the Cognitive Dissonance Theory of Festinger (1957) cited in Valkenburg et al. (2016), the dispositional paradigm contends that people will generally avoid the use of information that is contrary to their disposition, for example, their beliefs or attitudes and will rather seek information that encourages their disposition. However, the notion of cognitive dissonance was faulted,

because people seek information that may be contrary to their disposition when they perceive the benefits derivable from such information outweighs their biases against such information and that the notion favors political news items rather than items that are health related (Hart et al., 2009, cited in Valkenburg et al., 2016).

(2) *Development factors*: These factors imply that people are more prone to paying attention to messages that relate well with their age categories than media content that is discrepant to their developmental stages (Valkenburg and Peter, 2013a).

(3) *Social context factors:* These factors describe the social influence that institutions or parents wield to restrict or regulate media use. It also occurs when individuals base their actions on the norms of the social groups to which they belong, such as family, peer, religion, and subcultural groups (Valkenburg et al., 2016).

On the other hand, the Uses and Gratification Theory explains why and how people seek out specific media for self-gratification. The approach is anchored on the assumption that mass media have a significant impact on society by influencing individuals to change their behavior or belief about an issue. The theory argues that people are not passive consumers of media content but that they choose to interpret and integrate media content to address their desires and needs to achieve gratification.

West and Turner (2007) identified the unique assumptions of the Uses and Gratification Theory to include the following features:

(a) The audience is active and its media use is goal oriented;
(b) The initiative in linking need gratification to a specific medium choice rests with the audience member;
(c) The media compete with other resources for needs satisfaction;
(d) People have enough self-awareness of their media use, interests, and motives to be able to provide researchers with an accurate picture of that use; and
(e) Value judgments of media content can only be assessed by the audience. (West and Turner, 2007, p. 397)

The dynamism in media sources that situated social media networks ahead of other mass media sources in terms of coverage and use draws attention to the relevance of the Uses and Gratification Theory as applied to social media. In the first instance, the development of the mobile phones, equipped with diverse uses and motivations, especially the mobility component that allows one to interact with people in far climes in real time without necessarily being in the same environment with them and the social media platforms that complement the gratifications of the mobile phones, highlights the different types of gratifications that social media provide for the users. However, these gratifications may not necessarily be positive as some of the uses have also implied negative gratification, which is evident in the abuses that characterize social media networks. It becomes negative gratification if the motivation behind the use runs contrary to the gratification of others or the larger society, that is, if such benefits are inimical to the social well-being of other individuals or the general public. For instance, Leung (2013) identified some of the gratifications that motivate people to use social media to include social interactions and affection, the need to vent negative feelings, recognition, entertainment, and cognitive needs. Negative feelings may emerge from spoken or printed words transmitted to individuals who are acquaintances or friends in social interaction platforms. These may be expressed through cyberbullying aimed as a vengeful or malicious action against the bullied, spreading derogatory information as a way of discrediting an opponent or system, or spreading false information to mislead the public.

The effect of media on public perception and attitude has been widely researched. Media framing of news stories influences public perception and determines the responses that could lead to behavioral changes (Nwakpu, Ezema and Ogbodo, 2020). Media narratives contribute to the worsening of how social interactions are perceived, which have contributed to the circulation of negative, erroneous, and unverified information (Sayrum and Leon, 2015), and in describing how media content affects media news item, Egelhofer and Lecheler (2019) argued that even though the circulation of misinformation may be unintentional, the development of such media content may be intentional.

SOCIAL MEDIA AND COVID-2019 INFORMATION DISSEMINATION IN NIGERIA

The preservation of public health is a responsibility of not only the community but a global concern, especially for pandemics. The outbreak of a pandemic like COVID-2019 requires public education and awareness creation as a way of safeguarding public health as health information that is timely, accurate, and credible is key to stemming the socioeconomic impact of diseases on populations (Aryee, 2014). The increasing demand and dependence on mass media for health information put the social media at a focal point with regard to COVID-2019, due to the increasing use of social media platforms in social interactions globally, compared to other mass media sources in recent years.

The increasing number of mobile phone subscribers and Internet connectivity in Nigeria has greatly influenced the social interactions in the country, and with the COVID-2019 outbreak that led to a rise in information seeking and sharing about the disease, the number of Internet subscribers has been on the increase. The Global System of Mobile Communications (GSMA, 2018) reported that about half of the mobile phone users in Nigeria are Internet subscribers, with an estimated 53 million smartphone users, which is expected to increase to 144 million by 2025. NOIPolls (2018) reported that about 63 percent of mobile phone users in Nigeria use one form of social media networking site, such as Facebook, WhatsApp, and Twitter, with Facebook accounting for 91 percent representing 7.2 million daily active users and 97 percent accessing the social media platforms through their mobile phones for liking, sharing, and uploading messages and other social interactions. The outbreak of COVID-2019, which generated a lot of anxieties and a wave for information seeking and sharing, further increased the use of the Internet and social media platforms in Nigeria. Following the report of the index case of COVID-2019 in Nigeria, there was an increased circulation of information about the disease; creating public awareness on the symptoms of the disease, the need for hygiene and sanitation, and other measures that can help stem the spread of the disease were freely distributed through social media platforms. The increased use of social media is evident in the report of the NCC (2020) which revealed that mobile Internet subscriptions in Nigeria increased from 113.8 million in January 2019 to 143.3 million by June 2020.

In addition to the use of old electronic and print media sources for sensitizing the public about the disease, social media networking sites greatly contributed to informing the Nigerian public about the outbreak of COVID-2019 and the containment measures necessary for safeguarding public health. Social media greatly influenced the public knowledge about the disease compared to previous pandemics like influenza which spread quickly across the country due to poor communication dissemination (Adebowale, 2020). The Nigerian Centre for Disease Control (NCDC) explored the potentials of social media platforms by creating social media accounts in Facebook, WhatsApp, Twitter, and so on, which were used to provide credible information about the disease to the public. The agency also collaborated with Internet service providers who provided free Internet access to the websites of health stakeholders such as the NCDC, the World Health Organization, and the Presidential Task Force (PTF) as a way of ensuring the ease of delivery of health information to the public. Daily updates about COVID-2019 were also disseminated through Short Messaging Services (SMS), which has a wider reach to individuals that lack Internet connectivity and smartphones, particularly in rural areas. Civil society organizations and other private bodies as well as individuals who out of concern for the lives of family members and friends also maximized the potentials of social media networks to spread credible information about COVID-2019 in Nigeria.

The role of social media in creating public awareness about disease outbreaks is not new. Social media have been used in public health education and advocacy (Farnan et al., 2013), have also been used by public health departments and organizations in location-tracking technologies when responding to emergencies of public health (Househ, 2013; Saheed and Dumebi, 2020), and have also contributed to the social reinforcement of public health behaviors (George et al., 2013). The contributions of social media in enhancing public health behaviors notwithstanding, Lazer et al. (2018) argued that the ease of communication provided by social media makes it easy for spreading false, tailored, or unfiltered media contents that manipulate public behavior and perceptions.

SOCIAL MEDIA AND COVID-2019 MISINFORMATION AND MISCONCEPTIONS IN NIGERIA

The role of the media in the fight against COVID-2019 cannot be overemphasized. The high rate of spread and contagion of the virus, in the absence of accurate and informed reportage, spell doom for millions across the globe. The media is an integral part of the system in the fight against the pandemic. However, the role of the media in providing credible information to the public was marred by various conspiracy theories that heralded the COVID-2019 outbreak. Social media platforms were widely used to circulate various conspiracy theories, which resulted in a surge of misinformation and misconceptions about the disease with implications for the health security of the society.

The freedom of expression, association, and opportunities for anonymity that social media platforms provide made it easy for unverified information to be circulated using social media platforms. They provide individuals with the opportunity to choose media contents that satisfy their interest (Savrum and Leon, 2015), circulating such messages through sharing, liking, and retweeting, without verifying their sources. With the advantage of reaching a larger population within the shortest possible time, social media posed serious threats to the Nigerian public's perception, attitude, and responses to the COVID-2019 scenarios in the country. This is because social media platforms did not only carry the intended news but also circulated unverified narratives about the disease.

As the NCDC provided updates on the state of COVID-2019 in the country, the reportage was met with mixed reactions. When the disease first appeared in the country, the people's response was fear and panic because of the morbid stories, photos, and video clips from across the globe circulated through social media. With the lockdown measures imposed to stem the spread of the virus, tensions were reduced; but, the tensions increased again when the lockdown continued to affect the livelihoods of the people and the government made very little effort to mitigate the impact of the lockdown on them. The frustration that followed the handling of public needs and the poor management of palliatives which was ridden with misappropriations brought about public disbelief in the narratives of COVID-2019 as reported by the government. Doubts about the existence of COVID-2019 in the country, the spending on the treatment of cases and for purchases and coverage in the distribution of palliatives, and the rationale behind the closure of public places such as schools and religious centers abounded.

Unverified information that is fabricated and disseminated to misinform or deceive the public with false content such as rumors, myths, conspiracy theories, hoaxes, deception, and erroneous contents can be categorized as false or fake news stories (McGonagle, 2017; Wang et al., 2019). Fake news about COVID-2019 in Nigeria ranged from false information about medication for the treatment of COVID-2019, preventive measures, to conspiracy theories aimed at discrediting the efforts of the government. Hence, two dimensions of negative narratives about the COVID-2019 outbreak were circulated in Nigeria through social media platforms. Firstly, the perspective of false or fake information which was circulated to misinform the public and to create misconceptions about COVID-2019, and secondly, the aspersions that were cast on political and public office holders that deny or doubt the presence of the disease outbreak in the country due to lack of public trust in the government.

COVID-2019 Misinformation and Misconceptions in Nigeria

The increasing use of social media platforms for information dissemination is assuming a threatening position to factual and ratified information (Saheed and Dumebi, 2020). The hysteria that followed the outbreak of COVID-2019 in Nigeria led to the random circulation of unverified information through social media networks, without consideration for how such information will affect the physical, mental, social, and emotional well-being of the recipients. The authenticity or otherwise of these narrated scenarios about COVID-2019 went on in the social media spaces unhindered for a long time, until the intervention of the NCDC, which developed media messages to check the spread of fake news about the disease in Nigeria.

Public misinformation as regards public health issues in Nigeria is not new. Similar scenarios played out during the Ebola outbreak, where unverified treatment measures were circulated such as bathing with and drinking salt solution which led to the loss of several lives in the country (Adebimpe et al., 2015). Similar stories were equally circulated about COVID-2019 on social media platforms such as Facebook, WhatsApp, Twitter, and YouTube. People were made to believe that spraying alcohol on surfaces, including clothes, mobile phones, and keys, could reduce the possibility of contracting the disease and that using salt solution to bathe, drinking bleach, and taking vitamins are effective in preventing and treating COVID-2019 (Shahbaz and Funk, 2020; WhatsApp messages, 2020). Pineapple was also projected as a fruit that can prevent the spread of the virus, with the notion that it contains an antioxidant that boosts immunity, suppresses inflation, and contains an enzyme called bromelain that reduces respiratory problems such as coughs (WhatsApp messages, 2020).

High-profile citizens such as some state government officials and several other influential citizens who were isolated for COVID-2019 claimed they were treated with common malaria drugs such as azithromycin, hydroxychloroquine, vitamin C, and zinc, and they were advised to eat good food. Such claims went viral, such that panic buying was observed in the purchase of hydroxychloroquine (Akinpelu, 2020; Ibrahim, 2020), which led to a hike in the prices of the drug. For instance, 10 tablets of hydroxychloroquine were sold for as high as N25,000 during the lockdown period as individuals rushed to stockpile the drug. The implication is that people who need the drug and lack the financial resources were denied access to the drug as this further put their health status at risk. There was also a highly circulated message by a medical doctor who claimed to be trained in Nigeria but presently works in the United States. She condemned the use of face masks and argued that the high levels of deaths associated with COVID-2019 in the United States are unnecessary as the disease can be treated with hydroxychloroquine. The circulated message generated a lot of debates which were almost eroding the public trust of the Nigerian populace about the reality of the disease in some quarters and the potency of hydroxychloroquine in treating the disease in some other quarters, such that the Medical Association of Nigeria had to dissociate themselves from her claims as a way of dissuading the public from taking the drug which has not been scientifically proven as a curative drug for the disease.

Lack of Public Trust and COVID-2019 Misinformation in Nigeria

Another dimension of misinformation of the Nigerian public through social media platforms was evident in situations where the authenticity of the efforts of the government toward containing the spread of the disease was put to question. The negative stories that were circulated about the poor handling of the disease outbreak in the country were primarily fed by the long-standing problem of public distrust in the government due to the persistent levels of corruption evident in the diversion of public goods for personal use by public and political officeholders. Consequently, the existence of COVID-2019 in Nigeria was greatly doubted, and the popular opinion that appeared on social media was that the reported outbreak of the disease in the country was a hoax. Social media narratives also indicated that the compliance to measures that are meant to protect the public from COVID-2019 was taken lightly by sections of the society who believe the narratives about the reported cases of the pandemic in Nigeria are not factual, with the accusations that such narratives were meant to enrich public officeholders. Social media were also used to circulate videos of people who accused the government of neglect in isolation centers with little or no treatment as these media contents further reduced the public belief in the existence of COVID-2019 in Nigeria compared to situations in other parts of the world. Statements made by some state governors and other public figures who contracted the disease that they were treated with common malaria drugs raised a series of questions on social media about the government's transparency in informing the Nigerian public about the true state of the disease in the country (Akinpelu, 2020; Ibrahim, 2020). Popular opinion was that such revelations by discharged patients are indicative that most people who were isolated for COVID-2019 may only be suffering from malaria and that the continual denial by the government that the use of such malaria drugs is not ascertained as effective for the treatment of COVID-2019 may be due to vested interests (Ibrahim, 2020).

COVID-2019 was also misconceived as a disease for the elite and this notion was a result of the reportage of the number of political and high-profile public office holders that contracted the disease. This perspective, which was widely circulated in social media, led to situations where people took for granted the containment measures of proper sanitation and social distancing, with claims that COVID-2019 in Nigeria is a hoax that is meant to serve the greed of the privileged political and public office holders by exploiting the commonwealth of the country for the benefit of a few elites.

Where media frames tilt public perception in a way that puts public health at risk, the efforts made by governments at preventing the spread of COVID-2019 will be undermined (Lampos et al., 2020). Public health misinformation threatens the health of the public (Lazer et al., 2018) and the spreading of falsified or unverified health news puts the health of the public at risk since the possibility of practicing self-medication and the application of unverified medications as precautionary measures against COVID-2019 endanger public health (Pulido et al., 2020). Misconceptions that stem from misinformation about COVID-2019 could jeopardize public health (Frenkel et al., 2020;

Pennycook et al., 2020). The cost of ignoring the reality of a global pandemic like COVID-2019 is a threat to the health security of Nigeria as situations abounded where people engaged in behaviors that were contrary to measures that were meant to safeguard their health.

EFFECT OF SOCIAL MEDIA REPORTAGE OF COVID-2019 ON THE NIGERIAN POPULACE

While it is true that social media greatly influenced the attitudes of the Nigerian populace to the reality of the COVID-2019 outbreak in the country, the long-standing absence of public trust, which is due to the many unfulfilled promises of the government toward societal needs, and the high rate of corruption in the country provide a basis for such misinformation and misconceptions that were peddled by social media platforms to thrive in Nigeria.

The evidential instances where palliatives that were meant to mitigate the impact of COVID-2019 on the vulnerable and poor were swindled by government officials and political office holders, with accusations of misappropriation of funds meant to contain the disease, further cast doubt on the reportage of COVID-2019 cases in Nigeria. Persistently, questions were raised about the non-transparency and unaccountability of the government in the distribution of funds for the treatment of COVID-2019 patients and for social safety nets that were meant to mitigate the impact of the disease on the poor and vulnerable in society. For instance, following the youth uprising against police brutality in October 2020 that led to the killing of several people by the military in an attempt to disperse the protesters, several warehouses and private properties where palliatives that were meant to mitigate the impact of the disease on the people were discovered, stockpiled with foodstuff and other items in several states in the country. These items were carted away by angry youths, even though the affected state governments and individual political office holders involved in the issue attempted to explain away why such palliatives were not distributed. Can we say that these evidential realities justify the poor level of trust that the Nigerian public has about the government and confirm the diverse theories, rumors, and news that trailed the outbreak of COVID-2019 in the country? Do they justify the public denial of the presence of the disease in the country and the highly circulated messages in social media that portray the disease outbreak in the country as a figment of the creation of the political class to swindle public goods for self-benefit? In the absence of transparency in the administration of public goods for the benefit of all and the indigent, in particular, public trust will be eroded.

Narratives of how social media influenced public perception about COVID-2019, especially regarding misinformation about the disease, have been investigated in scholarly literature. Huynh (2020) noted that the high demand for COVID-2019 information in online sources led to increased consumption and circulation of misinformation about the disease, and in the view of Hou et al. (2020), as consumption of social media content about COVID-2019 increases, there will be a corresponding increased risk of how the public perceive the disease, and this will ultimately affect public attitude to the measures that are put in place to check the spread of the disease. Additionally, Pennycook et al. (2020) stated that the failure of the public to ascertain the authenticity of social media content before sharing contributed to the spread of false information about COVID-2019.

MANAGEMENT OF COVID-2019: MISINFORMATION AND MISCONCEPTIONS IN NIGERIA

The Internet and social medial platforms, which have greatly influenced the development of societies since their development, have also been used by fraudsters to perpetrate diverse forms of criminal activities, ranging from defaming messages, spreading of falsehood, theft, and cybercrimes, and have engendered hysteria at different times in Nigeria. Before the outbreak of COVID-2019, the rise in criminality in the use of social media networks led to the registration of SIM cards by network providers on the orders of the government, as a way of checking the social problems that are generated by social media platforms in the country.

The proliferation of false news accounts about the COVID-2019 in social media platforms, whether generated outside or within the Nigerian society, drew the attention of the government to the capacity of such misinformation to thwart efforts that are aimed at reducing the spread of the disease. Left unchecked, the false news could hamper the health security of the populace. To curb the trends in the spread of misinformation, the NCDC on several occasions called on the Nigerian public to seek information from credible sources of the government as the only authority that manages the public health of the Nigerian people. To stem this challenge, several measures were adopted by the government, as outlined in the subsections that ensue.

Advocacy and Awareness Creation

Public awareness is an important tool in discrediting fake news and misinformation, especially when issues that affect the generality of the public are concerned. While social media platforms have been effectively used to misinform the public and generate anxieties following the outbreak of COVID-2019 in Nigeria, credible information from reliable sources remains key in refuting such misinformation and restoring public trust in the efforts of the government toward curbing the spread of the disease.

As a way of providing credible information to the Nigerian public, the NCDC developed social media accounts with Facebook, Twitter, Telegram, and so on, in collaboration with network providers, who provide free Internet services to the websites of the Federal Ministry of Health, the NCDC, and the PTF in order to provide easy access to information in the country. Daily updates on awareness creation and sensitization were also sent through SMS on the deadliness of the disease, the need for proper sanitation and hygienic practices, use of protective masks, avoidance of large gatherings and social distancing measures, as well as encouraging the public to report suspected cases to the government through open lines made available to the public as a way of reducing community spread of the disease. Civil society organizations, community-based organizations, faith-based organizations, religious leaders, traditional leaders, and so on, were also mobilized to collaborate with the government as a way of creating public awareness and advocacy in Nigeria. Through the collaborative efforts of the NCDC and messaging services owned by Facebook, push notifications were also used to advise the public on the symptoms and prevention of the disease. Facebook also provided free advertisement spaces for the NCDC that is used for outreach about the pandemic (Naira Metric, 2020).

Media Censorship

The need for censorship of social media as a way of curbing the spread of fake news has been highly contested in Nigeria before the COVID-2019 outbreak. The government at various times has attempted to censor social media, which is alleged to be used as a tool for misinforming the public about the government by political opponents, who are believed to capitalize on the anonymity of social media to manipulate the public for political gain. While the need for censorship has gained momentum to the point of the passage of the hate speech and social media bills, the moves have been met with strict resistance by the Nigerian public and other interest groups.

The government had on several occasions blamed social media for the spread of politically motivated hate speech, especially the spate of unverified and derogatory information circulated through social media platforms that trailed elections in Nigeria, the inter-tribal and inter-religious disputes, several disputes between farmers and herders, which are believed to be fueled through poor reportage in social media networks (Ukpe, 2020). As a result of these, since 2015, the government had raised concerns over the use of social media platforms for public misinformation and derogatory comments targeted at the government, which is popularly described as hate speech in Nigerian parlance.

Two bills have been put forth as a way of restricting the use of social media in Nigeria. The "Hate Speech Bill," which is known as "the National Commission for the Prohibition of Hate speeches Bill 2019," stated that anyone who is found guilty of hate speech is liable to life imprisonment, and if it leads to the death of another, the guilty party should be sentenced to death by hanging (Paul, 2019). The second bill, which is the Social Media Bill, known as "Protection from Internet Falsehood and Other Related Matters Bill 2019" was meant to curb the spread of falsehood and fake news in Nigeria, which according to the government threatens the national unity and security of the country (Paul, 2019). The bill seeks to give the government control over conversations that are carried out on social media platforms (Onukue, 2020). The penalty for the social media bill is a fine of N300,000 ($826) or three years' imprisonment or both for an individual and a fine not exceeding N10 million ($27,550) for corporate organizations (Paul, 2019; Onukue, 2020).

The protests that followed the introduction of the bills stalled their passage. Firstly, the hate speech bill was vehemently resisted by the Nigerian public, as protesters argued that corrupt public office holders are hardly punished or held accountable for their misappropriation of public funds, and also raised questions as to who determines what constitutes hate speech since the definition of hate speech is based on the perspective of the government in power. Hence the attempt was condemned as an effort by the ruling party to stifle the voice of the opposition, thereby undermining the democratic principles of freedom of speech of the citizens. The public outcry against the social media bill similarly queried it as an attempt to stifle the voice of unbiased reportage of news stories, devoid of manipulations of the political class or the elite. The protesters against the social media bill also argued that most of the provisions made in the bill were already included in the Cyber Crimes Act of 2015 and the Nation's Penal Code (Onukue, 2020). Hence both bills were stalled at the national assembly.

The misinformation and misconceptions that trailed the COVID-2019 outbreak in Nigeria regenerated the issue of social media censorship to the front burner in the Nigerian political discourses. While social media censorship may be perceived to be healthy in the fight against the spread of misinformation about the disease that led to unhealthy misconceptions and responses to the pandemic outbreak, social media censorship has also been viewed as a means of closing the civic space in which the media operate.

Such censorship ranges from restrictions on reportage, intimidation, detention, harassment, seizure of broadcast licenses, and so on. Several arm-twisting approaches have been used both in Nigeria and other parts of the world to stifle the media in the reportage of COVID-2019 under the guise of spreading fake news. In Nigeria, for instance, the owner of the African Independent Television who contracted the virus was isolated; when discharged from the isolation center, he reported that he was treated with the regular malaria drugs while in isolation (Akinpelu, 2020; Nairaland, 2020). This news spread quickly through social media platforms with assertions aimed at discrediting the government. The main allegation was that despite the huge sum of money claimed to be spent for the care of patients in isolation centers, the government was not transparent in its report of the true state of the disease in the country and how the funds that were mobilized for the management of the disease were being spent. As a result of the circulated messages, and in an attempt to sanction the media house, the operating license of the media house was suspended by the Nigerian Broadcasting Commission. Additionally, through a collaboration with social media networks such as Facebook, unverified media contents with negative portrayal of COVID-2019 in the country and other harmful media content have been pulled down by Facebook, as a way of reducing the spread of fake news about COVID-2019.

Shahbaz and Funk (2020) argued that arresting people as a result of messages posted or deleting their media content could enhance conspiracy theories that powerful interests have something to hide about the pandemic. This view is also shared by Ibrahim (2020), who called to question the shrewdness of the Nigerian government over the outcry for clarifications as to why even though some public figures that were infected by COVID-2019 claimed that they were treated with malaria drugs, yet there has been a continual denial of the effectiveness of such drugs for the treatment of the disease.

Social media censorship is not peculiar to Nigeria as a crackdown against the allegedly spreading of COVID-2019 misinformation. Shahbaz and Funk (2020) noted that COVID-2019 is being used by several governments globally as a pretense for stifling freedom of expression and access to free information. They identified the following number of ways in which this is being achieved in several countries:

(1) *Blocking of websites and deleting unwanted information in social media platforms*: For example, 28 out of 65 countries assessed by Freedom on the Net blocked websites or forced Internet users, social media platforms, or online outlets to delete information that are deemed inimical to the governments. These moves are especially prevalent in China, Bangladesh, Egypt, Venezuela, Belarus, and so on (Shahbaz and Funk, 2020).

(2) *Keeping populations in the dark:* Internet shutdowns in at least 13 countries since January 2020 limited people's access to timely information about the disease or the use of digital tools for assessing healthcare,

education, and other services that are necessary to ensure their health security. This move is prevalent in Ethiopia (Shahbaz and Funk, 2020).

(3) *Network disruptions*: This has been used against specific ethnic and religious groups in Myanmar, Kyrgyzstan, Bangladesh, India, Pakistan, and so on (Shahbaz and Funk, 2020).

(4) *Banning criticism and arresting those who speak out*: A total of 45 out of the 65 countries assessed by the Freedom on the Net showed that journalists, activists, and members of the public were arrested or charged for criminal activities over comments made over COVID-2019 as such comments were claimed to cause panic, instigate violence, spread hate speech or aspersions against government officials, and so on. This measure has been applied in Zimbabwe, Thailand, the Philippines, Cambodia, Azerbaijan, Turkey, South Africa, and so on (Shahbaz and Funk, 2020).

(5) *Dangerous speech*: This played out through speeches by some leaders who discredited or disregarded the dangers posed by the virus or the promotion of unproven and ineffective treatments. The presidents of the United States and Brazil on several occasions commonized COVID-2019, comparing the disease to influenza, an opinion that is widely spread through social media platforms. Such misguided speeches led to the deaths of individuals in Nigeria, Vietnam, and Iran who consumed alcohol, bleach, hydroxychloroquine, and other self-medicated substances purportedly circulated as effective treatments for COVID-2019 (Shahbaz and Funk, 2020).

(6) *Promotion of conspiracy theories with COVID-2019 pandemic*: The pandemic has also been used for political gain by state and non-state actors in several countries. This has been evident in India, Sri Lanka, and so on (Shahbaz and Funk, 2020).

Similarly Amnesty International and Human Rights Watch reported censorship moves against several media houses. For example, in Madagascar, a journalist was accused of criticizing the response of the government to COVID-2019 in an article and charged with spreading fake news and incitement of hatred toward the president of the country (Amnesty International, May 3, 2020). In Zimbabwe, media workers faced various levels of harassment and intimidation in the line of doing their work (Amnesty International, May 3, 2020). In Ethiopia, the Human Rights Watch indicated that the government used COVID-2019 restrictions as a pretense to restrict freedom of speech, and reporters and media workers were detained for comments on social media that criticized the government's response to the COVID-2019 pandemic as well as spreading of fake news (Human Rights Watch, May 6, 2020).

CONCLUSION AND RECOMMENDATIONS FOR POLICYMAKERS

While it is true that the narratives of the spread of the COVID-2019 in Nigeria have been low and the rate of contracting the virus among the unbelieving masses has equally been low, there is no denying the fact that for Nigeria, distrust in government constitutes a greater risk in the management of the pandemic, as the consequences can be dire. The reactions of the Nigerian public to the government's approaches to curbing the spread of COVID-2019 engineered by social media stories, which may or may not be verified, throw up serious issues that could hamper the efforts of the government in preventing the spread of COVID-2019 in Nigeria.

Social media networks contributed significantly to the narratives about the global coronavirus pandemic outbreak, with both positive and negative perspectives of how social media networks presented media contents, particularly in the Nigerian space. Unlike previous pandemics reportage which was limited as a result of the type of media sources available at the time of their outbreak, the technological revolution that brought about the development of social media networks has redefined information dissemination and reduced the world to a global community.

Following the outbreak of COVID-2019 in Nigeria, social media reportage of the disease scenarios led to a series of agitations and frights engendered by unverified information that was freely circulated through social media networks which if not checked could jeopardize the health security of the Nigerian public. This formed the basis for this chapter which is aimed to interrogate the role of social media in disseminating COVID-2019 information in Nigeria, highlight the various perspectives of the disease outbreak as reported through social media networks, how these narratives affected the public perception and reactions to containment measures, and the efforts of the Nigerian government toward stemming the spread of misinformation about the disease outbreak in the country.

The study found that accurate and credible information about the novel COVID-2019 is necessary for the preservation of public health and that public education about the causes, effect, and preventive and containment measures is paramount to stem the spread of the pandemic. Social media played a very important role globally and in Nigeria in particular, in creating public awareness about the novel disease and necessary measures to prevent its spread. The revolution in mass media, birthed by the development of the Internet and social media networks, influenced the access to information about the disease in Nigeria, as the number of individuals with mobile phones and Internet connectivity greatly increased following the outbreak of the disease. The government also utilized the opportunities provided by social media to inform the Nigerian public about the disease through the creation of social media accounts through which messages were sent either directly to individuals or posted in the social media accounts of the NCDC for public consumption.

Nonetheless, social media networks were also used to misinform the Nigerian public as unverified media content about the likely effects of the disease, preventive measures and cures were freely circulated. This led to several people losing their lives who, out of fear of contracting the disease, used unverified self-medications. The freedom that social media networks offer was also leveraged to circulate information that questioned the authenticity of the claims of the government about the state of the disease in the country, as social media reportage portrayed the scenarios about the presence of the disease in the country as a hoax, which was only intended by the political class and other vested interest to appropriate public resources for self-gain.

Unverified information that was circulated through social media networks, either those which were meant to misinform the public or those that discredited the claims of the government about the status of the disease in the country or measures meant to stem the spread of the disease, played major roles in the perception and response of the Nigerian public toward COVID-2019 in Nigeria and globally. Such reportage led to situations where doubts were casts on the sincerity of the government to safeguard the health of the public as issues were raised about the accountability, transparency, and empathy of the government toward the populace since several pieces of evidence on the ground indicated that palliatives that were meant to mitigate the impact of the disease were poorly managed, while at the same time, the already poor level of trust which the citizens have about the government over the years was again put to test.

In a bid to address the spread of false information about the disease and the various narratives that put the government in a bad light, which were freely circulated through social media platforms, advocacy, awareness creation, and attempt to censor the social media space in the country were explored by the government. While advocacy and awareness creation through all media sources could be said to be effective in refuting some of the claims made in social media that misinformed the public and engendered misconceptions and unhealthy practices about the disease, attempts to censor social media were however resisted by the public and other interest groups who condemned the act as an attempt by the government to gag freedom of expression and deny the citizens of their fundamental rights to free speech.

Given the above, the study concludes that social media remain a veritable tool for public awareness and education, especially where the socioeconomic well-being of the public is concerned and this window of opportunity, which, as observed during the lockdown period, provides a new dimension of social interactions that can be maximized to reach individuals and societies that older media sources would ordinarily not be able to access. In addition, while it is acknowledged that social media have also been used to drive negative narratives which may be seen as running contrary to state efforts, censoring the media is far from addressing the challenges of the negative effect of the media. Therefore, this study recommends the following:

(a) As a way of checking the spread of misinformation and maximizing the efforts of the government, the need for verification of social media content is imperative. Continued effort should be made in awareness creation and advocacy on the harm of unverified information to the social security of the citizens.
(b) Even though the government believes media censorship is the solution to the spread of fake news, the role of social media platforms in providing credible information about the disease to the Nigerian public cannot be denied. Rather than closing the social space, the government should adequately utilize the potentials that social media networks offer through the proactive use of such networks for advocacy and public education to fast-track public awareness as a way of stalling misinformation.
(c) More collaboration with social media network service providers should be explored to regulate posted messages that are observed to contain unverified information.

Areas of Further Research

In light of the discoveries presented in the preceding sections, the following areas are suggested for further research:

(a) The long-standing issue of mistrust of government officials and political office holders has continued to undermine the positive perception, attitude, and response of the Nigerian populace to critical issues, especially social security in the country. Research is needed to operationalize and measure the impact of public mistrust on COVID-2019 efforts of government in Nigeria and globally.
(b) The impact of social media misinformation on Nigerian health security should be further researched.

REFERENCES

Adebimpe, W. O., Adeyemi, D. H. Faremi, A., Ojo, J. O. and Efuntoye, A. E. (2015). The relevance of social networking media in Ebola virus disease prevention and control in Southwestern Nigeria. *Pan African Medical Journal* 22(1):7. Retrieved on September 30, 2020 from https://doi.org/10.11694/pamj.supp.2015.22.1.6165.

Adebowale, O. (March 29, 2020). The Nigerian victory against the 1918 influenza pandemic and the 1897 epidemic. Guardian Nigerian newspaper. Retrieved on September 6, 2020 from http://m.guardian.ng/life/the-nigerian-victory-against-the-1918-influenza-pandemic-and-1897-smallpox-epidemic.

Akinpelu, Y. (May 18, 2020). Dokpesi directs AIT to stop airing own coronavirus claim. Retrieved on September 23, 2020 from www.premiumtimesng.com.

Amnesty International (May 3, 2020). Southern Africa: COVID-19 A pretext for surge in harassment of journalists and weakening of media houses by states. Retrieved on August 18, 2020 from www.amnesty.org.

Aryee, K. L. (2014). *The Role of the Mobile Phones in Health Education for Rural Communities in Ghana. An Explorative Study in Digital Technologies. Electronic Thesis and Dissertation Repository. Paper 2030.* Retrieved on October 17, 2020 from https://ir.lib.uwo.ca/etd/2030.

Borah, P. (2016). Media effect theories. Retrieved on November 7, 2021 from https://www.researchgate.net/publication/314119579_Media_Effects_Theory.

Boyd, D. M. and Ellison, N. B. (2008). Social network sites: Definition, history, and scholarship. *Journal of Computer-Mediated Communication* 13:210–230. Retrieved on August 15, 2020 from www.academic.oup.com.

Druckman, J. N. (2001a). The implications of framing effects for citizen competence. *Political Behavior* 23(3):225–256. Retrieved on October 27, 2020 from www.faculty.wcas.northwestern.edu.

Druckman, J. N. (2001b). On the limits of framing effect: Who can frame? *Journal of Politics* 63(4):1041–1066. Retrieved on October 27, 2020 from http://links.jstor.org.

Egelhofer, J. L. and Lecheler, S. (2019). Fake news as a two-dimensional phenomenon: A framework and research agenda. *Annals of the International Communication Association* 43(2):97–116. Retrieved on July 12, 2020 from www.researchgate.net.

Farnan, J. M., Snyder, S. L., Worster, B. K, Chaudhry, H. M., Rhyne, J. A. and Arora V.M. (2013). Online medical professionalism: Patient and public relationships: Policy statement from the American College of Physicians and the Federation of State Medical Boards. *Annals of Internal Medicine* 158(8):620–627. doi: 10.7326/0003-4819-158-8-201304160-00100. Retrieved on October 7, 2020 from www.acojournal.org.

Frenkel S., Alba, D. and Zhong, R. (March 9, 2020). Surge of virus misinformation stumps Facebook and Twitter: *The New York Times*. Retrieved on August 6, 2020 from www.nytimes.com.

George, D. R., Rovniak, L. S. and Kraschnewski, J. L. (2013). Dangers and opportunities for social media in medicine. *Clinical Obstetric Gynecology* 56(3):453–462. doi: 10.1097GRF.0b013e318297dc38. Retrieved on September 3, 2020 from www.researchgate.net.

Global System of Mobile Communications (GSMA). (2018). Spotlight on Nigeria. Delivering a digital future. Retrieved on August 3, 2020 from https://www.gsma

.com/publicpolicy/wp-content/uploads/2019/02GSMA-Potlight-on-Nigeria-Report-pdf.

Hou, Z., Du, F., Jiang, H., Zhou, X. and Lin, L., (2020). Assessment of public attention, risk perception, emotional and behavioral responses to the COVID-19 outbreak: Social media surveillance in China. doi:10.1101/2020.03.14.20035956. Retrieved on September 10, 2020 from www.papers.ssrn.com.

Househ, M. (2013). The use of social media in Healthcare: Organizational, clinical and patient perspectives. *Stud Health Technology Inform* 183:244–248. Retrieved on August 27, 2020 from https://books.google.com.ng/books?.

Human Rights Watch (May 6, 2020). Ethiopia: Free speech at risk amid COVID-19. Retrieved on August 18, 2020 from www.hrw.org.

Huynh, T. L. D. (2020). The COVID-19 risk perception: A survey on socioeconomics and media attention. *Economics Bulletin* 40(1):758–764. Retrieved on September 17, 2020 from www.researchgate.net.

Ibrahim, M. (24, May 2020). If Journalists were proactive and pragmatic in practice. Africa Media Development Foundation. Retrieved on September 16, 2020 from www.amdf-centre.org.

Lampos, V., Moura, S., Yom-Tov, E., Cox, I. J., McKendry, R. and Edelstein, M. (2020). Tracking COVID-19 using online search. *NPJ Digital Medicine* 93:4–9. Retrieved on November 11, 2020 from http:/arxiv.org/abs/2003.08086.

Lazer, D. M. J., Baum, M. A., Benkler, Y., Berinsky, A. J., Greenhill, K. M., Menczer, F., Metzger, M. J., Nyhan, B., Pennycook, G., Rothschild, D., Schudson, M., Sloman, S. A. and Suntein, C. R., Thorson, E. A., Watts, D. J. and Zittrain, J. L. (2018). The science of fake news. *Science* 359(6380):1094–1096. Retrieved on July 20, 2020 from www.researchgate.net.

Leung, L. (2013). Generational differences in content generation in social media: The roles of the gratifications sought and of narcissism. *Computers in Human Behavior* 29(3):997–1009. doi:10.1016/j.chb.2012.12.028. Retrieved on September 2, 2020 from www.dhi.ac.uk.

McGonagle, T. (2017). False fears or real concerns? *Netherlands Quarterly of Human Rights* 35(4):203–209. Retrieved on November 15, 2020 from https://journals.sagepub.com/doi/pdf/10.1177/0924051917738685.

Naira Land. (May 18, 2020). Dokpesi and his son clash over comment on COVID-19 – Health –Naira Land. Retrieved on October 12, 2020 from www.nairaland.com.

Naira Metrics. (2020). COVID-19: Nigeria, others to collaborate with tech giants to curb misinformation. Retrieved on October 12, 2020 from https://nairametrics.com/2020/04/02/covid-19-nigeria-others-to-collaborate-with-tech-giants-to-curb-misinformation/.

Nigerian Communications Commission (NCC). (2020). Statistics and reports. Retrieved on July 10, 2020 from http://www.ncc.gov.ng.

NOIPolls. (December 11, 2018). Facebook ranked No. 1 social media and online dating platform in Nigeria. Retrieved on November 25, 2020 from www.noipolls.com.

Nwakpu S. E., Ezema O. V. and Ogbodo, N. J. (2020). Nigeria media framing of coronavirus pandemic and audience response. *Health Promotion Perspectives*

2020 10(3):192–199. Retrieved on September 9, 2020 from https://doi.org/10.34172/hpp.2020.32.

Onukwue, A. (March 9, 2020). Nigeria's social media bill suffers its biggest defeat yet. Retrieved on November 21, 2020 from www.techcabal.com.

Paul, E. (November 28, 2019). Everything you need to know about Nigeria's social media bill and what you can do about it. Retrieved on November 16, 2020 from www.techpoint.africa.

Pennycook, G., McPhetres, J., Zhang, Y. and Rand, D. (2020). Fighting COVID-19 misinformation on social media: Experimental evidence for a scalable accuracy nudge intervention. *PsyArXiv Working Paper 1-24*. Retrieved on August 30, 2020 from www.researchgate.net.

Pulido, C. M., Vilarejo-Carballido, B., Redondo-Sama, G. and Gomez, A. (2020). COVID-19 infodemic: More retweets for science-based information on coronavirus than for false information. *International Sociology*. Retrieved on October 15, 2020 from https://journals.sagepub.com/doi/full/10.1177/0268580920914755.

Saheed, A. H. and Dumebi, O. (2020). Social media use and the challenges of information dissemination during emergencies: Experiences of library and information scientists on COVID-19 in Nigeria. *Library Philosophy and Practice (e-journal)* 4267. Retrieved on August 8, 2020 from https://digitalcommons.unl.edu/libphilprac.

Savrum, Y. M. and Leon, M. (2015). The role of the media in conflict, peacebuilding, and international relations. *International Journal on World Peace* 32(4):23–34. Retrieved on August 8, 2020 from http://www.rcmss.com.

Shahbaz, A. and Funk, A. (2020). Information isolation: Censoring the COVID-19 outbreak. Retrieved on November 10, 2020 from www.freedomhouse.com.

Ukpe, W. (November 1, 2020). End SARS: Social media must be regulated to prevent the spread of hate speech. Retrieved on November 10, 2020 from www.nairametrics.com.

Valkenburg, P. M., Peter, J. and Walther, J. B. (2016). Media effects theory and research. *Annual Research of Review of Psychology* 67. doi:10.1146/annurev-psych-122414-033608. Retrieved on August 27, 2020 from www.researchgate.net.

Wang, Y., Mckee M., Torbica, A. and Stucker, D. (2019). Social science & medicine systematic literature review on the spread of health-related misinformation on social media. *Social Science & Medicine*. doi: 10.1016/j.socsimed.2019.112552. Retrieved on August 27, 2020 from www.googleweblight.com.

West, R. and Turner, L. H. (2007). *Introducing Communication Theory: Analysis and Application*. New York: McGraw-Hill Higher Education. Retrieved on November 4, 2020 from https://polifilosofie.files.wordpress.com/.

WhatsApp Messages. (2020) Messages shared through WhatsApp communications.

Chapter 15

Corohistory

Hadizat Audu Salihu

This chapter on Corohistory examines how the histories of the deleterious effects of past pandemics have been used to characterize the emergence of the Coronavirus Disease (COVID)-2019 which has fomented hysteria among people. The outbreak and spread of pandemics have been part of human existence and narratives since the earliest times. Coronaviruses, which belong to a large family of viruses causing many illnesses in humans and animals, have been the cause of severe respiratory infections. They include the Middle East respiratory syndrome (MERS), the severe acute respiratory syndrome (SARS), and the COVID-2019. The family Coronaviridae encompasses a broad spectrum of animal and human viruses with distinctive morphology. Coronavirus virions are envelope- spherical-, disc-, kidney-, or rod-shaped (coronaviruses) (Burrell and Murphy, 2012).

Before 2003, members of the coronaviruses family were believed to cause only mild respiratory illness in humans; other coronaviruses before now were known in the livestock industry. But the emergence of severe acute respiratory-related coronavirus (SARS-Cov) in 2003 stimulated major research into these viruses. However many new coronaviruses have since been discovered, some with a zoonotic potential of causing serious outbreaks of disease in humans. The more recent emergence of Middle East respiratory syndrome coronavirus (MERS-CoV) is a typical example (Burrell and Murphy, 2012).

The chapter will therefore trace the history of coronaviruses before the outbreak of the COVID-2019 to isolate the latter variant's actual impact on the minds of people; also, an overview of some of the pandemics that have affected the world shall be discussed to create a clearer view of COVID-2019 pandemic in historical narratives.

Corohistory has been studied by many medical practitioners and medical historians. According to Kahn and McIntosh, the history of human coronaviruses began in 1965 when Tyrrell and Bynoe examined the proportion of viruses from patients with cold, and they found that cold could passage a virus named B814. This was found in human embryonic tracheal organ cultures obtained from the respiratory tract of an adult with a common cold. According to them, the presence of an infectious agent was demonstrated by inoculating the medium from these cultures intranasally in human volunteers; colds were produced in a significant proportion of subjects, but Tyrrell and Bynoe were unable to grow the agent in tissue culture at that time (Kahn and McIntosh, 2005).

At about the same time, other medical experts called Hamre and Procknow grew a virus with unusual properties in tissue culture from samples obtained from medical students with colds. Another expert, according to Kahn and McIntosh, reported the recovery of multiple strains of ether-sensitive agents from the human respiratory tract by using a technique similar to that of Tyrrell and Bynoe; these viruses were termed "OC" to designate that they were grown in organ cultures (Kahn and McIntosh, 2005). Tyrrell led a group of virologists working with the human strains and several animal viruses in the late 1960s on infectious bronchitis virus, mouse hepatitis virus, and transmissible gastroenteritis virus of swine, all of which had been demonstrated to be morphologically the same as seen through electron microscopy. This new group of viruses was named coronavirus (corona denoting the crown-like appearance of the surface projections) and was later officially accepted as a new genus of viruses (Kahn and McIntosh, 2005).

Before 2003, interest in human coronaviruses was primarily driven by having a role in relatively mild upper respiratory tract infections. Viral strains HCoV-229E and HCoV-OC43 were isolated from patients with upper respiratory tract infections in the 1960s. Shortly after the discovery of SARS-CoV in 2003, two new human coronaviruses were isolated, HCoV-NL63 in the Netherlands and HKU1 in Hong Kong (Burrell and Murphy, 2012).

From the foregoing, it is clear that coronaviruses have been identified and associated with cold in the 1960s which caused respiratory and intestinal infections in animals and humans. They were not considered to be highly pathogenic to humans until the outbreak of SARS in 2002 and 2003 in Guangdong Province, China, as the coronaviruses that circulated before that time in humans mostly caused mild infections in immunocompetent people.

Ten years after SARS, another highly pathogenic coronavirus, MERS-CoV, emerged in Middle Eastern countries; SARS-CoV and MERS-CoV were transmitted directly to humans from market civets and dromedary camels, respectively, and both viruses are thought to have originated in bats (Cui and Shi, 2019).

The chapter poses two major questions: (1) Why did coronavirus spread in 2019 despite advancements in medical technology and researches on the virus since the 1960s? (2) How were the previous pandemics managed and the applicability of methods used in curbing the spread of the COVID-2019 outbreak? In historical narratives, previous chains of activities are studied to understand the present trends and project future occurrences. It is however clear that coronaviruses in humans and animals had proven to be deadly and the rapidity of its spread is undoubted, therefore its management since the outbreak of COVID-2019 has shown that history is repeating itself despite past experiences from major pandemics.

The use of a qualitative research method was adopted in this chapter. It encompasses the use of primary and secondary variety of data sources, including Internet sources, oral interviews with key informants in the medical sectors, and researchers who carried out studies on the threat posed by the COVID-2019 pandemic.

The essence of investigating this topic came as a result of the quest to understand the novel coronavirus that is affecting global health. Furthermore, many people often believe that COVID-2019 started in Wuhan city of China in the year 2019 without the knowledge that the virus has been in existence long before 2019. This chapter is therefore important for several reasons. First, it is a pointer to the early outbreaks of pandemics which have affected the world in the twentieth century. Second, the chapter enables a historical study of coronaviruses before the 2019 outbreak which probes into the evolution of the coronavirus and its transmission from animal to the human body as well as its rapid transmission as a result of human contact. Third, for students of medical history and researchers interested in carrying out a study on coronavirus, it is vital to understand that the virus is not a twenty-first-century phenomenon rather its evolutionary processes started in the 1960s but its outbreak was not on a global scale and easily contained until 2019.

The chapter begins with the history of pandemics and medical advancement in the world before the outbreak of COVID-2019; this will allow for the historical context and understanding of medical researches and its attempt to cure and stop early pandemics that had ravaged the world. This is followed by an examination of globalization as one of the major determinant factors in the rapid spread of pandemics with a focus on COVID-2019. A critique of globalization enables us to locate the interconnectivity of the world, despite geographical differences and space, the role played by governments to ensure that borders are closed, and restrictions of movements put in place in response to the outbreak of a pandemic. The next section examines the North/South divide and its implication in infrastructural development with specific reference to medical facilities available in the less developed countries in the world. The concluding section of the chapter offers lessons learned and the way forward in terms of the spread and management of coronaviruses.

HISTORY: A THEORETICAL DISCUSSION

History as a concept plays a fundamental role in human thought; it invokes notions of human agency, change, the role of material circumstances in human affairs, and the putative meaning of historical events (Little, 2016). History helps in understanding our society in the present, by understanding the forces, choices, and circumstances that brought us to our current situation.

In its very earliest known uses in human society, history was simply a narrative account of past events. As a word, it entered the English language from the French formulation of *histoire*, the Latin notion of *historia*, and the Greek construction of *istoria*, each of which represented the basic sense of knowledge of the past (Nasson, 2009). In these early concepts, the sense of history encompassed both an imaginative story of events and a narrative or chronicle of past events.

History in the twenty-first century now began to take on the distinctive character or sense of an organized knowledge of the past. Through the development of this sense of history emerged the distinctly modern meanings and role of historian, historical, and historic. Writers on historiography and culture confirm that in contemporary English, this has become the predominant and lasting general sense of history. At the same time, it is important to note the growth of a further significant conception of history which goes beyond the basic meaning of an organized knowledge of past life. It is difficult to date or to define its intellectual source exactly, but it is the sense of history as something continuous, as human or self-development (Nasson, 2009). This particular stage of thinking is increasingly evident in European thought from around the eighteenth century and saw an early expression in the emergence of new forms of universal histories or world histories, based on the imperial sense of a "discovery" or physical charting of the world. Adopting the argument of the cultural critic, according to Raymond Williams, "the clearest way of projecting this newer post-eighteenth century sense of history is to say that past events are viewed not as specific or bounded histories, but as a continuous and connected process" (Nasson, 2009, pp. 216–218).

History is crucial to human development as any discipline of field of professional practice has a history, often extending back in time to a period before these practices of professions coalesced into anything resembling the current state of the discipline (Antony et al., 2013). It is imperative to note that "without history, it is difficult to know who one is, where one comes from or where one is headed" (Ferro, 2002, p. 1). Thus, having a history is important because what is articulated as having happened in the past profoundly affects all aspects of human lives in the present and the future (Antony et al., 2013).

The theory of history consists of "the philosophical examination of all the aspects of our descriptions, beliefs, and knowledge of the past" (Lorenz,

2011, p. 14). History and theory are both descriptive and normative. Historical theories pose questions concerning the characteristics of our knowledge of the past (epistemological); questions concerning how this knowledge is generated and what counts as "quality" and "progress" of historical knowledge (methodological); and questions concerning the mode of being of "the past" and those those concerning ethical, legal, and political uses of past knowledge (ontological or metaphysical) (Lorenz, 2011).

According to E. H. Carr, history, in the words of R. G. Collingwood, "is the past as created in the present" (Carr, 1961, p. 5). The past is an ocean of factual things, most of which are sunk out of sight into the depth of oblivion. The mere compilation of the facts has nothing to do with history, rather it is an activity whose source is to be looked for elsewhere, be it in the neurosis of nostalgia, an obsession with steady obliteration that time affects the known and knowable past (Carr, 1961).

The idea of history is that we can learn more about the past than the past knew about itself with the tool available and by the motivations which happen to provoke human curiosity. Another critique of the historical idea came from the fact that history deals with unrepeatable events. The theory of evolution, if ever a historical intrusion into natural science, does not lend itself to the prediction of its future course; history lies in the understanding of the process of evolution, it organizes our thoughts, it provides a narrative, and most importantly it provokes questions to be asked.

PANDEMICS BEFORE THE OUTBREAK OF COVID-2019

As human society grew and movement from one place to another ensued, so was the spread of infectious diseases. Over the years, there have been recorded pandemics that shaped human existence and development. These pandemics will be discussed according to how they affected human history before the outbreak of COVID-2019.

The History.com website provides us with a chronology and brief descriptions of earlier pandemics which can be easily accessed via the link provided in the References section of this chapter. These pandemics are as follows: (a) "in 430 BC, the earliest recorded pandemic happened during the Peloponnesian War in Athens"; (b) "the Antonine Plague in 165 AD was an early appearance of smallpox that began with the Huns"; (c) "the Cyprian Plague named after the first known victim the Christian Bishop of Carthage in 250 AD was another pandemic that spread wide and killed many people"; (d) "the Justinian plague of 541 AD, first appeared in Egypt and spread through Palestine and the Byzantine Empire, and then throughout the Mediterranean"; (e) "in the 11th Century, leprosy grew into a pandemic in Europe in the middle ages, resulting in the building of numerous leprosy-focused hospitals to accommodate the vast number of victims"; (f) "the 1350 Black Death, responsible for the death of one-third of the European population, was the second large outbreak of the bubonic plague possibly started in Asia and moved west in caravans"; and (g) "in the 15th Century, the age of exploration and the 1492 Columbian Exchange following the arrival of the Spanish in the Caribbean led to the outbreak of diseases such as smallpox, measles, and bubonic plague which were passed along to the native Indian populations by the European explorers and conquistadors" (History.com, 2019, p. 1). According to the study by Puritt: "Smallpox and measles caused the deaths of some 56 million Native Americans in the 16th and 17th Centuries, largely through disease, may have altered Earth's climate as vegetation growth on previously tilled land drew more CO_2 from the atmosphere and caused a cooling event" (Puritt, 2019, p. 1).

We also learn from the History.com website about (a) "the Great Plague of London in 1665 made a devastating appearance of the bubonic plague which led to the deaths of 20 percent of London's population"; (b) "in 1817, the first of seven cholera pandemics over the next 150 years broke out, this wave of small intestine infection originated in Russia, where one million people died"; (c) "the Fiji Measles Pandemic of 1875 broke out after Fiji ceded to the British Empire"; (d) "the Russian Flu started in Siberia and Kazakhstan in 1889, traveled to Moscow, and made its way into Finland and then Poland, where it moved into the rest of Europe"; (e) "in 1918, avian-borne flu known as Spanish Flu resulted in about 50 million deaths worldwide"; and (f) "immediately after the Spanish Flu, the Asian flu started in Hong Kong and spread throughout China and then into the United States, and a second wave of the Asian flu followed in early 1958, causing an estimated total of about 1.1 million deaths globally, with 116,000 deaths in the United States alone" (History.com, 2020, p. 1).

In more contemporary times, "the HIV/AIDS pandemic from 1981 till present is a disease that destroys a person's immune system, resulting in eventual death" (History.com, 2020, p. 1). In 2003, SARS was first identified in 2003 after several months of cases. SARS is believed to have possibly started with bats, spread to cats, and then to humans in China, followed by 26 other countries, infecting 8,096 people, with 774 deaths (History.com, 2019). SARS is characterized by respiratory problems, dry cough, fever, and head and body aches, and is spread through respiratory droplets from coughs and sneezes (Public Health Online, 2020).

As reported by Jarus, and the Centers for Disease Control and Prevention (CDC), "the 2009–2010 swine flu pandemic was caused by a new strain of H1N1 that originated in Mexico in the spring of 2009 before spreading to the rest of the world. In one year alone, the virus infected as many as 1.4 billion people across the globe and killed between 151,700 and 575,400 people" (CDC, 2019, p. 1; Jarus, 2020, p. 1). Jarus and the CDC add that the 2009 flu pandemic primarily affected children and young adults, and 80 percent of the deaths were in people younger than 65 (Jarus, 2020; CDC, 2020).

The Ebola virus was a disease that ravaged West Africa between 2014 and 2016, with 28,600 reported cases and 11,325 deaths. The first known cases of Ebola occurred in Sudan and the Democratic Republic of Congo in 1976, and the virus may have originated in bats. In December 2013, a case was reported in Guinea, then the disease spread to Liberia and Sierra Leone. The bulk of the cases and deaths occurred in those three countries. A smaller number of cases occurred in Nigeria, Mali, Senegal, the United States, and Europe, according to the CDC (Jarus, 2020; CDC, 2021). It is however sad that there is no cure for Ebola, although efforts at finding a vaccine are ongoing.

The Zika epidemic in South America and Central America from 2015 till the present is a virus that won't be known for several years. In the meantime, scientists face a race against time to bring the virus under control. The Zika virus is spread through mosquitoes of the *Aedes* genus, although it can also be sexually transmitted in humans that have been infected. While Zika is usually not harmful to adults or children, it can attack infants who are still in the womb and cause birth defects. The type of mosquitoes that carry Zika flourish best in warm, humid climates, making South America, Central America, and parts of the Southern United States prime areas for the virus to flourish (Jarus, 2020).

To contain the Zika virus, there was a high level of political and administrative commitment by the government of the affected countries. The epicenter and the area within a 3-kilometer radius (29 square kilometers) around this epicenter was mapped; teams of health workers attended to 50 households; and 350–375 teams constituted from different departments, comprising health, medical education, Integrated Child Development Services, and nursing colleges. They were responsible for implementing surveillance and vector control measures (BMJ Journals, 2021).

In 2019, the World Health Organization (WHO) announced that the COVID-2019 virus was officially a pandemic after barreling through 114 countries in three months and infecting over 118,000 people. COVID-2019 is caused by a novel coronavirus—a new coronavirus strain that has not been previously found in people. Symptoms of COVID-2019 include respiratory problems, fever, and cough, and can lead to pneumonia and death. Like SARS, it's spread through droplets from sneezes. The first reported case in China appeared on November 17, 2019, in the Hubei Province but went unrecognized. Eight more cases appeared in December with researchers pointing to an unknown virus (WHO, 2020).

Also, we learn from the History.com website that "many people learned about COVID-2019 when ophthalmologist Dr Li Wenliang defied government orders and released safety information to other doctors" (History.com, 2020, p. 1). The following day, China informed the WHO and charged Li with a crime. Li himself died from COVID-2019 just over a month later (Jarus, 2020). Without a vaccine available, the virus spread beyond Chinese borders and by mid-March, it had spread globally to more than 163 countries. On February 11, the infection was officially christened COVID-2019 (Public Health Online, 2020).

THE PLACE OF GLOBALIZATION IN THE SPREAD OF COVID-2019

"Globalization" is the term that is used interchangeably with terms such as "internationalization," "liberalization," "universalization," and "Westernization." However, some scholars believe that "a strict definition of globalization distinguishes between the cross-border and trans-border flow" (Saker et al., 2004, p. 5). Cross-border flow concerns the interactions across two or more countries, for example, the documented movement of people, official trade of goods and services, or capital flows such as foreign direct investment across national borders. Trans-border or transnational, in contrast, concerns the flow of people, goods and services, capital, values and ideas, and other entities in a way that does not recognize national borders. Lee (2003) argues that globalization is leading to changes in how we experience and perceive time.

Globalization is therefore shaping the time frame in which natural- and human-induced phenomena take place, as well as the time available and necessary for responding to the phenomena (Saker et al., 2004). With globalization, the time taken for some infectious diseases to spread across territorial space has become much quicker as a result of the increased amount, frequency, and speed of population mobility. Similarly, the potential capacity to detect and report the disease outbreak has quickened due to the advent of global information and communication systems (Saker et al., 2004).

Globalization influences how we perceive ourselves and our world due to the proliferation of a wide range of people and ideas within global reach. The use of mass media think tanks, research institutions, consultancy firms, advertising agencies, religious groups, educational institutions, and policy-making organizations has made it easy for people and ideas to cross over national boundaries. It is therefore clear that the above has led to the emergence of a "global culture" dominated by Western values and beliefs (Saker et al., 2004). According to them,

> globalization is a complex and multi-faceted set of processes that is having diverse and widespread impacts on human societies worldwide. Globalization

> can be a set of processes that are: changing the nature of human interaction across a wide range of spheres including the economic, political, social, technological and environmental . . . the process of change can be described as globalizing in the sense that boundaries of various kinds are becoming eroded. This erosion can be seen to be occurring along three dimensions; spatial, temporal, and cognitive. (Saker et al., 2004, p. 6)

Historically, infectious diseases contribute to a large proportion of deaths and disabilities worldwide. The process of globalization potentially influences a broad range of biological, environmental, and social factors that affect the burden of many important human infections (Saker et al., 2004). Globalization represents civilizational progress and it is highly intertwined with the decrease in the cost of moving people, goods, money, information, transportation costs more broadly. These allowed for the development of the "knowledge creation society," which is centered on global metropolises. However, this reduction of movement costs has facilitated the international spread of viruses, bringing infectious diseases to all of humankind. The current COVID-2019 crisis has manifested this inconvenient truth (Fujita and Hamaguchi, 2020).

China, where COVID-2019 originated from, has international commerce reflected in its exchange of people and products with almost all countries, and therefore its public health measures and the outbreak of COVID-2019 had devastating consequences on all nations. Mas-Coma, Jones, and Marty (2020) have criticized the developed countries of the Northern Hemisphere for not containing the spread of COVID-2019. Their thought is as follows:

> It is hard to understand why supranational agencies and expert institutions did not understand the magnitude of the risk posed by such a singular virus, nor of its capacity to take advantage of globalization with an astonishingly rapid worldwide spread. Indeed, the crucial characteristics of COVID-2019 lie in its transmission pathways, the existence of asymptomatic/presymptomatic carriers, and survival potential in the external environment, which were already explained and transmitted to the world by the Chinese colleagues since mid-January. (Mas-Coma, Jones and Marty, 2020, p. 9)

Mas-Coma, Jones, and Marty further stated that so many scientific publications during the last two decades about the capacity of globalization to facilitate the spread of infectious agents seem to have been ignored by health organizations and governments of respective countries. The worldwide spread of viruses following different transmission ways, such as HIV; Ebola virus; *Aedes* mosquito-borne viruses as those of Zika, Chikungunya, and dengue; yearly vaccine problems posed by the quick mutating seasonal flu viruses seem to have been useless models now in comparison to the very fast-spreading COVID-2019 (Mas-Coma, Jones and Marty, 2020).

In Africa, governments hastened to enforce measures designed to contain the spread of COVID-2019. Based on the realities of the continent's fragile health systems, several pertinent concerns arose regarding how socioeconomic development can be stimulated by globalization practices related to increased international trade. Another challenge posed by globalization to the African continent was how to reduce community transmission of COVID-2019 while also providing economic relief to families and businesses affected by physical distancing or 'lockdown' strategies (Yaya, Otu and Labonté, 2020).

Before the virus spread into Africa, the International Monetary Fund in mid-February 2020 warned the continent of the impending risk of an economic slowdown as China, where the virus emerged. China, however, is the largest trading partner and foreign investor of many countries in the African continent. It is worthy to note that many African countries are interconnected to the affected economies of the United States and the European Union. The growth deceleration in these major economies increased the price of goods exported from Africa such as mineral ores and metals (Yaya, Otu and Labonté, 2020).

The United Nations Development Programme estimates that the COVID-2019 pandemic could result in the loss of nearly half of all jobs in Africa where unemployment is already a major concern. This is likely to further aggravate Africa's fragile socioeconomic situation, one in which as many as 422 million people (one in three Africans) are estimated to be living below the international poverty line of $1.90 per day (Yaya, Otu and Labonté, 2020). Even though globalization represents civilizational progress, it also accelerated the spread of the COVID-2019 pandemic.

Fujita and Hamaguchi (2020) asserted that many countries took emergency measures to stop the propagation of the virus by blocking their national borders and restricting the internal movement of people. This restriction placed by the government of various countries affected the cost of moving people which rose sharply, and the flow of goods and money becomes unreliable, while online information exchange became more active than ever.

Fujita and Hamaguchi (2020) believe that the reorientation of globalization will be achieved "by responding successfully to challenges" as stated by Toynbee (1946), in the context of the growth of civilizations. Innovative responses to global problems are best promoted through international cooperation under unrestricted pluralism.

It is clear that globalization which contributes to the world's socioeconomic and political developments also harms the globe. In the case of infectious diseases such as COVID-2019, globalization has successfully aided its rapid spread to almost every part of the world, including the remote areas leading to the high death rate recorded since its outbreak in 2019.

RESPONSES TO COVID-2019 IN THE GLOBAL NORTH AND SOUTH

The novel coronavirus was not the first pandemic to struck mankind; however, the rapidity of its spread and death toll make it one of the deadly pandemics recorded in human history. Coronavirus can develop and replicate in the oral mucosa, and thus in the upper parts of the respiratory system, allowing for easy transmission similar to flu viruses. This upper respiratory involvement and high viremia at the beginning of the infection allowed for transmission to other subjects even before the appearance of symptoms, with additionally to subjects showing a very mild clinical symptom, poses a great epidemiological problem, which also happens with influenza viruses of asymptomatic/presymptomatic carriers. The difficulties in detecting asymptomatic carriers, who often do not know they are infected, undoubtedly facilitate the spread and appearance of unexpected disease foci whose traceability becomes impossible in several cases (Mas-Coma, Jones and Marty, 2020).

The outbreak of the novel coronavirus was faced with initial inaction, subsequent slow reaction, and lack of consensus agreements (memorandums of understanding) by neighboring countries, despite repeated warnings by WHO which suggest that the role of agencies put in place in the past precisely to prevent situations such as the present one will need to be re-analyzed (Mas-Coma, Jones and Marty, 2020). This is because too often governments focus their defense primarily against other nations and other ideological human actors. World leaders forget that Mother Nature is the most potent bringer of doom from massive cyclones, destructive wildfires, to horrific pandemics. However, in an attempt to fight COVID-2019, many countries adopted some international policy trends such as border closures, strict migration measures, imposition of quarantines, social distancing, and enforcement of stay-at-home orders (Yaya, Otu and Labonté, 2020). These measures embody the dialectical quality of contemporary globalization.

In the Global North, the deceptive presentation of countries within the European Union, with each one acting as if it were working alone, unavoidably poses the question about the usefulness of having a European Centre for Disease Prevention and Control (Stockholm). Similarly, the United States suffered from the same aspects as those of the European countries; they included a pronounced delay in developing tests, inexplicable delays in establishing testing criteria, and a strong reluctance by the U.S. CDC and U.S. government to accept new testing techniques (Mas-Coma, Jones and

Marty, 2020) to change the testing criteria significantly until mid-March, and the dearth of equipment including lack of needed personal protective equipment, including surgical masks and facemasks and insufficient quantities of mechanical ventilators for the patients and lack of surgical capacity for hospital beds and ICU space (Mas-Coma, Jones and Marty, 2020).

The devastating effects of COVID-2019 in the European Union and its Member States have fostered the spirit of cooperation, thereby acting together as "Team Europe" and taking comprehensive and decisive action to tackle the destructive impact of COVID-2019. The European Union supported efforts to halt the spread of COVID-2019 and helped other countries to strengthen their healthcare, water and sanitation systems. The goal was to provide fast and equitable access to safe, high quality, effective and affordable tests, treatments, and vaccines to combat the virus (European Commission, 2020).

In Africa, news of the COVID-2019 outbreak and spread was known, but many people believe it is not an African disease and therefore could not infect Africans; however, news of Africans in the diaspora who contracted and died from the virus proved that it was not limited to Asia, Europe, and America. At the end of 2019, almost all African countries had undertaken a Joint External Evaluation (JEE) of the International Health Regulations. This process helped countries identify the gaps in their ability to prevent, detect, and respond to public health threats when the virus spread to the continent (Ihekweazu and Agogo, 2020). Many countries had developed competencies in real-time surveillance and immunization, but overall, there was a pressing need for improving the resilience of the health sector to ensure an effective outbreak response. In response to recommendations from the JEEs, African countries were supported to develop a multi-sectoral National Action Plan for Health Security, addressing the gaps identified by the JEE and aligning with the various country sectorial plans (Ihekweazu and Agogo, 2020).

At the start of the pandemic in China, WHO's African regional office and the Africa Centres for Disease Control and Prevention provided guidance and technical and financial support to prepare countries for the effect of COVID-2019. Jack Ma, the founder of *Alibaba*, sent COVID-2019 prevention and test kits to many African countries to ensure that Africa is better prepared than ever (The Economic Times, 2020).

The first case of COVID-2019 was reported in the African region on February 14, 2020, in Egypt and Africa South of the Sahara on February 27, 2019, in Nigeria (Ihekweazu and Agogo, 2020). This was over one month after the first case of the disease was reported in China, giving the region the lead time to prepare for a large outbreak. Since then, more than 1 million cases were reported and every country on the continent has been affected. African governments were commended by the WHO for quick response to adopt public health measures in line with WHO guidelines and instituted other restrictions such as lockdowns and curfews. According to the WHO, "While most countries have been spared the exponential growth witnessed in other regions, these measures have come at a heavy social and economic cost and as countries have started to open their borders, some have started to see cases rise" (2020, p. 1).

Nonetheless, despite the widespread misinformation about the immunity of Africans to COVID-2019, overall poor health facilities, poor sanitation, high rate of slums, and many other factors increased the mortality in the continent. According to Ihekweazu and Agogo (2020), reports from other continents show higher morbidity and mortality in people of African heritage. While the observed disproportionality in adverse outcomes may be due to the impact of health disparities, poorer access to healthcare, and lower socioeconomic factors, the implication for African countries is therefore clear as stated as follows:

> As of November 23, 2020, the number of confirmed COVID-2019 cases in Africa amounted to 2,092,968, which represented around 3.5 percent of the infections around the world. By the same date, coronavirus cases globally were over 59.5 million, causing nearly 1.4 million deaths, while approximately 41.1 million people recovered from the disease. In the African continent, South Africa was the most drastically affected country, with more than 769.7 thousand infections, ranking as the sixteenth highest in several cases out of 213 countries worldwide. (Saifaddin Galal, 2020, p. 1)

In the United States, the first COVID-2019 case was reported in Washington State on January 21, 2020. Since then, it increased dramatically after expanded rapid testing for the virus in many centers around the country. As of April 3, 2020, seven nations have reported more than 40,000 cases, with the United States, Italy, and Spain leading the pack. Globally, there were 1,192,028 reported COVID-2019 cases and 64,316 deaths as of April 4, 2020 (Balogun, 2020). It is, however, ironic that South Korea and the United States had their first confirmed COVID-2019 case the same day, in late January this year. The South Korean government was more aggressive in community testing, contact tracing, and quarantining those exposed; the U.S. response was, however, delayed. The aggressive response by South Korea helped to reduce its death toll to less than 200 deaths, and the United States had 305,820 cases and 8,291 deaths, a figure that exceeded the September 11, 2001, terrorist attack fatalities (Balogun, 2020). South Korea conducted over 189,000 COVID-2019 tests, compared to 1,707 in the United States, although the two countries announced their first cases on the same day. Similarly, Sweden, on the other hand, delayed its response with a laissez-faire approach to the virus and had more infected cases and deaths than its neighbors, Denmark, and Norway, including Finland that locked down movements and sealed their borders early (Balogun, 2020).

In the United Kingdom, with about 140,000 people tested on the COVID-2019 virus, the number of confirmed cases rose, with nearly 42,000 people, which included Prime Minister Boris Johnson and Prince Charles. The United Kingdom recorded a total of 4,313 death cases with the disease. The precise number of people in the United Kingdom with a respiratory infection is estimated to be much higher among the National Health Service health workers and people in the hospital tested in the early stage of the pandemic by March 9, 2020 (Balogun, 2020).

It is clear that responses to COVID-2019 vary from one country to another because of the peculiarities and natures of societies. In Africa and other countries in the South, measures taken by the government such as lockdown, social and physical distancing did not go down well with the people due to the poverty, illiteracy, poor social infrastructures, belief system of the people, and corruption on the part of organization set up by the government to handle COVID-2019-related issues. COVID-2019 like the previous pandemic revealed the inadequacies in the aspect of readiness from government, research and medical advancement, poor policy formulation, and the WHO's failure to ensure the spread of the virus was curbed at the early stage.

CONCLUSION AND RECOMMENDATIONS

For over 100 years, enormous advances in technology including medical researches and communication have greatly influenced infectious diseases over time. Like other historical transformations through time and space, the modern technological revolution offers huge possibilities for improving as well as harming human health (Saker et al., 2004). The novel coronavirus has long been in existence since 1965 when it was first discovered by Tyrrell and Bynoe. Coronavirus continued to exist but not as pronounced among humans as in animals; in the 1960s, viral strains HCoV-229E and HCoV-OC43 obtained from patients with upper respiratory tract infections proved that humans were susceptible to contract and spread the virus. From the period, the virus was found in 2003 as two new human coronaviruses were isolated in the Netherlands and Hong Kong. This virus was not considered to be highly pathogenic to humans until the outbreak of SARS. A decade after, another coronavirus emerged in the Middle Eastern countries which was transmitted directly to humans from the use of animal extracts.

In 2009, a major pandemic was caused by SARS-CoV-2, also called COVID-2019. This virus first entered the human population in Hubei Province, China, in mid-November 2019 and manifested in Wuhan, the largest metropolitan area of Hubei. SARS-CoV-2 shares characteristics well known in other animal coronaviruses such as its capacity to survive for several days outside the host's body; this development helps explain how SARS-CoV-2 spreads by contact (Mas-Coma, Jones and Marty, 2020).

The outbreak and spread of the virus were not well managed by the Chinese government and the WHO, knowing the economic importance of China to the world and the high number of foreigners traveling in and out of the country. The virus sadly spread to other parts of the world and almost every country records new infections and death tolls daily. The rapidity of the spread of COVID-2019 and its effects on the socioeconomic structure of the globe made it one of the deadliest pandemic in human history.

The outbreak and spread of COVID-2019 have several implications for every aspect of human lives and the global economy. Coronavirus pandemic has affected day-to-day human lives and slowed down global economic activities. Many people are either affected or killed by the virus, according to the WHO. Globally, as of November 27, 2020, there have been 60,534,526 confirmed cases of COVID-2019, including 1,426,101 deaths. The most common symptoms of this viral infection are fever, cold, cough, bone pain, and breathing problems, and ultimately leading to pneumonia. This is a new viral disease affecting humans for the first time with no preventive vaccine. Thus, the emphasis is placed on taking extensive precautions such as extensive hygiene protocol (e.g., regularly washing of hands, avoidance of face-to-face interaction, etc.), social distancing, and wearing of masks (Haleem, Javaid, and Vaishya, 2020). This spread of the virus has led to countries banning international and local travels, gatherings of people, and strict quarantine to reduce the spread and break the exponential curve. The measures are good steps taken by the government of each country; however, they have dire implications on globalization which aim to bring people closer irrespective of distance.

The outbreak and spread of COVID-2019 have also affected day-to-day life, businesses, disrupted world trade, and movements. Most of the countries have slowed down the manufacturing of products due to restrictions on movement, low-income circulation, economic recession, loss of jobs, and reduction of tax generation, and so on. The various industries and sectors affected by the cause of this disease include the pharmaceuticals industry, solar power sector, tourism, information, education, and electronics industry. This virus creates significant knock-on effects on the daily life of citizens, as well as on the global economy (Haleem, Javaid and Vaishya, 2020).

The healthcare sector is one of the vital sectors that has been affected by the spread of the virus; there are a high number of patients that require diagnosis, quarantine, and treatment of suspected or confirmed cases, and in most cases, the facilities available cannot cater for the high number—this situation is most prevalent in the third world countries. Furthermore, to care for COVID-2019 patients, patients with other diseases and health problems were neglected. To compound the situation, medical officers were overworked and exposed to the virus while many have died due to exposure to the virus in the line of duty.

Recommendations for Policymakers and Future Research

Human history is laden with many socioeconomic and political developments and advancements, which aided the transformation of lives and global space into what it is today; however, there are challenges to development caused by humans themselves. Pandemics caused by infectious diseases are part of the challenges faced by humans which often affect historical narratives and development. COVID-2019 pandemic like every other pandemic discussed in this chapter had a devastating impact on the globe and it is yet to be overcome. The question that often comes to mind is, "why is history repeating itself?"

To avoid history repeating itself one must learn from past experiences. Thus, the following recommendations are suggested. First, governments are the major policymakers whenever there are emergencies such as the emergence of infectious diseases and natural disasters. As a major policymaker, the government of every country should be proactive in cases such as the outbreak of COVID-2019 by engaging all major stakeholders in decisions taken by the government to curb its spread. Also, governments of all countries should work together to finding a solution to curbing the spread of COVID-2019 instead of working separately. The government should also ensure fairness and accountability of bodies set up to handle COVID-2019 issues; this is because in Africa there are cases of fraud perpetrated by the CDC leading to mistrust of government policies and actions by the people.

Second, research institutions are set up with the sole aim of carrying out researches with a focus on finding the answer to some of the problems prevalent in society. This institution should be strengthened by the government through increased funding to enable it to function properly. Viruses and other infectious diseases should be researched upon and possible vaccines to protect people should be produced before the spread of the COVID-2019 and other forms of infectious diseases. Furthermore, heads of research institutions should treat any outbreak of the disease with the utmost alacrity even if such an outbreak is not in one's country. For example, when COVID-2019 broke out in Wuhan city of China and if research institutes of each country studied the virus to find a cure or vaccine without waiting for it to spread, the current situation may have been averted.

Third, health organizations such as the WHO and various health bodies in each country are the first point of contact between the government and the people. It is recommended that these health organizations should intensify the spread of awareness programs to the rural areas where are a large number of illiterates reside. Also, WHO should be responsible for curtailing the spread of any infectious diseases in any part of the world by spreading awareness of and risk of contracting such diseases. This would have positively and effectively forestalled the spread of COVID-2019 to other parts of the world.

Fourth, people have a very important role to play whenever there is an outbreak of infectious diseases. Obedience to the various preventive measures should be adhered to strictly without exemptions. Sanitation and cleanliness should be practiced religiously even after the curbing of COVID-2019. This is because most of the cases recorded were because of people flaunting preventive measures such as social distancing, wearing of facemask, constant hand washing, and restriction of movements.

Fifth, social infrastructures are poor and inadequate, especially in the Global South. As a result of this situation, there was a high spread of COVID-2019 in slums, public places, and transport terminals. Other social infrastructures which include the availability of water, food, access to medical treatment, and an uncrowded transport system should be made available. Although in the advanced nation of the Global North, there are higher cases compared to the South despite the provision of the aforementioned social amenities, this is perhaps due to the high number of aged people living in the cities in comparison to the South.

Sixth, and finally, religious institutions have a great role to play because, according to Karl Marx, "religion is the opium of the people." Thus, people then tend to listen more to their religious leaders than to the government or any other organization. The hysteria which is mostly associated with COVID-2019 has done more harm than the virus itself; many religious leaders believe the outbreak and spread of the virus is a punishment from God for all the sins committed by humans while others believe that it is a sign of the end of the world. All these misconceptions about the virus can be corrected if religious leaders address their followers and tell them the fact and truth needed to know about the pandemic.

REFERENCES

Balogun, J. A. (2020). Lessons from the USA delayed response to the COVID-19 pandemic. *African Journal of Reproductive Health* 24:14–21. Retrieved on

November 13, 2020 from https://www.ajrh.info/index.php/ajrh/article/view/2063 10.29063/ajrh2020/v24i1.2

Bryant, A, Black A., Land, F. and Porra, J. (2013). Information systems history: What is history? and why even bother with history? *Journal of Information Technology* 28(1):1–17. Retrieved on November 16, 2020 from https://doi.org/10.1057/jit.2013.3

Burrell, C. J. and Murphy, F. A. (2017). *Fenner and White's Medical Virology* (Fifth Edition), Academic Press, San Diego, United States: Elsevier Inc. Retrieved on November 15, 2020 from http://dx.doi.org/10.1016/B978-0-12-375156-0.00031-X

Carr, E. H. (1961). *What is History*? New York: Vintage.

Centers for Disease Control and Prevention—CDC. (2010). *H1N1 Flu*. The 2009 H1N1 Pandemic: Summary Highlights, April 2009–April 2010. Retrieved on November 15, 2021 from https://www.cdc.gov/h1n1flu/cdcresponse.htm#top.

Centers for Disease Control and Prevention—DCD. (2021). *Ebola (Ebola Virus Disease)*. What is Ebola Virus Disease? Retrieved on November 15, 2021 from https://www.cdc.gov/vhf/ebola/about.htmltop.

Cui, J., Li, F. and Shi, Z. (2019). Origin and evolution of pathogenic coronaviruses. *Nature Review Microbiology* 17:181–192. Retrieved on November 16, 2020 from https://doi.org/10.1038/s41579-018-0118-9.

European Commission, (October 2, 2020), E.U global response to COVID-19. Retrieved on November 16, 2020 from https://ec.europa.eu/international-partnerships/topics/eu-global-response-covid-19_en,23.

Fujita, M. and Hamaguchi, N. (August 16, 2020). Globalization and the COVID-19 pandemic: A spatial economics perspective. Retrieved on November 11, 2020 from https://voxeu.org/article/globalisation-and-covid-19-pandemic.

Galal, S. (December 17, 2020) Coronavirus (COVID-19) cases in Africa as of November 23, 2020, by country. Retrieved on November 24, 2020 from https://www.statista.com/statistics/1170463/coronavirus-cases-in-africa/.

Haleem, A., Javaid, M. and Vaishya, R. (April 10, 2020). Effects of COVID-19 pandemic in daily life. *Current Medicine Research and Practice* 10(2):78–79. Retrieved on November 27, 2020 from https://doi.org/10.1016/j.cmrp.2020.03.011.

History.com Editors. (January 30, 2020). Pandemics that changed history. Retrieved on November 6, 2020 from https://www.history.com/topics/middle-ages/pandemics-timeline.

Ihekweazu, C. and Agogo, E. (2020). Africa's response to COVID-19. *BMC Med* 18:151. Retrieved on November 23, 2020 from https://doi.org/10.1186/s12916-020-01622-w.

Jarus, O. (March 20, 2020). 20 of the worst epidemics and pandemics in history. *Live Science Contributor, all about history*. Retrieved on November 22, 2020 from https://www.livescience.com/worst-epidemics-and-pandemics-in-history.html.

Kahn, S. J. and McIntosh, K. (2005). History and recent advances in coronavirus discovery. *The Pediatric Infectious Disease Journal* 24(11):S223–S227. Retrieved on November 22, 2020 from doi: 10.1097/01.inf.0000188166.17324.60.

Little, D. (2017). Philosophy of history. *The Stanford Encyclopedia of Philosophy*. Retrieved on November 23, 2020 from https://plato.stanford.edu/archives/sum2017/entries/history/.

Lorenz, C. (2011). History and Theory. In *The Oxford History of Historical Writing, historical writing since 1945*. 5:13–36. Oxford University Press. Retrieved on November 23, 2020 from https://www.researchgate.net/publication/289802270_History_and_Theory_in_The_Oxford_History_of_Historical_Writing_vol_5_Historical_Writing_Since_1945_Oxford_University_Press_2011_13-36.

Mas-Coma, S., Jones, M. K. and Marty, A. M. (June 9, 2020). COVID-19 and globalization. *One Health (Amsterdam, Netherlands)*. Retrieved on November 23, 2020 from https://doi.org/10.1016/j.onehlt.2020.100132.

Nasson B. (2009). History; the meaning and role of history on human development. In Holton Robert and Nasson R. William (eds.), *World Civilization and History of Human Development*. Encyclopedia of life support system, Eolss Publisher, U.K. Retrieved on November 22, 2020 from https://www.eolss.net/sample-chapters/C04/E6-22-00-00.pdf

Nistha, S., Muhammad, Y. S., Osman U., Modasser, H. K, Ajlina, K., Uyen-Sa, D.T. Nguyen, Mahdi, B., Robert, W., Nasrin, A., Diana, C., Nahiduzzaman, K., Rafdzah, A. Z. and Ubydul, H. (2020). The impact of COVID-19 on globalization. *One Health* 11. Retrieved on November 23, 2020 from https://doi.org/10.1016/j.onehlt.2020.100180.

Public Health Online. (November 6, 2020). History's worst global pandemics: The history of pandemics: a telling story, Retrieved on November 23, 2020 from https://www.publichealthonline.org/worst-global-pandemics-in-history.

Puritt, S. (January 31, 2019). How colonization death toll may have affected earth's climate; did the mass death of the indigenous American's cool down the planet? Retrieved on November 10, 2020 from https://www.history.com/news/climate-change-study-colonization-death-farming-collapse.

Saker, L., Lee, K., Cannito, B., Gilmore, A. and Campbell-Lendrum, D. (2004). *Globalization and Infectious Diseases: A Review of the Linkages*. Social Economics, and Behavioral (SEB) Research, UNICEF/UNDP/World Bank/WHO. Geneva, Switzerland.

Singh, R., Gupta, V., Malhotra, B., Singh, S., Ravindran, P., Meena, P., Gupta, J., Mathur, V. K., Mathur, R. P., Singh, S., Sharma, P., Sharma, H., Bhandari, S., Gupta, N., Sapkal, G., Mourya, D. T. and Speer, M. D. (2021). Cluster containment strategy: Addressing Zika virus outbreak in Rajasthan, India *BMJ Global Health* 2019(4):e001383.

The Economic Times/Panache. (March 26, 2020). Jack Ma's coronavirus testing kits reach Nigeria. Retrieved on December 31, 2020 from https://economictimes.indiatimes.com/magazines/panache/jack-mas-coronavirus-testing-kits-reach-nigeria/articleshow/74829029.cms.

Tyrrell, D. A. and Bynoe, M. L. (1966). Cultivation of viruses from a high proportion of patients with colds. *Lancet* 1(7428):76–77. Retrieved on October 31, 2020 from doi: 10.1016/s0140-6736(66)92364-6. PMID: 4158999.

Walsh, B. (March 26, 2020). COVID-19: The history of pandemics. Retrieved on November 6, 2020 from https://www.bbc.com/future/article/20200325-covid-19-the-history-of-pandemics.

World Health Organization—WHO Africa. (August 13, 2020). COVID-19 in Africa: Marking six months of response; Communities, health workers, governments rally to combat the COVID-19 pandemic. Retrieved on November 23, 2020 from https://www.afro.who.int/covid-19-africa-marking-six-months-response.

Yaya, S., Otu, A. and Labonté, R. (June 24, 2020). Globalization in the time of COVID-19: Repositioning Africa to meet the immediate and remote challenges. *Global Health* 16:51. Retrieved on November 11, 2020 from https://doi.org/10.1186/s12992-020-00581-4.

Chapter 16

Corolaw

Osman Ibrahim Kabba

It was Rene Dubos who stated that any attempt to shape the world and modify human personality in order to create a self-chosen pattern of life involves many unknown consequences. Human destiny is bound to remain a gamble, because at some unpredictable time and in some unforeseeable manner nature will strike back (Dubos, 2018). From this proposition, it can be stated that everyone's fantasy is a utopia where diseases are conquered, and the only thing left is to die of old age (Dubos, 1959). As this pandemic has taught us, such a utopia is neither possible nor desirable. Dubos argued that organized species such as ants have established a satisfactory equilibrium with their environment and suffer no great waves of disease or changes in their social structure. But as for mankind, we are essentially dynamic, and our way of life constantly in flux from century to century. We experiment with synthetic products that change our diet, we build cities that breed rats and infection, we build automobiles and factories which pollute the air, and we construct radioactive bombs. As life becomes more comfortable and technology more complicated, new factors introduce new dangers; the ingredients for utopia are the agents of new disease. This may sound discouraging to a world looking for a cure-all in medical research, but actually it is affirmative—even hopeful. Once we accept the fact that complete freedom from disease and from struggle is almost incompatible with the process of living, we will know that our aspirations cannot be satisfied with health and easy life. The good news is we will stop panicking.

Indeed, globalization and interconnectedness have thrust upon the world many opportunities as well as challenges. Migration is an important part of human endeavor. So, as people move from place to place, like their culture, the diseases they also carry are transmittable as well. Such was the case with SARS-CoV-2, known as the novel coronavirus which began like all new viruses with an ordinary moment. As a group of patients admitted to a hospital with pneumonia turned out to have a new strain of coronavirus, the virus's high transmissibility made the epidemic in China turn into a global pandemic (Horton, 2020). With an ongoing daily briefing of new cases and deaths, panic and pandemonium set in. However, as fast as viruses spread, the detection of pandemics and taking early measures became much easier due to the advancement of science in today's world.

Yet, successful response by the world's industrialized nations in minimizing the transmission and containing its spread has depended to a greater extent upon many factors, least of which is not the form of governments under which the nations operate. Under a democracy, for instance, civil liberties and individual freedoms posed an obstacle to leadership in containing the virus. In an oligarchy, like Russia, very little if any resistance was encountered by Putin in deciding what was good for all people. The early responses and measures adopted by China, such as early reporting and situation monitoring, large-scale surveillance, and preparation of medical facilities and supplies, were all successful in reducing the epidemic in China generally and in the epicenter Wuhan specifically.

One of the foci of this chapter is the effectiveness of the measures taken by governments at every level in the United States, including federal, state, and municipal and to assess the response of the citizenry in stopping Coronavirus Disease (COVID-2019) from spreading, and by comparing those responses across states to SARS and COVID-2019 outbreaks, which will provide an example for the communities, health managers, and leaders of other countries to follow on how to prepare, detect, and respond to potential outbreaks.

The year 2020 has been a time quite unlike any other in the last century of human existence. Some families around the world have lost loved ones and livelihoods to the COVID-2019 pandemic, which continues to create extraordinary uncertainty about the future for millions. With no cure in sight and vaccines in their late-stage clinical trials, personal preventive measures mandated by governments and health experts to lessen the chain of transmission in the interim have for the most part being challenged at the federal, state, and municipal levels. At the individual and group levels, they have been drowned out by claims of individual liberties and political drumbeats. This in turn has exacerbated panic and hysteria.

Thus, the scope and the delimitation of this chapter need to be stated here. As mentioned earlier, COVID-2019 is quite unlike any pandemic the world has known. The mysteries surrounding its origin and how rapidly it has spread to become such a global contagion have exacerbated the uncertainties with which people and their national governments have responded either in cooperation with or against one another. Therefore, some actions taken by governments to protect their citizens from contracting and spreading the virus have been met with skepticism and fierce resistance. Hence, putting the chaos in context to make sense of it requires that clearly defined boundaries and demarcations are established. The scope and delimitations of this chapter therefore define the topic and set the boundaries within which the problem is explored. The scope, on the one hand, details the depth into which this chapter goes to explore the research question and the parameters within which it operates in relation to the population and time frame. The delimitation, on the other hand, establishes the parameters of what was studied and the factors not to be included in the investigation.

This chapter therefore examines the hysteria caused by the novel coronavirus in the wake of its outbreak in November 2019 and its devastating impact on all Americans, including America's political and civic life. It discusses further the influences of authoritative actions on the people, the economy, schools, and more.

The chapter also explains how ordinary citizens are coping not only with the spread of the virus, but also with the proliferation of mandates by their governments and how these coping mechanisms have turned into fear, anxiety, and even paranoia. Such conditions, even when the virus was at its initial subclinical stage, have tended to be a product of personal, predisposition factors, as well as shared cultural influences, including religious, literary, film, and gaming, all of which have led to emotional and less than rational responses. They have rendered people vulnerable to engage in implausible conspiracy theories about the causes of illness and governmental responses to it. They have also led the government and people to lend credibility to unsophisticated and unempirical misrepresentations about medications and devices which are claimed to prevent, treat, or cure disease. In short, such vulnerability has created predatory opportunities for the unscrupulous.

As Horton (2020) rightly observed, a pandemic like the novel coronavirus engages multiple triggers for anxiety and fear and carries particularly sensitive connotations—particularly because they bring with them the prospect of terrible numbers of fatalities. People's sense of trust is challenged by what is liable to be a pandemic of fear—not only are people afraid of the emerging infection but as Axe, Briggs, and Richards (2020) suggested, people become fearful of the state, the governments and institutions as though they are the sources of potential transmission of a fatal infection to us. Horton (2020) acknowledged that pandemics are universally disruptive. That they are associated with a score of psychosocial stressors, including health threats to oneself and loved ones. There may be severe disruptions of routines, separation from family and friends, shortages of food and medicine, wage loss, social isolation due to quarantine or other social distancing programs, and school closure. Additionally, hospital and medical facilities can break down under the pressure of the overwhelming number of patients to which they cannot cater. There can be a feeling that the fabrics of our communities are buckling, and social structures are faltering under the pressure of the medical crisis.

What is mass hysteria? In sociology and psychology, mass hysteria (also known as mass psychogenic illness, collective hysteria, group hysteria, or collective obsessional behavior) is a phenomenon that transmits collective illusions of threats, whether real or imaginary, through a population and society as a result of rumors and fear (Wolf, 1976). In medicine, the term mass hysteria is used to describe the spontaneous manifestation—or production of chemicals in the body—of the same or similar hysterical physical symptoms by more than one person (Bartholomew, Robert E.; Wesley, Simon, 2002). A common type of mass hysteria occurs when a group of people believe they are suffering from a similar disease or ailment, sometimes referred to as mass psychogenic illness or epidemic hysteria.

In this chapter, mass hysteria, interchangeably described as epidemic hysteria, is the quality of citizens' response to pandemic, not necessarily the fear of the disease itself, but the response to the emergency authority exercised by governments at all levels, including federal, state, and local authorities (Arnold, 2018). Hysteria can be defined as a feature of some conditions that involve people experiencing physical symptoms that have a psychological cause. It is a state that occurs between two or more people who share beliefs related to symptoms suggestive of an organic illness. Research suggests that real pandemics can lead to such mass hysteria. A key factor that creates hysteria around pandemics is that the population's ability to remain calm and react logically to the situation at hand is blurred and unfocused due to the anxiety and fear felt by large groups of people.

The issue of mass hysteria among citizens brought on by the confusion and uncertainties that ensued the uncoordinated response by governments at the federal, state, and local levels is the main focus of this study. I argue that while the spread of the virus and the ensuing death toll have undoubtedly spread fear and pandemonium among people, the governments' response to the virus through its arbitrary use of emergency authority has by comparison caused more hysteria than the pandemic itself. Instances of those rules and regulations enacted at the federal, state, and local level that may have contributed to the mass hysteria among citizens and communities in the United States are examined.

The pandemic hysteria is exacerbated by many factors. Key among those factors is the origin of the virus, which according to news accounts originated from a laboratory in the village of Wuhan in China. There were three factors which were dramatically accelerating the transmission of the new disease. First, according to official hedged reports from the Chinese government, people were getting the disease easily from other people, not just animals; otherwise called human-to-human spread. Second, it was being spread by people who didn't show any symptoms; this is called asymptomatic spread. Finally, by a conservative estimate, 50 percent of the people were infected but showed no symptoms. This meant a once-in-a-lifetime health emergency, a virus out of control with a vast amount of the spread not immediately detectable. And it had already traveled far from Wuhan, China, where the outbreak apparently began.

Despite concerted efforts by many infected nations to contain the spread of the disease, it spread rapidly like wildfire. In the prologue of his world-acclaimed book *Rage*, Woodward (2020) noted that the Chinese had essentially quarantined Wuhan, a city of 11 million people, larger than any American city. He stated that people could not travel within China, say from Wuhan to Beijing. But the Chinese government had not cut off travel from China to the rest of the world, including the United States. That meant a highly infectious and devastating virus was probably already silently streaming into the United States.

The number of cases in the United States alone (in 2021) had exceeded 10 million with over 250,000 dead, making the United States the world's most infected nation carrying 20 percent of the global caseload and 25 percent of the deceased. The devastating impact has been felt in all sectors of human endeavor. The economy has tanked with over 25 million unemployed. Small businesses, especially in the service industry, like gymnasiums, restaurants, and small retail stores have been forced to shut down, some temporarily and a majority permanently. According to the Centers for Disease Control and Prevention (CDC), over 7 million people have been infected and well over 200,000 have been reported dead. The situation according to experts could get worse. It is estimated that close to 400,000 lives could be lost by early 2021 (CDC, 2020) and nearly 2 million globally.

Every level of government in the United States, including federal, state, and local, invoked their emergency authorities granted to them by the constitution to act quickly to contain the spread of and eradicate the virus as quickly as possible. Since the federal government's jurisdiction under this circumstance is mainly at the diplomatic and foreign relations level, the president issued over 20 COVID-2019-related proclamations, which among others included travel into and exit from the United States and territories by foreign nationals. With exemptions for essential personnel, the U.S. State Department and the Department of Homeland Security issued restriction orders to all U.S. embassies and border personnel to prevent entry of non-essential personnel into the United States.

At the state and local levels, emergency laws and ordinances have been passed by state governors and municipal authorities to combat the disease while containing its person-to-person transmission and subsequent spread. To this end, governors in all 50 states have ordered the shutdown of most state buildings, and in particular state offices providing non-essential services. Those providing essential services are made to operate at the least minimally safe capacity. In New Jersey, for instance, some crucial but non-essential state operations, such as children and family welfare operations, have been carried out by employees working from their homes. Both non-profit and for-profit organizations with small business operations, particularly those with limited capacity to enforce safe distancing between their clients like gyms, restaurants and bars, mosques, synagogues, and churches in most states have been ordered to practice safe distancing or are told to shut down if they cannot.

There is an abundance of literature on the mass hysteria the coronavirus pandemic has caused among and across communities in most affected areas of the world, particularly the United States. Hitherto, very little if any literature exists on the contributory effects of the laws the federal, state, and local governments have passed at every level of government to combat, contain, and by and large eradicate the virus.

Thus, the concept of *Corolaw* that undergirds this chapter is a mixture of its two constituent words: (1) coronavirus and (2) law. Like the preceding and succeeding chapters in this book, it was coined for its phonetic and catchy appeal to readers. It is used to attract attention to those emergency laws, as distinct from non-emergency ones, that were enacted in response to the coronavirus pandemic.

The challenges of federalism and the legal developments between the federal government and the states, between one state and another state, and between governments at the various level within a state and their citizens made it difficult for governments to exercise their emergency authority in an effort to control, contain, and eradicate COVID-2019. Emergency authority was exercised through emergency laws exacted by federal, state, and local governments: international and domestic travel restrictions; laws governing quarantine of citizens; closure of public and private enterprises at the federal, state, and local levels; laws and ordinances with respect to public safety such as wearing mask; social distancing in public gatherings, schools, restaurants, parks, beaches; and business closures.

Consequently, Corolaw is probed in this chapter using two interconnected questions: (1) In what ways have federal, state, and municipal laws passed in response to COVID-2019 crisis impacted individual liberties? (2) In what ways have communities responded to these laws?

I argue in this chapter that notwithstanding the spirit and intent of these antiviral laws, that is, lockdown of service industries, social distancing in designated crowd-prone areas, and masking, these measures are not only infringement on civil liberties but also produce isolations and entrapment in communities. Consequently there has been an increase in suicide and drug addiction within communities. The author further argues that though well intentioned for the most part, many people believe these mandates are leveraged for political reasons. Furthermore, while the spread of the virus has obviously caused mass hysteria, the reasons previously cited are the main sources of much of the panic experienced by communities.

METHODOLOGICAL APPROACH

In political philosophy, a government's legitimacy and moral right to use state power is only justified and lawful when consented to by the people or society over which that political power is exercised (Nozick, 2014). It explains why the Constitution of the United States, for instance, starts with the infamous words "We the People." As such, the methodological approach by which the questions of this research were probed and answered must involve the citizenry, whose tacit consent provides the state to govern them. Historically, this theory of consent is contrasted to the divine right of kings and had often been invoked against the legitimacy of colonialism. Article 21 of the United Nations 1948 Universal Declaration of Human Rights states the following: "The will of the people shall be the basis of the authority of government." Quite often, the limit of state authority and the consent of the citizenry are tested under varying conditions and circumstances.

To this end, the appropriate methodological approach used in this study is the qualitative expert study. This method of qualitative empirical research has been a widely used qualitative method in political and social research since the early 1990s. Accordingly, while it emphasizes the importance of investigating experiences and perspectives of the interviewees for developing a better understanding of social reality, it also aims at exploring or collecting data about a specific field of interest (Edwards and Holland, 2013). This approach, therefore, will help us understand the role governments at every level have played in fermenting hysteria while trying to contain the spread and eradicate the virus. This methodological approach is the most appropriate approach that will examine these concepts through citizens the extent to which emergency authority may have exacerbated the hysteria caused by the COVID-2019. The data consisted of observational notes and semi-structured interviews of 21 residents of New Jersey with divergent political ideologies, views, practices, and participations. The data were analyzed using the method of content analysis and cross-verified through the process of data source triangulation.

The fundamental reason for employing this methodological approach to do this research was to comprehend the hysteria caused by the pandemic and to understand the extent to which federal, state, and local laws may have contributed to the hysteria. Also, as a tool for building knowledge, it is intended to enlighten readers about what is happening in their communities. In essence, it will expand the horizon of existing knowledge by filling the gaps in knowledge through the discovery of new information about the spread of the virus. Last, but by no means the least, it synthesizes a blueprint of how institutions should prepare to respond to emergency situations such as the one posed by the COVID-2019 pandemic. And while everyone should doubtlessly be taking coronavirus seriously, the hysteria surrounding the disease, on both social and governmental levels, has realistically done more direct damage to global quality of living than the disease itself. This chapter explains why that hysteria is so dangerous.

In the succeeding section of this chapter, the theoretical framework that underpins the study is discussed. This includes the theorist's ideas, support for, and critique of the main concepts and ideas. Then the synthesis of competing positions is discussed. Following the theoretical underpinning is an introduction of the case under review. Here, supporting, opposing, and competing views are enunciated. Following the theory, the actual case is described with supporting, opposing, and competing views enunciated.

THEORETICAL FRAMEWORK

In this section, the theories that inform the citizens' responses to the various laws instituted by federal, state, and local governments are expounded. The theoretical perspectives are couched on the following three rhetorical questions: (1) When society is hit with a problem as huge as this pandemic that requires collective efforts to resolve, should the state or government be the primary tool used to solve the problems? (2) How much responsibility is prudent to entrust to the state or government? (3) Are governments usually suited to solve the problems of society in the best manner possible, or does delegating more responsibility to the government or the state to deal with create more problems than its worth? To answer these questions, I draw upon the views of John Rawls and Robert Nozick, two leading American political philosophers of our time, in order to contextualize the responses of the people to the governments' collective instituted measures to the virus through their seminal works, namely a theory of *justice as fairness* (Rawls, 1999) and political liberalism (Rawls, 1996), and Nozick's *Anarchy, State, and Utopia* (Feser, 2005).

Rawls's Justice as Fairness Theory describes a society where free citizens with equal basic rights coexist within an egalitarian socioeconomic system. Then, his Political Liberalism Theory explains the legitimate use of political power in a democracy and envisions how civic unity might endure despite the diversity of worldviews that free institutions allow (Rawls, 1996, 1999).

However, Robert Nozick takes a binary approach in his political philosophy by recognizing state authority but sparingly relegating limited power and authority to states and government. In his *Anarchy, State, and Utopia*, Nozick presses the anti-consequentialist features of John Rawls's *A Theory of Justice* by arguing that respect for individual rights should be the key standard for assessing state action and, hence, that the only legitimate state is a minimal state that restricts its activities to the protection of the rights of life, liberty, property, and contract (Nozick, 1976).

The restrictive measures imposed on the citizens by governments in the wake of this pandemic across the world, and in the United States particularly, would clearly be challenged with Rawlsian precepts on state policy and popular welfare and Nozickian political philosophy on the minimal state. As the coronavirus spreads, initial appeals to the public and now enforced ordinances such as social distancing, washing one's hands, and wearing a mask in public gatherings, and the like appear to be focused primarily on the individual's self-interest and the public of not contracting the disease or spreading the disease to others for those already afflicted. While such appeals would seem to fit well within the context of Rawls's liberalism and its focus on individual rights, yet Rawls takes an issue with the imposition of a unified law on a diverse citizenry in that it raises two fundamental challenges. The first is the challenge of *legitimacy*: the legitimate use of coercive political power. Rawls argues that it would be impossible to use legitimate power to coerce all citizens to follow, say for instance one law in particular, given that citizens would inevitably hold quite different worldviews? The second challenge is the challenge of *stability*, which looks at political power from the perspective of the citizens. Why would a citizen willingly obey the law if it is imposed on her by a collective body many of whose members have beliefs and values quite dissimilar to their own? Yet, unless most citizens willingly and collectively obey the law, there will be no social order or stability but anarchy and hysteria.

Rawls responds to those challenges of legitimacy and stability with his theory of political liberalism. He argues that in a democracy, political power willingly given by consent is in essence the collective power of the people as a unified body. In light of the diversity within a democracy, what would it mean for citizens legitimately to exercise coercive political power over one another? Rawls's test for the acceptable use of political power in a democracy is his liberal principle of legitimacy:

Political power can be fully exercised if it based on a constitution that allows free and equal citizens to reasonably accept or reject. According to this principle, political power may only be used in ways that all citizens can reasonably be expected to endorse. The use of political power must fulfill a criterion of reciprocity: citizens must reasonably believe that all citizens can reasonably accept the enforcement of a particular set of basic laws. Those coerced by law must be able to endorse the society's fundamental political arrangements freely, not because they are dominated or manipulated or kept uninformed.

The liberal principle of legitimacy strengthens the challenge of legitimacy: how can any particular set of basic laws legitimately be imposed upon a pluralistic citizenry? What constitution could all citizens reasonably be expected to endorse? Rawls's answer to this challenge begins by explaining what it would mean for citizens to be reasonable.

The implications of Rawls's theoretical perspective are guided by his ideas of justice as fairness espoused by its two principles of justice: (1) that each person has the same indefeasible claim to a fully adequate scheme of equal basic liberties, with a one-size-fits-all scheme compatible to all regardless of their status in society; and (2) that social and economic inequalities are to satisfy the following conditions: that fundamental liberties are to be embodied in the political constitution, while the second principle applies primarily to economic institutions. Fulfillment of the basic constitutional right takes priority over actualization of the second principle, and within the second principle fair equality of opportunity takes priority over the difference principle.

The first principle affirms that all citizens should have the familiar basic rights and liberties: liberty of conscience and freedom of association, freedom of speech and liberty of the person, the rights to vote, to hold public office, to be treated in accordance with the rule of law, and so on. The first principle accords these rights and liberties to all citizens equally. Unequal rights would not benefit those who would get a lesser share of the rights, so justice requires equal rights for all, in all normal circumstances.

Rawls's first principle confirms widespread convictions about the importance of equal basic rights and liberties. Two further features make this principle distinctive. First is its priority: the basic rights and liberties must not be traded off against other social goods. The first principle disallows, for instance, a policy that would give draft exemptions to college students on the grounds that educated civilians will increase economic productivity. The draft is a drastic infringement on basic liberties, and if a draft is implemented then all who are able to serve must be equally subject to it, even if this means slower growth. Citizens' equal liberty must have priority over economic policy.

The second distinguishing feature of Rawls's first principle is that it requires *fair value of the political liberties*. The political liberties are a subset of the basic liberties, concerned with the right to hold public office, the right to affect the outcome of national elections, and so on. For these liberties, Rawls requires that citizens should be not only formally but also substantively equal. That is, citizens who are similarly endowed and motivated should have similar opportunities to hold office, to influence elections, and so on regardless of how rich or poor they are. This fair value proviso has major implications for how elections should be funded and run, as will be discussed below.

Rawls's second principle of justice has two parts. The first part, fair equality of opportunity, requires that citizens with the same talents and willingness to use them have the same educational and economic opportunities regardless of whether they were born rich or poor. He argues that in all parts of society there are to be roughly the same prospects of culture and achievement for those similarly motivated and endowed.

Robert Nozick takes a counter-approach to Rawls's binary approach of the maximin state. In that Nozick did not believe power should be relegated to the government. Instead Nozick argued that deference for individual rights is the key standard for judging state action and, hence, that the only legitimate state is a minimal state that restricts its activities to the protection of the rights of life, liberty, property, and contract.

In the first question, for instance, "When society is hit with a problem as huge as this pandemic that require collective efforts to resolve, should the state or government be the primary tool used to solve the problems?" Rawls will answer in the affirmative that big government could arbitrate societal problems. In his Justice as Fairness Theory, he lays out what he believes is the just distribution of social goods and then suggests that it's the state's duty to tax and redistribute accordingly to ensure that distribution remains equitable and balanced.

There are many thinkers who would disagree with Rawls that government isn't the best way to solve problems. This is the position of those who postulate that human beings began in the state of nature. As such, they do not believe that centralizing power into a single body called "the government" is going to produce any better results than what could otherwise be produced with private enterprises. Those thinkers are classified as anarchistic in their philosophical thinking.

Yet, the philosopher who struck a balance between Rawls and the anarchists was Robert Nozick. In his seminal work, *Anarchy, State, and Utopia*, Nozick distinguishes between three political philosophies: (1) anarchism, (2) the state, and (3) utopia (Herbjørnsrud, 2002).

In the first chapter on anarchy, Nozick establishes some complicity with the Anarchist's aversion to government but soon became circumspect ultimately at aspects that he deemed extreme. Nozick recognizes the libertarian nature of the anarchists and conceded that such a state was bound to be chaotic (Metcalf, 2011). In the second chapter on the state, Nozick then establishes the type of state he thought was best. Here we find that Nozick was not a fan of there being an organic state. How big should the government be and what exactly should it do? Nozick is a fan of what he would call "the minimal state." The best way to start understanding what he means by this is probably to contrast him with both the work of Rawls and the anarchists of his time.

Wolfe (2008) has argued that a large portion of Robert Nozick's *Anarchy, State, and Utopia* is dedicated to refuting the theories of John Rawls. Specifically, Nozick takes an exception to Rawls's conception of distributive justice as it pertains to economic inequalities. Rawls wrote that economic inequalities should only be permitted if they are to the benefit of society, and especially if they are to the benefit of its least advantaged members; this has come to be known as "the difference principle." Nozick believed that no one had any business "permitting" economic inequalities at all. To Nozick, as long as economic inequalities arise from voluntary exchange, they cannot be unjust.

In spite of the philosophical differences between John Rawls and Robert Nozick, they are nonetheless suitable for this analysis insofar as how they perceive the role of government ought to be, particularly in response to the COVID-2019 crisis. This is so because they both capture all the nuances through their contradictions and philosophical dissimilarities and distinctiveness and help us capture the broad contours of the popular responses. Communities in the United States exhibit dissimilar characteristics and behave differently based on race, social class, and political affiliation. As such, we can outline responses to the crisis into categories which are due to contextual variables that are consistent to each of the strata. For these reasons, we are inclined to adopt these theories for our expert analyses.

THE EMERGENCY POWERS OF GOVERNMENTS IN THE TIME OF THE COVID-2019 PANDEMIC

In this section, my focus is to establish the legal basis for government intervention in an emergency situation and we analyze citizens' response to those interventions. Our analysis will illustrate the challenges and tensions between the people and their governments as well as intergovernmental challenges. The analysis will illustrate the challenges and tensions within governments and between the people and governments.

As much that remains unknown about COVID-2019, there is also much that is known. It is generally accepted that COVID-2019 is a highly infectious and transmissible disease that can spread easily and quickly from person to person through respiratory droplets. While we are aware of the exponential rise in mortality rate, we are starkly aware that survival requires vigilance on the part of government and people to follow and abide by all stipulations made by government to contain the spread of the virus. Yet, as governments (federal, state, and local) try to assert their authority, the more resistance they encounter from the citizens and their local representatives.

Take, for instance, this report filed by the Associated Press reporters John Hanna and Heather Hollingsworth in the month of November 2020. State governor Laura Kelly issued a new mask mandate with hopes of lessening the spread of the coronavirus in Kansas after the state again reported another record seven-day increase in new cases. However, state law still allows the state's 105 counties to opt out of such an order especially from a Democratic governor, as most did when Kelly issued a similar order in July. But the state's rolling seven-day average for new coronavirus cases is now more than nine times higher than it was than when her first order took effect (Hanna and Hollingsworth, 2020).

Accordingly, the governor's order takes effect November 25, 2020, the day before Thanksgiving, and only in counties that do not yet have their own mask mandates, although that is still a majority of them. Kelly said she was giving counties without mandates a week to draft their own alternatives. Her order requires people to wear a "face covering" in indoor public spaces and in public spaces outdoors where social distancing is not possible (Hanna and Hollingsworth, 2020).

Also, in New York State, Governor Andrew Cuomo has imposed a new tab of restrictions on three key sources of COVID-2019 spread in New York, citing spiraling viral rates in the nation and across the globe that threaten to intensify numbers locally as the holidays loom. Announced on November 13, 2020, the governor's new measures took effect three days later. At that juncture, any establishment licensed by the State Liquor Authority, including bars, restaurants, and bowling alleys, must close dining areas at 10:00 p.m.; they can do curbside food-only pickup afterward. Gyms must also close at 10:00 p.m. (Chelsea, 2020).

Small social gatherings at private homes are also the target of Cuomo's restrictions. Citing these gatherings as the third "great spreader" identified by contract tracing, Cuomo indicated that those will be capped at 10, similar to the restriction Governor Ned Lamont recently put in place in Connecticut (Chelsea, 2020).

However, pushback did not emanate from the citizens but local government authorities when the governor conferred the task of enforcement on local governments. This has raised some contention between the New York State and local municipalities. A local sheriff, flat-out refused to carry out the governor's orders, citing invasion to privacy (Chelsea, 2020).

New York State and Kansas are not the only exceptions where challenges have been mounted against state authority. Some states refused to institute enforceable mandates out of concerns for a backlash as has been experienced in New York.

The New York Police Department will aid in enforcement in the city, Cuomo said, adding that after 10:00 p.m., "If the lights are on and people are drinking, they get a summons." The governor also said that the restrictions will last indefinitely and warned that the state could further tighten the health guidelines (Chelsea, 2020).

As of this writing, cases and mortality rate due to the disease have spiked exponentially. The CDC has reported that the number of cases in the United States has reached 10 million while the death rate has exceeded a quarter of a million. November 2020 saw the highest spike in both death and cases, with the CDC and health expert reporting that by spring mortality could rise to half a million (CDC, 2020).

Consequently, national and local governments have adopted extraordinary measures to counter the threat of infection and control and/or stop the chain of transmission. When faced with major crises—terrorist attacks, natural disasters, economic turmoil, or biological threats—the people look to their governments for protection, help, assistance, leadership, and assurance. As such, crises thrust upon the government both the motive and opportunity to act quickly to bring the crises to an end or under control.

According to the World Health Organization (WHO, 2020), the virus has now spread and encapsulated the entire globe, with well over 81 countries infected since its outbreak in Wuhan, China, in November 2019. There are now over 54,328,752 reported cases globally. In the United States, there are over 2,000,000 reported cases and well over 250,000 dead as of November 2020 (WHO, 2020). As is typically the case with contagious diseases, false news, overblown risk assessments, and conspiracy theories have spread quickly, inducing plague-level fears surrounding a disease that by all accounts whose actual origin is unknown.

Declaring a State of Emergency

To date, more than half of the world's democracies have declared a state of emergency in response to the coronavirus. In the United States, the secretaries of Health and Human Services and Homeland Security declared a public health emergency and emergency travel restrictions, respectively. On January 31, under the Public Health Service Act in response to COVID-2019, and, on March 13, President Donald Trump, invoking presidential powers under the constitution and the National Emergencies Act, declared that the COVID-2019 outbreak in the United States constituted a national emergency. In addition, all 50 states in the United States have declared a "state of emergency" in response to COVID-2019.

As Davis (2020) has observed, it is democracies that have been more likely to declare a state of emergency than nations with autocracies, with 54 percent of the world's democratic governments declaring a COVID-2019-related emergency compared with 33 percent of autocratic regimes. Unsurprisingly according to Davis (2020), when one considers it, autocracies already enjoy vast powers and do not need to declare an emergency to aggregate more power.

In the past few months, in the United States, we have witnessed numerous extraordinary measures adopted by various governments at every level, federal, state, and municipal in response to COVID-2019. While many of those measures make common sense, few have been challenged for their validation to limit or encroach upon fundamental rights such as freedom to assembly or freedom of movement in the face of COVID-2019. In several states, the obligation to wear face masks when going outside or, indeed, an order to stay indoors for a period of time, has also gone largely unchallenged. Certain limitations on the freedom of religion have been justified on the basis of preventing the congregants from spreading the virus during worship in churches, synagogues, and mosques. Other, more controversial measures such as enhanced surveillance and tracking, and contract tracing involve the right to privacy.

As Nozick (2002) argued, the government's ability to act swiftly, decisively (and, where needed, secretly) against major threats frequently becomes superior to limitations on governmental powers and to individual rights. Thus, crises tend to result in the expansion of governmental powers and the concentration of powers in the hands of the executive. They also result in derogations from, limitations imposed on, and contraction of individual freedoms and liberties. Some state governments have enthusiastically embraced such opportunities to extend their authorities.

However, the U.S. Constitution does not explicitly or implicitly make any references to states of emergency and to emergency powers. Nonetheless, the U.S. Constitution does not explicitly or implicitly make any references to states of emergency and to emergency powers, even though it allocates certain war-related powers both to Congress (declare war, raise armies, provide for a navy) and the Chief Executive (commander-in-chief). But where emergencies are concerned, the constitution is lacking in any detail and, in any event, it does not refer at all to nonviolent, non-war-related, emergencies.

The absence of clear constitutional provisions relative to emergencies was not the result of unintentional omission or lack of attention but rather of a conscious decision by the founding fathers. The rationale for their omission is explained by both Alexander Hamilton and James Madison, respectively.

Alexander Hamilton noted that it was impossible to foresee or to define the extent and variety of national emergencies, and the correspondent extent and variety of the means which may be necessary to satisfy them. The circumstances that endanger the safety of nations are infinite, and for this reason no constitutional shackles can wisely be imposed on the power to which the care of it is committed. This power ought to be coextensive with all the possible combinations of such circumstances (Chernow, 2005).

James Madison was concerned that if emergency powers were explicitly provided for in the constitutional document, attempts to restrain the use of such powers and to check potential abuses may be not only futile but outright dangerous, for it is in vain to oppose constitutional barriers to the impulse of self-preservation. This is because it implants into the constitution the usurpation of power.

Governments are conferred upon expansive emergency powers with the perception that the expansion and concentration of powers, and the contraction of rights, are likely to be temporally limited. Therefore, emergency powers are designed to respond to a particular exigency and then be removed as soon as, or shortly after, that emergency has been met successfully. The idea that extraordinary, even draconian, measures are to be temporary makes the nature of such measures easier to accept by the citizens.

In constitutional democracies like the United States, unexpected powers are conferred on the belief in the ability to separate crises from normality, and exceptional measures from ordinary legal rules and norms, confining the application of the former to extraordinary times, insulating periods of normality from the infringement of vast powers. Emergency must constitute no more than an exception to that rule—it must last only a relatively short time and yield no substantial permanent effects. Application of emergency powers is designed to be of a temporary nature, to serve as a bridge between pre-crisis and post-crisis normalcy.

Once brought to life, some emergency measures are not so easily terminable. Emergency powers thus become the norm, the ordinary state of affairs. Time-bound emergency legislation is often the subject of future extensions and renewals. It is commonplace to find on the statute books legislative acts that had originally been enacted as temporary emergency measures but subsequently transformed into permanent legislation. The same is true also with respect to legislation that, albeit not couched in terms of special emergency legislation, functions in similar ways with the attendant opportunities and dangers involved.

Consider, for example, a fairly benign example: the Defense Production Act (DPA). This act was first enacted in 1950 during the Harry Truman presidency to help his administration with the Korean War effort. It granted the authority to the executive branch to demand that private manufacturers give priority to defense production, to products related to critical infrastructure, homeland security, and stockpiling, so long as doing so was in the interest of national defense—as broadly defined (Else, 2009).

President Truman used the broad interpretations of the DPA to cap wages and impose price controls on the steel industry (after failing to takeover certain steel mills). Thereon the DPA has since been routinely used by the Department of Defense to ensure that military-related orders are given priority within the U.S. supply chain, and by Federal Emergency Management Agency to prioritize contracts for housing, food, and water in the wake of natural disasters. In the state of New Jersey, for instance, Governor Murphy has used emergency authority granted by the legislatures to keep state workers working from their homes with the prospect of making this permanent after the pandemic, rather than a temporary measure.

After initially refusing to invoke the DPA, President Donald Trump eventually decided to invoke the law and, on March 18, 2020, issued an executive order prioritizing and allocating health and medical resources to respond to the spread of COVID-2019. And on March 27, the president invoked the DPA to require General Motors to produce more ventilators and has later issued similar demands to other companies, including 3M. Now, demanding that the government's orders for supply of masks and ventilators makes a lot of sense. However, under the DPA, the executive may also waive, for example, anti-trust restrictions. A voluntary agreement could be used to coordinate production among several businesses even though such coordination would normally run afoul of anti-trust statutes (Else, 2009).

Invoking the act in times of emergency may make sense. Yet, it is part of our regular legal terrain and may be invoked in situations that do not amount to a true emergency in order to bypass the protections incorporated into the anti-trust legislation. This development is exactly what the Founding Fathers had predicted.

Governmental conduct during a crisis establishes a precedent for future emergencies as well as for normality. In a given future crisis, government will take as its starting point the experience of extraordinary powers and authority granted and exercised during previous emergencies. What might have been seen as sufficient "emergency" measures in the past may not be deemed enough for further crises as they arise. This process could be likened to the need to gradually increase the dosage of a medication past a tolerant level in order to experience the same level of relief, so too with respect to emergency powers. Government and its agents also grow accustomed to the convenience of emergency powers. Once they have experienced the ability to operate with fewer restraints and limitations, they are unlikely to be willing to give up such freedom. Emergency powers may also be used for purposes other than those for which they were originally granted. The farther we get from the original situation that precipitated its enactment, the greater are the chances that the norms and rules incorporated therein will be applied in contexts not originally intended.

Another pernicious effect that states of emergency entail refers here to the soothing effect that they have on the general public's critical approach toward extraordinary measures. In his world-acclaimed book, *Considerations on Representative Government* (2009), John Stuart Mill warns that a good despotism, in a country at all advanced in civilization, is more harmful than a bad one; for it is far more relaxing and enervating to the thoughts, feelings, and energies of the people. For example, the tyranny of Augustus prepared the Romans for Tiberius. If the whole tone of their character had not first been prostrated by nearly two generations of that mild slavery, they would probably have had spirit enough left to rebel against the more odious one.

A good case can be made that emergency situations, such as pandemic or natural disasters, offer a unique opportunity to liberate the polity from some state of paralysis, or some fixed status, thus holding governmental authority in pre-emergency times at an ineffectively low level. However, some believe that setting the balance between the powers of the state and the rights of individuals is particularly difficult, even with best intentions, in times of crisis. This is so particularly because emergencies require the valuation of action over deliberation—the need to respond quickly to major threats, as well as assuring the public that its government is acting decisively. This more often than not results in hasty governmental action and legislation, often without much deliberation and at times skipping over normal procedures.

Strong emotions such as fear, hysteria, and panic weigh heavy on people's idea of, and responses to emergency. That effect is further amplified and re-amplified as a result of hysteria. Individuals are highly responsive to emotions expressed by others. Some emotions, such as fear, are particularly spreadable.

The more serious a risk, the more dreaded people perceive a risk to be, and particularly if new and unknown like COVID-2019. Therefore, the more the demand increases for action, the more likely that something will be done, regardless the costs. And a risk triggers panic if people perceive it to be out of their control and potentially disastrous, and one over which they are powerless to control, particularly if it is unknown and not well understood.

MASKING, SOCIAL DISTANCING, AND CROWD RESTRICTIONS AS COVID-2019:PROTECTIVE MANDATES

The CDC has long advised people to take measures to stop the spread of the virus by wearing masks when outside the privacy of their homes and in the public, and in crowded areas, and if at all avoid crowded areas because they help prevent people who are infected from spreading the coronavirus. Yet there has been a series of resistances from a segment of the population that believes the mandates which according to experts are intended to break the chain of transmission are either an infringement on civil liberties or restrictive of individual freedom.

Mask Wearing: Misinformation and Hyperbole

Of all the personal protective measures recommended by health experts, including the CDC and the WHO, against contracting the virus, mask wearing has been the most controversial and challenging. It is usually a cloth with two stretchy bands at two ends. You put it on your face so you can cover your mouth and nose, and it acts as a barrier to the rest of the world. Masks, therefore, are very simple objects. But in the United States and many places around the world, they are a huge source of controversy. While many Americans follow public health recommendations and wear masks in public to limit the spread of COVID-2019, some citizens have passionately fought against wearing them, saying they impair individual freedom. In some countries, people have been made to believe in customs and religious beliefs in lieu of wearing protective gear or a mask.

In the United States, wearing face masks in public to lessen the chances of transmission of COVID-2019 was first suggested by the CDC in early April 2020 as a supplement to hygiene and appropriate social distancing. As the spread of the virus intensified, over the course of the pandemic, various states, counties, and municipalities issued mandates requiring the wearing of non-medical face coverings, such as cloth masks, in spaces and/or businesses prone to heavy human presence, and especially when physical distancing would not be possible. Some areas only mandated their use by public-facing employees of businesses such as supermarkets and retail outlets, although these flimsy orders have since been outdated as multiple states have passed a general more stringent mandate (Yan, 2020).

Federal officials, especially those in the Trump administration, had initially discouraged the general public from wearing masks for protecting themselves from COVID-2019. However, by early April 2020, some federal officials reversed their guidance, saying that the general public should wear masks to lessen transmission by themselves, particularly from asymptomatic carriers. Few public health experts like Anthony Fauci stated that mask wearing should have been recommended sooner. Others noted that U.S. government guidance lagged significantly behind mask recommendations in East Asian countries and likely exacerbated the scale of the pandemic in the United States (Jingnan, 2020).

In September 2020, Romm et al. (2020) reported that the government had contemplated leveraging the United States Postal Service to distribute free reusable masks nationwide as early as April, but later scrapped the plan due to concerns it could "create concern or panic." Wearing face masks, according to Samuels (2020), has become a highly contentious personal and political issue among Americans. While some have considered them a sign of vulnerability, attitudes among others have varied along political affiliations. Those who consider themselves as progressives or liberals, the so-called left, have been more amenable to wearing the mask out of respect toward others, while those on the right, the so-called conservatives, have largely considered mask mandates an infringement on individual liberties and a symbol of fear, control, and opposition toward President Donald Trump (Roberts, 2020).

President Trump, himself, according to news sources, had resisted wearing masks in public media appearances and had resisted mandating their use at his rallies and other public 2020 campaign events (O'Reilly, 2020). After briefly encouraging their use in mid-July, Trump continued to hold campaign events such as the 2020 Republican National Convention where masks were not widely used. Trump has mocked and ridiculed Joe Biden, his Democratic opponent in the 2020 presidential election, for wearing face masks in public appearances. Biden, House Speaker Nancy Pelosi, Michigan attorney general Dana Nessel, and others, mainly Democrats have openly criticized Trump's refusal, calling it dangerous and irresponsible. However, some supporters have pushed back that some of these critics themselves, such as Nancy Pelosi, have been caught in public spaces without masks. According to a report filed by the *Washington Post* reporters, Ann Gerhart and Lucio Villa, a lack of precautions (such as masks) taken during crowded White House ceremonies and receptions by Trump on September 26, 2020, were credited with having possibly resulted in a COVID-2019 outbreak at the White House, which included Trump himself (Gerhart and Villa, 2020).

Months leading up to general elections, mask wearing had become a toxic partisan issue. The *Washington Post* reporter Rachel Weiner (2020) reported that Republican-led states were, initially, less likely to impose health orders requiring the wearing of masks than Democratic-led states. Several states, including Arizona, Georgia, and Texas, took actions to block localized health orders requiring masks, but later softened their stances to help control local spikes.

According to European news sources, a Muslim cleric named Kohansal applied what he called the "Prophet's perfume" under the noses of coronavirus patients lying sick in a hospital in Northern Iran. He went into hiding after a warrant for his arrest was issued by the authorities. Esfandiari (2020) of Radio Free Europe reported that not wearing any mask or other protective gear, Kohansal appeared to suggest that the unknown tonic alone will cure those suffering from the COVID-2019 disease. He told one patient that he would feel better if he would sneeze, as the tonic induced sneezing.

One of the patients in the video died a few days after the unplanned visit. Iranian media reported that the cleric had trespassed the hospital without permission. Iranian Health Ministry spokesman Kianush Jahanpur accused Kohansal of interfering in the treatment of patients and "disturbing public opinion." He said he hoped the judiciary would take legal action against the cleric for trespassing and spreading false information. Iran is struggling to contain a deadly outbreak of the coronavirus that has officially killed thousands of people and infected over 50,000 by official health estimates. As some outside sources believe, those numbers are much lower than the actual numbers.

Why is there so much controversy surrounding mask wearing when health experts highly recommend everyone to wear mask as the primary defense against COVID-2019? Here's what we know about the resistance to wearing non-medical face masks in the United States: it was initially thought by some officials that masks did not protect the wearer as much as it protected the people with whom the masker came in contact with. For instance, the U.S. surgeon general Jerome Adams was known to have tweeted dissuading people from MASKS! He tweeted that masks were NOT effective in preventing the general public from catching the coronavirus (CDC, 2020).

Nonetheless, as some evidence suggested the contrary, Adams changed his tune. He has become an advocate for mask wearing. Adam pleaded in support of mask wearing that people should wear them when they cannot stay 6 feet away from others (CDC, 2020). The CDC recently released a statement that face masks do in fact offer protection to the wearer in addition to helping prevent the transmission of COVID-2019. Initially, it was thought that masks only prevented individuals from spreading the virus to others, but new research shows that exposure from infectious droplets is lowered through the filtration of masks.

Equally, the WHO early on had recommended against mask wearing for the general public, saying masks might lead to a false sense of security and that people who didn't know how to use them properly could infect themselves and others. In June, the WHO changed its stance, and now says people should wear them when they cannot be socially distant. So, if everyone wears a mask when social distancing is not feasible, the infection rate will be cut (CDC, 2020).

By mid-October 2020, the CDC added that masks can also protect wearers who are not infected, though to a lesser degree. The agency referred to a study led by Japanese researchers that found masks block about 60 percent of the amount of virus that comes out of an infected person. When an uninfected person wearing a mask is near an infected person who isn't wearing one, the amount of virus the uninfected person inhaled fell by up to 50 percent (CDC, 2020).

With so much controversy and uncertainty around non-medical mask wearing, many people tend to question the veracity of the reason health experts recommend wearing them. However, mask wearing, particularly in crowded settings, is one of the measures recommended for personal prevention and protections. The other two are social distancing and quarantine.

CONCLUSIONS AND RECOMMENDATIONS: CONTEXTUALIZING THE HYSTERIA

In this section, I conclude by contextualizing the response to the virus by the two most powerful nations, China and the United States, since these two nations found themselves enmeshed in controversy regarding the pandemic, with each pointing fingers at the other for being responsible for spreading the virus. In so doing, we acknowledge what they got right, show where and what mistakes were made and make recommendations on what ought to happen in a pandemic to assist governments in fighting the spread of the virus. In this effort, it is important we start from the beginning of the outbreak in Wuhan, China, and walk our way forward, to effectively trace our steps, in much the same as one would do to find a lost key. One is often asked to trace their steps from the beginning and walk their way forward.

However, this is neither a scorecard nor a comparative analysis. We acknowledge that no two nations are alike in structure or characteristics. Therefore, each nation's actions and responses are unique and consistent with their governmental and leadership structures. The United States is the greatest democracy in the world, while China is the greatest communist dictatorship in the world. These unique characteristics may be advantageous in some respects and disadvantageous in others. Approaches and methods of responding to a global pandemic of this magnitude may differ between the two nations, but the emergence of any infection within a nation can threaten public health security as it might cause serious health impacts and has the potential to interfere with international travel and trade. COVID-2019 has gained global attention from global health organizations and health regulatory authorities since its discovery.

The main issue with COVID-2019 disease is the high rate of human-to-human transmission regardless of the type of government people exist under. Transmission is inevitable due to interconnectivity and globalization. This should teach us to form alliances, no matter how much philosophical difference exists between governments.

The United States' Response to COVID-2019

Before we contextualize United States' response, it is important that we provide a brief synopsis of what happened in the wake of the pandemic.

Horton (2020), we learn that UN secretary-general Antonio Guterres declared COVID-2019 the greatest crisis since the Second World War. In the United States, state and federal governments have closed tens of thousands of small businesses—many never to return. Almost every school and college in the country sent its students home to finish the school year in front of their computers. Churches cancelled worship services, many before the government forced them to. Christians celebrated Easter in their homes, in front of screens. Overnight, "social distancing" went from an obscure medical term to a duty. Shaming of skeptics on social media was ratcheted up to ever-new heights. A walk in the park became a criminal act. In Brighton, Colorado, police handcuffed former state trooper Matt Mooney in front of his six-year-old daughter. Why? He was playing tee-ball with her in an otherwise empty field. Police cited a Pennsylvania woman "out for a drive" during stay-at-home orders. Michigan governor Gretchen Whitmer banned family visits between homes.

For many centuries, the United States has been a beacon of hope and strength to the rest of the world. But many health experts believe its response to the pandemic has put that hope in doubt. By some measures, the United States has handled the health crisis rather poorly than many affected countries. Although the United States represents only 4 percent of the world's population, it accounts for a quarter of all COVID-2019 cases and 22 percent of all deaths.

For a nation whose military and economic might powered a victory in the Second World War, and whose confidence and technological planted the first human being on the moon, it now finds itself as a reverse role model during the worst public health crisis in a century.

The United States' response to the COVID-2019 pandemic is the greatest science policy failure in a generation. We knew this was coming. Warnings about the threat of a new pandemic were passed on to the Trump administration during the most peaceful transfer of power. But as far back as in January it was clear that a dangerous new virus was causing a devastating human tragedy in China. And yet the Trump administration ignored the warnings. The question is, why? The United States' response, as Dr. Schaffner of Vanderbilt University put it quite simply, is a typical example of how to do it wrong. Relatively successful countries such as Denmark, Germany, Senegal, and Thailand put out messaging that was clear, consistent, and transparent with hardly any doubt and ambiguity in the minds of their people on what to do. They implemented nationwide policies guided by science rather than politics. And above all, they exerted strong national leadership. The first thing these nations did was to establish a coherent national strategy and a national policy. That national policy was decided on very quickly and it was communicated clearly and consistently and based on public health principles.

Of crucial importance in a fight against a pandemic is a concerted team effort rather than individualized and self-centered approaches. The one thing that struck many health experts as unique about the rest of the world compared to the United States is the lack of a sense of community, according to Dr. Krutika Kuppalli, vice chair of the Infectious Diseases Society of America's Global Health Committee, and an infectious disease doctor who has worked in Asia and on Ebola in Africa. In testimony submitted to the United States House of Representatives Select Subcommittee on the Coronavirus Crisis, he contended that the United States was much more about 'I' than 'we,' whereas in other countries the reverse approach was true (Kuppalli, 2020).

Apart from the lack of a sense of community, among citizens, the governments' initial responses were anything but coordinated, what stood out the most was the general attitude among groups and individuals which only help exacerbate the spread. Some countries that were worse off than the United States during the initial infestations now fair better than the United States, according to expert sources at the WHO. The author recognizes, however, many inhibiting factors that are present in the United States but absent in those nations. The size and scope of the U.S. society, its population, economy, and politics are often overlooked in these comparisons. For instance, the United States has over 332 million people while many of those countries have much smaller populations.

With that in mind, South Korea and the United States both recorded their first cases in January 20, 2020; yet, South Korea has held its outbreak level to 30 cases per 100,000 people, compared with the United States which currently stands at 3,655 per 100,000. In the month of November, New Zealand had gone 100 days without detecting a single example of community spread of the virus before encountering an outbreak that prompted the government to postpone the general election for a month. The United States surpassed 5 million cases and 160,000 dead around the same time, with cases mounting in six states and high transmission rates prevailing in more than a dozen others (Park Y, Choe Y, Park O et al., 2020)

Some countries with initial record highs in cases, such as South Korea and Denmark, have removed nearly all coronavirus-related restrictions. In the United States, authorities in numerous hot spots have either had to pause or roll back reopening some businesses. Hundreds of public health experts and medical professionals have called on the Trump administration for a national shutdown. According to STAT reporters Isaac and James Sebenius (2020), if the United States' response had been as effective as South Korea, Australia, or Singapore, fewer than 50,000 Americans would have died with well over 99 percent of those COVID-2019 deaths prevented (Sebenius and Sebenius, 2020). It all boiled down to the lack of decisive leadership at the helm to set the positive tone for citizens to follow.

Foreign Policy Analytics, an independent research and advisory division of the *Journal of Foreign Policy*, examined multiple metrics to gauge the performance of 36 nations in responding to COVID-2019. The United States was 31 out of the 36 nations graded. In addition to each country's death rate and case rate, researchers considered the state of each nation's public health system before the pandemic; the timeliness and stringency of its public health actions, such as closures, social distancing, testing and contact tracing; the consistency, effectiveness, and transparency of its communications; primacy of science in guiding policy; and coronavirus-related stimulus spending and public health funding (FP, 2020).

China's Response to COVID-2019

In this subsection, I assess China's response to the virus. China has a history of fighting against coronaviruses, such as SARS and MERS outbreaks. According to WHO (2002), China suffered from a SARS outbreak, one of the contagious coronaviruses that resulted in 8,098 infections and 774 deaths from 32 countries in late 2002 (WHO, 2002).

Although SARS was effectively contained, preparations of China and other countries were insufficient for the epidemic at that time in terms of late reporting to health officials, inadequate quarantine and isolation measures, poor hygiene precautions, and vulnerability of healthcare workers. Wuhan city, where the coronavirus originated, is the capital and largest city in Hubei Province in central China. It has a population of over 11 million and is considered a major industrial and economic part of central China. In December 2019, several cases of the emerging coronavirus, previously called 2019-nCoV, were reported in Wuhan. These cases, presenting with pneumonia, were thought to have one of the countless viruses that can create the same symptoms. Later on, in early and mid-January 2020, more cases started to appear in other provinces due to the population movement during the Chinese New Year holidays, and in other countries such as Thailand, the United States, South Korea, and Japan due to international travel (Wu and McGoogan, 2020).

The escalation in the number of infected cases in China and globally, and the reporting of deaths, made the Chinese authorities sense the abnormal situation and take immediate measures. Chinese authorities embarked upon three strategic actions that forever changed the landscape and put them in charge: (1) the Chinese authorities suppressed public opinion campaign by putting under house arrest the scientist who first raised the alarm, (2) the Chinese instituted a nationwide lockdown immediately and banned travel to and from affected areas immediately, and (3) China convened the best scientist to decipher the genetic code of the virus in a massive effort to create a vaccine. This was shared globally on the Internet (Wu and McGoogan, 2020). The authors argue that fighting and containing an outbreak of a novel pathogen with person-to-person transmission in a highly mobile world as China is a challenging task. Despite that, China's government and people were able to contain the outbreak within their country borders. After all the measures taken and people's commitment, a decline in the number of new cases and deaths was observed by the end of February 2020 and is still ongoing. The country has succeeded in reducing the numbers to hundreds and tens compared to thousands in previous months. This improvement can also be noticed in the very high recovery rate as more than 95 percent of the infected cases have recovered (Wu and McGoogan, 2020). The consequences are quite clearly devastating as far too many citizens are feeling the painful failures related to distrusting scientific facts and denying not only the existence of COVID-2019 but also failing to heed the recommendations of health experts to wear personal protective gear where social distancing cannot be possible.

Garrett (2020a) argues further that our reliant on the effectiveness of medical science and our public health system to protect us is at its highest level since the Ebola epidemic, and yet, current medical science and public health practices, because of their successes, have led to complacency and bureaucratic indifference and have helped to create the real biological peril in which we find ourselves. We live in a world in which new human pathogens emerge and old infectious diseases once thought conquered can resurface with a vengeance. It is sheer bluster to believe that we are now immune to these killers. But complacency in public health practices notwithstanding, conflicts in our political and lack of political will both carry the lion's share of the blames in the appropriate response to the current pandemic.

According to recent *Journal of American Medical Association* Network report, over 3 million new cases have been reported as hospitalizations reached a record high in November alone, a year since the virus was first reported. Consequently, more than 263,000 people have died in the United States alone because of severe acute respiratory syndrome caused by the coronavirus pathogen. This has brought the U.S. economy to a halt, resulting in more than 80 million people filing for unemployment, approximating numbers not seen since the Great Depression of the 1930s (JAMA, 2020).

This has coincided with the killing of several unarmed Black men and women—Ahmaud Arbery, Breonna Taylor, and George Floyd—spurring widespread civil unrest, with night after night of demonstrations demanding reform of systems of policing that have disproportionately harmed Black people for centuries. Ubiquitous fear and anxiety have accompanied the emergence of the new coronavirus cases leading to widespread limits on physical contact in attempts to mitigate the spread of the virus. There may not be any direct association between this pandemic and the social unrest we have witnessed in these few months, but they do conform to historic trends.

Nonetheless, the three events, the pandemic, massive unemployment, and civil unrest, have occurred concurrently while federal, state officials, and health experts offer daily summaries of COVID-2019 cases and deaths. At the same time, millions of people across the country are been adversely affected by unanticipated unemployment, with higher unemployment rates among Black and Hispanic workers compared with White workers. The resurgence of anger in a systemic long-standing racism and racial inequities has added to the anxiety and tension of the pandemic, creating a combustible scene of national civil unrest.

Deep political divisions have shaped the moment from the start. Partisan divisions have informed opinions around the extent of a national shutdown needed to mitigate pandemic spread, a pandemic that has disproportionately led to the deaths of Black people, and about how to address the legitimate concerns of thousands of individuals protesting the murder of Black men and women.

What we know, however, is that COVID-2019 is a highly transmissible virus that can spread easily from person to person through respiratory droplets. Like an enigma, some who carry the disease do not know they have it and those who contracted the disease do not know how it got transmitted to them.

Both what is known and the unknown have in and of themselves resulted in confusion and mass hysteria. Compounding that hysteria are the responses of national governments in adopting extraordinary measures to counter the threat of infection and to stop the virus from spreading. President-elect Joseph Biden said it best. "We are all in this together," Biden warns, and that we must remember that we are fighting against a common enemy, and not against each other. This is in sharp contrast to the sitting president, Donald J. Trump, who has politicized the response to this deadly disease and divided the nation into red and blue.

In his national best-selling book, *Ten Lessons for a Post-Pandemic World*, Fareed Zakaria reminds us of the Spanish Flu, the pandemic still lodged on our mind which hit the world in the midst of the First World War killing over 50 million people, more than twice the number of casualties of the war. According to Zakaria, the name Spanish Flu was a misnomer, since the flu did not originate in Spain but was only exclusively reported from Spain being that Spain was a noncombatant in war with no news censorship. Zakaria argued that science has progressed enormously since the early twentieth century. Back then, he contends that no one had ever seen a virus, let alone treat its infections. Electronic microscope had not been invented nor had antiviral drugs. He makes the case that the three most important guidelines from health experts—social distancing, mask wearing, and hand washing—remain three of the four most important mechanisms used today to slow the spread of the virus and save lives until the development of a vaccine. Regular testing is the fourth modern addition (Zakaria, 2020).

Dr. Anthony Fauci, who has spent nearly 40 years as head of the National Institute of Allergy and Infectious Diseases, is particularly well suited to reflect upon the lessons we have learned thus far. Fauci has helped steer the government response to a number of outbreaks, including the HIV/AIDS epidemic, and has now become one of the most prominent voices in the United States' response to the coronavirus pandemic. In the September 2020 issue of the *STAT* health magazine, Fauci's advice to citizens and authorities is that both entities become flexible enough to change and adapt to recommendations, guidelines, and policies depending upon the information and the data currently available. He cited the evolution of information: that what was known in February compared to what is known now (about COVID-2019) are a lot different with regard to the role of masks, the role of aerosol, the role of indoor versus outdoor, closed spaces. We've got to be humble enough to realize that we don't know it all from the get-go and even as time elapses (Gopalakrishna, 2020).

Finally, it appears that the world is in a protracted war with an unknown enemy. And, using the never-ending global war on terrorism as a backdrop, we still do not know when this crisis will be over. No cure has been found and it is uncertain when vaccines intended to fight against contracting and transmitting the virus will be distributed. Adding to the conundrum is the lack of leadership at the national level that would ameliorate the public's uncertainty about the medical experts being able to lessen the lethality of the virus. Indeed, we have met the enemy, and the enemy is us. As Garrett (2020a) argued in his recent work, decades of evidence have shown that scientific literacy rate in the United States in particular is far too low.

We saw how China responded with decisive collective and unified action in a modern city with more than 11 million people. Although some will say this might seem easy in a society or political system as that available in China, it is actually much easier in democratic systems to get this kind of passion, commitment, interest, and an individual sense of duty. But it requires political will and leadership. Even though there is currently a controversy regarding instituting mandates for lockdowns as cases spike, the policy may be acceptable if results indicate that many lives were actually saved.

In an article titled "Response to the COVID-19 Epidemic: The Chinese Experience and Implications for Other Countries," in the *International Journal of Environmental Research and Public Health*, the authors Wei Liu, Xiao-Guang Yue, and Paul B. Tchounwou stated that China's strict containment measures have significantly reduced the spread of the epidemic. China achieved this through the use of emergency control measures in the epidemic areas and the integration of resources from multiple systems, including business, community, technology, education, and transportation, across the country. They contend that in order to better understand how China has managed to reduce the public health and economic impacts of the COVID-2019 epidemic, they systematically reviewed the specific measures for infection prevention and control of the disease. Accordingly, the best practices for COVID-2019 eradication in China provide evidence-based strategies that could be replicated in other countries. The authors believe that China's response to COVID-2019 should be a model for all countries to emulate and start implementing prevention and control strategies immediately as each one is at risk of becoming the new virus epicenter. Considering that each country is unique, assessment should be done of the possible benefits and negative consequences of each strategy adopted. In addition, countries should work on enhancing their systems and personnel in order to be more prepared for future outbreaks and reduce consequences when they strike (Liu, Xiao-Guang, and Tchounwou, 2020).

Lessons Learned

In the June 18, 2020, publication of the Public Policy Institute of California newsletter, Mark Baldassare claimed that President Donald Trump's response to the COVID-2019 pandemic was creating headwinds not only for the incumbent president but also for Republican candidates in House elections (Baldassare, 2020). One issue he believes that resonated with the research community is the extent to which the current president and his administration meddled with science and scientific advice during the pandemic and misled the public into believing the virus was a hoax. That mix messaging, according to Gopalakrishna (2020), contributed to mass hysteria and pandemonium. Clearly, then, from where we started, it was apparent that we had nowhere to go but in the wrong direction. Whatever we may have learned from this may not bring back the close to 300,000 who have died by the time this book hits the bookshelves. However, it should be a moment of reflection for us as Horton (2020) consoles, in his book entitled, *The COVID-19 Catastrophe: What's Gone Wrong and How to Stop It Happening Again*, Horton wrote, "Those who died must not be summarized. They must not become lines on square pegs. They must not become mere rates used to argue differences between nations. Every death must count. A person who died in Wuhan is as important as one who died in New York" (Preface).

As Garrett (2020b) observed, it wasn't until the HIV emerged that the limits of, and imperatives for, globalization of health became obvious in a context larger than mass vaccination programs. From the moment it was discovered among gay men in New York, and California in 1981, AIDS became a prism through which the positive lights by which societies hoped to be viewed were splintered into thousands of disparate and glaring pieces. Through the AIDS prism it was possible for the world's public health experts to witness what they considered to be the hypocrisies, cruelties, failings, and inadequacies of humanity's sacred institutions, including its medical establishment, science, organized religion, systems of justice, the United Nations, and individual government systems of all political stripes. If HIV was our model, leading scientists concluded, humanity was in very big trouble. We hope this pandemic would be an exception (Garrett, 2020b).

REFERENCES

Arnold, C. (2018). *Pandemic 1918: The Story of the Deadliest Influenza in History*. New York: St. Martin's Press.

Axe, D., Briggs, W. and Richards, J. W. (2020). *The Price of Panic–How the Tyranny of Experts Turned A Pandemic into a Catastrophe*. New York: Regency Publishing.

Ball, P. and Maxmen, A. (2020). The epic battle against coronavirus misinformation and conspiracy theories. *Nature*. Retrieved May 18, 2020 from https://www.nature.com/articles/d41586-020-01452-z.

Baldassare, M. (2020) Informing and improving public policy through independent, objective, nonpartisan research – Public Policy Institute of California (PPIC). Retrieved June 18, 2020 from https://www.ppic.org/.

Bennett J. (1998). Fear of Contagion: A response to stress? ANS. *Advances in Nursing Science* 21(1):76–87. doi: 10.1097/00012272-199809000-00008. Retrieved November 20, 2020 from https://journals.lww.com/advancesinnursingscience/Abstract/1998/09000/Fear_of_Contagion__A_Response_to_Stress_.8.aspx.

Brennen J.S., Simon F., Howard P.N. and Nielsen R.K. (2020). Types, sources and claims of COVID-2019 misinformation. *Reuters Institute*. Retrieved on April 7, 2020 from https://reutersinstitute.politics.ox.ac.uk/types-sources-and-claims-covid-19-misinformation.

Brig B. (March 24, 2020) Joking in the time of pandemic: The 1889–92 flu and 2020 COVID-19. Nursing clio. Retrieved March 24, 2020 at https://nursingclio.org/2020/03/24/joking-in-the-time-of-pandemic-the-1889-92-flu-and-2020-covid-19/.

Broadhurst, R., Ball, M. and Jiang, C.J (2020). Availability of COVID-19 related products on TOR darknet markets. *Australian Institute of Criminology Statistical Bulletin* 24. 2020. Retrieved on April 7, 2020 from https://www.aic.gov.au/publications/sb/sb24.

Centers for Disease Control and Prevention CDC (2020). Retrieved on November 7, 2020 from https://wwwnc.cdc.gov/eid/article/26/10/20-1315_article.

Chelsea, D. (2020). *Albany Business Review*. Retrieved on November 13, 2020 from ttps://www.bizjournals.com/albany/bio/25841/Chelsea+Diana.

Chernow, R. (2004) *Alexander Hamilton*. New York: Penguin Random House.

Coleman, J. (2020). Pelosi: Nationwide mask mandate 'definitely long overdue.' *The Hill*. Retrieved on June 28, 2020 from https://thehill.com/homenews/sunday-talk-shows/504897-pelosi-definitely-long-overdue-to-mandate-wearing-masks-nationwide.

Cuthbertson, A. (2020). Coronavirus: Dark web market warns drug dealers selling fake COVID-19 vaccines. *The Independent*. Retrieved on April 3, 2020 from https://www.independent.co.uk/life-style/gadgets-and-tech/news/coronavirus-vaccine-cure-dark-web-drugs-market-covid-19-a9442671.html.

Davis, W. (2020). U.S. hits 11 million coronavirus cases, adding 1 million in a week. National Public Radio. Retrieved on November 16, 2020 from https://www.npr.org/sections/coronavirus-live-updates/2020/11/15/935229627/u-s-hits-11-million-coronavirus-cases-adding-1-million-in-a-week.

Debiec, J. (2020) Fear can spread from person to person faster than the coronavirus – But there are ways to slow it down. Retrieved on November 16 2020 from https://theconversation.com/fear-can-spread-from-person-to-person-faster-than-the-coronavirus-but-there-are-ways-to-slow-it-down-133129.

Dehority, W. (2020) Infectious disease outbreaks, pandemics, and Hollywood – hope and fear across a century of cinema. *Journal of the American Medical Association* 323(19):1878–1880. doi: 10.1001/jama.2020.7187.

Dubos, R. (2018). *Mirage of Health: Utopias, Progress and Biological Change*. New York: Pickle Partners Publishing.

Else, D. H. (May 14, 2009). Defense Production Act: Purpose and scope. *Congressional Research Service* 7–5700. Retrieved on November 16, 2020 from www.crs.gov RS20587.

Esfandiari, G. (2020). Prophet's Perfume & Gourd oil: Iran warns against quackery, Islamic medicine to treat coronavirus. Retrieved on November 16, 2020 from https://www.rferl.org/a/prophets-perfume-bitter-oil-drops-iran-warns-against-quackery-islamic-medicine-to-treat-coronavirus/30514396.html Radio Free Europe Radio Liberty.

Feser, E. (May 4, 2005). Robert Nozick (1938–2002). *Internet Encyclopedia of Philosophy*. Retrieved on November 16, 2020 from https://iep.utm.edu/nozick/.

Foreign Policy Analytics (FP). (2020) Retrieved on November 20, 2020 from https://foreignpolicy.com/fp-analytics/.

Garrett, L. (2020a). *Betrayal of Trust: The Collapse of Global Public Health*. New York: Hachette Books.

Garrett, L. (2020b). *The Coming Plague: Newly Emerging Diseases in a World out of Order*. New York: Farrar, Straus and Giroux Publishers.

Gerhart, A. and Villa, L. (2020). Attendees at Barrett nomination ceremonies. Retrieved on November 16, 2020 from https://www.washingtonpost.com/graphics/2020/politics/coronavirus-attendees-barrett-nomination-ceremony/.

Gopalakrishna, P. (2020). Anthony Fauci on lessons learned so far in the Covid-19 pandemic –STAT Exclusive analysis of biotech, pharma, and the life sciences. Retrieved on September 10, 2020 from https://pharmaceuticalintelligence.com/2020/10/18/the-lessons-from-the-covid-19-response-according-to-anthony-fauci/.

Gorter, J. (2020). Impact of coronavirus on EAPs: Managing the fear of communicable disease. *Journal of Employee Assistance*. University of Maryland, Baltimore. Retrieved on November 16, 2020 from https://archive.hshsl.umaryland.edu/handle/10713/12504.

Hana, J. and Hollingsworth, H. (November 19, 2020). Kansas governor issues new mask mandate as COVID cases surge. Alva Review Courier. Retrieved on November 19, 2020 from https://www.alvareviewcourier.com/story/2020/11/19/regional/kansas-governor-issues-new-mask-mandate-as-covid-cases-surge/67921.html.

Herbjørnsrud, D. (2002). *Leaving Libertarianism: Social Ties in Robert Nozick's New Philosophy*. Oslo, Norway: University of Oslo Press.

Horton, R. (2020). *The COVID-19 Catastrophe: What's Gone Wrong and How to Stop It Happening Again*. Medford, MA: Polity Press.

Jingnan, H. (2020). Why there are so many different guidelines for face masks for the public. National Public Radio. Retrieved on May 23, 2020 from https://www.npr.org/sections/goatsandsoda/2020/04/10/829890635/why-there-so-many-different-guidelines-for-face-masks-for-the-public.

Journal of American Medical Association (JAMA). (November 19, 2020) Retrieved on November 30, 2020 from https://jamanetwork.com/journals/jama.

Kuppalli K. (2020). Exposure notification and contact tracing: How AI helps localities

reopen safely and researchers find a cure. Retrieved on November 15, 2020 from https://financialservices.house.gov/uploadedfiles/hhrg-116-ba00-wstate-kuppallik-20200708.pdf.

Lee, J. D. (2014). *An Epidemic of Rumors: How Stories Shape Our Perception of Disease*. Boulder, CO: University of Colorado Press.

Liu, W., Xiao-Guang, Y and Tchounwou, P. B. (2020). Response to the COVID-19 epidemic: The Chinese experience and implications for other countries. *International Journal of Environmental Research and Public Health* 17(7):2304. doi: 10.3390/ijerph17072304

Mawson, A. R (2005). Understanding mass panic and other collective responses to threat and disaster. *Psychiatry: Interpersonal and Biological Processes* 68(2):95–113.

McDonald, S. M. (March 23, 2020). We can't let the coronavirus lead to a 9/11-style erosion of civil liberties. Retrieved on April 23, 2020 from https://www.theguardian.com/commentisfree/2020/mar/23/coronavirus-civil-liberties-authoritarian-measures.

Menzies, R.E., Menzies, R.G. and Iverach, L. (2018). *Curing the Dread of Death: Theory, Research and Practice*. Sydney, Australia: The Federation Press.

Metcalf, S. (June 19, 2011). The liberty scam: Why even Robert Nozick, the philosophical father of libertarianism, gave up on the movement he inspired. Retrieved on November 17, 2020 from https://slate.com/culture/2011/06/robert-nozick-father-of-libertarianism-even-he-gave-up-on-the-movement-he-inspired.html.

Nozick, R. (1974). *Anarchy, State, and Utopia*. Englewood Cliffs, NJ: Prentice-Hall, Inc.

Paakkan, L., Okan, O. (2020). COVID-19: Health literacy is an underestimated problem. *The Lancet Public Health* 5(5):249–250.

Park, Y., Choe, Y., Park, O., Park, S., Kim, Y., Kim, J., Kweon, S., Woo, Y., Gwack, J., Kim, S.S. and Jeong, E. (October 26, 2020). Contact tracing during coronavirus disease outbreak, South Korea, 2020. *Emerging Infectious Diseases*, Retrieved on October 26, 2020 from https://wwwnc.cdc.gov/eid/article/26/10/20-1315_article.

Pospelova S., Kamenskaya, N.A. and Pospelova S.V. (2020). Violation liability in the context of the spread of COVID-19: Russian Experience. *Journal of Law and Medicine* 27:877–895.

Rawls, J. (1971). *A Theory of Justice*. Cambridge, MA: Belknap Press of Harvard University Press.

Restuccia, A. (2020a). Trump's White House rally: Takeaways from the RNC's final night. *Wall Street Journal*. Retrieved on August 31, 2020 from https://www.wsj.com/articles/trumps-white-house-rally-takeaways-from-the-rncs-final-night-11598612414.

Restuccia, A. (2020b). White house defends trump comments on "Kung Flu" coronavirus testing. *Wall Street Journal*. Retrieved on August 31, 2020 from https://www.wsj.com/articles/white-house-defends-trump-comments-on-kung-flu-coronavirus-testing-11592867688.

Robertson, N. (July 19, 2020). Trump doesn't think US needs a national mask mandate. *CNN*. Retrieved on July 19, 2020 from https://www.cnn.com/2020/07/18/politics/trump-us-mask-mandate-coronavirus/index.html.

Romm, T., Bogage, J. and Sun, L. (2020) Newly revealed USPS documents show an agency struggling to manage Trump, Amazon and the pandemic. *The Washington Post*. Retrieved on September 17, 2020 from https://www.washingtonpost.com/us-policy/2020/09/17/usps-trump-coronavirus-amazon-foia/.

Samuels, A. (2020). For some, forgoing masks in public during the coronavirus pandemic has become a political statement. *The Texas Tribune*. Retrieved on June 6, 2020 from https://www.texastribune.org/2020/05/22/texas-coronavirus-masks/.

Spinney, L. (2017). *Pale Rider: The Spanish Flu of 1918 and How It Changed the World*. New York: Hachette Books.

Weiner, R. (2020). Republican governors who opposed mask mandates start to soften. *The Washington Post*. Retrieved on July 12, 2020 from https://www.washingtonpost.com/health/republican-governors-who-opposed-mask-mandates-start-to-soften/2020/07/10/465baf14-c070-11ea-b4f6-cb39cd8940fb_story.html.

Wolff, J. (2006). *An Introduction to Political Philosophy*. Oxford, UK: Oxford University Press.

Woodward, B. (2020) *Rage*. New York: Simon & Schuster.

World Health Organization (WHO). (March 20, 2020). Coronavirus disease (COVID-19) pandemic. Retrieved on November 14, 2020 from https://www.who.int/emergencies/diseases/novel-coronavirus-2019.

Wu, Z. and McGoogan, J. M. (2020) Characteristics of and important lessons from the coronavirus disease 2019 (COVID-19) outbreak in China: Summary of a report of 72 314 cases from the Chinese Center for Disease Control and Prevention. *Journal of the American Medical Association* 323(13):1239.

Yan, H. (2020). Why face mask guidance has changed so much and how wearing masks can protect the economy. *CNN*. Retrieved on November 6, 2020 from https://www.cnn.com/2020/07/19/health/face-masks-us-guidance/index.html.

Zakaria, F. (2020) *Ten Lessons for a Post-Pandemic World*. New York: W.W. Norton and Company.

Chapter 17

Coroexploitation

Henrietta Eshalomi

At different times in life, humans have defined a living pattern that suits their peculiarities. These living patterns are to ensure orderliness and normalcy in society. On the one hand, the normalcy that is often associated with organized and structured living can be ruptured when developments, planned and unplanned, come up. These often force society to adjust, yielding advantages to individuals or groups and vice versa. On the other hand, such adjustment can necessitate a restructuring. In most societies, the existence of laws and regulations is expected to carry through this period. Unplanned developments are not expected to turn society on its head, especially when there are laws and regulations in place to cater for such new developments. However, reality has shown that this is not often the case, as different interests play up during periods of unexpected developments. Some of these could be regarded as exploitation driven by non-altruistic objectives. This may create gains and advantages in the long run, forcing some sections of society on those who benefit from such unexpected developments. Examples of this are obvious during times of disasters and crisis such as natural and unnatural circumstances. These put different degrees of pressures and demands on the established codes of existence, as well as stretching the rules and regulations governing such societies.

In some cases, societies have been known to readjust their codes of engagement in tandem with the present and obtainable realities. In cases where this is not so, new shades and dimensions of interests often emerge, giving advantage to some individuals and groups of people who use the temporary situation to redirect the course of living, interaction, as well as development. Researchers have established that in these situations, new powers of influence often emerge to displace existing or established powers (Spash, 2020). From its initial outbreak in Wuhan, China, in 2019, the Coronavirus Disease

(COVID)-2019 pandemic wore on stealthily, and as it spread to different parts of the world, different scenarios and narratives came to the fore, especially the narrative of exploitation.

In a developing country like Nigeria with obvious socioeconomic indices of unemployment, poverty, corruption, infrastructural collapse, and poor healthcare facilities, among others, laws and regulation governing different aspects of human existence are often clouded with political considerations. This has continued to make the system malleable and open for exploitation (Abu and Staniewski, 2019). Unfortunately, the structures of the society are not necessarily empowered to withstand the vagaries of unexpected changes and new development. This was well amplified with the outbreak of the COVID-2019 pandemic and has upset the balance arrangement thereof. Consequently, ratification, exploitation, adaptation, and readjustments have become the new realities shaping the lives of people not only in Nigeria but also around the globe.

The diverse impacts have raised concerns and drawn attention to gray areas, incompetence, unpreparedness, and inhumanness of not just the government but as well as the private sector operators. The COVID-2019 pandemic unsettled governments across the world and caused them to institute measures to curb the spread. The pandemic had barely hit the country when the Nigerian government, like many other government around the world, imposed lockdown restrictions. These restrictions, on the advice of the World Health Organization, would help to contain the spread of the disease. However, the spontaneity and suddenness with which the government imposed these restrictions created other socioeconomic concerns that became more serious than the pandemic that informed the restrictions (Ozili, 2020). The short notice informing the masses in three principal locations—Lagos and Ogun states and Abuja, the Federal Capital Territory—of the planned lockdown allowed citizens less than 48 hours to prepare for an initial two weeks' lockdown. Many complained this move was wrong and responsible for the loud outcry that broke out, few days into the commencement of the lockdown. Notwithstanding, this development forced citizens into swift action to stock their homes with necessities, as much as their purchasing power could carry, for the period of the lockdown. Surprisingly, this stampede opened up opportunities for some business owners, wholesale and retail traders, service providers, and even the government to exploit the situation to their advantage. There was astronomical price hike of commodities and services, including other insensitive and inhuman ways as shall be explored later in this chapter.

The lockdown ordered by the government was aimed at curbing the spread of the virus. In recognition of the rude shock and discomfort that would arise from the lockdown, the Nigerian government institutionalized the provision of palliatives for the citizens. It was intended to cushion the harsh effects of the lockdown, especially its impacts on the socioeconomic activities of the populace. The government, in concert with individuals and other corporate organizations, designed and produced food items and other consumer essentials for the indigent and vulnerable members of society. This initiative was to further strengthen and justify the lockdown laws for not just effectively containing the spread of the virus but for quick comeback of the economy. In no small measure, profit-making organizations and other well-meaning Nigerians responded to this call to support humanity. While some supported the government with cash, others donated tangible essential materials. However, these initiatives with all their efforts were not without shortcomings as scores of residents raised alarm that the palliative materials did not get to the large majority of people (Vanguard, 2020).

Although a simple understanding of exploitation considers it as an occasion where one person takes undue advantage of another by reason of a particular transaction (Vrousalis, 2013), this study lifts this phenomenon from the narrow confinement and emboldens it within the context of spontaneity and emergency. The outbreak of the COVID-2019 was one unfortunate incident that threw the entire globe into a state of confusion. What started as a global health challenge soon became the proverbial cancer that spread to other aspects and institutions of the society especially socioeconomic, thus, creating other emergency concerns altogether.

Taking a cue for a lay understanding of exploitation, Cohen (1989) believes it is a situation with compelling attributes because of the 'extra-economic' demands on the exploited. Because of the compelling pressure it exerts on the exploited, Terray and Serrano (2019) say that exploitation is antagonistic, particularly because it denies the exploited justice and fairness on the one hand, while avails the exploiter domination and power on the other (Vrousalis, 2017). Sometimes, the exploited is not unaware of this compelling element yet gives what Vrousalis (2017) categorizes as irrational, unfree, and/or uninformed consent to the demands of the exploiter. Underlying these authors' positions with regard to the exploited being aware of the exploitation is that their desperation becomes their greatest undoing in such transaction.

The exploitation that occurred during the COVID-2019 restrictions in Nigeria validates Cohen's position of compelling economic costs. Following the less than 48 hours' notice announced by the government before the commencement of the lockdown, citizens had little or no choice but to accept the economic fate that befell them as a result of the pandemic. The widespread disorganization, rush, and panic buying by Nigerians exposed a character trait that rubbishes any shred of humanity. Prices of consumer commodities shot up as inflation rate spiked.

The kind of exploitative scenarios that played out in the Nigerian contexts allows us to review the narrowly confined view of exploitation that has dominated contemporary studies as involving two individuals in a particular transaction (Wollner, 2019), to a broader domain that touches on government, corporate organizations, and individual. Exploitation, in this work, is viewed against the backdrop of fundamental price influencers like increase in the pump price of gasoline, a factor that affects transportation and industrial production. Due to long years of irregular electric power supply, companies as well as individuals have resorted to gasoline generators as alternative power supply to achieve productivity. Another critical issue is that of wages in the country. Prior to the outbreak of the pandemic and up till the ease of the lockdown, the negotiation for the review of minimum wage persisted in the country. Rather than the expected increase of salaries, wages and salaries reduction swept across different industries.

Puzzled by the three salient questions—(1) What socioeconomic developments emerged from the COVID-2019 lockdown in Nigeria? (2) How did these developments affect the citizens? (3) What coping mechanisms were adopted to manage the situation—this chapter explores the exploitation dynamics that played out during the government's imposed restrictions to curb the spread of the coronavirus up till few months after the relaxation of these restrictions in Nigeria. Even though the lockdown and other restrictions are symbolically important in curbing the spread of the virus, it was imposed on a shaky and faulty socioeconomic foundation. With two fundamental themes emerging—structural and individual—sub-themes were deployed for precision and direction.

Responses by traders, government's officials, public and private transport operators, private school teachers and school owners, returnees, and service providers during the period of the restrictions reflected exploitation, and institutionalized corruption and inhumanness. This reality is established using responses of participants following an explorative method of data collection from randomly selected participants in selected states in the country. Secondary data including journal and newspaper articles, news media reports, as well as personal experience of the realities that characterized the moments of the COVID-2019 lockdown in Nigeria were deployed to deepen the discourse.

The realities that prevailed through social, political but particularly economic during the emergency COVID-2019 restrictions make this discussion invaluable to practically all and sundry across different levels of economic engagements in the society. First, government at all levels, corporate organizations, business owners, and individuals experienced the emergencies that came heavily on humanity due to the coronavirus. This is most important because price hike and inflation over time have been largely informed by salary increment, increase in pump price of Premium Motor Spirit following a pre-information or announcement notifying the masses of the intending development. Festive season like Christmas is another period when prices of goods and services experience a raise. For whatever informs the yuletide price hike, the generality of citizens is not new to the trend and have learned to prepare for its coming. At this point, it is convenient to say then that price hike may have always been a reality, but one that is always expected and prepared for. With that, the questions raised will shed more light on the dynamics of exploitation that manifested following the COVID-2019 lockdown restrictions, and how citizens managed the situation. The theory of exploitation is employed to foreground the study because it captures the uniqueness of the times as well as its context. Further discussion will unpack the economic realities in Nigeria in which gains were reversed, projections were cut, and new realities were put in place in a time of emergency like the one caused by COVID-2019.

THEORETICAL EXPLORATION OF EXPLOITATION

Exploitation, a social reality, is a concept with many dimensions particularly because it spans economic, political, health, social, cultural, and racial, among others. In what seems to be a matrix, scholars have in different contexts and circumstances used captions that engaged the logic of the concept of exploitation. Wollner's (2019) idea of exploitation basically refers to unfair advantage taken at the expense of another person for own or others' benefit. Such a position creates an advantage-disadvantage binary whereby the exploiter is the beneficiary of a self-styled opportunity (advantage) and the other person is the loser (disadvantage).

As a term largely discussed within economic and political domain, Terray and Serrano (2019) see it as social reality and social relations. For the economic, the authors argue that there is a deprivation of the direct laborers of a part of their productive labor, while unequal power distribution in society accounts for exploitation that exists within the political realm. Earlier, Marx (1992) had stated that the "laborers' productive labor" is a function of surplus labor, with laborer working extra time. For Marx, unequal distribution of labor with disproportionate surplus value is critical to exploitation because the exploiter has exploited something called an "unreciprocated labor" from the victim (Vrousalis, 2017). This line of argument underscores the logic of distributive justice posited by Walras (1926, p. 375). Walras contends that "prices of productive services are equivalent or proportionate to their marginal productivities." What this implies is that where there is labor justice manifested in correlate wages, exploitation is absent.

Terray and Serrano (2019) posit that exploiters are dominant, permitting that they are also controlling. By expanding their domain of domination and control beyond the political to economy, the concept of capitalism becomes clear. Since capitalism latches unto opportunities to increase wealth, power, and influence (Klein, 2007), both capitalism and exploitation share some interrelated characteristics. Though exploitation infers taking advantage of one at the expense of the other, capitalism with its subtle economic dominance is basically concerned with money flow through exchange (Spash, 2020). With the breakdown of financial flow following the shutdown of most societies of the world in the wake of the deadly COVID-2019, Spash highlights how economies are precariously configured for financial gains. At the heart of Spash's view is the prioritization of financial interest over human life. Such ideology is implicative of exploitation and injustice particularly for the disregard of humanity. To corroborate, Spash, Risse, and Wollner (2014) submitted that the situation like the concept is stripped of every sense of moral principle and constitutes all shades of wrong regardless of the gains.

The disregard exhibited by exploiters defies Baujard's fairness on humanity over circumstances (Baujard, 2010). For Baujard, social welfare is imperative and its maximization is made possible if individual utility is also maximized. Simply put, his position is an indication that communal good is a function of individual good. At the peak of a more general position that exploitation is unfairly taking advantage of a person, Vrousalis (2017) contends that this position is inconsistent as there can indeed be fair exploiting. Giving an analogy that explains distributive justice as one that shuns price for assets, the author argued that if the materiality of distributive justice is inconsequential, then distributive injustice cannot pass for exploitation.

Righting the wrong of exploitation demands the principle of fairness. The term fairness is imperative in concluding on human interaction with one another especially in an already chaotic situation because, above all, Baujard (2010) believes it is the greatest universal happiness. This line of thought appeals in an ideal society and is built on the principle of brotherliness and kindness that is non-discriminatory, non-partisan in rendering support to the people (Bentham, cited in Baujard, 2010). Accordingly, the realities that ensued during the COVID-2019 lockdown in Nigeria confirmed the flipside of an unideal society as expected. As much as Bentham's position is humanely stimulating, his position is shrouded in emotional sentiments.

Aside individual exploitation is the structural, allowing room for systemic exploitation (Wollner, 2019). He argued that the structure of a society allows reward and constraints people in either a coercive or non-coercive manner. His dogged position that structures are exploitative is instructive by the very sense in which he believes they shape the people's outlook to exploit. Similar argument had earlier been posited by Zwolinski (2012) on structural exploitation. Concurring to the injustice that defines the act of exploitation, the author argued that the exploitation that exists between employers and workers is not basically one of personal interaction but one enshrined in the political and economic institutions in the place where these interactions happen. Here, institutions that should regulate interactions and behavioral pattern of people have been ruptured, corrupted, or even collapsed, thereby availing loopholes and opportunities for unfairness, injustice, and wrongful exploitation.

Within the domain of politics, exploitation has become an albatross to the development of society. Abu and Staniewski (2019) show that indices such as corruption, mismanagement, poverty, oppression, and nepotism are a reflection of exploitation. Under such circumstance, government expresses lackluster insensitivity to the plight of the people, thereby making the system malleable and open for exploitation. Nuances of this are explored in the succeeding section.

STRUCTURAL EXPLOITATION

In this section, exploitations that are structural are highlighted. These exploitations transpired under different shades and guises in Nigeria during the sudden government-ordered lockdown that incidentally availed opportunists opportunities to exploit.

Exploitation Perpetuated by Government and Government Officials

Different aspects of Nigerian society were affected by the outbreak of COVID-2019. The first and widest response of the government was the need for education and enlightenment of the populace on everything concerning the virus. There was heavy concentration on the need for people to adjust, and this came with some form of restrictions and control of human circulation. The federal government-ordered initial two-week lockdown in three principal locations was the first stark realistic move that announced the arrival of a new normal in town. The total lockdown impacted the social, physical, and most importantly, economic aspects of the people in these three principal locations. Nigeria being a market-driven capitalistic economy had a huge challenge of addressing necessary survival necessities among the populace who in obedience to the lockdown orders had to stay indoor for two weeks. Save for essential service workers including health personnel, journalists, and law enforcement agents, schools, shops, offices, farms, and factories were locked down. And for the places where the lockdown was not ordered, the necessity of regulated and controlled socialization gave a near lockdown outlook.

With the preceding prevalent situation and the necessity of survival, a new level and shade of socioeconomic development emerged. On one hand, the government was constrained to come up with what became popular as palliatives to provide a cushion for the citizens who are not able to access and continue their regular socioeconomic activities. These packaged palliatives were in different forms and formats. This new word palliative connoted different things but most importantly, it meant support and gap-filling measures. The government at the federal, state, and even local levels developed different palliative packages including materials and cash. Food items were ingeniously packaged in different sizes for onward mass distribution to the populace in different areas, especially in those areas where there were enforced lockdown. In some other places, different organizations, including non-governmental organization, neighborhood and community groups, developed different types of palliative packages to ameliorate the situation and mitigate against hardship that may result from the enforced lockdown through government regulations.

It is important to note that even during the period of the enforced lockdown, different circumstances and social situations emerged across the nation. In no time, the government became greatly challenged and there was need to come up with new ways of spreading the palliatives around the country and making sure it got to people who needed it most. Under the office of the Minister for Humanitarian Affairs, the government embarked on a nationwide palliative distribution exercise. Government officials led by the minister for Humanitarian Affairs, Sadiya Umar Farouq, handed out COVID-2019 palliatives in cash, foodstuffs, and humanitarian materials, among others, to vulnerable and indigent Nigerians across the country. This initiative which received commendation soon ran into troubled waters as allegations of nepotism and political patronage were spread across the length and breadth of the nation. Despite the public show of cash distribution and as captured by leading television station, Channels Television, Nigerians across the board raised their voices against the unhealthy marginalization and exclusion that characterized the distribution. As their complaints steered toward individuals, Mayer (2007) cautions against such exclusivity and directs that complaints be made about structures.

Observations alongside media reports showed aggrieved Nigerians who pointed out that they only heard of the distribution of the palliative materials and could only point to very few beneficiaries in different communities across the country (Vanguard, 2020). In some cases, especially in the different states and local government councils, the palliative packages were channeled through elected public officials. That means these officials with their access to the grassroots populace were used as channels of transfer to the people in their different constituencies. The nobility of this process was variously challenged as the elected officials were accused of politicizing the distribution of the palliative packages or in some cases, keeping it to themselves with the intention to use them as electoral patronage inducement.

The outcry against this was far spread and was replicated across the different geopolitical zones of Nigeria. In some cases, politicians who got these palliative packages and were expected to transfer same to their constituents were accused of using these remedial packages to settle political scores, as those deem to be in opposing political camps were excluded even as the government did not design it for specific political supporters. In some other instances, as it happened in Lagos State specifically, the palliative packages became strong instruments of exploitation of the citizenry as the branded palliative packages, especially the ones including food staples like rice, flour, sugar, and salt, were diverted and sold in open markets. In spite of media reports of these diversions, there were no reported cases of investigation, arrest, or prosecution by the government. This lent credence to the narrative that the diversion of these life-saving packages was the contrived handwork of government officials and politicians.

To further cement the point of diversion and exploitation, especially of the COVID-2019 palliative packages, the widespread discovery and subsequent looting of different warehouses across the federation with large stock of COVID-2019 palliatives donated by corporate bodies in Nigeria comes to mind. Even when the government had scaled down the level of emergency of the COVID-2019 pandemic in Nigeria in the month of August–September 2020, a different sight greeted Nigerians when in the aftermath of a national protest over bad governance in the country escalated into looting and vandalism and different warehouses were discovered in which thousand tons of COVID-2019 palliative packages were hoarded (Sahara Reporters, 2020). Expectedly, it drew the ire of citizenry who saw this as grand deception and exploitation by the ruling elite, especially as the government itself had scaled down the pandemic and opened up the economy to normalcy. This situation is paradigmatic constituting wrongness of exploitation under the guise of respect theory, albeit, causing harm to rights (Vrousalis, 2017).

Besides this, COVID-2019 palliative materials that were packaged and given to politicians for onward distribution for their constituents were reportedly personalized, and in some cases, rebranded as birthday hampers and goody bags distributed as personal gifts to the people and not as government intervention packages. This came to light in Lagos State where two elected members of the state House of Assembly were accused of repackaging the government-issued COVID-2019 palliatives as their own personal intervention packages to the populace. Mr. Gbenga Osinowo, an elected parliamentarian in Lagos State whose house was looted by protesters, complained that the palliative packages were kept by him for distribution on his birthday that was scheduled to come up later in the year. Another parliamentarian, Jumoke Macaulay Ali, reportedly gave out goody bags filled with government-issued COVID-2019 palliative items on her birthday with the bags fully branded in her name and image (Sahara Reporter, 2020).

In Rivers State, there were media reports of a local government chairman who allegedly gave hundreds of cartons of COVID-2019 palliative items donated by corporate bodies to his constituency members with specific instructions on expected monetary returns after sale. Similar incident transpired in Kaduna State, where a supermarket was discovered with COVID-2019 palliative items on its shelves, displayed for sale even when these donated items were specifically designed to be given to the people free of charge. Obviously prominent in the explorative data are individuals taking advantage of a failed structure which further validates Wollner's (2019) position that the individual's action to exploit is not unconnected to the influence of the structure on such individual.

Experiences from the Education Sector

On another level, the period of the lockdown reflected a new form of exploitation, especially in the education sector. Prior to this time, the Nigerian educational sector had continued to battle different forms of crisis, especially the continuous breakdown of public education system. The near-collapse of the public education system, as evidenced by dilapidated infrastructures, low number of student, and unmotivated teaching force, had made the public school system less attractive. These irregularities have worked in favor of an increase in the number of private primary and secondary schools across the federation (Onuka and Arowoloju, 2008).

Although the education sector is still regulated by the government, there are fewer functional public schools with low level of enrollment and these ones grappled with the problem of low student enrollment (Onuka and Arowoloju, 2008). In contrast to that was the rise in increased number of private schools which had a corresponding effect of enhanced enrollment in these institutions. During the pandemic, schools were closed down and students forced to stay at home for long periods, especially those in the primary and secondary schools. The need for regulated social interaction made the closure of these schools necessary, and the government weighed down heavily on any form of infraction. By the end of the first month of the general lockdown, there was no talk of reopening of schools because of the logistic and health challenges associated with schools being in session.

The situation of the lockdown made educational planners, including owners of private institutions, to become creative as new methods of pedagogy were introduced. As a way of maintaining the momentum and continue with the curriculum, school owners moved the classroom into the virtual space. Students were made to link up with instructors virtually where lessons continued, even with minimal disruptions. As much as this was a major hit for continuity in curriculum, the flipside created a major problem that marred what would have been a success story in the education sector. Private primary and post-primary education system in Nigeria runs on funds and subscriptions which ultimately pay wages and salaries of teachers and other workers in the sector. The absence of students from the classroom created not only a curriculum continuity challenge but also the problem of finance, especially as it became difficult for school owners and operators to convince parents and guardians to pay the same fees for virtual classes like they would do for physical classes. Rather than lose everything, school owners were forced to adjust their fees, especially when parents made a case that they bore the expenses and cost of connection for the virtual classes.

In a popular and high-brow private school in Lagos, Atlantic Hall, parents reportedly protested the imposition of a $500 monthly virtual class fee. The parents complained bitterly of exploitation by the school authorities as they mentioned that contemporary schools with Atlantic Hall charged less than $200 for the same virtual classes (Premium Times, 2020). The aggrieved parents further complained that having paid in excess of $200 per child as fees, making them to part with this extra money amounted to exploitation by the school authority. The crisis which blew out in the open saw parents with children in many other private schools across the country rose to challenge this outrageous fee demanded by school owners (Guardian, 2020). The exploitation that ravaged the education sector in Nigeria, especially at the peak of the lockdown restrictions, highlighted the persistence of systemic exploitation (Wollner, 2019) and the dynamics of social exploitation (Spash, 2020). Such type of exploitation according to the authors is found with precarious working conditions, as witnessed with private school teachers detailed in this section.

Following the complaints by parents, there were reductions in the fees payable by students to reflect the exclusion of physical class essentials and items. One would have thought that this modification will reflect in the emoluments paid to teachers employed by these private school operators. However, the reverse appeared to be the case. For most part of the period of the lockdown when schools were shut, virtual classes went on and this serves as a bridge of the curriculum. So, students did not lose much but the same cannot be said of most teachers in the employment of private schools. Evidence of the financial crisis experienced by teachers of private schools was in the public domain for a long time. There were appeals from different quarters and in different ways, for public assistance to teachers of private schools who complained that they were not paid for the period of the closure of the school. The labor exploitation that was apparent therein was reflected in the fact that although schools made parents to pay for their students, albeit reduced fees, yet many teachers were not paid for the period of the closure. This precariousness of labor weighed heavily on most families and this forced many calls for appeal and assistance across the country. There were fundraising activities on social media platforms in support of teachers in private schools who were not earning any form of remuneration. Recall that since schools were shut, virtual lessons replaced physical classes yet teachers who moderated these virtual classes were paid low stipends that were not commensurate to their work, and in extreme cases, could not draw payment for work done (Interview, 2020). Even though the overall challenging situation threw humanity into confusion and almost rendered many helpless and vulnerable, this denial from distributive justice reinforces the argument that certain types of social system are culpable for exploitation (Zafirovski, 2019). This caused many private teachers to design survival strategies to assuage their situation.

One case that pulled and pooled the attention of Nigerians was a case of a teacher with a private school in Ikorodu, Lagos State, who went on Twitter and openly cried and appealed to kindhearted people to come to his aid as his family hungered. According to him, he and his spouse are private school teachers and with no income during the period of the lockdown, it had become a calamity in their home as they could not feed their children. The video of this helpless crying teacher went viral and in no time, funds were raised for him by Nigerians, a gesture he also publicly appreciated. His social media appeal opened the eyes of many to the plight of teachers and even other people whose form of livelihood had been temporarily halted due to the closure and restrictions on social activities. In order to forestall a situation of exploitation, anybody appealing for help in that wise was required to show evidence of employment as a teacher.

In what obviously validates 'extra-economic compulsion' by Cohen (1989) is the mandate imposed by Abia State University, a public university in southeastern Nigeria on returning students to pay what it called a "COVID-2019 Prevention Fee" (The Cable, 2020). This irregular payment was made compulsory and set as a condition for which students will be re-registered for a new academic session following school resumption. In spite of the public outcry that greeted this announcement, there were no clear indications that the school authority would back down from this directive. Similar incident transpired in another public university, the University of Port Harcourt directed that students would need to provide evidence that they are free of the coronavirus. This medical certification is listed as one of the conditions for readmission into the school after the lockdown. The school authorities added that it will only recognize certificates issued by specific health organizations approved by the school, not necessarily those approved by the government. This directive by the university authority reflects Vrousalis's (2017) exploitation versus vulnerability instrumentalization, as it underscores a condition shrouded in secrecy and economic gains.

Wage Adjustment as Exploitation

Wages and salaries like other economic variables were not spared from the effects of the COVID-2019 lockdown in Nigeria. Wages are critical variables by which economies are evaluated (Alatas and Cameron, 2003). What this means is that wages cannot function in isolation. It is largely determined and influenced by other economic factors. The level of economic growth in Nigeria prior to the lockdown had declined as the government had in 2019 ordered the closure of all of the country's borders. This had posed its own peculiar challenge to economic planning and projections as Nigeria's goods, products, and services were not allowed to go to other markets in the West Africa sub-region and vice versa. It was in this milieu that the government-ordered lockdown was effected. And one of the resultant effect of this was the constrained slash of wages and salaries of Nigerian workers across board, especially those in the private sector. This was widespread and affected manufacturing companies, consultancy agencies, small and medium enterprises, as well as sundry service providers.

In the banking sector, there were a good number of job losses, as some banks were forced to reconstruct their wage structures by reducing workers' salaries and wages while in some cases, branches of banks were closed down and the workers disengaged from service. The development in the banking sector did not go down well with many people. There were complaints that it was difficult to reconcile that the same banks that had made huge donations toward the federal government's drive to fight the coronavirus turned around to lay off workers. This was both a moral and economic question that needed answers and justification. Customers of these banks did not see the rationale for this as they could not marry the two opposing developments. On different social media platforms, banks were called out and accused of exploiting customers and patronizing the government at the expense of their workforce. The trolls that followed this action gained justification particularly because in addition to the expanded workload of the remaining staff, many branches shut down operations to curb the spread of the virus. This meant the few branches left to operate had more transaction to handle in a day, yet with a lesser salary. With more work to do, marginal productivity is disproportionate to labor and capital income and this passes for exploitation (Zafirovski, 2019).

In other sectors of the economy, employers of labor specifically made it clear that workers should be ready to take different degrees of pay cuts if their jobs must be preserved. In some cases, the cuts were imposed on the staff without any form of consultation or input by the workers. Many affected workers, forced to accept the reduced wages, complained that the cost of production and operation did not increase in many organizations, yet business owners exploited the situation by putting the workers in a tight position where they had to choose either a loss of job or a pay cut. This was viewed as a huge level of exploitation by different people who felt that employers of labor did this to preserve their bottom line and their profits at the expense of the workers who were forced to readjust to the new reality of either a pay cut or a job loss (Spash, 2020). This narrative cut across different sectors of the Nigerian economy with the exception of public service. In most cases, these organizations justified these on the ground of business survival and market enhancement expediencies. Despite the return of the economy into full-scale activities, and federal government's widespread support for business owners, as part of cushioning effects of the pandemic on businesses, most salaries that were reviewed downwardly have not been reversed.

Insane Fare Hike amid a Pandemic

Another area where the exploitation occasioned by the COVID-2019 pandemic was prevalent is in the transportation sector. The Nigerian public transport system is largely informal in the sense that there are more informal operators than government operators. Though highly regulated by the government, the different transport operators function under the umbrella of different trade unions. The largest of these trade unions in the transport sector is the National Union of Road Transport Workers (NURTW). There is also the Road Transport Employers Association of Nigeria as well as the National Association of Road Transport Owners. These three organizations control operations in the road transport sector. The NURTW, being the biggest of the three, has members all over the federation who drive buses, cars, trucks, and collect dues and fees from members operating in different motor parks across the federation. According to Agbiboa (2017), the NURTW controls up to 70 percent of road transport operators in Nigeria. This position tallies with Lawuyi (2012) and Madugu (2018) that the bulk of the business in the transportation sector in Nigeria falls within the category of road transport. In the light of this, it is evident that road transport workers and operators, especially those in the private sector, play critical roles in the movement of persons and goods in Nigeria.

Other informal forms of transportation including motorcycles popularly called *achaba* or *okada* as well as tricycles widely known as *Keke* have become important components of the road transport system in Nigeria. Because of the lax laws, road transport operators are often guilty of overloading of their vehicles, with reckless conducts on roads. A good number of these operators use mostly unkempt and decrepit vehicles for their operations. This makes them easy targets for corrupt law enforcement agents who prey on their illegalities to extort them. The corruption by the police also exacerbated the hike in the new fare regime, as transport operators factored these illegal payments into the fare charges.

At the outbreak of the pandemic, social distancing was one of the necessary measures promoted to deal with the spread of the virus. This process was carried into the transportation sector. Operators were mandated to observe and enforce necessary social distancing protocols, among their passengers. Thus, the carrying capacity of most vehicles, especially public transport, remained constant but the people carried was greatly reduced. In a country where prices and fares are arbitrarily fixed by the operators, most transport operators across the length and breadth of Nigeria decided to hike their fares without consideration for the economic hardship. According to one of the operators, the hike was to justify and bridge the gap occasioned by the forced reduced passenger numbers.

In Lagos, Nigeria's commercial nerve center and most populous city, the government had introduced the bus rapid transit (BRT) system as part of its reformation of public transportation in the city. The introduction of the BRT had reduced the overwhelming control of the informal operators who mostly use mini buses. These government-approved mini buses, popularly known as *danfo*, are designed to carry 10 passengers but operators often exceed this capacity by carrying 14 passengers. In order to mitigate losses or reduced income, occasioned by the forced reduction of number of passenger carried on each trip, transport operators arbitrarily hiked transport fares.

The hike caused untold hardship for passengers who were still grappling with the socioeconomic adjustments of the pandemic, and now forced to pay more for the same trip in the same vehicles. The outcry against the fare hike was not only in Lagos but it was also even worse and heavier on interstate passengers. Because close to 70 percent of movement of persons and goods are done via road, this increase in fares affected a good number of people. Within the period of the COVID-2019 pandemic, there was also a hike in the pump price of gasoline in Nigeria, and despite the initial hike based on reduced passenger numbers, road transport operators still added another level of increase on transportation cost. However, it can be argued that the conditions that necessitated the fare hike may not totally pass as exploitation because circumstances beyond operators' control warranted it and validated fair exploitation (Vrousalis, 2017).

The situation which caused passengers to cry out over this crushing cost of transportation saw operators justify the double increment on the ground of necessity of profit. Interestingly, public transport operators, from whom considerations were expected by the citizenry, also had their fares hiked.

Taking Lagos State as the point of focus, the fledging BRT system introduced and operated by the state government adapted to the new demands of social distancing among passengers riding on the buses. As mentioned earlier, BRT buses control a sizable fraction of the road transportation market in Lagos. One of the benefits and good point of the BRT system was the stable and fair cost of commuting. Owing to this, a good number of commuters can be found at the different bus termini, at different times of the day. The adjustment of the sitting arrangement in line with the new social distancing protocol was not the only change effected by the BRT operators. The main consideration of price was eventually thrown off board as the operators of the BRT buses jerked up the bus fares outrageously. This development caused a lot of disaffection among the populace and the government was called out for what was considered insensitivity and exploitation of the commuters in the state. Even after the sitting arrangement based on social distancing protocol was reversed, and the buses had gone back to carrying their normal passenger, according to their full capacities, the fare hike was not reversed. This established the fact, among commuters, that the government latched onto the opportunity of the pandemic to exploit commuters across the state. There is a sense in which this resonates with Wollner's (2019) argument that high-level insensitivity, unfairness, and the collapse of structures are responsible for such anomaly.

The Cankerworm of Security Exploitation

The complaints of the Nigerian populace concerning exploitation on the back of the COVID-2019 pandemic were not limited to private service providers, as government institutions and agencies were guilty of exploitation of the citizens in different ways. One critical institution that featured extensively in the picture of exploitation during the period of the pandemic is the principal law enforcement agency and more specifically, the Nigeria Police Force. There is a long history of corruption and underhand dealings involving the Nigerian police, to the point that the public confidence in this important and strategic law enforcement agency barely exists (Ahmed et al., 2013). There are widespread cases of corrupt practices among police officers and extrajudicial killings, aiding and abetting criminal activities, and creating an anti-trust system in different parts of the country. Because the lockdown came with restriction on movement and social gatherings, the Nigerian police as the number one law enforcement agency was saddled with the responsibility of ensuring compliance with the government directives. Evidence abounds to show that during this period, police officers exploited the populace in different ways and at different times. This can be looked at from different perspectives.

First, as the most essential law enforcement agency on the road, the Nigerian police is ubiquitous and a constant presence on Nigerian roads. That means there is a consistent interface between road users, especially transport operators, and officers of the Nigeria Police Force. As pointed out earlier, the Nigerian police do not enjoy wide popularity among the citizens, and the experience during the coronavirus lockdown only reinforced this sad reality, especially as outcry against police exploitation became more intense. Members of the police force being the prime security agency were also responsible for securing neighborhoods. However, they went beyond their mandate as they threatened to close business offices, premises, and shops. Police officers exploited and extorted traders who, in order not to fall victims, were forced to adjust their business hours in the face of the corona pandemic. At some point, the government of Ogun State, in Southwestern Nigeria, created specific days for the opening of markets. Markets were allowed to be opened on Tuesdays and Thursdays of each week. In spite of these government-approved opening days, police officers reportedly went into different markets, threatened to close down the markets, falsely accusing traders of breaching laid down regulations but willingly looked away once these traders ‘settled’ them (Interview, 2020). As would be discussed later, this forced cost was eventually loaded on prices by traders, especially those who deal in essential items like food and groceries.

NCDC Officials, Culpable Exploiters

On another level, officials of the National Center of Disease Control (NCDC) were accused of exploiting the unpleasant situation occasioned by the COVID-2019 lockdown in the country. Due to the peculiarity that characterized the virus, hospitals and clinics in the country were subject to approval by the NCDC before treating COVID-2019 patients. The same prerogative and authority empowered the agency to shut down hospitals and clinics that breached this directive. In fact, only specific public health facilities were authorized to treat patients who had contracted the disease. This was because the government had established specialized COVID-2019 treatment/isolation centers where members of the public could go for test, and if found positive, would be isolated in these places. So, no health facility, hospital, or clinic was authorized to treat anybody suspected of having COVID-2019. However, these regulatory and supervisory responsibilities opened doors of opportunities for exploitation by

NCDC officials. There were wide reports of NCDC officials who used this avenue to harass and exploit health operators, on the one hand, and patients on the other. According to an unnamed NCDC official, "it is just a matter of saying that XYZ clinic is treating COVID-2019 patients without reporting them to the NCDC and such facility would be penalized and in some extreme cases, shut down by the government" (Interview, Lagos NCDC official, 2020).

Something appears unclear in this whole saga, especially because testing is a critical phase that confirms infection or otherwise. Due to the ravaging corruption, health operators have become vulnerable, despite acknowledging the exploitative acts of these officials in the exploitation (Vrousalis, 2017). In comparison to other states in the country, this situation was prevalent especially in the city of Lagos which incidentally has the highest cases in the country (NCDC, 2020).

Closely connected to this is the issue of COVID-2019 test and certification especially as necessary requirement for people leaving or coming into the country. As a prerequisite for flight and inward mobility of people, the NCDC gave a standing rule that travelers into Nigeria as well as those leaving the country must undergo COVID-2019 screening. The screening was to be done in specific government-approved health facilities and certifications issued from these places are taken as part of necessary traveling documents. The good side of this initiative is the clearance and covering it gives to would-be travelers, while also doubles as a way of preventing infection and spread of the virus. However, the nobility of this gesture was upturned and opened to exploiters who used the opportunity to extort travelers. According to another anonymous official with NCDC, he said there were cases where some people did not undergo the test but were issued certification. In his words, some of our officials capitalize on their desperation to exploit their vulnerabilities. Although this response is colored with corruption, it is laced with exploitation.

Not a small controversy followed the introduction of this directive as many travelers complained of exploitation. This is premised on the fact that Nigerian-bound travelers were made to undergo COVID-2019 clearance test before coming to Nigeria and upon landing in Nigeria were made to go into isolation and pay for another round of testing regardless of their certification detailing their negative COVID-2019 status (Nairametrics, 2020). A returnee who participated in this study captures the process in a rather frustrating tone: "How can a structure be so inefficient and corrupt to the extent of being insensitive to people who have been on air for hours and some, even days?" (Interview, Lagos Returnee, 2020).

The bureaucratic process involved in the test and the isolation processes presented new opportunities for officials of the NCDC and Ministry of Health to exploit the people. Upon arrival in Nigeria, a passenger is mandatorily isolated, ironically, not in a government facility but in his/her own chosen space. The returnee is then expected to report at one of the designated test centers for necessary medical examination. This development is not unconnected to the pressure that had overwhelmed government facilities and the rupture in the health sector in the country. The result of this test coupled with the number of days that lapse before the tests are carried out, all created clumsy and exploitable processes that are openly exploited.

In spite of the shifting policies and compelling ridiculous charges on returnees in particular, for isolation and testing, the government of Nigeria failed to put in place a specific and straight testing and isolation protocols for them. Most returnees found the laborious testing process and attendant delays constricting and did not mind using the backdoor to access quick service. The subscription, by the returnees, to the unofficial and corrupt method of backdoor service resonates with the concept of vulnerability proffered by Vrousalis (2017) in the shadow of instrumentalization, which says that people are exploited when what they need is encumbered by other factors beyond their control. Besides, the returnees resorted to the backdoor approach as a form of coping strategy. The rationality of this is questioned in another way as it shows that the problem is not with the system but the people who sabotage the system for personal gains (Zwolinski, 2012).

Consumer Goods Exploitation

As noted earlier, the little time allowance between the announcement and commencement of the lockdown led many Nigerians into called panic buying. Nigeria, being a consuming society especially against the backdrop of its huge population, food commodities, and other consumer essentials, are always special areas of consideration and concern. There is always interest in the market prices of these items, particularly because they are often subjected to inflation and price variations. In anticipation of the announcement of the lockdown, and owing to past experiences, Nigerians turned to the market to stock up. However, it was with great shock that the prices of goods and essential commodities skyrocketed overnight, and this left many Nigerians near stranded at the beginning of the lockdown. People had expected that prices would remain the same, and they would be able to get items to sustain them while they are restricted indoor.

The situation is exacerbated by the federal government's limitation of the lockdown to three states because it created a market imbalance. Unfortunately, this impromptu market price increment of goods was not restricted to just the places that were under lockdown. Rather, the price hike spread across the federation even to areas where there were no forms of lockdown significant enough to affect production and transportation of goods and produces. In a country with a history of price hikes that are rarely reversed, people knew that it would be difficult to renegotiate a reversal even when things return to normal.

Prices of common food items like rice, beans, yam, and processed cassava generally called *garri* went through the roof across Nigeria. One such factor for pricing discrepancies for same product is location, but this discrepancy nationwide was heavily influenced by exploitation. Sellers latched onto the times and saw it as an opportunity to make more gains. Aware that they may also have bought at an increased rate, the new price regimes were extended to old stocks. There was no reason or justification for these because as a procurement officer for a pharmacy who rather remained anonymous said: "Only an insignificant increment was made but the management decided to add ridiculous margin profit to make more profit. Unfortunately, there is nothing I can do because many other pharmacies sell this product at an outrageous amount also." This situation defies the very essence of being health practitioners, whose first concern should be the preservation of humanity. But, again, the scenario is reminiscent of the social reality of non-producers controlling the means of production as much as they control sales (Terray and Serrano, 2019).

INDIVIDUAL EXPLOITATION

Like the structural exploitation discussed in the preceding section,, the realities that played out during the government's emergency lockdown impacted individuals negatively. For individual exploitation, as we shall see, the type of injustice that comes with exploitation is closer to home than the structural type.

Celebrity-"Sponsored" Giveaways as Exploitation

Away from the consumer goods price hike, the exploitation driven by the pandemic manifested in other areas. One of such is the indirect exploitation by celebrities who used their social acceptance status to exploit the populace during the period of the pandemic. One of the fallouts of the increase in social media use in Nigeria is the emergence of social media influencers who enjoy the status of celebrities, even in this virtual space. In most cases, these influencers are used to promote brands, causes, ideas, and processes. Because they enjoy good number of followership and they influence people's perceptions and opinions, they are often used to reach more people, in different ways. At some point, giveaways, financial support, and assistance increased on social media as celebrities or those who are given to philanthropy employed social media as good channels of extending support to needy Nigerians during the period of the lockdown. Such philanthropic gestures like cash giveaways are often pushed through the social media handles of celebrities who have good number of followers and fans. Thus, some philanthropists who do not command such followership push their philanthropic gestures and processes to these social media influencers and use their channels and clouts to reach more people, especially those in need.

During the period of the lockdown, a number of celebrities and social media influencers were alleged to have exploited their followers and the general public at large even when they were expected to use their social media handles for humanitarian support. One of such was Eniola Badmus, a popular Nigerian actress with a large followership in the social media space. She was allegedly approached by a philanthropist who wanted to give financial remedy to some Nigerians who were badly hit by the pandemic. The arrangement would see the actress give specific sum of money to randomly selected but needy followers. For this intermediary service, the popular actress reportedly demanded an outrageous commission. When the news broke on the social media, the actress was called out for exploiting the helplessness of Nigerians affected by the lockdown.

CONCLUSION AND RECOMMENDATIONS

Overall, this chapter stretches the concept of 'exploitation' from its narrowly deployed engagements of economies and governance and recast it as an assemblage of impromptu, spontaneous, and unprepared social realities. In doing so, the study stresses the unpreparedness of the government in containing the emergencies that came with the COVID-2019 lockdown restrictions in Nigeria. With its index case recorded in February 2020 being an Italian who arrived in Lagos and traveled to Ogun State where a company doctor suspected him of carrying COVID-2019 symptoms, the fear of the spread soon spread like wildfire. As new infected cases were reported and began to surge in Lagos and Ogun States as well as the Federal Capital Territory, the government in its wisdom and capacity ordered a lockdown to contain the spread of the deadly virus. This lockdown shut down almost all sectors of society except essential workers like health workers, security personnel, and media workers, among others. In what seems to be the solution to save humanity soon turned chaotic and compelling for the vast majority of citizens.

The lockdown orders necessitated citizens to stock their homes with essentials as it did the government to provide some welfare packages otherwise termed palliatives. Corporate organization joined in this gesture and supported the government with cash and essential items as a way of showing their solidarity (Nairametrics, 2020). Although it was expected that the palliative initiative would serve as cushion for the effect of the lockdown on the citizenry given its suddenness, the experiences, however, showed that these items were not transparently distributed. In some cases, access to them was tied to political patronage. This was a clear case of exploitation.

Experiences of exploitation during the pandemic were nuanced, thus expanding the discourse of exploitation. While government applauded itself for supporting the masses during the peak of its lockdown orders, counter-responses filed in from the citizens knocked the government's claim. Many complained they neither received nor know anyone that received government's palliatives. Months after the dust had settled and life had returned to normal, unrelated protests against police excesses resulted in the exposure of institutional/structural exploitation. One of the fallouts from the protests was the discovery of warehouses, in different parts of the country, stocked with branded palliative materials that were earmarked for distribution to Nigerians. Some other palliative materials were even discovered in homes of some government officials, who for their personal interests withheld essentials meant for the indigent and vulnerable in the society. As the discovery of these palliatives exposed the inhumanness of the government, the contradiction entirely destroys the very essence of governance and democracy, which is to serve and protect the interest of the people. Contrastingly, the government attitude confirmed Terray and Serrano's (2019) view on the concept of domination. The authors discuss this concept within the context of politics and drew conclusions that the government exercise dominion over people and resources. They argue that government's dominion is laced with exploitation of the public's common good. This did not come as a surprise as corruption, greed, insincerity, and insensitivity are apparent traits that characterize exploitation and form the foundation that has continued to be the bane of systems, structures, and institutions in developing countries like Nigeria.

At the instance of the order which plunged citizens into a state of anxiety due to the short period available for preparation, the situation was made worse by shortage or lack of funds by many. Panic buying became the order of the day for people who had the financial capacity to stock their homes with essential items. The situation automatically provided opportunity for exploiters, thereby leaving citizens to their mercy. From traders of essential products to service providers, the story was largely the same. Prices of food items shot up as well as transport fares. Fares went up because vehicles were forced to carry below their maximum passenger capacity, and operators used the increased fare as a bridge. For food and other essentials, the increase blew up for most essentials (Ozili, 2020). However, these were not reversed when activities returned to status quo prior to the adjustment.

Affected individuals designed coping strategies accordingly. While some sought help in the virtual space, some others preferred physical approaches by seeking help from family and friends. For many who experienced exploitation, especially returnees mandated to undergo COVID-2019 screening, they chose to sway with the bent rules by doing the illegal thing; it can be argued that this is not 'wholly' exploitation as Vrousalis (2017) believes, but they are compelled to go this route because of the unpleasant circumstances beyond their control.

Although the overwhelming realities limit the issues in their entirety and complexities, attention has been paid to critical issues that happened in Nigeria at the outbreak of the COVID-2019 and the months that followed after. With a deep-seated complexity, what is critical for a society like Nigeria to curtail a repeat is to do the following:

- Begin with a sincere movement or orientation program channeled to first and foremost put fairness and justice on the front burner of any human interaction and relationship. Cautious not to sound as an advocate, the term 'exploitation' in its sense negatively defies the principle of morality.
- Although there is a special task force team under the Federal Competition and Consumer Protection Commission saddled with the responsibility of monitoring and regulating pricing of goods and services, the exploitation that is prevalent during the COVID-2019 lockdown is an indication that they have not lived up to their responsibilities. Therefore, there is need for the government to strengthen this commission for quality service delivery.
- There is an urgent need for the government to improve the health sector to meet with the global standard.
- Have a transparent database: aside from the dilapidated health facilities and poor services that were exposed by the COVID-2019, the situation also uncovered incorrect and unavailability of citizens' record. Perhaps, if government were to have a transparent record with important and relevant demographics, managing the economic situation that played out during the peak of the COVID-2019 lockdown would have minimized the pressure.

REFERENCES

Abu, N. and Staniewski, M. W. (2019). Determinants of corruption in Nigeria: evidence from various estimation techniques. *Economic Research—Ekonomska Istraživanja* 32(1):3058–3082.

Agbiboa, D. (2017). No condition is permanent: informal transport workers and labor precarity in Africa's largest city. *International Journal of Urban and Regional Research* 24(1):44–65.

Ahmed, M., Muhammad, N., Mohammed, M. U. and Idris, Y. (2013). A GiS-based analysis of police stations distributions in Kano metropolis. *IOSR Journal of Computer Engineering* 8(4):72–78.

Alatas, V. and Cameron, L. (2003). The impact of minimum wages on employment in a low-income country: An evaluation using the difference-in-difference approach. Retrieved on November 11, 2020 from https://openknowledge.worldbank.org/handle/10986/18313.

Baujard, A. (2010). Collective interest versus individual interest in Bentham's felicific calculus. questioning welfarism and fairness, *The European Journal of the History of Economic Thought* 17(4):607–634.

Channels TV. (April 25, 2020). FG starts distribution of COVID-19 palliative in Abuja. Retrieved on November 1, 2020 from youtube.com/watch?v=6OGQsxq Zmpk.

Cohen, G. A. (1989). *History, Labor and Freedom: Themes from Marx*. Oxford, UK: Oxford University Press.

Guardian Newspaper. (June 18, 2020). As online learning fees pits parents against schools. Retrieved on October 10, 2020 from https://guardian.ng/features/education/as-online-learning-fees-pit-parents-against-schools.

Klein, N. (2007). *The Shock Doctrine: The Rise of Disaster Capitalism*. New York: Henry Holt and Company, LLC.

Lawuyi, O. B. (2012). The world of the Yoruba taxi driver: An interpretive approach to vehicle slogans. *Africa: Journal of the international African Institute* 58(1):1–13.

Madugu, Y. U. (2018). From motorcycle to tricycle: Security challenges and emergence of tricycle in Kano metropolis. *Kaduna Journal of Humanities* 1(1):280–300.

Mayer, R. (2007). Sweatshops, exploitation, and moral responsibility. *Journal of Social Philosophy* 38:605–619.

Nairametrics Online. (April 18, 2020). Updated: List of all companies and billionaires that have contributed to COVID-2019 relief fund. Retrieved on September 28, 2020 from https://nairametrics.com/2020/04/18/list-of-all-companies-and-billionaires-that-have-contributed-to-covid-19-relief-fund.

Nairametrics Online. (October 3, 2020). Fake labs, travel frustrations, passenger allege COVID-2019 test scams at airport. Retrieved on October 31, 2020 from https://nairametrics.com/2020/10/03/fake-labs-travel-frustrations-passengers-allege-covid-19-test-scams-at-airport.

Onuka, A. O. (2008). An evaluation of parents' patronage of private primary schools in Abeokuta, Nigeria. *International Journal of African and African American Studies* 2(2):58–70.

Ozili, P. K. (2020). Covid-19 pandemic and economic crisis: The Nigerian experience and structural causes. Electronic journal retrieved on November 3, 2020 from https://www.researchgate.net/publication/340439471.

Premium Times Newspaper. (May 13, 2020). Parents kick as Atlantic Hall imposes N175,000 monthly fees for online learning. Retrieved on October 12, 2020 from https://www.premiumtimesng.com/news/more-news/392527-parents-kick-as-atlantic-hall-imposes-n175000-monthly-fee-for-online-learning.html.

Risse, M. and Wollner, G. (2014). Three images of trade: On the place of trade in a theory of global justice. *Moral Philosophy and Politics* 1(2):201–225.

Sahara Reporters. (October 26, 2020). We hid palliatives ahead of second wave of COVID-2019, Nigerian governors say. Retrieved on October 21, 2020 from http://saharareporters.com/2020/10/26/we-hid-palliatives-ahead-second-wave-covid-19-nigerian-governors-sa.

Sahara Reporters. (October 30, 2020). Nigerians expose how Lagos assembly member, Alli-Macaulay, used COVID-2019 palliatives as birthday gift. Retrieved on November 2, 2020 from http://saharareporters.com/2020/10/30/nigerians-expose-how-lagos-assembly-member-alli-macaulay-used-covid-19-palliatives.

Spash, C. L. (2020). The economy' as if people mattered: Revisiting critiques of economic growth in a time of crisis. *Globalizations* 18(7):1–19.

Terray, E. and Serrano, J. (2019). Exploitation and domination in Marx's thought. *Rethinking Marxism* 31(4):412–424.

The Cable Newspaper. (May 11, 2020). Extra: Abia varsity asks students to pay N15k COVID-2019 prevention fee. Retrieved on October 11, 2020 from https://www.thecable.ng/extra-abia-varsity-asks-students-to-pay-15k-covid-19-prevention-fee.

Vrousalis, N. (2013). Exploitation, vulnerability, and social domination. *Philosophy & Public Affairs* 41:131–157.

Vrousalis, N. (2017). Exploitation. Electronic copy retrieved on October 18, 2020 from https://ssrn.com/abstract=3072032.

Vanguard Newspaper. (April 16, 2020). Lockdown palliatives a scam, residents fume. Retrieved on October 15, 2020 from https://www.vanguardngr.com/2020/04/lockdown-palliative-a-scam-residents-fume.

Walras, L. (1926). *Elements d'économie Politique Pure*. Paris, France: R. Pichon et R. Durand-Auzias.

Wollner, G. (2019). Anonymous exploitation: non-individual, non-agential and structural. *Review of Social Economy* 77(2):143–162.

Zafirovski, M. (2019). Exploitation in contemporary societies: An exploratory comparative analysis. *The Social Science Journal* 56(4):565–587.

Zwolinski, M. (2012). Structural exploitation. *Social Philosophy and Policy* 29:154–179.

Chapter 18

Coroweakstate

Emmanuel Vincent Nelson Kallon

On December 31, 2019, what was initially perceived as a localized epidemic in Wuhan, Hubei Province, China, gradually expanded beyond its border to become a global shock, following its declaration by the World Health Organization (WHO) a pandemic on January 30, 2020. WHO cautioned that it must be considered a global health threat and would be pernicious in societies with an existing feeble and deleterious health infrastructure (Sohrabi et al., 2020). Apart from this anticipated increase in the spread of the virus in the less developed and impoverished countries, which has yet to materialize, it is obvious that the emergence of the Coronavirus Disease (COVID)-2019 has created an atmosphere of unprecedented artificial barriers among countries across the globe, and is also having a retarding consequence on the foreign policies of countries relating to the promotion of social and economic integration.

Still, on a global scale, the COVID-2019 phenomenon has also impaired massive monetary activities. It has reduced a profound economic progression among and within societies, both developed and underdeveloped countries. The slowdown in many educational systems and people's lives caused by the virus remains (Yaya et al., 2020; World Bank, 2020; United Nations, 2020b; Walsh, 2020). For instance, in less than a year, on November 30, 2020, the destructive nature of COVID-2019 was noted by the Coronavirus Resource Center of Johns Hopkins University to have infected more than 63 million people globally (John Hopkins University Corona Resource Center, 2020). In addition, approximately a billion people within various school systems are noted to have been affected (Azzi-Huck and Shmis, 2020). These are a piece of considerable evidence indicating the magnitude of the virus's unpredictable threats globally. More importantly, at the national level, it uncovers the behavioral patterns of societies in their response approaches and how such could help us better understand the much-acclaimed reforms taking place within these countries.

Thus, this chapter aims to explain how weak states' characteristics are layered over time and how this connects with the heightened hysteria we are witnessing among people because of the COVID-2019. The chapter explains the pattern of institutionalized violence considered a core feature of a weak state when the violence becomes reified and prominent within nation-states, particularly in states once conceived as institutionally and democratically reformed when confronted with an internal difficulty. Thus, this study investigated the question: why did institutionalized violence a pattern formed in line with the state approach in curbing the COVID-2019 in Sierra Leone, a country that is acclaimed to have experienced institutional reforms? Building on the emergence of the COVID-2019 in the country as a litmus, the chapter argues that institutionally reformed nation-states can best be identified by their institutional, behavioral patterns when confronted with an internal dilemma and not a prior taken-for-granted practice.

One key feature of a weak state is its layered pattern of institutionalized structural violence. Institutionalized violence in this context would imply the physical violence exhibited by state organs in the execution of certain state functions and the state's systemic inability to guarantee the provision of requisite and mandatory socioeconomic opportunities to enhance the daily survival of the populace. The notion of an institutionally reformed and democratized state goes beyond the mere recycling of a political power exchange from one set of actors to the others. The exchange of power occasioned through systematic electoral processes is merely a symbolism of power contestations within the state's political power structure, which do not necessarily imply a strong linkage to any profound societal change. It is about how deeply rooted these exchanges of powers within the political space meaningfully reflect toward disintegrating those existential structural barriers in bringing about an equal opportunity that would cement the state's social stability.

The discussion of weak state in this chapter focuses on the relation between a state and its people and, more importantly, how a particular state that appears reformed or in its transition toward transformation has in fact become a weaker state in terms of its institutional and layered behavioral inadequacies, particularly when confronted with specific internal challenges. Analyzing this exemplary weak state phenomenon, the case of Sierra Leone provides a veritable standard, using the advent of the COVID-2019 case, to showcase how the response approach by the state toward curbing the COVID-2019 pandemic resulted in the reification of institutionalized violence.

Socioeconomic opportunities, like civil and political rights, are a tenet of a democratically reformed state, "albeit liberal and social democrats may have a dichotomized viewpoint" (see Hobson and Kurki, 2012, p. 7; Berkman and Erman, 2012). According to Shedrack C. Agbakwa, stability within countries is largely hinged on how the economic and social opportunities are made available across citizens (Agbakwa, 2003). In the developing countries, the emergence and continuity of many intra-state instabilities have not been unconnected to the wanton neglect by the state of this core responsibility. However, as noted by David M. Kotz, neoliberalism is a political ideology of a modern state system whose advocacy is hinged on the discountenance of the state from playing a significant role in the economic structure of society, as such would engender an "optimum efficiency, income distribution, and technological progress" (Kotz, 2005, p. 1). Nonetheless, the defectiveness of this maximalist construct would be that it could hardly be seen to have a huge impact on the poorer countries. These countries, precisely their governments, are the holder of economic power and, therefore, the leading distributor. Moreover, the process is highly centralized. Socioeconomic provision as a public good is thus the state's cardinal function and is a viable impetus that incrementally elevates the country from the weak state status quo in the transformative process.

Sierra Leone has severely remained a weak state because of its inability to ideally target and address this wide socioeconomic gap, which could be considered not only as an institutional weakness but an existentially institutionalized structural violence layered over time. This became conspicuous with the emergence of the COVID-2019 scourge in the country in alignment with other deeply rooted unaddressed societal challenges. As a weak state feature, the continuous maintenance of this institutionalized violence within the country because of the lack of socioeconomic opportunities would also be a political strategy that is sometimes tactically engaged and maintained within the political space for the rational benefit of political elites, as the maintenance of social vulnerability within society could become a hotbed for an engaged manipulation. In addition, it could be viewed that the over-dependency of countries on external supports has become so ingrained that domestically inward-looking approaches for solutions have been compromised, where state institutions are in dereliction of their roles because the external financiers have not danced to the tune in time. These factors help uncover the systemic nature of the weak-state nature of specific societies, as the case in Sierra Leone suggests.

As a qualitative study, this work utilizes a process tracing and institutional layering methodological approaches to locate knowledge of Sierra Leone's weak state structure, particularly from her recent political development in the post-conflict period. Through institutional layering methodological approach, the study showcases how what appeared to be reformed is an inherent pattern of the same system that has been layered over time, characteristic of the same weak state society. The study mainly used secondary sources from appropriate archival materials, academic literature, official documents, and Internet sources.

This study draws attention to the intricacies of reform process conceptualization within states and states in transition. The institutional behavioral patterns of the state and their relations with the populace are a critical pillar in conceptualizing reform patterns within the society. The remaining sections of this chapter are arranged as follows. The first section analyzed the conceptual framework, where it briefly looked at the weak state as a framework of analysis. In the second section, the study examined the emergence of COVID-2019 in Sierra Leone and the state's initial response mechanism. Next, the chapter succinctly analyzed the country's current state of health infrastructure to showcase how it presented a direct archetype of state weakness. In addition, the study then analyzed how institutionalized violence became manifested, particularly during the period of the statewide lockdown to curtail COVID-2019 transmission. The chapter ends with a conclusion and recommendations.

WEAK STATE THEORETICAL AND CONCEPTUAL DISCUSSIONS

Conceptual discussions on the weak state are incomplete without briefly locating how discussions about the state have evolved. In its philosophical and institutional evolution, one of the concepts associated with the state has been elaborated and advanced by a sociologist, Max Weber. Weber conceptualized state as an organized structure with an absolute "monopoly of the legitimate use of force" within its specified boundary (Anter, 2014, p. 11). From this sociological perspective, this standpoint had long been laid out by Niccolo Machiavelli, emphasizing the state's force as its central foundation (Di-John, 200). As a prior maximalist perspective, this historical conceptualization of the state was underpinned by the maintenance of state centric, and more importantly, in safeguarding the viability of the societal structure. Beyond state legitimization over the monopoly of the use of force, the modern state is characterized by "administrative and a legal order" (Whimster, 2004, p. 357). In addition, I. William Zartman chronicled a few essential characteristics of the state that includes "authority, population, territory, and government" (Zartman, 1995, p. 5).

In further clarification of the state, Joel S. Migdal asked whether "states make a difference in the lives of the people they seek to govern?"

(Migdal, 1988, p. xiii). This problematization of the state context exposed a desire for in-depth conceptual exploration, insofar as the identification of why states are topologized as weak or strong, particularly in the contemporary modern state discourse. As opined by Alberto Martinelli, this is integral as the meanings of the state have transcended beyond the mere internal and external domestic sovereign protection and maintenance to a broad spectrum of economic participation that addresses the socioeconomic requirements of its population (Martinelli, 2001). Thus, the differentiation in the analyses of a strong and weak state lies in their capacities and varies according to the applicability. Viewing from Westphalia's treaty that beckoned the notion of the modern state system, necessitating the commitment of rights and responsibilities between the state and the governed, weak states emerge in the context where the governing structure becomes incapable of adhering to their core obligated roles within the state. This phenomenon gained more salience in the latter part of the twentieth century (Mentan, 2004).

In this chapter, how sustainable the state has been positioned internally to the population's responsive needs showcases the difference, which is in line with what Robert I. Rotberg specified that nation-states' cardinal role, particularly in the contemporary context, is to ensure the availability of public goods to their governed within the demarcated geographical, political boundaries, and reiterated that the level of deliverability of these responsibilities lies in the identification of either a state is strong, weak, or failed (Rotberg, 2003).

From the internal domestic perspective of states, a weak state, or as often reference as a fragile state, where the state-people relations remain virtually displaced because of the vulnerability of state functional social responsibility, has been a phenomenon associated mainly with the developing countries (Eizenstat et al., 2005). Susan E. Rice and Stewart Patrick note that weak or fragile states are countries incapable of promoting a viable atmosphere favorable for the enhancement of an internal economic expansion. In addition, they are countries chiefly challenged with institutional openness, remain constrained by security challenges in protecting their populace, and in guaranteeing the availability of basic needs (Rice and Patrick, 2008, p. 3). Robert I. Rotberg argues that weak states are inhibited by the prevailing circumstances caused by "geological, physical, economic constraints . . . and they are weak because of the challenges in their management systems, the presence of greed, despotism, external attacks, and are societies characterized by identity tensions, situated along with ethnic, religious or linguistic patterns" (Rotberg, 2003, pp. 4–5). In addition, Robert I. Rotberg (2015) also indicates that weak states countries are noted for their insufficient provision of the required public goods needed within the state, and even those made available are of a low standard value.

Given that it is the systemic weakness within states that often transcend a country into a full-fledged failed state, Robert H. Jackson describes these kinds of societies as incapable of protecting modicum civil conditions of their citizenry within their domestic settings. He added that such countries are recognized worldwide as a sovereign state, but domestically they have minimal actual "political existence" (Jackson, 2000, p. 296). Beyond the incapability of meeting the population's needs domestically based on their intense capability problems, the conceptual analyses of weak states also capture its spillover effects that often affect regional and the global setting. Edward Newman indicates that weak states are countries that often experience noncompliant governmental leadership that is antagonistic and motivated in undermining the privileges of statehood. He further opined that, as a weak state, its fundamental challenge in ensuring regulatory measures often result in illegal linkages, and the deployment of "war economies" is probable. He asserted that a weak state has the characteristic of becoming a plausible hotbed for the generation of terrorism that constitutes a hindrance internally and externally (Newman, 2007, p. 466).

Notably, in Africa, the weak state phenomenon has remained permeated in many of the societal structures. Analyzing the case of West Africa, Jenifer J. Atiku-Abubakar and Yoku Saw-Taylor characterize a weak state as a society where there is a pervasiveness of "structural imbalance associated with a wide difference in economic access, cultural and political differences" (Atiku-Abubakar and Saw-Taylor, 2003, pp. 168–169). This pattern has been a prominent trend in the sub-Saharan African countries, which have stymied many of the government's programs over the decades. These imbalances, the authors note, generate the salience of ethnic classification and social boundary differences and undermine equal deliverability of state resources. The authors stress that these imbalances are not unconnected to threats that have often resulted within the state structure serving to undermine its authority (Atiku-Abubakar and Saw-Taylor, 2003, pp. 168–169). Within this structural analysis of state weakness in Africa, John Emeka Ekude notes that in the period of the evolution of the modern state in Africa, the process impeded the existence of a robust administrative system which rendered these societies overly dependent on external attachment, feeble and unable to cater for their inhabitants (Ekude, 2011).

As a framework of this study, institutionalized violence is a central element within societies characterized as internally weak. Within such societies, the obligation of the state to the population is compromised by their inability to ensure the basic livelihoods are guaranteed. The state organs become a source of repression and such stymies existing rights. Analyzing Sierra Leone's case with the advent of the COVID-2019 during the lockdown, issues of these became glaring, and therefore, instructive for scholarly inquiry.

SIERRA LEONE AND THE MILIEU OF COVID-2019 EMERGENCE

Sierra Leone within the Mano River Union was the last country in the region to register the COVID-2019 virus. It was one of those countries in West Africa that experienced the hardest hit of the Ebola epidemic between 2014 and 2016. The negative impacts of Ebola resulted in massive economic disruptions, extinction of a large number of limited trained and qualified medical professionals and ordinary citizens, and the extensive outgrowth of early child pregnancy (World Bank, 2015; Evans et al., 2015; Denney et al., 2015, Mason, 2016; UNFPA, 2018). Thus, the emergence of the first COVID-2019 index case was received in despondency by Sierra Leoneans, given the background of this negative shock bequeathed by the Ebola scourge.

The COVID-2019 declaration was made by the Government of Sierra Leone on March 31, 2020, following series preparedness and the identification of a confirmed case that traveled to the country (World Health Organization, 2020), amid the overwhelming existential gaps in the general health infrastructure. Before the outbreak, and given the trend that it was the only country left in the region without a case of the COVID-2019 virus, preparedness was mainly the "catchy phrase" used across the state structures while the country awaited its index case. Attempting to make do what was available, initial engagement and preparedness protocols targeted the country's international airport, being the main gateway, and emphasis was placed on vigorous screening of incoming travelers combined with quarantine measures for people arriving from countries specifically known to be COVID-2019 densely affected sites (Kamara, 2020).

As an early institutionalization of preventive measures, initial safety measures were communicated at the community level, which community leaders were to integrate into their local approaches to enhance the dissemination of COVID-2019 protective messages. At the same time, hand washing was to be intensified generally (Kamara, 2020). These preliminary measures were among some of the counteractive approaches instituted to stem the COVID-2019 virus permeation further countrywide.

In what appears to be a robust measure, the government declared a State of Public Emergency on March 24, 2020, and approved by parliament on March 26, for 12 months (Government of Sierra Leone, 2020a; Thomas, 2020a). This declaration resulted in the closure of the borders with the neighboring countries of Guinea and Liberia, and only movements with essential commodities were sanctioned. The COVID-2019 response team was constituted on March 31, 2020, to superintend the Emergency Operations Center, headed by a retired military brigadier who was also the country's Minister of Defense, and the task of the emergency center was to respond to issues related to testing and isolation of suspected cases, and to generally serve as the first respondent treatment facility hub for the country (Government of Sierra Leone, 2020b).

On April 1, 2020, the country registered its second COVID-2019 case, suspected to have had no contact with the first victim (Thomas, 2020b), a situation that further complicated prior information on the transmission patterns. Curtailing the rapid spread of the virus countrywide was conceived as imperative. Thus, the government announced a three-day national lockdown from April 5 to 7, 2020 (Shaban, 2020). Among some of the reasons for the lockdown as captured in the speech of the president was to "(1) strengthen surveillance, (2) contact tracing, test suspected cases, and detect, isolate and quarantine persons, (3) map out possible spread of COVID-2019 in Sierra Leone, (4) re-assess and strengthen COVID-2019 pillars and institutions, and (5) deploy additional expertise and resources" (Government of Sierra Leone, 2020c, para. 6). Another three-day lockdown was instituted from May 3 to 5, 2020, and this came because of a response to address what was named as a "community transmission of COVID-2019 virus in Sierra Leone" (Government of Sierra Leone, 2020d, p. 1), particularly, given the rapid spread and the increased registered cases in April and May.

On May 2, 2020, it was confirmed by the Government of Sierra Leone COVID-2019 update briefing team that the cumulative confirmed cases countrywide were 155, 72 female and 83 male, and from the time the country registered its index case to June 2020, the total confirmed cases had amounted to 1,462 (Thomas, 2020; World Health Organization, 2020). During the lockdown to curb the virus, curfew and movement between and among inter-districts became characteristic of the approach. In line with the prior public emergency declaration and the imposed lockdown, it gave enormous power to the state actors while at the same time maximally limited the movement of people within vicinities and across districts during these periods.

The 1991 Constitution of Sierra Leone, section 29, and its subsidiary sections empower the Government of Sierra Leone for actions to be taken during a period of emergency, like in the case of COVID-2019, and the Public Health Ordinance of 1960 (Government of Sierra Leone, 1991, 1960). However, what remained much conspicuous was the actions taken, the lockdown measure to combat the ailment, and how that badly resulted in worsening as well as revealing the despicable existential state of the socioeconomic and sustenance livelihood of the majority of the ordinary population, who continuously remained subjected at the poverty continuum by the state, a phenomenon considered institutionalized violence, as a tenet of a weak state.

With the emergence of COVID-2019 in Sierra Leone, every district across the country has been without a recorded number of the virus, albeit substantial variation remains among districts on infection patterns. The situational

Table 18.1 Summary of COVID-2019 Cases in Sierra Leone as of September 28, 2020

Districts	*Confirmed Cases*	*Cumulative Confirmed Cases*	*Proportion of Total Cases (%)*	*New Deaths*	*Cumulative Deaths*	*Days since Last Confirmed Cases*
Western Area (Urban)	0	1,059	47.8	0	59	1
Western Area (Rural)	0	261	11.8	0	1	1
Port Loko	0	105	4.7	0	0	6
Kenema	0	125	5.6	0	4	12
Tonkolili	0	82	3.7	0	0	2
Bombali	0	49	2.2	0	4	44
Bonthe	0	87	3.9	0	0	52
Bo	0	108	4.9	0	2	29
Koinadugu	0	36	1.6	0	0	62
Falaba	0	11	0.5	0	0	50
Kailahun	0	79	3.6	0	0	6
Moyamba	0	58	2.6	0	0	37
Pujehun	0	29	1.3	0	0	34
Kono	0	75	3.4	0	2	28
Kambia	0	30	1.4	0	0	83
Karene	0	11	0.5	0	0	66
Incoming Cases	0	10	0.5	0	0	1
Total	0	2,215	100.0	0	72	-

Source: Sierra Leone Ministry of Health and Sanitation Situational Report (2020).

report by the Government of Sierra Leone corroborated this fact. Table 18.1 shows the cumulative cases of COVID-2019 captured in each of the districts across the country, and the total death cases, as of September 28, 2020.

OVERVIEW OF THE STATE OF HEALTH INFRASTRUCTURE IN SIERRA LEONE

For several years, Sierra Leone has been ranked one of those countries notable for the highest records of child and maternal mortality rate globally (Assaf and Winter, 2015; Reid, 2017, Amnesty International, 2009). In 2019, country analysis of maternal mortality, for instance, among the Mano River Countries shows that "Sierra Leone has a maternal mortality rate at 1120, Liberia at 661, and Guinea at 576, and Ivory Coast at 617" (World Health Organization, 2019). Besides the ranking within the MRU region, Sierra Leone is also noted for being among the countries with the highest maternal mortality rates in the world (Ministry of Health and Sanitation, 2016). Beyond this ranking, the nature of the entire health infrastructure was no longer subjected to denial by the political structure when the Ebola epidemic shocked the country in 2014. According to the Centers for Disease Control and Prevention, Sierra Leone has 14,124 Ebola cases, the highest compared with Liberia and Guinea from 2014 to 2016 (Centers for Disease Control and Prevention, 2019).

It is unarguable that the context behind this continued high medical challenge that has always claimed numerous lives of vulnerable inhabitants to preventable ailments in the country cannot be unconnected to the general poor health infrastructure, including the inaccessibility of the requisite medical facilities like medicines, and the limited availability of trained and qualified staff, and their maintenance. This cataclysmic ambience of the country's medical infrastructure has negatively shrouded the population's efficient obtainability of urban and rural medical attention.

The devastation caused by Ebola in Sierra Leone was equally an opportunity that uncovered the general state of the medical environment and the need for a total national restoration of the whole sector. Nonetheless, the notion of whether the country was able to learn meaningfully, particularly from the carnage occasioned by the Ebola scourge from 2014 to 2016, as a result of the deteriorated health infrastructure until the emergence of the COVID-2019 in 2020, would be conceived to have remained a governmental dereliction toward its core national development agenda of the state.

The state of the country's health infrastructure is fractured by a persistent lack of sufficient, trained, and qualified medical personnel. This was conspicuous in the existing data published by the government. For instance, the report indicated that out of a "10,000 population countrywide the availability of doctors was 0.18%; while out of 10,000 population the availability of Community Health Officers (CHOs) was 0.6% and also, for every 10,000 population the nurses available were at 0.6 %" (Government of Sierra Leone, 2016a, p. 26; Sharples, 2015, p. 6). Beyond the national challenge of medical personnel insufficiency, there has also remained an intense disparity in the availability of health workers between the country's rural and urban settings (Barr et al., 2019). As noted, the rural setting with a population strength of 62 percent has only 30 percent of the available healthcare workers, while the urban setting comprising 38 percent of the population has 70 percent of the healthcare workers. In addition, the situation is even complicated by the limited incentives structure that could motivate health personnel into rural settings (Government of Sierra Leone, 2016b). Across the country, this phenomenon has been one of the significant underpinning conditions for the lack of an attentive healthcare provision in these densely inhabited locations. The research conducted by Vijay Narayan on Sierra Leone's healthcare system in 2015 showcases that out of the "90 health care workers interviewed comprising 58 from the rural and 32 from urban settings, 71% of the rural health care workers respondents registered their disillusionment with their jobs, while 52% of the urban and 61% of the rural health workers were inclined to relinquish their current jobs" (Narayan, 2015, p. 11).

The state of Sierra Leone medical infrastructure is also convoluted by an existential threat of an enormous funding gap, resulting in the unavailability of essential medical equipment and medicines. This situation has caused a disappointment among the majority of the available medical personnel within the health system. The majority of the healthcare service providers are without remuneration. At the same time, the country has remained heavily dependent on external assistance for funding to enhance the management and operations of the medical system (Barr et al., 2019, Government of Sierra Leone, 2016). Between 2004 and 2007, the "total government public health spending were 16.8%, 17.9%, 25.2% and 21.2%, while external supports were at 83.2%, 80.3%, 68.9% and 78.1% respectively" (Ensor et al., 2008, p. 17). The Abuja Declaration agreed upon in 2001 mandated African countries the commitment of 15 percent of their national budget to the health sector for its enhancement; in 2016, Sierra Leone projected budgetary support to the health sector was below this targeted threshold, "with the capacity of only 6% as its commitment" (Government of Sierra Leone, 2017, p. 52; Organization of African Unity, 2001). These prevailing conditions intensely indicate a huge challenge of access. In the absence of a sufficient national budget to strengthen the entire infrastructure of the medical system, corruption has also been a common phenomenon (Pieterse and Lodge, 2015, Amnesty International, 2011). Thus, limited access to the majority of the vulnerable population who would only need these services for survival further compounded the state of the health infrastructure.

Thus, enhancing access to the country's medical system as it directly links to the socioeconomic challenge of the vulnerable population in the majority was a veritable venture by the government in conjunction with support by the development partners. On this basis, a Free Health Care Initiative (FHCI) was launched in 2010 by the government meant to cater mainly for lactating mothers, pregnant women, and children under five. The impetus for this initiative included the deeply rooted challenge of accessibility to health facilities by citizens considered to be the most vulnerable in society, an attempt to reduce the increasing complication of child and maternal mortality rates, and a general intervention to address some of the structural issues of the health system.

While the initiative itself has been laudable, the process has been entirely occasioned on a donor-driven project (Witter et al., 2016). It is noted that 60–80 percent of the financial support toward the FHCI implementation has been externally dependent, particularly from the Department for International Development and the Global Fund (Witter et al., 2016, p. xii). Nonetheless, while it is generally apparent that external collaboration is imperative in such a pivotal national post-war development project, yet, the pattern undermines the long-term durability of the government's frantic willingness to build its national infrastructure. In that, the country's general over-reliance on external support is informed by the state's fragile nature to boldly embark on an inward income generation mechanism that could be broadly sustainable and can address significant development issues. In addition, its over-reliant can also be maximizing opportunity due to the proliferation of aid donors in which robust accountability compliance no longer appears to be the concrete norm associated with much foreign aid provision not to compromise international bilateral cementation.

The launch of the FHCI in 2010 was carried out without overwhelmingly addressing the significant existential infrastructural gaps within the medical system. The system of policy development was asymmetrical, which undermined the significant involvement of the local constituents. A decade after the launch of the Free Healthcare System, the state of the health system has remained deplorable. With the emergence of COVID-2019, the overdependence on external aid to enhance the government's response with the required treatments to curtail its massive spread across the country has increased. From the realist point of view, the pattern of the society's excessive dependency level and its inability toward the provision and stabilization of core state roles indicate the strength of the magnitude of how weak the country has remained nationally and its role at the international scene.

The lack of inclination on the part of the political system in restoring such an essential societal pillar to make the society a healthy state is engineered by the pattern in which governance and political administration are intersected within the political space, and such a system has been characteristic of fragrant neglect of significant internal institutional development by successive regimes. Within the political system the entrenched nature of the elite capture has made almost everything to be taken for granted. Accountability and transparency have remained taken for granted, not necessary and deeply considered as a vital tenet of an ideal governance system for national transformation and development. The impact of elite capture in Sierra Leone has undermined the bond between the state and the citizens, particularly where the citizens establish members of the state government, and in return, the state commits to the availability of the necessary protections and guarantees the population's well-being that ensures the state's smooth running and strengthening of its robust system.

SIERRA LEONE AND THE EXISTENTIAL SOCIAL STRUCTURAL INEQUALITY

Social structural inequality is a phenomenon associated with nation-states, with its particular salience gained following the Westphalia sovereign state system's advent, where the notion of modern states emerged. Within such a state system appears countries' sovereign rights over their territories, a pattern conceived differently from the ancient state system (Diener and Hagen, 2012). In the current modern state system, states' sovereign rights have increasingly intensified to imply countries' internal responsibilities in the protection of citizens (Glanville, 2010). Thus, internally, stratified inequalities associated with nation-states remain a challenging issue and have widely remained debatable among academics and policymakers, as the state's social stability is conceived as critical (see Grusky and Kricheli-Katz, 2012; United Nations Development Programme, 2013).

The historical understanding of the pattern of inequality within a state system is traceable to many classical scholars: one of such widely referenced is Karl Marx in his work on Structural Theory of Class. The analysis is mainly on the context of how instituted structural patterns of the state engendered inequality by the capitalist system, particularly how certain groups within the state system with the means of power to own and control asymmetrically had commanding influence over the vast majority of others, who merely were powerless of ownership and control (Sorensen, 1996; Wright and Perrone, 1977; Peet, 1975). Such structural existence led to the systemic preservation of the impoverished proletariats under the abuse of the bourgeoisie, and the class struggle argued by Marx was absolute to break such a deeply rooted structural system (Marx, 1973).

In the contemporary context of inequality, Anis Dani and Arjan De-Haan characterize this phenomenon within states as a situation associated with the emerging uneven privileges possessed by a certain kind of group relative to the others visible through access to opportunities, their participation, and responsibilities. The authors further reiterated that in societies classified as not developed, inequality occurs by the varied nature of their social structures in conjunction with extreme prejudices, oppositions, and classified organizational patterns of their customary systems (Dani and De-Haan, 2008). Uncovering the perspective of inequality in Africa, Nicolas Van De-Walle emphasizes that it commenced as a result of practices associated with class construction with its direct linkage to the formation of the state originating from the economic patterns of the prior periods of these colonial state systems (De-Walle, 2009).

Economic, social, and political aspects mostly appear as indicators captured in the analyses of inequality. Lucas Chancel, Denis Cogneau, Amory Gethin, and Alix Myczkowski assert that African countries are with the uppermost crack on income inequality issues. The authors stated that in the economic circulation within the continent there is harshly low income found at the bottom than that compared to the top (Chancel et al., 2019). The report of the United Nations also notes that the current burgeoning inequality trend does not only further affect those already impoverished but can undermine the safety of society in general. Because of the permeated pattern of inequality within contemporary societies, the report referenced that it has resulted in social dissatisfaction and intensified divisiveness within political systems, which has the proclivity to produce instability within states (United Nations, 2020a, p. 20). Likewise, it has also been noted that the permeated nature of inequality within states could negatively affect the decision-making process within the political system of nation-states and can constrict the general participatory process in the governance systems (United Nations Development Programme, 2013).

Nonetheless, Dzodzi Tsikata notes that inequality within the state could not be unconnected to the nature of state policy systems' failures combined with the discrimination rooted in the political structure (Tsikata, 2015). In addition, Simon Kuznets argues that inequality is associated with the growing nature of the state's economies, particularly in the early periods, and becomes more pronounced as development entrenched. However, he noted that it diminishes as the prosperities of these countries become consolidated. He also based his arguments on the modification from an agricultural to an industrial-based system within the state, making inequality inevitable (Kuznets, 1955).

Indeed, cognizant of the above perspectives, social structural inequality is a pattern of institutionalized violence often characterized negatively in the weak state system. Sierra Leone, beyond the periods of her institutional development stages from the colonial era, has mostly remained with characteristic patterns of social structural inequalities. Social inequality is situated within the country's political, social, and economic structure and taken for granted as a normalized pattern. The political, economic, and social combination to expatiate how the patterns of inequality are produced in Sierra Leone is unique in that, in the post-conflict political system, these have remained inseparable. Access to the political system has concomitantly rendered the readily accessible and available economic opportunity over the vast majority of the population. Therefore, it also adds to the social status, privileges, roles, and functions within society. The majority of Sierra Leoneans remain part of the state system but far removed from its governance processes, and this is apparent in the aspect of social, economic, and political rights as well as participation, because of the socially constructed system which privileged only a few political class and those within the tight clientelistic networks.

Generally, those without economic strength are deprived of participating in mainstream politics, as it is through economic strength as opposed to logical policy ideas that have emerged to constitute the determinant of attaining power. For instance, the Sierra Leone Public Elections Act 2012, section 46 (1) and 60 (5) mandated aspiring candidates to pay nomination fees as a mandate for their eligibility to be endorsed by the institution of the National Electoral Commission (Government of Sierra Leone, 2012; Carter Center, 2012; European Union, 2018). This pattern has inhibited an open and general participatory space and process and nurtured a social tension within the political space. The majority of the youths and women, who are mainly classified within the current state structure as the economic underdogs, are confronted with participatory limitations, a pattern that has consistently shaped the continuity of the systemic gerontocratic political entrenchment.

Access to economic opportunity is asymmetrically endemic. Only a limited category within the political class controls the state resources at the expense of the vast majority of the population living in penury. The report on Sierra Leone Poverty Index for 2017, capturing several clusters on living standard, housing, health, and education, specified that about 64.8 percent of Sierra Leoneans were in multidimensional poverty, where 86.3 percent of the population live in the rural area while 37 percent live in the urban area (United Nations Development Programme, 2019). This was at the period when concentration of development aid in the country was on the increase, intended to bolster peacebuilding consolidation and the stabilization of the state (Foday et al., 2012). This wide nature of post-conflict inequality as evident within the current societal structure undermines any existence of stable peace intended to serve as a solid pillar for state's development and transformation. This apparent inequality pattern has served as one of the variables for the high electoral tensions within the political space in the country's post-conflict period. This has contributed to the state's gradual polarization through a strong salience of ethnic and regional attachment. Elite capture has made accountability untenable. The pattern has silenced institutional regulatory actions, and state institutional corruption remains well established, all of which constitute a weak state's characteristics.

INSTITUTIONALIZED STRUCTURAL VIOLENCE IN PERIODS OF COVID-2019 LOCKDOWN

The pattern of institutionalized structural violence is a phenomenon characteristic of a weak state system. This characteristic has been part of Sierra Leone's state system in response to the COVID-2019 virus curtailment across society. One significant way this became manifested was during periods of lockdown. The declaration of lockdown to curtail the spread of COVID-2019 was the institutionalized model taken as an approach by countries to limit the widespread of the virus across many societies. In Sierra Leone, the state adoption of this universal model did not give much cognizance to the inherent income and livelihood gaps but revealed how patterns of institutionalized violence have remained entrenched within the state structure. Though in the context of Weber, the state monopoly of force to ensure compliance is legitimate; however, in countries where the state is unable to ensure the stabilization of the population's well-being, compliance of monopolistic force becomes a feature of the weak state, particularly with the modern state system.

The invocation of the lockdown in Sierra Leone warranted people to forcefully stay home in which primary livelihood for the majority could not be attained or guaranteed. Nearby shops to access groceries were inaccessible, and there were penalties for the defaulters of the lockdown measures, often in certain occasions, such measures were often accompanied by brutal police arrest followed by detention. It is a country where the majority of the population only survives on the daily routine of the day to upkeep their families and homes. The invocation of the lockdown by the state widely left the majority of these populations unprotected and more vulnerable. According to Julio S. Solis Arce, Macartan Humphreys, Niccolo Meriggi, Maarten Voors, and Emilie Yam, during the pandemic in conjunction with the lockdown, "income plummeted to 57% of households and with an increase of 16% food price" (Arce et al., 2020, para. 12). The majority of the homes are not well fixed and have no running water. The population became subject to institutionalized state violence, caught in between efforts to escape the virus, yet gravely constrained and affected by livelihood issues. As considered a weak state, decision-making within such a society is asymmetrical, with less participation, and the state actors are taken as supreme and absolute. During the lockdown, the state attempted to reach a few vulnerable inhabitants within some deprived communities with livelihood cash support. As a weak state, such a largesse, as with all successive regimes in periods of crisis, has not been founded on a comprehensive remedy approach to address these plights other than a mere political gimmick for political gains. Unequivocally, the state dereliction of these fundamental responsibilities in enhancing and ensuring internal protection of all citizenry at all times implies the level and magnitude of transformation and the institutional gaps within such a society.

As the lockdown became unbearable for some families, given the unavailability of water and food at homes in most of the communities, particularly in the capital, Freetown, for instance, staying at homes became distasteful and anathema, as well as in adherence to rules. Police brutality became increased on poor citizens, who merely seek to survive, culminating in pockets of violence (Dumbuya, 2020).

In post-conflict Sierra Leone, there remains a wide-ranging ineffectiveness inherent within state institutions in the actualization of core state responsibilities. Some of this ineffectiveness is a result of the inappropriate prioritization of policy development framework and implementations. The challenges of most of the policy processes are not unconnected to the emerged contentious political engagements within the political space that has now incrementally resulted in a stark polarization of the country along ethnic and regional identity blocs, covertly operating within political parties as ethnic symbols rather than actual modern state political parties. The institutionalized structural violence within the state which has resulted because of the inability of the government on its general commitment toward the state is a broad phenomenon underpinned by the pattern of the post-conflict political party mobilization pattern situated along stronghold consolidation for political interest as against nationally striving efforts for sustainable development and transformation. The institutionalized violence within the political system is a phenomenon taken for granted and a normalized characteristic of the political superstructure which has been layered over time. These implications provide a conceptual understanding related to why the political structure of Sierra Leone has remained undermined, in which the weak features of the state remain pronounced.

CONCLUSION AND RECOMMENDATIONS

There have remained many societies complicated by structural challenges. Ingrained structural challenges associated with states are internally produced, utilized, and sometimes have come to be taken for granted and normalized within the state system, making reforms complex to effect necessary societal structural changes. This study highlights such a complex internal challenge, using the case of Sierra Leone by answering the question, why institutionalized violence was formed in line with the government's approach in the fight against COVOD-2019 during the state of lockdown? As a weak state, institutionalized violence was not merely an outgrowth that became manifest during the COVID-2019 lockdown but a layered state pattern. Amid the extensive institutional reform and democratic openings in the aftermath of the post-conflict peacebuilding process, the need for a more concerted and steady effort to work and change the system's nature and the pattern is imperative. Challenged by its post-war devastation gap, a collectively genuine national development approach that allows the space to enhance a general participatory process would effectively mitigate the profound state institutionalized violence.

Internally generated institutionalized violence that becomes inherent within state structures is an outgrowth of complex human interactions. Such interactions hardly become eliminated within the state structure, and therefore, has become a fundamental challenge to the transformation of societies. Thus, the chapter outlines three recommendations as significantly imperative for Sierra Leone's institutionalized structural challenge-response mechanism to make the country a viable state. The first one is "institutional performance." "Institutional performance refers to the extent to which commitment to and the faithful enactment of institutional roles result in the collectively desired institutional outcomes" (Messner et al., 2013, pp. 409–410). Institutional performance in Sierra Leone has not produced the desired outcome that serves the collective interest of everyone. Recognizing this gap and its considerations within the political structure as its core pillar for social integration would significantly reduce institutionalized violence within the state structure. The second is "strengthen and empowerment" (Webb, 2019, p. 59). The majority of the state population in Sierra Leone would fundamentally be faced with unending challenges in trying to escape the socially constructed dilemma of the state's institutionalized violence. Thus, empowerment and strengthening of such category through attentive need response mechanism would fundamentally yield crucial dividend, and such would have the proclivity of safeguarding the state from extreme polarization. Finally, "strong civil society." "It is believed that civil society involvement in monitoring and accountability is critical to ensure development effectiveness" (Malena et al., 2004, pp. 14–15). In post-conflict Sierra Leone, a vibrant role of civil society would have a direct impact that may lead to an institutionalized violence reduction within the societal structure. This would be realized through civil society role in effective monitoring and reporting and social awareness-raising. The three highlighted recommendations are part of the everyday societal structures of the state. When their usefulness within the state becomes recognized as an essential tool for development, institutionalized violence becomes less pronounced.

REFERENCES

Agbakwa, S. C. (2003). A path least taken: Economic and social rights and the prospect of conflict prevention and peacebuilding in Africa. *Journal of African Law* 47(1):38–64.

Amnesty International. (2009). Out of reach. The cost of maternal health in Sierra Leone. London, UK: Amnesty International. Retrieved on November 26, 2020 from https://www.amnesty.org/download/Documents/44000/afr510052009eng.pdf

Amnesty International. (2011). At a crossroads: Sierra Leone's free health care policy. London. Retrieved on November 25, 2020 from https://www.amnestyusa.org/files/pdfs/sierral_maternaltrpt_0.pdf.

Anter, A. (2014). *Max Weber's Theory of the Modern State. Origins, Structure and Significance* (translated by Keith Tribe). Hampshire, UK: Palgrave Macmillan.

Arce, J. S. S., Humphreys, M., Meriggi, N., Voors, M. and Yam, E. (2020). Sierra Leone lockdown early to contain COVID-19 but at a high price. Retrieved from International Group Center on November 29, 2020 from https://www.theigc.org/blog/sierra-leone-locked-down-early-to-contain-covid-19-but-at-a-high-price/.

Assaf, S., and Winter, R. (2015). Trends in maternal health indicators in Sierra Leone, 2008–2013. DHS further analysis reports No.97. *Maryland ICF International.* Retrieved on November 26,2020, from https://www.dhsprogram.com/pubs/pdf/FA97/FA97.pdf

Atiku-Abubakar, J. J. and Shaw-Taylor, Y. (2003). An empirical profile of weak states in Sub-Saharan Africa. *African Development* 28(3/4):168–185.

Azz-Huck, K., and Shmis, T. (March 18,2020). Managing the impact of COVID-19 on education systems around the world: How countries are preparing, coping and planning recovery. *World Bank Blogs.* Retrieved on December 31, 2020 from https://blogs.worldbank.org/education/managing-impact-covid-19-education-systems-around-world-how-countries-are-preparing.

Barr, A., Garrett, L., Marten, R. and Kadandale, S. (2019). Health sector fragmentation: Three examples of Sierra Leone. Retrieved from Globalization and Health on November 26, 2020 from https://globalizationandhealth.biomedcentral.com/track/pdf/10.1186/s12992-018-0447-5.pdf.

Beckman, L. and Erman, V. (2012). Introduction. In L. Beckman and E. Erman (eds.), *Territories of Citizenship* (pp. 1–6). Hampshire, UK: Palgrave Macmillan.

Cater Center. (2012). Sierra Leone 2012 general elections. Carter Center reports transparent and orderly process; urges Sierra Leone to await results. Retrieved on November 27, 2020 from:https://www.cartercenter.org/resources/pdfs/news/peace_publications/election_reports/sierra-leone-prelim-111912.pdf.

Centers for Disease Control and Prevention. (2019). 2014–2016 Ebola outbreak in West Africa. Retrieved on November 25, 2020 from https://www.cdc.gov/vhf/ebola/history/2014-2016-outbreak/index.html.

Central Intelligence Agency. (2015). Country comparison. *The World Factbook*. Retrieved on November 26, 2020 from https://www.cia.gov/library/publications/the-world-factbook/rankorder/2223rank.html.

Chancel, L., Cogneau, D., Gethin, A. and Myczkowski, A. (2019). Inequality in Africa, 1990–2017. *World Issue Brief* 2009/6. Retrieved on November 29, 2020 from https://wid.world/document/income-inequality-in-africa-1990-2017-wid-world-issue-brief-2019-06/.

Corona Resource Center. (2020). Global confirmed cases, Johns Hopkins University. Retrieved on November 30, 2020 from https://coronavirus.jhu.edu.

Dani, A.A., and De-Haan, A. (2008). Social policy in a development context: Structural inequalities and inclusive institutions. In A. A. Dani and A. De-Haan (eds.), *Inclusive States: Social Policy and Structural Inequalities* (pp. 1–37). Washington, DC: World Bank.

Denney, L., Gordon, R., and Ibrahim, I. (2015). *Teenage Pregnancy After Ebola in Sierra Leone: Mapping Responses, Gaps and Ongoing Challenges*. Working Paper 39. London, UK: Overseas Development Institute.

De-Walle, N.V. (2009). The institutional origins of inequality in Sub-Saharan Africa. *The Annual Review of Political Science* 12:307–327.

Diener, A.C., and Hagen, J. (2015). *Borders. A Very Short Introduction*. New York: Oxford University Press.

Di-John, J. (2008). Conceptualizing the causes and consequences of failed states: A critical review of the literature. *Crises States Working Papers Series No. 2*. London, UK: DESTIN Development Studies Institute.

Dumbuya, M. (April, 24, 2020). Op-Ed: Ruling out violence as a means of achieving compliance with COVID-19 measures in Sierra Leone. *Politico online*. Retrieved on November 30, 2020 from https://jhr.ca/op-ed-ruling-out-violence-as-a-means-to-achieving-compliance-with-covid-19-measures-in-sierra-leone.

Eizenstat, S. E., Porter, J. E., and Weinstein, J. M. (2005). Rebuilding weak states. *Foreign Affairs* 84(1):134–146.

Ekude, J. E. (2011). Weak states and security threats in West Africa. In Brauch, H. G. Spring, U. O., Mesjasz, C. Grin, J. Kamei-Mbote, P. Chourou, B, Dunay, P and Birkmann, J. (eds.). *Coping with Global Environment Change, Disaster and Security: Threats, Challenges and Vulnerabilities and Risk*. Berlin, Germany: Springer-Verlag.

Ensor, T., Lievens, T., and Taylor, M. (2008). Review of financing of health in Sierra Leone and development of policy options. *Final Report by Oxford Policy Management*. Retrieved on November 27, 2020 from https://citeseerx.ist.psu.edu/viewdoc/download?doi=10.1.1.394.7144&rep=rep1&type=pdf.

European Union (2018). Sierra Leone. European Union elections observation mission. Final report. Presidential, parliamentary and local council elections 2018. Retrieved on November 19, 2020 from http://www.epgencms.europarl.europa.eu/cmsdata/upload/c6e03970-dda2-45c8-9d36-48c885b72f97/Sierra-Leone _presidential-parliamentary-local-elections_7-March-2018_EU-EOM-report.pdf.

Evans, D. K., Goldstein, M., and Popova, A. (2015). The next wave of deaths from Ebola? The impact of health care worker mortality. *Policy Research Paper 7344, World Bank Africa Region, Office of the Chief Economist*. Retrieved on November 25, 2020 from http://documents1.worldbank.org/curated/en/408701468189853698/pdf/WPS7344.pdf.

Foday, Y., Addision, D., and Petrie, M. (2012). Sierra Leone: PIM in a donor dependent post-conflict economy. *World Bank*. Retrieved on November 29, 2020 from https://openknowledge.worldbank.org/bitstream/handle/10986/21047/933610WP0P1200000Sierra0Leone0Final.pdf?sequence=1&isAllowed=y.

Gborie, S., and Boakye-Agyemang, C. (March 31, 2020). Sierra Leone confirms first case of COVID-19. *World Health Organization (WHO)*. Retrieved on November 24, 2020 from https://www.afro.who.int/news/sierra-leone-confirms-first-case-covid-19

Glanville, L. (2010). The antecedent of sovereignty as responsibility. *European Journal of International Relations* 17(2): 233–255.

Government of Sierra Leone (March 24, 2020a). Declaration of a state of public emergency by His Excellency, Dr. Julius Maada Bio, president of the Republic of Sierra Leone. *State House Media and Communication Unit*. Retrieved on November 25, 2020 from https://statehouse.gov.sl/wp-content/uploads/2020/03/Declaration-of-a-State-of-Public-Emergency-by-His-Excellency-Dr.-Julius-Maada-Bio-President-of-the-Republic-of-Sierra-Leone—24-March-2020.pdf.

Government of Sierra Leone (March 31, 2020b). Statement by His Excellency, Dr. Julius Maada Bio, president of the Republic of Sierra Leone at the second press conference on COVID-19. *State House Media and Communication Unit*. Retrieved on November 26, 2020 from https://statehouse.gov.sl/wp-content/uploads/2020/03/Statement-by-His-Excellency-Dr-Julius-Maada-Bio-President-of-the-Republic-of-Sierra-Leone-at-the-Second-Press-Conference-on-COVID-19.-State-House-Freetown-31-March-2020.pdf.

Government of Sierra Leone (April 8, 2020c). Statement by His Excellency, Dr. Julius Maada Bio, president of the Republic of Sierra Leone at the third press conference on COVID-19. *State House and Media Communication Uni*t. Retrieved on November 25, 2020 from https://statehouse.gov.sl/wp-content/uploads/2020/04/Statement-by-His-Excellency-Dr-Julius-Maada-Bio-President-of-the-Republic-of-Sierra-Leone-at-the-Third-Press-Conference-on-Covid-19.-State-House-Freetown-8-April-2020.pdf.

Government of Sierra Leone (April, 30, 2020d). Statement by his Excellency, Dr. Julius Maada Bio, president of the Republic of Sierra Leone on the three-day lockdown—30 April. *State House Media and Communication Unit*. Retrieved on November 24, 2020 from https://statehouse.gov.sl/wp-content/uploads/2020/04/Statement-by-His-Excellency-Dr-Julius-Maada-Bio-President-of-the-Republic-of-Sierra-Leone-on-the-Three-Day-Lockdown-30-April-2020.pdf.

Government of Sierra Leone (2017). National health sector strategic plan,2017–2021. *Ministry of Health and Sanitation*. Retrieved on November 18, 2020 from https://

extranet.who.int/countryplanningcycles/sites/default/files/planning_cycle_repository/sierra_leone/sierra_leone_nhssp_2017-21_final_sept2017.pdf.

Government of Sierra Leone (2016a). Annual health sector performance report 2016. *Ministry of Health and Sanitation.* Retrieved on November 27, 2020 from https://www.afro.who.int/sites/default/files/2017-08/Sierra%20Leone%20Health%20Sector%20%20Performance%20Report%202016.pdf.

Government of Sierra Leone (2016b). Human resources for health country profile. Sierra Leone country profile. *Directorate of Human Resources for Health, Ministry of Health and Sanitation.* Retrieved on November 21, 2020 from https://www.afro.who.int/sites/default/files/2017-05/hrhprofile16.pdf.

Government of Sierra Leone (2012). The public elections act, 2012. Supplement to the Sierra Leone gazette, vol. CXLIII, No. 26. Retrieved on November 29, 2020 from http://aceproject.org/ero-en/regions/africa/SL/sierra-leone-the-public-elections-act-2012-1.

Government of Sierra Leone (1991). Constitution of Sierra Leone, Act No.6 of 1991. Retrieved on December 25, 2020 from https://www.wipo.int/edocs/lexdocs/laws/en/sl/sl003en.pdf.

Government of Sierra Leone (1960). Public health ordinance, Act No. 23. Retrieved on November 20, 2020 from http://sierra-leone.org/Laws/1960-23.pdf.

Grusky, D.B., and Kricheli-Katz, T. (2012). *The New Gilded Age. The Critical Inequality Debates of our Time.* Stanford, CA: Stanford University Press.

Hobson, C., and Kurki, M. (2012). Introduction: The conceptual politics of democracy promotion. In Hobson, C. and M. Kurki, M. (eds.), *The Conceptual Politics of Democracy Promotion.* London, UK and New York: Routledge.

Jackson, R.H. (2000). *The Global Covenant: Human Conduct in a World of States.* Oxford, UK: Oxford University Press.

Kamara, A. B. (2020). Responding to COVID-19 in fragile states: The case of Sierra Leone. *International Growth Center.* Retrieved on November 24, 2020 from https://www.theigc.org/blog/responding-to-covid-19-in-fragile-states-the-case-of-sierra-leone/.

Kotz, D. M. (2005). The role of the state in economic transformation: Comparing the transition experiences of Russia and China. *Economic Department Working Paper 67.* Retrieved on November 17, 2020 from https://scholarworks.umass.edu/cgi/viewcontent.cgi?article=1064&context=econ_workingpaper.

Kuznets, S. (1955). Economic growth and income inequality. *The American Economic Review* 45(1):1–28.

Malena, C., Forster, R., and Singh, J. (2004). Social accountability. An introduction to the concept and emerging practice. Social Development Papers, Participation and Civil Engagement. Paper No.76. *World Bank.* Retrieved on December 31, 2020 from http://documents1.worldbank.org/curated/en/327691468779445304/pdf/310420PAPER0So1ity0SDP0Civic0no1076.pdf.

Martinelli, A. (2001). Weak state/strong society. In Caplow, T. (ed.), *Leviathan Transformed: Seven National States in the New Century.* Montreal, Canada: McGill-Queen's University Press.

Marx, K. (1973). *Karl Marx on Society and Social Change* (edited by Neil. J. Smelser). Chicago, IL: The University of Chicago Press.

Mason, H. (2016). A second chance at schooling for pregnant teenagers in Ebola-affected Sierra Leone. *UNICEF*. Retrieved on November 23, 2020 from https://www.unicef.org/stories/second-chance-schooling-pregnant-teenagers-sierra-leone.

Mentan, T. (2004). *Dilemmas of Weak States: Africa and Transnational Terrorism in the Twenty-First Century*. London, UK: Routledge.

Messner, S., Rosenfeld, R., and Karstedt, S. (2013). Social institutions and crimes. In Cullen, F. T and Wilcox, P. (eds.), *The Oxford Handbook of Criminological Theory*. New York: Oxford University Press.

Migdal, J. S. (1988). *Strong Societies and Weak States: State-Society Relations and State*. Princeton, NJ: Princeton University Press.

Ministry of Health and Sanitation. (2016). Maternal death surveillance and responses. Annual report. *Government of Sierra Leone*. Retrieved on November 11, 2021 from https://www.afro.who.int/sites/default/files/2017-06/mdsrreport.pdf.

Narayan, V. (2015). Sierra Leone's health care workforce crisis. Drivers of sub-optimal distribution and poor retention of primary healthcare workers in rural areas. *Master's Thesis*. Washington, DC: University of Washington. Retrieved on November 26, 2020 from https://digital.lib.washington.edu/researchworks/bitstream/handle/1773/33072/Narayan_washington_0250O_14121.pdf?sequence=1&isAllowed=y.

Newman, E. (2007). Weak States, States Failure and Terrorism. *Terrorism and Political Violence* 19(4):463–488.

Organization of African Unity (2001). African summit on HIV/AIDS, tuberculosis and other related infectious diseases. *OAU/SPS/Abuja/3*. Retrieved on November 21, 2020 from https://au.int/sites/default/files/pages/32894-file-2001-abuja-declaration.pdf.

Peet, R. (1975). Inequality and poverty: A Marxist-geographic theory. *Annals of the Association of American Geographers* 65(4):564–571.

Pieterse, P., and Lodge, T. (2015). When free healthcare is not free. Corruption and mistrust in Sierra Leone's primary healthcare system immediately prior to the Ebola outbreak. *International Health* 7(6): 400–404.

Reid, A. (2017). (2017). *Sierra Leone's Latest Maternal Deaths and Surveillance Today at a Launch in Freetown. Launch of the Health Sector MDSR report*. Retrieved on November 26, 2020 from https://sierraleone.unfpa.org/en/news/sierra-leone's-latest-maternal-death-and-surveillance-report-mdsr-released-today-launch

Rice, E. S., and Patrick, S. (2008). *Index of State Weakness in the Developing World*. Washington, DC: The Brookings Institution.

Rotberg, R. I. (2015). Failed and weak states in theory and practice. *Oxford Bibliographies*. Retrieved on November 19, 2020 from https://www.oxfordbibliographies.com/view/document/obo-9780199756223/obo-9780199756223-0119.xml.

Rotberg, R. I. (2003). Failed states, collapsed states, weak states: Causes and indicators. In Rotberg, R. I. (ed.), *State Failure and State Weakness in a Time of Terror*. Washington, DC: Brookings Institution Press.

Shaban, A. R. A. (October 7, 2020). Sierra Leone coronavirus: Places of worship, main airport to reopen. *Africa News*. Retrieved on November 26, 2020 from https://www.africanews.com/2020/07/10/virus-free-sierra-leone-records-covid-19-scuffles-over-quarantine-at-airport/.

Sharples, N. (2015). Health revenues: How the extractive industry can support universal health coverage in Sierra Leone. *Health Poverty Action*. Retrieved on November 15, 2020 from https://www.healthpovertyaction.org/wp-content/uploads/2018/12/Healthy-Revenues-extractives-industry-Sierra-Leone-report-June-2015.pdf.

Sierra Leone Ministry of Health and Sanitation. (2020). Coronavirus disease (COVID-19) situational report No. 182. *Government of Sierra Leone*. Retrieved on November 26, 2020 from https://mohs.gov.sl/2020/09/28/covid-19-situation-report/.

Sohrabi, C., Alsafi, Z., O'Neil, N., Khan, M., Kerwan, A., Al-Jabir, A, Losifidis, C., and Agha, R. (2020). World Health Organization declares global emergency: A review of the 2019 novel coronavirus (COVID-19). *International Journal of Surgery* 76:71–76.

Sorensen, A.B. (1996). The structural basis of social inequality. *Journal of Sociology* 101(5):1333–1365.

Thomas, A. R. (March 26, 2020a). Sierra Leone parliament approves coronavirus state of public emergency. Sierra Leone Telegraph. Retrieved on November 24, 2020 from https://www.thesierraleonetelegraph.com/sierra-leone-parliament-approves-coronavirus-state-of-public-emergency/.

Thomas, A. R. (April 1, 2020b). Sierra Leone records its second case of COVID-19. *Sierra Leone Telegraph*. Retrieved on November 23, 2020 from https://www.thesierraleonetelegraph.com/sierra-leone-records-its-second-case-of-covid-19/.

Thomas, A. R. (May 2, 2020c). Sierra Leone records highest daily number of COVID-19 cases. *Sierra Leone Telegraph*. Retrieved on November 27, 2020 from https://www.thesierraleonetelegraph.com/sierra-leone-records-highest-daily-number-of-new-covid-cases/.

Tsikata, D. (2015). Understanding and addressing inequality in the context of structural transformation in Africa. A synthesis of seven country studies. *Development* 58(2–3):206–229.

United Nations Development Programme. (2019). Sierra Leone multidimensional poverty indeed 2019. Retrieved on November 29, 2020, from https://ophi.org.uk/wp-content/uploads/Sierra_Leone_MPI_2019_final.pdf.

United Nations Development Programme (2013). Humanity divided: Confronting inequality in developing countries. *Bureau for Development Policy*. Retrieved on November 29, 2020 from https://www.refworld.org/pdfid/52fcc3fe4.pdf.

United Nations. (2020a). Inequality in a rapidly changing world. World social report. *Department of Economic and Social Affairs*. Retrieved on November 28, 2020 from https://www.un.org/development/desa/dspd/wp-content/uploads/sites/22/2020/01/World-Social-Report-2020-FullReport.pdf.

United Nations. (2020b). Policy brief: education during the COVID-19 and beyond. Retrieved on November 19, 2020 from https://www.un.org/development/desa/

dspd/wp-content/uploads/sites/22/2020/08/sg_policy_brief_covid-19_and_education_august_2020.pdf.

United Nations Fund for Population Activities. (2018). Recovering from the Ebola virus disease: Rapid assessment of pregnant adolescent girls in Sierra Leone. Retrieved on November 17, 2020 from https://sierraleone.unfpa.org/sites/default/files/pub-pdf/Rapid%20Assessment%20of%20Pregnant%20Adolescent%20Girls.pdf.

Walsh, C. (September 29, 2020). Marking the passing of a grim pandemic milestone for the nation. *Harvard Gazette*. Retrieved on November 24, 2020 from https://news.harvard.edu/gazette/story/2020/09/how-do-we-mourn-the-growing-number-of-deaths-from-covid-19/.

Webb, R. J. (2019). Addressing structural violence: Reforming our perspectives. In Vahakangas, A., Angel, S. and Johansen, K. H. (eds.), *Reforming Practical Ideology. The Politics of Body and Space. Vol. I.* (pp. 53–60). Oslo, Norway: International Academic of Practical Theology Conference Series.

Whimster, S. (2004). *The Essential Weber: A Reader*. London, UK: Routledge.

Witter, S., Brikci, N., Harris, T., Williams, R., Keen, S., Mujica, A., Jones, A., Murray-Zmijewski, A., Bale, B., Leigh, B. and Renner, A. (2016). Sierra Leone free healthcare initiative (FHCI): Process and effective review: Retrieved on November 16, 2020 from https://core.ac.uk/download/pdf/141197533.pdf.

World Bank. (2020). The global economic outlook during the COVID-19 pandemic: A changed world. World Bank group flagship report. Retrieved on November 18, 2020 from https://www.worldbank.org/en/news/feature/2020/06/08/the-global-economic-outlook-during-the-covid-19-pandemic-a-changed-world.

World Bank. (2015). Most African countries avoid major economic loss but impact on Guinea, Liberia, and Sierra Leone remains crippling. Press Release. Retrieved on November 25, 2020 https://www.worldbank.org/en/news/press-release/2015/01/20/ebola-most-african-countries-avoid-major-economic-loss-but-impact-on-guinea-liberia-sierra-leone-remains-crippling.

World Health Organization. (2020). COVID-19: Situation update for the World Health Organization Africa Region. External situation report 18. Retrieved on November 27, 2020 from https://apps.who.int/iris/bitstream/handle/10665/332929/SITREP_COVID-19_WHOAFRO_20200701-eng.pdf.

World Health Organization. (2019). Trends in maternal mortality 2000 to 2017: Estimates by world health organization, united nations international children's emergency fund, united nations population fund, world bank group and the united nations population division. Geneva, Switzerland. Retrieved on November 11, from https://www.unfpa.org/sites/default/files/pub-pdf/Maternal_mortality_report.pdf.

Wright, E. O., and Perrone, L. (1977). Marxist class categories and income inequality. *American Sociology Review* 42(1):32–55.

Yaya, S., Out, A., and Labonte, R. (2020). Globalization in the time of COVID-19: repositioning Africa to meet the immediate and remote challenges. *Globalization and Health* 16(1):51.

Zartman, I. W. (1995). Introduction: posing the problem of state collapse. In Zartman, I. W. (ed.), *Collapsed States. The Disintegration and Restoration of Legitimate Authority* (pp. 1–13). Boulder, CO: Lynne Renner Publisher.

Chapter 19

Cororacism

J. P. Afamefuna Ifedi

The aim of this chapter is to offer a critical analysis of the intersection of the Coronavirus Disease (COVID)-2019 pandemic hysteria and racism in the United States. The study will identify and examine official, institutional, public, and nativist responses and reactions to the pandemic. The COVID-2019 pandemic, which rapidly spread across the world, has literarily changed the world as we know it. It has not only posed a challenge to the world in unprecedented ways but has also revealed how racism can be a crucial factor in how COVID-2019 pandemic impacts the minority communities in America.

COVID-2019 was first identified in December 2019 in Wuhan, Hubei Province, China. It was declared a Public Health Emergency by the World Health Organization in January 2020 and declared a pandemic in March 2020 (WHO, 2020). As of October 2, 2020, more than 34.3 million cases and 1.02 million deaths attributed to COVID-2019 have been reported worldwide (The New York Times, 2020). It should be noted that the actual number of cases is probably much higher than the number that has been reported.

COVID-2019 is a new disease, and it is caused by a novel (or new) coronavirus that has not previously been noticed in humans. The virus is spread as respiratory droplets are expirated when an infected person coughs or sneezes. These droplets can land in the mouths or noses of people who are nearby, which is why transmission is more likely when people are within about 6 feet of one another. It may also be transmitted via contaminated surfaces, although this has not been conclusively proven.

The coronavirus can survive in the host for up to two days prior to symptom onset and can also be spread by hosts who are asymptomatic. The host can remain infectious for up to two weeks post-infection. The incubation period of the disease can also range from 1 to 14 days.

Its common symptoms include fever, cough, and fatigue; shortness of breath or breathing difficulties; and loss of smell (WHO, 2020). Complications from the disease can include anything from pneumonia to acute respiratory distress. There is currently no known specific antiviral medication, but many promising efforts to find workable vaccine are underway, and some, such as the Pfizer, Moderna, Oxford, and AstraZeneca vaccines, have yielded impressive results and are being administered after receiving emergency use authorization by the U.S. and UK governments.

This chapter would analyze the racialization of the incidence of COVID-2019 pandemic in relation to group ostracism, harassment, and stigmatization of non-White minority communities in America, mainly African Americans, Latino Americans, and Asian Americans, especially those of Chinese descent. This analysis would focus on the racist social, political, institutional dispositions; commentaries; and actions in relation to COVID-2019 pandemic in America. In the United States, the hysteria, angst, fear, unrest, and difficulties associated with the pandemic have exposed the compromising effects of racism and racist attacks on non-White minority communities; racism toward these groups has exacerbated their experience with the COVID-2019, relative to health issues, access to healthcare, jobs, residence, exposure to infection, dietary choices, access to proper nutritional foods, and death rate.

Racism in America is essentially a deterministic factor in the socioeconomic conditions of African Americans and other minorities. Historically, de jure and de facto racism has created social and economic, as well as political conditions which have posited minorities in the lower totem pole of American society in virtually all spheres of life, manifesting vulnerabilities upon which the novel coronavirus pandemic attaches; hence, wrecking disproportional havoc among African Americans and other minorities. It is essentially racism, institutional and social, that has located minorities to a place where their employment, area of residence, access to healthcare, dietary preferences, and social and economic options make them more vulnerable to infection and fatality at a disproportional rate.

Inequality between Whites and African Americans, as well as other minorities, is present in almost all spheres of society, portending deleterious economic, political, and social implications. Such inequalities and disadvantages leave African Americans and other minorities with poorer education, less wealth, poorer health, shorter life spans, among a coterie of other social ills. These disparities are reflective of systemic racism; and, although, demonstrably, some measurable progress has been made in the general effort to end or reduce institutional racism, wide gaps remain, rooted in the legacy of slavery, discrimination, and segregation. Furthermore, the legacy of racism has salient implication for the way that the coronavirus pandemic has impacted African Americans and other minorities.

The coronavirus pandemic has accentuated, exposed, and highlighted several inequalities in the American social system. For example, people in white-collar occupations—workers who belong to a class of employees known for earning higher average salaries doing highly skilled work, not by performing manual labor, such as corporate executives, advertising and public relations professionals, architects, lawyers, professors, doctors, engineers, and stockbrokers—could work from home, but the lower cadre and "essential" workers—delivery drivers, garbage collectors, hospitality, meat packers, and such—must continue to ply and toil in their trades outside the relative safety of their homes in public spaces where the pandemic thrives.

Although, in absolute numbers, more White Americans have died of COVID-2019, more African Americans and other minorities have been infected and died in larger numbers relative to the proportion of their number in the general population. The rate at which African Americans and other minorities are dying serves as an abject lesson in racial inequality. Essentially, African Americans and other minorities are more likely to die of the pandemic because they are more likely to present with pre-existing health conditions that make the coronavirus especially deadly to them. Health conditions such as asthma, diabetes, heart disease, and obesity, as well as socioeconomic factors like income, access to healthcare, place of residence, and type of occupation are critical factors that have important connection to the lingering effects and persistence of COVID-2019 on minorities in America. In the United States, people of color are more likely than Whites to work in contagion-exposed, low-skilled, "essential" occupations; they are more likely to live in crowded tenements and inner-city conditions, and also more likely to have comorbidities such as obesity and diabetes. Furthermore, the economic consequences of lockdowns have impacted African Americans and other minorities in worse ways than White Americans.

Consequently, racism's attendant socioeconomic manifestations are important in understanding the cause of the prevalence of the coronavirus infection and death among African Americans and other minorities, such as Asian Americans and Latino Americans, who also tend to have many health-compromising socioeconomic attributes in common. The effects of the coronavirus pandemic on the minority community and the role which racism plays in it will be examined, following a theoretical discussion which is meant to posit the discussion within a theoretical framework. This research did not excavate any contrarian issues and/or positions on the effects of the coronavirus pandemic on the minority community. Hence, there is no serious critical or opposing view on the impact of coronavirus on the minority community in America which calls for analytical attention or synthesis.

THEORETICAL DISCUSSION

Theory is important to understanding and explaining the material and symbolic elements of racial phenomena and race relations; in this case, the theory of race is meant to fasten and explain the nature and nuances of the impact of COVID-2019 on African American and other non-White minorities, namely the Latino and Asian Americans. Functionally, racism is an attitude, action, or institutional structure which subordinates a person or group because of their color (Downs, 1968). As applied in this study, it is an interpretation of all individual and societal events according to deeply embedded attitudes and beliefs. It pervades every facet and aspect of life. Hence, some form of racism is present in the sociopolitical and economic life in America (Crain, 1968). So, essentially, all consequential social decisions in public affairs become racial in nature and very likely to be influenced overtly, covertly, and tacitly by the fact of race. This can be ever so subtle that even the racist themselves(s) could not fully be aware of it.

Powerful racialized institutional and social factors have traditionally been at play to ensure that minorities were kept from social and economic advancement; hence, locating them in the lower strata of society where they suffer from exposure to the vagaries of economic and social life. Indeed, "the concept of racial [color] stigma aims to probe beneath the cognitive acts of individuals and investigate the structure of social relations within which those individuals operate" (Loury, 2020, p. 2). Available research supports the assertion, by this writer, that there is no genetic or biological basis for distinction within humanity. There is only one human race.

The idea of separate human races is a construct in the modern era developed by Europeans. It was crafted in order to justify exploitation of other peoples. Also, the idea of different races has a long standing in academic literature. It is in addition an institutional and social reality that has been deeply ingrained into the human psyche, as well as in political and social culture; hence, it has taken on a life of its own. But in the context of objective analysis, there is no objective ground for racial taxonomy. However, "such a false construct and lack of objective racial taxonomy has neither prohibited the use of skin color as racial categories nor has it diminished its influence in America and elsewhere. It is enough that many social actors hold schemes of racial classification in their minds and act accordingly [for racism to continue to thrive and influence public policy and social life]" (Loury, 2002, p. 2).

The phenomenon of racism has been subjected to extensive investigation, analysis, speculation, and theoretical scrutiny. The idea of differentiation in a lot of humans set up by the Europeans is a pervasive element in the cognitive patterning of Western thought and experience (Smedley and Smedley, 2012). European colonial conquests and domination have created a status of "Whiteness" which was attained through conquest, while imposing the lower status to other peoples. This apartheid social and ideological sociopsychological formation led to horrendous human misery that reached places the world over. The idea of race and racism, as it is formed and expressed in the Americas, a recent worldview in human history, emanated with colonial expansion across the world, "especially with European world's contact with the African world, starting in the 15th Century during which conquest, exploitation, and enslavement characterized the world. Hence, racism is a modern conception, for, prior to the XVIth century, there was nothing in the life of the West that can be described as racist" (Smedley and Smedley, 2012, p. 14). Race is, essentially, a conqueror's cultural construct which was developed in order to justify domination and expansion in lands and places far removed from the European world of their origin. Furthermore,

> race cuts across the social relations of class, power, religion, ethnicity, occupation, age, gender, culture, as well as such other socio-economic differences and takes priority over them. The racial social expressions and theory have intensified on the grounds of socio-economic and/or political dynamics, forces that alter the social arrangements. The racial worldview originated, incidentally, not as a product of scientific investigation, but as a folk concept. (Smedley and Smedley, 2012, p. 24)

Also, once people notice that their society classifies them on racial grounds, they naturally, over time, adopt such racial constructs to classify and identify themselves, further perpetuating, entrenching, validating, and transmitting that racial myth intergenerationally. As denoted earlier, there are no racial differences within people, as ascertained by serious research. Modern genetics has shown that there are no "races" as such, and some critics such as Paul Gilroy have therefore argued that social, political, and economic analysts and commentators should abandon the use of racial categories (Cavalli-Sforza, 2000; Gilroy, 2000, Loury, 2002).

It is important to state that, in many cases, there might not be observable evidence of racism, but it can work very subtly and be deeply embedded in the symbolic and expressive life of the society, where racial distortions and acculturation have endured for a long time. Evidently, de facto and de jure racism can be instinctual in racist institutions and/or individuals.

In the interim, racism is a salient construct for an understanding of the Black person and other minority's disproportionate vulnerability to social ills that might afflict the general population. This is exemplified by the extremely deleterious impact of COVID-2019 pandemic on the minority population. As various studies and data evinces, the coronavirus pandemic has impacted African Americans and other minority communities more severely than the White population in America. Incidentally, it is the socioeconomic position in which African Americans and other minorities have been forced into by racism, as was made practical in slavery, virulent, and persistent institutionalized de jure and de facto racist policies, which account for their choice of profession, jobs, as well as the health conditions that are advantageous to the COVID-2019 infections and fatalities. The Black person is more likely than a White person to be poor, have less access to primary healthcare, be less educated, reside in food deserts, more likely to hold an "essential" job, and more likely to be compelled to work in jobs that inescapably expose them to COVID-2019 infections and disproportionately likely death.

A significant amount of research and literature in the social sciences has solidified the place of color (race) centrally in the patterns of social relations that mediate and intercede in social life in the United States. Hence, racism theory has been a critical framework for understanding and explaining social, economic, and political life in America. The process of race-based social exclusion and marginalization has created a significant socioeconomic gap in essentially all matters of value in America. Self-evidently, social connections and resources play a vital role in social mobility and status and "who gets what," as well as what one can get in any society. Social segregation along color lines tended to stigmatize African Americans and determine their socioeconomic status. Essentially, racism, founded on racial stigma, was a hindrance to the ability of African Americans to realize their full human potential. Regarding the COVID-2019 incident, the disparity in infection and treatment of the disease in hospitals evinces that racial stigma, and racism is very much at play, whether intended, unintended, or structural.

Critically observing, racism does not require the presence of empirically determinable cultural differences. Nonetheless, many mainstream White scholars tend to frame and exonerate systemic racism logic in the racism theory, especially as the basis for the social disparities between Whites and African Americans, as well as other minorities. They often point out that race theory, in general, is usually subjective and anecdotal and not generally open to rigorous empirical investigation. Often, they completely relegate, to the point of apologies, the role of racism in the American culture and institutions, as well as public policy. But many scholars point out that racism in American society is so self-evident that it does not require the presence of empirically determinable cultural differences (Smedley and Smedley, 2012). The study would now turn to examination of the effects of the coronavirus pandemic on the selected minority groups that were identified earlier.

THE COVID-2019 RACISM AND AFRICAN AMERICANS

Although, essentially, all minority groups in America have and continue to experience racism from the dominant White community, African Americans have suffered the heaviest brunt of racism in contemporary times in America. Daniel Thompson describes this assertion as follows:

> No other group has had such a wide variety of socio-cultural experience as have African Americans . . . from the very beginning of the nation until the present, African-Americans have undergone a whole set of personal and socio-cultural experiences entirely their own. Such experiences range all the way from slavery and total segregation in a bi-racial system, to the often subtle, yet very real, system of institutionalized racism that is so deeply rooted in every major aspect of the American society. (Thompson, 1974, p. ix)

Furthermore, African Americans "are systematically deprived of all citizenship rights and privileges and subjected not merely to prejudice and ethnic discrimination, but to an atrocious racism that declare them to be virtually sub-human" (Genovese, 1971, p. 58). This level of racism and its attendant institutional and personal exclusion from any meaningful social and/or material progress set up the foundation of the vulnerabilities that the COVID-2019 pandemic has leveraged to wreak havoc in the African American community.

Essentially, the racist social and economic strictures to which African Americans have for so long been exposed to have predisposed them to the ravages of COVID-2019, as aptly noted by the following observation: "African America was already sick before coronavirus . . . they carry the highest burden of chronic diseases like high blood pressure, heart disease, diabetes, asthma, even obesity. Healthcare institutions in predominantly black neighborhoods are often underfunded and provide lower quality care than in other neighborhoods and nearly one-third of blacks lost someone they know to coronavirus" (Buchwald, 2020, p. 1). Hence, the novel coronavirus appears to be infecting and killing African Americans and other minorities in extraordinarily high rates. The statistics speak for themselves; compared to White Americans, Black Americans are 2.6 times more likely to contract COVID-2019. COVID-2019 hospitalizes Black people 4.7 times more than Whites, and Blacks are more than twice as likely to die from the coronavirus (CDC, 2020). These facts are the grim reality of this deadly disease relative to its impact on the African American community. There are several factors that culminate in this situation for African Americans. One factor is the disparities between Blacks and Whites relative to underlying health conditions, such as obesity, hypertension, and diabetes. African Americans are at a greater risk of having these health conditions because of decisions to locate grocery stores that are apparently based on racism and often lead to what is referred to as "food deserts."

Food deserts are regions where access to healthy and affordable food is limited. This is common to fairly all places in urban areas where African Americans predominantly domicile. Historically, fast-food restaurants have flooded African American communities, and many do not have grocery stores or may only have one in the community. An example of a food desert would be Southeast, Washington, DC. Of the 49 grocery stores located in Washington, DC, only 3 are in the Southeast neighborhood even though there are more than 160,000 residents in Southeast, Washington, DC. There are more grocery stores in a 0.1-mile stretch of streets in Columbia, the Heights section of Washington, DC, which is outside of the African American community, than in the entire Southeast quadrant of the city. Black people compose 75 percent of everyone in Southeast, Washington, DC (Caporuscio, 2020). Since there are so few grocery stores in the neighborhood, people must turn to unhealthy food that is cheap and available; sugary and fatty foods dominate most fast-food menus. Consumption of foods that are high in sugars and fats often leads to obesity, diabetes, and hypertension.

Many large grocery store brands with a national presence chose not to set up stores in an impoverished area because they do not expect to make as great of a return as they would make in higher-end areas (Kurzius and Simons, 2020). Another reason why Black Americans are suffering disproportionately from COVID-2019 may be because Black Americans are exposed to it at a much higher rate due to the occupations that are available to them, such as "essential" service jobs that compel them to work outside their homes and in close quarters with other peoples and contaminable materials.

In March 2020, public health officials and both local and state politicians implemented their most robust stay at home orders. People were urged to stay at home as much as possible in order to avoid the coronavirus infection and only to leave their house for essential activities. Schools were closed, many restaurants and businesses were closed, and the only people that could work were people that were "essential" workers. Many of these essential workers include healthcare professionals, as well as supply chain workers, and other businesses that were deemed essential for society to function. African Americans tend to dominate these "essential" occupations. This view is further elucidated by the following assertion:

> People of color make up most essential workers in the food and agriculture industry, fifty percent; and, in industrial, commercial, residential facilities and services, fifty-three percent. Black people specifically make up twenty-two percent of all the workers within the warehouse, transportation, and delivery sector. People of color are disproportionately at risk by being essential workers. Some

> businesses are being operated remotely and others have offered paid time off. But the essential workers are not afforded the luxury of staying home but instead are exposed to the virus while working long hours. Because of this increased exposure, more positive COVID cases, more hospitalizations, and more deaths arise. (McNicholas and Poydock, 2020)

As alluded to earlier, the novel COVID-2019 has ravished Americans in general, accounting for millions of infections and hundreds of thousands of deaths. But it has disproportionally impacted African Americans. Available statistics evince that there is a stark difference in the effect of COVID-2019 in the African American community compared to the White community. As the novel coronavirus sweeps across the United States, it appears to be infecting and killing African Americans at a disproportionately high rate. A *Washington Post* analysis of the available data and census demographics shows that counties that are majority African American have three times the rate of infections and almost six times the rate of deaths as counties where White residents are in the majority (Wan, 2020). A review of some cities with large African American population validates this assertion, as illustrated by the citations to follow, worth citing at length:

> In Milwaukee County, home to Wisconsin's largest city, African Americans account for 73 percent of the dead but just 26 percent of the population. The disparity is similar in Louisiana, where 70 percent of the people who have died were black, although African Americans make up just 32 percent of the state's population. In Michigan, where the state's 845 reported deaths outrank all but New York's and New Jersey's, African Americans account for 33 percent of cases and 40 percent of deaths, despite comprising only 14 percent of the population. The state does not offer a breakdown of race by county or city, but more than a quarter of deaths occurred in Detroit, where African Americans make up 79 percent of the population. And, in Illinois, a disparity nearly identical to Michigan's exists at the state level, but the picture becomes far starker when looking at data just from Chicago, where black residents have died at a rate six times that of white residents. Of the city's 118 reported deaths, nearly 70 percent were black—a share 40 points greater than the percentage of African Americans living in Chicago. (Thebault, 2020, p. 1)

Furthermore, African Americans are more likely to not have medical insurance. The access barriers facing uninsured people mean they are less likely to receive preventive care, are more likely to be hospitalized for conditions that are preventable, and are more likely to die in the hospital than those with health insurance; lack of access exacerbates the impact of the coronavirus outbreak.

Healthcare is not readily accessible to people who do not have a job which comes with healthcare benefits or service jobs that have no healthcare benefits. These types of jobs account for a significant proportion of jobs that are open to African Americans. Therefore, their main access to healthcare is usually urgent care or the emergency room. What the limited access to healthcare for African Americans evinces is that there is still a wide gap between the races regarding healthcare, which also explains the differences in care and mortality for African Americans relative to COVID-2019 deaths. The same disparity can be seen in employment for African Americans; they have limited job security and tend to experience higher job loss than White Americans due to the coronavirus pandemic. The following statistical evidence explains and underscores this assertion:

> It is estimated that the true rate of unemployment is likely 20.7% for African Americans rather than the official rate of 4.1% . . . workers, as opposed to the official rate of 6%. Also, African American . . . workers are less likely to be able to work from home. He said that the higher unemployment rates for minorities and young workers is primarily because the sectors in which they typically work will be more affected by current lockdown policies in much of the country. It just comes down to the fact that in the United States there's still a lot of occupational segregation by race and ethnicity. For example, she said, there's a large concentration of Hispanic workers in construction and a large concentration of black workers in service sector jobs. The economists' analysis notes that most low-wage workers can't telework. (Thebault, 2020, p. 1)

Furthermore, coronavirus spreads faster in high density urban areas, such as inner cities. African Americans are more likely to live in urban counties than suburban or rural ones. And within those areas, African Americans are more likely to have lower incomes, which may press them into crowded living situations. Health officials recommend that infected people isolate themselves from others, but it may not be possible for people living in housing projects, homeless shelters, or prisons and jails—all places with disproportionate Black populations. Data in Chicago, for example, shows that Black non-Latino people were more likely to be infected with coronavirus and to die of it. Black non-Latino people made up 52 percent of all coronavirus cases in the city, and adjusted for population, this group was more than twice as likely to be infected as White non-Latino people (Thebault, 2020). Allison Arwady, commissioner of the Chicago Department of Public Health, said that these racial health disparities were evident in Chicago before the COVID-2019 outbreak. The following statistical evidence supports this view:

> In Illinois, for example, there were 12,262 coronavirus cases Monday and 307 deaths, according to the state's Department of Public Health. Of the confirmed

> cases, 29.4% were black, 27.5% white, 9.4% Hispanic, 3.34% Asian and 24.4% were left blank. Of the deaths, 42% were black, 37.1% white, 7.5% Hispanic, 7% blank and 4.2% Asian. Roughly 15% of the state's population is black, while whites make up 77% of the state, according to the Census. In Michigan, the numbers were also bleak, with African Americans accounting for just 14% of the state's population, but 33% of COVID-2019 cases and 41% of deaths. In Louisiana, one of the hardest hit states in the country, 70% of the deaths related to coronavirus were African American and 29% were white, according to the state's health department. As of Monday, there were 14,867 cases across the state and 512 deaths. African Americans make up 32% of the state's population. Louisiana Gov. John Bel Edwards called the disparity "disturbing." (Berry, 2020, p. 2)

The study turns next to an analysis of the incidence of coronavirus and racism within the Asian American community.

COVID-2019 AND RACISM TOWARD ASIAN AMERICANS

Asian Americans have suffered from intense racism and bigotry since their immigration to the United States. Asian immigration to America commenced in a significant way in the mid-1700s. Filipinos began to immigrate to Louisiana in the 1760s. Chinese immigrants began to enter Hawaii in the 1780s and then the mainland of America in the 1820s. The immigration of people of Asian descent triggered a sense of nativism within White America. Asians began to experience increasing resentment as their number increased. This racial resentment and discrimination, as well as cultural clashes, have continued to date, usually intensified in times of economic or social dislocation, such as in the coronavirus pandemic. Laws and public policies were enacted to keep Asians out of the American mainstream or to codify discriminatory practices against them.

Some salient laws which practicalized a general sense of racism and xenophobia toward Asian Americans include the Asian Exclusion Act of 1882 and the Oriental Exclusion Act of 1924, which were designed by White Americans to limit the number of Asians. Many White Americans felt threatened and upset that Asian immigrants were competing with them for jobs. Soon, thereafter, this manifested into propaganda directed at stereotyping, dehumanizing, and degrading Asian immigrants in order to effectively keep Asians out of the United States and or the economy. This resentment of Asians has not subsided and has re-manifested significantly in the wake of the COVID-2019 pandemic, despite their contributions to the industrialization, growth, and development of America.

During the period of America's industrial revolution, many Asians worked in mines, railroads construction, or the agricultural fields, as there was an immense need for cheap labor. America needed skilled construction workers during the era of railroad construction, especially those with know-how and willingness to work with explosives; the railroad companies faced natural obstructions due to the Rocky and Appalachian Mountains which had to be cut through with explosives. The U.S. railroad companies recruited individuals of Asian descent that have expertise in the use of dynamite, which was vital in blasting through the mountains. Soon, thereafter, the Asian population of the entire workforce, of railroad production, comprised about 80 percent of the Central Pacific's workforce, according to Harvard University's Library of Open Collections Program (Namratha and Nilay, 2020). The railroad companies viewed Asian workers as diligent and skilled labor, needed to accomplish the goals of developing the necessary infrastructure for economic development of the country. Despite their contributions, Asians were accorded little to no respect and continue to suffer implicit bias and racism up to the present time.

Furthermore, the fact that the virus originated from China has brought about intense racist reaction toward Americans of Asian descent, especially those from China. Although racism toward Asian Americans is historical, the emanation of coronavirus from China has served as an excuse for renewed racist backlash on the Asian American community and businesses. The pandemic has showcased a positive relationship between health and racism. This correlation has resulted in an increase in racial profiling of the Asian community. They have been subjected to racial slurs, derogatory remarks, and violent actions and even accused of bearing and causing the spread of the disease.

Assumption that the virus is being spread by the Asian community has become a central facet of racist public reactions and statements by politicians who attribute the blame to Asians in general, ostensibly to foster their own political aims; this attitude is fanned by leading politicians like President Trump who has often referred to COVID-2019 as the "China-Virus" and the "Kung-Flu." Hostile remarks by the president of the United States influence and encourage elected officials such as Secretary of State Mike Pompeo who has referred to COVID-2019 as the "Wuhan virus." These comments have proved to be dangerous and inappropriate, as it further justifies the exposure of members of the Asian community to racial animosity and attacks. These official negative expressions by high officials of the U.S. government have normalized and given impetus to fringe elements who harbor racist intentions toward Asian Americans, as the following observation explains:

> Due to official and unofficial racist disposition of the American White community, Asian Americans, especially those of Chinese descent, have witnessed

> widespread racist reactions, remarks and targeting by the White community in America, to include boycott of Chinese grocery stores and restaurants. Across the U.S., Asian Americans have become the target of xenophobic and bigoted attacks as the pandemic wreaks havoc on American community. Experts said the scapegoating is fueled by harmful rhetoric from politicians, including the president, who . . . repeatedly called the COVID-2019 the "Chinese virus" . . . people of Asian descent—not just Chinese Americans—have been shunned, verbally abused, name-called, coughed and spat on, even physically assaulted. (Larsson, 2020, p. 2)

The escalation of racially motivated attacks on the Asian community has left lasting effects on them both economically and socially. These incessant race-motivated attacks on Asian Americans are reflected in the following observation:

> According to the Asian Pacific Policy and Planning Council, in March, over 600 racist instances were reported in one week and there have been countless reports of assault, racial slurs, threats, harassment and discrimination over the last several months. Pew Research has indicated that over 31 percent of Asians have experienced discrimination specifically involving COVID-2019 slurs over the last few months. In the United States, racially motivated attacks on the Asian community have been hate filled and much more violent in nature. The Federal Bureau of Investigation (FBI) has reported a spike in violations and hate crimes reported since the beginning of the pandemic. There have been countless reported attacks that are all racially motivated and result in the physical assault of people of Asian descent. (Kim, 2020, p. 1)

These racist attacks against members of the Asian community are a result, in part, of favorable disposition in the White community for a racist ideology, which is expressed, perpetuated, and acknowledged by the president of the United States and his supporters, as they encourage the racist tendencies that are already prevalent in the society, with negative implications for Asian businesses (Liu, 2020).

Coronavirus completely disrupted and altered economic fortunes of Asian-owned and operated businesses, which have suffered from significantly lower revenue stream and spike in unemployment. In large metropolitan areas in the United States, Chinatowns have been noted as being eerily empty even as cities have made strides to reopen. Some cities have dishonestly reported that there are corona outbreaks in Asian neighborhoods and Chinatowns across the country. These false reports have wreaked havoc on the restaurant industry, especially restaurants operated by Asians and even Asian cuisine (Knowles, 2020). White Americans have associated the Asian community with COVID-2019 in a very negative and racist manner, with negative implication for their restaurant businesses. Asian cuisine, noted by the *Washington Post* as the fastest growing takeout industry in the United States, which grew substantially over the last 20 years has suffered significantly. As an industry, the revenue from Asian restaurants had exceeded $150 billion annually. So, with the economic distress caused by racist reaction to coronavirus, Asian American businesses have experienced substantial economic losses (Wan, 2020). Furthermore, apart from restaurant businesses, many other Asian businesses have been affected by the economic shutdown, leading to a sharp decline in revenue.

Many Asian American businesses are struggling financially as Asian-dominated businesses are not patronized at the same rate as they were prior to COVID-2019. As the pandemic continues to disrupt and take the lives of thousands of Americans daily, many continue to look at this pandemic through xenophobic lenses. Reporters and commentators allude to the fact that Asian Americans complain that they have been refused entry into businesses, excluded from hotel rooms, cab rides, and Uber taxis. The ramifications of these instances of racist treatments are irreparable damage, not only to the individuals who experience these direct attacks, but also the entire Asian community. Discrimination in the form of verbal harassment, slurs, physical assault, workplace, and everyday bias directed at the Asian community has created such stressful and disturbing experiences that will have long-lasting effects.

The intersection of racism and COVID-2019 has left the Asian community unprotected and more susceptible to targeted attacks; it has further exacerbated the socioeconomic inequities within the United States for them. This analysis would pivot to analysis of the effects of racist reaction to the Latino community due to the COVID-2019 pandemic.

COVID-2019 AND RACISM IN THE LATINO AMERICAN COMMUNITY

As in the case of African American and Asian American communities, the coronavirus pandemic has led to a heightened incidence of overt racism toward the Latino American community. The Latino community is experiencing disproportionately high infection and mortality rate. Dr. Peter Hotez said in a virtual Congressional Hispanic Caucus briefing that "What we're seeing really is the historic decimation among the Hispanic community by the virus" (Gamboa, 2020, p. 1). Dr. Anthony Fauci, America's leading infectious disease expert who has been at the forefront of the COVID-2019 medical response in the United States, said that as of September 19, hospitalizations among Latinos were "359 per 100,000 compared to 78 in whites. Deaths related to Covid-19 are 61 per 100,000 in the Latino population compared to 40 in whites, and Latinos represent 45 percent of deaths of people younger than 21" (Gamboa, 2020, p. 1).

This points out the palpable disparity in healthcare experienced by the Latino community. This is because they have a higher incidence of comorbidities, which is a critical risk factor. In other words, clearly there is no health equity relative to Latino Americans and the larger White American community, as is also the case in other minority communities (Gamboa, 2020, p. 1). Health equity is where everyone has a fair and just opportunity to live their healthiest life possible (Ramirez, 2020). Health is somewhat dependent on where people reside. Inequitable city planning, redlining, and other discriminatory practices created racialized wealth and residential neighborhood disparities, creating a poor racial class that is vulnerable and unable to protect itself from the coronavirus pandemic in a way that White Americans could.

As a result, many communities of color lack critical health-promoting assets and infrastructure. The Latino community specifically struggles with access to healthy food, green spaces for physical activity, affordable housing, and social support (Ramirez, A., 2020). These social amenity deficits have long made communities of color more susceptible to illnesses like diabetes, asthma, obesity, hypertension, and kidney disease. The COVID-2019 impacts those with underlying conditions more significantly. People of color, therefore, being predisposed to such underlying pre-existing illnesses find themselves at a higher risk of contracting and succumbing to the coronavirus. The COVID-2019 pandemic has highlighted a worsening historical healthcare inequity, consequently producing disproportionate number of infections and deaths in the Latino American community.

Health inequities are exacerbated during times of crisis. The coronavirus pandemic demonstrates how important health equity is and supports the case for why systemic policy changes are critical. Not only is general health inequity systemic, but it is also the reason for disproportionate infection rate among Latino Americans. It is evident that infection rates are higher in big cities like New York, urban settings where there are normally more diverse populations living in close quarters. In the interim, Latino people across the country have been disproportionately affected by the coronavirus, throughout hundreds of counties in urban, suburban, and rural areas, as well as across all age groups (Oppel, 2020). To further undergird this point, in 206 counties across the nation with at least 5,000 Latino residents, the *New York Times* found that 178 have higher infection rates for Latino residents than for White residents (Oppel, 2020). Part of the reason for this is that Black and Brown people are overwhelmingly represented in the category of essential jobs;

(Public Health Law Watch, 2020). These recommendations are designed to offset future disparities. Lastly, but equally important, is the fact that we as a nation need to identify racism as a public health crisis. The disparities in healthcare we see in Latino and other communities of color are systemic and can only be eliminated by enacting a coherent policy.

CONCLUSION AND RECOMMENDATIONS

Racism can be a decisive factor in American life; it is insidious, pervasive, and affects all aspects of life in America. It is de jure, de facto, institutional and characterizes many important public policies, with serious implication for the African American, Asian American, Latino American, and other minorities. Racism is a veritable factor in explaining and understanding the rules of motion of issues in American sociopolitical and economic life. Clearly important and salient impact of the coronavirus pandemic on the lives of minorities is strongly tethered to racism. The impact of racism in minority population of America has created social, economic, and political conditions which have placed them in a lower socioeconomic stratum, affecting the occupations that are available to them, education quality, health options, access to healthcare, availability of medical insurance, choice of and availability of nutritious food, and so on.

The COVID-2019 emanated from Wuhan, China, in early 2020 and quickly became a global pandemic, reaching virtually all corners of the world including the United States, bringing with it strong social reactions of angst, fear, economic and political disruptions, which rapidly became politicized and integrated into the racist animus of America's majority population and institutions; it also leveraged socioeconomic vulnerabilities of the American system to the extent that it reflected negatively on the health of the minority peoples, mainly due to the social place reserved for them by the legacy of historical racism, segregation, and rampant discrimination.

The pandemic has had its most devastating impact on America. More than over 300,000 Americans have succumbed to the disease to date and the number is likely to climb even further. America's long-standing racism against minorities, which has made their relative upward mobility and development prohibitive, as well as the manner in which effort to stem the disease has been politicized by those in positions of power and responsibility to manage it, has contributed to the high level of infection and morality of the disease; they largely failed to warn or properly advise the general public to heed the guidance of scientists and medical experts on how to protect themselves from the disease. The effect of the pandemic on the general population of America, especially the minority population, has been devastating in all ramifications.

This is attributable to the consequences of debilitating poverty and social dislocations occasioned by racism, which has historically been decisive in the lives of minorities in America.

Pervasive racism has literarily trapped minorities in a socially disadvantageous position which has lent itself to the worst effects of the COVID-2019 pandemic. Racism has laid down a bedrock foundation of societal inequities, which can be surmounted only by a sustained series of public policies directed at addressing economic and social inequities that is structural to the social, political, and economic system.

The effect of the pandemic on the African American, Latino Americans, and Asian Americans serves as a salient reminder of the outrightly dangerous economic, occupational, health-related conditions that they find themselves in within a racist system. It shows that the issue of racism has created various socioeconomic vulnerabilities which even an incidental pandemic can leverage to the detriment of minority populations.

It is therefore important that public policy prescriptions be orchestrated to address long-standing race-based social system that has long been a problem for minorities. The impact of the pandemic on the minority population indicates that the history of racism is continuing to affect minorities in America, and that previous effort to address it has not been fully effective, hence calling for more work to be done in that regard.

Public policy decisions should be made to ensure that minorities are able to gain access to good healthcare, have support to receive lucrative education, and elevate themselves to position of lucrative employment. The income disparity must be addressed to enable minorities earn enough income to afford better housing which would facilitate their escape from crowded tenement housing.

Public policy efforts should also be made to combat the issue of racism in all aspects of life to ensure that minorities enjoy the full rights of citizenship without hindrance from personal and institutionalized racism. It also demonstrates that the vestiges of slavery, segregation, and discrimination are still in place, with serious socioeconomic consequences for minorities. This is exemplified in the case of the coronavirus COVID-2019 pandemic in America, and concerted effort should be made to end it.

REFERENCES

Berry, D. B. (March 28, 2020). Black people are overwhelmingly dying from coronavirus in cities across the US. *USA TODAY*. Retrieved on November 15, 2020, from https://www.usatoday.com/story/news/nation/2020/04/07/who-dying-coronavirus-more-black-people-die-major-cities/2961323001/.

Blight, D. G. B. (June 26, 2020). Perspective: Black people aren't naturally vulnerable to COVID-19. That's junk race science. *The Washington Post*. Retrieved on November 15, 2020 from https://www.washingtonpost.com/outlook/black-people-arent-naturally-vulnerable-tocovid-19-thats-junk-race-science/2020/06/25/d04a5f98-b5d2-11ea-a8da693df3d7674a_story.html.

Buchwald, E. (July 1, 2020). Dispatches from a pandemic. *Market Watch*. Retrieved on November 15, 2020 from https://www.marketwatch.com/column/dispatches-from-a-pandemic.

Caporuscio, J. (June 22, 2020). Food deserts: Definition, effects, and solutions. *Medical News Today*. Retrieved on November 15, 2020, from https://www.medicalnewstoday.com/articles/what-are-food-deserts.

Centers for Disease Control and Prevention (CDC). (March 2, 2020). Tuskegee Study: Timeline. Retrieved on November 15, 2020, from https://www.cdc.gov/tuskegee/timeline.htm.

Centers for Disease Control and Prevention (CDC). (December 10, 2020). COVID-19 hospitalization and death by race/ethnicity. Retrieved on November 15, 2020, from https://www.cdc.gov/coronavirus/2019-ncov/covid-data/investigationsdiscovery/hospitalization-death-by-race-ethnicity.html.

Coronavirus Cases: (n.d.). Retrieved on October 03, 2020, from https://www.worldometers.info/coronavirus/?utm_campaign=homeAdvegas1%3F%22.

Crain, R. L. (1968). *The Politics of Segregation*. Chicago, IL: Aldine Publishing Company.

Despres, C. (August 31, 2020). Report: U.S. failed miserably in policy response to COVID-19 but has a path forward for future pandemics. *Salud America*. Retrieved on November 15, 2020, from salud-america.org/report-u-s-failed-miserably-in-policy-response-to-covid-19-but-hasa-path-forward-for-future-pandemics/.

Doubek, J. (April 7, 2020). Louisiana Sen. Cassidy addresses racial disparities in coronavirus Deaths. *National Public Radio*. Retrieved on November 15, 2020, from https://www.npr.org/sections/coronavirus-live-updates/2020/04/07/828827346/louisiana-sen-cassidy-addresses-racial-disparities-in-coronavirus-deaths.

Downs, A. (November 22, 1968). The nature of racism in America and how to combat it. Unpublished Manuscript Written for the US Civil Rights Commission, Washington, DC.

Egede, L. (September 17, 2020). Author affiliations from the division of general internal medicine. Retrieved on October 03, 2020, from https://www.nejm.org/doi/full/10.1056/NEJMp2023616.

Gamboa, S. (September 30, 2020). Coronavirus is causing the historic decimation of Latinos, medical expert says. *NBCNews.com*. Retrieved on November 15, 2020, from www.nbcnews.com/news/latino/coronavirus-causing-historic-decimation-latinos-medical-expert-says-n1241576.

Genovese, E. D. (1971). *In Red and Black*. New York: Vintage Books.

Hannah, K. K. (May 16, 2020). Fear sent her Chinatown restaurant spiraling: The challenges to reopening feel just impossible. Retrieved on October 03, 2020, from https://www.washingtonpost.com/nation/2020/05/16/asian-american-businesscoronavirus/.

Kim, J. (April 09, 2020). Report: Sam's Club stabbing suspect thought family was Chinese. Retrieved on November 15, 2020, from https://www.ktsm.com/news/report-sams-club-stabbing-suspect-thought-family-was-chinese-infecting-people-with-coronavirus/.

Krogstad, J. M. and Lopez, M. H. (August 26, 2020). Coronavirus economic downturn has hit Latinos especially hard. *Pew Research Center's Hispanic Trends Project*, Pew Research Center. Retrieved on October 3, 2020, from https://www.pewresearch.org/hispanic/2020/08/04/coronavirus-economic-downturn-has-hit-latinos-especially-hard/.

Kurzius, R. and Simons, S. A. (April 25, 2019). Residents in Southeast D.C. look to expand food options with co-op. WAMU. Retrieved on November 15, 2020, from https://wamu.org/story/19/04/23/residents-insoutheast-d-c-look-to-expand-food-options-with-co-op/.

Larsson, P. (September 06, 2020). Anti-Asian racism during coronavirus: How the language of disease produces hate and violence. Retrieved on October 3, 2020 from https://theconversation.com/anti-asian-racism-during-coronavirus-how-thelanguage-of-disease-produces-hate-and-violence-134496.

Liu, O. (April 11, 2020). Covid-19 has inflamed racism against Asian-Americans: Here's how to fight back. Retrieved on October 3, 2020, from www.cnn.com/2020/04/10/opinions/how-tofight-bias-against-asian-americans-covid-19-liu/index.html.

McNeir, D. K. (March 4, 2020). Food deserts continue within DC's Southeast-based environs. *The Washington Informer*. Retrieved on November 15, 2020, from https://www.washingtoninformer.com/food-desertscontinue-within-d-c-s-southeast-based-environs/.

McNicholas, C. and Poydock, M. (May 19, 2020). Who are essential workers? A comprehensive look at their wages, demographics, and unionization rates. *Economic Policy Institute Working Blog*. Retrieved on November 15, 2020, from https://www.epi.org/blog/who-are-essential-workers-a-comprehensive-look-at-their-wages-demographics-and-unionization-rates/.

Namratha, K. and Nilay, S. (July 24, 2020). Asian Americans invisible in COVID-19 data and in public health response. Retrieved on October 3, 2020, from https://www.chicagoreporter.com/asian-americans-invisible-in-covid-19-data-and-in-publichealth-response/.

Oppel, R. A., Gebeloff, R. and Rebecca, K. K. (July 5, 2020). The fullest look yet at the racial inequity of coronavirus. *The New York Times*. Retrieved on November 15, 2020, from www.nytimes.com/interactive/2020/07/05/us/coronavirus-latinos-african-americans-cdc-data.html.

Phillips, K. (March 22, 2020). They look at me and think I'm some kind of virus: What it's like to be Asian during the coronavirus pandemic. *Providence Journal*. Retrieved on November 15, 2020, from https://www.providencejournal.com/zz/news/20200330/they-look-at-me-and-think-im-some-kind-of-virus-what-its-like-to-be-asian-during-coronavirus-pandemic.

Public Health Law Watch. (August 2020). Assessing legal responses to COVID-19. *Public Health Watch*. Retrieved on November 15, 2020, from https://www.publichealthlawwatch.org/covid19-policy-playbook.

Ramirez, A. (May 28, 2020). 19 ways to ensure health equity for Latinos during (and after) COVID-19. *Salud America*. Retrieved on November 15, 2020, from https://salud-america.org/19-ways-to-ensure-health-equity-for-latinos-during-and-after-coronavirus/.

The New York Times. (January 28, 2020). Covid world map: Tracking the global outbreak. *The New York Times*. Retrieved on November 15, 2020, from https://www.nytimes.com/interactive/2020/world/coronavirus-maps.html.

Thebault, R. (April 7, 2020). The coronavirus is infecting and killing Black Americans at an alarmingly high rate. *The Washington Post*. Retrieved on November 15, 2020 from https://www.washingtonpost.com/nation/2020/04/07/coronavirus-is-infecting-killing-black-americans-an-alarmingly-high-rate-post-analysis-shows/?arc404=true.

Thompson, D. C. (1974). *Sociology of the Black Experience*. Westport, CT: Greenwood Press.

Thuy, L. T. (November 02, 2016). *Social and Cultural Analysis*. New York: New York University Press.

Wan, W. (September 15, 2020). Coronavirus kills far more Hispanic and Black children than White youths, CDC study finds. *The Washington Post*. Retrieved on November 15, 2020, from https://www.washingtonpost.com/health/2020/09/15/covid-deaths-hispanic-blackchildren/.

World Health Organization (WHO). (January 13, 2020). Novel coronavirus—China. Retrieved on November 15, 2020, from http//www.who.int/csr/don/12-january-2020-novel-coronavirus-china/en/.

Chapter 20

Coroadaptation

Feyisitan Ijimakinwa

In the history of humanity and the existence of many human societies, there are events and developments that occur and result in changes and alterations—both temporary and permanent. These changes affect history and narratives about such societies and the age of their occurrence. Aside from these, in order to negotiate these developments, different things come into play, necessitating planned and sometimes unplanned changes, as well as adaptations that are found necessary for a negotiated continuous existence (Soyinka, 2020).

At different points in human history and existence, there have been diverse forms of challenges that have tasked humanity on different fronts. Revolutions, wars, disease outbreaks, pandemics, plagues, and natural disasters are some of the problems that different human societies have had to face, and have informed different survivalist approaches by human beings, in order to sustain their existence. In the modern age of humanity, there have been scourges of diseases like river blindness, polio, measles, acquired immune deficiency syndrome, Ebola, bubonic plague, bird flu, Zika, and other lesser diseases and outbreaks. Aside from these, there have been political, social, and economic developments that have had widespread impacts on the human race. These include, but not limited to, the First and Second World Wars, global economic recessions, the Cold War, terrorism, climate change, and other issues that affected large numbers of people across the globe.

The structure and order of human society as we know it was to change in December 2019 when a new strain of the coronavirus was discovered in Wuhan, China. In the months that followed, Coronavirus Disease (COVID)-2019, so named because of the year of the discovery of the new strain of the virus, spread from China to other parts of the world, creating what became the most widespread health challenge faced by humanity in the modern age.

The rate of infection was rapid and left huge fatalities in its wake. This forced different countries to evolve strategies and protocols aimed at stemming the spread and rate of infection. In most countries, people were constrained to comply with new and unwelcome government regulations that affected every facet of human society (CNN, 2020).

On February 4, 2020, the first reported case of COVID-2019 infection in Africa was recorded in Egypt. As the pandemic drew nearer home, the government in Nigeria decided to take proactive steps to forestall the spread of the disease in the country (African Statesman, 2020). The federal government in Nigeria announced and advised on the necessity of wearing protective face masks, good sanitary procedures like washing of hands, and more importantly, strict observance of social distancing protocols, especially in public places across the country. In addition to these, enlightenment programs on different media platforms and channels were actively carried out, in order to alert Nigerians to the new realities of COVID-2019 (This Day, 2020).

On February 27, 2020, Nigeria recorded its first COVID-2019 case when an Italian citizen, who arrived in the country two days earlier, tested positive for the virus. That incident marked the beginning of COVID-2019 cases in the country. This new development presented a new reality check to the citizenry as the practice of wearing masks and other social distancing protocols had not been widely accepted and practiced, even when it had been made mandatory in public spaces. By mid-March, the number of infected people in Nigeria had risen to 32, and these were concentrated in three principal locations—Lagos and Ogun states as well as the nation's capital city, Abuja. In the wake of the rising figure of infected people, President Muhammadu Buhari, in a nationwide broadcast, announced an initial total lockdown of the three affected areas—Lagos, Ogun, and Abuja—to last for two weeks. This was extended for another two weeks, and on the sides, different states' governments across the country announced and put in place different forms of restrictions and lockdowns that lasted for months. The lockdown affected and altered different aspects of people's lives and engagements (Kalu, 2020).

This chapter takes a critical look at how Nigerians, in the light of the strict and extensive lockdowns, restrictions, alterations, and changes, negotiated and adapted to the new realities that came with the COVID-2019 pandemic. As government's restrictions and regulations threw up new challenges, especially their impacts on the sociocultural, political, and economic lives of the people, among others, Nigerians evolved different methods of adapting to these imposed changes, even as they maintained continuity of their daily existence and engagements, with little or no alteration or disruption.

What is *Coroadaptation*? A dictionary definition of adaptation speaks of the modification of a person or group of people, or their parts that make them more fit for existence under the conditions of their environment. This means that adaptation is about what is done to adjust to present realities without disruptions. Nilsson (2002) points to the need for survival and continuity as a major driver of adaptation, and this is often achieved through sacrifices. This mirrors the experience of many Nigerians who had to, swiftly but sacrificially, adjust to the new realities of life in the COVID-2019 era. Therefore, in the context of this study, necessary adjustments were made to different aspects of Nigerian life by the people themselves, and these happened because of the government's impromptu regulations on social engagements and interactions. This is what is referred to as *Coroadaptation*, that is, the inevitable changes informed by the pandemic and the coping mechanisms and processes developed and practiced by the people to negotiate the changes and this is substantiated by Heimlich and Ardoin (2008).

This study searched out different aspects of the Nigerian life affected by the pandemic and how the people creatively adapted to the new environment and the end result of these adaptations. These tally with Terziev's (2019) position that the relationship between the individual and the group (community) is characterized primarily by the individual's conscious and voluntary compliance with social norms, as well as legal norms put in place to guide conducts and engagements.

THE NEW NORMAL

Using a panoramic view, the chapter highlights not just the adaptive activities but the implications of these on what became the new normal, in a society that had had to deal with something similar, though on a lower scale but as widespread. The term—new normal—was to become associated with the adaptations and reformation of lifestyle and existence that came on the heels of the pandemic. The coinage gained currency and wide use as news media organizations repeatedly use it as an umbrella term for new approaches and dimensions of existence that people were constrained to adopt in the wake of the global pandemic. The term presupposes that there was a pre-existing normal or norm that had been established over time and taken as the ideal way (Adebowale, 2020).

I employed the dual approaches of non-participant observation as well as descriptive exploratory research design for the study. It was practical to observe because some of the occurrences continued well beyond the period of the investigation, and with the descriptive design, I was able to gather data using secondary sources to get a robust understanding of the subject matter. The choice of secondary data enabled me to draw on the resources of other works that had been done and data previously gathered by other researchers. These data were derived from publications including books, journal articles, monographs, newspapers and magazines, broadcast media reports, as well as government and non-governmental publications. These helped me to get an in-depth understanding of the subject matter.

It was important to investigate how Nigerians adapted to the demands and necessities of existence in the wake of the disruptions that came with COVID-2019. This is made profound because of the large informality of Nigerian society. The country has a history of widespread non-compliance with government's regulations and directives by the citizens. These non-adherences are often premised on the mostly factitious but deeply rooted sociocultural beliefs, traditions, and leanings of different groups in the country (Siollum, 2009). Thus, this study presented an interesting opportunity to study the reaction and adaptation of the Nigerian society to a global pandemic, especially one that is different from the previous disease outbreaks and emergencies that the people may have been familiar with. On the other hand, this also presented an opportunity to see the level of government's influence and power in extracting strict compliance from the populace, even with the unexpected disruptions to the social and economic lives of the people. The results of this study served the purpose of throwing more light on the dialectics of development, especially against the backdrop of forced but needful changes, such as was thrown up by COVID-2019.

Nigeria's healthcare sector has a long history of challenges and continues to grapple with the institutional problems of inadequacy of essential work tools and equipment, ill-motivated workforce, and other policy gaps. By the time the lockdown had spread across the federation, the National Centre for Disease Control (NCDC) was constrained to start a daily monitoring report service that briefed Nigerians on issues surrounding the pandemic. There were daily briefings as well as releases in the mass media by the NCDC, which highlighted the number of reported cases in different states and fatalities where they had occurred. All these were aimed at giving a general balance picture of the fight against COVID-2019 in Nigeria. The first four weeks of lockdown and restrictions necessitated some constrained adjustments by everybody, including employers, families, service providers, public officials, students, and many more. Unlike any health scare or emergency that the nation had faced before, there was huge fear about COVID-2019, especially because there was no known cure. This made Nigerians to heed the counsel of the NCDC, and the daily figures released by the agency were diligently followed and broadcast widely, especially through various social media channels. On another level, being forced to stay at home with necessary modification to everyday existence, Nigerians became agitated and this was reflected in the widespread appeal to the government for support (palliatives) to help the populace negotiate the protracted losses of income, occasioned by the cessation of economic activities, the socioeconomic realignment, and more importantly, the danger and fear of infection. In response to this, the federal government came up with the idea of COVID-2019 palliatives which came in the form of material supports, including different food items—rice, sugar, salt, pasta—given to families and homesteads. There were also cash donations, distribution of foods that were undertaken by both government and organizations, all aimed at cushioning the effect of the lockdown on the people across the country (Kalu, 2020).

Because the lockdown was ordered by the federal government, and with its weight and apparatus behind the order, it was fairly successful in restricting movements, cutting down human-to-human contacts and engagements, which in the long run, went a long way in keeping the number of infection low. In other states where the federal government did not order a lockdown, the states government, at different times, gave their orders on lockdowns and restriction of movements. By the end of April 2020, a full month into the federal government-ordered lockdown in Lagos, Ogun, and Abuja, Nigeria had entered a new phase of existence and social engagement processes. At this point, there was little or no mention of reopening of schools or public institutions as the number of infected persons continued to rise, although still perceptibly low when compared with other countries, especially in the Global North.

The reformatted mode of existence owing to COVID-2019 resulted in adaptations that were not envisaged, but become necessary for the continuous existence of people in this environment (Vanguard, 2020). It must be noted that as the virus ravaged the world, some of the adaptations that came into play were translocated from one part of the globe to another, while some others were local and indigenous to different societies and communities across the globe. In Nigeria, the adaptations ran through the economic, social, religious, political, as well as educational aspects of the country, among others. The rest of this chapter will examine the multidimensional alterations that occurred in Nigerian society, in the wake of COVID-2019 pandemic, and the different forms of adaptations employed in negotiating these changes.

CONCEPTUAL CLARIFICATION OF SOCIAL ADAPTATION

Adaptation, as it concerns human beings, is mostly within the terrain of sociality, and means that adaptation of any individual is mostly social. In the light of this, sociality therefore becomes the most critical element in defining any individual. This is so because the absence of sociality puts a valid question of legitimacy on the definition of a person as a living being. Therefore, it is not out of place to say that the lack of sociality or its total loss, according to

Terziev (2019), is virtually impossible because an individual, who is without his or her basic mental function such as consciousness, can be successfully adapted to live as a diligent member of the human society. This means that such an individual has his or her place in the society and can be counted as a member of that society. While the concept of adaptation is grounded in the response of organisms to the environment and other stimuli, social adaptation of human beings is principally the work of responses to new, and sometimes pre-existing, conditions that now dictate new ways of engagement within the community or society. Thus, social adaptation becomes necessary and is often beneficial, especially when it has to do with functioning under stated laws or regulations that should be properly understood in order to be counted as a stakeholder in that community.

It is also important to point out that social adaptation can also be defined as the process of establishing compliance, especially one that is based on specific approaches that overcome artificial restrictions. This is strategic because of the recognition of obstacles and challenges that may be at variance with set characteristics and ways of conduct and engagement. Therefore, a proper definition and understanding of the concept of social adaptation would take into cognizance the clear interaction between the individual and the social environment. Furthermore, the pattern of development between the individual and the society in which he or she operates is not significantly altered because existence is negotiated, without any alteration that may drop the relevance in that society. With these, the needs of the individual, as well as his aspirations, are fully embedded and accommodated within the larger spectrum of society. This strengthens the compliance elements of social adaptations, just as organisms modify themselves in response to stimuli and their environment. In further understanding the concept of social adaption, and as made popular by Terziev (2019), it must be established that social adaptation is, in itself, about the satisfaction of the needs of the individual, in spite of the many needs of such an individual, at any given time. The importance of understanding and defining social adaptation as a critical element of the development of any individual within a given society is informed by objectives, scope, and survival. What this means is that necessary adjustments, whether ordered or premeditated, reflect the level of comfortability of the individual, with the necessary demands of the society.

The forced lockdown and restrictions that came with the COVID-2019 pandemic in Nigeria made the people differentiate between contravention and survival. It became easy for most people to adjust their objectives and comfort to align with the specific modified conditions prevalent in society. This may be different to what Cordell (2014) describes as selective adaptation where he pointed out that survival is not as important as domination; hence, organisms that have better chances of domination adapt to such environment that favors them. However, this stands in opposition to the concept of consumer adaptation, as made popular by Hankers (1999), that says that consumers will always adapt to market forces that complement them, more than the ones that put them below. However, Ellenoch (2013) stands with Terziev (2019) that social adaptation is a holistic process that is continually restructured by emerging forces, interests, and influence. Thus, human beings will always find a place of convenience, within the ambit of requirements, in order to perpetuate themselves and sustain their happiness.

These strengthened the adaptations that became necessary following COVID-2019, especially in Nigeria where the populace were unprepared for the forced lockdown and other restrictions that were ordered without adequate preparation, both mentally and otherwise. Dullard (1999) sees adaptation through the lens of satisfaction of needs and explains that the needs of an individual cannot be superimposed over the larger societal needs. Thus, anyone who fails to align with the bigger needs of the society is labeled an enemy of the people and a deviant that has no place in the community. Dullard (1999) argues further that this does not remove personal ambitions and desires which many people tend to suppress. He makes a case for the greater needs and benefits of society above individual desires. Terziev (2019) believes that the satisfaction of needs is the most essential criterion in achieving balance, inclusion, adaption, rationality, and development. But, he believes that the human need can only be accommodated but not satisfied by an imposed set of rules without special recognition of distinct, individual needs. Still, Dullard (1999) and Terziev (2019) agree that proper social adaptation can only be achieved when an individual is developed and satisfied to its maximum potentialities.

THE MULTIFARIOUS ADAPTATIONS

As mentioned earlier, the outbreak of COVID-2019 led to alterations to everyday existence of people across the world. These were extensive and affected the sociocultural, economic, political, and religious departments of Nigerian society. Following the initial rude shock of the impromptu lockdown and restrictions, Nigerians soon recovered to evolve diverse social adaptation processes. These adaptations are discussed in the subsections that follow.

Call to Worship

The unintended but necessary social adaptations that came with the COVID-2019 opened a new chapter in human affairs, especially as this affected every aspect of human existence. The general human need for continuity of life and engagement made social adaptations, in the wake of COVID-2019, necessary, strategic, and applicable to the generality of humanity, regardless of race, gender, political belief, and philosophy and taste, among others. These adaptations were not only necessary but also important for the continuous existence of humanity, without allowing the disruptions associated with the pandemic to alter lives, engagements, and other human activities (Spencer, 2020).

In Nigeria, Africa's most populous country, with an estimated population of 190 million people, the outbreak of COVID-2019 spelled different things for different people, in different ways that necessitated different reactions, using different approaches. This was most apparent in the area of religion, a very sensitive and often divisive factor in Nigeria. Though a secular state, most Nigerians are adherents of the two Abrahamic faiths—Islam and Christianity—and a negligible few being practitioners of African Traditional Religion (Afatakpa, 2016).

The government-ordered restrictions and lockdowns impacted the fundamental freedom of association, especially under the canopy of worship. The lockdown barred the assemblage of Christians and Muslims in their different places of worship. Religion, as a sensitive issue in Nigeria, has been known to be a sore and sticky point, especially as the country is often divided along religious lines (Kukah, 2018). Thus, the issues of these two religions are often viewed deeper than the surface. In fact, people often interrogate government's policies and actions with the lenses of religion. The Muslims dominated the northern part of Nigeria, and the largely Christian south are often conflicted on who seem to get more of government's protection and patronage. So, when the lockdown order came, it raised a fundamental question of "will the government favor or give concessions to one religion, over the other?" In a bold declaration, the government repeatedly affirmed that the lockdown and order on non-assemblage included religious gathering in places of worship. Confronted with this new reality, the Christian and Muslim faithful were constrained to adapt and evolve new ways and methods of worship without contravening the lockdown order.

In the first week of the lockdown, most Christian faithful were left in a bind. Many Christians decided to hold worship services in their individual homes, especially because there were no clear-cut instructions from their mother churches on how to negotiate the blanket lockdown orders. In different homes across the country, there were widespread cases of families that gathered to hold individuated church worship services. In most homes, the fathers as heads of families assumed the roles of priests and coordinated the 'home/family church.' These impromptu 'pastors' re-enacted church and tried their hands on preaching messages to their minuscule congregation of mostly less than 10 people, depending on the size of the family. In order to give it a full semblance of a church, the whole processes are made complete with other church liturgies and rituals such as communal prayers, tithes, offering praise and worship, and even announcements and invitations for deeper commitments to God. These 'altar calls' are mostly used as evangelistic invitations to congregants for them to commit their lives to God. The idea of payments of tithes and offerings in these 'makeshift' home churches threw up interesting posers such as (a) where were the monies collected as offerings remitted to? (b) who had the oversight function of accounting for the monies collected from 'home worshippers' during the period of the lockdown? (Aligbe, 2020).

After the initial shock of the forced lockdown that jolted church leaders across the nation, and as the days wore on and the lockdown extended to other states in the federation, different churches moved their activities into the virtual space, as they began to stream their services to their followers. Some of the most used channels by churches were YouTube, Facebook, and Instagram. Church members had the opportunity to join in live worship sessions that were streamed live at designated times (Sunday Punch, 2020). This adaptation method was widely used by churches as a way of keeping their members focused on obligatory communal worship.

Although initially a drag this new method soon gained ground and acceptance across different denominations, and for larger meetings, platforms and tools such as Zoom, Hopin, Google Meet, and Webex, among others were deployed. Some churches recorded their worship sessions and messages and these were made available on specific platforms for members.

In order to bridge the gap occasioned by the prohibition of physical gathering of people, most churches publicized their bank account details for members to make necessary payments, including tithes, offerings, and pledges through electronic transfers. This is interesting because prior to this period, most churches did not encourage the electronic payment option as they put emphasis on members bringing the cash to church for payment, especially where it concerns tithes and offerings. On another level, smaller groups within churches turned to holding virtual meetings on social media platforms (Akinyomi, 2020). Churches with small congregation also used WhatsApp and Telegram platforms. Muslims too adapted to the new normal as congregational and communal worship was stepped down and there was noticeable absence of the mandatory call to worship by the *Muezzins*. Instead, Islamic devotionals, call to worship, music videos, prayers and passages of the Quran, all aimed at encouraging the faithful, were shared on social media platforms and pages.

Learning in the Air

Adaptation in the age of coronavirus was not limited to just the issues of faith and belief. Also, the critical sector of education was affected across the globe. In Nigeria, educational institutions found a way to adapt, with as little disruption as possible, especially in keeping to the timetable and schedule of activities as laid down and regulated by the ministries of education at the federal and state levels.

Nigeria runs the 6–3–3–4 education system. The first six years is for primary education, followed by three years of junior secondary education and another three years of senior secondary school education. The last leg involves four years of tertiary education. The terminal examination at the end of six years of primary school education is called the National Common Entrance examination, centrally organized and conducted for pupils across the federation. The West African Senior School Certificate Examination is the standard test at the end of secondary education. This test is organized and coordinated annually by the West African Examinations Council for candidates in secondary schools across West Africa, in the months of May/June. However, the COVID-2019 altered this long-standing tradition as schools were locked down and students were unable to attend physical classes which in itself impacted negatively on their preparations for these important examinations. On the other side, the lockdown and restrictions affected the planning, preparations for, as well as the organizations of this important examination. Thus, on both sides of the divide, the examinations were affected (Obiozor, 2020).

In keeping with the continuity of the school calendar and curriculum, most schools moved their classes to the virtual space as a way of adapting to the new reality of social distancing and non-assemblage in public spaces. Private and public schools organized online classes for their students, and these were moderated by teachers from the schools. Parents were made to pay for these virtual classes (This Day, 2020). The fees charged for the virtual classes were lower than the regular school fees. The necessity of connecting and keeping abreast of the online classes forced many parents to procure necessary gadgets such as smartphones, tablets, and laptops to facilitate connectivity for their wards and children. In some cases, some schools even went beyond the normal classes to provide extra after school hour classes which used to be done physically, but now made virtual.

Further to this, the government also used the mass media channels of television and radio to organize classes and lessons for students, especially those in public schools to bridge necessary gaps that may have arisen as a result of the lockdown. Special attention was given to students in terminal classes such as the last classes of primary, junior, and senior secondary schools. The classes and the lessons were run using the government-approved curriculum and were rendered in English language. However, this mass media initiative did not fully answer the question of exclusion, as there were some states of the federation which did not do this, and public school students in these areas were left in limbo (This Day, 2020).

Graduation, which is an important tradition in the education system, especially in Nigeria, was forced to adapt to the new normal. Most schools reformatted their graduation processes and ceremonies to virtual events. Only graduands who observed necessary COVID-2019 protocols gathered in the schools for the graduation rite and such ceremonies were only streamed or broadcast to members of the public through designated social media channels (Adeifa, 2020). On another level, the social media platforms, especially like YouTube, WhatsApp, and Telegram, became new centers of learning and interaction for students who leveraged the technology to keep abreast of developments in learning.

Different groups moved their conferences, workshops, trainings, symposiums, meetings, interactions, and engagements online. It is instructive to note that even though the option of virtual participation in conferences and associated matters was available prior to the outbreak of the COVID-2019, it was an option that was rarely taken up and only used in the light of unavoidable logistic challenges and encumbrances. However, online mode of participation became the preferred mode for most meetings, especially academic and interactive conferences, workshops, and trainings. Where Internet penetration and connection constituted challenges, as time went on, people found ways around this by enhancing their Internet connectivity as well as their mastery of the use of online options for meetings and connections. The disruption occasioned by restrictions of movements and interaction was not allowed to linger on for too long before connection and normalcy were integrated for continuity, especially in education and knowledge development (AAJS, 2020).

SOCIAL ADAPTATIONS

The most interactive aspect of humanity has to do with sociality, and it is easy to gauge the effects of restrictions and alterations on social engagements and activities of people. The lockdown had varied effects on the social interactions and activities of Nigerians, and they devised new ways of maintaining social continuity and these persisted beyond the lockdown.

New Venue, Same Music

Nigerians are characteristically known for their colorful splendor, especially in social spaces (Osori, 2017). There are accounts of Nigerians standing out by the reason of their right and colorful outfits: formal or informal. In a country made up of over 360 distinct cultures (Ugbachi, 2018), a commonality shared by most of the different cultures is sartorial splendor. So, when the restriction on social gathering came into place as a result of the COVID-2019 pandemic, one of the areas that bore the effect was the social department of Nigerian public life. Normally, parties, celebrations, and even somber gatherings like funerals are often marked with fanfare, dances, and colorful procession by different Nigerian cultures. According to Ugbachi (2018) and Adinobi (2017), a good number of Nigerian tribes, characteristically, have a part of the colorful social life integrated into their cultural fabric. Although a country heavy on religion as evidenced by the huge population of Christians and Muslims, Nigerians are unanimously united in their disposition and preferences for loud, colorful, and vibrant social gatherings and celebrations. It therefore became a challenge to see how this informal yet deeply ingrained aspect of the people was going to be lived out in the face of this global new normal. According to Adonrai (2007), adjustment to culture and the exigencies that may arise lends credence to the fact that culture in itself is not static, but is constantly negotiated and having new faces within new time frames, involving new people. Adonrai's (2007) position is a viable premise and explanation for the creative adaptation of Nigeria's sociocultural life as celebrations including parties were moved into the virtual space. Hitherto large and colorful parties like wedding and birthday ceremonies were marked spectacularly on available online platforms, especially Zoom, Webex, Facebook, and Instagram, among others.

Popular Nigerian thespian, Rita Dominic who clocked 45 years in July 2020, at the height of the lockdown, was the first Nigerian celebrity to have a Zoom party to mark her birthday (Naija Avenue, 2020). It was reported that over 3,000 people joined in the online celebration at different times, while it lasted. Other notable names in Nigerian world of celebrities that had Zoom parties include Mercy Johnson and Innocent Idibia, popularly called Tuface Idibia. Even government officials like Nigeria's minister for transport, Rotimi Amaechi, celebrated his 55th birthday in the virtual space. However, one birthday celebration that was remarkable was that of the popular publisher of Nigeria's leading celebrity magazine, Dele Momodu. This publisher of *Ovation* magazine turned 60 and for someone whose glossy photo-magazine records the social celebrations and lives of the rich and famous across Africa, his landmark birthday could only be celebrated online. According to leading tabloid, *The Nation*, in spite of the relative novelty of the virtual party, Dele Momodu's birthday lasted over 5 hours on Zoom and was attended by over 6,000 people who signed in at different times and were part of the proceedings (Netadvoc, 2020).

Indeed, these showed that Nigerians swiftly and ingeniously filled the social gaps created by the pandemic and the lockdown restrictions. This social adaptation was not only common with celebrities as regular people too held virtual birthday celebrations, wedding parties, marriage solemnizations, baby christening, and other forms of celebrations that would have attracted colorful social gathering but now held online. This was not just about lively and effervescent parties, as somber events like funerals were not left out as they were held online and people joined (Aligbe, 2020). In fact, during the period of the lockdown and even after this had been eased, online access particulars had become a normal component of invitations for social events. Thus, it is now normal to see information on Zoom access printed on invitations for social events. Since such events are streamed virtually, invited guests have the option of joining remotely or attending physically.

As part of creating continuity, without allowing for disruptions in the social lives of the people, broadcast media organizations creatively enhanced their content by designing and broadcasting live musical performances in the mode of what obtains at live social parties. These were broadcast to viewers who are enjoined to dress up colorfully and gaily and party from their respective homes, just as they would have done if it was a physical party in a public place. Cable television service provider in Nigeria, DSTV, created a program called *Owambe Saturday*, loosely translated as Saturday party, to reflect the local parlance for parties in Nigeria, and Saturday being the day that is commonly regarded as the day for socialization, parties, and social festivities in Nigeria. On the program, a live band plays from the studio, with no audience, and belt out different songs from most of the ethnic groups in the country. While *Owambe Saturday* remained on the air even after the lockdown had eased, and hosted by a popular comedian who catered to the old generation, another program—*Turn Up Friday*—was designed and broadcast in response to the yearnings of members of the young generation who mostly go to nightclubs on Friday evenings (This Day, 2020). A disc jockey plays popular tunes from the studio, and viewers at home are encouraged to send short videos showing them partying at home. These programs were hailed widely and received huge acceptance among television viewers in Nigeria. The popularity of these two programs stems from the fact that they reinforced the spirit and culture of celebration that are common with many Nigerians. This is made more profound by the fact that it mediated the gaps, disruptions, and discomforts that arose from COVID-2019 and the lockdown that followed. The peculiarity of these interventions was reflected in the remote connection of viewers with the studio, thus bridging the gap of non-physical assemblage of people, while continuing with the practice of social parties, a common cultural denominator acceptable across the Nigerian society.

Broadcast Media Outputs

Necessity, the saying goes, is the mother of invention. This was played out in how the Nigerian society, in different ways, adapted itself to the necessity of the new normal, especially as it concerned the restrictions on the physical congregation of people in a place. This development was extended to popular media reality shows that attract huge viewership. The auditioning and screening processes that precede these reality shows draw huge number of interested contestants. According to Multichoice Nigeria, the organizers of Big Brother Naija, over 20,000 people took part in the audition that preceded the show in 2019. The auditioning exercises were held at four different locations across the country. Owing to the prize money and attendant celebrity status that the show confers on participants, it has become a major hit among young people in the country. Adaptation became a necessity in year 2020 as the organizers of the show, in response to the COVID-2019 pandemic, decided to take the auditioning for Big Brother Naija Season Five online (Punch, 2020). This novel approach and departure from the usual put many people who were counting on impressing the judges at physical auditions in tight spots. The exigencies of social distancing made the organizers to request would-be housemates to make 2 minutes videos of themselves and send in as part of the audition process (Premium Times, 2020). At the close of the entry process, Multichoice announced that over 30,000 people, the highest number of entries ever in the five seasons of the show, submitted short homemade videos for consideration (Premium Times, 2020). Of these lots, 20 entries were picked as successful and made their way into the house when Big Brother Naija Season Five premiered on July 19, 2020, for the period of 71 days that the show lasted. The peculiarity of Big Brother Naija 2020 was not limited to the virtual audition.

The weekly eviction show is an integral part of the Big Brother show and it used to be live, packed with audience to welcome any evicted housemate. However, it took a new form this year as the eviction show featured only the anchor, a disc jockey, and simulated voices and pictures of audience, all to make it as real as possible.

A number of popular reality shows like Naija Sings, Maltina Dance, and Peak Factor also used the remote auditioning processes over regular physical auditioning processes. In the same vein, media appearances especially on television were remodeled, as guests were mostly brought in via virtual connection, away from the normal physical presence in the studio or designated places. Before COVID-2019 appeared on the scene, Nigeria's leading news station, Channels Television, regularly invite guest analysts for appearances on their news broadcasts and other current affairs programs. During the period of the COVID-2019 lockdown and the months that followed, the station changed the mode of guest appearances as it moved away from physical appearance to virtual connection. This, in no small way, helped the news station to improve on its remote connectivity with guests and other people who were able to make appearance without the encumbrance of distance and related logistics. This trend subsequently spread to other broadcast media organizations, especially television stations across the country.

The virtual dimension to broadcast media was not only limited to news and program appearances. The necessity of continuity, especially in the creative industry, extended to film production. A Nigerian filmmaker, Obi Emelonye, in response to the peculiarities of the time, and against the pre-COVID-2019 style of gathering actors in a film location, shot a short film that reflected a good degree of novelty and creative ingenuity. The film, *Heart to Heart*, is a love story of two people in a relationship but separated by distance, but overcame this through their own creative ingenuity in leveraging technology. It was shot through the virtual connecting platform of Zoom as the different cast members self-recorded their different parts of the script and these were put together by the director. The end result was the first virtual film shot and produced via Zoom. The feat of Emelonye was hailed as a major milestone in film production (Channels, 2020).

NOVEL GOVERNANCE STYLE

Governance and its processes were not left out of the necessary adaptation that came in the wake of COVID-2019. Across the world, we saw that meetings, including those which involved critical political figures and personalities, were forced to toe the line of strict social distancing protocols. In many instances, physical assemblage was totally removed and remote connection took its place (Al Jazeera, 2020). During this period, the United Nations conducted most of its businesses virtually. The UN General Assembly is the biggest regular convocation of world leaders in one single place. However, proceedings including speeches and addresses by Heads of Government of member nations during the 2020 General Assembly of the UN were delivered remotely and beamed to the rest of the world. The African Union also conducted its General Assembly sessions via remote connections by leaders of member states. The Economic Community of West African States followed the same trend for its meetings. It is important to note that this option of remote connectivity was sparingly used in the past, but this became the most ideal form of connection in establishing continuity of proceedings (Africanews, 2020).

In Nigeria, the Federal Executive Council (FEC) is the highest decision-making body, made up of the president, the vice president, and the cabinet ministers, and it meets weekly to take important decisions on the running of the Nigerian state. The FEC meeting is presided over by the president. In the eventuality of the absence of the president, the vice president sits over the meeting. Strategic and critical decisions that impact the government and the people of Nigeria are taken during this meeting. However, owing to the COVID-2019 pandemic and the need for strict social distancing protocol, the FEC meeting went virtual, as the president connected virtually with other members of the council in deliberating on critical matters. This was widely advertised and promoted via the media and showed a strong example of a government that adhered to its own regulations. Because of the action of the highest decision-making body in the country, it was easy for other states and organizations to buy into this and adopt the same style and mode for their meetings and engagements. According to a foremost social policy analyst in Nigeria, Reuben Abati who spoke on Arise Television:

> The necessary adaptations that came as a result of the coronavirus pandemic allowed for the creative elements in every society to be woken as a way of bridging the disruptions that could have arisen from necessary adaptations and alignments. It shows that humanity can go beyond itself to cover any hole that may sink it, but emerge better on the other side of the divide. (Arise Television, 2020)

This means that human beings have capacities to creatively and resourcefully respond to daunting situations by digging deep to come up with solutions. The necessity of continuity and consolidation became the catalyst for the adaptations that greeted the restrictions and lockdowns of COVID-2019.

No Usual Business

If the adaptation of the FEC was commendable, then it was easy for the change of mode of operation to extend beyond government circle. With the forced change of lifestyle because of the pandemic, the new normal soon extended to the formal and informal labor sectors. In Nigeria, the informal labor sector constitutes 42 percent of the labor market and this is made up of small and medium enterprises which averagely employ about four people (NBS, 2019). The human need for survival meant that a disruption could not be allowed, especially as it concerned the day-to-day economic activities and this was the reason why, in no time, the necessity of adaptation overtook even the labor sector. Most businesses that hitherto would not have considered virtual connection as an option soon turned in this direction and devised means of plugging in and making the best out of the situation. During the period of the COVID-2019 pandemic, there was an upsurge in online business activities. A large number of business owners went online to bridge gaps created by the lockdown order, as well as for business continuity and sustenance of connection with their customer base. Different businesses even offered extra service of delivery (Adebowale, 2020). This way, many businesses that would have been cut off from their customers continued with little or no disruption, and the advantage of this is that beyond the COVID-2019 period, online business activities and processes became an integral component of doing business in Nigeria.

For those who could not work remotely, and still needed public connection, accessing public places had new rules. Citizens were expected to wear masks, sanitize their hands, and have their temperatures taken before they could enter any public place. Owners of business premises were also mandated by the government to make facilities for sanitizing the hands—hand sanitizers/water and soap/hand wash—available on their business premises, specifically at the entrance. This increased the people's awareness about COVID-2019 as new markets sprang up for producers and retailers of essential materials like masks, face shields, gloves, sanitizers, hand wash, and so on. Another set of people who benefited from the constrained adaptation to the coronavirus pandemic are website developers and designers who experienced remarkable upsurge in the demand for their services and had to come up with quick and inexpensive website designs and e-commerce platforms for increasing number of people. Aside from this, demands for knowledge of website designs and do-it-yourself webpage designs increased and more people showed interest in the acquisition of these skills.

Ride Space for Less

One of the critical sectors of Nigerian society has to do with transportation. As important as this sector is, it is one that is often bedeviled by intractable difficulties. The Nigerian transportation sector involves private and public owners and operators. However, over time, public transportation which is mostly dominated by road transport has largely been overtaken by private owners and operators who own and operate buses, taxis, cars, tricycles, motorbikes, and trucks, among others. The government has largely concerned itself with the provision of road infrastructures while the operations in this sector are largely dominated by private operators. This does not mean that government's ownership or operation is non-existent but it has continued to diminish across the different states of the federation. In their places, private ownership and informal transport operations have been on the ascendancy in most states.

Road transportation is the biggest and the most widely used transport system in Nigeria. This cuts across the urban and rural areas in all states in the country. As new settlements and communities open up, different forms of informal transport system are used by people in these areas; hence, the popularity of motorbikes and tricycles that are often preferred for their low passenger carrying capacity and their ease of getting into remote areas, with little or no access to roads. With the COVID-2019 pandemic and the social distancing protocols that followed, adjustments were introduced into road transport passenger carriage systems in Nigeria. Prior to this, passenger overload was a common feature of road transport systems in Nigeria. It was not uncommon to see buses and taxis carrying more passengers than the advised maximum capacity. Most times, law enforcement officers compromise and willingly turn blind eyes to the traffic infractions by these drivers.

With the corruption of the system, transport operators have perfected ways of bribing police and transport officials to look the other way while they carry excess passengers. In spite of years of outcry against this practice of passenger overload, it has been difficult to change this as different government initiatives in regulating and checking passenger overload have been largely ineffective and unsuccessful. However, with the social distancing protocols that came with the pandemic, government made a last dash at effecting necessary changes within the transportation sector, especially as it concerns number of passengers that are carried in most public transport vehicles. Before the pandemic, mini buses, designed to carry 12 passengers including the driver, are often filled with 20 occupants, including the driver. But this was to change when the government used the opportunity of the social distancing protocols to institute and effect changes in the number of passengers these mini buses are allowed to carry. A very strict regulation was put in place to ensure that mini buses do not carry more than nine passengers. According to Maduka (2020), this new regulation met with initial stiff resistance, especially among those who operate interstate road transport services. In spite of the opposition, the government across the federation used the instrumentality of the Federal Road Safety Corps (FRSC), the federal agency responsible for the regulation and enforcement of road laws and regulations across the country, to make the new rule work effectively. The FRSC alongside the Nigerian Police ensured that road transport operators carried only the number of passengers approved by the government. It is important to point out that the introduction of this new passenger capacity regime changed the face of transportation as attendant fare increment greeted this new development. However, owing to the long period of the COVID-2019 restrictions and the fact that transport fares were increased based on the reduced number of passengers that could be carried, the fare hike soon became a new normal with passengers. Thus, what the government had struggled to achieve for years, in spite of different regulations and laws, was easily achieved and adapted to by the populace including the operators.

This adjustment was not only limited to vehicles owned by private operators but it also was extended to the few public transport owned and operated by the government. A very good example of this is the Bus Rapid Transit (BRT) system in Lagos, the most populated state in Nigeria, which is highly popular and preferred in the movement of people from one part of the state to another. According to Otunola et al. (2019) as of 2019, BRT buses in Lagos were moving an average of 18,000 daily between the operational hours of 5 a.m. and 9 p.m. As popular as the BRT is, this world-class transport system is only in its second phase of a 25-year-long plan. However, in accordance with the new social distancing laws and regulation, the sitting and standing arrangement on the BRT buses was reconfigured to reflect the new realities of social distancing. While on one hand, one can hail this as the government setting examples with its own ventures, it must also be recognized that this created a shortfall that was evident in increased number of passengers who were stranded and forced to readjust their schedules or go with other means of transportation. The fallout of this was that other forms of transportation such as ferries as well as ride hailing service providers like Bolt and Uber recorded upsurges in patronage. For example, Lagos being a littoral state had a good number of people turning to water transport as ferries and boats were increasingly used to connect different parts of the city. A study by the Nigerian motorway sector of the National Insurance Association showed that Uber and Bolt, the two leading ride hailing service providers in Nigeria, recorded significant increase in their operations, and this was attributed to the significant number of people who could not travel with the BRT.

CONCLUSION AND RECOMMENDATIONS

Overall, the social adaptation that came in the wake of the COVID-2019 and the forced lockdown, by the federal government in Nigeria, can be attributed to the need for survival by the populace. That was the most viable route opened for continuous involvement, and it was easy for members of the society to negotiate the difficulties and the new realities that were thrust upon them by external forces and factors beyond their control. Social adaptation was made easier because the alternatives that were open could considerably accommodate the desires, opinions, and processes. Most aspects of the Nigerian life easily adapted to the new normal and the availability of technology made this easier. This was evidently clear in how educational and training activities easily transited from the physical to the virtual space, with minimal hitch. This shows that these options can be leveraged for enhanced productivity and betterment of society with little or no alterations to everyday life.

The easy adaptation by the populace lends credence to the fact that human resourcefulness holds the answer to all human problems. Opposition to necessary adaptive mechanisms and necessities arose not because this was necessary but because of some need for human perpetuation. Church worship was moved to the virtual space and this bore evidence that showed that people could hold their own, retain their communion without necessarily gathering in a physical building. However, it is curious to find out that one of the most vociferous oppositions to government-ordered lockdown and restrictions were church leaders who 'strangely' framed the lockdown and restrictions as a deliberate onslaught against the church by the state. It is interesting also that some members of the two Abrahamic faiths did not see any value in remote or virtual worship. As far as they were concerned, it is either physical congregation or nothing.

Beyond this, the adaptations that occurred established the resourcefulness and creative ingenuity inherent in human beings and available in society. The government can benefit from this novel and remarkable development especially in areas or sectors that are groaning under the pressure of limited capacity to handle crowd or human traffic. Instead of being on the road to attend that party or celebration, the necessity of fraternity can still be achieved even if the virtual option is taken up. Not everyone should and must be within the four walls of classroom when the same curriculum can be taught virtually and other necessity of learning achieved via the same medium. Since a number of infections thrive with close human contact and engagement, the responses that came in the wake of COVID-2019 lockdown have shown that nothing is impossible as long as you set your mind to it. It also affirms that there is always another route to achieve your aim and purposes without any infraction or alteration to normalcy.

It is recommended that the federal government strengthen the online study system as a strategic component of Nigeria's educational system. The disruptions that came as a result of the lockdown caught many schools unprepared, especially as remote learning had not been a part of the school learning system in Nigeria, and this reflected in the initial problems that most schools faced when the lockdown and other social distance protocols made physical classes and lessons impracticable. Nonetheless, the effectiveness/ineffectiveness of online or remote learning in tertiary institutions could not be ascertained because public universities, which make up 65 percent of tertiary institutions in Nigeria, were inoperative during the period of the lockdown due to a labor strike by university lecturers in the country.

Also, it is important for the government to ensure that the backbone for the growth and development of information technology in Nigeria be strengthened. This is necessary in order to drive the veritable and viable option of doing diverse activities online. Internet penetration and connectivity should be given top priority attention by the government as this is one of the strategic necessities in leveraging maximal opportunities available to different sectors of the economy and the Nigerian life in the virtual space.

The social adaptations that came in the wake of COVID-2019 showed that a new order can be institutionalized in Nigeria. The government can use this as a springboard for the enthronement of a new social order and work this into the framework for nation building. Previous attempts at social reforms in Nigeria have been largely unsuccessful but COVID-2019 showed clearly that a new order is achievable in the country, and the government can leverage this to jumpstart the much-needed social recalibration in the society, especially as it concerns attitudes and perceptions to social orders.

REFERENCES

Adebowale, A. (2020). Emerging platforms for businesses during and after COVID-19 in Nigeria. *Paper Presented at the 3rd International (Online) Conference of the African Association for Japanese Studies (AAJS)*. October 2–3, 2020.

Adeifa, B. (2020). The new normal and global social processes. *African Political Review* 15(2):46–57.

Adinobi, S.I. (2017). Living in bondage: Exploring the narratives of contempt and mistrust in inter-group relationships in Nigeria. *Journal of African Political Science* 8(1):13–22.

Adonrai, S. (2007). A short history of the military and Nigerian politics (1979–2000). *Journal of Military History* 45(4):20–38.

Afatakpa, O. F (2016). An African monotheism: The Igbe religion of the Urhobo and the economic importance of Ore—Isi Festival. In Nolte, I and Ogen, O. (eds.), *Mobile Populations, Fluid Boundaries: Community, Trade, and Religion in Coastal Yorubaland and Western Niger Delta*. Ondo City, Nigeria: Adeyemi College of Education Press.

Africanews. (April 23, 2020). ECOWAS leaders meet to discuss impact of Covid-19. *Africanews*. Retrieved on October 18, 2020 from https://www.africanews.com/2020/04/23/ecowas-leaders-meet-to-discuss-impact-of-covid-19/.

African Association for Japanese Studies (AAJS). (October 3, 2020) Report of the 3rd International (Online) Conference of the African Association for Japanese Studies (AAJS). *African Association for Japanese Studies (AAJS)* Retrieved on October 16, 2020 from https://youtube.com/XJWwoQ7Sc4M0.

African Statesman. (March 6, 2020). Can Africa survive another pandemic? *African Statesman*. Retrieved on October 13, 2020 from https://www.african-statesman.com/can-africa-survive-another-pandemic-/.

Akinyomi, N. (2020). The conflicts of religions in a new world. *Journal of Faith and Law* 3(1):34–42.

Al Jazeera. (September 15, 2020). The new face and phase of international meetings. A Special Report on the 75th Session of the United Nations' General Assembly. *Al-Jazeera*. Retrieved on September 30, 2020 from https://www.aljazeera.com/news/2020/9/15/the-new-face-and-phase-of-international-meetings.

Aligbe, C. (2020). We are always connected: Exploring the realms of virtual connectivity in social celebrations in Nigeria. *African Studies Review* 12(2):14–29.

Arise Television. (September 26, 2020). Covid19: A re-invention is necessary for Nigeria. *Arise Television*. Retrieved on October 2, 2020 from https://www.arise.tv/covid-19-a-re-invention-is-necessary-for-nigeria/.

Cable News Network (CNN). (August 16, 2020). COVID-19: The scourge of a pandemic. *CNN*. Retrieved on October 12, 2020 https://edition.cnn.com/2020/8/16/health/covid-19-the-scourge-of-a-pandemic/index.html.

Channels Television. (May 9, 2020). Nollywood's Obi Emelonye shoots first film directed by Zoom. *Sunrise on Channels Television*. Retrieved on October13, 2020 from https://www.youtube.com/watch?v=jEKMmuP8L1A.

Cordell, A. (2014). Domain and dominations: A study of behavioral change in the construction industry. *Psychology Reflections* 8(2):113–147.

Dullard, J. (1999). Motivating sustainable adaptation: A review of evidence on college students' behaviour and behavioural change. *Journal of Canadian Sustainable Development* 13(2):16–41.

Ellenoch, B. N. (2013) Conceptual clarifications of social productivity. *Journal of Occupational Therapy* 33(2):65–84.

Hankers, J. (1999) Social adaptation among migrant workers in the auto industry. *Journal of Occupational Therapy* 13(2):14–31.

Heimlich, J. E. and Ardoin, N. M. (2008). Understanding behavior to understand behavior change: A literature review. *Environmental Education Research* 14:215–237.

Kalu, B. (2020). Covid I9 in Nigeria: A disease of hunger. *The Lancet* 8(6):556–557.

Kukah, M. H. (June 16, 2018). Threats to the Christian faith in contemporary Nigeria. Keynote address at a conference of the Catholic Men's Guild, Archdiocese of Lagos, Lagos, Nigeria.

Lirtell, J. H. and Girvin, H. (2002). Stages of change: A critique. *Behaviour Modification* 26:223–273.

Maduka, J. S. (2020). Reappraising transportation and road infrastructures in Lagos, Nigeria. *Journal of African Development* 18(1):16–23.

Naijaavenue. (July 13, 2020). Nollywood actress, Rita Dominic, holds online birthday bash. *Naijaavenue*. Retrieved on October 16, 2020 from https://www.naijaavenue.com/rita-dominic-sets-new-record-as-she-becomes-first-nigerian-actress-to-hold-birthday-party-on-zoom/.

Nigeria Bureau of Statistics (NBS). (November 2019) Small and medium scale enterprises report, third quarter, 2019. *NBS*. Retrieved on September 16, 2020 from https://www.nigerianstat.gov.ng/page/reports.

Nilsson, D. H. (2002). What's the 'problem'?: A conceptual and empirical exploration of adjustment to health condition and adjustment to hospitalisation as Indicators for intervention for social workers in health-care settings. Unpublished Doctor of Social Work Thesis, La Trobe University, Melbourne, Australia.

Netadvoc (May 17, 2020). Dele Momodu defies coronavirus, hosts virtual party. *NetAdvoc*. Retrieved on September 24, 2020 from https://netadvoc.com.ng/dele-momodu-defies-coronavirus-hosts-virtual-party/.

Obiozor, W. T. O. (September 21, 2020). The politics of Covid-19 and universal education. A Keynote Address Delivered at the Ngwa Education and Scholarship Board Retreat, Umuahia, Abia State, Nigeria. September 21–24, 2020.

Osori, A. (2017). *Love Does Not Win Elections*. Abuja, Nugeria: Hazelnut Books.

Otunola, B., Kriticos, S. and Harman, O. (2019). The BRT and the Danfo: A case study of Lagos' transport reforms from 1999–2019. *IGC Cities that Work Case Study*. London, UK: International Growth Centre.

Premium Times. (July 17, 2020). BBNaija 2020 organizers announce season 5 audition dates. *Premium Times*. Retrieved on September 13, 2020 from https://www.premiumtimesng.com/news/393793-bbnaija-2020-organisers-announce-season-5-premiere-date.html.

Punch. (July 16, 2020). COVID-19 and Nigeria's new values. *Punch*. Retrieved on October 24, 2020 from https://www.punchng.com/covid-19-and-nigeria's-new-values/.

Soyinka, W. (September 3, 2020). The first light after dark. A Paper presented at the 13th African Leadership Initiative Conference, Lagos, Nigeria. September 3, 2020.

Siollum, M. (2009). *Oil, Politics and Violence: Nigeria's Military Coup Culture (1966-1979)*. New York: Algora Publishing.

Spencer, B. (2020). Bouncing against the wall: The imperatives of socio-cultural engagements and a post pandemic world. *Journal of Socio Cultural Pedagogy* 13(2):13–32.

Sunday Punch. (April 5, 2020). Government bars churches from reopening. *Sunday Punch* Retrieved on April 5, 2020 from https://www.punchng.com/government-bars-churches-from-reopening/.

Terziev, V. (2019). Conceptual framework of social adaptation. *Proceedings of INTCESS 2019- 6th International Conference on Education and Social Sciences*, February 4–6, 2019- Dubai, United Arab Emirates.

This Day. (May 15, 2020). Turn up Friday with Pepsi launches on Africa magic channels. *This Day*. Retrieved on September 12, 2020 from https://www.thisdaylive.com/index.php/2020/05/15/turn-up-friday-with-pepsi-launches-on-africa-magic-channels/.

This Day. (May 24, 2020). Retooling Nigeria's health Sector for the coronavirus pandemic. Retrieved on September 12, 2020 from https://www.thisdaylive.com/index.php/2020/05/24/retooling-nigeria's-health-sector-for-the-coronavirus-pandemic/.

Ugbachi, N. O. (2018). Recharting Nigeria's political experiences (1996–2018). *Pan African Journal of Contemporary Developments* 4(1):13–27.

Vanguard. (May 18, 2020). Covid -19: The exigencies of new realities. *Vanguard*. Retrieved on August 24, 2020from https://www.vanguardngr.com/2020/05/covid-19-the-exigencies-of-new-realities/.

Chapter 21

Coropoliticaldiscourse

Rachael M. Rudolph

An unusual year deserves an unconventional beginning, harkening back to when I was still in China. The month was December and the semester was nearing its end. A student was in my office talking about finals and asking of my plans for our two-month break. I had started the semester with travel to India and had just returned (right before finals) from a business trip in Italy. Blowing my nose from a cold I caught immediately after returning, I replied that I had planned to meet with my daughter (who was living in South Korea) in January in Macau for the New Year and then would be traveling to Central America with another colleague for some field research. She had told me to take care and to make sure I got some rest because, if not, I might end up sicker than I was. A flu had already been making its rounds on campus for a few weeks. I promised her that I would take care.

A week later, I was certain my cold had turned into flu. The same student, whose father was a doctor, asked me if I was okay. Her dad suggested some antibiotics for me to take, which she kindly picked up from the pharmacy and brought them to my apartment. A few days afterward I was feeling well and back to normal. When she came to see me one more time before departing for her home town up north I had queried her about new flu that seemed to be circulating in the northern provinces. She asked me where I heard of it, so I showed her the news article I read. The flu referred to in the article was not COVID-2019; and, thankfully, neither myself nor any of my students came down with either of those two viruses.

After leaving Macau in January, I briefly stopped in the United States before heading to Central America. My American mobile phone had been stolen in Italy, so I needed to stop at home in Florida to pick up the new one I had ordered before heading to El Salvador, which is where I would stay for most of January and the first two weeks of February. There are was a short couple-day trip to Guatemala in that time period. During that entire time, international news was filled with reports of COVID-2019.

Initially, we read the reports daily because both my colleague and I planned to return to China in mid-February; our lives were tightly connected to the events that were unfolding—from the lockdown in China to the border closure to flights coming to and from China to the United States. Meanwhile, we had to report daily to work via WeChat or e-mail, completing forms on our location changes, the number of people we were in contact with, and so on. As the hysteria in the global media increased and fear began to take hold as the virus spread both inside and outside of China, the news soon became something we avoided.

A decision had been made right before we left El Salvador in February. I returned to the United States to prepare to teach online while my colleague traveled to South America. Since the travel restrictions were already in place before my return and with Chinese residency and visa stamps in my passport, I got pulled in for questioning by airport security in Houston, Texas. Airport security asked me where I was coming from, why I had been there, when was the last time I was in China, why was I in China, how long I would be staying in the United States, where I would be staying and with whom, and for the telephone number and address where I could be reached? I ended up missing my flight back to Florida.

From Florida, I watched news and listened to an array of accounts regarding the virus. It was still something distant in my mind and remained as such until my daughter notified us that someone whom she worked with in South Korea had been exposed to the virus. It became a little more real at that point. I cancelled my flights to both South Korea and Japan for March and remained in Florida for the rest of the year. As I write this chapter, I am sitting in a hotel room in Dallas, Texas, waiting to take the required tests to enable me to travel back to China. The testing requirements to return are quite stringent. I must be tested (blood and nasal swab), have the results certified by the Chinese ministry, and travel within a 48-hour period. Airplane prices are quite expensive, too. Whether this becomes the new normal remains to be seen, but there is no escaping the fact that COVID-2019 has altered all of our lives in many ways. Crises usually do, however.

In the field of policy studies, we learn and teach (for those of us who do) that crises provide windows of opportunity to facilitate change in policy direction if there is a will among policymakers to do so. COVID-2019 has impacted people, businesses, and governments far and wide. It has been significant enough to facilitate policy change within the United States and across the globe, altering the nature of relations and type of engagement on a variety of levels. It has also contributed to the further deterioration in American Chinese relations, which had already been on shaky ground since the opening of the trade war under the Trump administration. Many think tank events examined how COVID-2019 was likely to impact U.S.-China relations. A few of them even capitalized on the outbreak of virus to advocate for the complete decoupling of relations and the adoption of a confrontational approach, the latter which has been the preferred choice for the clique known globally as the China hawks. Other scholars dismissed the potential they could have in altering policy in this period. Still in my mind though were the lessons learned and those which I teach on about how when crises are significant enough and there is political will, the direction of policy can be altered in ways where there can be no turning back. This reality provided the background for wanting to examine whether COVID-2019 was being used by U.S. policymakers to facilitate or induce behavior change: that is, whether they were using the China threat narrative like some of the individuals from the NGO think tanks in the United States and other countries to induce policy change in United States-China relations. Could the fear of the virus and its suspected origin from China, coupled with an already tense relationship, provide the opening the China hawks needed to drive U.S.-China relations to the point of no return?

The China threat thesis has been around for quite some time, and it is usually coupled with discussions on America's decline. The first section of this chapter provides readers with an overview of the existing literature on both theses. Because they have been around and prevalent in the literature since the 1990s, it is nothing new for policymakers, who are so driven, to use those theoretical prisms to drive their cause for change. After all, every policymaker engages in the act of framing an issue in order to gain support for the cause-at-hand and to generate enough momentum to mobilize support for formulating legislation to effect the desired change in either policy or behavior. New though would be the use of COVID-2019 and the convergence of political discourses of the threat thesis and the virus to drive or induce behavior change. Although I am examining it within a single case—the China threat—it is plausible that COVID-2019 is being used more widely to induce change, thus opening the door to the potential for a wider study on "coropoliticaldiscourse." Used in such a context, coropoliticaldiscourse refers to the use of written or spoken communication or debate about COVID-2019 to exploit fear, hatred, and/or discord within a given context and directed toward a specific audience for the purpose of advancing a political narrative. This study seeks to examine whether it was used and exploited to advance fears of America's decline, China's rise, and the perceived threat of the latter to a Western-dominated geopolitical global order.

THEORETICAL FRAMEWORK

Scholars, policymakers, and the media have been debating America's relative decline in power since the end of the twentieth century (Strange, 2001; Nye,

2002–2003; Wallerstein, 2003; Oppenheimer, 2008; Richter, 2009; Quinn and Kitchen, 2019). Some scholars have focused on debating the causes and consequences of the decline, while others have refuted their arguments, positing that, in fact, America is not in decline when assessing its power capabilities in relation to emerging powers. Decline scholars highlight the loss of America's influence and support for its policies and positions over time by allies and the latter's reluctance to cooperate with Washington; the loss of economic superiority over its allies in the Cold War period, political hegemony in the post-Cold War period, and ideological support in the post-September 2001 period; and open and growing opposition to U.S. policies and positions by emerging powers and outright hostility toward them by adversaries. Scholars countering the decline thesis tend to adopt a traditionalist perspective, focusing specifically on America's economic, political, and military primacy. They conjecture that there is no other emerging power (allied or adversary) capable of assuming the role played by the United States in the global community. America's structural advantages such as its alliance arrangements, dollar primacy, vast military, and financial and commercial clout ensure its primacy now and for a long time to come.

Other scholars have rooted their scholarship in the decline literature but concentrated on the rise of emerging powers generally or within specific regions, and/or on the rise of countries like China and their impact on global order (Nye, 2002–2003; Houweling and Amineh, 2003; Ross, 2006; Williams, 2007; Richter, 2009; Parisot, 2013; Afridi, Yousef and Ahmad, 2015; Quinn and Kitchen, 2019). They concur with the aforementioned scholars that none of the emerging powers at this time have the capabilities nor the desire to play the role that America has played, and their rise is simply a product of and necessitated by the changing nature of global order from a unipolar, American and Western-centric order to a multipolar, more democratic order that varies regionally. They argue the shifting nature of order has contributed to the reemergence of geoeconomic, geopolitical, and geostrategic competition among global and regional powers, with it being more evident at the regional rather than the global level except for American Chinese global economic competition. American Chinese competition is felt globally due to Beijing's economic rise within a declining American-liberal economic order coupled with a shift from an American-centered political hegemonic order to a democratic, hegemonic political order. China's rise has been the main scholarly focus since the end of the twentieth century (Zhang, 2010; Zhang, 2013; Acharya, 2014; Liang, 2018). Scholars have examined Western perceptions of its rise, its impact on regional order, and within the context of U.S.-China relations. Most scholars conclude that its rise presents both opportunities and challenges for the United States, the West, and global and regional order.

A few scholars posit that the underlying debate of all the aforementioned assumptions is about power; and, more specifically, its nature and how it is measured by scholars focusing on both America's decline and China's rise. Definitions of power and how it has been measured have varied over time (Nye, 2002–2003). Hard power has traditionally referred to the possession and use of military and economic capabilities to induce others to change their behavior or policy. Soft power refers to the ways and means of influence or persuasion, including the ability to frame debates; set political agendas; and/or attract others to one's beliefs, ideas, or values. As Nye and others have argued, both hard and soft power reinforce each other, and how they are wielded (used) matters in advancing and navigating a state's position in the global order. Richter (2009) has focused more on the role of influence given its importance to both types of power. He defines power as the ability to influence domestic and international issues or regions in relation to others by military, political, economic, and social means. His definition recognizes there is variance by the type of means, thereby suggesting some will or could be considered more powerful than others. This is important when contemplating the debate on America's decline and China's rise in relation to the dimensions of global order, namely economic, political, and security. Quinn and Kitchen (2019) build on the traditional and more nuanced ways of defining and measuring power to develop a framework that systematizes the underlying structure of disputes over the shift in power in global order, focusing specifically on America's decline and China's rise. This study draws from and builds on the assumptions cited by these scholars to code and analyze a sample of articles for the purpose of understanding how American policymakers used political discourse immediately before and after COVID-2019 was declared a pandemic. Table 21.1 summarizes the assumptions by the decline and rise theses and measures of power.

Scholars studying the China Threat Theory have examined how it has been studied, used, and advanced within academic scholarship, think tank and political elite publications, and traditional conservative American news media outlets (Broomfield, 2003; Turner, 2011; Yang and Liu, 2012; Dong, 2014; Goodman, 2017; Pavlicevic and Kratz, 2018). Some scholars focused on American foreign policy while others looked at either specific regions (e.g., Southeast Asia and Latin America), countries (e.g., Australia and America), or issues (e.g., high-speed railway diplomacy). They all look at the threat within the context of one or more of the threat dimensions—economic/trade, ideological/political, military/security, and geopolitical. Pavlicevic and Kratz (2018) take the categorization of the threat one step further by breaking the dimensions into soft and hard threats. Soft threats refer to what is perceived to be China's intentions and can be broken down into two categories, namely those that seek to advance Beijing's geopolitical, geoeconomic, and

Table 21.1 America's Decline, Emerging Powers, and China's Rise by Measure of Power

Decline/Rise Theses	*Hard Power*	*Soft Power*
America's Decline	Loss/decline of economic and/or military superiority	Loss of ideational and/or political influence for America's policies, positions, and/or support for actions by allies
	Inability of the America to use its economic and/or military capabilities to influence others	Opposition and/or hostility to America's policies, positions, and/or action by adversaries
	Perceived inability of America to project her hard power	Inability of America to gain support for its actions within multilateral institutions/ initiatives
		Perception of emerging powers replacing America's leadership role
Emerging Powers and/ or Rise of China	Growing economic and/or military capabilities in relation to America's capabilities	Ideational: Ability to frame beliefs, ideas, values, and discourse on issues and/or positions
	Use of such capabilities to challenge America	Political: Ability to frame political agendas, deploy persuasive rhetoric, and actively encourage behavior or positions that are favorable to the emerging power or its positions and in opposition to America
	Perceived ability to project hard power	Network: Growing cooperation with other countries and/or multilateral institutions outside or in absence of America
		Structural: Ability to shape frameworks within which states relate to each other (e.g., institutions, voting power, financing)

Source: Self-generated by the author using measures extrapolated from the cited studies.

geostrategic aims and others that advance its domestic economic, political, and national security aims. Hard threats refer to China's capabilities to attain those intentions and to influence host countries and/or the regional and global environments. The capabilities can be broken into two categories, namely the use of China's economic growth and strength to attain its domestic, regional, and global aims and specific economic tools to advance its interests in pursuit of those aims. Both the dimensions and threat categories identified in the cited literature are adopted and expanded on and used in this study to code and analyze the sampled articles. However, they have been broadened to be applicable to more than just China. By broadening them as such, it is easier to tease out perceptions of America's leadership role in the sample of articles.

Table 21.2 provides a breakdown of the data extracted from the cited studies by dimension and threat categories.

To assess whether coropoliticaldiscourse was used and exploited, this study examines America's decline, China's rise, and the China threat theses in a sample of domestic and international newswires or newspapers retrieved from *NexisUni* from October 1, 2019, to June 1, 2020. *NexisUni* is a subscription-based database that provides researchers with access to newswires and newspapers across the globe. From the database, newswire services were preferred because of the role they play in shaping the public's perceptions on specific issues via their use by domestic and mainstream media and their common use as one of several sources by global intelligence agencies for *Open Source Intelligence* analysis.

For domestic sources, both the wire services *States News Service* and *United States Federal News* were selected to capture American policymakers' perception and framing of China and its perceived threat as well as America's position in the world. *States News Service* is a newswire service providing Washington, DC, government coverage to about 80 media outlets across the United States, while *United States Federal News* provides verbatim transcripts and other news material, including speeches, congressional hearings, interviews, and news articles published by government officials. These services are additionally picked up by *Associated Press International*, and thus disseminated to international news outlets covering U.S. government-related news and positions on issues. They are used by international sources to understand Washington's position and thinking on the direction of U.S. domestic and foreign policies.

For international sources, *Agence France Presse*, *Xinhua General News Service*, and *Russian Newswire Services* were selected due to their availability in *NexisUni*. There was a minor exception in retrieving Chinese newswires between December 1, 2019, and February 29, 2020. *China Daily*, an outlet of the Communist Party of China, was used since wires were not available for those dates. Wires were available for the other two temporal periods, however. Also, there were no Russian wires or newspapers available between March 11, 2020, and May 30, 2020. The Chinese and Russian sources were selected to investigate whether there was variation in Western versus non-Western coverage of COVID-2019 and because of the strategic partnership that has formed as a result of the U.S.-China rivalry and rising geopolitical competition among major powers in the periods of concern in this study.

A search of both domestic and international sources in the *NexisUni* database was conducted using the search terms "China" AND "U.S." OR "United States" AND "threat" for three different temporal periods—September 1, 2019, to November 30, 2019; December 1, 2010, to March 10, 2020; and March 11, 2020, to May 30, 2020. The first period covers the pre-COVID-2019 period, the

Table 21.2 Perceptions of Threats by Dimension and Type

Threat Dimensions	*Soft Threats*	*Hard Threats*
Economic/Trade	Alter or threaten the peace and security of America, its allies, and the Indo-Asia Pacific region	Economic strength and growth to facilitate economic overdependence, coerce or influence domestic, regional, and global actors and/or policies
	Pursue regional and global expansion; alter the regional and global balance of power	Unfair trade practices including artificially low pricing to undercut or undersell competitors, undervaluing its currency, system of subsidies and tariffs to protect domestic markets, and giving unfair advantage to its companies in foreign/global markets
	Influence great power diplomacy	Trade imbalance/deficit; infiltration of capital markets
	Dominate domestic, region, and global economic markets	Financing, loans, and investments that facilitate debt crises or drain the recipient state's budget
	Expand the government's regional and global linkages	Use of the wealth by the diaspora community in key strategic states to advance the country's economic sphere of influence
	Avoid or defend against negative criticism of its policies (e.g., human rights)	
	Finance military modernization	
	Enable technology transfer	
	Obtain natural resources	
Ideological/Political	Expand its political and ideological influence in the region and around the globe	Political coercion
	Use of soft power to leverage and secure support from countries in the region and across the globe to support its domestic, regional, and global political aims	Engage in corrupt practices Use of the diaspora community to expand political ideology and influence Nationalism and anti-Americanism

(*Continued*)

Table 21.2 Perceptions of Threats by Dimension and Type (*Continued*)

Threat Dimensions	*Soft Threats*	*Hard Threats*
Military/Security	Gains in relation to host countries' national security Challenge America's security and the survival of democracy throughout the world	Controlling or owning host country's land and/or infrastructure Military modernization, WMD proliferation, weapons sales to America's adversaries including state and non-state actors, and regional and global projection of military power
	Military/security domination Expansion of foreign intelligence activities	Provocative actions and aggressive behavior Espionage activities to extract military and business secrets and technological advancements Information warfare targeting both the military and the American people Pursuit of dual use technology
Geopolitical	Attain superpower/major power status	Challenge norms and rules of international system Regional domination Population and territory expansion

Source: Self-generated by the author using measures extrapolated from the cited literature.

second period covers its outbreak in China, and the last one covers the first couple months after it was declared a pandemic by the World Health Organization (WHO). They were broken down into such periods to capture changes in the perceived threats and COVID-2019 discourses. A total of 606 articles covering the three temporal periods were retrieved from the database, and 65 percent of them covered domestic sources while the remaining 35 percent covered international sources. Of the 606 articles, 188 of them contained references to COVID-2019. Sixty-four percent of the articles referencing the virus covered domestic sources while the remainder of them covered international sources.

Each article was manually coded using the threat dimensions listed in table 21.2 and categorized to identify narrative themes. The themes were then used to construct a narrative for each dimension (e.g., economic and trade, ideological and political, etc.) and discussed in relation to the theoretical assumptions made regarding America's decline and the rise of emerging powers (China) in the first case. Table 21.1 was used as a guide for this analytical process. The articles in the second and third periods were also manually coded for the virus narrative for the second case. They were then categorized according to narrative themes (e.g., impact and consequences of the virus, actions taken and by whom, mention of the virus in relation to the threat dimension, and politicization). Politicization refers to the use of the discourse to facilitate or induce behavior change or to advance a political narrative for the purpose of advancing a specific agenda. The findings were discussed in relation to how the COVID-2019 discourse was used politically relative to the China threat and America decline theses, with the latter focusing more specifically on U.S. global leadership.

THE CHINA THREAT NARRATIVE: U.S. POLICYMAKERS' EVOLVING PERCEPTIONS FROM THE PRE-TO-COVID-2019 PERIOD

The China threat and America declines theses remain quite prevalent in academic debates today, and they are both topics of wide discussion by political pundits on talk shows, social media, and events held by nongovernmental think tanks. China has consistently pushed back against such discussions, claiming that it neither poses a threat nor does it seek to replace America. Despite its claims, most scholars, policymakers, and lay audience watched officials from the U.S. government under the Trump administration pursue a political agenda designed to challenge China. Then, with the outbreak of COVID-2019, the Trump administration initially downplaying its potential global and domestic impact, and fear and hysteria spreading among not just the American public but also global audiences, the anti-China rhetoric from both the China hawk policymakers and mainstream media increased. This sensationalized discourse provoked some questions, namely: Do American policymakers really perceive China as a threat? If so, how is the threat framed? Would COVID-2019 open the door to them using it to advance their anti-China agenda? Using the theoretical framework outlined in the preceding section, this section begins to answer some aspects of these questions to better understand how American policymakers perceive the China threat prior to its outbreak in China, after its outbreak, and in the first three months after it was declared to be a pandemic. It is not possible to answer the question as to whether American policymakers used the discourse to advance their agenda until first establishing how they perceive the China threat.

The perceived threat is broken down in this section according to each dimension. The cross-tabulation of the frequency results of the sources reveals the military and security dimension to be salient (32.5 percent). It was followed by the ideological and political dimension (25 percent), geopolitical dimension (22 percent), and economic and trade dimension (20.5 percent). There are, of course, variations by each source. For the U.S. domestic sources, the order stays the same. For the French sources, the military and security dimension was followed by the economic and trade dimension. Both the ideological and political and geopolitical dimensions in the French sources were ranked of equal value, thus ranking them third. The military and security dimension was followed by the geopolitical and ideological and political dimensions for the Russian sources. The economic dimension was not present for that source. For China, the ideological and political dimension was referenced more. It was followed by the geopolitical, economic and trade, and military and security dimensions.

A closer examination of the U.S. domestic sources by entity finds that government sources comprise 64.5 percent of the coverage. Of that coverage, the legislative branch makes up 69 percent and the executive branch comprises 31 percent. Republican members of Congress comprise most of the legislative coverage. Nongovernmental sources make up the remaining 35.5 percent of the domestic sources. U.S. nongovernmental think tanks comprise 51 percent of that coverage, while the other 49 percent includes civil society organizations, media, foreign diplomats, and academia. The narratives constructed below are derived from the government sources to capture American policymakers' perceptions.

The Economic and Trade Threat Narrative

U.S. government officials perceive China's growing economic linkages across the globe to be a threat to America's interests and its allies. Many officials cite the potential for Beijing to use economic statecraft to influence countries' economic and political interests in its favor. However, when looking more closely at the government sources across the three temporal periods, a better understanding of the perceived threat emerges.

In the first temporal period, economic assistance and energy purchases used as geopolitical weapons, unfair trade practices including predatory investments and currency manipulation, and the undermining of American businesses were all mentioned by policymakers as economic threats. These threats were expanded upon in the second period to include China's social credit system and its impact on American businesses; emphasis on the moral duty of those businesses to ensure they are not engaging or assisting in anyway Chinese theft of intellectual property or the persecution of ethnic and religious minorities and political dissidents; and the need for American businesses, academic institutions, and others working in China and for Chinese companies to be cognizant of the national security consequences of "doing business in a country controlled by the Communist Party." In the third temporal period, China's growing technological dominance and the need to protect American supply chains, and to decouple key economic sectors from China were emphasized.

There are three important takeaways from the above narrative. First, the three policy concerns for American policymakers are China's trade practices, technological dominance, and using both the economy and energy purchases as geopolitical weapons. Second, policymakers believe the U.S. government should take action to reduce America's dependence on China by protecting key economic sectors and supply chains critical to national security. Lastly, they place onus on Americans, American businesses, and academia who work in or are connected to China to set aside economic interests for national security interests and human rights concerns.

The Ideological and Political Threat Narrative

China's expanding cultural influence via Confucius Institutes; talent recruitment programs; financial contributions to universities, colleges, and research institutions in America and abroad; and its use of soft power to leverage and secure support from countries and their population in furtherance of its domestic, regional, and global aims elicit fear among American policymakers, particularly those who are advocates of human rights. Congress has always led on human rights in U.S. foreign policy, and it has been quite vocal against perceived adversaries in general and on China in particular.

In all three periods, American policymakers emphasized Beijing's perceived human rights violations and coercive and non-coercive measures adopted within the country against minorities and dissidents and against international organizations, policymakers, and states who criticize its policies. Hong Kong; lack of religious freedom; media and information suppression; treatment of prisoners; and use of technology to surveil, harass, and intimidate individuals within China and the Chinese living abroad dominated all the sources. References to these perceived human rights abuses were uttered within a context of highlighting the political differences between America and China and their implications for a global order dominated by Beijing.

Inferred from the coverage was that Beijing's treatment of its own population as such exemplified how it would lead the global community in response to massive human rights violations in other parts of the world. That is, Beijing would turn a blind eye to such abuses and the instability they could cause regionally and globally when left unchecked or overlooked. Human rights also provided an opportunity for American policymakers to highlight Beijing's failure to uphold international norms. The language employed by some congressional members was quite provocative, which was noted in the nongovernmental sources. Taking the rhetoric one step further, policymakers intentionally engaged in behavior that they knew would provoke a more aggressive response by Chinese policymakers, thereby enabling them to reify their stance on the inconsistency between Beijing's words and actions and reinforce perceptions that it is acting in ways that are contrary to the liberal-based international order.

There are four important takeaways from the above narrative. First, human rights are a major policy concern for American policymakers. It is an area where there is convergence between the executive and legislative branches when it concerns adversaries; and, one where both Congress and the Trump administration saw eye-to-eye when it came to China. Second, human rights have been a consistent point of tension between China and Congress. Third, the rhetoric employed by policymakers resonates with the American public and both the domestic and international nongovernmental organizations and rights community. Finally, this issue area allows American policymakers to draw a sharp distinction between American-style democracy and the Chinese political governance system, thereby allowing them to leverage the perceived soft power threat Beijing poses to both America and international order.

The Military and Security Narrative

American policymakers fear the loss of America's military and security primacy to China. It should be no surprise then that military and security threats were quite prevalent in the threat narrative across all three temporal periods. However, when looking closely across the periods, there was variation in the threat narrative. A greater emphasis was placed on the perceived military threat than the security threat in the first two periods. The security threat became more pronounced in the third period, particularly as concerns over espionage, intellectual property theft, and China's technological dominance among policymakers grew.

For the military threat, policymakers raised China's theft of military technology, the use of information warfare and propaganda to target and influence the American public, and both the militarization of the Indo-Asia Pacific and its potential military expansion beyond the region to Africa and South America as major concerns in the first period. In the second period, the threat narrative expanded to include concerns over China's perceived militarization of space and the importance of non-traditional security concerns to national security. Greater emphasis was also placed on the multidimensionality of the threat China poses to America and its allies. The third period witnessed emphasis on China's growing cyberwarfare capabilities and the civil-military fusion program. China's civil-military fusion program is designed to harness the civilian sector to promote simultaneously civilian and military technological developments.

Unlike the military concerns, security threats did not vary much across the three temporal periods, but there was a greater emphasis placed on them and the introduction of two new types of non-traditional security threats in the third temporal period. The concerns raised by policymakers across the temporal periods included cyber-enabled campaigns targeting critical national infrastructure, data security, espionage, intellectual property theft, technology, and telecommunications. Technology, telecommunications, and data security concerns were raised in relation to the espionage concern. Health and economic insecurities were the two new non-traditional security issues raised in the third period.

From the above narrative, there are four key takeaways. First, the security challenges posed by China to U.S. national security and America's global position are growing in the minds of policymakers. There are concerns about China's gains over that of America's capabilities and the potential for the Department of Defense to maintain its dominance in the near future. Second, policymakers are increasingly viewing Beijing's military and security actions as hostile or aggressive. The perceived aggressive actions are no longer simply limited to China's military modernization program and actions in the Indo-Asia Pacific. They now encompass its growing security relations with countries in other regions that are participating in the Belt and Road Initiative. The latter helps to explain greater emphasis being placed on both traditional and non-traditional security concerns. Third, an emphasis on non-traditional security concerns also corresponds to a shift in U.S. national security, intelligence priorities, and hybrid warfare to include both traditional and non-traditional challenges. Finally, great power competition between the United States and China exacerbates the perceived military and security threats.

The Geopolitical Narrative

The geopolitical narrative recognized China as a global power, emphasized great power competition, and included both the soft and hard challenges that Beijing's rise posed to America and the international community. There was also recognition by executive branch personnel that the challenges stem from the ongoing change in international order. A change in the existing international order and the challenge it posed to America's global leadership were predominant in all government sources. The concern increased in the third temporal period. Interestingly, as will be noted below, there was only a direct questioning of America's global leadership in European sources.

In the domestic sources, American policymakers made numerous references to the threat Beijing poses to the rules-based order, highlighting its failure to act "normally" and "consistently" within established international norms. Members of Congress emphasized that America has a duty to work in concert with its allies to contain Beijing's more aggressive behaviors in the Indo-Asia Pacific and apply both economic and political pressure for it to behave in a manner that is consistent with the existing international order. On the European front, they emphasized the importance of working with allies in concert to protect the Western, liberal-based order and to defend against the challenge posed by revisionist states like China who are perceived to want to mold the international system in its own vision.

In the international sources, European policymakers raised questions about U.S. leadership, to which the Department of State defended, stating that Washington has no intention of retreating from multilateral engagement. State department personnel went further to highlight the role played by the United States in NATO. French sources also noted the challenge posed by the U.S.-China trade war to existing order. Neither Russian nor Chinese sources directly questioned American leadership, but they did highlight the inconsistencies in Washington's rhetoric and behavior. Washington's behavior under the Trump administration is more consistent with a revisionist power since it actually does challenge the existing rules-based order they countered.

From the narrative above, it is quite evident that all countries are concerned about the shift in international order and its implications for global leadership and relations between countries. American policymakers seem to be more concerned about losing their primacy to Beijing, while the international community is more concerned about Washington's trend toward unilateralism rather than multilateral engagement. European leaders seem less concerned about China's growing global influence. Chinese leaders were keen on asserting that they have no intention to challenge America's leadership nor do they want to play the role that Washington has been playing in international affairs. They place greater emphasis on the need for multilateralism and promote a more democratic rules-based order. Scholars argue the latter is more consistent with a multipolar order.

To conclude, the findings across the sources within this case support and run contrary to some of the theoretical assumptions in the literature regarding America's decline, China's rise, and perceived threats to both the U.S. and international order. First, U.S. domestic coverage does not recognize nor highlight the loss of Washington's influence and support for its policies and positions by allies and their reluctance to cooperate. The international sources do, however. Second, both the domestic and international sources recognize there is open and growing opposition to America's policies and positions by emerging powers, while the domestic sources also recognize hostility by adversaries, thereby tacitly recognizing America's leadership in international relations is waning. The nongovernmental domestic and international sources highlight the challenge posed by the perceived decline of U.S. global leadership under the Trump Administration. Third, the nongovernmental domestic sources and all international sources recognize that U.S.-China competition and the confrontational approach adopted under the Trump administration are having a negative impact on international order. None of them, however, attribute this to the shift from a quasi-unipolar to a multipolar international order. Finally, though the United States seems to fear being replaced by China as a dominant actor in the Indo-Pacific region and/or global order, others in the international community don't have a similar concern nor is the perception that there will be a transfer of power from Washington to Beijing.

AN EVOLVING COVID-2019 NARRATIVE: FROM THE TIME OF ITS OUTBREAK IN CHINA TO THREE MONTHS AFTER THE WHO DECLARED IT A PANDEMIC

COVID-2019 broke out in Wuhan, China, in December 2019, and it was declared a public health emergency of international concern by the WHO on January 30, 2020. Japan, South Korea, and Thailand were the first countries to report known cases on January 20. One day later, the first known case was reported in the United States. Washington imposed travel restrictions limiting travel from China to the United States on February 2, which happens to be the same day of the first reported virus death outside of China; the gentleman was Filipino and from the Philippines. The spread of the virus in countries outside of America and actions taken by Washington to assure the American people there was no need to fear or that there was minimal risk to the country at that time dominated domestic coverage between February and March. It would not be until after it was declared a pandemic when the coverage changed.

The narrative described in this section has been constructed from the same domestic and international sources used for the threat narrative; thus, it does not capture the full scale of the virus narrative nor how it evolved. Instead, it seeks to understand how the virus narrative was constructed and used within the confines of the boundaries imposed on this case study, which were outlined in the theoretical section. It is divided into two parts—the first part focuses on the period prior to it becoming a pandemic and the second part covers the period after it was declared a pandemic by the WHO. Part one provides an overview of the U.S. narrative, narrowing in on how it was used by policymakers, the differences in that narrative, and whether it was politicized; how the narrative evolved in the international sources; and, finally, whether there was criticism of Washington's leadership. Part two reports the results from the frequency analysis and then focuses more specifically on the nuanced ways in which the political discourse was used by American policymakers. As the discussion from two periods highlights, the narrative went from being relatively neutral in the first period to it being overtly politicized in the second period.

The Outbreak in China: From December 1, 2019, to March 10, 2020

In this period, there were a total of 52 articles containing references to COVID-2019, and 54 percent of them came from international sources and 46 percent from domestic sources. Of the domestic sources, 25 percent of the coverage was politicized. Eighty-three percent of that politicized coverage either mentioned or discussed the virus within the context of the China threat narrative, while 17 percent reflected a U.S. policymaker's intentional use of the virus narrative to advance his political agenda. Therefore, it can be concluded that coverage was relatively neutral in this period and not overtly politicized.

Most of the domestic coverage consisted of updates regarding the virus situation in America and China, calls by members of Congress for either government updates or action plans, and actions taken by the government, including imposing travel restrictions on non-U.S. citizens (excluding foreign nationals with permanent resident status) traveling from China to America; screening procedures at airports and other entry points into the United States; government assistance to China and other countries to help with the health crisis resulting from the virus; and the actions taken by foreign governments including China to manage the virus outbreak. Nongovernmental domestic sources highlighted the economic impact of the virus on China's economy as well as other countries that are dependent on Chinese tourism.

A turning point in the coverage occurred in February, which is when members of Congress began questioning whether China was providing accurate information on the scope and scale of the problem and sharing accurate information with global officials and health organizations. Then, on February 11, a press release was issued following the passage of a bipartisan piece of legislation honoring Dr. Li Wenliang—the doctor who first identified the severity of the problem in China and was reprimanded by Chinese authorities for doing so, and later died from the virus. The bill was critical of the Chinese government and called for greater openness and transparency. In those calls for greater openness and transparency, references were made to media censorship and lack of freedom of speech in China, which is commonly cited in the domestic sources highlighting the political dimension.

Shortly after the passage of the legislation honoring Dr. Li, other U.S. government officials from the Department of Health and Human Services reiterated the risk to the American public remained relatively low and highlighted the measures the government was taking to protect Americans. They also expressed hope that American experts will be able to work on the ground with their Chinese counterparts. Personnel from both the State and Defense departments highlighted assistance the government was providing to China and other countries; they also noted this is an area where the two countries can cooperate. There were only a few references from the executive branch that mentioned the virus within the context of discussing the threats posed by China. However, they did not intentionally use the narrative to advance an agenda. Both the secretary of state and military officials attempted to keep the two types of discourse separate.

There was only one reference that attempted to intentionally use the virus to advance a political agenda. A member of Congress known for his anti-China position and who considered to be a China hawk in Chinese sources highlighted the virus outbreak, China's refusal to be transparent, and the threat it poses to the American healthcare industry in a press release and linked them to legislation he had proposed to curb America's dependence on China. He had long been advocating for curbing America's dependence on China, and the outbreak of the virus provided for and was used by him to renew his call for legislation to address the matter. Though the legislation would be proposed later in the next period, his politicization of the narrative at this time cannot be construed as reflective of the U.S. government; it must be interpreted as a position adopted and expressed by a single member of Congress. These findings are interesting because of the references made in this period by Chinese sources of what they perceived to be an information warfare campaign waged against their country and its policymakers by Western media and some American policymakers. Although this study does not examine mainstream outlets it can conclude that, at least in terms of the releases of information and transcripts issued by American policymakers and published in both *States News Service* and *United States Federal News*, there was not widespread politicization of the virus narrative by policymakers at that time.

International coverage in this period highlighted the economic impact of the virus on China and expressed concern should it spread throughout the United States like it did in China, the actions Washington has taken and Beijing's criticism of them, inconsistency in America's narrative, and the need for international cooperation. Both Chinese and French sources focused on the economic impact of the virus, but they differed in context. There was a global discussion on whether the virus would be declared a pandemic following the WHO's declaration of it as an international concern on January 30. Beijing warned against too hastily declaring the virus an international concern and a pandemic because of the impact it could have on the global economy. French sources, on the other hand, noted the impact the virus was having on China's economy, particularly after parts of the country went on full lockdown to stem the spread of the virus. French and other European policymakers were concerned about what could happen to global economy should the virus spread similarly in America and if the government reacted as China did. All sources noted the actions taken by Washington, namely imposing travel restrictions and entry guidelines, and highlighted the inconsistency in the discourse at the local, state, and federal levels of government on the seriousness of the virus and the measures needed to be taken by both the government and public to prevent the spread of the virus in the United States. Beijing's criticism of Washington's actions was covered by both Chinese and Russian sources. Chinese sources also complained about what they perceived to be an information warfare campaign against their country by Western media outlets including American mainstream outlets; a lack of sympathy for and recognition of the actions their country took to combat the virus; and some actions taken by American governmental officials, which were construed as intentionally exploiting the virus to advance an anti-China agenda. All international sources called for and noted the absence of international cooperation to manage the spread of the virus. There were no overt references questioning or critiquing U.S. global leadership in this period other than the highlighting Washington's inconsistency and the lack of and need for international cooperation to manage the global health crisis.

COVID-2019 Is Declared a Pandemic: The Period of March 11, 2020, to May 30, 2020

In this period, there were a total of 136 articles containing reference to COVID-2019, and 71 percent of them came from domestic sources and 29 percent from international. Of the domestic sources, 75 percent of the coverage was politicized. This is an increase of 50 percent from the first period. Sixty-five percent of domestic coverage during this period came from government sources, with the legislative branch comprising 82 percent of that coverage, 17 percent from the executive branch, and 1 percent from state and local government. Members of the Republican Party continued to dominate the legislative coverage. The remaining 35 percent of the coverage was nongovernmental. U.S. nongovernmental think tanks comprised 61 percent of that coverage and 39 percent came from media, academia, or other civil society organizations. Unlike in the previous period, there were far greater instances of American policymakers using the discourse to advance their political agendas and there were more instances of U.S. leadership being questioned. The narrative constructed below mainly focuses on the nuanced ways in which the political discourse was used by policymakers, as it was really in this period when the Chinese threat and virus narratives converged.

Several themes emerged in this period. They include narratives on the impact and consequences of the virus, a war of words between Beijing and Washington, the questioning of both Beijing's and Washington's leadership, American policymakers' targeting of the WHO at the height of both the war of words and as criticism of Washington's leadership at home and abroad, and both the actions taken by American policymakers' use of the virus narrative to attempt to induce domestic and international behavior change toward Beijing.

Domestic sources highlighted the economic impact on Indo-Pacific countries due to supply chain disruptions, lack of materials for industry operations, and loss of jobs; America's susceptibility to supply chain disruptions and dependence on China for health supplies and the government's unpreparedness for dealing with both the economic and health implications of the virus; and how the virus impacts both American and Chinese economies and people and their importance for the global economy. International sources also focused on the economic impact of the virus, but they took note of how the war of words was exacerbating tensions between the two countries and how the latter negatively impacts the global economy. The amplification of political divisions because of heightened America-China tensions and the growing disconnect between the two countries were focused on by both domestic and international sources.

U.S.-China tensions reached a peak during the war of words between policymakers in both countries. American policymakers blamed Beijing for the spread of the virus and conspiracy theories over the origin of the virus, while some of Beijing's diplomats did the same to America. From slogans calling it the "American coronavirus" in China to the "Chinese" or "Wuhan" virus in America to Chinese diplomats claiming it could have been brought to China by the American military and American policymakers stating it could have originated from the Wuhan virology laboratory, chaos and discord were sown by both sides. Australian and European diplomats cited in international sources noted that no one is to blame and to focus on that hinders international efforts to combat the major global crisis. NGO think tanks and media outlets attempted to dismiss policymakers from both countries, stating they are both attempting to deflect blame for their failures to manage the health crisis and its economic, political, and social impacts on their population and global community. Their war of words campaigns and the chaos they brought domestically and internationally shifted to concerted information campaigns, with both sides attempting to better manage the narratives; put forward their interpretation of the narrative; and highlight the fact that each side was indeed engaging in media, information, and propaganda operations.

With international criticism increasing among Europeans over the behavior of both China and America and the impact it was having on sowing chaos, division, and discord beyond the geographical boundaries of both countries, American and Chinese policymakers shifted their tactics and focused instead on using the narratives to facilitate change at home and abroad. It should be noted that international criticism of American policymakers increased following the latter's shift to targeting not just the leadership in China but also that of the WHO around March 31, 2020. Chinese policymakers focused on facilitating international cooperation to manage the health and economic crises all countries were facing, while American policymakers focused on drafting legislation to blame and penalize China, promote the economic decoupling of the two countries, and rallying support from anti-Chinese political pundits at home and abroad for their political agendas. Both domestic nongovernmental sources and international sources questioned American leadership at home and abroad, while American policymakers questioned Chinese leadership and their handling of the virus as well as their motives for wanting to facilitate international cooperation.

Another set of themes emerged when examining more closely how the narrative was used to either facilitate or induce behavior change both inside America and China. They include American policymakers pressing for and proposing legislation to hold China and its officials accountable for the spread of the virus (e.g., sanctions and legislation authorizing Americans to sue China) and to better protect American supply chains and to reduce America's dependency on China for critical supplies (e.g., America Supply Chain and National Security Act and offering tax incentives for reshoring critical supply chain businesses); partnering with allies like Israel (whom American policymakers can trust) to shift production out of China; calling for China to close its wet markets; and generating attention on China's human rights abuses (e.g., suppression of information and individuals who spoke out against China's handling of the virus and the restrictions Beijing imposed on reporting on the virus and the imprisonment of individuals such as the pastor in China imprisoned for his religious practices). They also highlighted Chinese coercive practices including a Chinese consular staff who sent a letter pressing for the State of Wisconsin's legislature to commend China for its handling of the virus, the targeting of American policymakers with sanctions of its own and the use of trolls and bots to target them on social media, and penalizing Australia for calling for an independent investigation into the handling of the virus.

The narrative supporting these actions was situated within the context of the threat dimensions, with American policymakers highlighting that the virus is just one of many threats America and the world face from China. They used China's handling of the virus (or what they perceived as its mishandling of it) to illustrate why it is incapable of being a responsible great power, ignoring and downplaying its calls for a multilateral response to combat the virus and deal with the outcomes and consequences of its impact on developing countries; linked some of its actions to other human rights abuses to reinforce the perception that China holds values, beliefs, and political practices contrary to America and the norms of the international community; raised concerns of potential theft of vaccine research through hacking and talked about that within the context of known cases of intellectual property theft and economic espionage; and reinforced why America needs to adopt a different approach to China than the one it has pursued in the past. Some argued that Beijing would use the outbreak of the virus to supplant America and pursue world domination.

American policymakers' politicization of the virus narrative and their conflation of that narrative with the China threat narrative were noted in the international sources. Chinese sources attempted to deconstruct the narratives and respond to American policymakers' claims. French sources like the Chinese sources covered the narratives of both American and Chinese officials but emphasized how they both are having a destabilizing impact on global affairs. There were no Russian sources available for this period. At the end of the day, the way in which American policymakers discursively approached the COVID-2019 crisis once it became a pandemic and the manner in which they framed their actions to mobilize support for the anti-China legislation led to actors in the international community and a growing number of other members of Congress to question the U.S. leadership abroad. There has been bipartisan support for much of the anti-China legislation passed under the Trump administration. Congress had long criticized past presidential administrations for not being "tougher on China," but the manner in which the campaigns were waged by some policymakers in this period led to some of them shying away and withdrawing their support for some policy actions. What this means though for the long term is that American policymakers must be more cognizant of how they use crises and frame issues because, as long as America continues to play a leading role in international affairs, its domestic politics and the policy actions it takes will have an impact on the international community and the perception of Washington as a global leader.

CONCLUSION AND RECOMMENDATIONS

This chapter explored what is being coined "coropoliticaldiscourse" within a specific case study. As will be recalled from the introduction, coropoliticaldiscourse refers to the use of written or spoken communication or debate about COVID-2019 to exploit fear, hatred, and/or discord within a given context and directed toward a specific audience for the purpose of advancing a political narrative. The political narratives investigated here were derived from the China threat and American decline theses. American policymakers used the economic, ideological and political, and geopolitical narratives from those theses, as constructed in the first case in this study, to exacerbate existing fears about the origins of the virus and its economic and political consequences for America and Americans; to capitalize on existing and growing anti-Chinese sentiment among the American population; and to wage media, information, and propaganda operations (albeit in response to those waged by Beijing) for the purpose of advancing both the China threat narrative and mobilizing support for legislation that advanced their own political agenda.

While the legislature primarily used the narratives to mobilize and gain support among the American population, other members of the U.S. government used the narratives to seek support among allies for support of their anti-China foreign policy agenda. Some valid points were raised by American policymakers and some of the proposed and actual legislation is in American interest (e.g., reducing America's dependency on foreign suppliers for critical needs), but the manner in which they were raised and the campaigns waged to garner support for them and their failure to balance leadership roles at home and abroad had a negative impact on perceptions of American leadership. By being so overtly anti-China in their rhetoric, they lost sight of the underlying concerns of Americans, allies, and others. The lesson to be drawn from this is that perceptions matter and they are formed from the political discourse used, so American policymakers have to be cognizant of how they frame policy issues and take into consideration the domestic and global audience if they seek to continue to play a leading role in international affairs.

Questions about U.S. leadership have become far more rampant since 2017, and what is perceived by many American allies is an America in retreat. American policymakers' handling of the virus and their politicization of it, as was demonstrated more specifically in the French sources citing European leaders, have increased concerns and reinforced that perception. A confrontational approach in such a context, particularly in times of global crises, does not demonstrate strength; instead, it demonstrates weakness. America need not worry about competing with China for global leadership with such a politicized, confrontational approach because it will end up ceding power to other great powers (not necessarily China), as the global leaders will move on because both economic and health insecurities, which are critical non-traditional security issues, require cooperation and multilateral engagement even with adversaries. Economic and health insecurities are two global security issues that have the potential to create social, political, and economic instability far and wide, and a unilateral or bilateral approach simply will not suffice in a globally interdependent community comprised of both state and non-state actors.

Given everything that has been covered in this chapter—from American policymakers' perceptions of the threat narrative to the politicization of COVID-2019 by them and the impact they have on global perceptions of America's global leadership role—there are several policy recommendations or, rather, advice that should be taken into consideration. They are as follows:

- First, although foreign policy is the constitutional prerogative of the executive branch, the legislature has a key role to play in the foreign policy process generally and on certain issues more specifically. As the United States transitions from an almost exclusive emphasis on military and security issues in its foreign policy toward an equal emphasis on both traditional and non-traditional security issues, the legislature will have a greater impact on foreign policy issues pertaining to economic security, energy, technology, and trade. This means that future presidential administrations and their principles are going to need to place greater emphasis on executive-legislative relations. Executive-legislative relations are likely to have a greater impact on the White House's ability to pursue its foreign policy agenda and the actual implementation of that agenda.
- Second, the legislature is going to need to be more cognizant of its impact on how its statements (though not public law) and domestic policy actions impact leaders around the world and the global public perceptions of America and its global leadership. Policymakers should no longer assume that their political discourse is for their domestic constituency only. This means they should wield wisely the use of political discourse as a tool for the purposes of opposing their domestic political adversary and in gains against the White House in periods of heightened executive-legislative tensions. Otherwise, American leadership abroad will continue to suffer.
- Third, there is no debating that American policymakers' approach toward China in the trade war and Washington's lack of leadership on COVID-2019 have negatively impacted perceptions of America's role as a global leader. European leaders from allied countries consistently highlighted the negative impact the confrontational approach toward China and the U.S.-China trade war were having on global peace and security. Then, with the lack of leadership on COVID-2019 and, as they highlighted, the inconsistency in both words and actions by all levels of the U.S. government, European leaders turned away to focus on how to deal with the global health and economic security crises facing the global community without Washington. The politicization of the global crises at home and abroad has challenged American leadership more so than the perceived China threat. A different approach toward both China and the global health and economic

crises resulting from COVID-2019 is warranted. Economic and health insecurities should not only be considered national security concerns but also global security concerns. America cannot turn inward on them or it will cede global leadership to other countries (again, not necessarily China).

- Fourth, American policymakers should understand that most non-traditional security issues (i.e., corruption, economic insecurity, health insecurity, and terrorism to name a few) are intermestic issues, that is, they have both domestic and foreign policy implications. Therefore, they have to use a multidimensional lens when contemplating domestic legislation and its impact at home and abroad. Wise leaders are those who can navigate multidimensionally. There are so many military manuals talking about viewing and operating through such a lens; and, throughout the liberal arts education curricula in secondary and tertiary education critical thinking is emphasized. Yet, so many present-day political leaders in each level of the American government view both issues and the world from one dimension. America is not the world, but it is a global leader in a global world; thus, a one-dimensional perspective is not going to suffice for it to retain its leadership role.

REFERENCES

Acharya, A. (2014). Power shift or paradigm shift? China's rise and Asia's emerging security order. *International Studies Quarterly* 58:158–173.

Afridi, M. K., Yousufi, M., and Ahmad, M. (2015). Power interest and rivalry of major powers (United States, Russia and China) in Central Asia. *FWU Journal of Social Sciences* 1:25–36.

Broomfield, E. V. (2003). Perceptions of danger: The China threat theory. *Journal of Contemporary China* 12(35):265–284.

Dong, C. (2014). Who threatens whom? The Chinese threat and the Bush doctrine. *Journal of East Asia and International Law* 7(1):31–49.

Goodman, D. S. G. (2017). Australia and the China threat: managing ambiguity. *Pacific Review* 30(5):769–782.

Houweling, H., and Amineh, M. P. (2003). The geopolitics of power projection in U.S. foreign policy: From colonization to globalization. *Perspectives on Global Development and Technology* 2(3/4): 339–389.

Liang, C. (2018). The rise of China as a constructed narrative: Southeast Asia's response to Asia's power shift. *The Pacific Review* 31(3): 279–297.

Nye, J. (2002–2003). Limits of American power. *Political Science Quarterly* 117(4): 545–559.

Oppenheimer, M. F. (2007). The end of liberal globalization. *World Policy Journal* 24(4):1–9.

Pavlićević, D., and Kratz, A. (2018). Testing the China threat paradigm: China's high-speed railway diplomacy in Southeast Asia. *Pacific Review* 31(2):151–168.

Parisot, J. (2013). American power, East Asian regionalism and emerging powers: In or against empire? *Third World Quarterly* 34(7):1159–1174.

Quinn, A. and Kitchen, N. (2019). Understanding American power: Conceptual clarity, strategic priorities, and the decline debate. *Global Policy Volume* 10(1):5–18.

Richter, T.M. (April 27, 2009). Is U.S. power in decline? *E-International Relations.* Retrieved on November 25, 2020 from https://www.e-ir.info/2009/04/27/is-us-power-in-decline/.

Ross, R. (2006). Balance of power politics and the rise of China: Accommodation and balancing in East Asia. *Security Studies* 15(3):355–395.

Sexton, J. (2019). From triumph to crisis: An American tradition. *Diplomatic History* 43(3):405–417.

Strange, S. (1988). The future of the American empire. *Journal of International Affairs* 42(1):1–17.

Turner, S. (2011). A rather climactic period: The Sino-Soviet dispute and perceptions of the China threat in the Kennedy administration. *Diplomacy and Statecraft* 22(2): 261–280.

Wallerstein, I. (2003). *The Decline of American Power: The U.S. in a Chaotic World.* New York: The New Press.

Williams, M. J. (2007). The empire writes back (to Michael Cox). *International Affairs* 83(5):945–950.

Yang, Y. and Liu, X. (2012). The China threat through the lens of U.S. print media: 1992–2006. *Journal of Contemporary China* 21(76):695–711.

Zhang, L. (2010). The rise of China: media perception and implications for international politics. *Journal of Contemporary China* 19(64):233–254.

Zhang, Y. (2013). China anxiety: Discourse and intellectual challenges. *Development and Change* 44(6):1407–1425.

Chapter 22

Coroinfodeluge

Collence T. Chisita, Nyarai P. Chibanda, Cecilia T. Olugbara, and Moeketsi Letseka

A pneumonia of unknown cause detected in Wuhan city of China was first reported to the World Health Organization (WHO) Country Office in China on December 31, 2019. The disease, caused by a novel coronavirus, was subsequently named the Coronavirus Disease (COVID-2019) and declared a public health emergency of international concern on January 30, 2020. The outbreak of COVID-2019 in late December 2019 led to loss of lives, businesses came to a standstill in most countries, and lockdown was imposed in several countries that created panic, fear, anxiety, and unease globally. The disease which initially broke out in Wuhan was labeled a global pandemic by the WHO on March 11, 2020 (Perillat and Baigrie, 2020). Southern Africa was not exempted from the effects of the COVID-2019 pandemic and infodemic as evidenced by the loss of lives, lockdowns, and closure of businesses and accompanying large volume of information about the disease that were freely distributed.

It has become a pre-ordained ritual that the outbreak of a pandemic triggers a cloud of confusion, uncertainty, loss of life, and disruption of socioeconomic activities arising from misinformation and disinformation which are detrimental to the socioeconomic stability of the society (Takaingenhamo, 2020; Zarocostas, 2009). Due to the outbreak of the disease, many unverified sources of information on infectious cases were freely disseminated. Mortality rates were not spared, resulting in panic, with most nations forced to make instantaneous decisions.

Organizations such as the WHO rose up to the challenge by responding through the provision of information and advocating for a two-pronged approach to fight the epidemic and infodemic. The WHO director emphasized the seriousness of the COVID-2019 pandemic and the associated infodemic when he stated: "We're not just fighting an epidemic; we're fighting an infodemic. Fake news spreads faster and more easily than this virus, and is just as dangerous" (WHO Director General, 2020).

The COVID-2019 pandemic caused unprecedented and excruciating experiences in the lives of many people throughout the world. This unprecedented scenario forced Higher Education Institutions (HEIs) to re-strategize on best practices that will ensure their teaching, learning, research, and other activities are carried out on a daily basis, without truncating the educational progress.

In Zimbabwe, COVID-2019 outbreak greatly changed the educational system in the country. In line with what was obtainable in other countries where institutions of learning were closed down to reduce the spread of the disease, HEIs in Zimbabwe were initially closed down. However, since HEIs cannot be permanently closed, the pandemic notwithstanding, the COVID-2019 pandemic and infodemic forced HEIs in Zimbabwe to re-think and re-strategize in order to ensure that the country's educational system is not grounded and that credible information about the disease is provided to students and other stakeholders of the higher education community. Learning and research have to continue even under these difficult times.

Moreover, the responsibility of providing credible information to students of higher learning, especially in view of the infodemic that followed the outbreak of the COVID-2019, rests with the libraries, making it a critical challenge to the academic communities in Zimbabwe. One move that was adopted by academic libraries to circumvent the problems that were created by the COVID-2019 and infodemic was the shift to online services as a way of supporting continuous teaching, learning, and research.

In view of the above, this chapter seeks to answer the following three key questions: (1) How has COVID-2019 pandemic affected academic libraries in Zimbabwe? (2) What is the role of academic libraries in dealing with the Coroinfodeluge? (3) How can academic libraries contribute toward managing the Coroinfodeluge? These questions will underpin the chapter. The questions are important because they capture the key themes that will be examined and they will guide the chapter by giving it a clear purpose and focus.

Zimbabwe imposed a nationwide lockdown on March 30, 2020, to mitigate and prevent the spread of COVID-2019 (Gardaworld, 2020). The pandemic outbreak was characterized by emergency regulations and delegated personnel to mitigate and prevent the deadly disease (Parwada, 2020). The national lockdown in Zimbabwe started with a 21-day nationwide shutdown and was further extended until May 16, 2020, before an indefinite extension (Parwada, 2020). It is interesting to note that the COVID-2019 pandemic received support from the current government and the opposition because the issue at stake concerns national survival. Slowly the government started to ease the lockdown with the opening of key sectors such as the mines and some businesses in order to avoid a total meltdown of the economy. Some sectors such as higher education were identified under the essential services category because the institutions needed to open and offer solutions to the pandemic through making protective clothing such as face masks and sanitizers that the nation was in urgent need of in order to curb the spread of the pandemic.

The government of the Republic of Zimbabwe's COVID-2019 curfew took effect from July 22, 2020, from 6 p.m. to 6 a.m., although essential services were exempted from the curfew (Xinhua, 2020). The government also designated local universities and other institutions of higher learning to provide temporary quarantine services for all returning residents as part of efforts to contain the spread of COVID-2019 and intensified measures to ensure that the 21-day lockdown was a success (Maponga, 2020). As a way of ensuring that the universities are equipped to provide the needed support toward the containment of COVID-2019 in Zimbabwe, Mukeredzi (2020) reported that the government of Zimbabwe released an initial ZW$33 million (US$ 1.3 million, according to the official exchange rate) in seed capital to selected state universities to produce personal protective equipment including face masks and sanitizers which were in short supply and highly needed to combat the coronavirus.

The COVID-2019 pandemic and the subsequent indefinite lockdown became a global norm, causing unprecedented coroconfusion, corohysteria, and coroinfodeluge. These aforementioned portmanteau words are beginning to make their entry into the lexicography of the COVID-2019 pandemic. The outbreak of the COVID-2019 pandemic also precipitated an equally dangerous infodemic characterized by an increase in the volume of information generated by the print and digital media. This chapter is premised on the argument that academic libraries have a key role to play in managing the avalanche of information produced as well as empowering users with digital literacy skills so that they make judicious use of the available information resources. The researchers use document analysis, Internet sources, including personal knowledge of the institutions as they responded to the threat posed by the COVID-2019 pandemic.

The significance of this chapter is that it delves into the experiences and responses of academic institutions to the COVID-2019 pandemic and infodemic. The chapter generates new knowledge on how COVID-2019 pandemic and infodemic can be addressed. The chapter confronts the COVID-2019 pandemic from the perspective of Library and Information Science (LIS). It brings the LIS practitioner and educators to the frontline of the battle against COVID-2019 pandemic. The chapter provides a praxis-oriented response to combat COVID-2019 by offering strategies that are needed to address the infodemic through the frontiers of the library. The chapter challenges academic librarians on the need for innovativeness by proffering solutions that will assist users in dealing with the COVID-2019 pandemic and infodemic.

The chapter begins with a brief overview of the higher education systems in Zimbabwe followed by the institutions' experiences in trying to combat the spread of COVID-2019 pandemic, while at the same time providing services to its stakeholders. It also provides recommendations that are necessary to enhance the services of academic libraries amid the COVID-2019 pandemic and infodemic.

BACKGROUND OF THE CHAPTER

Zimbabwe, in the previous years, has faced economic challenges that resulted in the slow development of some of its HEIs. Isaac (2007) stated that "the Zimbabwean economy has been beset with crises, characterised by an unsustainable fiscal deficit, an overvalued exchange rate, and rampant inflation (which stood at 1,000% in 2006)." However, despite these economic challenges, the government of Zimbabwe has rolled out various programs to situate the Zimbabwean economy through digital technologies. Computers were donated to ensure that Internet services providers promote the production of desired commodities at reasonable pricing models. In addition, the Zimbabwean government adopted a national Information and Communication Technology (ICT) policy in 2005 modeled after the Harvard University-guided e-readiness survey that showed that the country was not uniformly e-ready (Isaac, 2007). The main reasons for adopting the policy were to support the development of ICT architectures, provide training programs on the use of ICT equipment, produce knowledge workers and qualified personnel and promote skills training, and encourage equitable access to ICTs. According to Chisita (2012), the government of Zimbabwe developed an ICT strategic plan for the years 2012–2015. The strategic plan sought to ensure total digitalization of various government institutions. According to the World Economic Forum's Global Information Technology Report, Zimbabwe was ranked 122 out of 139 economies in 2016 based on networked readiness index.

Internet access in Zimbabwe is offered through wired and wireless networks. Mobile phones have the highest use and these are largely dominated by the younger generation. Mobile phones ensure quick access to information through wireless connections which are used by most academic institutions. Most of the academic institutions in Zimbabwe have invested in the provision of desktop computers as mandated by the country's higher education governing board, which is the Zimbabwe Council for Higher Education

(ZIMCHE). It calls for this in its quality assurance standards on infrastructure, ICT and library resources (Zimbabwe Council for Higher Education, 2006).

The Higher Education System in Zimbabwe

The ZIMCHE Act of 2006 defined higher education as the education which is provided by HEIs. The institutions include the following: (a) technical or polytechnic college offering degrees, (b) public or private universities or a university college and its associate or affiliate institutions, and (c) arms of a foreign institution of higher education that awards degrees (Zimbabwe Council for Higher Education Act, 2006).

According to UNECA (2018), Zimbabwe has the highest levels of literacy in Africa, with the levels reaching an excess of 94 percent. The higher education system in Zimbabwe started with the establishment of the University College of Rhodesia and Nyasaland in 1955. The institution was later renamed the University of Zimbabwe (UZ) upon gaining independence. The country currently has 24 registered universities with ZIMCHE, out of which 14 are public and funded by the state in terms of salaries and 10 private owned that are largely funded by Christian organizations. In addition, and consistent with the Zimbabwean definition of HEIs, 5 out of the 12 polytechnics, 3 out of the 15 teachers' colleges, and over a hundred public and private colleges offer degree programs in association with registered universities under various models of affiliated relationships.

The Ministry of Higher and Tertiary Education, Science and Technology in Zimbabwe also developed a new strategic plan (Ministry of Higher and Tertiary Education, 2019) that focused on the Education 5.0 philosophy. The strategic plan added two pillars—innovation and industrialization—to its old strategic plan which previously had only three pillars—research, teaching, and community engagement. This new development made all the HEIs in Zimbabwe to revise their strategic plans in sync with this new philosophy, which is deeply rooted in innovation, information communication technologies, industrialization, and the commercialization of products. The Zimbabwe University Libraries Consortium (ZULC), which is a consortium of academic institutions in Zimbabwe, was not spared in the re-design of strategic plan in line with their parent institutions as well as that of their line ministry.

Value of Information in the Fight against COVID-2019 Pandemic and Infodemic

Tangcharoensathien et al. (2020) argued that people need accurate information during epidemics to adjust their behavior and protect themselves, their families, and their communities against infections. According to the aforementioned authors, an infodemic cannot be eliminated but it can be managed. Tangcharoensathien et al. (2020) contended that similar to epidemics, information spreads farther and faster, propagated by the interconnected ways in which information is disseminated and consumed through the web, digital and social media, chat apps, TV, radio, and other communication channels. Radu (2020) noted that since the outbreak of COVID-2019, the proliferating digital media have been both the culprits of and antidotes to misinformation. According to Radu (2020), many governments around the world adopted and implemented priority COVID-2019 actions; for example, measures that reflected the heightened importance of combating fake news, such as (a) criminalizing malicious coronavirus falsehood (Hungary, South Africa), (b) establishing special units to combat misinformation (European Union, United Kingdom), and (c) providing guidance to social media companies to take down contentious pandemic content (e.g., India). The Zimbabwe government is also in the process of enacting the Cyber Security and Data Protection Bill (2019). The bill is meant to strengthen data protection, consolidate cyber-related offenses, and promote a technology-driven business environment. The relevance of the bill in this chapter is Clause 164C in particular, which criminalizes the spread of false information online.

Chisita and Ngulube (2020) noted that the misuse of social media has resulted in governments promulgating laws to ensure sanity amid the menacing COVID-2019 pandemic and infodemic. While the new COVID-2019 legislation and regulations might sound draconian, it should be noted that in times of emergencies, government usually have no option but to take such measures as long as they will benefit the nation.

The South Africa's Regulations issued in terms of Section 27(2)0 of the Disaster Management Act, 2002 section 11 subsection 5 stipulate that

> any person who intentionally misrepresents that he, she or any other person is infected with COVID-19 is guilty of an offence and on conviction liable to a fine or to imprisonment for a period not exceeding six months or to both such fine and imprisonment. . . . Any person who publishes any statement, through any medium, including social media, with the intention to deceive any other person about—(a) COVID-19; (b) COVID-19 infection status of any person; or (c) any measure taken by the Government to address COVID-19, commits an offence and is liable on conviction to a fine or imprisonment for a period not exceeding six months, or both such fine and imprisonment. (Section 27(2)0 of the Disaster Management Act, 2002 Section 11 Subsection 5)

The aforementioned legislation clearly stipulates the offenses and penalties for flouting COVID-2019 regulations in the Republic of South Africa. The government of Botswana promulgated the Statutory Instrument No. 61 of

2020 Emergency Powers Act (CAP. 22:04), Emergency Powers (COVID-19) Regulations, whereby Section 30 subsection 1 states that

> any person who relays any information to the public about COVID-19 from a source other than the Director of Health Services, and the WHO commits an offence and is liable to a fine not exceeding P100 000 or to imprisonment for a term not exceeding five years, or to both . . . (3) A person who publishes any statement, through any medium, including social media, with the intention to deceive any other person about. (Emergency Powers Act (Cap. 22:07), 2020)

> Emergency Powers (COVID-19) Regulations, 2020 whereby Section 30 subsection 1). The above highlighted legislation clearly outlines the offences and penalties for peddling false information relating to the COVID-19 pandemic and infodemic (Emergency Power Act, CAP. 22:07, 2020).

Zimbabwe gazetted the Statutory Instrument (SI) 83 of 2020 (CAP. 15:17 Public Health (COVID-19 Prevention, Containment and Treatment) (National Lockdown) Order, 2020) which criminalizes the publication and communication of fake news relating to COVID-2019 pandemic (Machivenyika, 2020). Madhuku (2020) cited in Machivenyika (2020), a constitutional law expert cited in the *Herald* (2020), hinted that the promulgation of SI was constitutional. Globally, countries that have declared lockdown have had to promulgate laws to justify their actions. Just like South Africa and Botswana, Zimbabwe's legislation is clear on the offenses and penalties for peddling false information which is stated as follows:

> Any person who publishes or communicates false news about any public officer, official or enforcement officer involved with enforcing or implementing the national lockdown in his or her capacity as such, or about any private individual that has the effect of prejudicing the State's enforcement of the national lockdown, shall be liable for prosecution . . . and liable to the penalty there provided, that is to say a fine up to or exceeding level fourteen or imprisonment for a period not exceeding twenty years or both. (CAP. 15:17 Public Health COVID-19 Prevention, Containment and Treatment, National Lockdown Order, 2020).

Gupta et al. (2020) argued that while established scholarly platforms continue to publish and disseminate peer-reviewed and validated items on the new coronavirus, numerous online channels with variable quality checks are emerging and supplying their users with statements, instructions, and recommendations on various aspects of COVID-2019. The paucity of highly skilled professionals, primarily physicians with diverse interests in virology, immunology, and thrombology, capable of moderating the unprecedented flow of information via the established and alternative communication channels paves the way for circulation of poorly checked and misleading hypotheses, ideas, and research outcomes (Gupta et al., 2020). Llewellyn (2020) contended that while lay public and professionals scramble to gather more about the current situation, the massive fluidity of unverified information created uncertainties due to the infodemic and putting thousands of lives at risk globally.

The proliferation of digital technologies caused COVID-2019-related information to spread quickly around the world. While the Internet provides powerful channels for real-time information sharing over geographic barriers (Yao et al., 2020), the disadvantage of enhanced connectivity was revealed; it partially contributed to an escalation in the devastating global effects of the disease, a situation that was termed an "infodemic" (Zarocostas, 2009). Love et al. (2020) stated that an infodemic is characterized by false news, misinformation, and conspiracy theories that impose extra uncertainties and threats on people's daily lives. According to the authors, the COVID-2019 pandemic and infodemic have seen an escalation in the volumes of inconsistent and incorrect information spread, even resulting in many deaths.

Tangcharoensathien et al. (2020) described an infodemic as an overabundance of some accurate and inaccurate information that occurs during an epidemic. According to the authors, an infodemic spreads between humans via digital and physical information systems, thus making it hard for people to find trustworthy sources and reliable guidance when they need it. The misinformation arising from the COVID-2019 pandemic leads to coroconfusion about cures and prevention or public behavior, can be harmful to life and can exacerbate the outbreak of the disease (Tangcharoensathien et al., 2020). This precarious scenario, termed Coroinfodeluge (Chisita, 2020), can be more challenging to manage when health information messages and facts are incorporated into political narratives and online commentary that are not grounded in verified facts and evidence (Tangcharoensathien et al., 2020).

THEORETICAL FRAMEWORK

The chapter is underpinned by several theories that are related to information overload and information deluge, such as the Magical Number Seven, Plus or Minus Two (Miller, 1956). Miller (1956) highlighted the limitation with regard to the number of times items can be held in instant memory. The choice of this theory is premised on its explanation of the phenomenon of Coroinfodeluge. The concept of information deluge is dynamic and complex; hence, studies that are related to the phenomenon will equally be considered such as the works of Roetzel (2019), Eppler and Mengis (2004), Toffler (1970), Giuseppe and Benedetto (2020), and Cowan (2001) 4 ± 1 Chunks Theory. The aforementioned studies underpinning the theoretical framework will provide a solid intellectual basis on which the concept of Coroinfodeluge will be grounded in relation to the COVID-2019 outbreak in Zimbabwe.

Eppler and Mengis (2004) and Roetzel (2019) argued that information overload occurs when decision-makers face a level of information that is greater than their information processing capacity. Toffler (1970) coined the term "information overload" in his classic book *Future Shock*. The book analyzed the experiences of people in a dynamic futuristic technology and information-driven age. It highlighted how the transition from the industrial to the super-industrial age would overwhelm citizens. This phenomenon is as old as history; for example, Blair (2011) stated that during the thirteenth century, scholars complained of the key ingredients of the feeling of overload which are still with us today—described as the multitude of books, the shortness of time, and the slipperiness of memory.

In a similar vein, Levine (2017) argued that social scientists who used the term information overload were concerned with the internal dynamics of information flow in social systems as much as any perceived external threat of a superabundance of reading material. According to Levine (2017), social scientists were primarily concerned with unveiling the reasons why there is breakdown or less efficient communication in a given system, and what strategies could be employed to restore it.

Giuseppe and Benedetto (2020) on their part contended that prior to the enormous spread of computer technology, information was far from complex. They noted that the development of digital technologies shifted the paradigm: from individuals who faced scarce and costly information to individuals who face massive amounts of information accessible at low costs. According to the authors, the current age of information is synonymous with big data characterized by high volumes of information. Miller (1960) viewed information overload as a pathological disease described as an increasingly hectic world of media with many blatant and competing sources of information such as radio, television, movies, magazines, and newspapers which are contributing to the increased tension that characterize our age. For example, in a movie picture, a person who breaks down emotionally is depicted as seeing whirling bright lights coming toward him, loud noises, and other information overloads, as if these were the subjective experience of patients in this plight (Miller, 1960).

In addition, Giuseppe and Benedetto (2020) stated that several studies on the human brain provided evidences on the limited information elaboration capacity of the human mind. These studies included Miller's (1956) argument that every individual possesses a limited span of immediate memory estimated to be, for several reasons, about seven items in length. Klingberg (2000) contended that human beings can only retain a restricted amount of information in working memory (WM), and when one attempts to perform several tasks at the same time, performance declines. In the same vein, Bawden and Robinson (2008) stated that before pushing large amounts of data to the receivers, it is important to consider cognitive limitations, as attempting to retain too much information in the mind at once may cause information overload and impaired performance.

Finding the optimal balance of information availability and reliability without outstripping the limits to human processing capabilities is a critical research area. Gambel et al. (2018) argued that the capacity limits with regard to processing and retaining information are better comprehended and apprehended by relating it to WM capacity (Mathy and Feldman, 2020). Miller (1956) viewed WM capacity as 7±2 items, while Cowan (2001) postulated the 4 ± 1 chunks.

The use of aids or information sources (or mnemonics) can help to improve performance. Academic librarians have the knowledge and skills to develop mnemonic devices in the form of indexes, abstracts, classification numbers, and catalogs. These devices have been used in traditional librarianship but currently, digital technology has been incorporated as evidenced by the proliferation of digital catalogs, metadata, and active links that support access to online content.

Cowan (2001) argued that while Miller's Magical Number Seven Plus or Minus Two Theory summarized evidence that people can remember about seven chunks in short-term memory (STM) tasks, contrarily, that number was more or less a rough estimate and a rhetorical device than as a real capacity limit.

Cowan (2001) also noted a number of other limits of cognition that point to a Magical Number Four which is different from Miller's Magical Number Seven Plus or Minus Two, which stirred debate on whether the phenomenon was a magic number or magic spell (Schweickert and Boruff, 1986). The theory of Cowan (2001) is based on the notions that (a) the focus of attention is capacity limited; (b) the limit in this focus averages about four chunks in normal adult humans; (c) no other mental faculties are capacity limited, although some are limited by time and susceptible to interference; and (d) any information that is deliberately recalled, whether from a recent stimulus or from long-term memory, is restricted to this limit in the focus of attention.

Miller's (1956) Magical Number Seven Plus or Minus Two Theory states that there is an upper limit of seven plus or minus two elements in our capacity to elaborate information. The basis of Miller's theory is premised on the assumptions that (a) the span of absolute judgment and the span of immediate memory impose unembellished limitations on the amount of information that the human mind is able to receive, process, and remember; (b) the process of recoding is very important and deserves much more explicit attention than it has received; this process encapsulates the kind of linguistic recoding that people have, that is, the very lifeblood of the thought processes; (c) the concepts and measures provided by the theory of information provide a quantitative way of finding answers to the phenomenon of learning and memory; and (d) the Magic Number Seven (plus or minus two) provides confirmation for the capacity of STM, for example, most adults can store between five and nine items in their STM.

The key factors spurring the rapid increase in the availability of information and the decrease in information search-related costs include Gutenberg galaxy and the rise of information technology (IT). While information overload prior to the industrial revolution was felt more among the academics and nobles or aristocrats who had access to knowledge, in the modern era the proliferation of digital technologies has democratized access to information on a wider and deeper scale (Blair, 2011).

Baddeley (1986) contradicted Miller's (1956) findings, arguing that there was no limit in storage capacity per se, but a limit in the duration for which an item can remain active in STM without rehearsal. The information overload relates to the experience of a decision-maker when overwhelmed by information as highlighted as follows: "a wealth of information (which) creates a poverty of attention and a need to allocate that attention efficiently among the overabundance of information sources that might consume it" (Simon, 1971).

Bawden and Robinson (2008) argued that while the information overload phenomenon has been under the radar of researchers, the information age and subsequent digital technologies have significantly increased the amount of information available and consequently the degree of misinformation has reached a crescendo. Levintin (2014) showed concern about the problem of information overload when he stated that "the information age is drowning us with an unprecedented deluge of data." Another classic example of how researchers can misinform society was the fraudulent article published by the *Lancet* in 1998 that implied a nexus between the measles, mumps, and rubella (MMR) vaccine and a "new syndrome" of autism and bowel disease. The article misinformed parents as they believed that the MMR vaccine was likely to lead to autism.

UNIVERSITIES' RESPONSES TO THE COVID-2019 PANDEMIC IN ZIMBABWE

Following a recommendation from the national COVID-2019 Response Task Force, all HEIs were requested by the parent ministry to reopen institutions in August so that students could continue with their studies. However, the continuation of the studies was based on a new model of teaching, which was online. Face-to-face classes were suspended. Most of the universities were caught unaware by this move. The only university that was not severely affected was the Zimbabwe Open University which, by its nature, is a distance learning institution that offers distance learning programs through extensive use of open education resources. The rest of the academic institutions offers face-to-face teaching programs.

The aforementioned scenario saw the birth of many new innovative responses and activities, committees, and library services within the institutions and these required huge investments of both human and financial resources to fully implement them. Universities such as the Midlands State University (MSU) had to quickly put in place a COVID-2019 Response Task Force which was meant to work as the institution's link to the National Task Force in terms of information dissemination. The University Response Task Force, which was chaired by the Dean of the Faculty of Medicine, has its key objective of ensuring that the institution's staff and students remained safe from the virus, by putting in place measures that will ensure prevention of cases and early detection considering that the university's learning and teaching activities had resumed, though remotely online. A limited number of administrative staff were permitted to work from the campus in order to attend to administrative work as well as support the e-learning platforms.

Most of the universities such as the MSU, Women's University in Africa, the National University of Science and Technology, and Great Zimbabwe University adopted the Google classroom platforms, while some such as Africa University adopted Moodle. The UZ adopted Zoom, while the Harare Institute of Technology uses both Google classroom and Moodle.

In addition, universities' libraries in Zimbabwe had to quickly invest in new services and technologies such as the use of self-check units, drop boxes for those returning books they had borrowed before the lockdown, and adoption of social media platforms to communicate with students and staff. The constant shifts in technology necessitate the adaptation of metaliteracy as a pedagogical framework for developing critical thinking skills among users of information in an era of information disorder. Metaliteracy has been recommended for adaptation by academic institutions because of its all-encompassing nature in empowering information users to deal with the complexities of an increasingly information-driven twenty-first century. It provides a unified and comprehensive core for engaging with individuals and ideas in digital information milieus (Mackey and Jacobson, 2011). The model is befitting to help information users tackle the complexities of the Coroinfodeluge in the wake of COVID-2019 pandemic and infodemic. The access to the physical collections was closed for all the university libraries. As a result of these, students and staff have to heavily depend on electronic collections and information. Access to the electronic collections was made possible through the efforts of the ZULC. In order to ensure access to the e-resources, ZULC also put together a workgroup to work on developing a consortium framework for information literacy training programs in universities. The main objective of establishing the workgroup was for the consortium to ensure that all university students become more self-directed and assume control over their own learning. Information literacy skills also promote and stimulate thinking skills such as finding information and evaluating the sources. Information literacy skills will enable an individual to identify what is true and relevant, not just for one's studies but even for life and work. Information literacy skills promote human development.

According to the Association of College and Research Libraries' Information Literacy Competency Standards for Higher Education, information literacy skills enable one to access the needed information effectively and efficiently. It also enables one to evaluate information and its sources critically (Iannuzzi, 2000). Most universities in Zimbabwe have adopted the ZULC curriculum in offering information literacy although some institutions modified the framework. Some universities such as the MSU made the curriculum compulsory for all first-year students. Others use it upon request. Due to the information overload currently experienced globally it is of paramount importance that universities ensure that training on information retrieval and evaluation skills is made compulsory.

Radia and Stapleton (2008) contended that constant increase of online information resources should be matched by the necessary information needed by literate students to circumnavigate and access information from digital platforms. The authors warned that heavy reliance on Internet sources would ultimately negatively affect the quality of learning, teaching, and research among students and researchers.

The COVID-2019 pandemic and infodemic provide academic libraries the basis to reposition themselves by providing praxis-oriented mitigation and preventive solutions in the form of Information Literacy Competencies (ILC). The overwhelming volumes of information on COVID-2019 as a pandemic and infodemic and the accompanying regulations oblige innovative librarians to assist users to deal with the Coroinfodeluge. ILC was defined as the sum total of skills that are required to navigate and use information from various sources in order to meet information needs (Hajam, 2017; Osahon et al., 2020). The Chartered Institute of Library and Information Professionals (CILIP) viewed ILC as the ability to critique and judiciously utilize the available information (Coonan et al., 2018).

With ILC, people are able to fully engage society with informed views as well as make sound decisions. In addition to CILIP's interpretation of ILC, other theories and models have been developed by researchers to further examine the concept. According to the definition of the SCONUL Working

Group on Information Literacy (2011), ILC requires an understanding of how information and news are gathered, used, managed, synthesized, and created in an ethical way. In the SCONUL model, the core skills that are the goals of ILC were defined; each of the core competencies can transform undergraduates from novices to experts in detecting fake news. The model explicitly presented ILC as having seven pillars: ability to identify a need for information, assess current knowledge and identify gaps, construct strategies for locating information and data, locate and access the information and data they need, evaluate information and data, ethically organize information, and apply the acquired knowledge.

With the universities having access to e-resources, the need to revamp the university library systems, by providing the tools and skills required to properly adapt to the new models of providing library services without compromising on quality, becomes imperative. Libraries were faced with the need to establish research support units with clear terms of references which included tracking and extracting COVID-2019 key information and distributing the information through robust e-marketing platforms in order to assist in the sharing of credible information. This also means that the universities have to set up online training programs for both students and staff on information retrieval skills as well as how one can evaluate information resources that are obtained from the Internet and other media platforms, especially those that are transmitted through social media platforms which have flooded the society globally.

The university librarians in Zimbabwe hosted webinars that fully focused on discourses of COVID-2019 pandemic which were moderated by personnel from the health sector. These webinars were greatly appreciated by the university stakeholders as credible information and information retrieval skills were discussed and shared at length. The use of webinar as discussion forums on national issues is new to many. Information literacy programs were also redesigned to suit the new methodology of training that is provided through platforms such as the Google classroom and Zoom. Online media platforms such as social media have played key roles in the spread of COVID-2019 information.

The MSU used its Facebook page to disseminate information pertaining to the pandemic. Most of the information was extracted from the WHO global website. Pamphlets on COVID-2019 safety guidelines were also designed and spread to the university community through various online platforms such as the university's website, Facebook page, and students' e-learning platforms. Daily statistics on infections and deaths were also extracted from the Ministry of Health and Childcare website, repackaged and distributed through WhatsApp to various internal and external stakeholders of the university. This was done in order to ensure that stakeholders are kept abreast with the correct information in order to contain panic and distress among its principal stakeholders. Information provided by WHO included advice to the public and technical guidelines on travel across the globe. Situation reports and updates on vaccines were also disseminated by sharing the WHO link to key stakeholders.

The websites of organizations such as the U.S. Centers for Disease Control and Prevention, Africa Centres for Disease Control and Prevention, and WHO AFRO were also integrated into the university's open access collections for easy access to credible information. E-marketing platforms such as Libguides were created to ensure that the libraries are fully marketed as well as make it easy to access some of these open access resources that contain credible information.

This also means that institutions have to invest in mobile data for both students and staff. For most of the public-funded institutions, this strategy was a tall order as they heavily relied on fees to offer such services. Negotiations with Internet Service Providers such as NetOne and Econet were also accomplished through IT directors as well as the parent Ministry in an effort for universities to be given access to subsidized data bundles for students and staff and for universities' websites to be zero rated. Despite the subsidized rates which were finally offered by the service providers, most students still could not afford the bundles. Some universities using their own third stream income resources could only afford to buy data bundles for their academic staff. Hence, lack of funds needed to acquire data bundles remains a major drawback to access to credible information on COVID-2019 that were extracted by the universities' libraries in Zimbabwe.

Polytechnics and Colleges' Responses to the COVID-2019 Pandemic in Zimbabwe

Similar to the experiences of the universities in Zimbabwe, all polytechnics were also closed following the country president's pronouncement to close all businesses and institutions in the country in an effort to contain the spread of COVID-2019. When the directive to reopen educational institutions online was announced, most of the polytechnics were ill-prepared; they had no capacity to adapt to the new normal. Most of them lack adequate IT infrastructures and their libraries were equally lacking in robust e-resource collections. These made it very difficult for the libraries to fully support the online teaching and learning process. Some of the colleges, however, moved to the use of open platforms such as Google classrooms for teaching. Nevertheless, most of the students could not afford the cost of the data bundles, forcing lecturers to adopt other cheaper platforms such as WhatsApp. Students gradually returned to their institutions in smaller groups. Some of the support services in the colleges such as library physical buildings were gradually opened as well since there had not been serious investment in electronic collections.

The polytechnics and colleges were greatly affected as most of them could not afford the subscription due to high cost of electronic resources. The implication is that there was limited distribution of COVID-2019 information, even though some efforts were made by posting safety guidelines on some websites. It was also noted that most of the polytechnics and colleges were not offering information literacy training programs that are needed to equip their library users with lifelong information retrieval and evaluation skills.

SUMMARY, CONCLUSION, AND RECOMMENDATIONS

The COVID-2019 pandemic and infodemic have awakened academic libraries and related institutions to the need to have an emergency or contingent plan in place in order to manage emergencies. The provision of information literacy skills to students and staff has contributed to human capacity development with regard to independent or liberated learning. Miller's (1956) Magical Number Seven, Plus or Minus Two provides a theoretical basis for the chapter, with the argument that learners' capacity to learn are limited. The response of academic libraries confirms Miller's argument that information overload is a pathological disease that requires strategies, including knowledge and skills, that empower learners and researchers to navigate e-resources without any hindrances (Miller, 1960).

The COVID-2019 pandemic and infodemic are wake-up calls to governments in developing countries to support the development of robust digital technologies in order to build fifth-generation libraries and users supported by fifth-generation technologies (5G). These technologies are useful in facilitating democratic access to information by closing the gap between resource-endowed and resource-starved institutions. Emerging digital technologies, including integrated digital library systems, cloud storage forensic bibliographic reconstruction, and virtual reality, have been useful in ensuring that teaching, learning, and research continue irrespective of the limitations of time and space. Modern digital technologies for libraries have brought digital mnemonic devices to aid memory, for example, digital catalogs with digital metadata standards and the use of Libguides and digital institutional repositories that preserve information in digital format.

The proactive and praxis-oriented responses by academic librarians to the Coroinfodeluge or overabundance of information about COVID-2019 serves as an affirmation of Miller's (1956) and Giuseppe and Benedetto's (2020) assertions that the human brain has limited information elaboration capacity. While Roetzel (2019) and Eppler and Mengis (2014) linked information overload to the limited information processing capacity of decision-makers, the availability of a developed interoperable information ecosystem helps to manage and process vast chunks of information for the benefit of individuals and formal organizations including academic institutions.

Indeed, the COVID-2019 pandemic and infodemic have been a litmus test for academic libraries and related institutions as they encountered challenges in providing unfettered access to learning, teaching, and research resources during a crisis. While the pandemic has exposed the gap between resource-endowed and resource-poor institutions, it has also provided academic libraries with an opportunity for innovation as evidenced by the provision of services through digital platforms. The COVID-2019 pandemic and infodemic continue to serve as wake-up call for academic librarians to re-think, re-strategize, and re-profile their relevance in an age of digital information avalanche (Coroinfodeluge).

The skills and knowledge of academic librarians have become more useful in helping users deal with the Coroinfodeluge characterized by massively disorganized information on the Internet. While many concur that Google is everything, the COVID-2019 pandemic and infodemic have shown that the world of Google becomes more meaningful if one is equipped with information and the digital literacy skills that are required to manage the Coroinfodeluge and fake news. Information and digital literate citizens are the first and most important front in the combat against COVID-2019 pandemic and infodemic. Without information literate citizens, developing countries risk being trapped in a vicious cycle of unverified information and information illiterate citizens that lack the knowledge and skills to make judicious and optimum use of information amid the escalating Coroinfodeluge.

In light of the findings in the preceding sections and the conclusion drawn, a number of recommendations are tendered here. First, there is a need for academic libraries to ensure that necessary measures are put in place in order to curb the spread of false information among their key stakeholders, especially during times of crisis. The libraries should source adequate information from reputable organizations, repackage the information, and make them easily available to their constituency. Credible information about COVID-2019 will assist institutions and their stakeholders in decision-making.

Second, libraries should fully embrace the use of social media platforms, including Social Network Sites and Academic Social Network Sites, in service delivery so that information can be distributed easily. Libraries can create viral content to assist in distributing information during a crisis, as people are usually displaced when there is a crisis. Social media allow one to reach large audience within a short period of time. Social media also give the library room to create organic content that is specific to the targeted audience. They provide opportunity for the library to connect directly with the targeted audience. When library users are provided with better customer services, the value of the library and related impact on the community amid the COVID-2019 pandemic will be enhanced.

Third, there is a need for institutions to make information literacy skills' training programs compulsory for all students. This will ensure that even after college or university, the students will be equipped with adequate life-long skills. Additionally, when confronted with excessive information, the students will be able to evaluate the information and their sources in order to distinguish credible from unverifiable sources. The information literacy skills will also promote thinking skills, with ability to ask questions, retrieve useful information, evaluate sources, and make decisions based on the ability to distinguish between credible and untrusted sources. Information and e-Health literacy skills are useful in helping users evaluate the content and its source in order to ensure judicious use of information.

Fourth, academic libraries should establish robust research support units in their establishments. This will allow the gathering of credible information and ensure quick distribution to the institutions' communities.

Fifth, information and digital literacy programs should be enhanced to equip users including students and staff with requisite skills and knowledge to tackle Coroinfodeluge. This is critical for enhancing best practices.

REFERENCES

Baddeley, A. (1986). Working memory. In *Working Memory. Oxford Psychology Series, 11*. London, UK: Clarendon Press/Oxford University Press.

Bawden, D. and Robinson, L. (2008). The dark side of information: Overload, anxiety and other paradoxes and pathologies. *Journal of Information Science 35(2) 180–191*. Retrieved on September 14, 2020 from https://doi.org/10.1177/0165551508095781

Blair, A. (2011). Information overload's 2,300-year-old history. *Harvard Business Review*. Retrieved on September 14, 2020 from https://hbr.org/2011/03/information-overloads-2300-yea.html.

Chisita, C. T. (2012). Knotting and networking agricultural information services through Web 2.0 to create an informed farming community: A case of Zimbabwe. *World Library & Information Congress: 78th IFLA General Conference & Assembly. May* 1–21. Retrieved on August 12, 2020 from http://www.ifla.org/past-wlic/2012/205-chisita-en.pdf.

Chisita, C. T. (2020). Libraries in the midst of the Coronavirus (COVID-19). Researchers experiences in dealing with the vexatious infodemic. *Library Hi Tech News* 37(6): 11–14. Retrieved on August 15, 2020 from https://doi.org/10.1108/LHTN-03-2020-0022

Chisita, C. T. and Ngulube, P. (2020) A framework for librarians to inform the citizenry amidst COVID-19 pandemic. *IFLA Journal* (unpublished).

Coonan, E., Geekie, J., Goldstein, S., Jeskins, L., Jones, R., Macrae-Gibson, R., Secker, J., and Walton, G. (2018). CILIP definition of information literacy. *CILIP-The Library and Information Association* 1–8. Retrieved on June 16, 2020 from https://infolit.org.uk/wp-content/uploads/2018/03/CILIP-Definition-Doc-Final-for-website.pdf.

Cowan, N. (2001). The magical number 4 in short-term memory: A reconsideration of mental storage capacity. *Behavioral and Brain Sciences*, 24(1) 87–185. Retrieved on June 10, 2020 from https://doi.org/10.1017/S0140525X01003922.

Cyber Security and Data Protection Bill, (2019). Retrieved on July 2, 2020 from http://veritaszim.net/sites/veritas_d/files/Cyber%20Security%20and%20Data%20Protection%20Bill.pdf.

Emergency Power Act (cap.22:07). (2020). Emergency Powers (COVID-19) Regulations (Cap. 22:04 (Sub. Leg.)) Botswana Extraordinary Government Gazette 215 (2020).

Eppler, M. J. and Mengis, J. (2004). The concept of information overload: A review of literature from organization science, accounting, marketing, MIS, and related disciplines. *The Information Society*, *20*(5) 325–344. Retrieved on October 15, 2020 from https://doi.org/10.1080/01972240490507974.

Gamble, K. R., Cassenti, D. N. and Buchler, N. (2018). Effects of information accuracy and volume on decision making. *Military Psychology*, *30*(4) 311–320. Retrieved on November 2, 2020 from https://doi.org/10.1080/08995605.2018.1425586.

Gardaworld. (March 27, 2020). Zimbabwe government to impose nationwide lock-down for 21 days from March 30. Gardaworld. Retrieved on September 22, 2020 from https://www.garda.com/crisis24/news-alerts/327176/zimbabwe-government-to-impose-nationwide-lockdown-for-21-days-from-march-30-update-3.

Giuseppe, P. and Benedetto, T. (2020). A theory of information overload applied to perfectly efficient financial markets. *Review of Behavioral Finance: Vol. ahead-of-p* (Issue ahead-of-print). Retrieved on August 25, 2020 from https://doi.org/10.1108/RBF-07-2019-0088.

Gupta, L., Gasparyan, A. Y., Misra, D. P., Agarwal, V., Zimba, O. and Yessirkepov, M. (2020). Information and misinformation on COVID-19: A cross-sectional survey study. *Journal of Korean Medical Science 35*(27) e256–e256. Retrieved on July 17, 2020 from https://doi.org/10.3346/jkms.2020.35.e256.

Hajam, M. (2017). Users' information literacy competencies: A study with reference to scholarly community of Kashmir university. *DESIDOC Journal of Library and Information Technology* 37:153–157.

Iannuzzi, P. (2000). Information literacy competency standards for higher education. *Community and Junior College Libraries* 9(4):63–67. Retrieved on November 29, 2020 from https://doi.org/10.1300/J107v09n04_09.

Isaacs, S. (2007). ICT in education in South Africa. *Survey of ICT and Education in Africa: South Africa Country Report 21–29, June 2007*. Retrieved on October 8, 2020 from https://doi.org/10.1080/02680930903314269.

Klingberg, T. (2000). Limitations in information processing in the human brain: neuroimaging of dual task performance and working memory tasks. In: Uyling, H. B. M., Van Eden, C. G., De Bruin, J. P. C., Feenstra, M. G. P. and Pennartz, C. M. A. (eds.), *Cognition, Emotion and Autonomic Responses: The Integrative Role of the Prefrontal Cortex and Limbic Structures* 126:95–102. Retrieved on October 10, 2020 from https://doi.org/https://doi.org/10.1016/S0079-6123(00)26009-3.

Levine, N. (2017). The nature of the glut. *History of the Human Sciences* 30:32–49.

Levitin, D. J. (2014). *The Organized Mind : Thinking Straight in the Age of Information Overload*. New York: Penguin.

Llewellyn, S. (2020). Covid-19: how to be careful with trust and expertise on social media. *BMJ* 368:m1160. Retrieved on September 30, 2020 from https://doi.org/10.1136/bmj.m1160.

Love, J. S., Blumenberg, A. and Horowitz, Z. (2020). The parallel pandemic: Medical misinformation and COVID-19: Primum non nocere. *Journal of General Internal Medicine* 35(8):2435–2436. Retrieved on November 5, 2020 from https://doi.org/10.1007/s11606-020-05897-w.

Machivenyika, F. (March 31,2020). Spreading fake Covid-19 news attracts jail term. *The Herald*. Retrieved on May 28, 2020 from https://www.herald.co.zw/spreading-fake-covid-19-news-attracts-jail-term/.

Maponga, G. (13 April, 2020). Universities offer quarantine sanctuary. *The Herald*. Retrieved on May 31, 2020 from https://www.herald.co.zw/universities-offer-quarantine-sanctuary/.

Mackey, T. P. and Jacobson, T. E. (2011) Reframing information literacy as a metaliteracy. *College and Research Libraries* 72(1):62–78.

Mathy, F. and Feldman, J. (2012). What's magic about magic numbers? Chunking and data compression in short-term memory. *Cognition* 122(3):346–362. Retrieved on November 19, 2020 from https://doi.org/10.1016/j.cognition.2011.11.003.

Miller, G. A. (1956). The magical number seven, plus or minus two: Some limits on our capacity for processing information. *Psychological Review* 63(2):81–97. Retrieved on August 23, 2020 from https://doi.org/10.1037/h0043158.

Miller, J. G. (1960). Information input overload and psychopathology. *The American Journal of Psychiatry* 116:695–704. Retrieved on August 16, 2020 from https://doi.org/10.1176/ajp.116.8.695.

Ministry of Higher and Tertiary Education, Science and Technology Development. (2019). *The MHTESTD, Strategic Plan 2019–2023*.

Mukeredzi, T. (April 6, 2020). Government ropes in universities to fight COVID-19. *University World News : Africa Edition*. Retrieved on November 2, 2020 from https://www.universityworldnews.com/post.php?story=20200406073439527.

Osahon, I. M., Omorodion, O. and Oluwaseye, A. J. (2020). Information literacy competence in curtailing fake news about the COVID-19 pandemic among undergraduates in Nigeria. *Reference Services Review: Vol. ahead-of-p* (Issue ahead-of-print). Retrieved on November 2, 2020 from https://doi.org/10.1108/RSR-06-2020-0037.

Parwada, C. (2020). COVID-19 outbreak lockdown and its impacts on marketing of horticultural produces in Zimbabwe. *International Journal of Horticultural Science* 26:38–45. Retrieved on October 20, 2020 from https://doi.org/10.31421/ijhs/26/2020/6178.

Perillat, L. and Baigrie, B. (2020). COVID-19 and the generation of novel scientific knowledge in a dangerous time. Part A: Research questions and study designs.

Authorea. Retrieved on October 20, 2020 from https://europepmc.org/article/ppr/ppr257335.

Radia, P. and Stapleton, P. (2008). Unconventional Internet genres and their impact on second language undergraduate students' writing process. *The Internet and Higher Education* 11:9–17. Retrieved on June 17, 2020 from https://doi.org/10.1016/j.iheduc.2007.12.004.

Radu, R. (2020). Fighting the 'infodemic': Legal responses to COVID-19 disinformation. *Social Media and Society 6*(3). Retrieved on November 18, 2020 from https://doi.org/10.1177/2056305120948190.

Republic of South Africa. (2002). *The Disaster Management Act 2005* 451(57).

Roetzel, P. G. (2019). Information overload in the information age: A review of the literature from business administration, business psychology, and related disciplines with a bibliometric approach and framework development. *Business Research* 12(2):479–522. Retrieved on July 7, 2020 from https://doi.org/10.1007/s40685-018-0069-z.

Schweickert, R. and Boruff, B. (1986). Short-term memory capacity: Magic number or magic spell? *Journal of Experimental Psychology: Learning, Memory, and Cognition* 12(3):419–425. American Psychological Association. Retrieved on August 11, 2020 from https://doi.org/10.1037/0278-7393.12.3.419.

SCONUL Working Group on Information Literacy. (2011). *The SCONUL Seven Pillars of Information Literacy: Core Model for Higher Education*. Retrieved on August 11, 2020 from https://www.sconul.ac.uk/sites/default/files/documents/coremodel.pdf.

Simon, H. (1971). Designing organizations for an information rich world. *Computers, Communications, and the Public Interest* 37–72. Retrieved on August 11, 2020 from https://digitalcollections.library.cmu.edu/awweb/awarchive?type=file&item=33748.

Statutory Instrument (SI) Order. (2020). 2020-083 Public Health (COVID-19 Prevention, Containment and Treatment) (National Lockdown) Order, 2020. Retrieved on November 9, 2020 from http://www.veritaszim.net/node/4046.

Takaingenhamo, C. C. (2020). Libraries in the midst of the Coronavirus (COVID-19): Researchers experiences in dealing with the vexatious infodemic. *Library Hi Tech News* 37(6):11–14. Retrieved on November 15, 2020 from https://doi.org/10.1108/LHTN-03-2020-0022.

Tangcharoensathien, V., Calleja, N., Nguyen, T., Purnat, T., D'Agostino, M., Garcia-Saiso, S., Landry, M., Rashidian, A., Hamilton, C., AbdAllah, A., Ghiga, I., Hill, A., Hougendobler, D., van Andel, J., Nunn, M., Brooks, I., Sacco, P. L., de Domenico, M., Mai, P. and Briand, S. (2020). Framework for managing the COVID-19 infodemic: Methods and results of an online, crowdsourced who technical consultation. *Journal of Medical Internet Research* 22(6):1–8. Retrieved on November 14, 2020 from https://doi.org/10.2196/19659.

The Herald. (March 31, 2020). Spreading fake Covid-19 news attracts jail term. Retrieved on May 20, 2020 from https://www.herald.co.zw/spreading-fake-covid-19-news-attracts-jail-term/.

Toffler, A. (1970). *Future Shock*. New York: Random House.

UNECA. (2018). *Zimbabwe Country Profile for 2017.* Addis Ababa, Ethiopia: UNECA Publications.

WHO Director-General. (2020). *Munich Security Conference.* Retrieved on November 13, 2020 from https://www.who.int/director-general/speeches/detail/munich-security-conference.

Xinhua. (July 22, 2020). Zimbabwe imposes dusk-to-dawn curfew amid spike in local COVID-19 infections. Retrieved on August 28, 2020 from http://www.xinhuanet.com/english/2020-07/22/c_139230485.htm.

Yao, X., Zhang, C., Qu, Z., and Tan, B. C. Y. (2020). Global village or virtual balkans? evolution and performance of scientific collaboration in the information age. *Journal of the Association for Information Science and Technology* 71(4):395–408. Retrieved on November 12, 2020 from https://doi.org/https://doi.org/10.1002/asi.24251.

Zarocostas, J. (2009). World Health Organization declares A (H1N1) influenza pandemic. *BMJ* 338:b2425. Retrieved on June 13, 2020 from https://doi.org/10.1136/bmj.b2425.

Zimbabwe Council for Higher Education. (2006). *Quality Assurance Standards for Higher Education* 1–19. Retrieved on June 25, 2020 from http://library1.nida.ac.th/termpaper6/sd/2554/19755.pdf.

Zimbabwe Council for Higher Education Act (Chapter 25–27). (2006). Public Law 25:08.

Chapter 23

Corolockdown

John Idriss Lahai

What is *Corolockdown* (Coronavirus-2019 Lockdown)? It is a medical advisory legitimated by political actors and enforced through *militarized* strategies that are politically *Janus faced.* It is paradoxically more about political control and less about the emergent scientific accounts of how lockdowns help advance medical knowledge on the behaviors of the Coronavirus Disease's (COVID-2019) pathogenic strains (and other serotypes of virulent diseases with similar *coro-characteristics*). As such, any pure medical narrative on the definition of corolockdown should be interrogated for political contradictions, especially where the impact of corolockdown is experienced differently by different sub-groups, populations, private sector institutions, and governments.

That is not all. Corolockdown comes in various forms. These 'other' forms relate to the World Health Organization's (WHO) alternatives to 'lockdown.' These alternatives, which can best be summarized as the 'softening' of the penological character of corolockdown, have attempted to use the concepts of "civic duty," "corporate social responsibility," "duty-of-care" (for self and others), and "public information/education" to relax corolockdowns without displacing the psychological and physical coercive powers of state actors. The enforcement of social distancing rules, the insistence on hand sanitizers in public, and the closure of mass gathering sites (religious centers, schools, cinemas, pubs, stadiums, etc.) are 'softer' forms of corolockdown.

These public measures do not discredit the effectiveness and associated dangers of "stay-at-home" lockdowns. Instead, they represent the subtle reconfiguration and expansion of corolockdown sites—to encompass both the physical space (the homes, schools, offices, etc.) and the psychological space (people's mindsets).

As a result of this reconfigured expansion, public education/information is instrumentalized. People are now required to learn how to wash their hands; learn how to use their eyes to measure the 1.5-meter safe distance; and remember to abandon their *cultured* ways of saying hello with handshakes, kisses, and hugs. They should learn how to use mobile/computer applications to enable them to virtually meet, greet, dine, weep, and celebrate.

Consequently, these "soft" corolockdown alternatives have contributed to creating new forms of burden-laden demands that further entangle people in the politicized and militarized web of medical knowledge and control. In this web, there is no escape, and there are only two predators, the government and the mainstreamed biomedical and scientific community; and there are many preys (the people), whose bodies, whether they are coro-diseased or not, must not be offered as platforms for the promotion of anti-corolockdown oppositional attitudes.

Therefore, it is essential to note that corolockdown has the following features. Firstly, it is an outcome of either an actual or perceived incident of the COVID-2019 outbreak and the hysteria caused by fears that, if militarized corolockdown measures are not adopted, the number of coro-deaths will reach unprecedented levels.

Secondly, its severity level is suggested to governments by the medico-science community that conforms to acceptable political norms. The views of non-conformist epidemiologists, medical doctors, and scientists do not matter. In fact, they are considered an accomplice of the coronavirus.

Thirdly, it is regulated by governments. Finally, due to the government's securitized approach, there are a growing number of anti-corolockdown movements globally. Prominent among these movements is the 'Great Barrington Declaration' Movement (GBDM), which began in the United States. It was signed at the American Institute for Economic Research in Great Barrington, Massachusetts (BBC News, 2020; Kulldorff et al., 2020). The GBDM explains in the preamble of its declaration that "as infection disease epidemiologists and public health scientists [they] have grave concerns about the damaging physical and mental health impacts of the prevailing COVID-2019 [lockdown] policies" (Kulldorff et al., 2020, p. 1). They conclude their declaration with a call on governments to suspend all lockdown measures.

Therefore, irrespective of whether a country has weak or strong democratic institutions and human rights norms, I argue that the adoption of lockdown measures or policies is not solely about saving people from self and others. They are about justifying, in the first instance, the securitization of hysterical attitudes toward human freedoms. In the second instance, where it is necessary, the men/women-in-boots can apply force to discredit oppositional knowledge.

These characteristics should be seen as *inputs* and *outputs* of power (power-over), sociopolitical class difference, racialized identities, and the epistemological framing of epidemiological knowledge that go beyond the biomedical and scientific justifications for adopting all forms of lockdown measures. As such, we should not lose sight of the factors that shape the relationship between medicine and politics (including its militaristic dimensions). The intersectional positioning of the two creates the necessitating conditions for the nuances surrounding the patterns of acceptance and rejection of lockdown measures across the world.

To interrogate these two, I adopt a Foucauldian penological (discipline and punishment) perspective. I contend that lockdowns are mechanisms that unnaturally situate people as an existential threat to power. Hence, there is a need for the state to invoke its securitized control over its subjects. That said, in part one of this chapter, I contend that lockdowns represent a crisis produced by the unethical convergence of medico-political modernism. In part two, I explore conditional uses of lockdowns to transform people into an existential threat to power. In part three, I examine how the leaders of governments and their mainstream medical and scientific communities are using 'class' and 'knowledge' to regulate oppositional attitudes and knowledge to lockdown. I argue that this regulation's performative functions are aimed at the oppressive and discriminatory case management and discreditation of these oppositional attitudes that have gained friction with the rise of the GBDM movements.

However, before moving on to the next section, I should state here that the analysis presented in this chapter is not aimed at an outright dismissal of the public health gains in the solitary confinement spaces for the infected. I recognize the personal sacrifices and successes of the frontline health workers. They are our heroes and heroines: our 'unsung' lifesavers who deserve more than just a Nobel Prize.

That said, what this chapter does is provide answers to the following fundamental questions: Are corolockdowns an outcome of the failed promises of medico-political modernism? Why the securitization of lockdown measures? How does it feel like to be placed in an involuntary coro-instigated lockdown? What has medical/political hysteria got to do with it? Does the breaking of corolockdown rules by the political class a far more serious attack on our liberty than the lockdown itself?

COROLOCKDOWN: AN OUTCOME OF A CRISIS OF FALSE MODERNISM AND A SECURITIZED MEDICO-POLITICAL CONVERGENCE

Drawing from a range of country-specific experiential accounts, it has been argued that lockdowns are aimed at stopping the coronavirus from entering the 'community transmission' phase, where it would be challenging to do contact tracing, testing, isolation, and treatment, as well as to take stock of the number of mortalities. With initial advice from 'the pioneers' of medical modernism—such as the WHO, the Centers for Disease Control and Prevention, and the vaccine manufacturing companies—those (administrators and scientists) with monitoring and regulatory responsibility for infectious diseases at country levels got their governments to adopt penological containment strategies following the eruption of the COVID-2019 pandemic in Wuhan, China.

These strategies called for prioritizing both the use of 'men/women-in-boot' (militaries) and frontline health workers as risk management instruments and low-cost agents of control. The goal is to prevent people from pointing out the shortcoming of medico-political modernism when drawing a binary between their anti-lockdown protests and their everyday quest for survival during the COVID-2019 pandemic. This crisis of medico-political modernism began following the pandemic's eruption in many countries around the world. Western governments that were exercising hegemonic control of the world's health systems because they thought they had the best public health and disease control systems were (like the countries in the Global South with inadequate systems) unable to prevent millions of people's deaths.

Angered by the growing numbers of deaths, and the need to address the deficiency of medical modernism, medical choices and strategies took a political turn, and counter-narratives and actions that would otherwise strengthen the tenets of democracy are retributively (be it in expressive or physical) coerced into silence. Through this silencing, the contain-and-cure medical ideals that would, in normal circumstances, characterize the concept of 'hospitalization' are either reconfigured and mainstreamed or outrightly abandoned. In its place emerged narratives and actions that situate the state (used here interchangeably with 'government') as the one in need of protection from the 'diseased bodies' of its citizenry.

The schematic intention for projecting the state as the one in need of protection is to create the enabling environment where the 'given' conventional medical wisdom should feel convenient when throwing its support behind the experientially authoritarian policies that force people to accept lockdowns as the solution to the problems posed by the coronavirus. In countless protest tweets, many people, including President Donald Trump, have voiced similar fears that while lockdowns may slowdown the spread of the virus, they will also suppress people's movement, which could lead to other health (psychological and physical) and economic problems.

This oppositional theorization of the shortcomings of both the crisis of medico-political modernism and the dangers posed by lockdowns is sensitive to the question of inequality. It explains how the structural trends of inequalities will play out on the economic front, particularly on people's purchasing power—the ability to feed and pay their bills—during a lockdown. These considerations are, in themselves, determinants that can be used to understand and analyze (as well as predict) lockdown outcomes in the sites of their experimentation: the homes, communities, and countries.

In part, there are possibilities that lockdowns will produce conflicting (intended and unintended) outcomes. Moreover, these outcomes reflect assumptions around the increasing convergence between human rights practice and neoliberal medical ideals. It also exposed the connection between lockdowns and excessive drug abuse (Mallet et al., 2020; Volkow, 2020), sexual and gender-based violence (Every-Palmer et al., 2020; Gosangi et al., 2020; Roesch et al., 2020), acute depression, and anxiety disorder (Benke et al., 2020), and suicide (Caballero-Domínguez et al., 2020), and its gendered dimensions (Standish, 2020).

It also reveals a broader pattern in society whereby militaries and civilian medical practitioners work in sites that should not be militarized. For the military, to defend the state against innocent civilians (who are carriers or suspected carriers of the COVID-2019 pathogens) within the country presents a sense of psychological disconnection from their usual 'place' of work and a demoralizing displacement of their conventional understanding that armies defend against internal and external aggression, and not against their own people who should be seen as victims of an airborne virus.

For the frontline health workers, the sense of having to transform the whole country into hospital sites has the tendency of creating the necessitating conditions for them to cooperate with non-medical military personnel—while operating—within an improvised lockdown site. In these sites, it is the expectation that the frontline health worker will (and must) allow politicians and their militaries to replace medical ethics with inhumane militarized interventions that are born out of elevated existential political speech acts to justify the militarization of the failed attempts at medico-political modernism before and during the COVID-2019 pandemic.

This convergence of the political and the medical in the production of corolockdowns is understood, for present purposes, just as clearly as the corpus of work, which has explored the connection between the psychology of control and the severity of solitary confinement (be it in a hospital, a prison, or the home) (see Cloud et al., 2020; Franco-Paredes et al., 2020; Stanojoska and Ilik, 2020), with a view of moving beyond the superficialities of health-based discourses to the political meanings of lockdowns, isolations, and confinement.

This shift (from the medical to the political), which I am calling for in this chapter, is essential. In that, it exposes, in part, the thin line between (a) political security and health security and (b) public (government) and private (the scientific-pharmaceutical industries) sectors in the case management of lockdowns. This exposure is also made possible by a number of factors: (1) a country's political system and the regime's ideological underpinnings; (2) the sociocultural belief systems within a country; (3) the role of national identities, including discourses of race and racism in the development, trial, and deployment of vaccines; (4) the nature of state secrets on biosecurity; (5) the levels of corruption within the country and how it influences the relationship between the government and the medical and scientific communities; and (6) the responsiveness of state bureaucracies to both the government and the people (people's competing needs).

With a focus on this thin line of convergence (which makes it impossible to trivialize the aforementioned factors), we can use the 'Scandinavian experience' as an example of a situation whereby the forces that would have necessitated unprecedented lockdown were weighed against several factors: the individualistic understanding of rights and health, the welfare-oriented ideological positions of the regimes, and the pro-people political choices of the bureaucracies, to project a legitimate argument against the political justifications to securitize or militarize medical interventions. Although the country-specific health systems in Scandinavia presented a false promise of modernism and has failed to prevent COVID-2019-related deaths, these Nordic countries saw no reason to take the militant's path (Christensen and Lægreid, 2020).

In other non-Nordic Western European countries, say, Italy, there was a clear justification for lockdowns (seen from the number of coronavirus deaths). However, they were experientially tolerant and receptive to the truth that their health systems were built under the false premise of 'modernism' (Capano, 2020). To have refused to acknowledge this failure, and at the same time take steps to militarize the face of the frontline health workers, the crisis could have resulted in more deaths. In the United States, the institutionalized objections to President Trump's refusal to encourage states to adopt punitive lockdown measures did not come so much from the country's pre-COVID-2019 racialized social systems and incarceration histories (Desai et al., 2020; Franco-Paredes et al., 2020; Henry, 2020; Meyer et al., 2020). Instead, it was due to the refusal to acknowledge the negative impact of political divisions on the American health systems (Mellish et al., 2020). Some have argued that this failure stems from the flaws in the United States' economic model of public health governance pandemic regulation (Galvani et al., 2020).

In Africa, particularly in the countries that are located South of the Sahara, one can identify several broad factors that created similarities (a) between corolockdowns and the curfews that are triggered by general political unrest, military coups, and civil war and (b) between home-based corolockdowns and prison-based penological confinement. Overcrowding (in confined spaces at homes), sexual violence (Sierra Leone, for example, had to declare a state of emergency on rape crimes in 2019) (Srivatsa, 2020), and food rationing (or the search for it) are some of the penal/prison conditions visible in the non-prison conditions of home-based corolockdown. Concerning the latter (i.e., people's quest for food during lockdown), people risked their lives when they escaped from their homes searching for drinkable water. Several instances are there on YouTube and other social media sites. They show real-time cases in which these water-searching *escapees* are caught by armed security (military and paramilitary) personnel enforcing the lockdown. The armed personnel physically abused them like they would the real prison inmate escapees.

This country-specific African case that I have presented raises another critical issue. It is a fact that the health systems of African countries, South of the Sahara, are yet to be modernized. Access to health still is a significant challenge for over 70 percent of the continent's population. Despite this unfavorable characterization, the continent was able to escape mass COVID-2019-related deaths.

The question, then, is: What explains Africa's relative success in averting uncontrolled COVID-2019 deaths in 2020? This question has attracted many assumptions. Some have pointed to the role of political leadership and African governments' willingness to embrace the science-based facts about the virus without resorting to postcolonial narratives that would have reduced the virus's discursive representation as a virus meant for non-Africans.

For some, it was due to the willingness of Africans (in Africa) and the leaders of their political groups (say political parties) to allow—or rather, create the governance space—for governments to take authoritarian steps to prevent community transmission. African governments declared states of national emergency with bipartisan and inter-tribal support.

For others, it was the adoption of grassroots or community-based engagement strategies. These strategies are characterized by the socialized uses of traditional political authority. Building awareness of and compliance with government policy on COVID-2019 at the grassroots level requires an approach that does not sway too far from people's relationships with their traditional authorities or rulers. In Africa, the governance structure of traditional rulers (the Kings/Paramount Chiefs, Mammy Queens/Queen Mothers) has, for centuries, been providing the institutional pathways for the transition of knowledge and information from the central government to the people within the communities (Abraham, 1978; Acemoglu et al., 2014; Jackson, 2005; Lahai, 2016; Rashid, 2000). By empowering these traditional rulers, the governments were able to decentralize the infrastructure to regulate knowledge about and interventions on COVID-2019. These community-level traditional rulers created bylaws that reflected national policies on social distancing and hygiene.

Some believe that Africa got lucky. With references to Africa's weak health systems, they say, Africa was spared, not by science but by mere luck. Those who embody this thinking believe that African countries should understand that if 'luck' had not played a role, the coronavirus could have re-written the medical histories of Africa's human societies.

Others have pointed to the pre-existing social and emotional pillars of resilience in Africa. Communicable and non-communicable, tropical and non-tropical diseases have been with us (in Africa) for as long as one can remember. So, to the Africans (in Africa), the coronavirus's lethality is connected to the fear factor. By treating the virus as just another pandemic, they demonstrated the kind of fearlessness some of us saw (and wrote about) in our communities during the Ebola pandemic (see Lahai, 2017).

Finally, some believe Africans (in Africa) had developed the natural antibodies to the plasmodium parasite that causes malaria. This argument remains contentious because of the lack of biomedical scientific research. However, those who believe in this argument say the existence of the malaria antibodies in the morphology and anatomical makeup of the people in sub-Saharan Africa, who are without other pre-existing conditions such as asthma, heart disease, sickle cell, and HIV/AIDS, can withstand the coronavirus. Since this argument has not been scientifically proven, I always advise people to ignore this headless unscientific knowledge until there is a convincing number of research findings that will ascertain its validity.

In North Korea, despite the challenges of getting a clear picture of the country's handling of the pandemic, one can pre-empt a scenario-based argument (that draws from available data) that the historic, albeit institutionalized, structures of societal servitude and the state's insistence on universal respectability for central political authority may have resulted in a general societal acceptance of corolockdown as a solution for the false hopes of medical modernism.

In South Korea, a psychiatric ward (with a COVID-2019 outbreak) during the lockdown became a medical disaster. Measures were later taken to contain the virus and prevent lockdown-induced suicides (by closing all windows and jumping points). But, Min Joo Kim, writing in the *Washington Post* (in February 2020), tells us that there were concerns that patients were looking for ways to kill themselves—one of such ways (though ineffective) was the drinking of hand sanitizers (Kim, 2020). To the patients in the hospitals, the imposition of lockdowns as forms of medical modernism was dismissive of 'ethical consideration.'

In Australia, the interplay between (a) the tension-ridden relationships between state premiers that began with the suspension of interstate travels, and (b) the connections between the humid environment and food spoilage, forced Prime Minister Scott Morrison's federal government to announce exceptions. Among them, the relaxation of lockdown measures to enable people (all 'panic buyers') to wrestle at the Wesfarmers (the big agro-food industries and retailers of raw farm produce) and the shopping malls (the sellers of toiletries and BBQ appliances) (Arafat et al., 2020; for more on COVID-2019-induced "panic buying" in Australia, see Prentice et al., 2020). Of course, panic buying is not a determinant of medical modernism in Australia. However, the Morrison government's social sanctions imposed to case-manage food scarcity and the fears that food shortage imposed on people brought its health-related problems. Acute depression, anxiety disorder, and eating disorder (and its impact on the circle of paranoic compulsive buying) are among the issues that emerged during the early-to-mid phases of the COVID-2019 pandemic in Australia (Phillipou et al., 2020). And there were human rights concerns too for persons with mental and cognitive impairments, who were subjected to coercive powers in Australia (Wilson, 2020).

Despite these country-specific differences/similarities, one of the visible features that cut across all these corolockdown scenarios is that the interplay of the crisis of false modernism and the attempts to impose medico-political alternatives led to the politicization of interventions. Through this (save for the Scandinavian countries), governments' political decisions (and decisiveness) can hardly be said to be tolerant of disruptive attitudes. Attempts at fusing the political and the medical to case-manage lockdowns and human behaviors resulted in the elevation of corohysteria to the point where it became a political necessity to transform the people into an existential threat to the powers of the state.

COROLOCKDOWN: THE TRANSFORMATION OF PEOPLE INTO AN EXISTENTIAL THREAT TO POWER

The outbreak of the COVID-2019 in December 2019 unmasked more than just the unpreparedness of countries (both developed and developing) (Capano, 2020; Chehrehgosha, 2020; Lo and Hsieh, 2020). For most countries, the COVID-2019 pandemic also created problems relating to the dilemma of not knowing whether the application of policies explicitly designed for complex political emergencies will achieve the same output when applied to regulate public health emergencies and pandemics.

With no biosecurity policies and weak disease regulatory institutions, governments, especially those in the Global South, are left with no option but to show how non-medical political policies can be applied to case-manage the pandemic. In trying to make sense of which approach will address what, how, when, and where, uncertainties gave rise to the narratives that would eventually place the people as threats to the state's political survival.

Existential securitized discourses are elevated over people's (who are now suspects) human rights entitlements (Keilitz, 2020; Liu et al., 2020; Shani, 2020). Decrees and states of emergency (SOE) are not only adopted to contain the pandemic. Using SOEs to regulate people's lives (i.e., dictate what they can say, where they can go, what they can do, and when they should be freed from involuntary confinement/lockdown), governments are saying they have the sole necropolitical power to determine who lives and dies. In such a tense political environment, the state's survival eclipses all considerations for people's individualistic rights. It is the survival of the state, the regime, which was at stake, not the diseased bodies of the contained individuals.

With the state's survival at stake, people are required to recognize the ultimate power of the state over them. This means that the state's "power-over" the people goes beyond the attendant socio-relational, economic, and medico-scientific drivers of uncertainties. The performative character of this state power is that it serves a dual function. First, it forces people to open up their private spaces (homes; the new coronavirus sites) for governments to validate the SOEs that they have hurriedly put together to contain both the people and the coronavirus.

Within this space, people should accept that the real intention is to save them (from themselves). In reality, it is not just about saving lives. It is about serving—on the dish of 'undemocratic' constitutionality and governmentality—the food that governments desire most, which is the powers to adopt policies that override constitutional limitations that often prevent governments from restricting people's movement. Governments, whose rogue political desires were 'imprisoned' by constitutional checks and balances (including those imposed by the curious eyes/ears of the fourth estate, the media), are now free to do as they see fit without risking being accused of constitutional wrongdoing.

For obvious reasons, my assessment of the SOE-induced lockdowns of a select group of governments (in Africa, Europe, the Americas, the Tasman Sea, the Pacific, and South Asia) reveals alarming deficiencies. Firstly, these lockdowns (whether they are relaxed or harsh) reflect governments' autocratic tendencies, irrespective of the ideological orientation of those who adopted and implemented them. Governments' projected political reasonings justified using their SOEs to engage in 'site capture.'

In this captured site (i.e., the public spaces, which can either be under a lockdown or prone to a lockdown), governments use punitive penological methods to selectively imprison their populations. In these sites, whereas discipline and punishment (*inputs* of power) are the main instruments of control, *care* is reserved (or so it seems) for only to the dying, and *comfort*, which suddenly becomes a luxury, should be merited. Here, merit is determined, in part, by class difference. The subaltern class (the powerless, the poor, the marginalized) must show unreserved obedience to the state to deserve this comfort. For the powerful class (politically influential and economically affluent), their only obligation is to point out their connections to and positions within the political establishment to merit this comfort that will remove them from the list of those who posed a threat to the powers of the state.

Within this captured space, 'governments' authoritarian tendencies make it less likely for their punitive use of *power-over* to be about governance quality (which does affect people's quality of life). Instead, it is about the survival of the political regime, whose interpretation of people's reaction to the state's handling of the pandemic is driven by their fears that the people will call for regime change.

Secondly, what happens during corolockdowns is an outcome of the intersectional collision of governments' official policy, the individualized political rhetoric of politicians, and the socialized forms and levels of people's (i.e., the citizens) resistance (or acceptance) of lockdowns (how it affects their freedoms). Regarding the latter, it is unusual for people to accept restrictions to their movements willingly.

As such, it is the temporality or longevity of corolockdowns that will determine the potency (or the lack of it) of any socialized resistance of the people against involuntary confinement, isolation, and lockdown. Based on this observation, I argue that governments have used 'timing' as an instrument for transforming the people as an existential threat to power. The longer the lockdown lasts, the higher the tendencies for anti-government rhetoric to take a violent turn, and, in tandem, the greater the chances that the government will try, at first, to use soft power to get the people to do self-discreditation of the legitimacy of their resistance to governmental authority. When that fails, and in most cases, it does, then the government will, in the final instance, use disproportionate force to get the people to conform to the dictates of state power.

Observably, one can predict the intended outcome of official government lockdown policies—to transform people as threats to state power—by looking at politicians' public statements and rhetoric. Their political 'statements' impact, after all, depends on whether they are in a collision course with or in favor of official government policies and elevated political speech acts. Here, opposition parties and their followers will be on a collision course, and those in government (and their supporters) will favor these policies.

Using this analytical framing of the relationships between policy, rhetoric, and resistance/acceptance, I discovered, during the course of researching this chapter, that, in some countries, it is only because of the insistence of WHO that governments must follow international best practices, guidelines, and regulations that make it possible for their self-serving lockdown policies not to obscure the processes that would lead to the classification of state-led interventions as actions aimed at containing the virus.

From South Sudan to India, from Ethiopia to the Philippines, from Somalia to Venezuela, from Afghanistan to Syria, and from Yemen to Guinea (Conakry), there are accusations of selective interventions that are borne out of the government's existential security threat concerns. For example, regions considered strongholds of the opposition parties are deprived of monies (to pay workers) and medical equipment—ventilators, personal protective equipment, and ambulances—needed to manage health concerns during (blanket or partial) lockdowns effectively. The aim is not to kill people, per se, but to prevent any form of localized ownership in the fight against the pandemic and, with it, to create a docile population out of the deprived.

The problem becomes more protracted when the government (in compliance with its obligations to the WHO directives) offers its assistance to these 'rebellious' regions. The political uses of oppositional ideological incompatibility and ego (ego induced by tribal/racial differences) have led to instances whereby people in the deprived, rebellious regions have rejected the central/federal government's assistance.

Whereas WHO country-level reports have given an impression of governments' commitment to de-securitize and re-commit to the people's health and welfare, first-hand accounts of lockdowns counter all fanciful characterization contained in some of the reports. Ideals of governmental 'duty-of-care' were never embedded in the securitized interventions, leading to gross disparities between commitment to WHO directives and what is happening on the ground. Countries are designing policies (including securitized lockdown policies) that reflect their historic culture-centric objection to the universal application of liberal, albeit Western civilizational norms.

Thus, while WHO may insist on 'ethics' (founded on respectability and individuality), countries are developing anti-pandemic lockdown strategies that are highly intrusive and oppressive. Notably, televised reports from China's Wuhan Province (the first site in the world to experience military-controlled corolockdown) suggest that 'Black' African were forced to undergo many COVID-2019 tests. Even when these tests returned a 'negative,' they (the Black Africans) were still forced into state/military-controlled facilities to "spend time" under observation (an outcome of ethno-selective lockdown). From these Wuhan files, we see that a lockdown policy (with militarized transformative powers that change innocent civilians into security threats) can be racially and disproportionally used against those seen as 'aliens' or racially 'different.'

But, of course, China is not the only country that has been accused of racialized corolockdown. The anti-coronavirus policies of most countries are exclusionary. Governments do not rely so much on internationally (WHO) recognized best practices that frown against the political uses of biological, racial, and country-of-origin differences. No country can claim a moral high ground and boast of having a quarantine/lockdown policy that does not apply bio-racialized differences. The only thing that guides against public acknowledgment of the uses of these differences (to either exclude or devise a 'special' approach of treatment) is the existence of WHO's international regulatory policies and directives.

Drawing from the preceding disparities, it is not helpful to conflate COVID-2019 investment in the form of material resources pumped into the management of a lockdown with people's quality of life in isolations sites, especially in poor countries where governmental preference is on the payment of politicians' salaries and not on the welfare of the epidemiologists. People's quality of life in a lockdown situation matters much in sustaining governmental power and control. The story (at least from my experience in Sierra Leone during the cholera and Lassa fever pandemics in the 1980s and 1990s) goes this way. When a government places its citizens in deprived conditions and limit their access to alternative sources of sustenance, and, then, after a prolonged period of deprivation expand government's humanitarian assistance in the form of rationed food packages, the people will be tamed by the lack of food and other basic amenities. In such a situation, open critics are transformed into subservient followers for as long as the conditions of deprivation, confinement, and lockdown last—and, of course, with the backing of SOEs or other laws that allows for the government's use of brute force on protesters.

Nonetheless, for the sake of want of fresh air, we can point to Scandinavia's welfare states, where lockdown investment reflects people's quality of life. In these countries, the social services delivery to 'effect' 'power-over,' rarely occurs; and, where the severity of a pandemic calls for the adoption of a lockdown measure, power politics can only go as far as to replace external humanitarian assistance with transformative interventions that focus, in the interim, on their citizens. This is due to (a) the long history of governmental commitment to the welfare system's perfection and (b) the positive relationships between the people and the government. As previous studies on the politics, laws, and economics of the Nordic welfare states have demonstrated (Castles et al., 2010; Greve et al., 2020; Kvist et al., 2012; Kvist and Greve, 2011; Pedersen and Kuhnle, 2017), I argue that the substance of a political regime is in the equitable delivery of its governance mandate (translated into pro-people policies, post-elections) to its people. Likewise, the relationship between the government and, say, frontline workers go as much as to determine whether long- or short-term lockdowns will be characterized as humane and sensitive to engender differences. Away from the Nordic region and into Africa, whether a lockdown policy will positively impact the quality of state/

government power depends on (1) the political understanding of the limits of power, (2) government's knowledge about its responsibilities, and (3) citizens' appreciation of their rights and civic duties.

Fourth, during lockdowns, the most definitive and calculable measures of the extent to which government can apply state power during a public health emergency, with the resultant effect of transforming the people into dangerous beings, get us only as far in appreciating the experiential meanings of the tenets of responsive public health policies (of the welfare state orientation) that are far more distinct than most metrics can explain. Some of its principles can be found in WHO's directives, particularly Article 3 of its International Health Regulation (2005). These policies (which should teach governments 'how to put people in a corolockdown without killing somebody') should be regarded as input and output measurement indicators of the impact of de-securitizing lockdowns. They include the following: (1) government's commitment to providing the highest standards of health to its citizens, (2) support for the vulnerable population, and (3) assurances (with actions to show for it) that quarantine and lockdown measures are in compliance with the law (laws that do not negate from international laws, conventions/protocols, and WHO's regulations and directives) and are within a clear set of objectives aimed at achieving legitimate goals through proportionate means that are neither arbitrary nor discriminatory (WHO, 2020).

Notwithstanding these indicators mentioned above, the impact of 'power-over' in the state's enforcement of lockdown will also depend on people's preferences. During the course of my research (for this study), I spoke to many people—in Sierra Leone and other African countries. Some told me they find "home-site-sharing" (sharing a house with others) preferable to "hospital-site-sharing" (sharing a hospital ward with other patients). This is because in countries with hospital sites that lack the structures, human resource expertise, and equipment, life in such a securitized lockdown setting will be unbearable. Others said they would value lockdowns and solitary confinement over the dangers of community transmission.

These points are valid. The way people experience lockdown depends, firstly, on their interpretation of "place." What is being prevented by placing people in militarized lockdowns will always come with its psychological impact. Imagine being in a lockdown situation surrounded only by military personnel (soldiers and medic) in a country with a long history of civil wars. Without someone (a civilian) to provide clinical psychological support to you, the outcomes will be trauma, depression, anxiety (with the constant reoccurrence of freeze, fight, and flee modes), and possibly suicide.

Secondly, it also depends on people's expectations. In countries with autocratic governments, people in militarized lockdowns anticipate that there will be a 'deprivation continuum.' In that, there are no noticeable differences between the pre-COVID-2019 penological systems (of prisons, curfews, sieges, and lockdowns) and the COVID-2019 lockdowns, save for the pandemic, which is, but, one of the many infectious diseases affecting an already oppressed population. As such, they may feel less bothered with the penalization of their lives during COVID-2019.

Conversely, in pro-rights, pro-people welfare states, people will continue to feel worse-off as the level of the state's extrajudicial lockdown-induced control measures increases. The lesser people's sense of control over their private spaces of lockdown or isolation, the higher their chances of losing their sense of entitlement. And where there is no long history of governmental commitment to the people's well-being (physical and psychological), the regime will exploit people's loss of entitlement by taking steps to unleash and consolidate their self-serving model of governance that will outlive the pandemic. For this reason, I suggest we look beyond accounts of lockdown that focus only on the medico-scientific justifications for lockdown. To trivialize the role of 'power-over' is to diminish the value of politics. If not for anything, there should be the recognition that the 'political' has hegemonic control (*input*) over the apolitical *biomedical* interventions (output).

COROLOCKDOWN: CLASS (AS *PRACTICE*) AND KNOWLEDGE (AS *EPISTEMOLOGY*) IN THE FIGHT TO INVALIDATE OPPOSITIONAL ATTITUDES

The analysis presented thus far is not aimed at an outright dismissal of the public health gains from corolockdowns (and in the solitary confinement spaces for the infected). Instead, it answers the fundamental question about what it feels like to be placed in an "involuntary" COVID-2019-instigated lockdown. Several studies have drawn from the disciplines of medicine, psychology, psychiatry, sexuality studies, philosophy, criminology, race relations, statistics, human rights, and terrorism studies in their attempts to understand the implications of involuntary confinement, isolation, and lockdowns on people and society.

I will focus on the *necropolitical* management of oppositional attitudes by those seeking to protect the medical, jurisprudential, and political justifications for corolockdown. I employ Achille Mbembe's necropolitics. However, rather than focus on his original idea of how necropolitics is used to determine who lives and dies (Mbembe, 2008), I will put a twist into it, for present purposes. I define the necropolitical management of anti-lockdown attitude as the use of socialized (class), political (power), medical (science), and knowledge-framing (epistemology) power to determine who and what matters, and how what matters should either be accepted or rejected.

In practical and epistemological terms, the relevance of this necropolitical management of oppositional, anti-corolockdown attitudes is seen from the backdrop of the functions of class and knowledge in the configuration, legitimation, and institutionalization of calls for the removal of corolockdown policies for reasons that the GBDM has highlighted.

The Instrumentalization of George Orwell's *Animal Farm* in the Validation of Capitulatory Lockdown Privileges and How the Subalterns Are Resisting

In practical terms, the role of class in the production of anti-corolockdown protests (oppositional attitudes) is not far-fetched. Let us start with examples from the United States to understand the place of George Orwell's *Animal Farm* in the validation of oppressive class relations. In November 2020, California's governor, Gavin Newsom, who for months was calling on Californians not to violate the "soft" and "hard" corolockdown rules, broke these rules (which he had passed into law), when, on November 6, 2020, he attended a large birthday party gathering at the "posh French Laundry Restaurant in the wine country north of San Francisco" (Ronayne, 2020, para. 2). What is also noteworthy about Governor Newsom's Orwellian action is that "three days after the party, [he] held his usual Monday news conference on the virus and spoke about how the state's cases were at their highest levels in months and attributed it to social gatherings, including at Halloween" (Ronayne, 2020, p. 1). The questions to ask then are: did ordinary people who violated these rules go unpunished? The answer is a resounding "no"! did he (Newsom) go unpunished? The answer is yes!

In New York (the epicenter of the COVID-2019 outbreaks), Governor Andrew Cuomo announced, during a radio interview, on November 23, 2020, that his 89-year-old mother, Matilda, was traveling to join him (and other group of invitees) for Thanksgiving at a time when New Yorkers were either dying of coronavirus or were struggling with grief, substance abuse, domestic violence (including sexual violence), acute depression and anxiety disorder, and suicidal thoughts and attempts. What followed was a public outcry (a form of protest against the class-based indifference of the political class). In response, Richard Azzopardi, one of Cuomo's top advisers, issued a statement (on Twitter) that his boss had decided to do a virtual Thanksgiving with mama Matilda. Whether he kept his promise, we do not know. What is known (or what is public knowledge) is that Governor Cuomo had issued a special authorization for Matilda to travel after he had placed New York on corolockdown.

In Washington, DC, Mayor Muriel Bowser was on record defending her trip to Delaware to attend a 'Joe Biden post-election celebration.' This

Delaware merrymaking travels occurred after she had placed "soft" corolockdown (in the form of travel advisory) on DC residents. This advisory told all DC residents to stay at home. In Oklahoma, Governor Kevin Stitt, and in Missouri, Governor Mike Parson are also on record for violating the corolockdown measures they had imposed on their 'states' residents. They hosted large crowds for private parties and dinners.

In Britain, the controversial Dominic Cummings, when he was senior adviser to Prime Minister Boris Johnson, violated both the travel ban and corolockdown rules when he visited his family in May 2020. In New Zealand, the health minister (at the time), David Clark, is also on record for violating the stringent corolockdown measures he (and his ministry) had imposed on the people in New Zealand. In India, the governor of the State of Assam, Jagdish Mukhi, was on record for violating the corolockdown rules, when in May 2020, he visited the city of Kokrajhar in Bodoland. At the time of his travels, India was under one of its most stringent corolockdown periods.

In the Philippines, in April 2020, three state governors and two mayors faced presidential queries following public outcry for putting themselves above the corolockdown laws they had imposed on their people. To the penalized Filipino population, there should be no preferential treatment for those with political power. These unnamed governors and mayors did things to make the people angry. They broke the prohibition against mass gatherings. They failed "to strictly implement social distancing measures." They refused to allow Filipino workers (returning from overseas and stranded at airports) to return to their homes (despite their coronavirus negative test results). They refused to grant travel passes to the essential workers, including personnel operating the industries that were vital to food security. It was after they had imposed these corrosive corolockdown measures that they (these governors and mayors) gave themselves the right to bend the laws for their self-gratification (Cabico, 2020).

In South Africa, a government cabinet minister, Stella Ndabeni-Abrahams, also violated the corolockdown rules when she went out to do what columnists have dubbed "lockdown lunch" (Heiberg and Winning, 2020). However, following public outcry, President Cyril Ramaphosa suspended her for two months and took a one month pay off her annual salary (gross salary) (Heiberg and Winning, 2020, para. 1).

The stories about top government officials violating corolockdown rules are the same for Sierra Leone, Scotland, Japan, South Sudan, Nigeria, Spain, Italy, Zimbabwe, Liberia, Guinea, among many other countries. It was this Orwellian (privileged-based) characterization of the violation of lockdown rules that promoted the editor of *The Conversation*, Misha Ketchell, to write an eye-opening essay, which he titled "Why Leaders Breaking Rules Is a Far More Serious Attack on Our Liberty than the Lockdown Itself." He argues that

> recent developments in the politics of the coronavirus pandemic have shown that threats to our liberty are not always what they seem. Over the past few weeks, armed protestors have occupied public spaces in the US, demanding an end to lockdown rules, and protests have occurred in major British cities. The issue of whether the Government can expect you to wear a face mask has been co-opted into a "culture war." (Ketchell, 2020, p. 1)

Ketchell adds:

> These protesters claim lockdowns are intolerable violations of their freedom. The problem is that this argument relies on a facile conception of liberty. They should be looking instead at the many examples of people in power bending the rules. The COVID-2019 pandemic has revealed that many of those in power believe themselves to be above the law. That jeopardizes liberty in a far more profound way than being instructed to wear a face mask. (Ketchell, 2020, pp. 1–3)

In all of these aforementioned case studies, class difference was instrumental in creating a sense of Orwellian capitulatory privileges for those on top of the political hierarchy. In essence, those below the ladder (the subalterns; the powerless masses) should aspire to accept their designated position as the ones who should experience discipline and punishment in the form of coro-confinement and corolockdown. After all, being an involuntary 'subject' for the securitization of civil spaces, the subaltern must see him or herself as the one whose body poses a medico-political threat to power. For this reason, the intersectionality of class-based difference should not be ignored. It is only by interrogating it will we be able to adjust some of the lenses through which we (a) imagine and experience life under coronavirus's "lock and key" and (b) understand the discriminating nuances surrounding the use of corolockdown as an input and output of power.

The Instrumentalization of Knowledge to Invalidate Oppositional Attitudes toward Corolockdown

Regarding knowledge production and its uses in the case management of oppositional attitudes, we should note the following. Firstly, the subalterns do not have a social contract (of either the Lockean or Hobbesian theorization) with the coro-private-sector, coro-marketeers, coro-profiteers, and coro-biomedical scientists (in the private sector).

Secondly, these actors are driven by the desire to make profits from the coronavirus. However, should they remember their cooperate social responsibilities, they will contribute to pro-poor public health humanitarian projects to save lives.

Thirdly, they are the ones that have access to power and, therefore, can suggest to governments when and for how long corolockdowns should last. Armed with their scientific knowledge and reassured by their access to power, the mainstream private medico-scientific companies have enthralled governments (and the international community) not to entertain—by way of legitimizing—oppositional attitudes toward lockdown measures.

Why the apprehension? An answer to this question is not far-fetched. Thousands of scientists and health experts have joined the subalterns in their protests against corolockdowns. These scientists and health experts have encouraged the grassroots anti-corolockdown protest movements to be socially responsible and purposeful in their activism. Among them are oncologists, epidemiologists, health informaticians, geneticists, pediatricians, clinical ethicists, microbiologists, statisticians, psychologists, historians, environmentalists, and so on.

What is also interesting is that they are affiliates of the United States' Ivy League and United Kingdom's Russell Group universities, and many other research-intensive universities and *proto*-academic institutions around the world. Their entry into the anti-lockdown movement brought with it its scientifically robust counter-narratives that were lacking in these movements before their arrival. To explain this better, I need to quote (at length) the critical sections of the GBDM (which was signed on October 4, 2020, in Great Barrington, Massachusetts, USA), one of the global movements with over 6,000 members from all disciplines in the medical, scientific, applied social science, and humanities across the world. The declaration reads thus (with the italics embedded for emphasis): "The Great Barrington Declaration—As infectious disease epidemiologists and public health scientists we have grave concerns about the *damaging physical and mental health impacts of the prevailing COVID-2019 policies* and recommend an approach we call *Focused Protection*" (Kulldorff et al., 2020, p. 1).

Coming from both the left and right, and around the world, they furthered that they have devoted their careers to protecting people. As such, based on their experience in public health governance, the current lockdown policies are producing *devastating effects on short- and long-term public health*. The results (to name a few) include lower childhood vaccination rates, worsening cardiovascular disease outcomes, fewer cancer screenings, and deteriorating mental health—leading to greater excess mortality in years to come, with the working class and younger members of society carrying the heaviest burden.

With a focus on the impact of corolockdown on the human rights of the youthful populations, the framers of the GBDM went on to state that "keeping students out of school is a grave injustice. Keeping these measures in place until a vaccine is available will cause irreparable damage, with the underprivileged disproportionately harmed." That said, they called on governments to reopen schools and universities for in-person teaching. Not wanting to appear insensitive to individual choices, they went on to state that sports should be resumed and people who are more at risk may participate in corolockdown if they wish. However, the participation of the vulnerable populations in these corolockdowns should not prevent those who have built up herd immunity, enjoying rights to be free from militarized lockdown measures that have been adopted until the arrival of vaccines.

Thus, and by way of a suggestion, the GBDM called on governments to ensure that

> [their] goal should . . . be to minimize mortality and social harm until we reach herd immunity. The most compassionate approach that balances the risks and benefits of reaching herd immunity is to allow those who are at minimal risk of death to live their lives normally to build up immunity to the virus through natural infection, while better protecting those who are at highest risk. Those who are not vulnerable should immediately be allowed to resume life as normal. (Kulldorff et al., 2020, pp. 1–8)

In line with this 'compassionate approach,' the GBDM developed what it called "focused protection." What this means is that the adoption of measures to protect the vulnerable should be the central aim of public health responses to COVID-2019. For example, nursing homes should use staff with acquired immunity and perform frequent PCR testing of other staff and all visitors. Staff rotation should be minimized. Visiting family members should meet the nursing home residents outside rather than inside. Furthermore, a comprehensive and detailed list of measures, including (a) approaches to multigenerational households and (b) hygiene measures such as hand washing and staying home when sick should be practiced by everyone to reduce the herd immunity threshold, can be implemented. But their implementation should be within the scope and capability of public health professionals (Kulldorff et al., 2020, pp. 1–8).

Soon after the publication of this declaration, the mainstream medico-scientific community issued a detailed counter-warning to governments. In a letter to the British government on October 7, 2020, it pointed out that (a) a more targeted approach (the GBDM suggested) could make it difficult to entirely protect vulnerable people, (b) the risk of long-term complications from the COVID-2019 virus means many others are also at risk, and (c) the "soft" and "hard" lockdown policies should remain until a vaccine is found (BBC News, 2020, p. 1).

In response to this mainstream medico-scientific community, the GBDM wrote a letter (titled "Health Harm Letter"), dated November 7, 2020, to the

British minister of health and social care, Rt. Hon Matt Hancock MP (BBC News, 2020, p. 1). Some of the signatories of this letter are prominent TV doctors (including Drs. Phil Hammond and Rosemary Leonard) and medics (some of whom had held senior roles at the British Medical Association). They include Dr. Sunetra Gupta (an epidemiologist at Oxford University), Professor Ellen Townsend (self-harm expert at Nottingham University), and Dr. Paul McKeigue (a disease modeler at Edinburgh University) (BBC News, 2020, p. 1). Back to the "Health Harm Letter," in it, they emphatically stated (with statistical figures and data from several robust biomedical and scientific studies) that the "risk from coronavirus is 1,000 times greater for the old and the infirm [especially heart disease and cancer patients], with children more at risk from flu than COVID-2019." And that, if governments do not release the world's populations from their securitized "hard" (stay-at-home) corolockdown measures, the impact will have "irreparable damage, with the underprivileged disproportionately harmed" (BBC News, 2020, p. 1).

The mainstream medico-scientific community objected to the arguments of the GBDM. They called on the governments in the United Kingdom and elsewhere not to give credence to the "headless" medical, psychological, and scientific conclusions of the GBDM. Governments accepted their argument against the GBDM. Their reliance on "state power" to discredit the GBDM's "Health Harm Letter," I suggest, calls for intellectual self-reflection and public conversation about the contemporary politicized, albeit militarized, issues that have held 'knowledge' (the input and output of power) in captivity. In this captor's space, knowledge is produced (by some), validated (for some), represented (through Orwellian means), *disseminated* (in diluted forms to the subalterns), and *securitized* (to defend it against the oppositional attitudes and protests of the learned and illiterate, experts and non-expert subalterns).

This powerful mainstream medico-scientific community refuses to see the centrality of the "underprivileged" people's needs and concerns, for whom and by whom the GBDM owes its legitimacy. Why the attempts to invalidate the voice of the underprivileged? This is what I think is the underlining issue. By silencing the disadvantaged and the subalterns (experts and non-experts), the mainstream medico-scientific community is trying to prevent people from escaping the predicament their bio-securitized positioning of the diseased bodies has created for the common man and woman, and child (boy and girl).

As such, the problem is in the positionality of hegemonic knowledge (of the powerful mainstream medico-scientific community) and its intersectional connection to state power in silencing the GBDM, the voice of the voiceless. The UN conventions on human and people's rights have created a space (however precarious) for reflections and conversations on matters that affect people. However, to the mainstream medico-scientific community, an oppositional attitude to corolockdown poses a danger to the laboratories of power, mainstreamed epidemiological knowledge, and hysteria. But the GBDM understands that, by mixing power, epidemiological knowledge, and hysteria within these militarized laboratories (i.e., governments), politicians (and their mainstreamed medico-science community) can create the structures that validate the use of corolockdown to penalize the underprivileged.

In epistemological terms, we should know the underprivileged class's oppositional attitudes as partly aimed at the performative positioning of invented notions of epidemiological power. In the process of coming to terms with their diseased bodies, people are expected to recognize their powerlessness and accept the militarized biomedical/scientific calls for the epistemological colonialization of all terrains. The goal is to ensure that no neutral space is left for the subalterns to voice their oppositional views to corolockdown. Without this space, they will be left with no option but to embrace the mainstream medico-scientific community's 'imperial' knowledge and accept the Orwellian colonizing powers of governments that see their people as existential threats to their power.

Within this colonialized epistemological space, the knowledgeable and unknowledgeable, the powerful and the powerless, the peoples of the Global North and the Global South alike are expected to understand the issues surrounding corolockdown measures through the categories and conceptual systems immersed in a hegemonic epistemological order. Despite the factual statistics and scientific data presented by the GBDM, the gatekeepers of this colonialized epistemological space have ruled out any form of compromise. They have decreed that any oppositional knowledge is subaltern in outlook and, therefore, lacks political legitimacy. Without this political legitimacy, I argue, it will be challenging for people (even for the elites within GBDM) to transcend their subalternate marginal status in the fight for freedom from corolockdown.

CONCLUSION AND RECOMMENDATIONS

In epistemological and practical political terms, countries are an intermediate space for the explosive political use of corolockdown measures. In this intermediating space, corolockdown is a platform that bears the markers of an oppressed class, the subalterns. On this penological platform, people's being and knowing—of what the pandemic means to them—is constrained by the hybridized (half-political and half-medical) formations of power.

As I have argued throughout this chapter, this power is the outcome of the Orwellian palimpsestuous political intertextual inscriptions of various 'conventionally acceptable' (though not necessarily 'just') medical and scientific tendencies, attitudes, institutional practices, and identities. In this corolockdown space, issues of identity matter too. After all, it was at the height of corolockdowns, amid the search for a medical cure, that two French doctors suggested (during a televised radio talk show) the *positional* inclusion of Africans—in Africa—in the historic space of the proverbial lab rat. Of course, corolockdown measures were to play a role here. They should have created an opportunity to select a large number of people from the immobile African population to test the efficacy of the promising COVID-2019 vaccines being manufactured in the West.

The problem then is that there is no "uncontrolled" space, politically, epistemologically, and medico-scientifically, for the subalterns to invent and take steps to validate their oppositional anti-corolockdown attitudes. To the neutral scholars writing on corolockdown, a problem is worth investigating. But, even if we can show how our research subjects (the subalterns) are navigating the dangerous terrains of corolockdown, the question of validation remains.

We can suggest ways for the subalterns to reclaim knowledge—by writing about their corolockdown gains, fears, and pains. This knowledge will enable people in situations of corolockdown to own their stories and discredit the medico-political hysteria surrounding the dangers posed by their diseased bodies to state power. However, there are two questions we must answer. Can the subaltern be able to reclaim knowledge (his lived experiences) on corolockdown in the constrained space of SOE laws—developed to (a) contain the COVID-2019 and (b) control the physical and psychological sites of corolockdown? Even if they transcend the limitations imposed by SOEs and reclaim knowledge, how do we know precisely that this reclaimed corolockdown knowledge has not been 'doctored' by the elaborate power structures (and the associated mainstream medico-scientific community) and systems?

In a nutshell, the corolockdown policies are colonizing measures that adopt specific aspects of Orwellian power and governance structures that have transformed human societies forever. Through the introduction and expansion of institutional, legal, procedural, and structural changes to our human relationships (not forgetting the virtualization of relationships), the problem goes beyond hygiene-related modifications of the corolockdown sites. People's social contract with their governments is now in the hands of the private sector of coro-profiteers, coro-marketers, and coro-scientists. For this reason, some may say it will be difficult for people to reclaim their governments without risking the dangers of being categorized as an existential threat to state power.

Notwithstanding societal misgivings, by adopting the following recommendations, governments should be able to address the complex issues surrounding the corolockdown. First, governments should introduce strict rules on mask wearing in public spaces. Governments must ensure that all people, irrespective of their influence and affluence, always wear masks in all public places. There must not be any "sacred cows" in this process. Everyone should adhere and comply with this rule, from the president right down to the least workers. When the public sees this, they will understand and appreciate the process's seriousness and importance and will follow the same. Moreover, Sierra Leoneans comply with what they see, not what they hear.

Second, hand washing should also take center stage just as in the days of the Ebola. Washing of hands should be made mandatory in all public spaces. There should be soap and water (in open areas, where everyone can see) on all public buildings and public spaces to wash their hands and sanitize them before gaining access to these buildings/spaces. People should not be allowed access to these spaces if they do not follow this rule.

Third, in crowded areas like markets and motor parks, the government should establish temporary entrance and exits points (with the constant provision of soap, water, and hand sanitizers). These entrances should be staffed by civilian personnel. The rationale behind having military personnel operating these places has not always worked well in countries that have experienced (within the last two decades) civil wars and military coups. Replacing military personnel with civilians helps prevent people from reliving their war/junta time traumatic experiences.

Fourth, governments should work closely with the private sector (including the public transport sector) to ensure they comply with existing COVID-2019 safety rules and regulations regarding people's movements and adjust swiftly as new ones are being implemented to protect the general public.

Fifth, there should be active and accurate public communication and civic education. Governments should ensure that the public is aware of all the latest updates as they fight against the diseases through daily public sensitization. They should be putting out the statistics and regularly updating the people on the rules and regulations. This can be done through transparent engagement with the media throughout the country. COVID-2019 messages must be made accessible and understandable by all.

Sixth, most importantly, citizens must see this fight as their own. They must all be their neighbor's keepers by adhering and following all the prescribed rules and regulations to keep themselves, their families, their communities, and their nations safe and free from this unwanted stranger called COVID-2019.

These recommendations are aimed at de-securitizing the pandemic. They will enable governments to flatten the curve without corolockdown, which cuts people off their sources of livelihood and diminishes their sense of security during such a precarious time.

REFERENCES

Abraham, A. (1978). *Mende Government and Politics under Colonial Rule: A Historical Study of Political Change in Sierra Leone, 1890–1937*. Oxford, UK: Oxford University Press.

Acemoglu, D., Reed, T., and Robinson, J. A. (2014). Chiefs: Economic development and elite control of civil society in Sierra Leone. *Journal of Political Economy* 122(2):319–368. Retrieved on November 20, 2020 from https://doi.org/10.1086/674988.

Arafat, S. Y., Kar, S. K., and Kabir, R. (2020). Possible controlling measures of panic buying during COVID-19. *International Journal of Mental Health and Addiction* 2020:1–3.

BBC News. (2020). Coronavirus: Health Experts Join Global Anti-lockdown Movement. *British Broadcasting Corporation.* Retrieved on November 20, 2020 from https://www.bbc.com/news/health-54442386. on December 9, 2020.

Benke, C., Autenrieth, L. K., Asselmann, E., and Pané-Farré, C. A. (2020). Lockdown, quarantine measures, and social distancing: Associations with depression, anxiety and distress at the beginning of the COVID-19 pandemic among adults from Germany. *Psychiatry Research* 293, 113462. Retrieved on November 20, 2020 from https://www.ncbi.nlm.nih.gov/pmc/articles/PMC7500345/.

Caballero-Domínguez, C. C., Jiménez-Villamizar, M. P., and Campo-Arias, A. (2020). Suicide risk during the lockdown due to coronavirus disease (COVID-19) in Colombia. *Death Studies* 1–6. Retrieved on November 20, 2020 from https://pubmed.ncbi.nlm.nih.gov/32589519/.

Cabico, G. K. (2020). DILG issues show cause orders to 3 Governors, 2 mayors for violating quarantine rules. *Philstar.Com.* Retrieved on November 20, 2020 from https://www.philstar.com/headlines/2020/04/15/2007508/dilg-issues-show-cause-orders-3-governors-2-mayors-violating-quarantine-rules.

Capano, G. (2020). Policy design and state capacity in the COVID-19 emergency in Italy: If you are not prepared for the (un) expected, you can be only what you already are. *Policy and Society* 39(3):326–344.

Castles, F. G., Leibfried, S., Lewis, J., Obinger, H., and Pierson, C. (2010). *The Oxford Handbook of the Welfare State.* Oxford, UK: Oxford University Press.

Chehrehgosha, M. (2020). The unpreparedness of the healthcare system for the management of COVID-19 pandemic leading to the mistreatment of the elderly: A newly emerging moral dilemma. *The Journal of Nutrition, Health and Aging* 2020:1–6. Retrieved on November 20, 2020 from https://www.ncbi.nlm.nih.gov/pmc/articles/PMC7275658/.

Christensen, T., and Lægreid, P. (2020). Balancing governance capacity and legitimacy-how the Norwegian government handled the COVID-19 crisis as a high performer. *Public Administration Review.* Retrieved on November 20, 2020 from https://onlinelibrary.wiley.com/doi/full/10.1111/puar.13241.

Cloud, D. H., Ahalt, C., Augustine, D., Sears, D., and Williams, B. (2020). Medical isolation and solitary confinement: Balancing health and humanity in US jails and prisons during COVID-19. *Journal of General Internal Medicine* 35(9):2738–2742.

Desai, A., Durham, K., Burke, S. C., NeMoyer, A., and Heilbrun, K. (2020). Releasing individuals from incarceration during COVID-19: Pandemic-related challenges and recommendations for promoting successful reentry. *Psychology, Public Policy, and Law.* Retrieved on November 20, 2020 from http://dx.doi.org/10.1037/law0000279.

Every-Palmer, S., Jenkins, M., Gendall, P., Hoek, J., Beaglehole, B., Bell, C., Williman, J., Rapsey, C., and Stanley, J. (2020). Psychological distress, anxiety, family violence, suicidality, and wellbeing in New Zealand during the COVID-19 lockdown: A cross-sectional study. *PloS One* 15(11):e0241658. Retrieved on November 20, 2020 fromhttps://journals.plos.org/plosone/article?id=10.1371/journal.pone.0241658.

Franco-Paredes, C., Jankousky, K., Schultz, J., Bernfeld, J., Cullen, K., Quan, N. G., Kon, S., Hotez, P., Henao-Martínez, A. F., and Krsak, M. (2020). COVID-19 in jails and prisons: A neglected infection in a marginalized population. *PLoS Neglected Tropical Diseases* 14(6):e0008409. Retrieved on November 20, 2020 from https://www.ncbi.nlm.nih.gov/pmc/articles/PMC7307724/.

Galvani, A. P., Parpia, A. S., Pandey, A., Zimmer, C., Kahn, J. G., and Fitzpatrick, M. C. (2020). The imperative for universal healthcare to curtail the COVID-19 outbreak in the USA. *EClinicalMedicine*. Retrieved on November 20, 2020 from https://www.ncbi.nlm.nih.gov/pmc/articles/PMC7231536/.

Gosangi, B., Park, H., Thomas, R., Gujrathi, R., Bay, C. P., Raja, A. S., Seltzer, S. E., Balcom, M. C., McDonald, M. L., and Orgill, D. P. (2020). Exacerbation of physical intimate partner violence during COVID-19 lockdown. *Radiology* 298(1). Retrieved on November 20, 2020 from https://pubs.rsna.org/doi/full/10.1148/radiol.2020202866.

Greve, C., Ejersbo, N., Lægreid, P., and Rykkja, L. H. (2020). Unpacking Nordic administrative reforms: Agile and adaptive governments. *International Journal of Public Administration* 43(8):697–710.

Heiberg, T., and Winning, A. (2020). South African minister disciplined for "lock-down lunch." *Thomson Reuters*. Retrieved on December 9, 2020 from https://www.reuters.com/article/us-health-coronavirus-safrica/south-african-minister-disciplined-for-lockdown-lunch-idUSKBN21Q1D8.

Henry, B. F. (2020). Social distancing and incarceration: Policy and management strategies to reduce COVID-19 transmission and promote health equity through decarceration. *Health Education and Behavior* 1090198120927318. Retrieved on December 9, 2020 from https://pubmed.ncbi.nlm.nih.gov/32390473/.

Jackson, P. (2005). Chiefs, money and politicians: Rebuilding local government in post-war Sierra Leone. *Public Administration and Development* 25(1):49–58.

Keilitz, I. (2020). Illiberalism enabled by the coronavirus pandemic: An existential threat to judicial independence. *IJCA*, *11*, 1. Retrieved on December 9, 2020 from https://www.iacajournal.org/articles/10.36745/ijca.339/.

Ketchell, M. (2020). Why leaders breaking rules is a far more serious attack on our liberty than lockdown itself. *The Conversation*. Retrieved on December 9, 2020 from https://theconversation.com/why-leaders-breaking-rules-is-a-far-more-serious-attack-on-our-liberty-than-lockdown-itself-139405.

Kim, M. J. (2020). How a South Korean psychiatric ward became a "medical disaster" when coronavirus hit. *The Washington Post*. Retrieved on December 9, 2020 from https://Www.Washingtonpost.Com/World/Asia_pacific/How-a-South-Korean-Psychiatric-Ward-Became-a-Medical-Disaster-When-Coronavirus-Hit/2020/02/29/Fe8f6e40-5897-11ea-8efd-0f904bdd8057_story.Html.

Kulldorff, M., Gupta, S., Bhattacharya, J., and Medical and Public Health Scientists and Medical Practitioners. (2020). *Great Barrington Declaration*. The American Institute for Economic Research. Retrieved on December 9, 2020 from https://gbdeclaration.org/.

Kvist, J., Fritzell, J., Njorn, H., and Kangas, O., eds. (2012). *Changing Social Equality: The Nordic Welfare Model in the 21st Century*. London, UK: The Polity Press.

Kvist, J., and Greve, B. (2011). Has the Nordic welfare model been transformed? *Social Policy and Administration* 45(2):146–160.

Lahai, J. I. (2016). *Gender in Practice: Culture, Politics and Society in Sierra Leone* (vol. 1–14). Oxford, UK: Peter Lang Ltd.

Lahai, J. I. (2017). *The Ebola Pandemic in Sierra Leone: Representations, Actors, Interventions and the Path to Recovery*. New York: Palgrave Macmillan.

Liu, H.-Y., Lauta, K., and Maas, M. (2020). Apocalypse now? Initial lessons from the Covid-19 pandemic for the governance of existential and global catastrophic risks. *Journal of International Humanitarian Legal Studies* 1:1–16.

Lo, M.-C. M., and Hsieh, H.-Y. (2020). The "societalization" of pandemic unpreparedness: Lessons from Taiwan's COVID response. *American Journal of Cultural Sociology* 2020:1–21. Retrieved on December 9, 2020 from https://www.ncbi.nlm.nih.gov/pmc/articles/PMC7500988/.

Mallet, J., Dubertret, C., and Le Strat, Y. (2020). Addictions in the COVID-19 era: Current evidence, future perspectives a comprehensive review. *Progress in Neuro-Psychopharmacology and Biological Psychiatry* 110070. Retrieved on December 0, 2020 from https://www.ncbi.nlm.nih.gov/pmc/articles/PMC7420609/.

Mbembe, A. (2008). Necropolitics. In Morton, S. and Bygrave, S. (eds.), *Foucault in an Age of Terror*. New York: Palgrave Macmillan.

Mellish, T. I., Luzmore, N. J., and Shahbaz, A. A. (2020). Why were the UK and USA unprepared for the COVID-19 pandemic? The systemic weaknesses of neoliberalism: a comparison between the UK, USA, Germany, and South Korea. *Journal of Global Faultlines* 7(1):9–45.

Meyer, J. P., Franco-Paredes, C., Parmar, P., Yasin, F., and Gartland, M. (2020). COVID-19 and the coming epidemic in US immigration detention centres. *The Lancet Infectious Diseases* 20(6):646–648.

Pedersen, A. W., and Kuhnle, S. (2017). The Nordic welfare state model. In Knutsen, O. P. (ed.), *The Nordic Models in Political Science. Challenged, but Still Viable?* Stockholm, Sweden: Fagbokforlaget.

Phillipou, A., Meyer, D., Neill, E., Tan, E. J., Toh, W. L., Van Rheenen, T. E., and Rossell, S. L. (2020). Eating and exercise behaviors in eating disorders and the general population during the COVID-19 pandemic in Australia: Initial results from the COLLATE project. *International Journal of Eating Disorders*. Retrieved on December 9, 2020 from https://www.ncbi.nlm.nih.gov/pmc/articles/PMC7300745/.

Prentice, C., Chen, J., and Stantic, B. (2020). Timed intervention in COVID-19 and panic buying. *Journal of Retailing and Consumer Services* 57, 102203. Retrieved on December 9, 2020 from https://www.ncbi.nlm.nih.gov/pmc/articles/PMC7414736/.

Rashid, I. O. D. (2000). Patterns of rural protest: Chiefs, slaves and peasants in north-western Sierra Leone, 1896–1956. PhD Dissertation, McGill University, Canada. Retrieved on Deember 9, 2020 from http://digitool.library.mcgill.ca/R/?func=dbin-jumpfull&object_id=35051&local_base=GEN01-MCG02.

Roesch, E., Amin, A., Gupta, J., and García-Moreno, C. (2020). *Violence against Women during Covid-19 Pandemic Restrictions*. London, UK: British Medical Journal Publishing Group.

Ronayne, K. (November 14, 2020). California governor went to party, violated own virus rules. *The Associated Press*. Retrieved on December 9, 2020 from https://apnews.com/article/birthdays-coronavirus-pandemic-california-napa-gavin-newsom-9426bc09f958ae9865309dd71a04aa97.

Shani, G. (2020). Securitizing 'bare life'? Human security and coronavirus. *E-International Relations*. Retrieved on December 9, 2020 from https://www.e-ir.info/2020/04/03/securitizing-bare-life-human-security-and-coronavirus/.

Srivatsa, S. I. (2020). *Action on Covid-19 and Gender: A Policy Review from Sierra Leone*. Freetown, Sierra Leone ALiGN/Overseas Development Institute. Retrieved on December 9, 2020 from https://www.alignplatform.org/sites/default/files/2020-07/sierra-leone-brief.pdf.

Standish, K. (2020). A coming wave: Suicide and gender after COVID-19. *Journal of Gender Studies* 30:114–118.

Stanojoska, A., and Ilik, G. (2020). Penitentiary institutions and Covid-19: How to stop the virus and guarantee human rights? *Journal of Liberty and International Affairs* 6:80–92.

Volkow, N. D. (2020). Collision of the COVID-19 and addiction epidemics. *Annals of Internal Medicine* 173(1):61–62.

WHO. (2020). *Addressing Human Rights as Key to the COVID-19 Response*. World Health Organization (WHO). Retrieved on December 9, 2020 from https://www.who.int/publications/i/item/addressing-human-rights-as-key-to-the-covid-19-response.

Wilson, K. (2020). The COVID-19 pandemic and the human rights of persons with mental and cognitive impairments subject to coercive powers in Australia. *International Journal of Law and Psychiatry* 73, 101605. Retrieved on December 9, 2020 from https://www.ncbi.nlm.nih.gov/pmc/articles/PMC7318936/.

Selected Bibliography

Adams, H. E. and Sutker, P. B., eds. (1984). *Comprehensive Handbook of Psychopathology*. New York: Springer.

Bailey, R. (April 6, 2020). U.S. fever trends suggest COVID-19 rates could soon decline. Retrieved on April 19, 2020 from https://reason.com/2020/04/06/u-s-fever-trends-suggest-covid-19-rates-could-soon-decline/

Beattie, M. and Lenihan, P. (2018). *Counseling Skills for Working with Gender Diversity and Identity*. London, UK: Jessica Kingsley Publishers.

Bogousslavsky J. and Dieguez S. (2014). Sigmund Freud and hysteria: The etiology of psychoanalysis? *Frontiers of Neurology and Neuroscience* 35:109–125. Retrieved on May 2, 2020 from https://www.ncbi.nlm.nih.gov/pubmed/25273494

Cascella, M., Rajnik, M., Cuomo, A., Dulebohn, S. C. and Napoli, R. D. (April 6, 2020). Features, evaluation and treatment of coronavirus (COVID-19). Retrieved on April 19, 2020 from https://www.ncbi.nlm.nih.gov/books/NBK554776/

Cassoobhoy, A. (April 17, 2020). Symptoms of coronavirus: Early signs, serious symptoms and more. Retrieved on April 18, 2020 from https://www.webmd.com/lung/covid-19-symptoms#1

Centers for Disease Control and Prevention—CDC (2020a). Situation summary. Retrieved on April 4, 2020 from https://www.cdc.gov/coronavirus/2019-ncov/cases-updates/summary.html#emergence

Centers for Disease Control and Prevention—CDC. (2020b). *CDC Self Study Text*. Retrieved on April 19, 2020 from https://www.cdc.gov/

Freedman, J. L. (1978). *Introductory Psychology*. Boston, MA: Addison-Wesley Publishing Company.

Gilman, S. L. et al. (1993). *Hysteria Beyond Freud*. Berkeley, CA: University of California Press.

Gray, R. T. (2016). Freud and the literary imagination. University of Washington Faculty Web Server. Retrieved on May 2, 2020 from http://courses.washington.edu/freudlit/Hysteria.Notes.html

Health and Human Services (HHS) Office & Public Affairs. (March 27, 2020). HHS Coronavirus (COVID-19) updates. Retrieved on April 19, 2020 from https://www.hhs.gov/about/news/coronavirus/index.html

Jones, E. (1964). *The Life and Work of Sigmund Freud*. London, UK: Penguin Books.

Lennon, J. and Shah, R. (March 31, 2020). Investigation of COVID-19 clusters in Singapore. Retrieved on April 18, 2020 from https://www.2minutemedicine.com/investigation-of-covid-19-clusters-in-singapore/

Lewis, D. K. L. (April 4, 2020). How does cardiovascular disease increase the risk of severe illness and death from COVID-19? Retrieved on April 18, 2020 from https://www.health.harvard.edu/blog/how-does-cardiovascular-disease-increase-the-risk-of-severe-illness-and-death-from-covid-19-2020040219401

Maines, R. P. (1999). *The Technology of Orgasm: "Hysteria," the Vibrator, and Women's Sexual Satisfaction*. Baltimore, MD: The Johns Hopkins University Press.

Mayo Clinic. (April 15, 2020). Coronavirus disease 2019 (COVID-19). Retrieved on April 18, 2020 from https://www.mayoclinic.org/diseases-conditions/coronavirus/symptoms-causes/syc-20479963

Nicholson, C. (November 16, 2017). Why Freud was right about hysteria. *The Conversation*. Retrieved on May 2, 2020 from https://theconversation.com/why-freud-was-right-about-hysteria-86497

Nicholson, T. R. et al. (2016). Life events and escape in conversion disorder. *Psychological Medicine* 46(12):2617–2626.

O'Brien, J., ed. (2009). *Encyclopedia of Gender and Society*. Thousand Oaks, CA: Sage Publications.

Oren, O. L., Kopecky, S. J., Gluckman, T. J., Gersh, B. S. and Blumenthal, R. (April 6, 2020). Coronavirus disease 2019 (COVID-19): Epidemiology, clinical spectrum and implications for the cardiovascular clinician. Retrieved on April 19, 2020 from https://www.acc.org/latest-in-cardiology/articles/2020/04/06/11/08/covid-19-epidemiology-clinical-spectrum-and-implications-for-the-cv-clinician

Pittalwala, I. (April 6, 2020). Epidemiologist answers questions on COVID-19 ranging from grocery store visits to wearing masks and gloves. Retrieved on April 19, 2020 from https://news.ucr.edu/articles/2020/04/06/epidemiologist-answers-questions-covid-19-ranging-grocery-store-visits-wearing

Tasca, C. et al. (October 19, 2012). Women and hysteria in mental health. *Clinical Practice and Epidemiology in Mental Health* 8:110–119. Retrieved on April 30, 2020 from https://www.ncbi.nlm.nih.gov/pmc/articles/PMC3480686/

World Health Organization—WHO. (March 20, 2020). Coronavirus disease 2019 (COVID-19), *Situation Report—61*. Geneva, Switzerland. Retrieved on April 18, 2020 from https://www.who.int/docs/default-source/coronaviruse/situation-reports/20200321-sitrep-61-covid-19.pdf

Index

About the Contributors

Yakub Adams has a PhD in linguistics and is a senior lecturer at Maseno University in Kenya. He has excellent skills in research and postgraduate education. He is the author of 1 book and 25 academic papers in recognized peer-reviewed journals in Linguistics, Media, and Communication. He is also involved in advancing good governance and public policy, especially in advocacy activities involving balancing the Kenyan constitutional and African traditional views on women's rights as broadcasted through the local radio stations. His most recent research involved assessing UNESCO's Media Policy Dialogues for Improved Media Landscape in Kenya.

Cecy Edijala Balogun is a doctoral candidate of rural sociology in the Department of Agricultural Extension and Rural Development at the University of Ibadan, Nigeria. She is a research fellow in the Nigerian Institute of Social and Economic Research (NISER), Ibadan, Nigeria. She is coauthor in the book titled *African-Centered Theories* being published by the CODESRIA College of Mentors and a few scholarly articles. She is a prestigious scholar of the CODESRIA College of Mentors 2019 Cohorts. She has also worked with a nongovernmental organization where she coordinated youth empowerment programs for youth development and is highly interested in youth development and rural sociology studies.

Abdul Karim Bangura has five PhDs in political science, development economics, linguistics, computer science, and mathematics. He is a researcher-in-residence of Abrahamic Connections and Islamic Peace Studies at American University's Center for Global Peace. He is the author and editor of 104 books and the author of 707 scholarly articles. Many of these works have won eminent awards, in addition to more than 50 other distinguished national and international awards. He has served as president and then ambassador to the United Nations for the Association of Third World Studies and is fluent in a dozen African and six European languages.

Isatu Ramatu Bangura's first degree is in computer graphics design and her second degree is in mathematics; she is working on her PhD in mathematics. During the past summers, she worked at various U.S. government agencies designing mathematical models for their operations. Many of her writings have won major national awards. She has designed many book covers, and some of her artworks have been displayed for public viewing and won prestigious awards. She is also the lead trumpet player for her school and community concert, marching and jazz bands.

Nyarai P. Chibanda holds a master's degree in library and information science from the National University of Science and Technology in Zimbabwe and is currently studying for a PhD in information science at the University of KwaZulu—Natal in South Africa. She is currently the university librarian for the Midlands State University in Zimbabwe. She is an emerging researcher who has published one article in a refereed journal. She is also an active member of the Zimbabwe International Book Fair General Council and holds a number of leadership positions in the library fraternities nationally and internationally.

Collence T. Chisita holds a PhD (University of Pretoria) in information science. He is a research fellow at the University of South Africa's (UNISA) College of Human Sciences in the Department of Information Sciences in South Africa. Chisita has authored 2 books, edited 3 books, written 21 journal articles and 20 book chapters, and participated in 15 international conference proceedings. Chisita has done webinars in the field of Information Science and the impact of COVID-2019 pandemic and infodemic on academic libraries Higher Education. He has served as keynote speaker for regional and international conferences.

Henry Chigozie Duru holds a PhD in mass communication with specialization in journalism and political communication. He has published 15 scholarly articles in national and international journals, as well as authored eight book chapters. He lectures in the Department of Mass Communication at Nnamdi Azikiwe University in Nigeria, after having worked as a full-time journalist for over a decade.

Henrietta Eshalomi is a doctoral candidate of diaspora and transnational studies in the Institute of African Studies at the University of Ibadan in

Nigeria. She is a member of the CODESRIA College of Mentors 2019 cohort. Currently, she is an awardee of the University of Ibadan postgraduate scholar award for Teaching and Research Assistant. Henrietta was also part of the research team for the UNESCO project, Irregular Migration from Nigeria: Causes, Risks and Policy Implications, published in 2019. Several other publications of hers are currently under review by peer-reviewed journals.

Chinwe Beatrice Ezeoke holds a PhD in mass communication. She is a lecturer in the Department of Mass Communication at Nnamdi Azikiwe University, Awka, in Nigeria. She has written over 17 scholarly articles and had a full scholarship as a mentee to attend the first CODESRIA College of Academic Mentors Institute convened in Nairobi, Kenya, in 2017.

Harrison Adewale Idowu is a PhD candidate in political science at the Obafemi Awolowo University in Ile-Ife, Nigeria. His research interests are predominantly on democratization and democracy, electoral politics, comparative studies, and development studies. Harrison is the author of over 17 scholarly articles, including chapter contributions in edited books. He has won several national and international grants to attend and present his research findings at various conferences. Presently, he lectures in the Department of Political Science and Public Administration at Adekunle Ajasin University in Akungba-Akoko, Nigeria.

J. P. Afamefuna Ifedi lectures political science at Howard University and previously at Lincoln and Bowie State Universities. He has published extensively in various scholarly peer-reviewed journals in political science. He is the executive director of the Council on African World Affairs, an organization dedicated to educating the public on African world issues. His PhD is from Howard University. He also completed post-doctoral studies in international political economy as an Institute for British and Irish Studies Summer Fellow at St. Anthony's College, Oxford, and Trinity College.

Feyisitan Ijimakinwa is a doctoral candidate of diaspora and transnational studies in the Institute of African Studies at the University of Ibadan in Nigeria. He is also a research fellow of the Institut Francais de Recherche en Afrique (IFRA-Nigeria) with research interests in diaspora connections, environmental migration, anthropology, trans-atlantic slave trade, as well as cultural diplomacy. His works have been presented in national and international conferences and he has published in the *Journal of African Studies*, *African Historical Review*, *Migration Studies*, and *KUJUUA*. He is also a regular social and political analyst on radio and television in Nigeria.

Osman Ibrahim Kabba holds a PhD in public administration with a concentration in law and public policy. He is a senior administrative analyst at the New Jersey State Department of Children and Families where he reviews, analyzes, and appraises state policies, administrative procedures, and practices. He is a veteran of the U.S. Navy with tours of duty in Europe, Africa, and the Middle East. He served as instructor and adviser, and is a recipient of many military awards, including the highest award, the Navy Achievement Medal, National Defense, and Navy's Commendation Medal. A proponent of conflict resolution, he believes that the nexus between development and security in a nation emerging from conflict is ethnic group cooperation.

Emmanuel Vincent Nelson Kallon holds a PhD in political science. He is a research associate at the African Studies Center, Tokyo University of Foreign Studies in Tokyo, Japan. He is the author of four scholarly articles and two book chapters. He was the MEXT Scholarship recipient and has lectured (part-time) at the Tokyo University of Foreign Studies. His research interests include identity politics, comparative politics, peacebuilding theories, public policy, and research methods.

Joseph Lansana Kormoh has a PhD in peace and conflict studies from the University of Bradford in the United Kingdom. He was a Fulbright Scholar at New York University in the United States and also a commonwealth scholar in the United Kingdom. He is a lecturer in the Department of History and African Studies at Fourah Bay College, University of Sierra Leone. He is currently a freelance researcher in the United Kingdom. His book chapters have been published by Palgrave Macmillan and Routledge, and he has also published a book with Arthur House, United Kingdom, among other reputable publishing houses.

Alie Kunda holds a PhD in political science. He is a research associate at the African Institution in Washington, DC. He is the author of 5 books and more than 60 scholarly articles, some of which have won major scholarly awards. He is the recipient of more than 20 other prestigious national and international scholarly and community service awards. He has lectured and done television and newspaper interviews in many countries across the globe. He is also fluent in many African and several European languages and enjoys computer programming.

John Idriss Lahai has a PhD in applied development studies and is currently pursuing a second doctorate in International Security Law. He is the author of 14 scholarly books and 24 journal articles and book chapters. He is a senior research fellow at the University of England in Australia and an international consultant (working for governments, international agencies, and think tanks in Africa and the South Pacific). He has held academic positions at research/teaching-intensive universities in Australia, the United States, and New Zealand. Before becoming a full-fledged academic and consultant, he held civil service positions in Sierra Leone's government.

Moeketsi Letseka is professor of philosophy of education and African philosophy at the UNISA, where he is also the holder of the endowed United Nations, Educational, Scientific and Cultural Organization Chair on Open Distance Learning. Letseka is editor-in-chief of *Africa Education Review*, an international scholarly journal that is jointly published by UNISA Press and Taylor & Francis in the United Kingdom. He is chairperson of the Task Force on Distance Education in the World Council of Comparative Education Societies (WCCES). He is also co-chairperson of the WCCES's Finance Standing Committee.

Ishmael I. Munene holds a PhD in higher education administration and policy studies and is a professor of higher education, research, and educational foundations at Northern Arizona University in the United States. He is also the current executive secretary of the African Studies and Research Forum. He has authored, edited, and co-edited many books, book chapters, and articles in referred journals and commentaries in leading opinion periodicals on African higher education. He also serves on the editorial boards of several journals. He has held fellowships from the Carnegie African Diaspora Fellowship Program, Organization of Social Science Research in Africa, and the Catholic University of Eastern Africa. He has consulted and trained for the Council for the Development of Social Science Research in Africa.

Jafred Muyaka holds a PhD in comparative education and international studies. He is a lecturer at the University of Eldoret in Kenya where he teaches courses in educational foundations. He has over the years developed research interest in higher education, gender, and technology. He has written over 10 scholarly articles in refereed journals and has coauthored a book on complexity of masculinity in Africa. He is an active member of a number of professional bodies, including the African Network for Internationalization of Education, the Council for the Development of Social Science Research in Africa, and the Women Educational Researchers of Kenya.

Pamela Anyango Oloo holds a PhD in linguistics. She is a senior lecturer and chairperson in the Department of Linguistics at Maseno University in Kenya. She is a DAAD scholar and author of 1 book and 20 scholarly articles in recognized peer-reviewed journals. She also holds various postgraduate professional development certificates. Her research interests include Discourse Analysis, Language and Gender, and Health Communication. Her most recent research activity entailed investigating the role of leadership in the use of innovative pedagogies for learning and research outputs in Kenyan public universities.

Cecilia T. Olugbara is a post-doctoral research fellow at the UNESCO Chair on Open Distance Learning at the University of South Africa. She is a researcher with a doctorate in Science and Technology Education. She lectured Life Science at the University of Zululand and Tshwane University of Technology in South Africa. Her research interests include Language in Science, Information Communication Technology in Science Teaching and Learning, and Quantitative Methods. She has published in international scholarly journals.

Simon Gisege Omare holds a PhD in religious studies. His area of interest is sociology of religion. He is a senior lecturer at Moi University in Kenya. He is the author of *Witchcraft Scapegoat: Abagusii Beliefs and Violence against 'Witches'* and *Religion and Environment Conservation: Role of Isukha Religious Beliefs and Practices in the Conservation of Kakamega Forest, Kenya*. He has written 5 book chapters and more than 10 scholarly articles. He also enjoys reading and writing about the nexus between religion and humans.

Omosefe Oyekanmi is a doctoral candidate of political science at the University of Ibadan in Nigeria. She is a research fellow at the NISER in Ibadan cum academic facilitator at the University of Ibadan Distance Learning Center. A recipient of a number of scholarly awards, she is a PhD Mentee of the Council for the Development of Social Science Research in Africa. With over 20 articles, cutting across development, public policy, gender issues, and international peacebuilding, she is an ardent believer of liberty, equality, freedom, and morality, as essential drivers of a just and peaceful society.

Rosemary Oyinlola Popoola holds a PhD in international relations from Covenant University in Ota, Ogun, Nigeria. She has close to a decade of experience in teaching and research at Covenant University. She is the recipient of the 2018 Early Career Fellowship at African Doctoral Academy, Stellenbosch University, South Africa; 2019 Best Doctoral Thesis in Lagos Studies by Lagos Studies Association; and 2019 University of Michigan African Presidential Programme postponed to Fall 2021 due to COVID-2019 restrictions. She has attended significant academic conferences, roundtable discussions, training, and workshops in Nigeria, Kenya, South Africa, and the United States and published 12 peer-reviewed articles, 1 book chapter, and 10 conference papers.

Rachael M. Rudolph holds a PhD in political science. She is an assistant professor for a joint program between Bryant University and the Beijing Institute of Technology, Zhuhai in China. She also serves as an advisory board member for the New York Center For Foreign Policy Affairs, which is headquartered in New York and has an office in Washington, DC. She is the author of 4 books, more than 10 scholarly articles, and numerous media articles. She has lived in the Indo-Asia Pacific region for eight years and traveled for fieldwork to Africa, Central America, Europe, and the Middle East.

Hadizat Audu Salihu is a PhD candidate in the History and International Studies Department of the University of Ilorin in Nigeria. She teaches international-related courses such as United States, Southern America, and British History in the Department of Religions, History and Heritage Studies at Kwara State University in Malete, Nigeria. She has published more than 10 scholarly articles in books and journals. She is a member of prestigious academic bodies such as CODESRIA, Lagos Studies Association, Historical Society of Nigeria, and Society for Peace Studies and Practice in Nigeria. Her areas of specialization include socioeconomic history, maritime, and gender studies.

Gregory Obinna Ugbo holds a PhD in mass communication. He is an early career scholar. He lectures in the Department of Mass Communication at Federal University in Oye-Ekiti, Nigeria. He is an avid researcher with particular interests in journalism and media studies, conflict communication, and gender studies. He has published over 14 scholarly articles in reputable international and national journals. He is a member of several academic associations, including the International Association for Media and Communication Research, the African Council for Communication Education, and the Association of Communication Scholars and Practitioners of Nigeria.